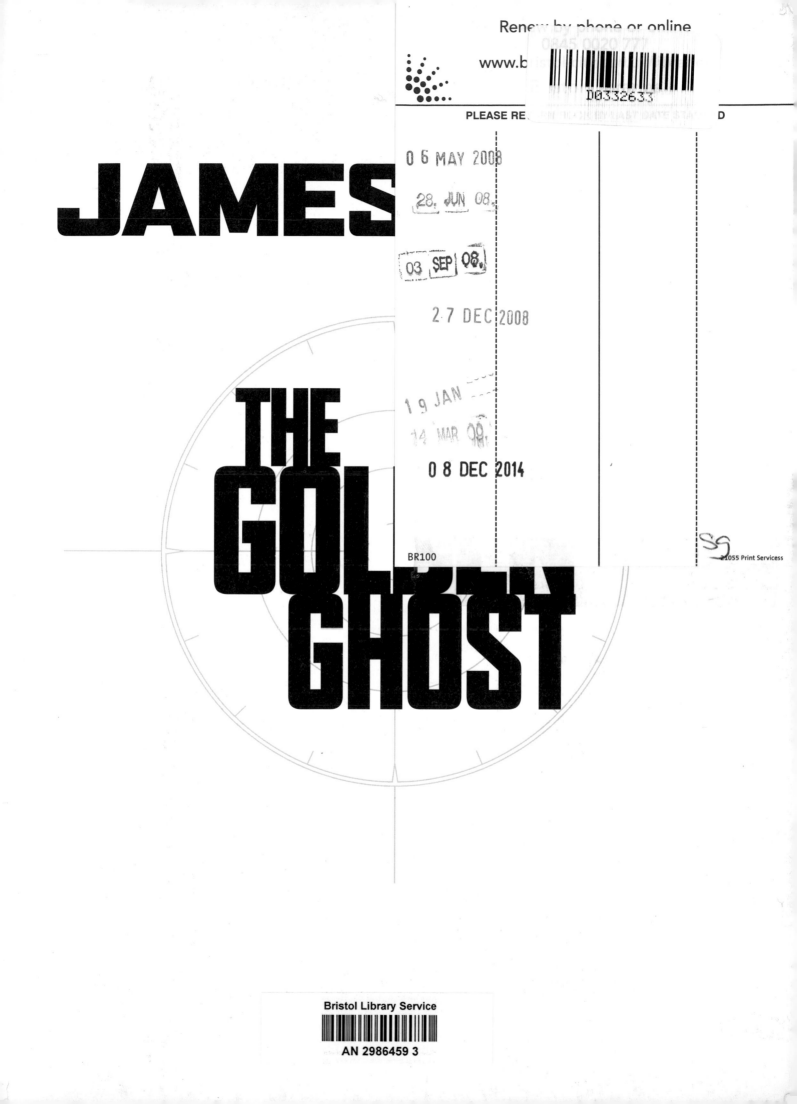

JAMES

THE GOLDEN GHOST

JAMES BOND 007:
THE GOLDEN GHOST

ISBN 1 84576 261 4
ISBN-13: 9781845762612

Published by Titan Books,
a division of Titan Publishing Group Ltd.
144 Southwark St
London SE1 0UP

A CIP catalogue record for this title is available from the British Library

First edition: April 2006
1 3 5 7 9 10 8 6 4 2

Printed in Italy.

Also available from Titan Books:
James Bond: The Man with the Golden Gun (ISBN: 1 84023 690 6)
James Bond: Octopussy (ISBN: 1 84023 743 0)
James Bond: On Her Majesty's Secret Service (ISBN: 1 84023 674 4)
James Bond: Goldfinger (ISBN: 1 84023 908 5)
James Bond: Casino Royale (ISBN: 1 84023 843 7)
James Bond: Dr No (ISBN: 1 84576 089 1)
James Bond: The Spy Who Loved Me (ISBN: 1 84576 174 X)
James Bond: Colonel Sun (ISBN: 1 84576 175 8)

Huge thanks to John Abbott at the Daily Express, everyone at http://www.mi6.co.uk, Peter Knight
at Knight Features, Bryan Krofchok at bondian.com, David Anthony Kraft, Vipul Patel, Zoe Watkins
and Fleur Gooch, without whom this book would never have happened.

Introduction © Richard Kiel 2006
'James Bond's Cars – The Ian Fleming Era' article by David Leigh © David Leigh 2006
'James Bond's Cars – The John Gardner Era' article by James Page © James Page 2006

Picture credits: Richard Kiel photo © EON Productions/Richard Kiel Collection.
SAAB advert and 'Silver Beast' images © SAAB Automobile AB.

What did you think of this book? We love to hear from our readers.
Please email us at: readerfeedback@titanemail.com, or write to us at the above address.
You can also visit us at www.titanbooks.com

Much of the comic strip material used by Titan in this edition is exceedingly rare.
As such, we hope that readers appreciate that the quality of the materials
can be variable.

JAMES BOND 007

THE GOLDEN GHOST

IAN FLEMING

JIM LAWRENCE 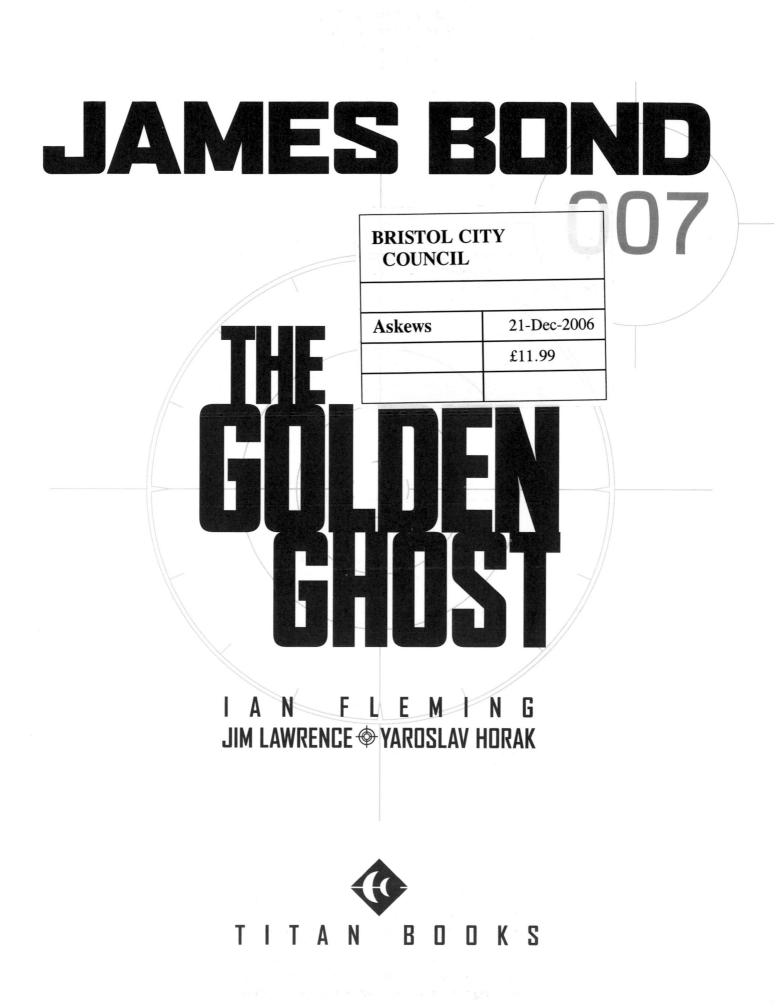 YAROSLAV HORAK

TITAN BOOKS

BITING BACK

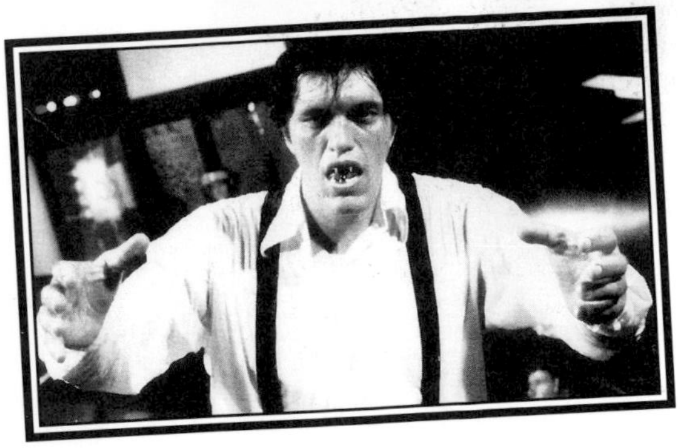

Introduction by RICHARD KIEL

After seventeen years of being a successful working actor in America, I found myself doing my first *James Bond* film, *The Spy Who Loved Me*, and suddenly becoming an overnight international success. I had gone from being one of those actors whose face you knew – but not the name – to becoming known all over the world.

The *Bond* films opened the door to many international commercials, from Shredded Wheat in the UK to a high-speed drill bit commercial in France. I found myself doing Water Pik commercials alongside the people with beautiful teeth – except mine were chrome! I became the spokesperson for Sharp Electronics in Japan, and also did a milk commercial there for Gilco Milk. In America I was doing Mug Root Beer and Mountain Dew commercials for PepsiCo. In between shooting the two *Bond* films, I did feature films in Italy, Taiwan and America, as well as the critically acclaimed *Force 10 from Navarone*, which was filmed in Yugoslavia.

So needless to say I was very fortunate that Cubby Broccoli had a vivid imagination and, with his writers, created a brand new story with brand new characters from Ian Fleming's novel *The Spy Who Loved Me*. In reading and looking at the strips drawn by Horak, I realise now that not only was Jaws an original idea but the whole concept of the story was changed. I quite liked the strip version as it kept me hooked right until the last page; I really admired how the scriptwriter tied the title to Vivienne's final words in the strip, 'I'll never ever forget the spy who loved me.'

As good as the strips and novels were, I can't help but think that Cubby and the writers improved the story in *The Spy Who Loved Me*: by introducing the beautiful Russian spy Anya; incorporating Stromberg and his underwater city; and by bringing yours truly into the picture. Of course, I can't help but be prejudiced.

The film of *Moonraker* is also completely different to Fleming's novel and the strip version. It is no longer a German's revenge against London but, rather, a megalomaniac out to destroy the world so that he can remake it as he wishes. Jaws doesn't exist in the *Moonraker* novel, and I see he replaced Krebs as Drax's chief henchman. Of course, the novel was without space stations or shuttles, but rather the technology of the day with V2-type rockets, etc. Despite the dated technology, I enjoyed the strip version just as much as the film as I grew up during WWII, and as such the story has resonance for me.

After the two movies had been filmed, I was invited along with my wife, Diane, to a very special *James Bond* event in Jamaica. One of the highlights of that experience was being invited to a party at Goldeneye, sitting at Ian Fleming's desk in front of his typewriter and looking out at the view of the ocean. What a peaceful way to write! I have to get up at 5am – before the phones start ringing – in order to achieve that kind of tranquility.

As a writer, I was impressed by the first-person approach used in the *Moonraker* strip. The illustrations by John McLusky bring the characters to life and Bond is very Roger Moore-ish, as he is an extremely handsome and heroic figure. I particularly liked the Gala Brand character and – after all the kissing – the surprise ending where she tells 007 that she has a fiancé and Bond is left somewhat disappointed and lonely.

It was interesting to see how both artists incorporated sex into their strips, through events like shower scenes, and to see how so many of the men – and women – smoked cigarettes. Times have changed and so has James Bond, but it is as enjoyable to read the strips now as it had to have been when they were first published.

So I hope you enjoy this adventure and the others as much as I have; the strips bring a new and different Bond to light, just as the electronic games have. No matter the medium, it seems that we will always enjoy the exploits of James Bond.

Richard Kiel
California, 2006

Richard Kiel is a massive presence in the world of cinema. His 7'2" build has seen him in great demand to play giants, but his movie credits reveal a far more diverse actor, having appeared in *The Nutty Professor*, *The Longest Yard*, *Cannonball Run II*, Hong Kong smash *Aces Go Places III*, *Pale Rider*, *Happy Gilmore* and many more. His TV work includes *The Man From U.N.C.L.E.*, *Land of the Lost*, *Barbary Coast* and *The Wild Wild West*.

JAMES BOND'S CARS

THE IAN FLEMING ERA

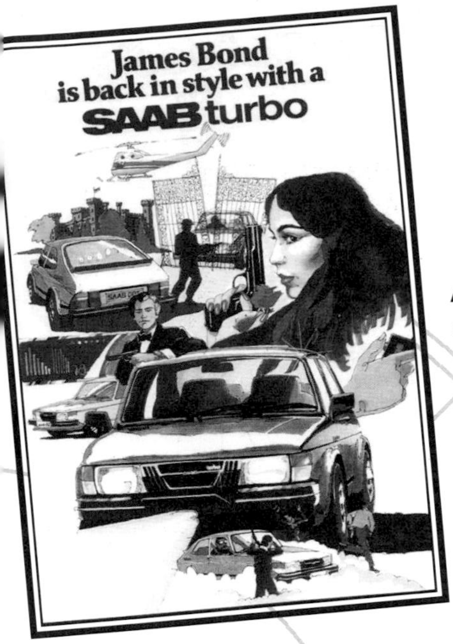
James Bond
is back in style with a
SAAB turbo

Left: A SAAB advert featuring Bond's 'Silver Beast'.

Although James Bond will forever be associated with Aston Martin, the literary character is very much a Bentley man. The first time we meet him in *Casino Royale*, Bond is driving one, and while he is to be found behind the wheel of a secret service Aston Martin in *Goldfinger*, he owns a total of three Bentleys in Ian Fleming's books.

Bond's first Bentley is a 4.5-litre Convertible coupé in battleship-grey with an Amherst Villiers supercharger. This particular model was known as the 'blower Bentley', developed specifically for racing. With a huge supercharger mounted on its nose and large French Marchal headlamps it certainly was distinctive-looking, although rather unsuccessful as a racer.

According to *Casino Royale*, Bond bought the car in 1933 and had kept it in storage during the Second World War. However, in *You Only Live Twice* — published eleven years after *Casino Royale*, in 1964 — we learn that he joined the armed forces in 1941, when he was seventeen. How Bond bought his first car at the age of nine remains one of the great mysteries of the series.

Although the car was badly damaged in *Casino Royale*, repairs were made in time for *Moonraker*. Its reappearance was short-lived, though, as the car was soon wrecked by the release of fourteen tons of newsprint from the back of a lorry. Bond must have cursed his luck as only fifty-four 'blowers' were ever made. At the end of *Moonraker*, Bond purchases his second Bentley, a new 1953 Mark VI with an open touring body. Again, it was battleship-grey with dark blue leather upholstery. After a test-drive, Bond agrees to buy the car on the condition that it is at the Calais ferry terminal the following evening. Quite a different car from the 'blower', Fleming never referred to the Mark VI again and it, too, must remain a mystery.

James Bond's final Bentley first appears in 1961's *Thunderball*. Having bought the wreck of a Mark II Continental with the R-type chassis — its previous owner having written it off against a telegraph pole — he had the chassis straightened and upgraded the engine to the Mark IV. Bond also commissioned Mulliners to remove the original sports saloon body and transform the car into a rather square two-seater convertible; in those days it was common to commission

JAMES BOND'S CARS (IN ORDER OF FIRST APPEARANCE)

• Bentley 4.5-litre:	*Casino Royale* (1953)
	Moonraker (1955)
• Bentley Mark VI:	*Moonraker* (1955)
• Aston Martin DB III:	*Goldfinger* (1959)
• Bentley Mark II Continental:	*Thunderball* (1961)
	On Her Majesty's Secret Service (1963)
• SAAB 900 Turbo:	*Licence Renewed* (1981)
	For Special Services (1982)
	Icebreaker (1983)
• Bentley Mulsanne Turbo:	*Role Of Honour* (1984)
	Nobody Lives For Ever (1986)
	Scorpius (1988)
• SAAB 9000 CD Turbo:	*Never Send Flowers* (1993)
	Seafire (1994)
• Bentley Turbo R:	*The Facts Of Death* (1998)
• Jaguar XK8:	*The Facts Of Death* (1998)
	High Time To Kill (1999)

coachbuilders, such as Mulliners, to design and build car bodies. Again the car is battleship-grey, this time upholstered in black leather. Bond's customisation doesn't end there, though, as the car is fitted with two-inch exhaust pipes and a large, octagonal silver bolt in place of the Bentley winged 'B'.

Two years later, in *On Her Majesty's Secret Service*, we find the same Bentley with a new improvement. Although Rolls-Royce had advised Bond that the crankshaft bearings wouldn't cope with the additional strain, he had fitted an Arnott supercharger controlled by a magnetic clutch. Bond finally gets a chance to try his new toy on the way to Royale-Les-Eaux while racing a girl headed the same way. Activating the supercharger by flipping up a red switch on the dash, he takes the car up to 125 mph — the engine is undamaged and the girl eventually becomes Mrs Bond.

In fact, Ian Fleming had written to Rolls-Royce back in 1957 requesting information for Bond's new car. Wanting a hybrid somewhere between a Bentley Continental and the Ford Thunderbird — Fleming owned two Thunderbirds in succession — he was directed to Mulliners, who had been commissioned for a similar project. When the Mulliners design proved too expensive, the Portuguese owner chose Henri Capron to build the car in France instead. The resulting car is perhaps closer to Fleming's request than the Mulliners design, with a long Thunderbird-like boot.

When not in his own car, 007 is sometimes reduced to borrowing or renting his transport, and on one occasion even driving a company car. When he arrives in Jamaica in *Live And Let Die*, for instance, he drives an unspecified small car brought up from Kingston by Quarrel, a Cayman islander who assists him on his mission. In *Dr No*, again accompanied by Quarrel, he drives the black Sunbeam Alpine belonging to Commander Strangways — whose disappearance Bond is sent to investigate — which also appears in *The Man With The Golden Gun*. And in the short story *From A View To A Kill* he borrows a battered black Peugeot 403, as well as making a brief appearance on the two wheels of a Royal Corps of Signals BSA.

It is in *Goldfinger*, though, that at long last we find Bond in an Aston Martin provided to him by his employer. From Kent he tails Goldfinger's Rolls-Royce across the English Channel and through France into Switzerland. The Aston Martin is fitted with a number of extras by 'Q' branch, although nothing like the ejector seat fitted to the DB5 in the film. Described as a battleship-grey DB III, it is more correctly an Aston Martin DB Mark III - the third incarnation of the DB 2/4 which had a new front grille, based on that of the DB3S racing car. But for all the associations we draw between James Bond and Aston Martin, the car fails to reappear in the books.

Crossing the Atlantic, Bond pours scorn on American cars whenever the opportunity arises. In *The Living Daylights* he compares drab West Berlin's glossy veneer with the chrome trim on American cars and although he appears impressed when Felix Leiter drives an old Cord in *Live And Let Die* — Bond considers it has personality compared to other American cars — he is quick to point out the faults of Leiter's car in *Diamonds Are Forever*. However, this is short-lived: when Leiter floors the throttle of his 'Studillac', Bond is stunned by the acceleration.

Although the Studillac sounds like pure fantasy, Fleming had come across a similar car owned by William Woodward Jr, who he met while staying with mutual friend Ivar Bryce on a research trip for *Diamonds Are Forever*. The Studillac was the product of renowned French designer Raymond Loewy, who was also responsible for such icons as the packaging of Lucky Strike cigarettes, the Greyhound bus and the Shell logo. The car consisted of a Studebaker with modified suspension and a powerful Cadillac engine. According to Andrew Lycett's biography, *Ian Fleming*, Fleming was pulled over by the local sheriff while test-driving Woodward's car; he was let off when the sheriff could barely understand his upper-crust English accent.

Ian Fleming's whole attitude to American cars was very different to that of his creation and when he received £6,000 for the film rights to *Casino Royale*, he immediately bought a Ford Thunderbird. He loved the car so much that he bought another to replace it and appears to have been so obsessed by it that that his wife even nicknamed Fleming 'Thunderbird'. Bond drives a hired Thunderbird in *The Spy Who Loved Me* — actually, the only reason that he is involved in the story at all is because of a puncture — and it is surely no coincidence that Fleming named the hotel in *The Man With The Golden Gun* after the car.

Nevertheless, after his second Thunderbird, Fleming decided a change was called for. His final car was a black Studebaker Avanti, a fibreglass-bodied model also designed by Raymond Loewy.

David Leigh

Remote Starter unit
A four-speaker self-seeking stereo
(Electrically heated front seats)
Air conditioning
CO_2 gas-operated compartment for Oxygen kit (under passenger seat)
Black leather upholstery
Bullet proof glass
Cruise control
Infra-red goggles (simulated)
(Electric wing mirrors)
SAAB 007
Tear gas (4ducts)
CO_2 gas-operated compartment for gun (indashboard)
Specially developed engine
Halogen lamp (beneath moving numberplate)

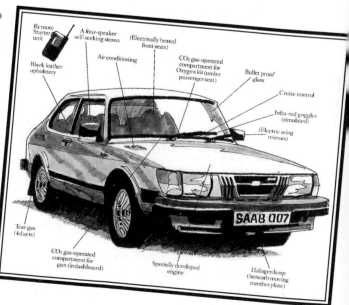

Right: SAAB's design for the real-life 'Silver Beast', a concept car produced in 1982.

THE JOHN GARDNER ERA

John Gardner took over the 007 literary torch in 1981 after a long hiatus since Kingsley Amis' one *Bond* novel, *Colonel Sun*. Gardner continued the legacy by producing an astounding fourteen original novels and two movie novelisations. In his first 007 adventure in 1981, *Licence Renewed*, he let Bond venture away from his traditional 'Q' branch vehicles to a new brand — the SAAB 900 Turbo 'Silver Beast' — a moniker given to the souped-up car by the author's son.

The SAAB 900 Turbo saw Bond depart from his earlier Bentleys and Aston Martins, as well as having his own car personally modified by the real-life multinational security firm Communication Control System, rather than the fictional 'Q' Branch.

Launched in 1980, the 900 Turbo was seen at the time as a car which broke new ground, offering the public high-end performance and practicality. SAAB's prestige and automotive credibility were raised to levels shared by other Bond thoroughbreds — Bentley, Aston Martin and Lotus.

Following *Licence Renewed*, which was published to great critical acclaim, the new 'Silver Beast' went on to see action again in two more Gardner titles in 1982's *For Special Services* and 1983's *Icebreaker*.

In a recent interview, John Gardner talked about his use of the SAAB 900 Turbo in his Bond novels, and why he chose the brand over 007's previous vehicles: 'The Bentley was ridiculous. In many ways so was the Aston Martin, because I regarded it as a fairly flash motor car. I had to get away from that, and I liked the SAAB, it was a very safe motor car indeed. You could clock up the miles on it, you could clock up the speeds on it. I had a SAAB right up until I stopped driving two years ago, and loved them.'

When Gardner was penning his fourth 007 novel in 1983, his contact at SAAB left the company for Bentley, and promptly invited the author to try out their latest model — the Mulsanne Turbo. After a convincing test drive, Gardner switched Bond's car of choice back to Bentley, with no mention of the 'Silver Beast' in *Role Of Honour* (1984). As per Bentley's request, no special modifications were made to the Mulsanne Turbo other than the installation of a long-range telephone.

The SAAB would return, though, with Gardner putting Bond back behind the wheel of a 900 Turbo in 1986's *Nobody Lives For Ever*, when 007 stumbles across his familiar ride at a rental car office for his undercover trip near Salzburg. Bond also rents a SAAB in the subsequent novel *No Deals, Mr. Bond* (1987) whilst on a mission in Dublin. Four years and four novels later, his boss, M, gets behind the wheel of a SAAB 9000 CD in *The Man From Barbarossa* (1991), an endorsement that must have rubbed off on 007, as Bond uses the same model in *Never Send Flowers* (1993) and Gardner's penultimate novel, *Seafire* (1994).

In 1982, SAAB specially created a car based on Gardner's depiction of Bond's customised 'Silver Beast' the previous year in *Licence Renewed*. The car was a fully working version of its fictional cousin, including a specially developed turbo-charged engine with water injection, raising the power to 240bhp from 2000cc and providing acceleration of 0-60mph in less than seven seconds.

James Page

007'S SAAB 900 TURBO 'SILVER BEAST' MODIFICATIONS

- Top speed in excess of 170mph
- Four external tear gas outlets
- CO_2 gas-operated, under-seat compartment containing oxygen mask
- Armour plating and bulletproof glass
- Gas filter in cabin to prevent external attack
- Dunlop Denovo tyres: self-resealing, puncture- and split-proof
- Reinforced stressed steel ramming bumpers
- V L 22H countersurveillance receiver
- Pen alarm
- Small ultrasonic transmitter to protect the SAAB from sabotage
- Hidden compartments within the dashboard, containing:
  - Unauthorised heavy Ruger Super Blackhawk
  - Magnum .45
  - Unauthorised Browning hand gun
  - TH70 Nitefinders goggles for lightless driving
- Halon 12 fire extinguishing system and fireproofing
- Heads-up digital instrument display
- Side gun port
- Black leather upholstery
- Remote starter unit
- Cruise control
- Air conditioning
- Self-seeking sound system
- Radio telephone
- Rotating license plates
- Two front halogen lamps
- High-power aircraft headlight concealed behind front license plate

THE GOLDEN GHOST

At the beginning of this mission, Moneypenny gets a welcome break from the office when Bond asks her to be his observer, but her involvement is cut short when S.P.E.C.T.R.E's plans go awry.

American writer Jim Lawrence seems to struggle with early attempts at establishing Bond's British accent, transforming him into a London cockney with a rash of 'luvs' and 'mates'. 007's regular alias Mike Hazard becomes 'Mark Hazard', who is employed initially by Transworld Consortium and later Transworld News.

Some sequences in this adventure may seem familiar to *Bond* fans. When 007 is to be made an example of in front of his fellow hostages, the villain opts to tow him through shark-infested waters, in a very similar sequence to the keel-hauling in *Live And Let Die*. The final showdown between Bond and the villain in the ship's galley is akin to the kitchen sequence from the movie *The Living Daylights*, and is equally brutal in its use of culinary equipment!

Finally, take a second look at the South Atlantic island where the Golden Ghost is anchored — it is visually similar to Tracy Island, from the late '60s hit television series *Thunderbirds*!

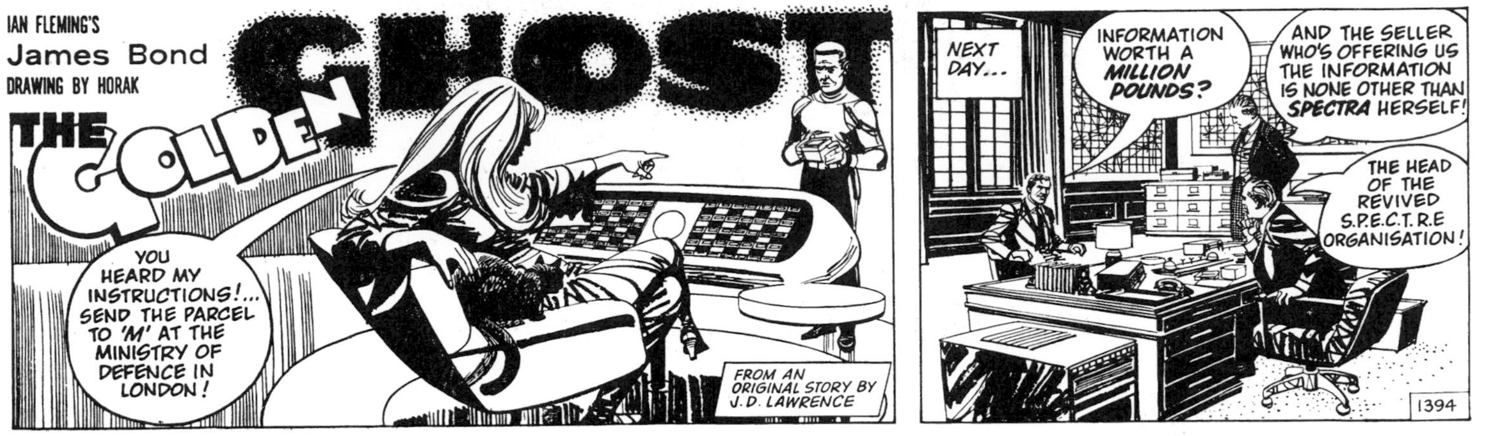
IAN FLEMING'S
James Bond
DRAWING BY HORAK
THE GOLDEN GHOST
YOU HEARD MY INSTRUCTIONS!... SEND THE PARCEL TO 'M' AT THE MINISTRY OF DEFENCE IN LONDON!
FROM AN ORIGINAL STORY BY J.D. LAWRENCE
NEXT DAY...
INFORMATION WORTH A MILLION POUNDS?
AND THE SELLER WHO'S OFFERING US THE INFORMATION IS NONE OTHER THAN SPECTRA HERSELF!
THE HEAD OF THE REVIVED S.P.E.C.T.R.E ORGANISATION!
1394

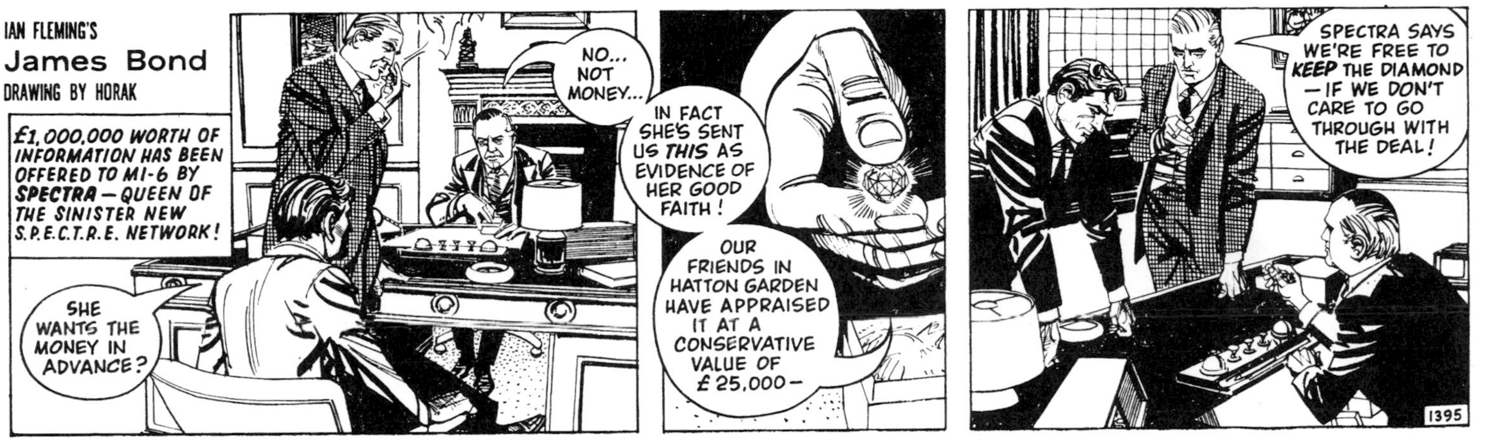
IAN FLEMING'S
James Bond
DRAWING BY HORAK
£1,000,000 WORTH OF INFORMATION HAS BEEN OFFERED TO MI-6 BY SPECTRA — QUEEN OF THE SINISTER NEW S.P.E.C.T.R.E. NETWORK!
SHE WANTS THE MONEY IN ADVANCE?
NO... NOT MONEY...
IN FACT SHE'S SENT US THIS AS EVIDENCE OF HER GOOD FAITH!
OUR FRIENDS IN HATTON GARDEN HAVE APPRAISED IT AT A CONSERVATIVE VALUE OF £25,000 —
SPECTRA SAYS WE'RE FREE TO KEEP THE DIAMOND — IF WE DON'T CARE TO GO THROUGH WITH THE DEAL!
1395

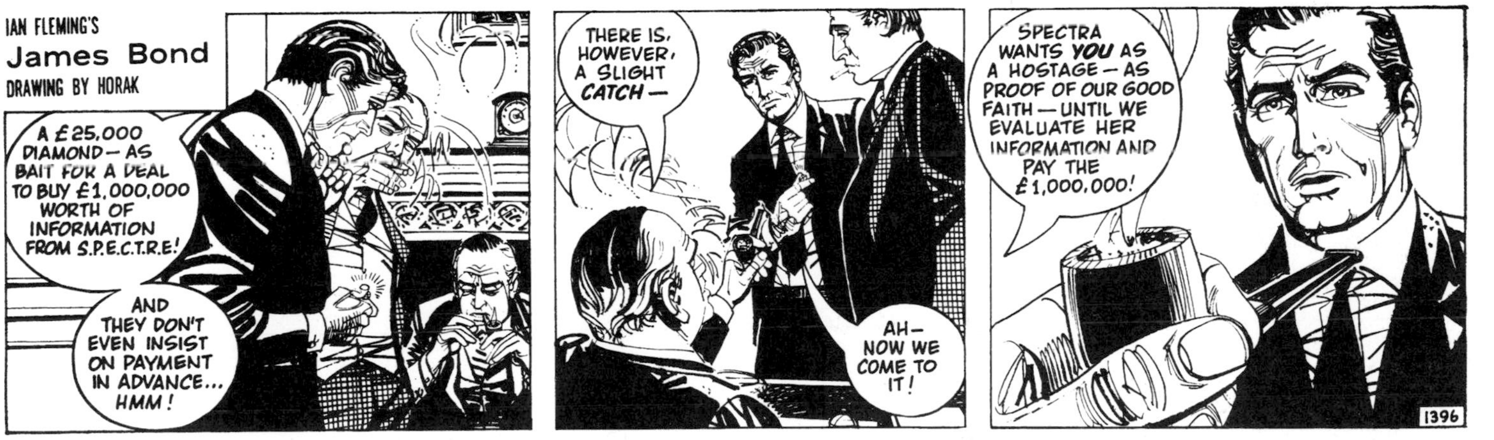
IAN FLEMING'S
James Bond
DRAWING BY HORAK
A £25,000 DIAMOND — AS BAIT FOR A DEAL TO BUY £1,000,000 WORTH OF INFORMATION FROM S.P.E.C.T.R.E!
AND THEY DON'T EVEN INSIST ON PAYMENT IN ADVANCE... HMM!
THERE IS, HOWEVER, A SLIGHT CATCH —
AH — NOW WE COME TO IT!
SPECTRA WANTS YOU AS A HOSTAGE — AS PROOF OF OUR GOOD FAITH — UNTIL WE EVALUATE HER INFORMATION AND PAY THE £1,000,000!
1396

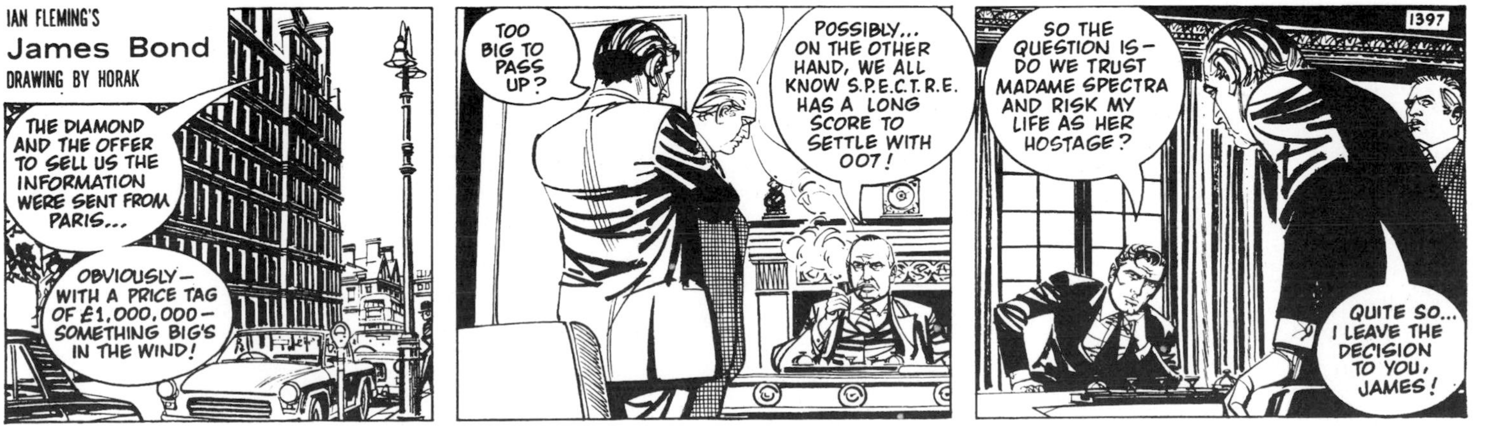
IAN FLEMING'S
James Bond
DRAWING BY HORAK
THE DIAMOND AND THE OFFER TO SELL US THE INFORMATION WERE SENT FROM PARIS...
OBVIOUSLY — WITH A PRICE TAG OF £1,000,000 — SOMETHING BIG'S IN THE WIND!
TOO BIG TO PASS UP?
POSSIBLY... ON THE OTHER HAND, WE ALL KNOW S.P.E.C.T.R.E. HAS A LONG SCORE TO SETTLE WITH 007!
1397
SO THE QUESTION IS — DO WE TRUST MADAME SPECTRA AND RISK MY LIFE AS HER HOSTAGE?
QUITE SO... I LEAVE THE DECISION TO YOU, JAMES!

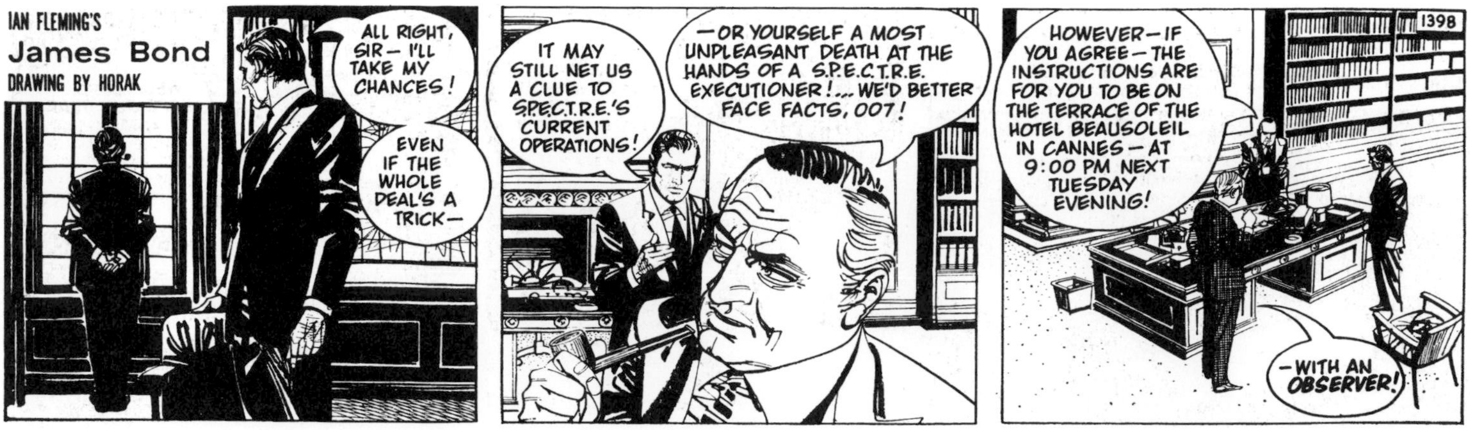
IAN FLEMING'S
James Bond
DRAWING BY HORAK
ALL RIGHT, SIR— I'LL TAKE MY CHANCES!
EVEN IF THE WHOLE DEAL'S A TRICK—
IT MAY STILL NET US A CLUE TO S.P.E.C.T.R.E.'S CURRENT OPERATIONS!
—OR YOURSELF A MOST UNPLEASANT DEATH AT THE HANDS OF A S.P.E.C.T.R.E. EXECUTIONER!... WE'D BETTER FACE FACTS, 007!
1398
HOWEVER—IF YOU AGREE—THE INSTRUCTIONS ARE FOR YOU TO BE ON THE TERRACE OF THE HOTEL BEAUSOLEIL IN CANNES—AT 9:00 PM NEXT TUESDAY EVENING!
—WITH AN OBSERVER!

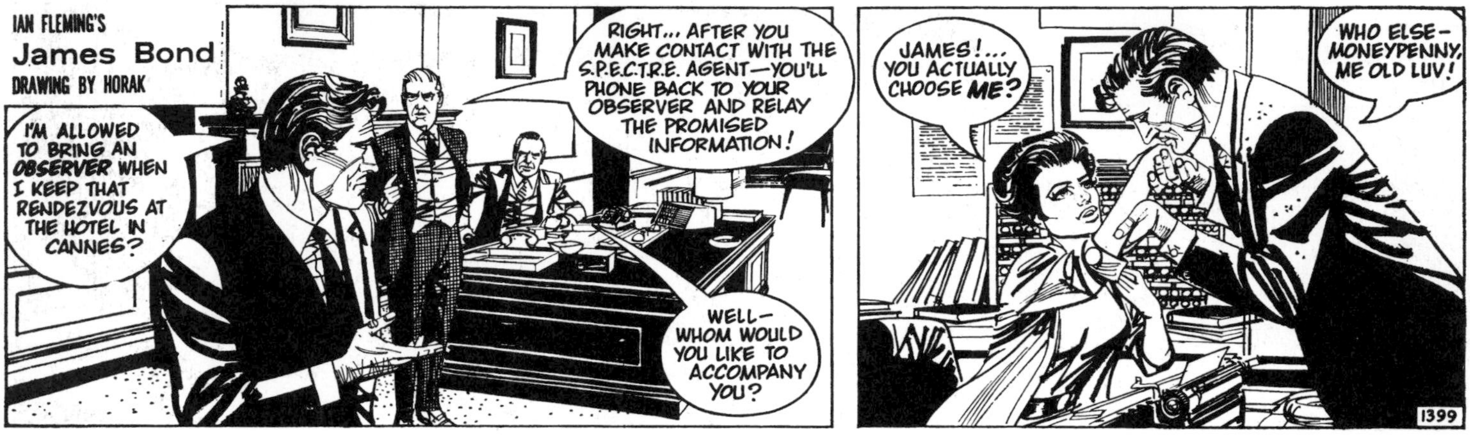
IAN FLEMING'S
James Bond
DRAWING BY HORAK
I'M ALLOWED TO BRING AN OBSERVER WHEN I KEEP THAT RENDEZVOUS AT THE HOTEL IN CANNES?
RIGHT... AFTER YOU MAKE CONTACT WITH THE S.P.E.C.T.R.E. AGENT—YOU'LL PHONE BACK TO YOUR OBSERVER AND RELAY THE PROMISED INFORMATION!
WELL— WHOM WOULD YOU LIKE TO ACCOMPANY YOU?
JAMES!... YOU ACTUALLY CHOOSE ME?
WHO ELSE— MONEYPENNY, ME OLD LUV!
1399

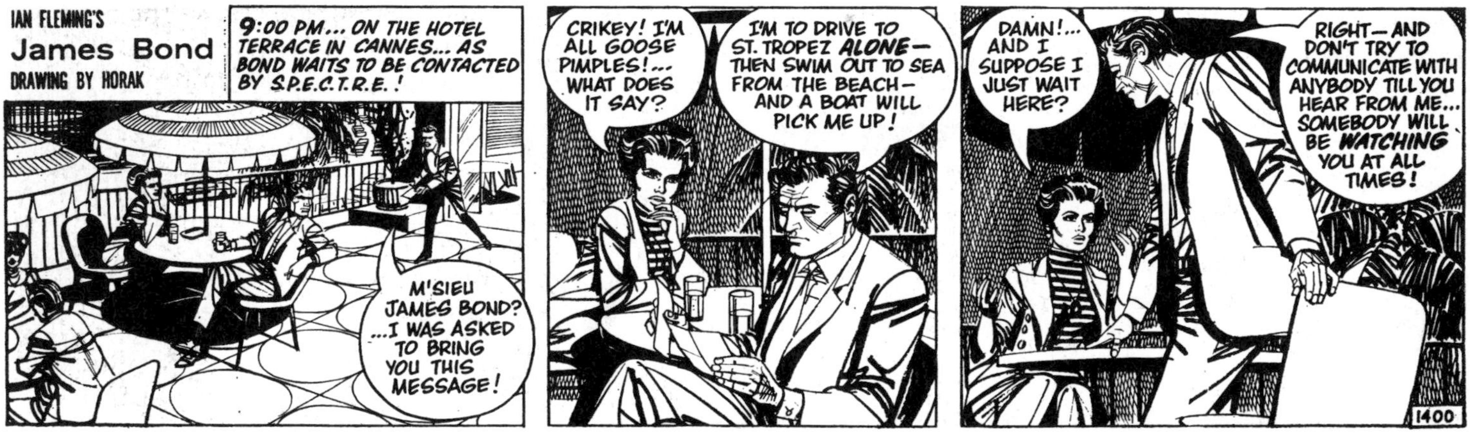
IAN FLEMING'S
James Bond
DRAWING BY HORAK
9:00 PM... ON THE HOTEL TERRACE IN CANNES... AS BOND WAITS TO BE CONTACTED BY S.P.E.C.T.R.E.!
M'SIEU JAMES BOND? ...I WAS ASKED TO BRING YOU THIS MESSAGE!
CRIKEY! I'M ALL GOOSE PIMPLES!... WHAT DOES IT SAY?
I'M TO DRIVE TO ST. TROPEZ ALONE— THEN SWIM OUT TO SEA FROM THE BEACH— AND A BOAT WILL PICK ME UP!
DAMN!... AND I SUPPOSE I JUST WAIT HERE?
RIGHT— AND DON'T TRY TO COMMUNICATE WITH ANYBODY TILL YOU HEAR FROM ME... SOMEBODY WILL BE WATCHING YOU AT ALL TIMES!
1400

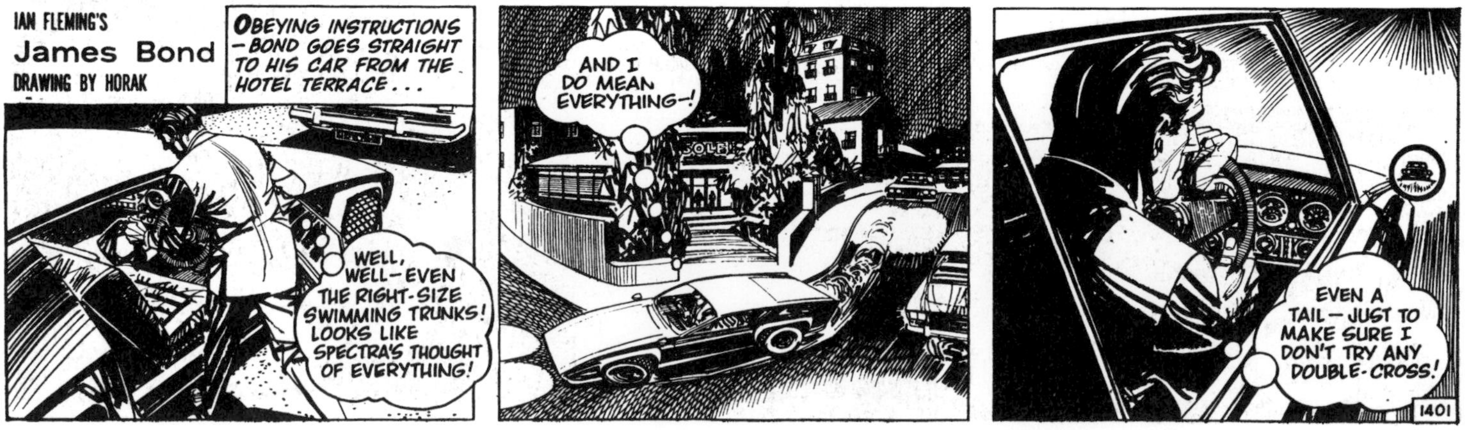
IAN FLEMING'S
James Bond
DRAWING BY HORAK
OBEYING INSTRUCTIONS —BOND GOES STRAIGHT TO HIS CAR FROM THE HOTEL TERRACE...
WELL, WELL—EVEN THE RIGHT-SIZE SWIMMING TRUNKS! LOOKS LIKE SPECTRA'S THOUGHT OF EVERYTHING!
AND I DO MEAN EVERYTHING—!
EVEN A TAIL— JUST TO MAKE SURE I DON'T TRY ANY DOUBLE-CROSS!
1401

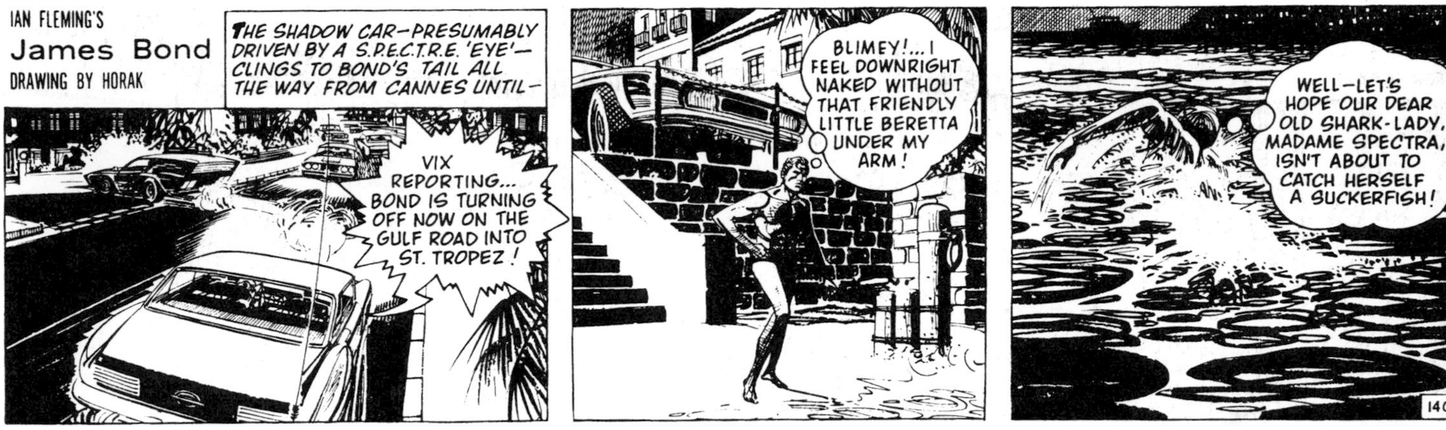
IAN FLEMING'S
James Bond
DRAWING BY HORAK
THE SHADOW CAR—PRESUMABLY DRIVEN BY A S.P.E.C.T.R.E. 'EYE'—CLINGS TO BOND'S TAIL ALL THE WAY FROM CANNES UNTIL—
VIX REPORTING... BOND IS TURNING OFF NOW ON THE GULF ROAD INTO ST. TROPEZ!
BLIMEY!... I FEEL DOWNRIGHT NAKED WITHOUT THAT FRIENDLY LITTLE BERETTA UNDER MY ARM!
WELL—LET'S HOPE OUR DEAR OLD SHARK-LADY, MADAME SPECTRA, ISN'T ABOUT TO CATCH HERSELF A SUCKERFISH!
1402

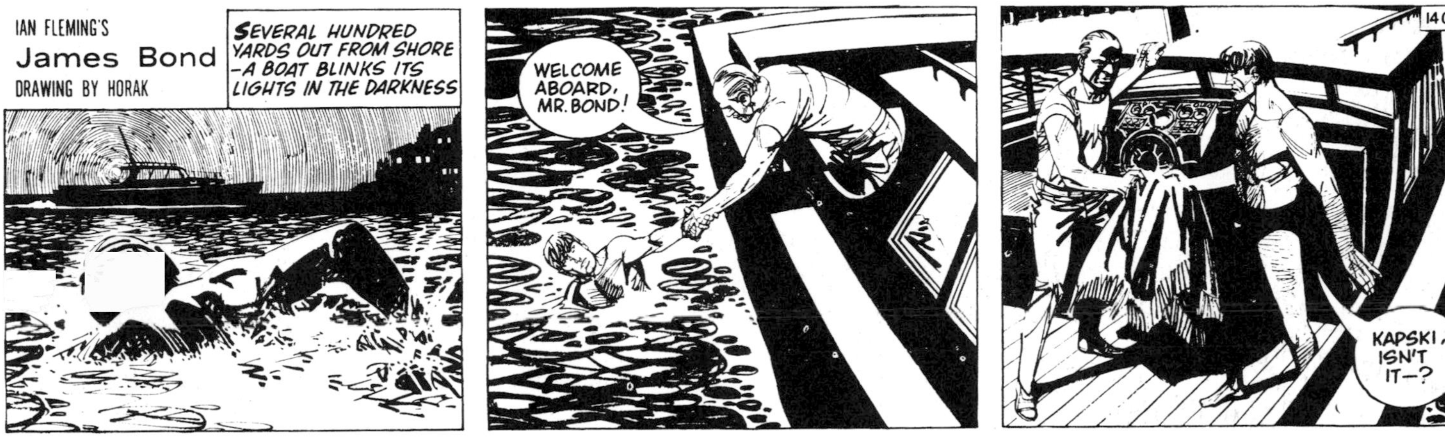
IAN FLEMING'S
James Bond
DRAWING BY HORAK
SEVERAL HUNDRED YARDS OUT FROM SHORE —A BOAT BLINKS ITS LIGHTS IN THE DARKNESS
WELCOME ABOARD, MR. BOND!
1403
KAPSKI, ISN'T IT—?

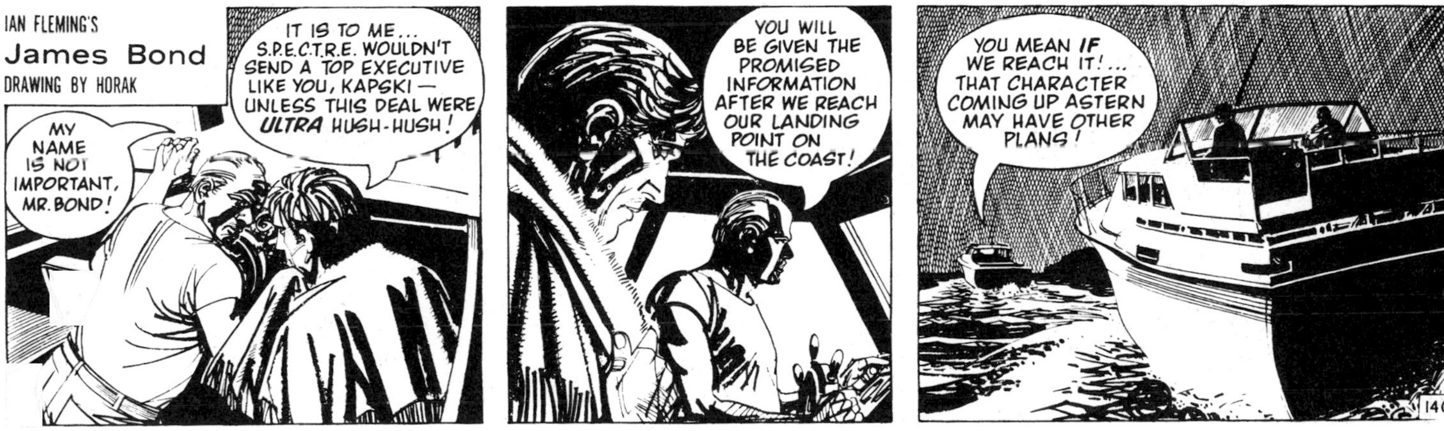
IAN FLEMING'S
James Bond
DRAWING BY HORAK
MY NAME IS NOT IMPORTANT, MR. BOND!
IT IS TO ME... S.P.E.C.T.R.E. WOULDN'T SEND A TOP EXECUTIVE LIKE YOU, KAPSKI — UNLESS THIS DEAL WERE ULTRA HUSH-HUSH!
YOU WILL BE GIVEN THE PROMISED INFORMATION AFTER WE REACH OUR LANDING POINT ON THE COAST!
YOU MEAN IF WE REACH IT!... THAT CHARACTER COMING UP ASTERN MAY HAVE OTHER PLANS!
1404

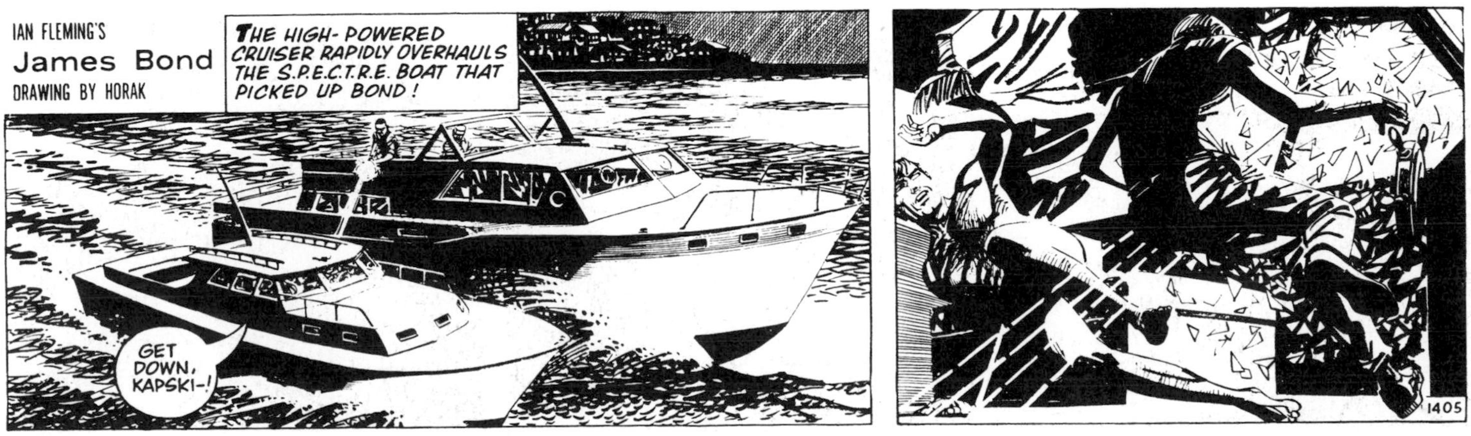
IAN FLEMING'S
James Bond
DRAWING BY HORAK
THE HIGH-POWERED CRUISER RAPIDLY OVERHAULS THE S.P.E.C.T.R.E. BOAT THAT PICKED UP BOND!
GET DOWN, KAPSKI-!
1405

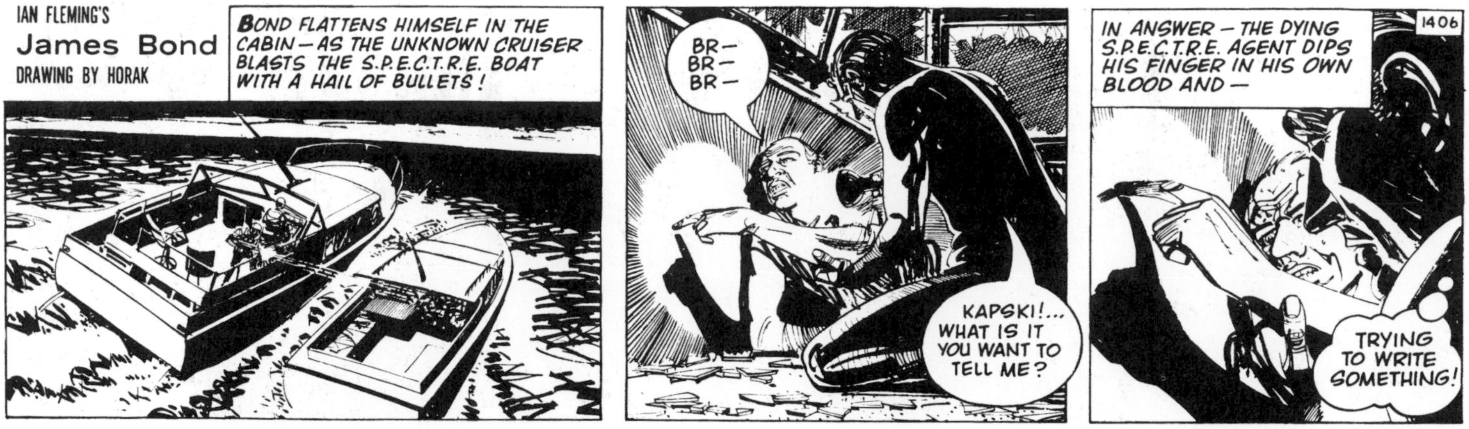
IAN FLEMING'S
James Bond
DRAWING BY HORAK
BOND FLATTENS HIMSELF IN THE CABIN—AS THE UNKNOWN CRUISER BLASTS THE S.P.E.C.T.R.E. BOAT WITH A HAIL OF BULLETS!
BR—
BR—
BR—
KAPSKI!... WHAT IS IT YOU WANT TO TELL ME?
1406
IN ANSWER—THE DYING S.P.E.C.T.R.E. AGENT DIPS HIS FINGER IN HIS OWN BLOOD AND—
TRYING TO WRITE SOMETHING!

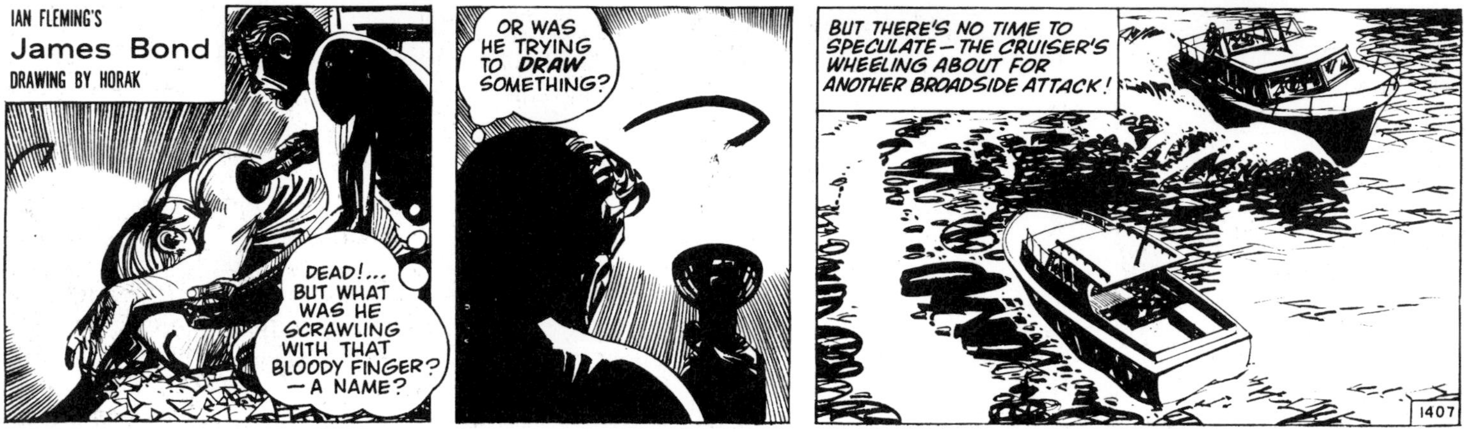
IAN FLEMING'S
James Bond
DRAWING BY HORAK
DEAD!... BUT WHAT WAS HE SCRAWLING WITH THAT BLOODY FINGER? —A NAME?
OR WAS HE TRYING TO DRAW SOMETHING?
BUT THERE'S NO TIME TO SPECULATE—THE CRUISER'S WHEELING ABOUT FOR ANOTHER BROADSIDE ATTACK!
1407

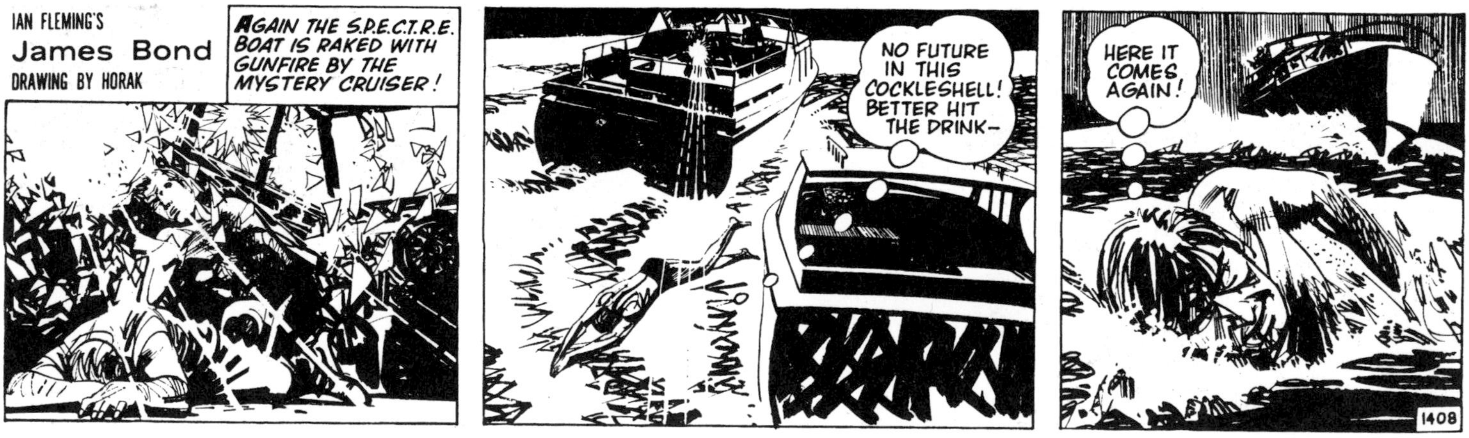
IAN FLEMING'S
James Bond
DRAWING BY HORAK
AGAIN THE S.P.E.C.T.R.E. BOAT IS RAKED WITH GUNFIRE BY THE MYSTERY CRUISER!
NO FUTURE IN THIS COCKLESHELL! BETTER HIT THE DRINK—
HERE IT COMES AGAIN!
1408

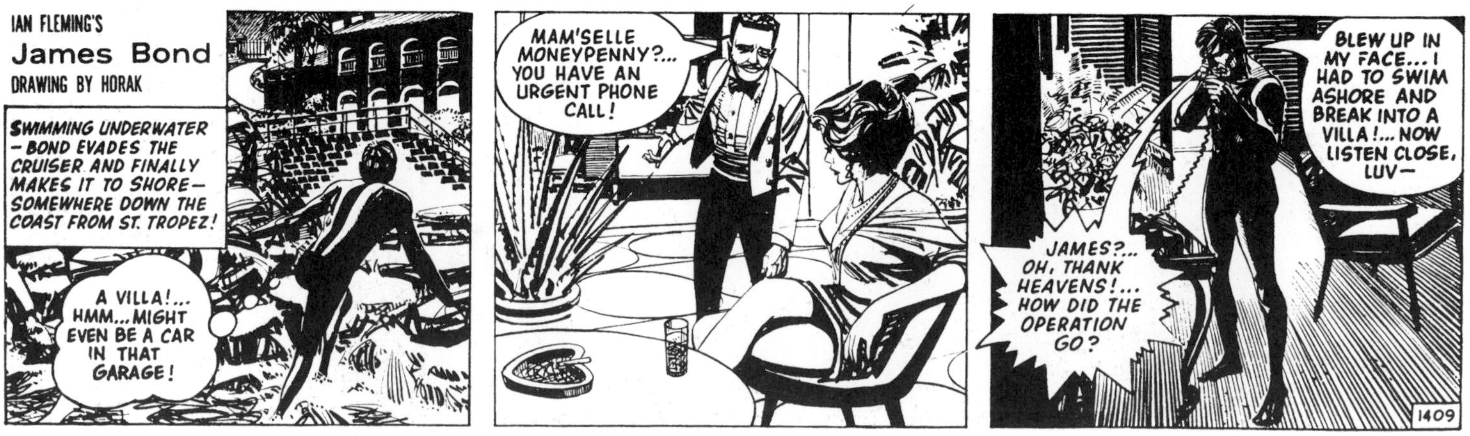
IAN FLEMING'S
James Bond
DRAWING BY HORAK
SWIMMING UNDERWATER—BOND EVADES THE CRUISER AND FINALLY MAKES IT TO SHORE—SOMEWHERE DOWN THE COAST FROM ST. TROPEZ!
A VILLA!... HMM... MIGHT EVEN BE A CAR IN THAT GARAGE!
MAM'SELLE MONEYPENNY?... YOU HAVE AN URGENT PHONE CALL!
JAMES?... OH, THANK HEAVENS!... HOW DID THE OPERATION GO?
BLEW UP IN MY FACE... I HAD TO SWIM ASHORE AND BREAK INTO A VILLA!... NOW LISTEN CLOSE, LUV—
1409

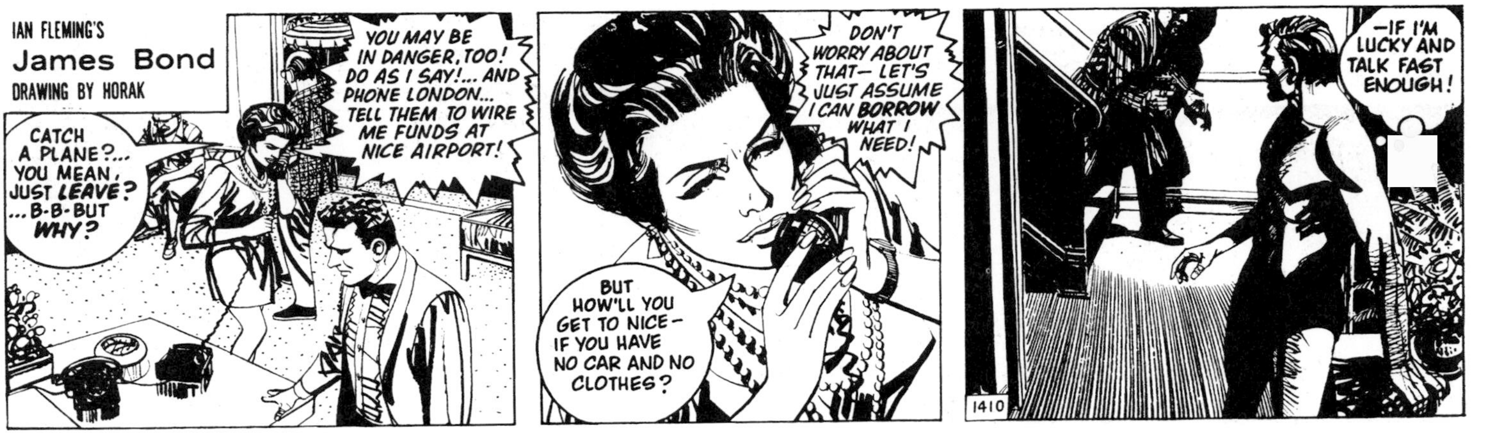
IAN FLEMING'S
James Bond
DRAWING BY HORAK
CATCH A PLANE?... YOU MEAN, JUST LEAVE? ...B-B-BUT WHY?
YOU MAY BE IN DANGER, TOO! DO AS I SAY!... AND PHONE LONDON... TELL THEM TO WIRE ME FUNDS AT NICE AIRPORT!
BUT HOW'LL YOU GET TO NICE— IF YOU HAVE NO CAR AND NO CLOTHES?
DON'T WORRY ABOUT THAT— LET'S JUST ASSUME I CAN BORROW WHAT I NEED!
—IF I'M LUCKY AND TALK FAST ENOUGH!
1410

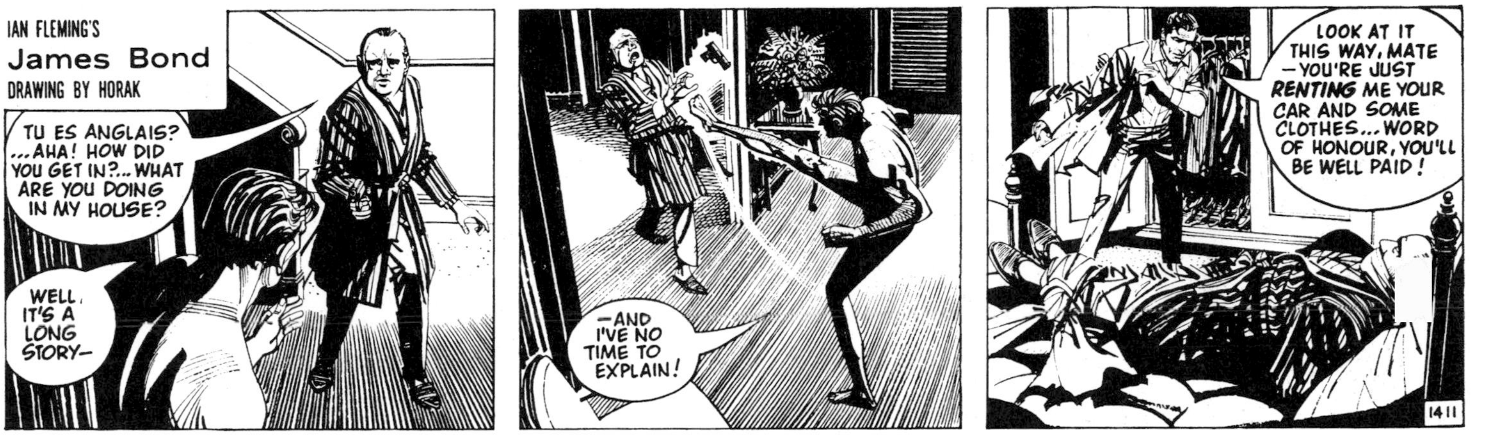
IAN FLEMING'S
James Bond
DRAWING BY HORAK
TU ES ANGLAIS? ...AHA! HOW DID YOU GET IN?... WHAT ARE YOU DOING IN MY HOUSE?
WELL, IT'S A LONG STORY—
—AND I'VE NO TIME TO EXPLAIN!
LOOK AT IT THIS WAY, MATE —YOU'RE JUST RENTING ME YOUR CAR AND SOME CLOTHES... WORD OF HONOUR, YOU'LL BE WELL PAID!
1411

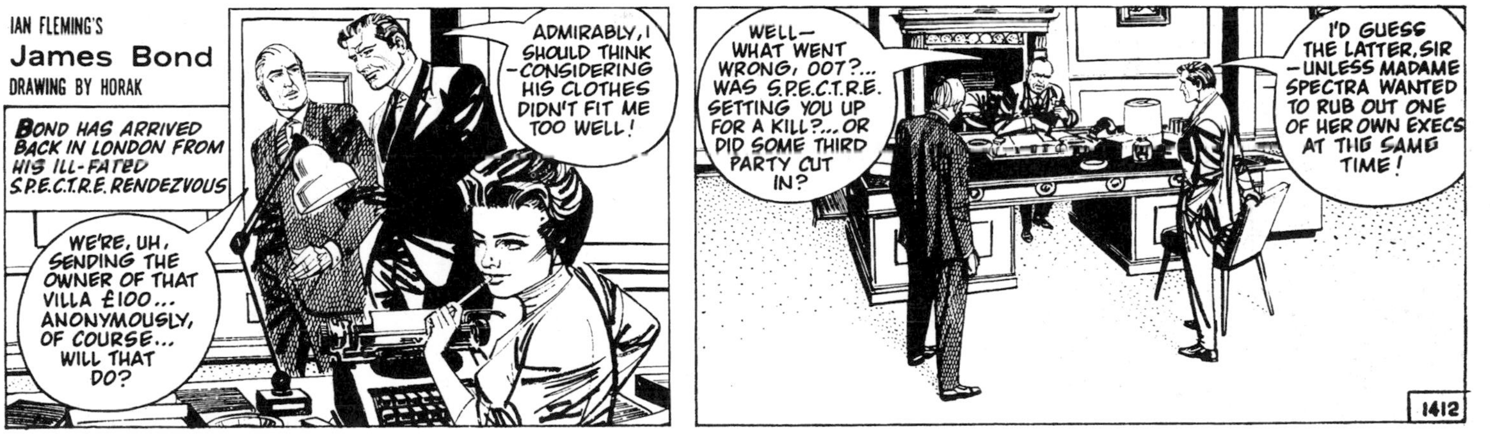
IAN FLEMING'S
James Bond
DRAWING BY HORAK
BOND HAS ARRIVED BACK IN LONDON FROM HIS ILL-FATED S.P.E.C.T.R.E. RENDEZVOUS
WE'RE, UH, SENDING THE OWNER OF THAT VILLA £100... ANONYMOUSLY, OF COURSE... WILL THAT DO?
ADMIRABLY, I SHOULD THINK —CONSIDERING HIS CLOTHES DIDN'T FIT ME TOO WELL!
WELL— WHAT WENT WRONG, 007?... WAS S.P.E.C.T.R.E. SETTING YOU UP FOR A KILL?... OR DID SOME THIRD PARTY CUT IN?
I'D GUESS THE LATTER, SIR —UNLESS MADAME SPECTRA WANTED TO RUB OUT ONE OF HER OWN EXECS AT THE SAME TIME!
1412

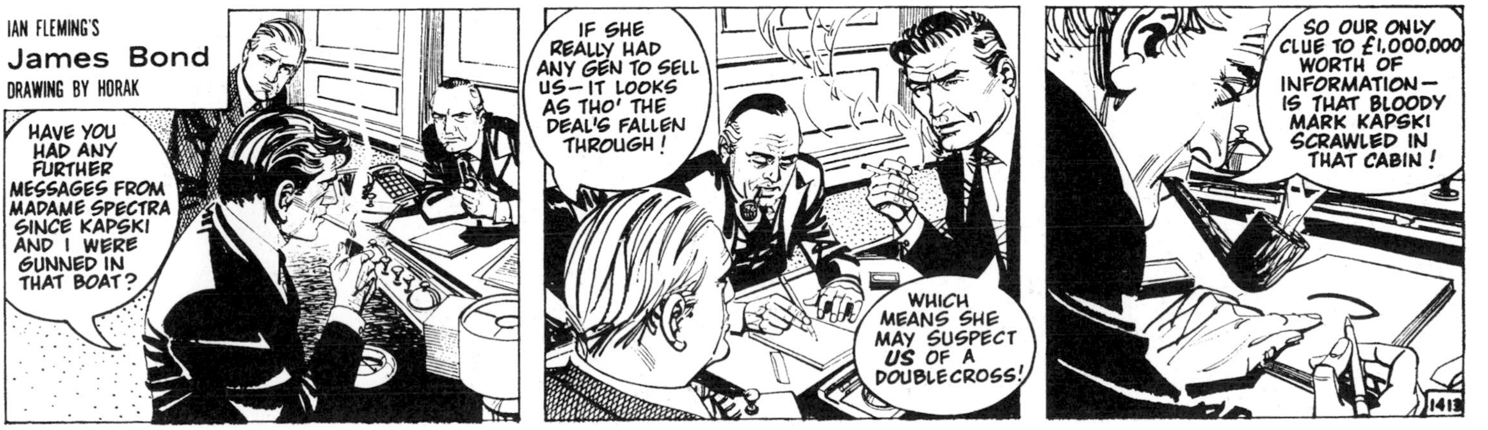
IAN FLEMING'S
James Bond
DRAWING BY HORAK
HAVE YOU HAD ANY FURTHER MESSAGES FROM MADAME SPECTRA SINCE KAPSKI AND I WERE GUNNED IN THAT BOAT?
IF SHE REALLY HAD ANY GEN TO SELL US—IT LOOKS AS THO' THE DEAL'S FALLEN THROUGH!
WHICH MEANS SHE MAY SUSPECT US OF A DOUBLECROSS!
SO OUR ONLY CLUE TO £1,000,000 WORTH OF INFORMATION— IS THAT BLOODY MARK KAPSKI SCRAWLED IN THAT CABIN!
1413

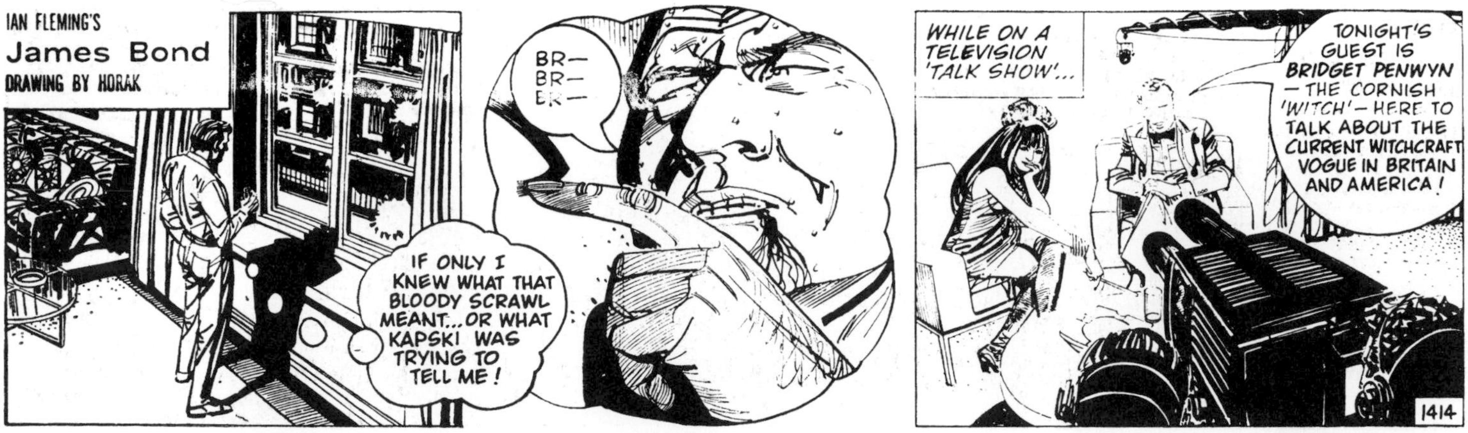
IAN FLEMING'S
James Bond
DRAWING BY HORAK
BR—
BR—
BR—
IF ONLY I KNEW WHAT THAT BLOODY SCRAWL MEANT...OR WHAT KAPSKI WAS TRYING TO TELL ME!
WHILE ON A TELEVISION 'TALK SHOW'...
TONIGHT'S GUEST IS BRIDGET PENWYN — THE CORNISH 'WITCH' — HERE TO TALK ABOUT THE CURRENT WITCHCRAFT VOGUE IN BRITAIN AND AMERICA!
1414

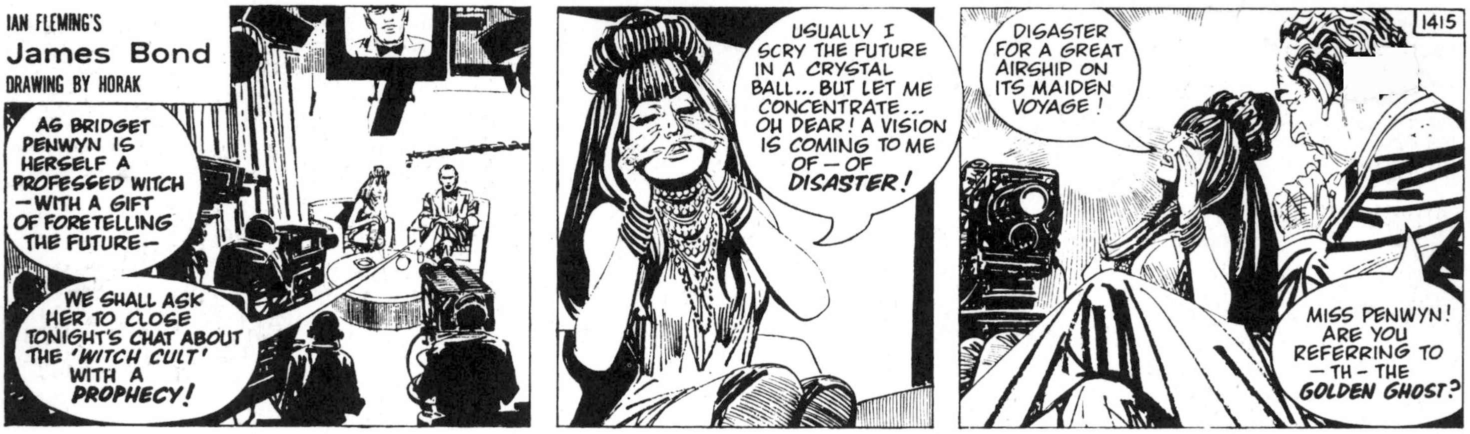
IAN FLEMING'S
James Bond
DRAWING BY HORAK
AS BRIDGET PENWYN IS HERSELF A PROFESSED WITCH — WITH A GIFT OF FORETELLING THE FUTURE—
WE SHALL ASK HER TO CLOSE TONIGHT'S CHAT ABOUT THE 'WITCH CULT' WITH A PROPHECY!
USUALLY I SCRY THE FUTURE IN A CRYSTAL BALL... BUT LET ME CONCENTRATE... OH DEAR! A VISION IS COMING TO ME OF — OF DISASTER!
1415
DISASTER FOR A GREAT AIRSHIP ON ITS MAIDEN VOYAGE!
MISS PENWYN! ARE YOU REFERRING TO — TH — THE GOLDEN GHOST?

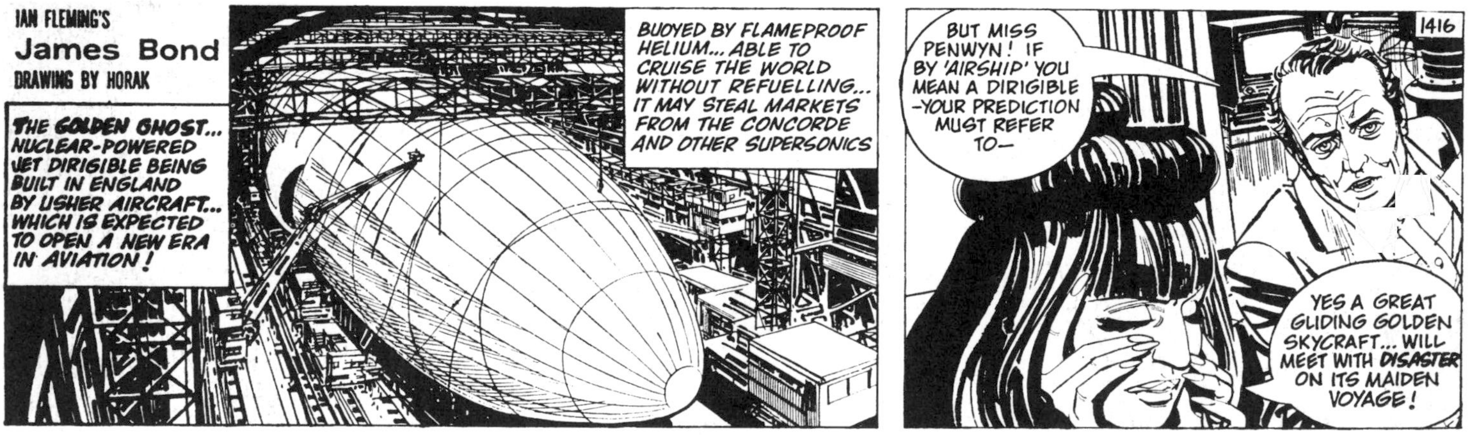
IAN FLEMING'S
James Bond
DRAWING BY HORAK
THE GOLDEN GHOST... NUCLEAR-POWERED JET DIRIGIBLE BEING BUILT IN ENGLAND BY USHER AIRCRAFT... WHICH IS EXPECTED TO OPEN A NEW ERA IN AVIATION!
BUOYED BY FLAMEPROOF HELIUM... ABLE TO CRUISE THE WORLD WITHOUT REFUELLING... IT MAY STEAL MARKETS FROM THE CONCORDE AND OTHER SUPERSONICS
1416
BUT MISS PENWYN! IF BY 'AIRSHIP' YOU MEAN A DIRIGIBLE — YOUR PREDICTION MUST REFER TO—
YES A GREAT GLIDING GOLDEN SKYCRAFT... WILL MEET WITH DISASTER ON ITS MAIDEN VOYAGE!

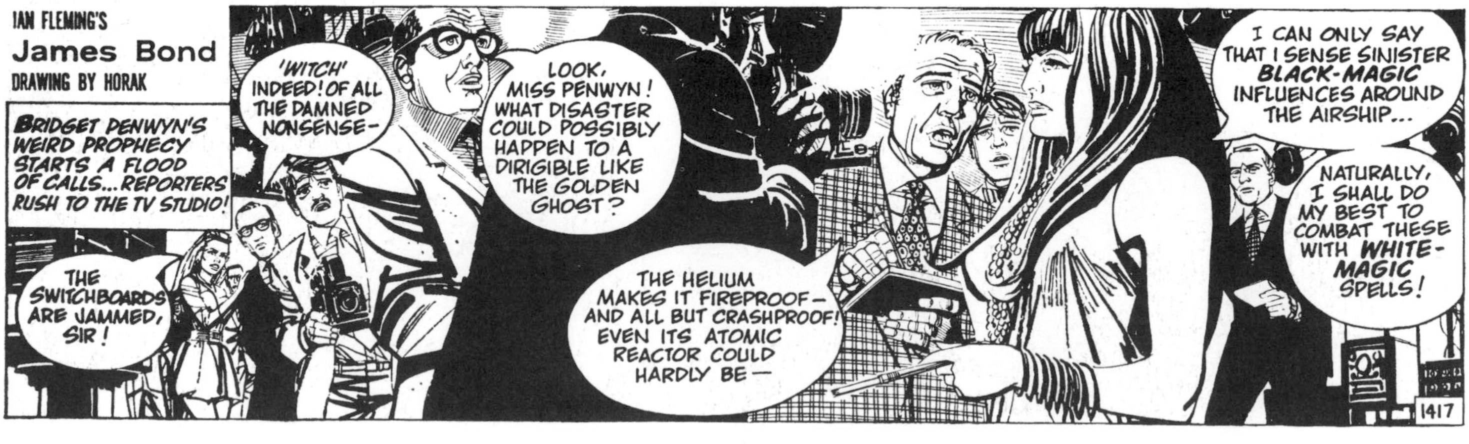
IAN FLEMING'S
James Bond
DRAWING BY HORAK
BRIDGET PENWYN'S WEIRD PROPHECY STARTS A FLOOD OF CALLS... REPORTERS RUSH TO THE TV STUDIO!
THE SWITCHBOARDS ARE JAMMED, SIR!
'WITCH' INDEED! OF ALL THE DAMNED NONSENSE—
LOOK, MISS PENWYN! WHAT DISASTER COULD POSSIBLY HAPPEN TO A DIRIGIBLE LIKE THE GOLDEN GHOST?
THE HELIUM MAKES IT FIREPROOF — AND ALL BUT CRASHPROOF! EVEN ITS ATOMIC REACTOR COULD HARDLY BE—
I CAN ONLY SAY THAT I SENSE SINISTER BLACK-MAGIC INFLUENCES AROUND THE AIRSHIP...
NATURALLY, I SHALL DO MY BEST TO COMBAT THESE WITH WHITE-MAGIC SPELLS!
1417

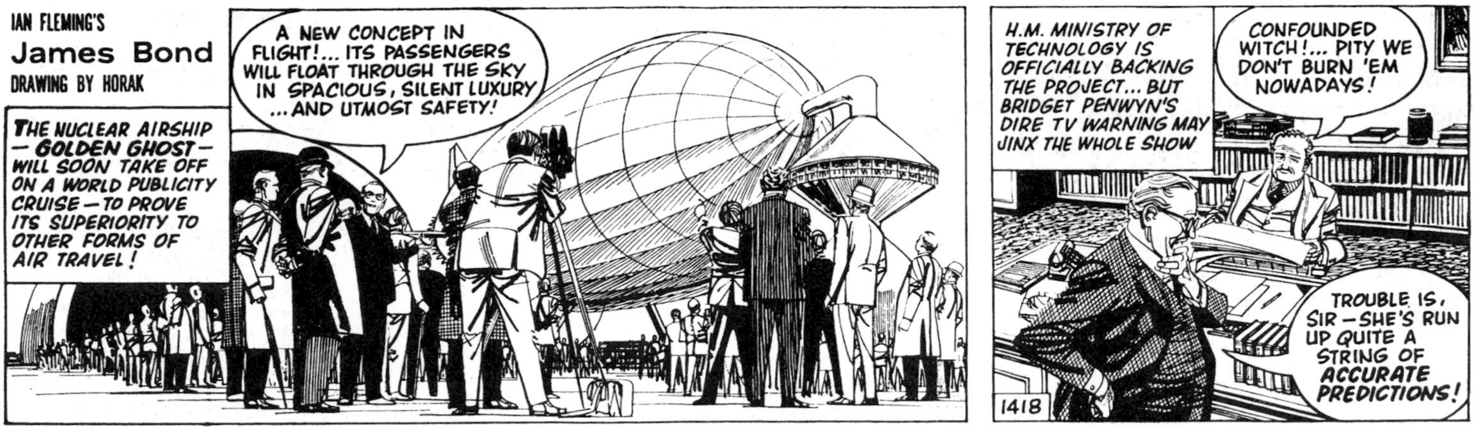
IAN FLEMING'S
James Bond
DRAWING BY HORAK
THE NUCLEAR AIRSHIP — GOLDEN GHOST — WILL SOON TAKE OFF ON A WORLD PUBLICITY CRUISE — TO PROVE ITS SUPERIORITY TO OTHER FORMS OF AIR TRAVEL!
A NEW CONCEPT IN FLIGHT!... ITS PASSENGERS WILL FLOAT THROUGH THE SKY IN SPACIOUS, SILENT LUXURY ... AND UTMOST SAFETY!
H.M. MINISTRY OF TECHNOLOGY IS OFFICIALLY BACKING THE PROJECT... BUT BRIDGET PENWYN'S DIRE TV WARNING MAY JINX THE WHOLE SHOW
CONFOUNDED WITCH!... PITY WE DON'T BURN 'EM NOWADAYS!
TROUBLE IS, SIR — SHE'S RUN UP QUITE A STRING OF ACCURATE PREDICTIONS!
1418

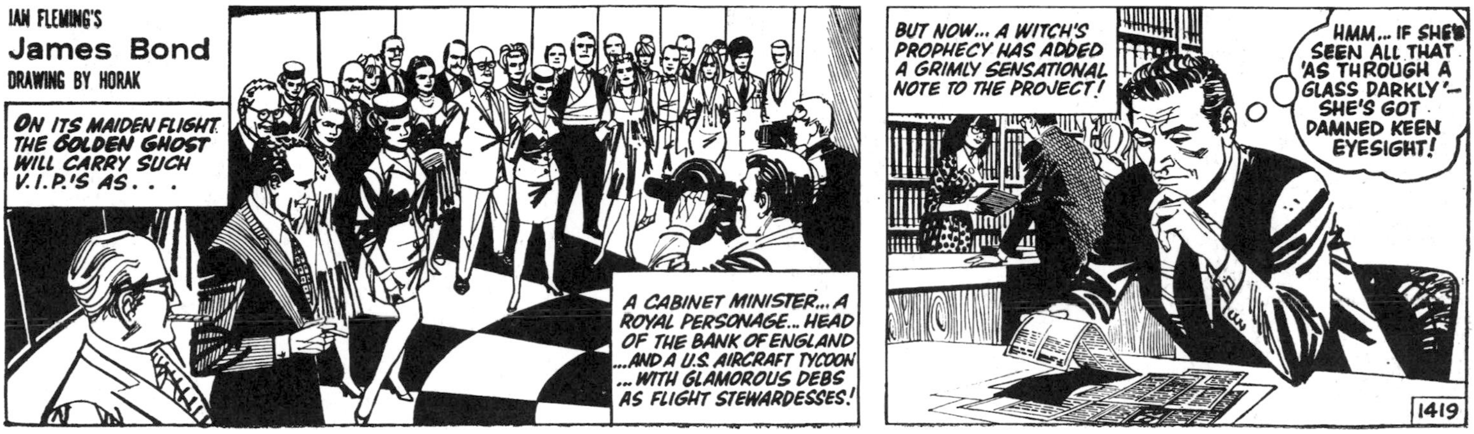
IAN FLEMING'S
James Bond
DRAWING BY HORAK
ON ITS MAIDEN FLIGHT THE GOLDEN GHOST WILL CARRY SUCH V.I.P.'S AS . . .
A CABINET MINISTER... A ROYAL PERSONAGE... HEAD OF THE BANK OF ENGLAND ... AND A U.S. AIRCRAFT TYCOON ... WITH GLAMOROUS DEBS AS FLIGHT STEWARDESSES!
BUT NOW... A WITCH'S PROPHECY HAS ADDED A GRIMLY SENSATIONAL NOTE TO THE PROJECT!
HMM... IF SHE'S SEEN ALL THAT 'AS THROUGH A GLASS DARKLY' — SHE'S GOT DAMNED KEEN EYESIGHT!
1419

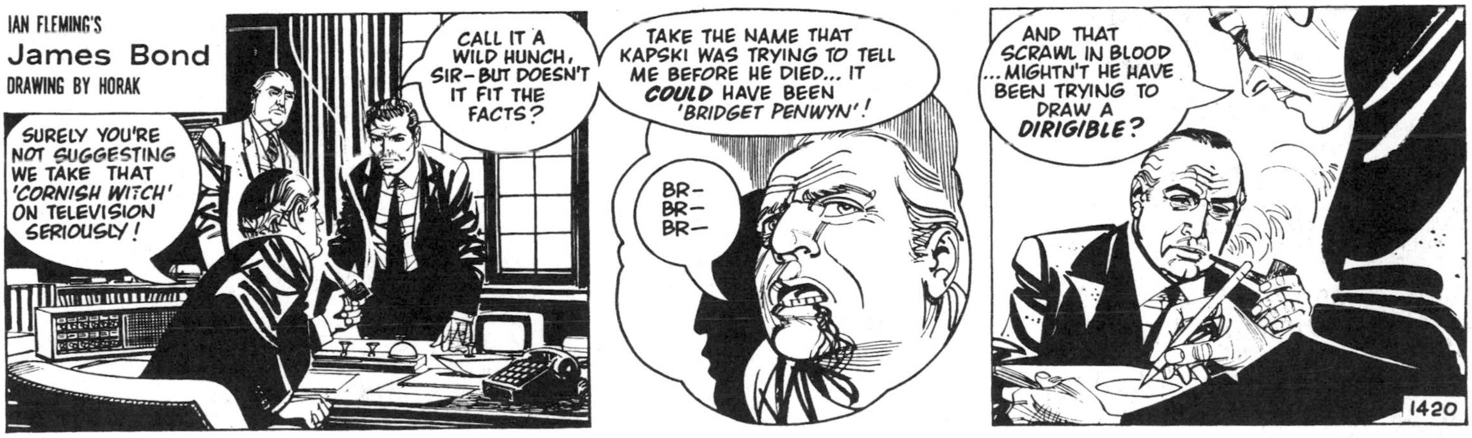
IAN FLEMING'S
James Bond
DRAWING BY HORAK
SURELY YOU'RE NOT SUGGESTING WE TAKE THAT 'CORNISH WITCH' ON TELEVISION SERIOUSLY!
CALL IT A WILD HUNCH, SIR — BUT DOESN'T IT FIT THE FACTS?
TAKE THE NAME THAT KAPSKI WAS TRYING TO TELL ME BEFORE HE DIED... IT COULD HAVE BEEN 'BRIDGET PENWYN'!
BR- BR- BR-
AND THAT SCRAWL IN BLOOD ... MIGHTN'T HE HAVE BEEN TRYING TO DRAW A DIRIGIBLE?
1420

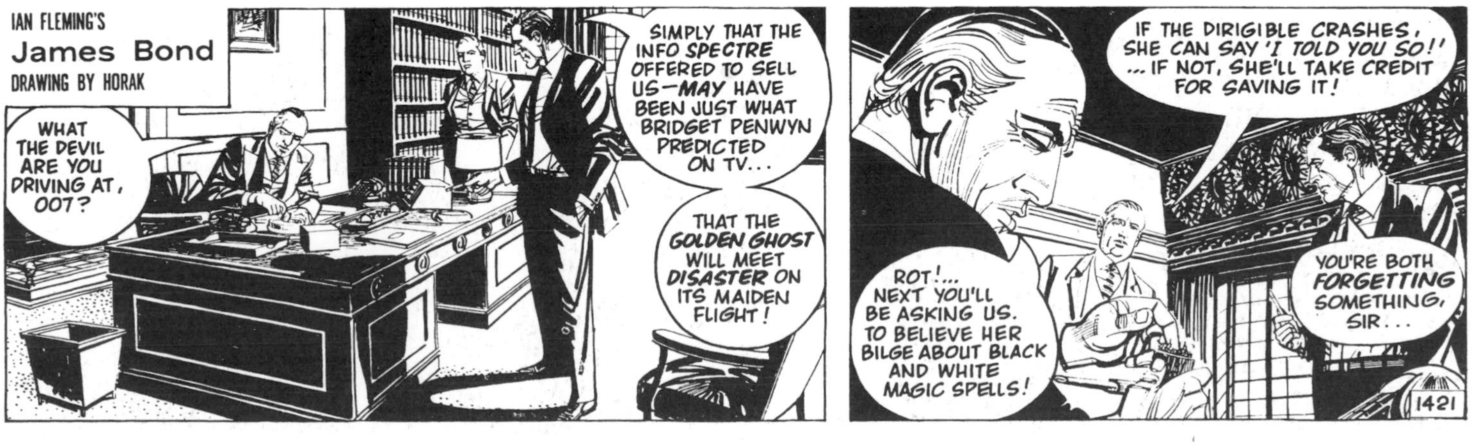
IAN FLEMING'S
James Bond
DRAWING BY HORAK
WHAT THE DEVIL ARE YOU DRIVING AT, 007?
SIMPLY THAT THE INFO SPECTRE OFFERED TO SELL US — MAY HAVE BEEN JUST WHAT BRIDGET PENWYN PREDICTED ON TV...
THAT THE GOLDEN GHOST WILL MEET DISASTER ON ITS MAIDEN FLIGHT!
IF THE DIRIGIBLE CRASHES, SHE CAN SAY 'I TOLD YOU SO!' ... IF NOT, SHE'LL TAKE CREDIT FOR SAVING IT!
ROT!... NEXT YOU'LL BE ASKING US TO BELIEVE HER BILGE ABOUT BLACK AND WHITE MAGIC SPELLS!
YOU'RE BOTH FORGETTING SOMETHING, SIR...
1421

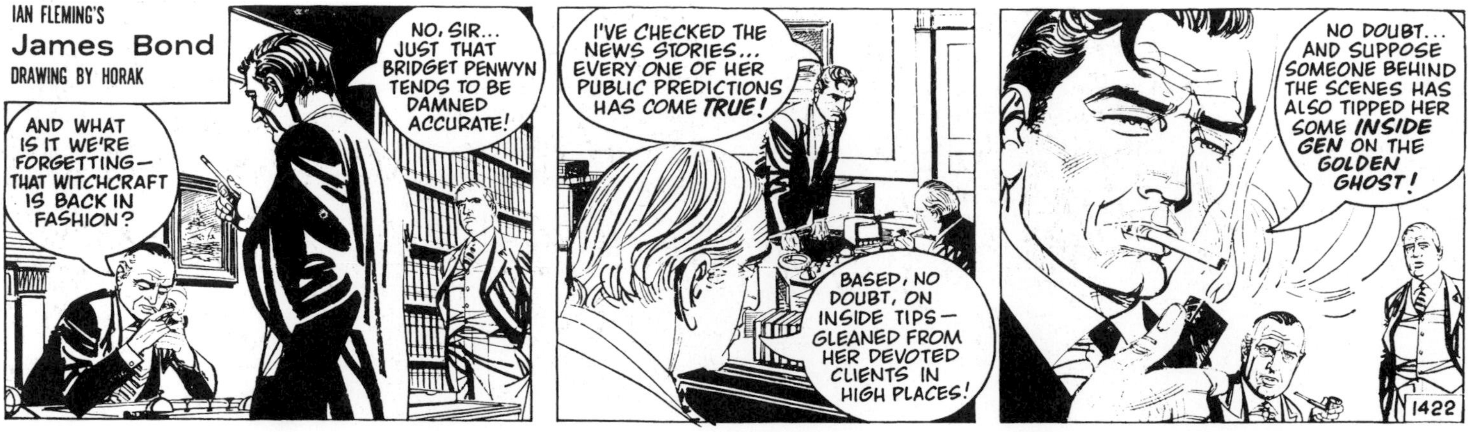
IAN FLEMING'S
James Bond
DRAWING BY HORAK
AND WHAT IS IT WE'RE FORGETTING— THAT WITCHCRAFT IS BACK IN FASHION?
NO, SIR... JUST THAT BRIDGET PENWYN TENDS TO BE DAMNED ACCURATE!
I'VE CHECKED THE NEWS STORIES... EVERY ONE OF HER PUBLIC PREDICTIONS HAS COME TRUE!
BASED, NO DOUBT, ON INSIDE TIPS— GLEANED FROM HER DEVOTED CLIENTS IN HIGH PLACES!
NO DOUBT... AND SUPPOSE SOMEONE BEHIND THE SCENES HAS ALSO TIPPED HER SOME INSIDE GEN ON THE GOLDEN GHOST!
1422

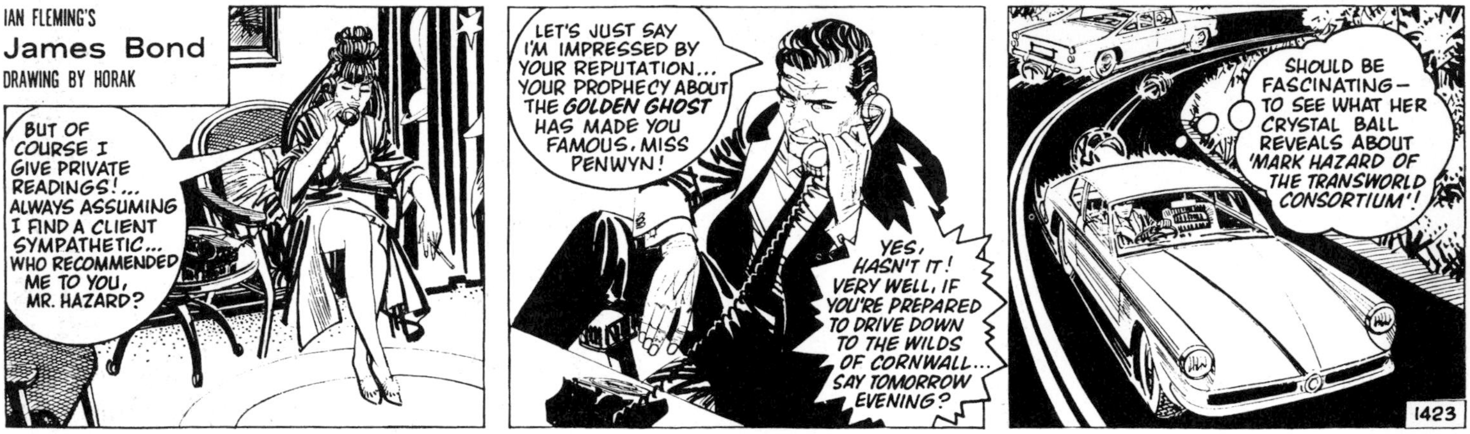
IAN FLEMING'S
James Bond
DRAWING BY HORAK
BUT OF COURSE I GIVE PRIVATE READINGS!... ALWAYS ASSUMING I FIND A CLIENT SYMPATHETIC... WHO RECOMMENDED ME TO YOU, MR. HAZARD?
LET'S JUST SAY I'M IMPRESSED BY YOUR REPUTATION... YOUR PROPHECY ABOUT THE GOLDEN GHOST HAS MADE YOU FAMOUS, MISS PENWYN!
YES, HASN'T IT! VERY WELL, IF YOU'RE PREPARED TO DRIVE DOWN TO THE WILDS OF CORNWALL... SAY TOMORROW EVENING?
SHOULD BE FASCINATING— TO SEE WHAT HER CRYSTAL BALL REVEALS ABOUT 'MARK HAZARD OF THE TRANSWORLD CONSORTIUM'!
1423

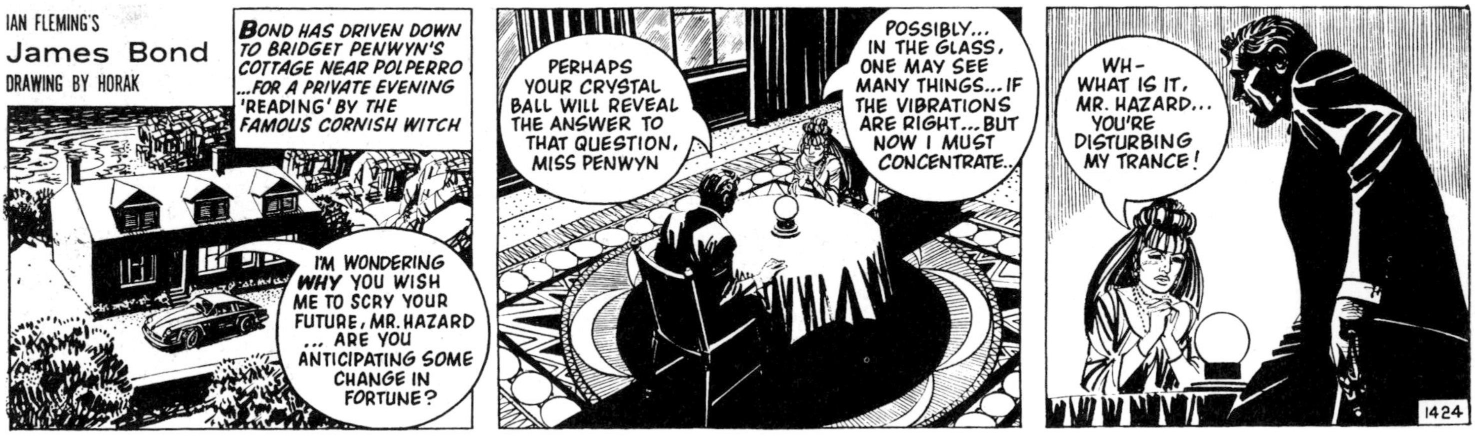
IAN FLEMING'S
James Bond
DRAWING BY HORAK
BOND HAS DRIVEN DOWN TO BRIDGET PENWYN'S COTTAGE NEAR POLPERRO ...FOR A PRIVATE EVENING 'READING' BY THE FAMOUS CORNISH WITCH
I'M WONDERING WHY YOU WISH ME TO SCRY YOUR FUTURE, MR. HAZARD ... ARE YOU ANTICIPATING SOME CHANGE IN FORTUNE?
PERHAPS YOUR CRYSTAL BALL WILL REVEAL THE ANSWER TO THAT QUESTION, MISS PENWYN
POSSIBLY... IN THE GLASS, ONE MAY SEE MANY THINGS... IF THE VIBRATIONS ARE RIGHT... BUT NOW I MUST CONCENTRATE..
WH- WHAT IS IT, MR. HAZARD... YOU'RE DISTURBING MY TRANCE!
1424

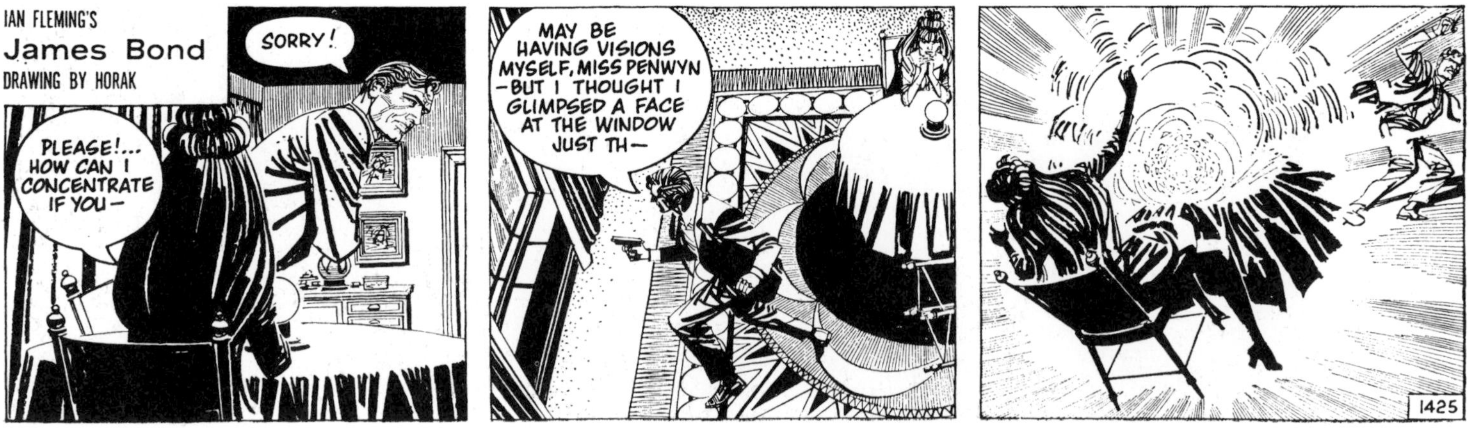
IAN FLEMING'S
James Bond
DRAWING BY HORAK
PLEASE!... HOW CAN I CONCENTRATE IF YOU—
SORRY!
MAY BE HAVING VISIONS MYSELF, MISS PENWYN —BUT I THOUGHT I GLIMPSED A FACE AT THE WINDOW JUST TH—
1425

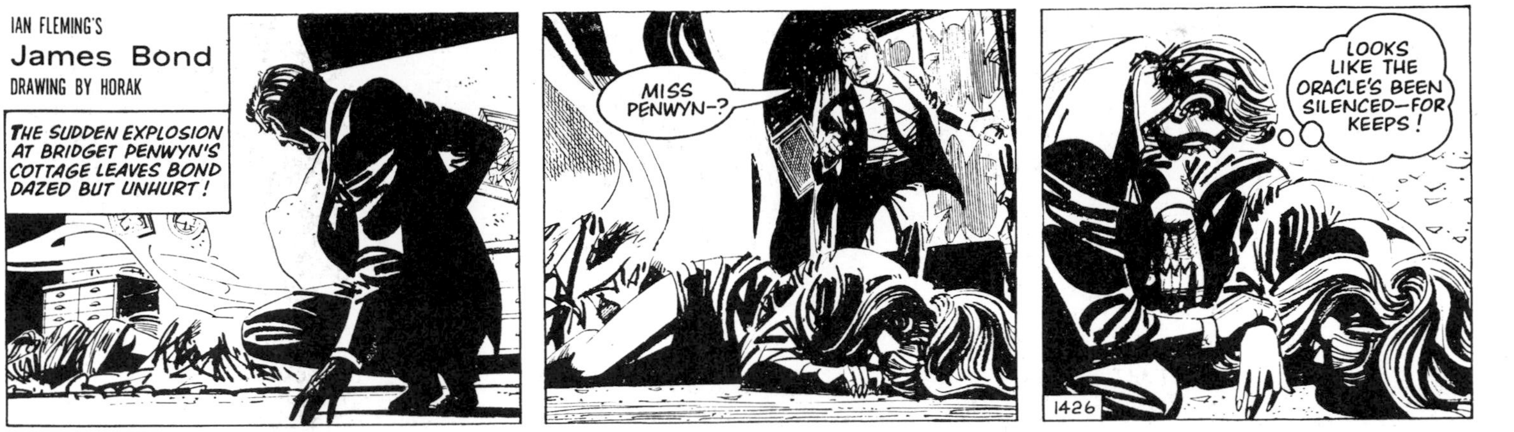
IAN FLEMING'S
James Bond
DRAWING BY HORAK
THE SUDDEN EXPLOSION AT BRIDGET PENWYN'S COTTAGE LEAVES BOND DAZED BUT UNHURT!
MISS PENWYN-?
LOOKS LIKE THE ORACLE'S BEEN SILENCED—FOR KEEPS!
1426

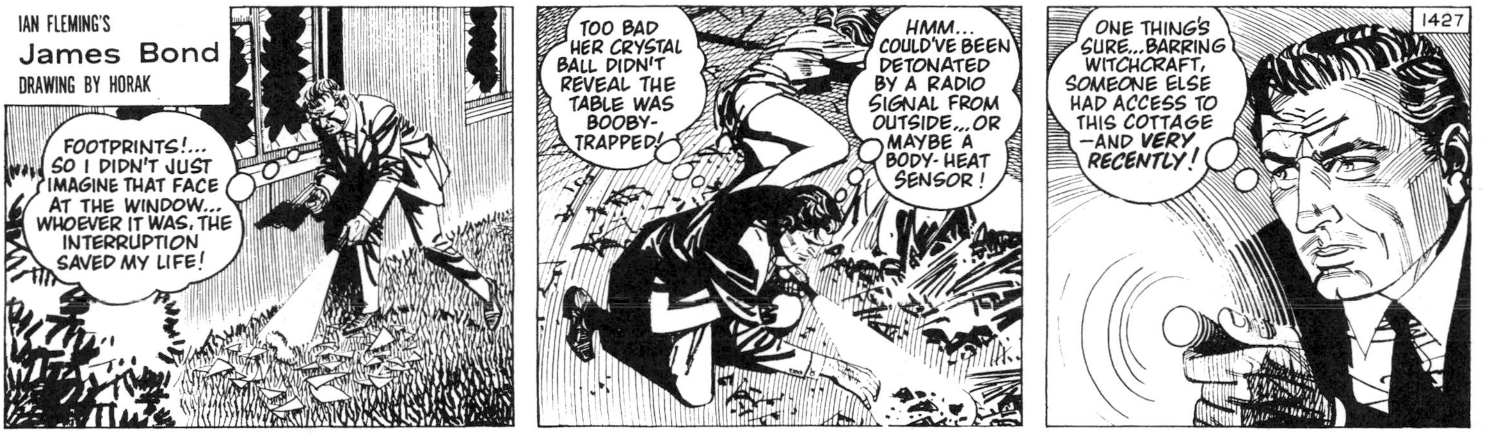
IAN FLEMING'S
James Bond
DRAWING BY HORAK
FOOTPRINTS!... SO I DIDN'T JUST IMAGINE THAT FACE AT THE WINDOW... WHOEVER IT WAS, THE INTERRUPTION SAVED MY LIFE!
TOO BAD HER CRYSTAL BALL DIDN'T REVEAL THE TABLE WAS BOOBY-TRAPPED!
HMM... COULD'VE BEEN DETONATED BY A RADIO SIGNAL FROM OUTSIDE... OR MAYBE A BODY-HEAT SENSOR!
1427
ONE THING'S SURE... BARRING WITCHCRAFT, SOMEONE ELSE HAD ACCESS TO THIS COTTAGE —AND VERY RECENTLY!

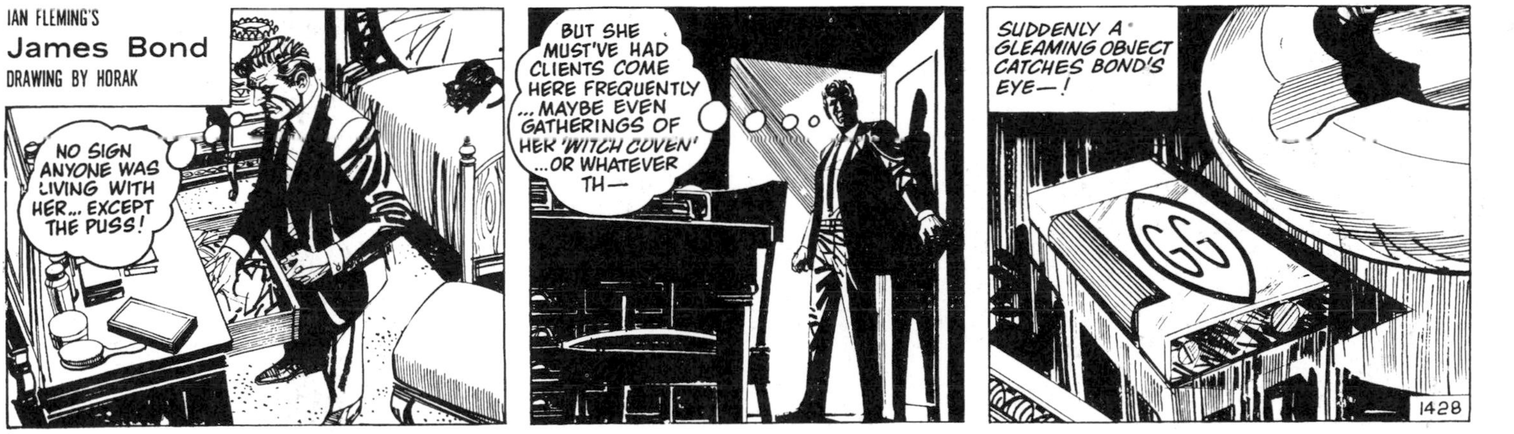
IAN FLEMING'S
James Bond
DRAWING BY HORAK
NO SIGN ANYONE WAS LIVING WITH HER... EXCEPT THE PUSS!
BUT SHE MUST'VE HAD CLIENTS COME HERE FREQUENTLY ... MAYBE EVEN GATHERINGS OF HER 'WITCH COVEN' ...OR WHATEVER TH—
SUDDENLY A GLEAMING OBJECT CATCHES BOND'S EYE—!
1428

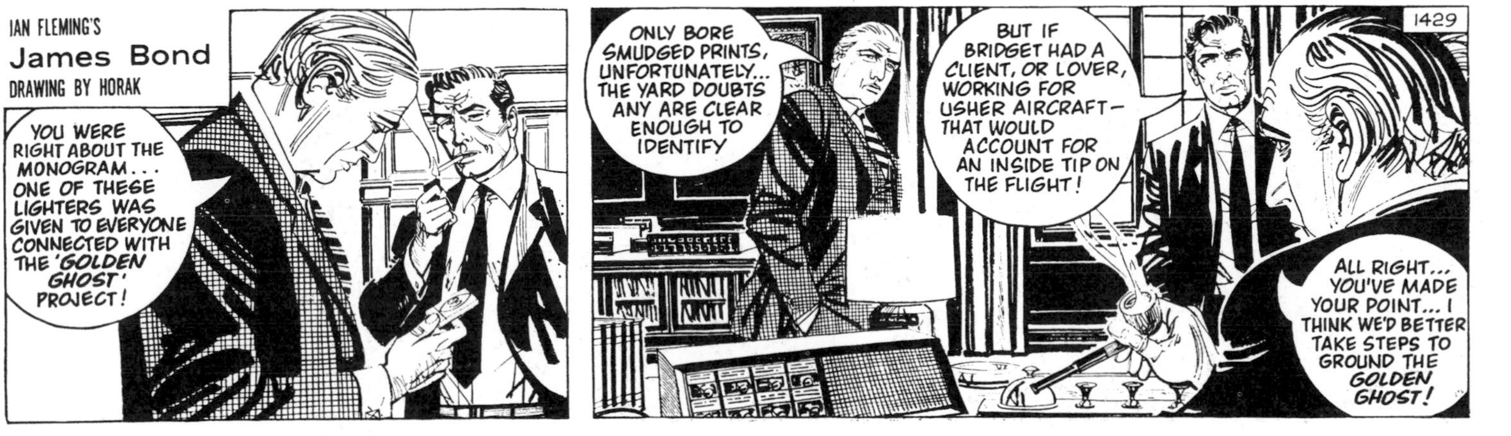
IAN FLEMING'S
James Bond
DRAWING BY HORAK
YOU WERE RIGHT ABOUT THE MONOGRAM... ONE OF THESE LIGHTERS WAS GIVEN TO EVERYONE CONNECTED WITH THE 'GOLDEN GHOST' PROJECT!
1429
ONLY BORE SMUDGED PRINTS, UNFORTUNATELY... THE YARD DOUBTS ANY ARE CLEAR ENOUGH TO IDENTIFY
BUT IF BRIDGET HAD A CLIENT, OR LOVER, WORKING FOR USHER AIRCRAFT— THAT WOULD ACCOUNT FOR AN INSIDE TIP ON THE FLIGHT!
ALL RIGHT... YOU'VE MADE YOUR POINT... I THINK WE'D BETTER TAKE STEPS TO GROUND THE GOLDEN GHOST!

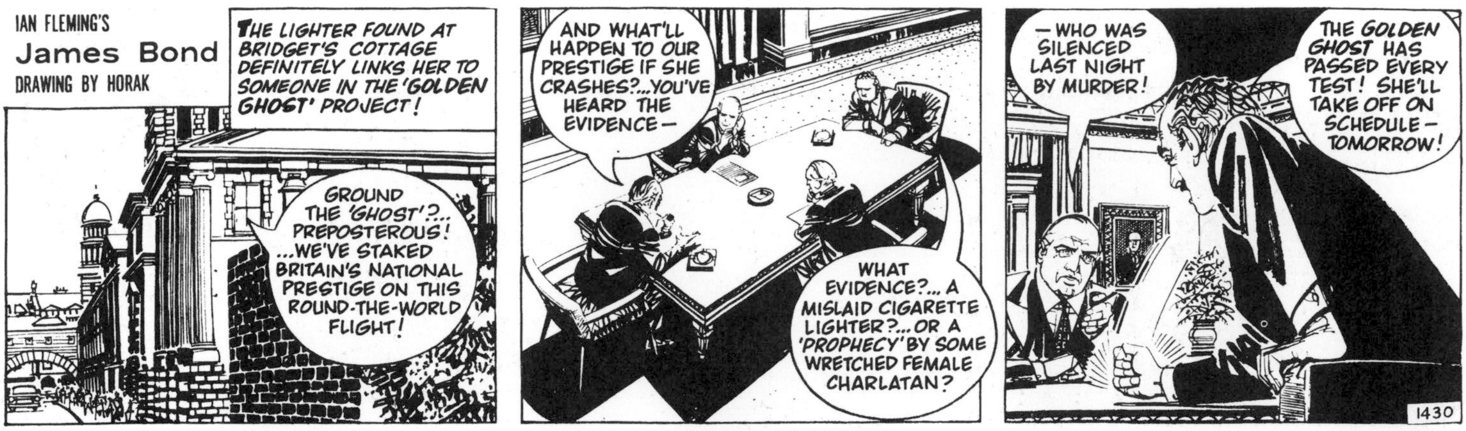
IAN FLEMING'S
James Bond
DRAWING BY HORAK
THE LIGHTER FOUND AT BRIDGET'S COTTAGE DEFINITELY LINKS HER TO SOMEONE IN THE 'GOLDEN GHOST' PROJECT!
GROUND THE 'GHOST'?... PREPOSTEROUS! ...WE'VE STAKED BRITAIN'S NATIONAL PRESTIGE ON THIS ROUND-THE-WORLD FLIGHT!
AND WHAT'LL HAPPEN TO OUR PRESTIGE IF SHE CRASHES?...YOU'VE HEARD THE EVIDENCE—
WHAT EVIDENCE?... A MISLAID CIGARETTE LIGHTER?...OR A 'PROPHECY' BY SOME WRETCHED FEMALE CHARLATAN?
—WHO WAS SILENCED LAST NIGHT BY MURDER!
THE GOLDEN GHOST HAS PASSED EVERY TEST! SHE'LL TAKE OFF ON SCHEDULE—TOMORROW!
1430

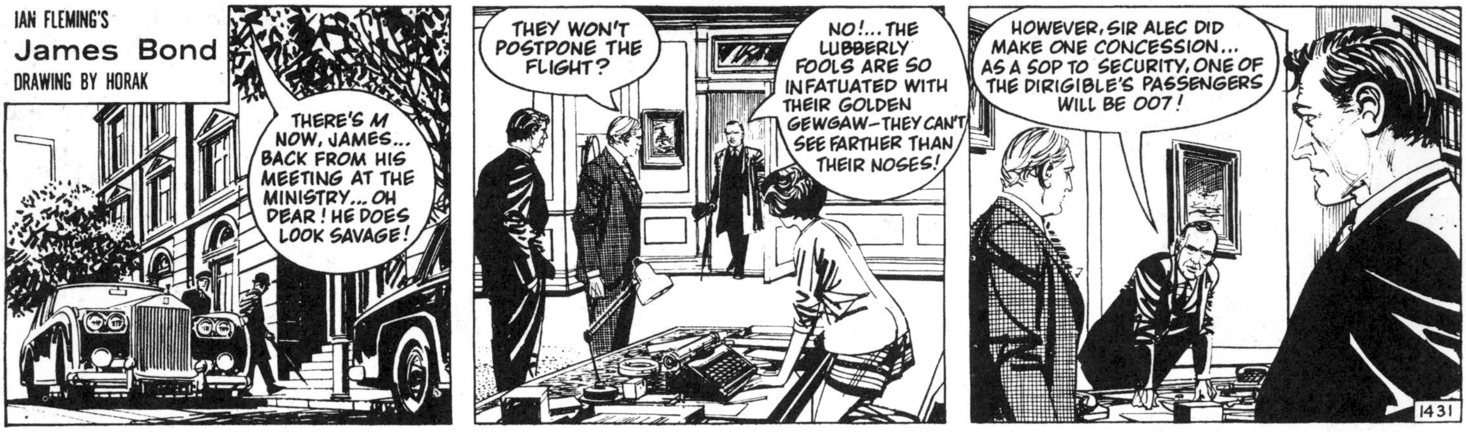
IAN FLEMING'S
James Bond
DRAWING BY HORAK
THERE'S M NOW, JAMES... BACK FROM HIS MEETING AT THE MINISTRY... OH DEAR! HE DOES LOOK SAVAGE!
THEY WON'T POSTPONE THE FLIGHT?
NO!... THE LUBBERLY FOOLS ARE SO INFATUATED WITH THEIR GOLDEN GEWGAW—THEY CAN'T SEE FARTHER THAN THEIR NOSES!
HOWEVER, SIR ALEC DID MAKE ONE CONCESSION... AS A SOP TO SECURITY, ONE OF THE DIRIGIBLE'S PASSENGERS WILL BE 007!
1431

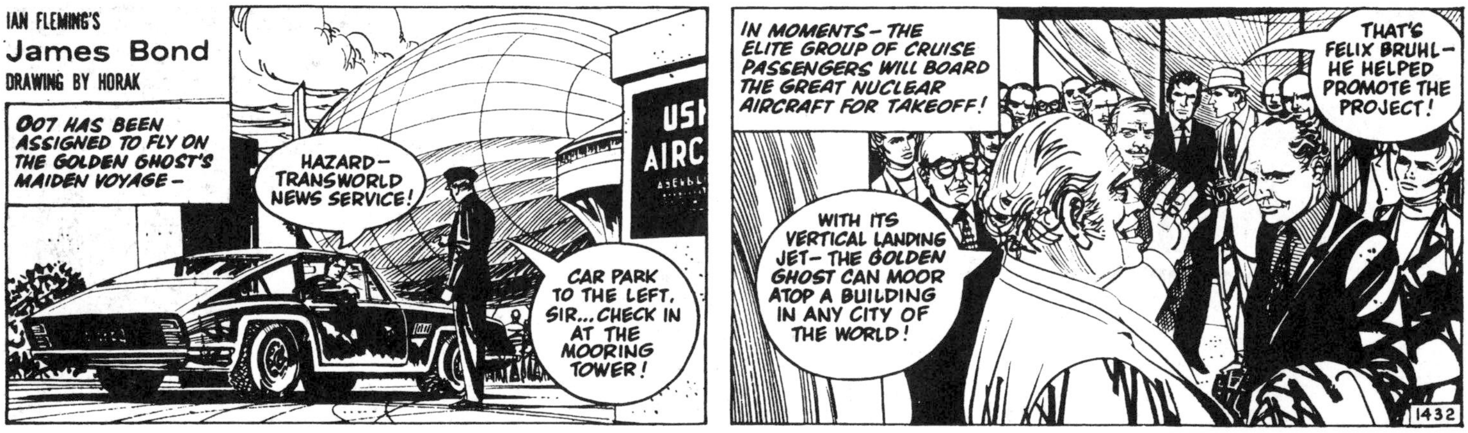
IAN FLEMING'S
James Bond
DRAWING BY HORAK
007 HAS BEEN ASSIGNED TO FLY ON THE GOLDEN GHOST'S MAIDEN VOYAGE—
HAZARD—TRANSWORLD NEWS SERVICE!
CAR PARK TO THE LEFT, SIR... CHECK IN AT THE MOORING TOWER!
IN MOMENTS—THE ELITE GROUP OF CRUISE PASSENGERS WILL BOARD THE GREAT NUCLEAR AIRCRAFT FOR TAKEOFF!
THAT'S FELIX BRUHL—HE HELPED PROMOTE THE PROJECT!
WITH ITS VERTICAL LANDING JET—THE GOLDEN GHOST CAN MOOR ATOP A BUILDING IN ANY CITY OF THE WORLD!
1432

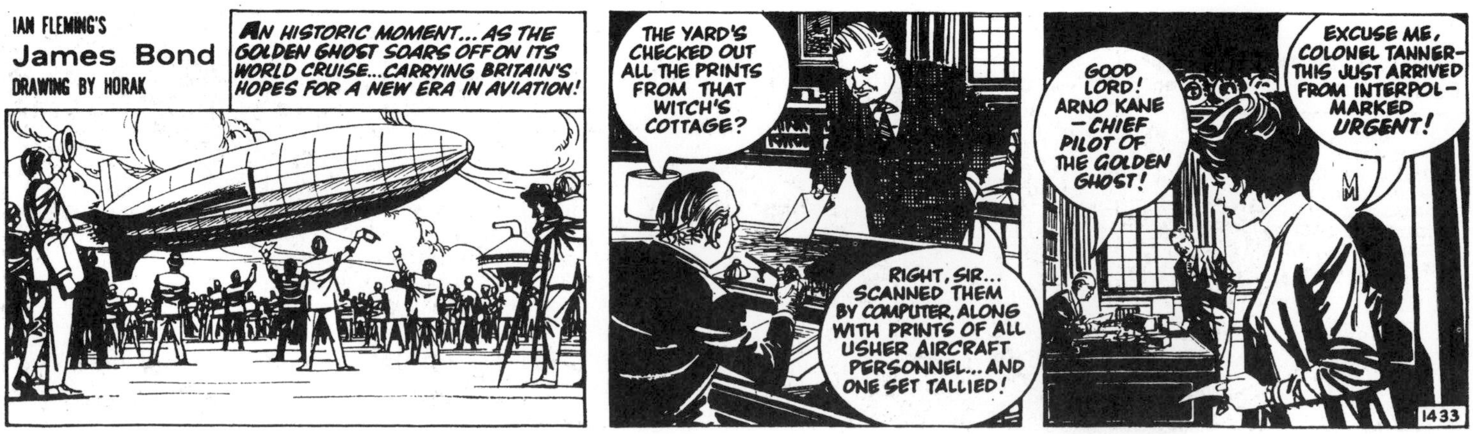
IAN FLEMING'S
James Bond
DRAWING BY HORAK
AN HISTORIC MOMENT... AS THE GOLDEN GHOST SOARS OFF ON ITS WORLD CRUISE...CARRYING BRITAIN'S HOPES FOR A NEW ERA IN AVIATION!
THE YARD'S CHECKED OUT ALL THE PRINTS FROM THAT WITCH'S COTTAGE?
RIGHT, SIR... SCANNED THEM BY COMPUTER, ALONG WITH PRINTS OF ALL USHER AIRCRAFT PERSONNEL... AND ONE SET TALLIED!
EXCUSE ME, COLONEL TANNER—THIS JUST ARRIVED FROM INTERPOL—MARKED URGENT!
GOOD LORD! ARNO KANE—CHIEF PILOT OF THE GOLDEN GHOST!
1433

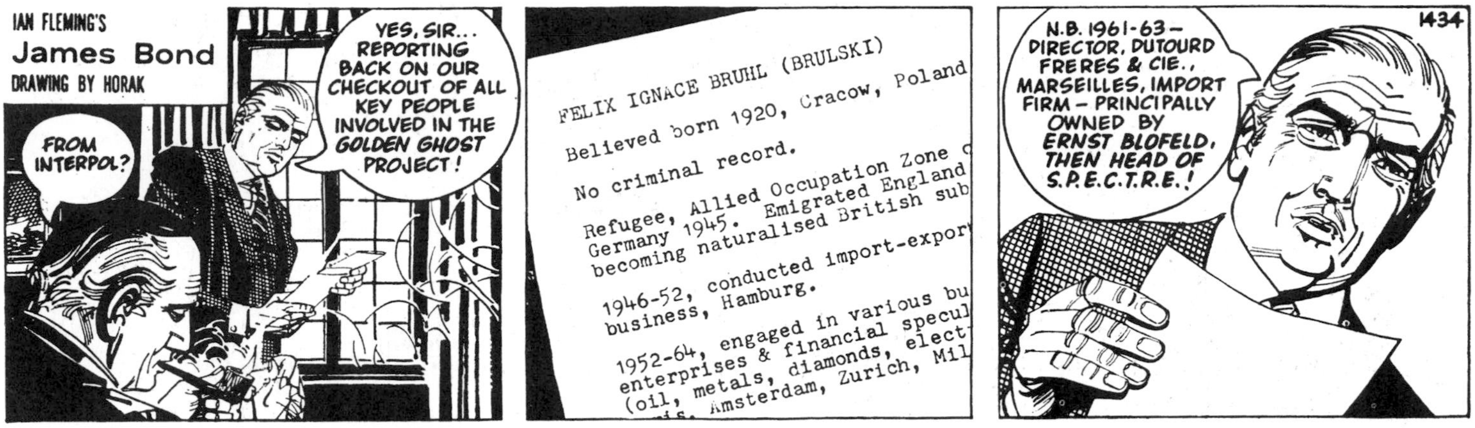
IAN FLEMING'S
James Bond
DRAWING BY HORAK
FROM INTERPOL?
YES, SIR... REPORTING BACK ON OUR CHECKOUT OF ALL KEY PEOPLE INVOLVED IN THE GOLDEN GHOST PROJECT!
FELIX IGNACE BRUHL (BRULSKI)
Believed born 1920, Cracow, Poland
No criminal record.
Refugee, Allied Occupation Zone c
Germany 1945. Emigrated England
becoming naturalised British sub
1946-52, conducted import-expor
business, Hamburg.
1952-64, engaged in various bu
enterprises & financial specul
(oil, metals, diamonds, elect
Amsterdam, Zurich, Mil
1434
N.B. 1961-63 — DIRECTOR, DUTOURD FRERES & CIE., MARSEILLES, IMPORT FIRM — PRINCIPALLY OWNED BY ERNST BLOFELD, THEN HEAD OF S.P.E.C.T.R.E.!

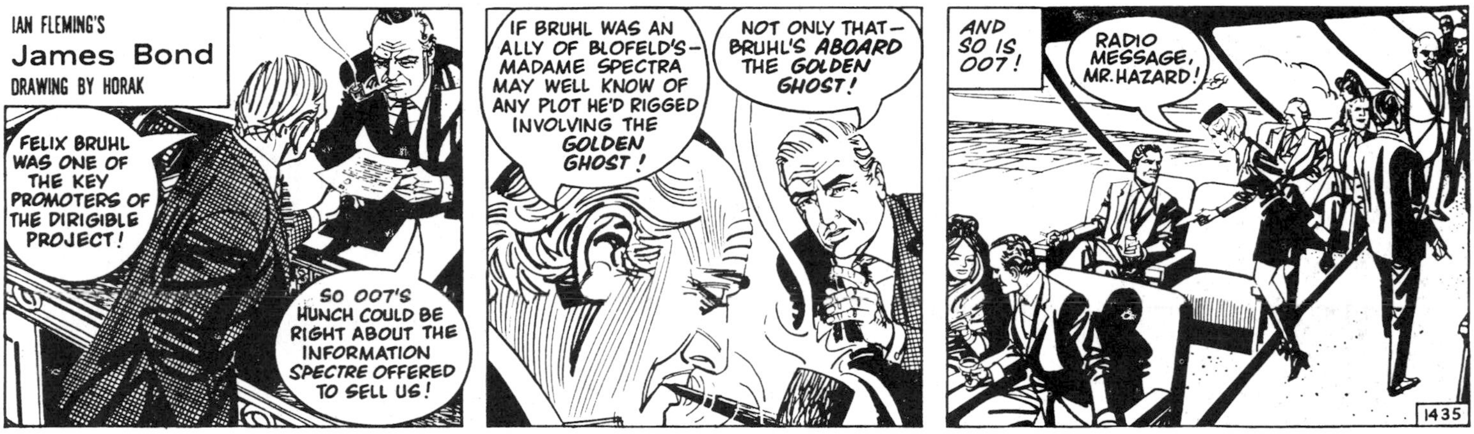
IAN FLEMING'S
James Bond
DRAWING BY HORAK
FELIX BRUHL WAS ONE OF THE KEY PROMOTERS OF THE DIRIGIBLE PROJECT!
SO 007'S HUNCH COULD BE RIGHT ABOUT THE INFORMATION SPECTRE OFFERED TO SELL US!
IF BRUHL WAS AN ALLY OF BLOFELD'S — MADAME SPECTRA MAY WELL KNOW OF ANY PLOT HE'D RIGGED INVOLVING THE GOLDEN GHOST!
NOT ONLY THAT — BRUHL'S ABOARD THE GOLDEN GHOST!
AND SO IS 007!
RADIO MESSAGE, MR. HAZARD!
1435

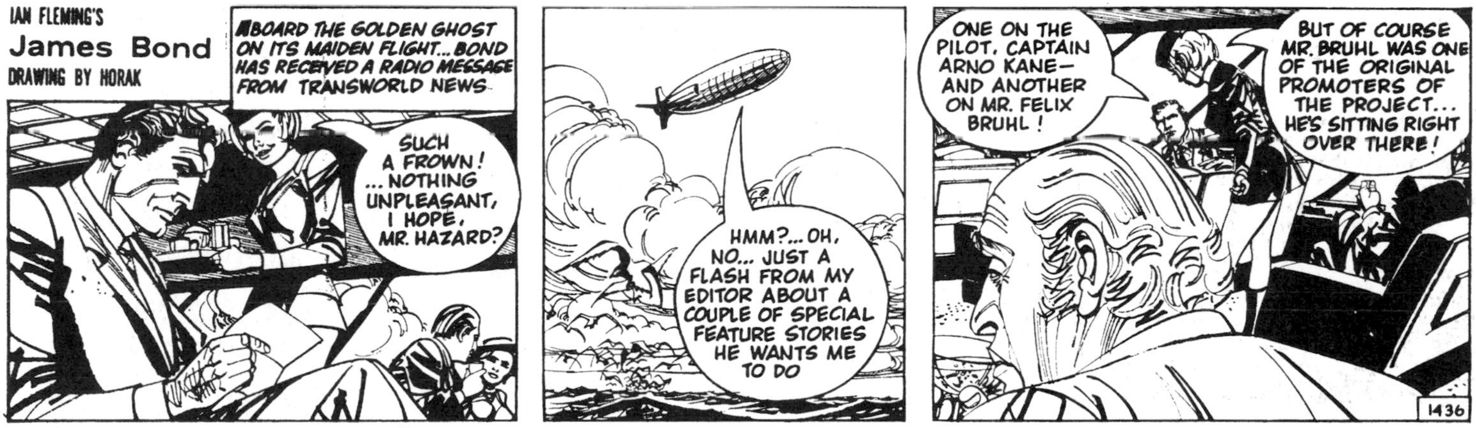
IAN FLEMING'S
James Bond
DRAWING BY HORAK
ABOARD THE GOLDEN GHOST ON ITS MAIDEN FLIGHT... BOND HAS RECEIVED A RADIO MESSAGE FROM TRANSWORLD NEWS
SUCH A FROWN! ...NOTHING UNPLEASANT, I HOPE, MR. HAZARD?
HMM?... OH, NO... JUST A FLASH FROM MY EDITOR ABOUT A COUPLE OF SPECIAL FEATURE STORIES HE WANTS ME TO DO
ONE ON THE PILOT, CAPTAIN ARNO KANE — AND ANOTHER ON MR. FELIX BRUHL!
BUT OF COURSE MR. BRUHL WAS ONE OF THE ORIGINAL PROMOTERS OF THE PROJECT... HE'S SITTING RIGHT OVER THERE!
1436

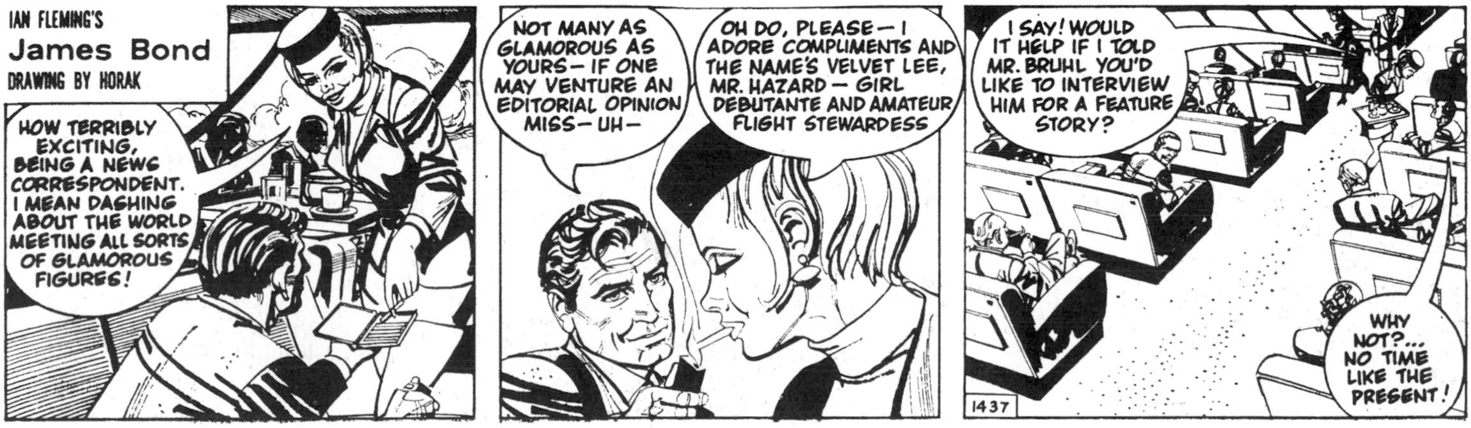
IAN FLEMING'S
James Bond
DRAWING BY HORAK
HOW TERRIBLY EXCITING, BEING A NEWS CORRESPONDENT. I MEAN DASHING ABOUT THE WORLD MEETING ALL SORTS OF GLAMOROUS FIGURES!
NOT MANY AS GLAMOROUS AS YOURS — IF ONE MAY VENTURE AN EDITORIAL OPINION MISS — UH —
OH DO, PLEASE — I ADORE COMPLIMENTS AND THE NAME'S VELVET LEE, MR. HAZARD — GIRL DEBUTANTE AND AMATEUR FLIGHT STEWARDESS
I SAY! WOULD IT HELP IF I TOLD MR. BRUHL YOU'D LIKE TO INTERVIEW HIM FOR A FEATURE STORY?
WHY NOT?... NO TIME LIKE THE PRESENT!
1437

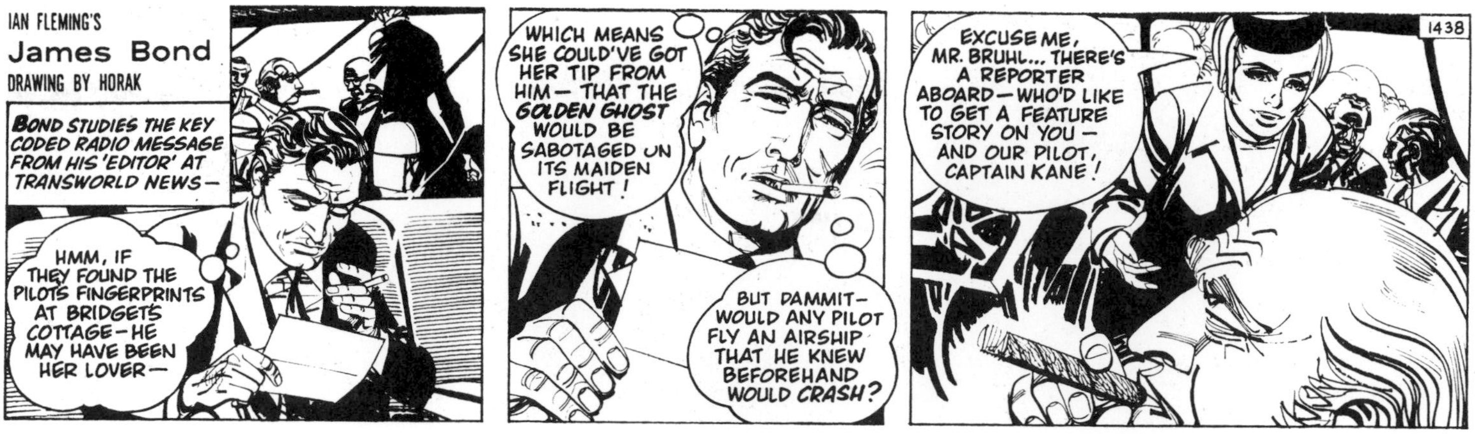
IAN FLEMING'S
James Bond
DRAWING BY HORAK
BOND STUDIES THE KEY CODED RADIO MESSAGE FROM HIS 'EDITOR' AT TRANSWORLD NEWS—
HMM, IF THEY FOUND THE PILOTS FINGERPRINTS AT BRIDGETS COTTAGE—HE MAY HAVE BEEN HER LOVER—
WHICH MEANS SHE COULD'VE GOT HER TIP FROM HIM—THAT THE GOLDEN GHOST WOULD BE SABOTAGED ON ITS MAIDEN FLIGHT!
BUT DAMMIT—WOULD ANY PILOT FLY AN AIRSHIP THAT HE KNEW BEFOREHAND WOULD CRASH?
1438
EXCUSE ME, MR. BRUHL... THERE'S A REPORTER ABOARD—WHO'D LIKE TO GET A FEATURE STORY ON YOU—AND OUR PILOT, CAPTAIN KANE!

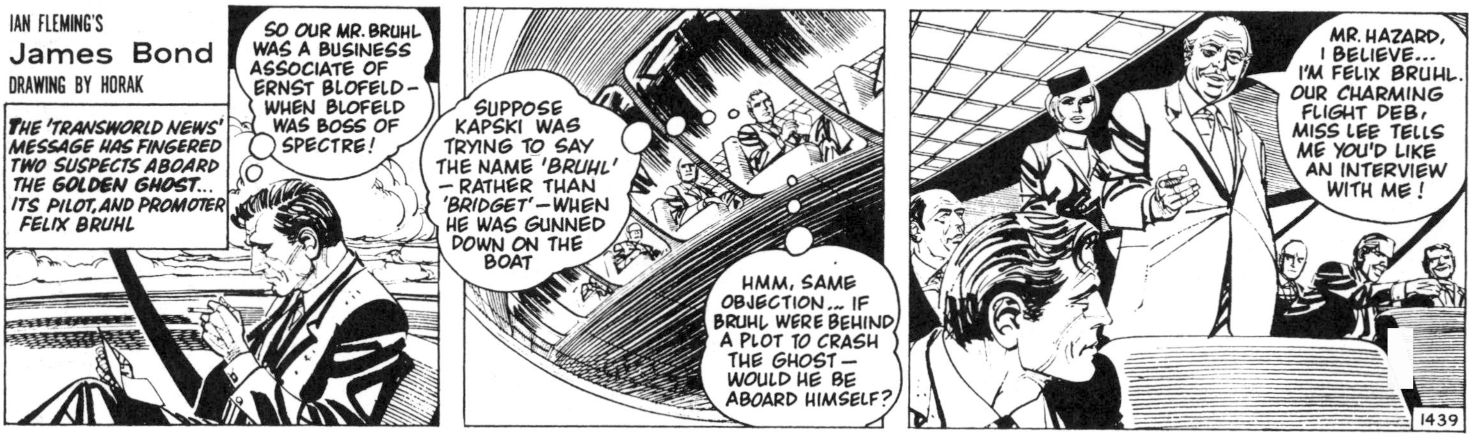
IAN FLEMING'S
James Bond
DRAWING BY HORAK
THE 'TRANSWORLD NEWS' MESSAGE HAS FINGERED TWO SUSPECTS ABOARD THE GOLDEN GHOST... ITS PILOT, AND PROMOTER FELIX BRUHL
SO OUR MR. BRUHL WAS A BUSINESS ASSOCIATE OF ERNST BLOFELD—WHEN BLOFELD WAS BOSS OF SPECTRE!
SUPPOSE KAPSKI WAS TRYING TO SAY THE NAME 'BRUHL'—RATHER THAN 'BRIDGET'—WHEN HE WAS GUNNED DOWN ON THE BOAT
HMM, SAME OBJECTION... IF BRUHL WERE BEHIND A PLOT TO CRASH THE GHOST—WOULD HE BE ABOARD HIMSELF?
MR. HAZARD, I BELIEVE... I'M FELIX BRUHL. OUR CHARMING FLIGHT DEB, MISS LEE TELLS ME YOU'D LIKE AN INTERVIEW WITH ME!
1439

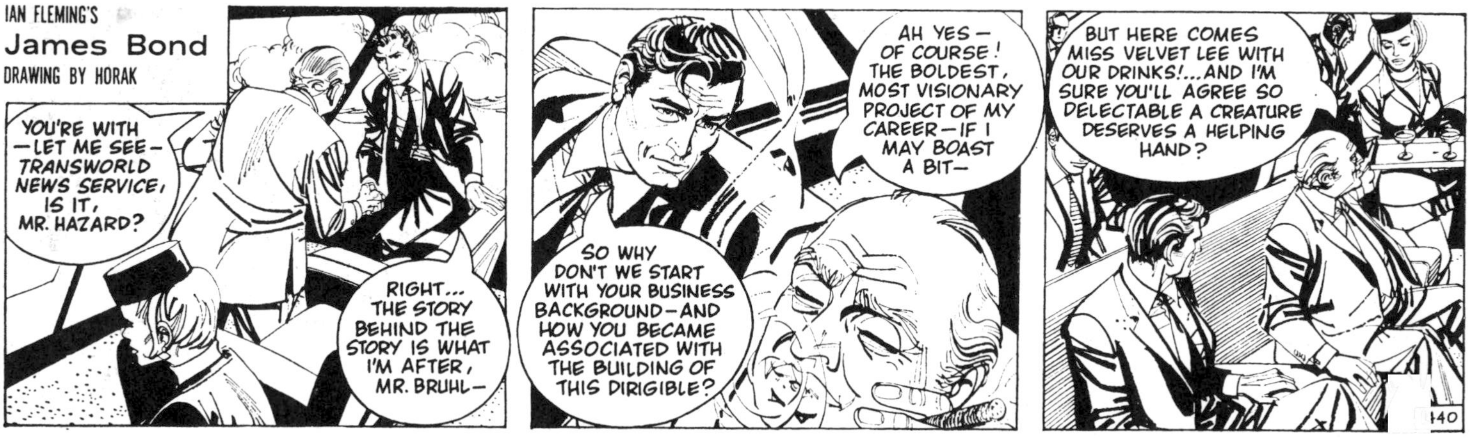
IAN FLEMING'S
James Bond
DRAWING BY HORAK
YOU'RE WITH—LET ME SEE—TRANSWORLD NEWS SERVICE, IS IT, MR. HAZARD?
RIGHT... THE STORY BEHIND THE STORY IS WHAT I'M AFTER, MR. BRUHL—
SO WHY DON'T WE START WITH YOUR BUSINESS BACKGROUND—AND HOW YOU BECAME ASSOCIATED WITH THE BUILDING OF THIS DIRIGIBLE?
AH YES—OF COURSE! THE BOLDEST, MOST VISIONARY PROJECT OF MY CAREER—IF I MAY BOAST A BIT—
BUT HERE COMES MISS VELVET LEE WITH OUR DRINKS!...AND I'M SURE YOU'LL AGREE SO DELECTABLE A CREATURE DESERVES A HELPING HAND?
1440

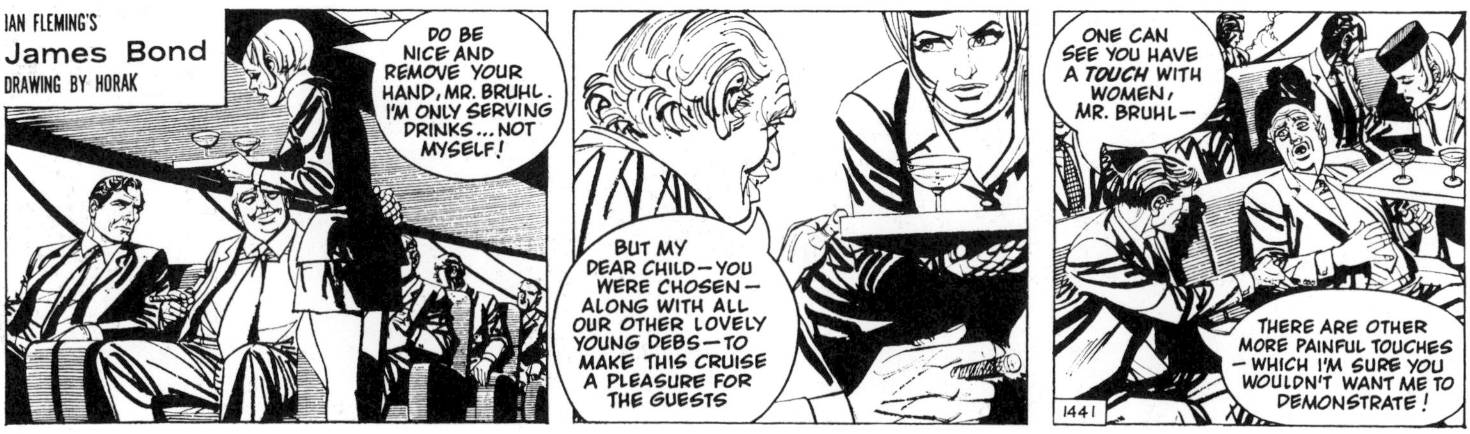
IAN FLEMING'S
James Bond
DRAWING BY HORAK
DO BE NICE AND REMOVE YOUR HAND, MR. BRUHL. I'M ONLY SERVING DRINKS... NOT MYSELF!
BUT MY DEAR CHILD—YOU WERE CHOSEN—ALONG WITH ALL OUR OTHER LOVELY YOUNG DEBS—TO MAKE THIS CRUISE A PLEASURE FOR THE GUESTS
1441
ONE CAN SEE YOU HAVE A TOUCH WITH WOMEN, MR. BRUHL—
THERE ARE OTHER MORE PAINFUL TOUCHES—WHICH I'M SURE YOU WOULDN'T WANT ME TO DEMONSTRATE!

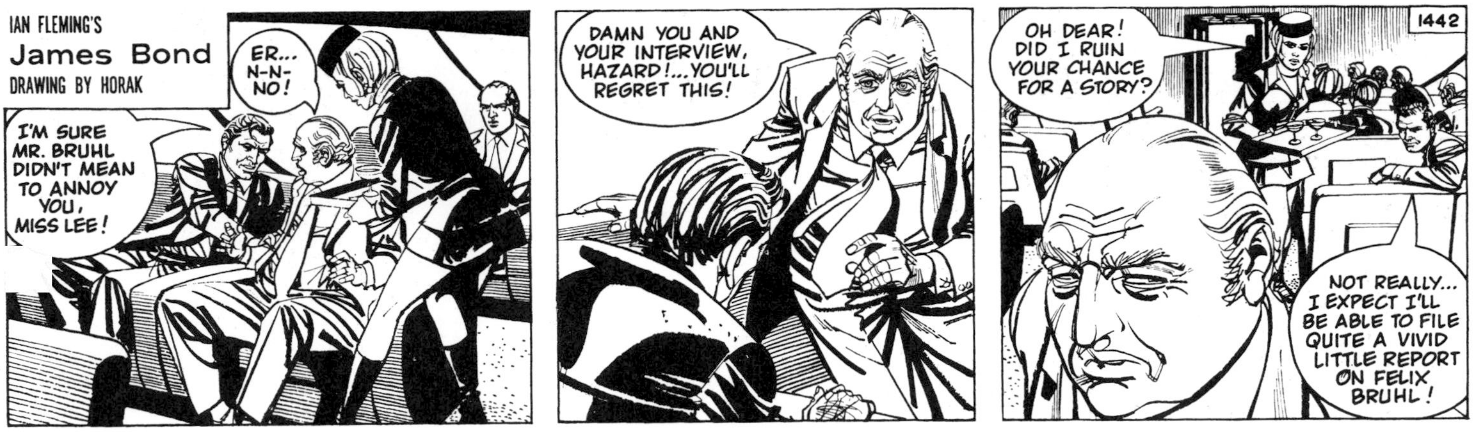
IAN FLEMING'S
James Bond
DRAWING BY HORAK
ER... N-N-NO!
I'M SURE MR. BRUHL DIDN'T MEAN TO ANNOY YOU, MISS LEE!
DAMN YOU AND YOUR INTERVIEW, HAZARD!... YOU'LL REGRET THIS!
1442
OH DEAR! DID I RUIN YOUR CHANCE FOR A STORY?
NOT REALLY... I EXPECT I'LL BE ABLE TO FILE QUITE A VIVID LITTLE REPORT ON FELIX BRUHL!

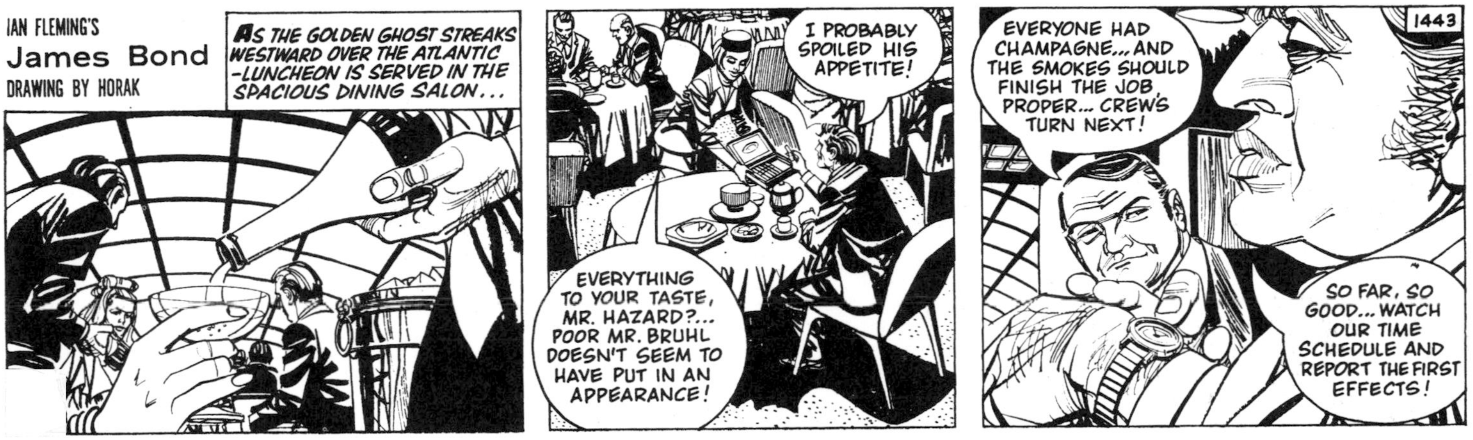
IAN FLEMING'S
James Bond
DRAWING BY HORAK
AS THE GOLDEN GHOST STREAKS WESTWARD OVER THE ATLANTIC -LUNCHEON IS SERVED IN THE SPACIOUS DINING SALON...
I PROBABLY SPOILED HIS APPETITE!
EVERYTHING TO YOUR TASTE, MR. HAZARD?... POOR MR. BRUHL DOESN'T SEEM TO HAVE PUT IN AN APPEARANCE!
1443
EVERYONE HAD CHAMPAGNE... AND THE SMOKES SHOULD FINISH THE JOB PROPER... CREW'S TURN NEXT!
SO FAR, SO GOOD... WATCH OUR TIME SCHEDULE AND REPORT THE FIRST EFFECTS!

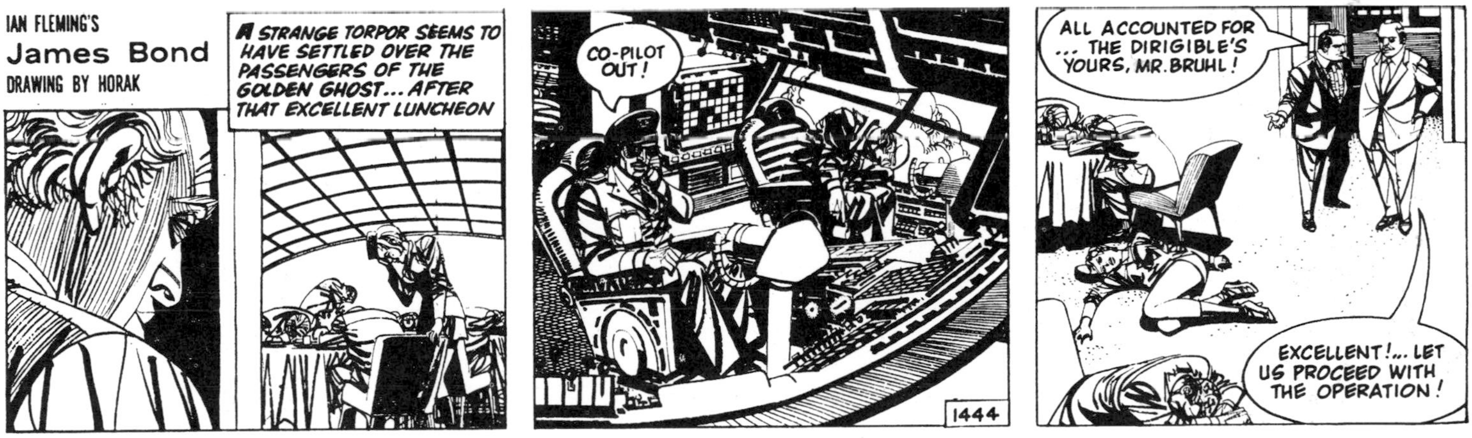
IAN FLEMING'S
James Bond
DRAWING BY HORAK
A STRANGE TORPOR SEEMS TO HAVE SETTLED OVER THE PASSENGERS OF THE GOLDEN GHOST... AFTER THAT EXCELLENT LUNCHEON
CO-PILOT OUT!
1444
ALL ACCOUNTED FOR ... THE DIRIGIBLE'S YOURS, MR. BRUHL!
EXCELLENT!... LET US PROCEED WITH THE OPERATION!

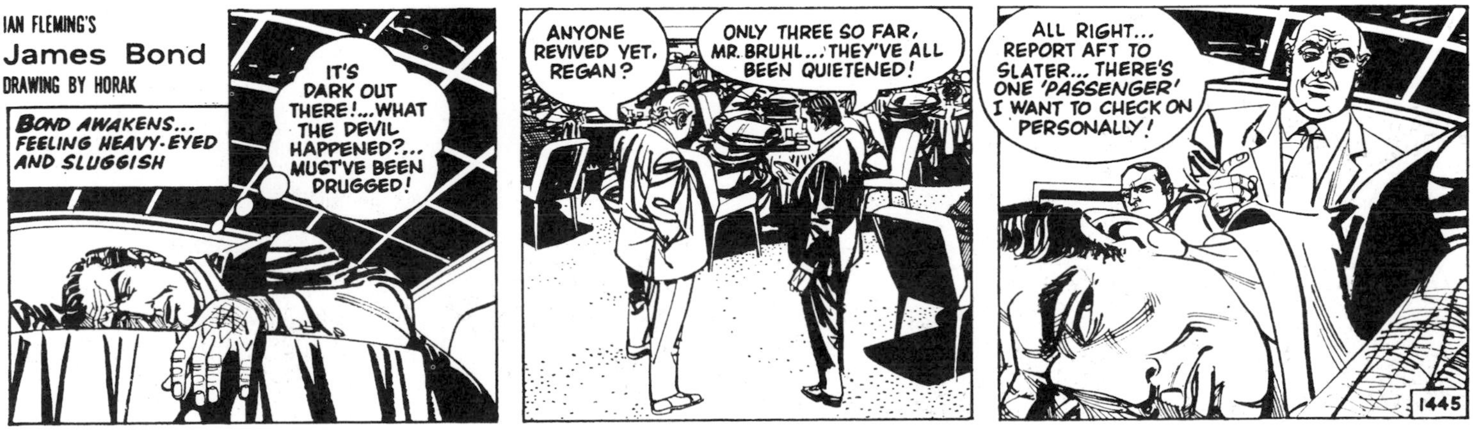
IAN FLEMING'S
James Bond
DRAWING BY HORAK
BOND AWAKENS... FEELING HEAVY-EYED AND SLUGGISH
IT'S DARK OUT THERE!... WHAT THE DEVIL HAPPENED?... MUST'VE BEEN DRUGGED!
ANYONE REVIVED YET, REGAN?
ONLY THREE SO FAR, MR. BRUHL... THEY'VE ALL BEEN QUIETENED!
ALL RIGHT... REPORT AFT TO SLATER... THERE'S ONE 'PASSENGER' I WANT TO CHECK ON PERSONALLY!
1445

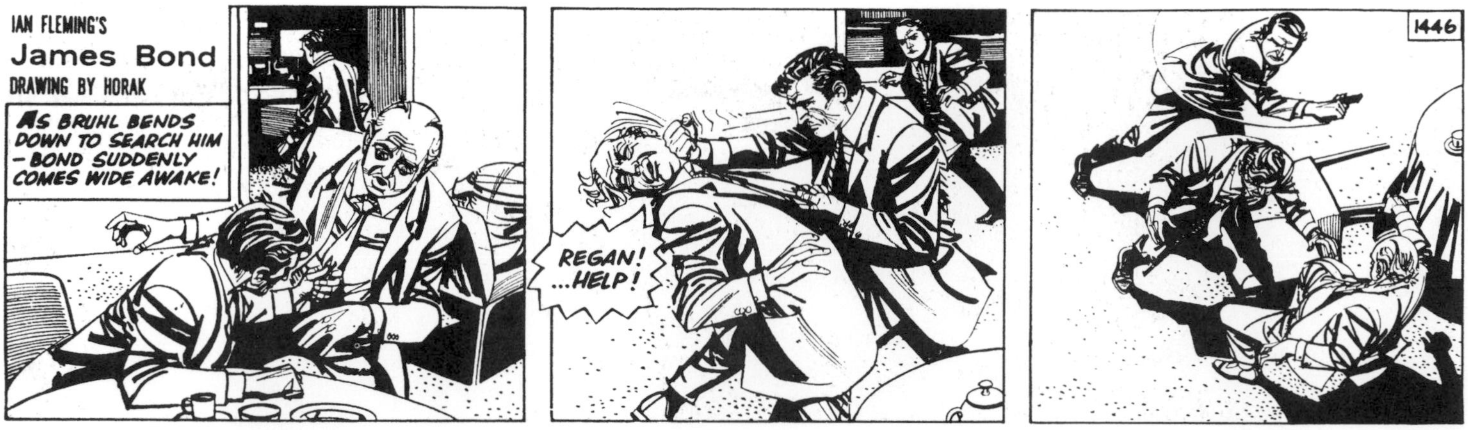
IAN FLEMING'S
James Bond
DRAWING BY HORAK
AS BRUHL BENDS DOWN TO SEARCH HIM – BOND SUDDENLY COMES WIDE AWAKE!
REGAN! ...HELP!
1446

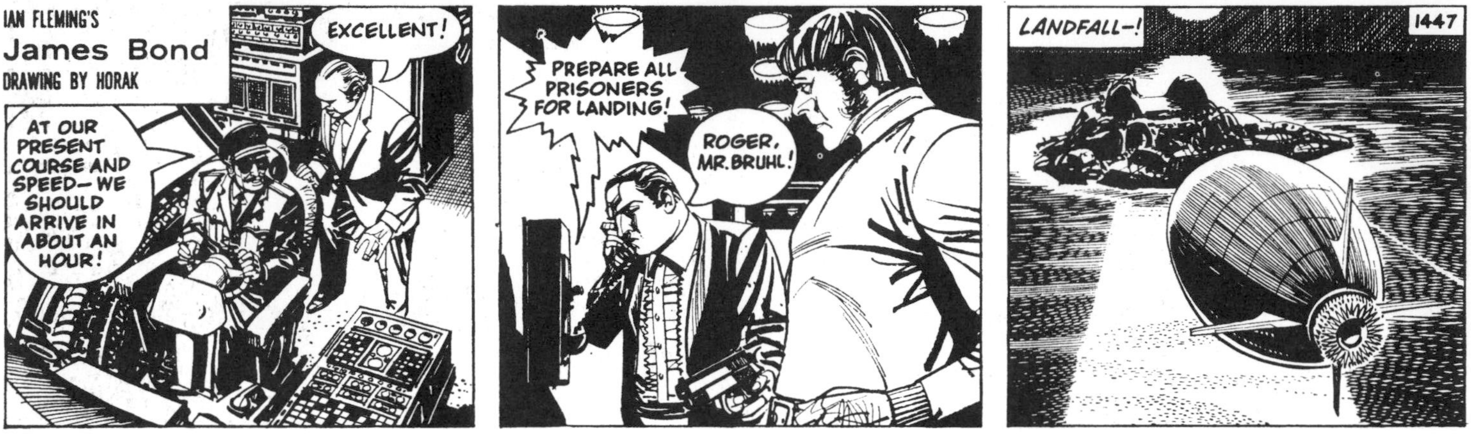
IAN FLEMING'S
James Bond
DRAWING BY HORAK
EXCELLENT!
AT OUR PRESENT COURSE AND SPEED– WE SHOULD ARRIVE IN ABOUT AN HOUR!
PREPARE ALL PRISONERS FOR LANDING!
ROGER, MR. BRUHL!
LANDFALL–!
1447

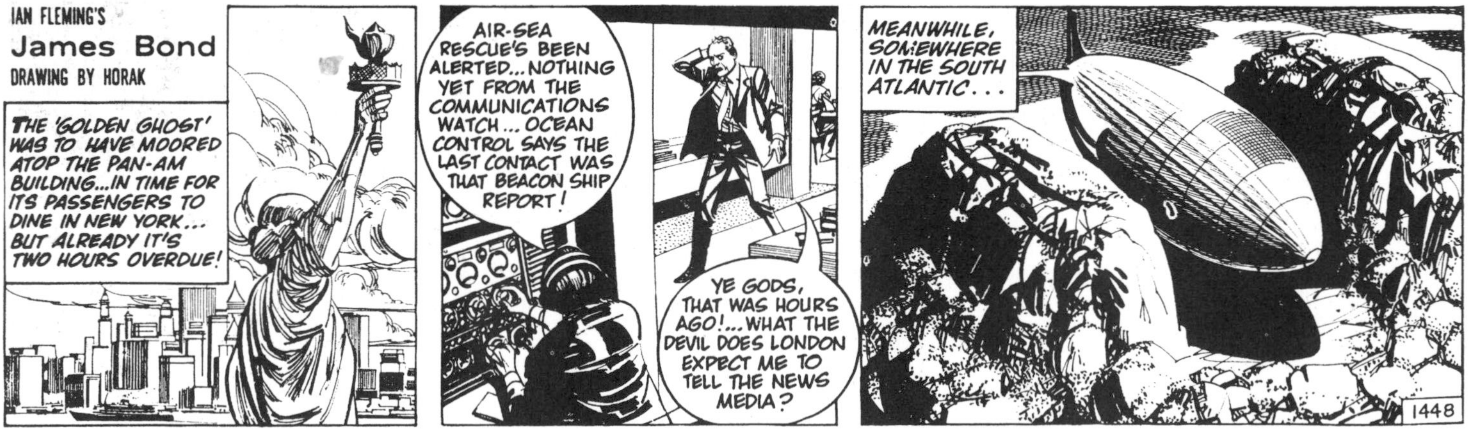
IAN FLEMING'S
James Bond
DRAWING BY HORAK
THE 'GOLDEN GHOST' WAS TO HAVE MOORED ATOP THE PAN-AM BUILDING... IN TIME FOR ITS PASSENGERS TO DINE IN NEW YORK... BUT ALREADY IT'S TWO HOURS OVERDUE!
AIR-SEA RESCUE'S BEEN ALERTED... NOTHING YET FROM THE COMMUNICATIONS WATCH... OCEAN CONTROL SAYS THE LAST CONTACT WAS THAT BEACON SHIP REPORT!
YE GODS, THAT WAS HOURS AGO!... WHAT THE DEVIL DOES LONDON EXPECT ME TO TELL THE NEWS MEDIA?
MEANWHILE, SOMEWHERE IN THE SOUTH ATLANTIC...
1448

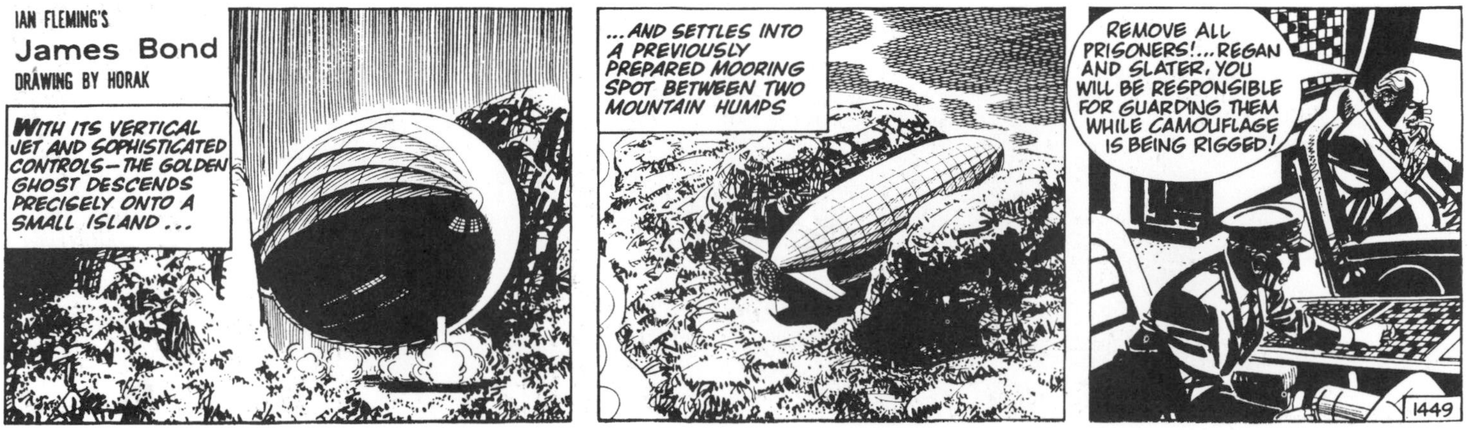
IAN FLEMING'S
James Bond
DRAWING BY HORAK
WITH ITS VERTICAL JET AND SOPHISTICATED CONTROLS – THE GOLDEN GHOST DESCENDS PRECISELY ONTO A SMALL ISLAND...
...AND SETTLES INTO A PREVIOUSLY PREPARED MOORING SPOT BETWEEN TWO MOUNTAIN HUMPS
REMOVE ALL PRISONERS!... REGAN AND SLATER, YOU WILL BE RESPONSIBLE FOR GUARDING THEM WHILE CAMOUFLAGE IS BEING RIGGED!
1449

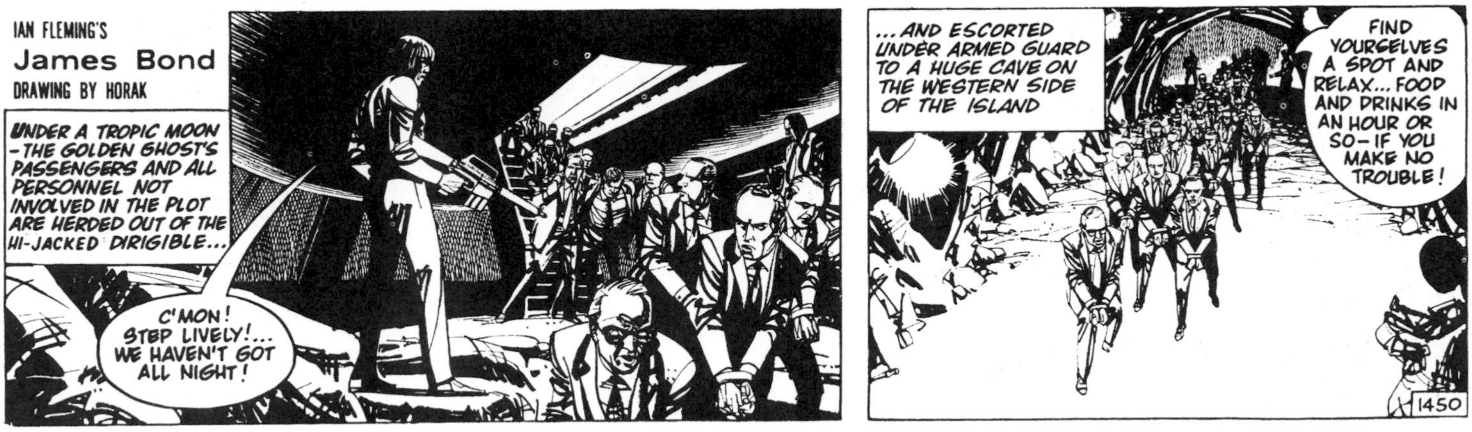
IAN FLEMING'S
James Bond
DRAWING BY HORAK
UNDER A TROPIC MOON —THE GOLDEN GHOST'S PASSENGERS AND ALL PERSONNEL NOT INVOLVED IN THE PLOT ARE HERDED OUT OF THE HI-JACKED DIRIGIBLE...
C'MON! STEP LIVELY!... WE HAVEN'T GOT ALL NIGHT!
...AND ESCORTED UNDER ARMED GUARD TO A HUGE CAVE ON THE WESTERN SIDE OF THE ISLAND
FIND YOURSELVES A SPOT AND RELAX... FOOD AND DRINKS IN AN HOUR OR SO—IF YOU MAKE NO TROUBLE!
1450

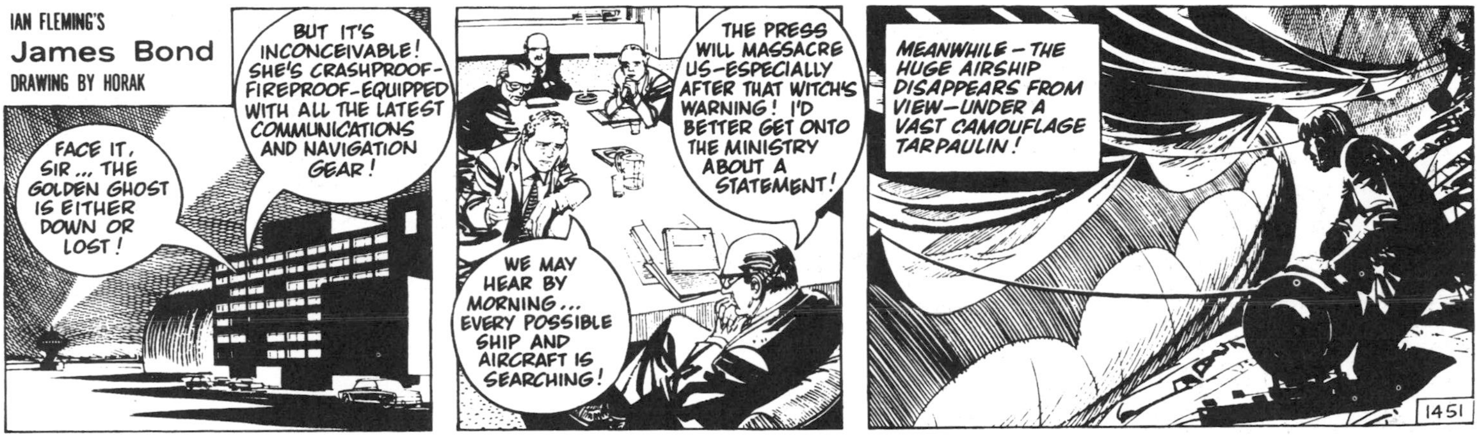
IAN FLEMING'S
James Bond
DRAWING BY HORAK
FACE IT, SIR... THE GOLDEN GHOST IS EITHER DOWN OR LOST!
BUT IT'S INCONCEIVABLE! SHE'S CRASHPROOF-FIREPROOF-EQUIPPED WITH ALL THE LATEST COMMUNICATIONS AND NAVIGATION GEAR!
THE PRESS WILL MASSACRE US—ESPECIALLY AFTER THAT WITCH'S WARNING! I'D BETTER GET ONTO THE MINISTRY ABOUT A STATEMENT!
WE MAY HEAR BY MORNING... EVERY POSSIBLE SHIP AND AIRCRAFT IS SEARCHING!
MEANWHILE—THE HUGE AIRSHIP DISAPPEARS FROM VIEW—UNDER A VAST CAMOUFLAGE TARPAULIN!
1451

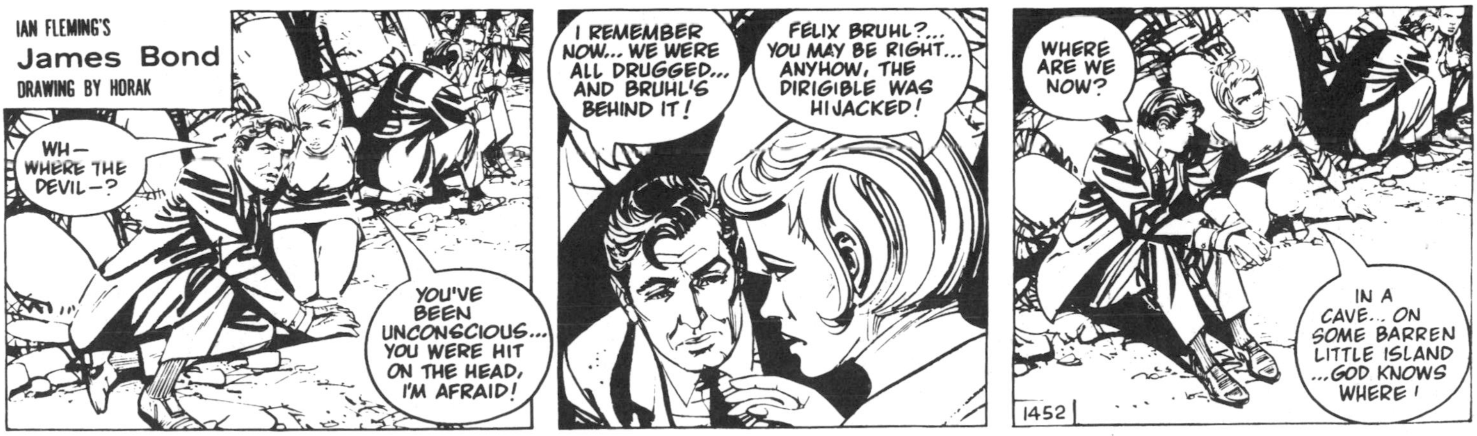
IAN FLEMING'S
James Bond
DRAWING BY HORAK
WH— WHERE THE DEVIL—?
YOU'VE BEEN UNCONSCIOUS... YOU WERE HIT ON THE HEAD, I'M AFRAID!
I REMEMBER NOW... WE WERE ALL DRUGGED... AND BRUHL'S BEHIND IT!
FELIX BRUHL?... YOU MAY BE RIGHT... ANYHOW, THE DIRIGIBLE WAS HIJACKED!
WHERE ARE WE NOW?
IN A CAVE... ON SOME BARREN LITTLE ISLAND ...GOD KNOWS WHERE!
1452

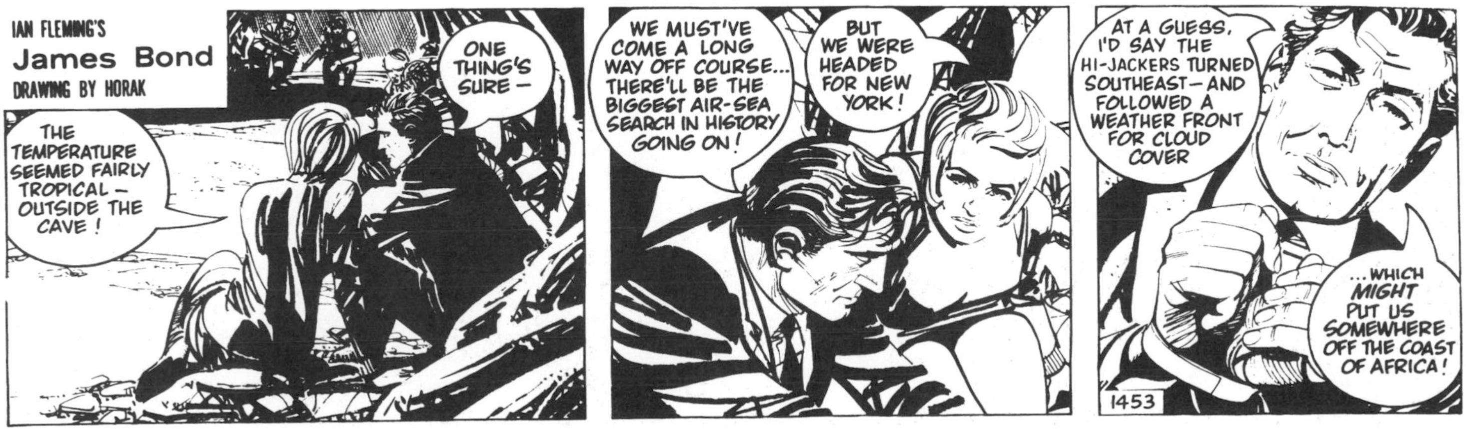
IAN FLEMING'S
James Bond
DRAWING BY HORAK
ONE THING'S SURE—
THE TEMPERATURE SEEMED FAIRLY TROPICAL— OUTSIDE THE CAVE!
WE MUST'VE COME A LONG WAY OFF COURSE... THERE'LL BE THE BIGGEST AIR-SEA SEARCH IN HISTORY GOING ON!
BUT WE WERE HEADED FOR NEW YORK!
AT A GUESS, I'D SAY THE HI-JACKERS TURNED SOUTHEAST—AND FOLLOWED A WEATHER FRONT FOR CLOUD COVER
...WHICH MIGHT PUT US SOMEWHERE OFF THE COAST OF AFRICA!
1453

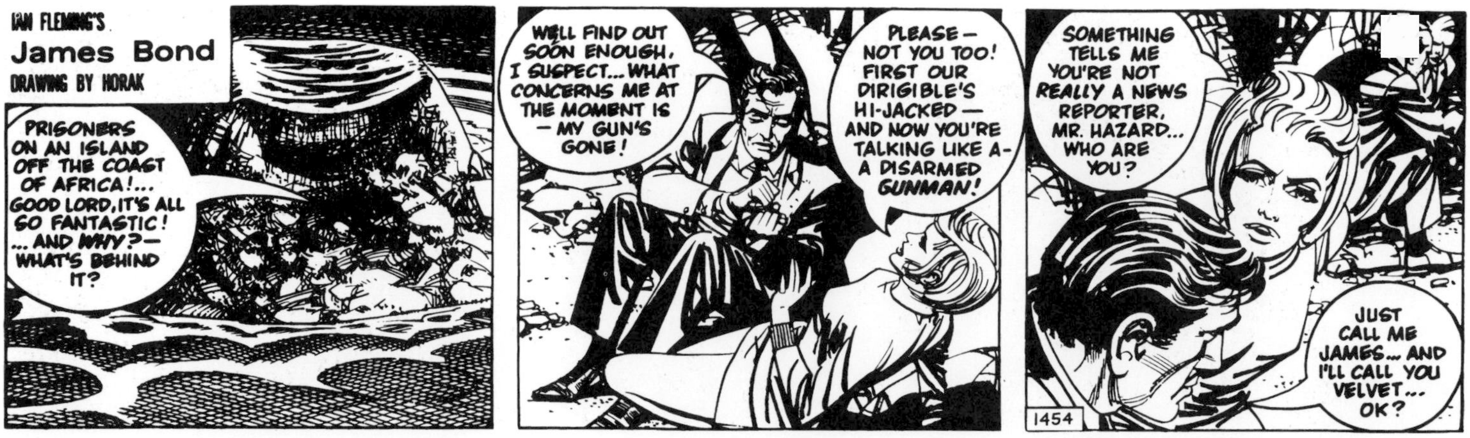
IAN FLEMING'S
James Bond
DRAWING BY HORAK
PRISONERS ON AN ISLAND OFF THE COAST OF AFRICA!... GOOD LORD, IT'S ALL SO FANTASTIC! ... AND WHY?— WHAT'S BEHIND IT?
WE'LL FIND OUT SOON ENOUGH, I SUSPECT... WHAT CONCERNS ME AT THE MOMENT IS — MY GUN'S GONE!
PLEASE— NOT YOU TOO! FIRST OUR DIRIGIBLE'S HI-JACKED— AND NOW YOU'RE TALKING LIKE A DISARMED GUNMAN!
SOMETHING TELLS ME YOU'RE NOT REALLY A NEWS REPORTER, MR. HAZARD... WHO ARE YOU?
JUST CALL ME JAMES... AND I'LL CALL YOU VELVET... OK?
1454

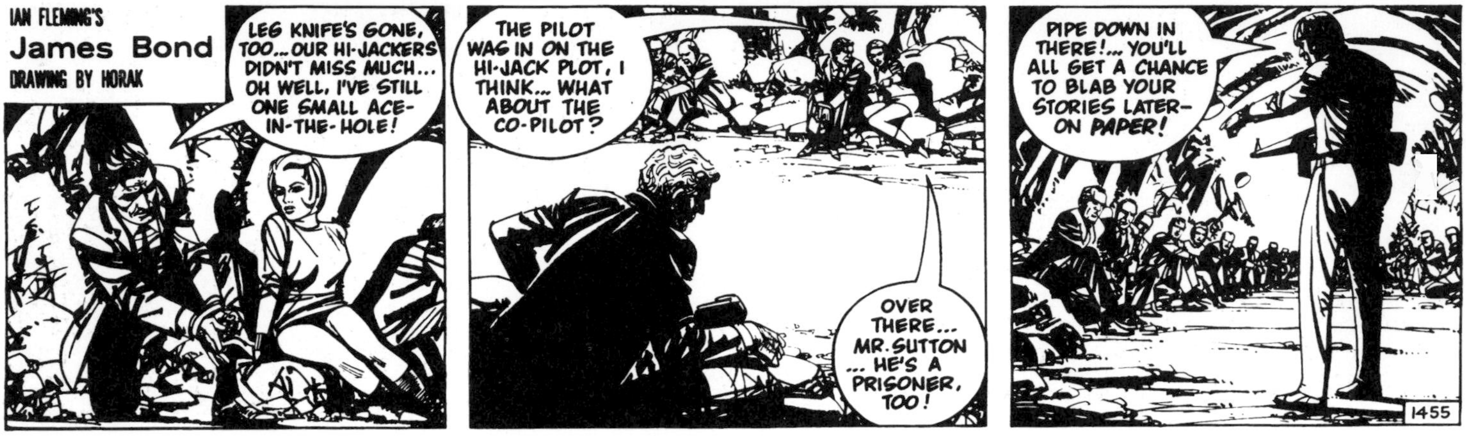
IAN FLEMING'S
James Bond
DRAWING BY HORAK
LEG KNIFE'S GONE, TOO... OUR HI-JACKERS DIDN'T MISS MUCH... OH WELL, I'VE STILL ONE SMALL ACE-IN-THE-HOLE!
THE PILOT WAS IN ON THE HI-JACK PLOT, I THINK... WHAT ABOUT THE CO-PILOT?
OVER THERE... MR. SUTTON ... HE'S A PRISONER, TOO!
PIPE DOWN IN THERE!... YOU'LL ALL GET A CHANCE TO BLAB YOUR STORIES LATER— ON PAPER!
1455

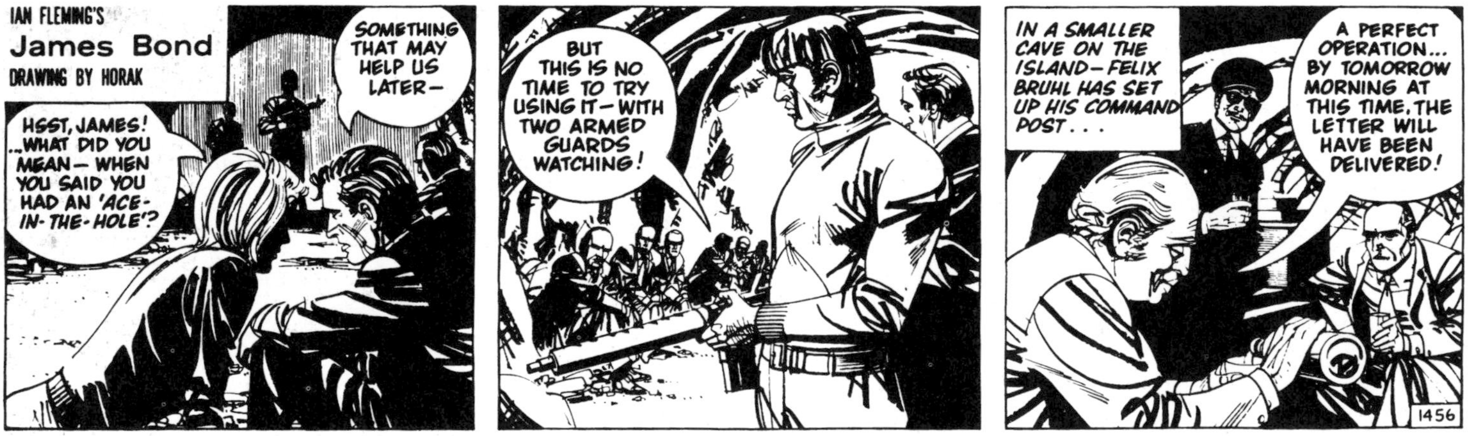
IAN FLEMING'S
James Bond
DRAWING BY HORAK
HSST, JAMES! ...WHAT DID YOU MEAN— WHEN YOU SAID YOU HAD AN 'ACE-IN-THE-HOLE'?
SOMETHING THAT MAY HELP US LATER—
BUT THIS IS NO TIME TO TRY USING IT— WITH TWO ARMED GUARDS WATCHING!
IN A SMALLER CAVE ON THE ISLAND— FELIX BRUHL HAS SET UP HIS COMMAND POST . . .
A PERFECT OPERATION... BY TOMORROW MORNING AT THIS TIME, THE LETTER WILL HAVE BEEN DELIVERED!
1456

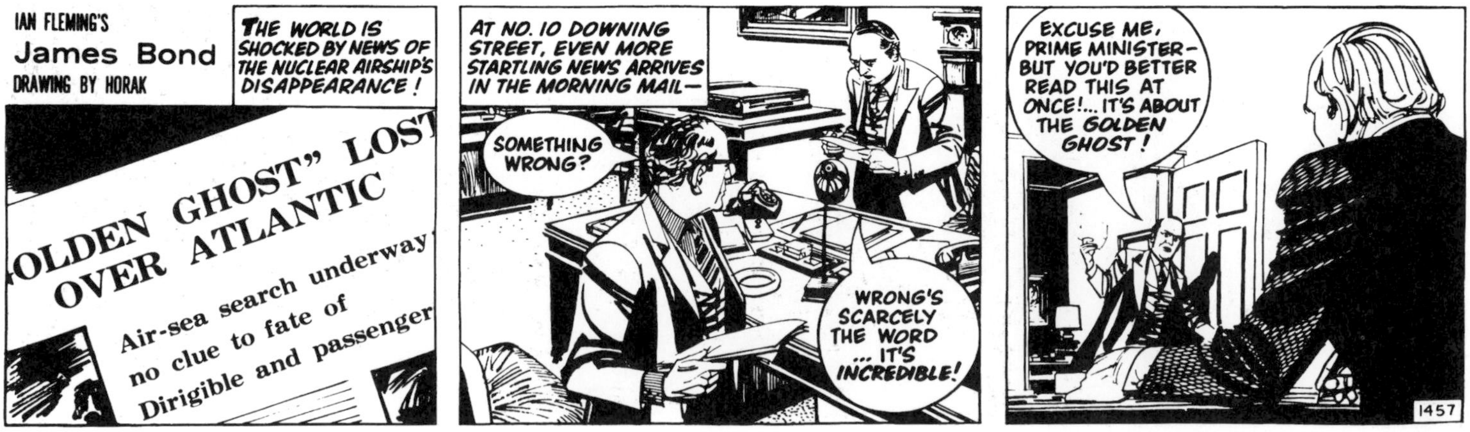
IAN FLEMING'S
James Bond
DRAWING BY HORAK
THE WORLD IS SHOCKED BY NEWS OF THE NUCLEAR AIRSHIP'S DISAPPEARANCE!
OLDEN GHOST" LOST OVER ATLANTIC
Air-sea search underway
no clue to fate of
Dirigible and passenger
AT NO. 10 DOWNING STREET, EVEN MORE STARTLING NEWS ARRIVES IN THE MORNING MAIL—
SOMETHING WRONG?
WRONG'S SCARCELY THE WORD ... IT'S INCREDIBLE!
EXCUSE ME, PRIME MINISTER— BUT YOU'D BETTER READ THIS AT ONCE!... IT'S ABOUT THE GOLDEN GHOST!
1457

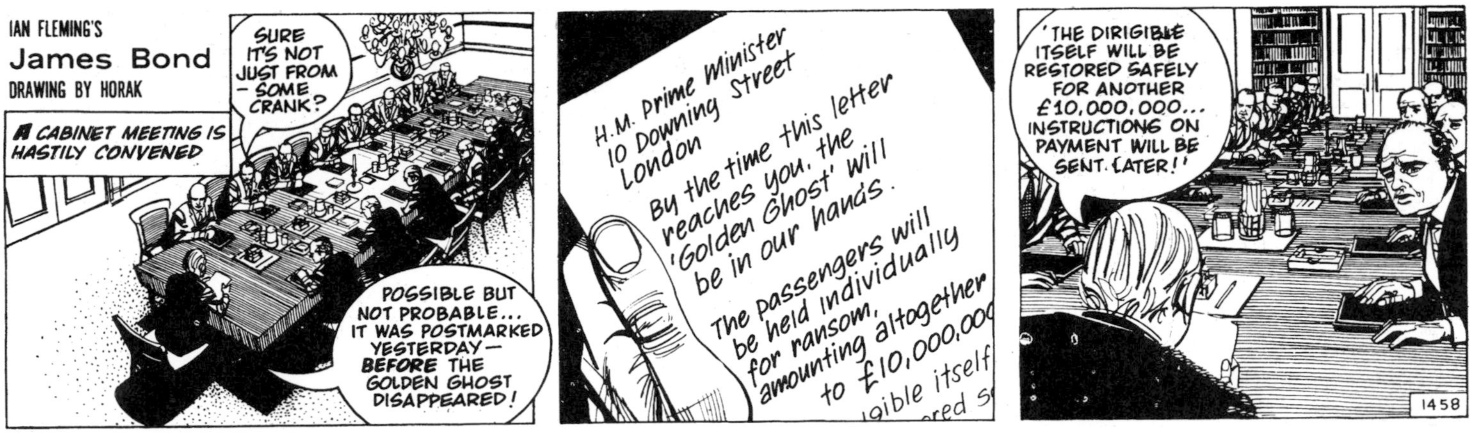
IAN FLEMING'S
James Bond
DRAWING BY HORAK
A CABINET MEETING IS HASTILY CONVENED
SURE IT'S NOT JUST FROM —SOME CRANK?
POSSIBLE BUT NOT PROBABLE... IT WAS POSTMARKED YESTERDAY— BEFORE THE GOLDEN GHOST DISAPPEARED!
H.M. Prime Minister
10 Downing Street
London
By the time this letter reaches you, the 'Golden Ghost' will be in our hands.
The passengers will be held individually for ransom, amounting altogether to £10,000,00
'THE DIRIGIBLE ITSELF WILL BE RESTORED SAFELY FOR ANOTHER £10,000,000... INSTRUCTIONS ON PAYMENT WILL BE SENT LATER!'
1458

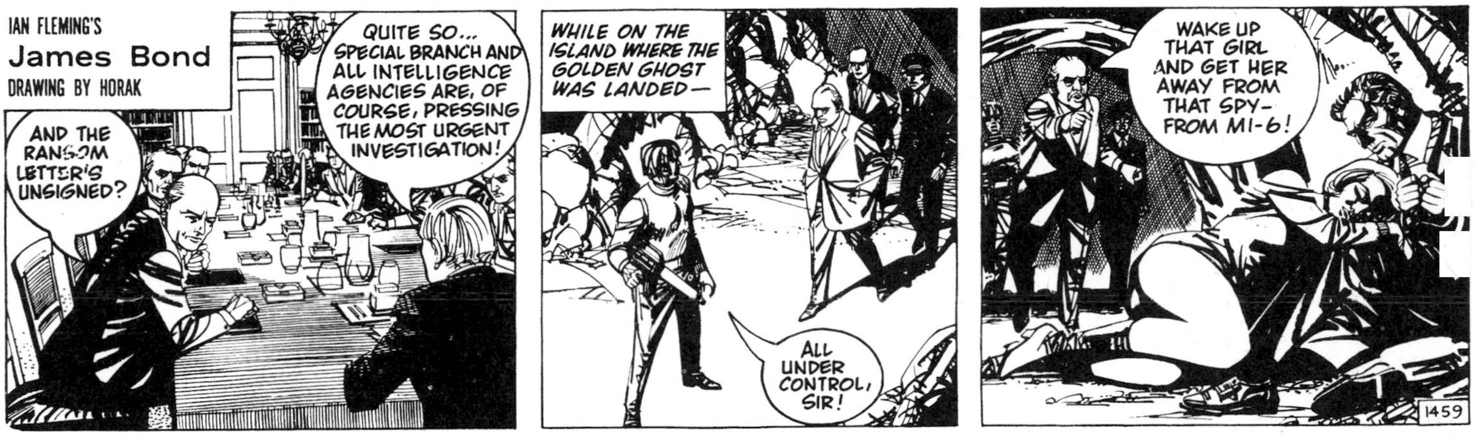
IAN FLEMING'S
James Bond
DRAWING BY HORAK
AND THE RANSOM LETTER'S UNSIGNED?
QUITE SO... SPECIAL BRANCH AND ALL INTELLIGENCE AGENCIES ARE, OF COURSE, PRESSING THE MOST URGENT INVESTIGATION!
WHILE ON THE ISLAND WHERE THE GOLDEN GHOST WAS LANDED—
ALL UNDER CONTROL, SIR!
WAKE UP THAT GIRL AND GET HER AWAY FROM THAT SPY— FROM MI-6!
1459

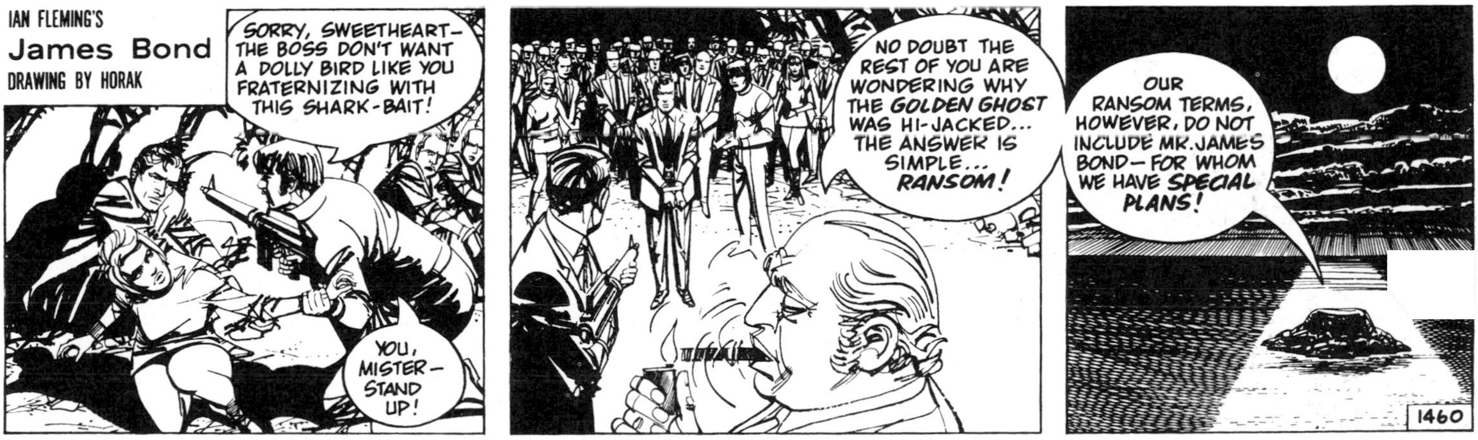
IAN FLEMING'S
James Bond
DRAWING BY HORAK
SORRY, SWEETHEART— THE BOSS DON'T WANT A DOLLY BIRD LIKE YOU FRATERNIZING WITH THIS SHARK-BAIT!
YOU, MISTER— STAND UP!
NO DOUBT THE REST OF YOU ARE WONDERING WHY THE GOLDEN GHOST WAS HI-JACKED... THE ANSWER IS SIMPLE... RANSOM!
OUR RANSOM TERMS, HOWEVER, DO NOT INCLUDE MR. JAMES BOND— FOR WHOM WE HAVE SPECIAL PLANS!
1460

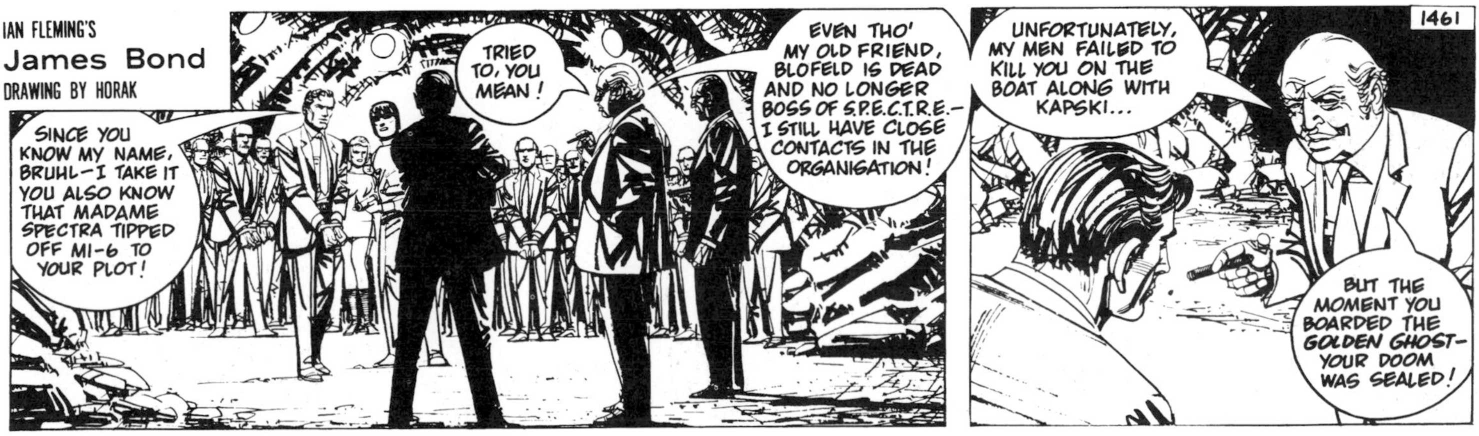
IAN FLEMING'S
James Bond
DRAWING BY HORAK
SINCE YOU KNOW MY NAME, BRUHL—I TAKE IT YOU ALSO KNOW THAT MADAME SPECTRA TIPPED OFF MI-6 TO YOUR PLOT!
TRIED TO, YOU MEAN!
EVEN THO' MY OLD FRIEND, BLOFELD IS DEAD AND NO LONGER BOSS OF S.P.E.C.T.R.E.— I STILL HAVE CLOSE CONTACTS IN THE ORGANISATION!
1461
UNFORTUNATELY, MY MEN FAILED TO KILL YOU ON THE BOAT ALONG WITH KAPSKI...
BUT THE MOMENT YOU BOARDED THE GOLDEN GHOST— YOUR DOOM WAS SEALED!

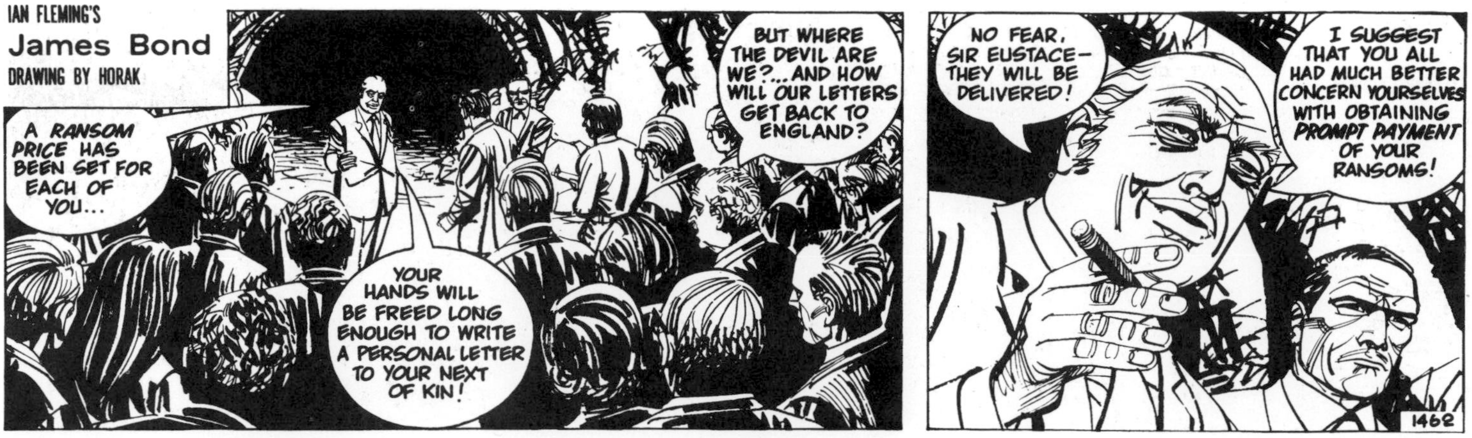
IAN FLEMING'S
James Bond
DRAWING BY HORAK
A RANSOM PRICE HAS BEEN SET FOR EACH OF YOU...
BUT WHERE THE DEVIL ARE WE?...AND HOW WILL OUR LETTERS GET BACK TO ENGLAND?
YOUR HANDS WILL BE FREED LONG ENOUGH TO WRITE A PERSONAL LETTER TO YOUR NEXT OF KIN!
NO FEAR, SIR EUSTACE— THEY WILL BE DELIVERED!
I SUGGEST THAT YOU ALL HAD MUCH BETTER CONCERN YOURSELVES WITH OBTAINING PROMPT PAYMENT OF YOUR RANSOMS!
1462

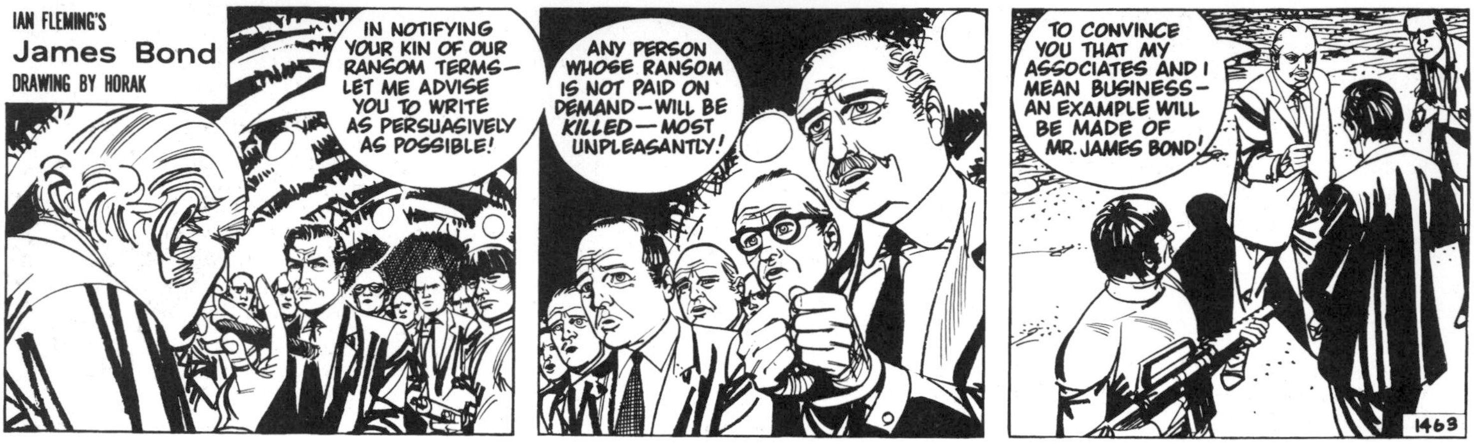
IAN FLEMING'S
James Bond
DRAWING BY HORAK
IN NOTIFYING YOUR KIN OF OUR RANSOM TERMS— LET ME ADVISE YOU TO WRITE AS PERSUASIVELY AS POSSIBLE!
ANY PERSON WHOSE RANSOM IS NOT PAID ON DEMAND—WILL BE KILLED—MOST UNPLEASANTLY!
TO CONVINCE YOU THAT MY ASSOCIATES AND I MEAN BUSINESS— AN EXAMPLE WILL BE MADE OF MR. JAMES BOND!
1463

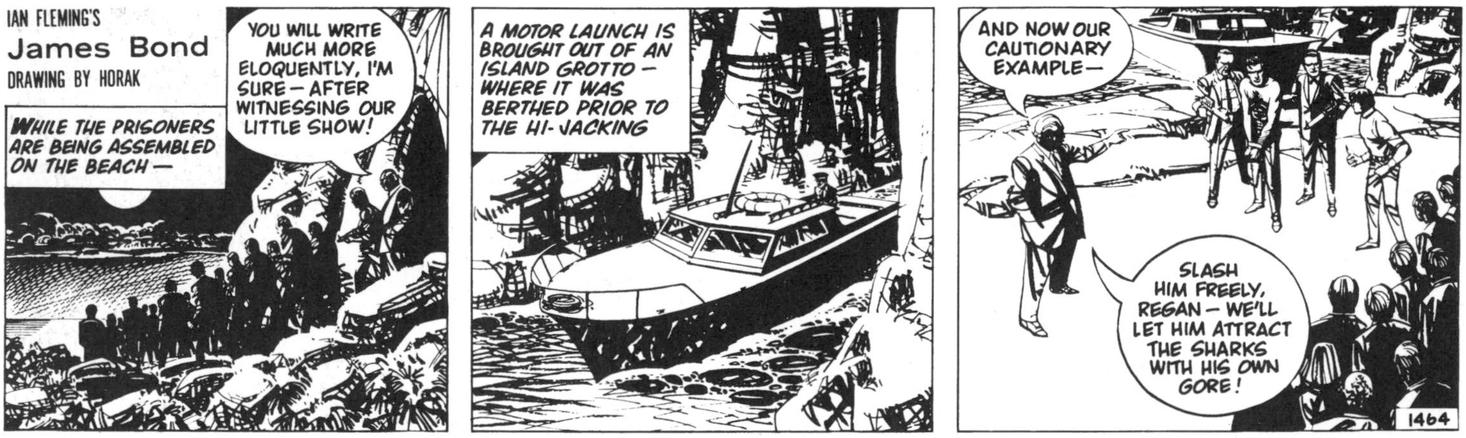
IAN FLEMING'S
James Bond
DRAWING BY HORAK
WHILE THE PRISONERS ARE BEING ASSEMBLED ON THE BEACH—
YOU WILL WRITE MUCH MORE ELOQUENTLY, I'M SURE—AFTER WITNESSING OUR LITTLE SHOW!
A MOTOR LAUNCH IS BROUGHT OUT OF AN ISLAND GROTTO— WHERE IT WAS BERTHED PRIOR TO THE HI-JACKING
AND NOW OUR CAUTIONARY EXAMPLE—
SLASH HIM FREELY, REGAN— WE'LL LET HIM ATTRACT THE SHARKS WITH HIS OWN GORE!
1464

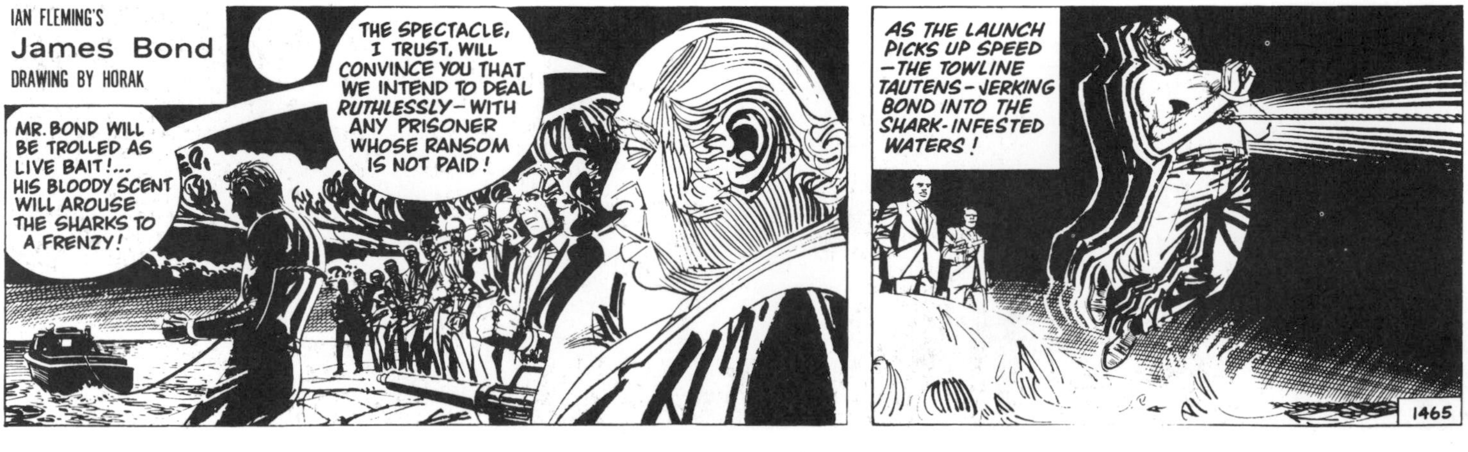
IAN FLEMING'S
James Bond
DRAWING BY HORAK
MR. BOND WILL BE TROLLED AS LIVE BAIT!... HIS BLOODY SCENT WILL AROUSE THE SHARKS TO A FRENZY!
THE SPECTACLE, I TRUST, WILL CONVINCE YOU THAT WE INTEND TO DEAL RUTHLESSLY—WITH ANY PRISONER WHOSE RANSOM IS NOT PAID!
AS THE LAUNCH PICKS UP SPEED —THE TOWLINE TAUTENS—JERKING BOND INTO THE SHARK-INFESTED WATERS!
1465

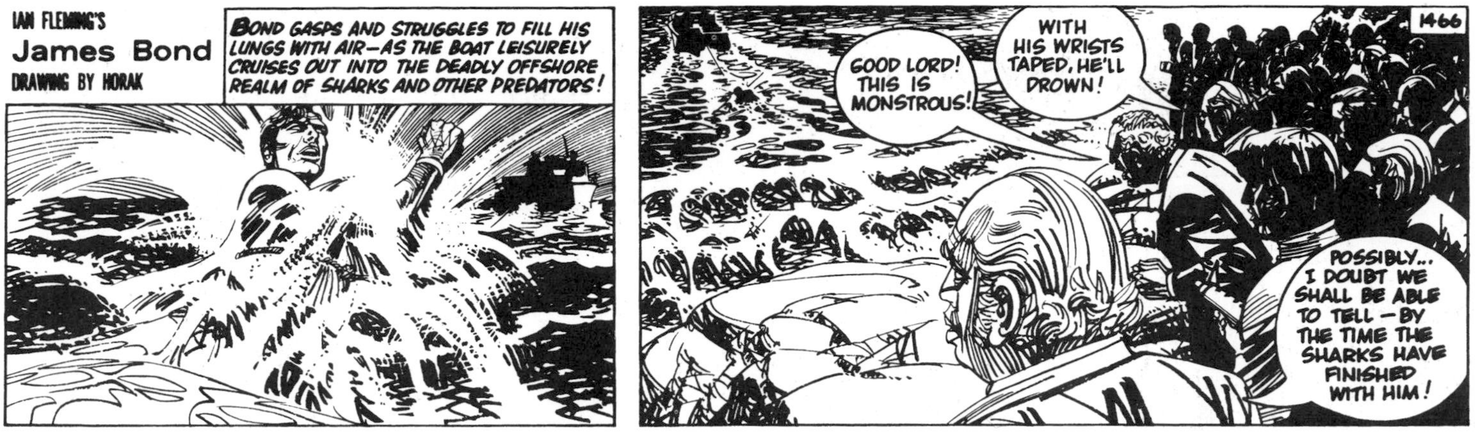
IAN FLEMING'S
James Bond
DRAWING BY HORAK
BOND GASPS AND STRUGGLES TO FILL HIS LUNGS WITH AIR—AS THE BOAT LEISURELY CRUISES OUT INTO THE DEADLY OFFSHORE REALM OF SHARKS AND OTHER PREDATORS!
1466
GOOD LORD! THIS IS MONSTROUS!
WITH HIS WRISTS TAPED, HE'LL DROWN!
POSSIBLY... I DOUBT WE SHALL BE ABLE TO TELL—BY THE TIME THE SHARKS HAVE FINISHED WITH HIM!

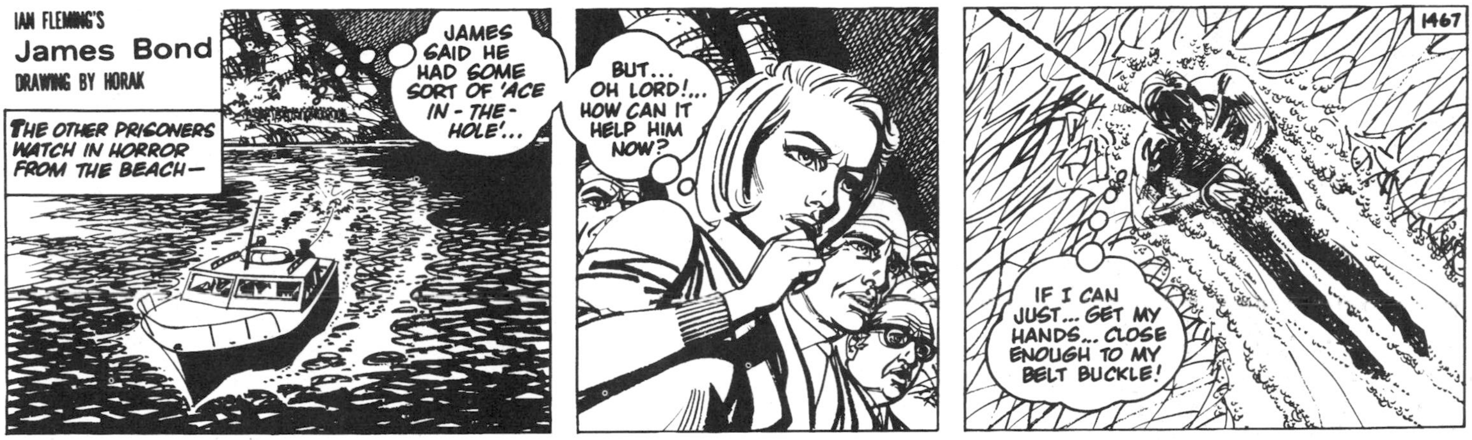
IAN FLEMING'S
James Bond
DRAWING BY HORAK
THE OTHER PRISONERS WATCH IN HORROR FROM THE BEACH—
JAMES SAID HE HAD SOME SORT OF 'ACE IN-THE-HOLE'...
BUT... OH LORD!... HOW CAN IT HELP HIM NOW?
1467
IF I CAN JUST... GET MY HANDS... CLOSE ENOUGH TO MY BELT BUCKLE!

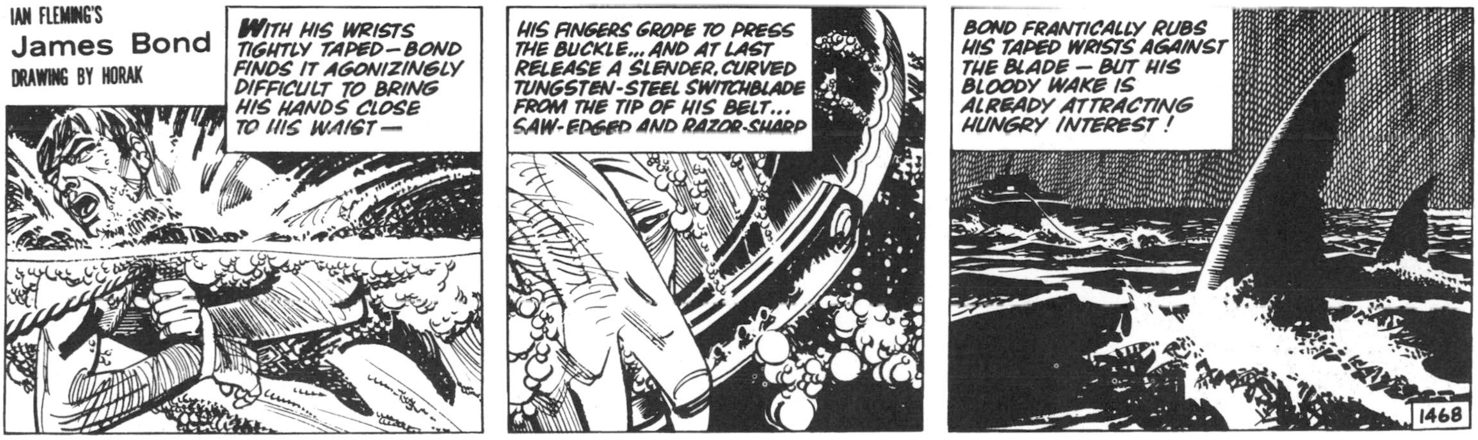
IAN FLEMING'S
James Bond
DRAWING BY HORAK
WITH HIS WRISTS TIGHTLY TAPED—BOND FINDS IT AGONIZINGLY DIFFICULT TO BRING HIS HANDS CLOSE TO HIS WAIST—
HIS FINGERS GROPE TO PRESS THE BUCKLE... AND AT LAST RELEASE A SLENDER, CURVED TUNGSTEN-STEEL SWITCHBLADE FROM THE TIP OF HIS BELT... SAW-EDGED AND RAZOR-SHARP
BOND FRANTICALLY RUBS HIS TAPED WRISTS AGAINST THE BLADE — BUT HIS BLOODY WAKE IS ALREADY ATTRACTING HUNGRY INTEREST!
1468

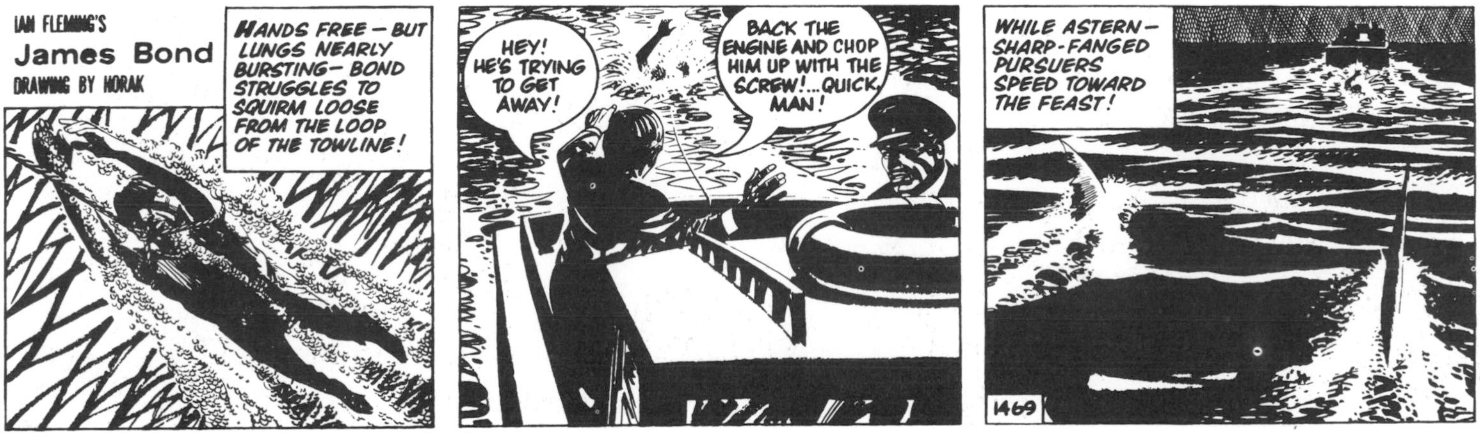
IAN FLEMING'S
James Bond
DRAWING BY HORAK
HANDS FREE—BUT LUNGS NEARLY BURSTING—BOND STRUGGLES TO SQUIRM LOOSE FROM THE LOOP OF THE TOWLINE!
HEY! HE'S TRYING TO GET AWAY!
BACK THE ENGINE AND CHOP HIM UP WITH THE SCREW!... QUICK MAN!
WHILE ASTERN—SHARP-FANGED PURSUERS SPEED TOWARD THE FEAST!
1469

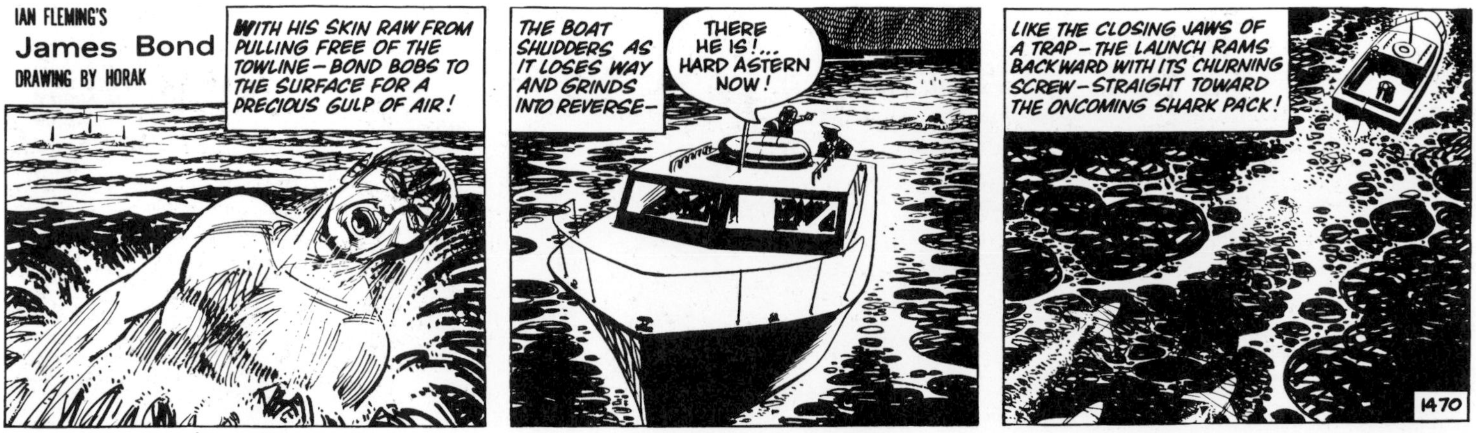
IAN FLEMING'S
James Bond
DRAWING BY HORAK
WITH HIS SKIN RAW FROM PULLING FREE OF THE TOWLINE—BOND BOBS TO THE SURFACE FOR A PRECIOUS GULP OF AIR!
THE BOAT SHUDDERS AS IT LOSES WAY AND GRINDS INTO REVERSE—
THERE HE IS!... HARD ASTERN NOW!
LIKE THE CLOSING JAWS OF A TRAP—THE LAUNCH RAMS BACKWARD WITH ITS CHURNING SCREW—STRAIGHT TOWARD THE ONCOMING SHARK PACK!
1470

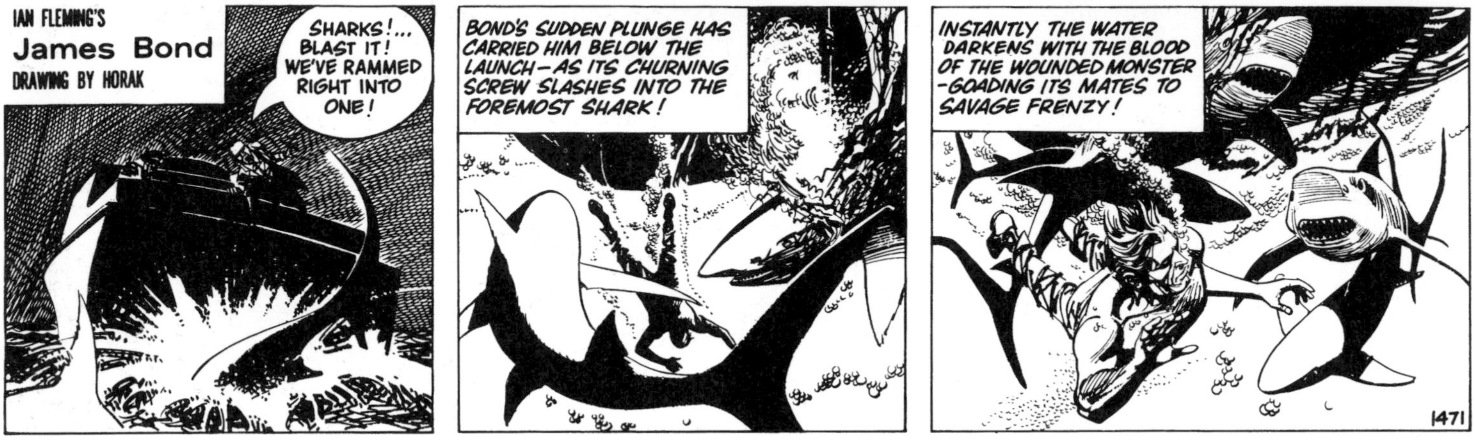
IAN FLEMING'S
James Bond
DRAWING BY HORAK
SHARKS!... BLAST IT! WE'VE RAMMED RIGHT INTO ONE!
BOND'S SUDDEN PLUNGE HAS CARRIED HIM BELOW THE LAUNCH—AS ITS CHURNING SCREW SLASHES INTO THE FOREMOST SHARK!
INSTANTLY THE WATER DARKENS WITH THE BLOOD OF THE WOUNDED MONSTER—GOADING ITS MATES TO SAVAGE FRENZY!
1471

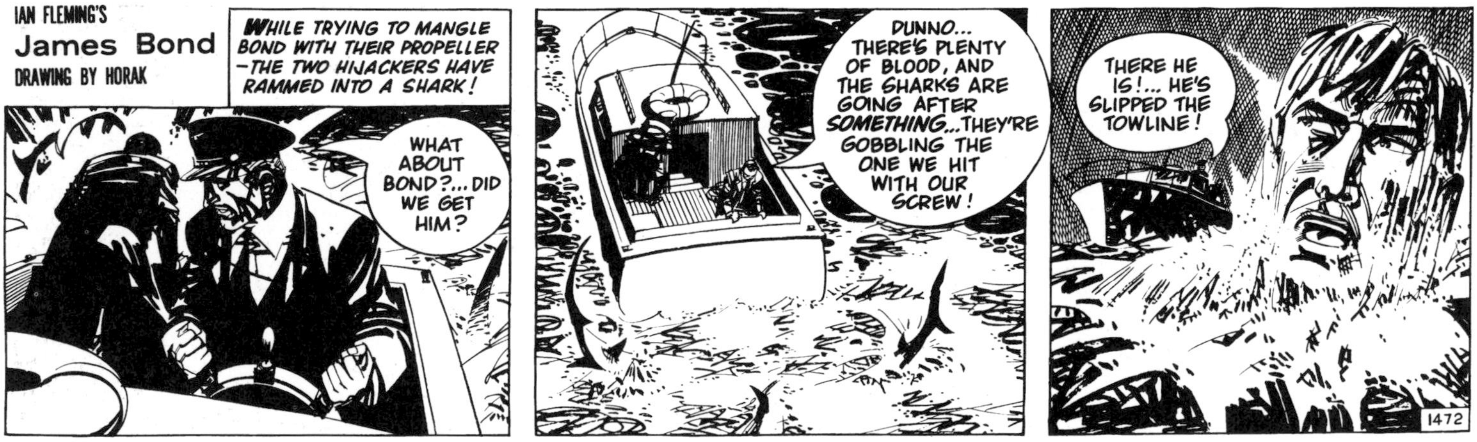
IAN FLEMING'S
James Bond
DRAWING BY HORAK
WHILE TRYING TO MANGLE BOND WITH THEIR PROPELLER—THE TWO HIJACKERS HAVE RAMMED INTO A SHARK!
WHAT ABOUT BOND?... DID WE GET HIM?
DUNNO... THERE'S PLENTY OF BLOOD, AND THE SHARKS ARE GOING AFTER SOMETHING... THEY'RE GOBBLING THE ONE WE HIT WITH OUR SCREW!
THERE HE IS!... HE'S SLIPPED THE TOWLINE!
1472

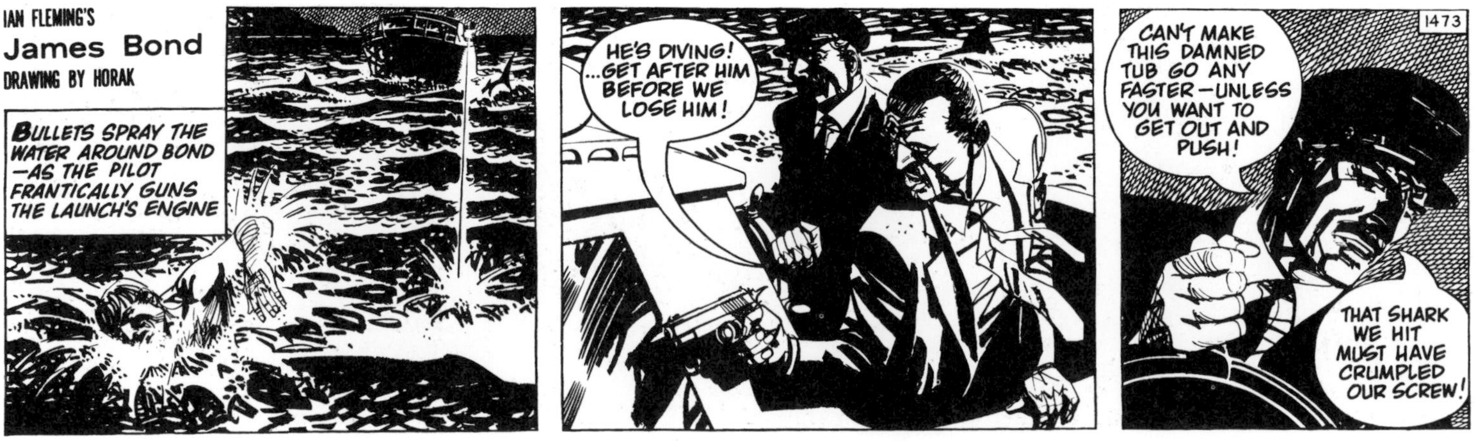
IAN FLEMING'S
James Bond
DRAWING BY HORAK
BULLETS SPRAY THE WATER AROUND BOND—AS THE PILOT FRANTICALLY GUNS THE LAUNCH'S ENGINE
HE'S DIVING! ...GET AFTER HIM BEFORE WE LOSE HIM!
1473
CAN'T MAKE THIS DAMNED TUB GO ANY FASTER—UNLESS YOU WANT TO GET OUT AND PUSH!
THAT SHARK WE HIT MUST HAVE CRUMPLED OUR SCREW!

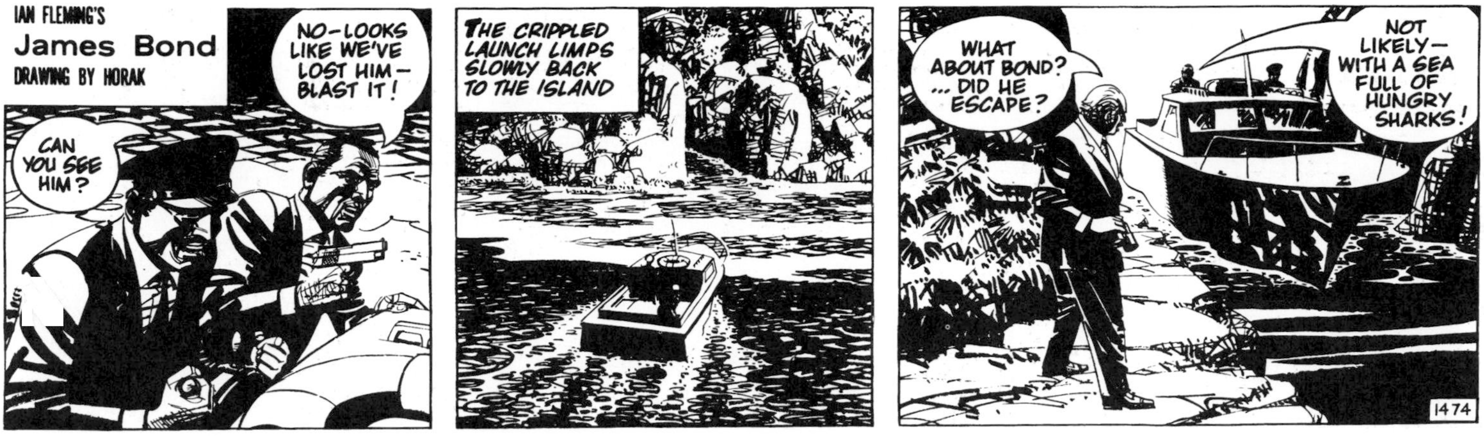
IAN FLEMING'S
James Bond
DRAWING BY HORAK
NO-LOOKS LIKE WE'VE LOST HIM-BLAST IT!
CAN YOU SEE HIM?
THE CRIPPLED LAUNCH LIMPS SLOWLY BACK TO THE ISLAND
WHAT ABOUT BOND? ... DID HE ESCAPE?
NOT LIKELY-WITH A SEA FULL OF HUNGRY SHARKS!
1474

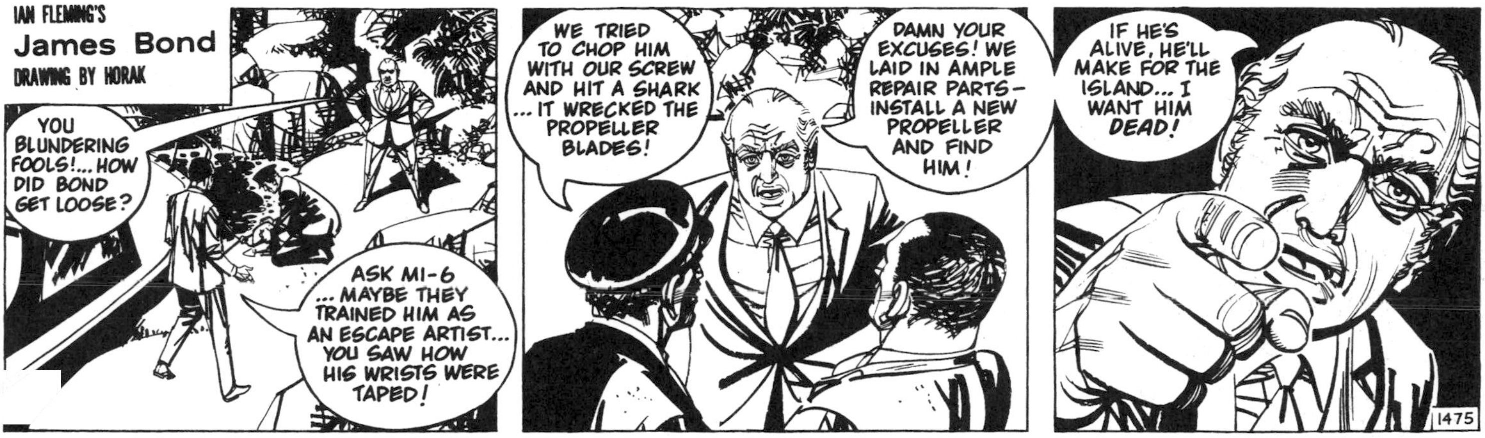
IAN FLEMING'S
James Bond
DRAWING BY HORAK
YOU BLUNDERING FOOLS!... HOW DID BOND GET LOOSE?
ASK MI-6 ... MAYBE THEY TRAINED HIM AS AN ESCAPE ARTIST... YOU SAW HOW HIS WRISTS WERE TAPED!
WE TRIED TO CHOP HIM WITH OUR SCREW AND HIT A SHARK ... IT WRECKED THE PROPELLER BLADES!
DAMN YOUR EXCUSES! WE LAID IN AMPLE REPAIR PARTS-INSTALL A NEW PROPELLER AND FIND HIM!
IF HE'S ALIVE, HE'LL MAKE FOR THE ISLAND... I WANT HIM DEAD!
1475

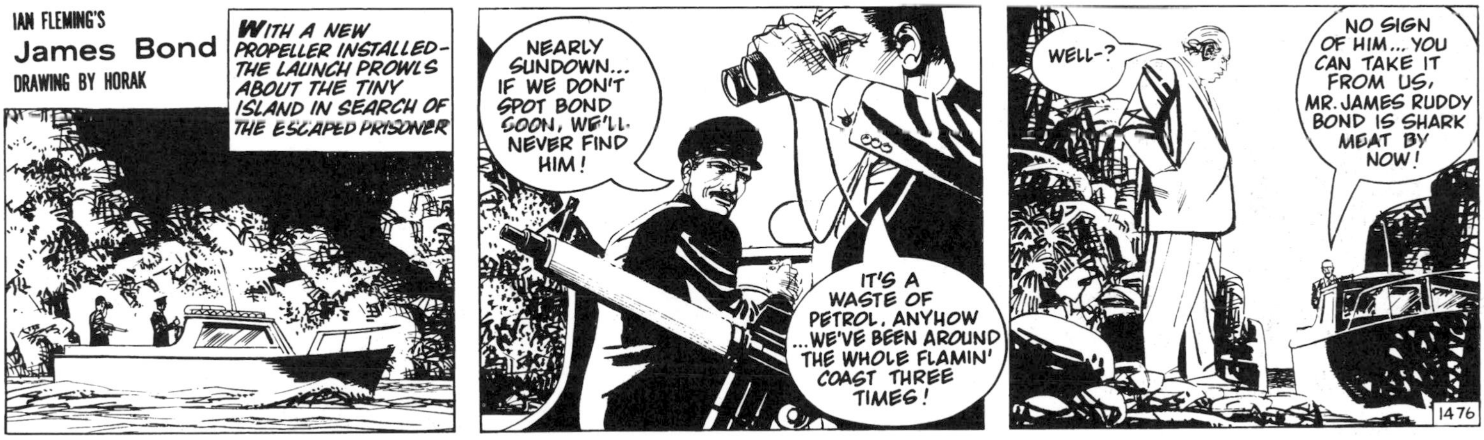
IAN FLEMING'S
James Bond
DRAWING BY HORAK
WITH A NEW PROPELLER INSTALLED-THE LAUNCH PROWLS ABOUT THE TINY ISLAND IN SEARCH OF THE ESCAPED PRISONER
NEARLY SUNDOWN... IF WE DON'T SPOT BOND SOON, WE'LL NEVER FIND HIM!
IT'S A WASTE OF PETROL, ANYHOW ...WE'VE BEEN AROUND THE WHOLE FLAMIN' COAST THREE TIMES!
WELL-?
NO SIGN OF HIM... YOU CAN TAKE IT FROM US, MR. JAMES RUDDY BOND IS SHARK MEAT BY NOW!
1476

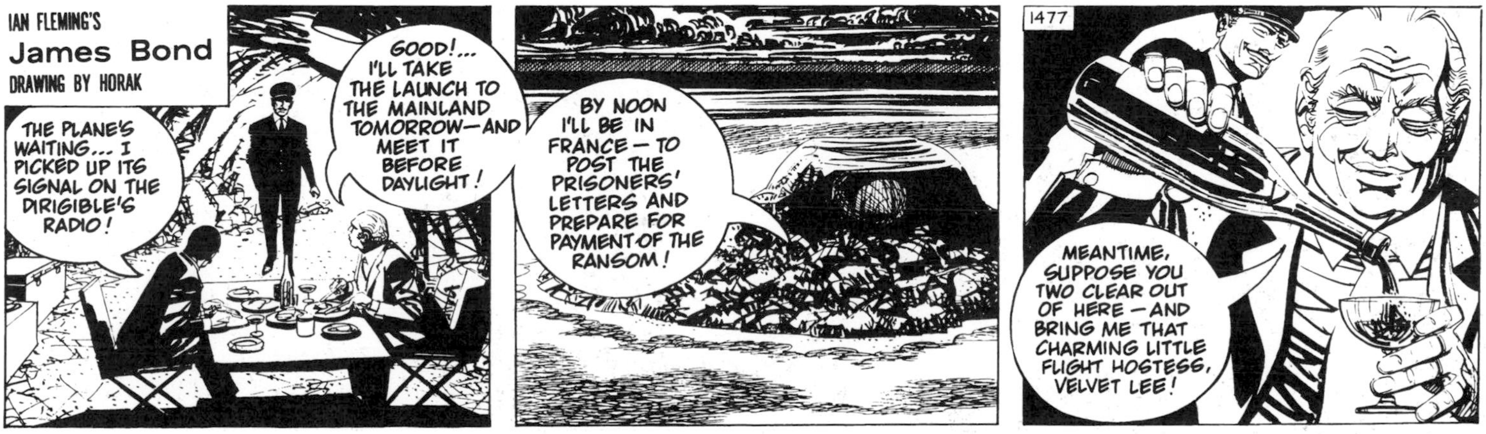
IAN FLEMING'S
James Bond
DRAWING BY HORAK
THE PLANE'S WAITING... I PICKED UP ITS SIGNAL ON THE DIRIGIBLE'S RADIO!
GOOD!... I'LL TAKE THE LAUNCH TO THE MAINLAND TOMORROW-AND MEET IT BEFORE DAYLIGHT!
BY NOON I'LL BE IN FRANCE-TO POST THE PRISONERS' LETTERS AND PREPARE FOR PAYMENT OF THE RANSOM!
1477
MEANTIME, SUPPOSE YOU TWO CLEAR OUT OF HERE-AND BRING ME THAT CHARMING LITTLE FLIGHT HOSTESS, VELVET LEE!

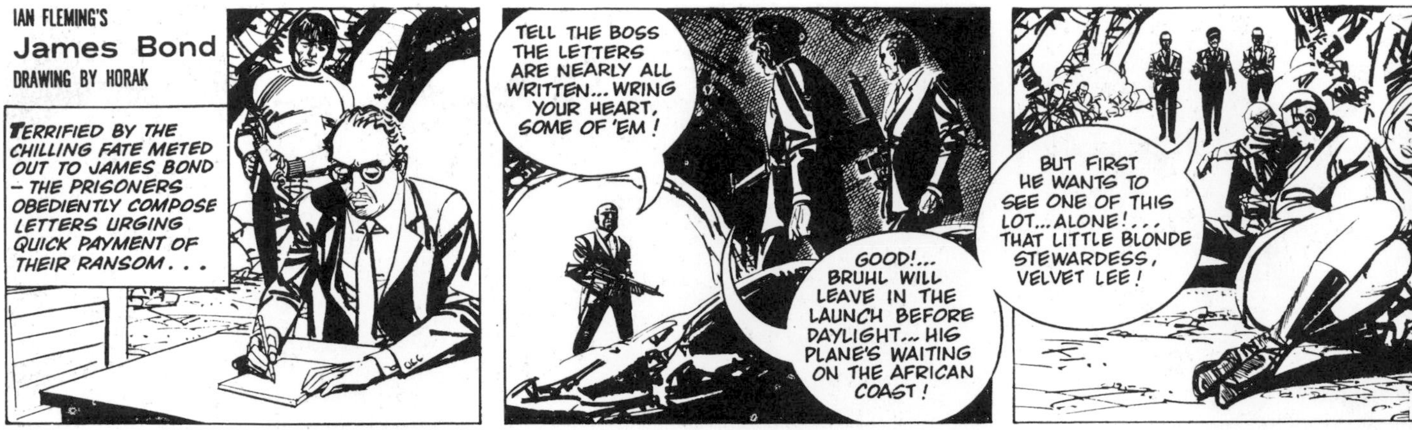
IAN FLEMING'S
James Bond
DRAWING BY HORAK
TERRIFIED BY THE CHILLING FATE METED OUT TO JAMES BOND – THE PRISONERS OBEDIENTLY COMPOSE LETTERS URGING QUICK PAYMENT OF THEIR RANSOM . . .
TELL THE BOSS THE LETTERS ARE NEARLY ALL WRITTEN... WRING YOUR HEART, SOME OF 'EM!
GOOD!... BRUHL WILL LEAVE IN THE LAUNCH BEFORE DAYLIGHT... HIS PLANE'S WAITING ON THE AFRICAN COAST!
BUT FIRST HE WANTS TO SEE ONE OF THIS LOT... ALONE!... THAT LITTLE BLONDE STEWARDESS, VELVET LEE!
1478

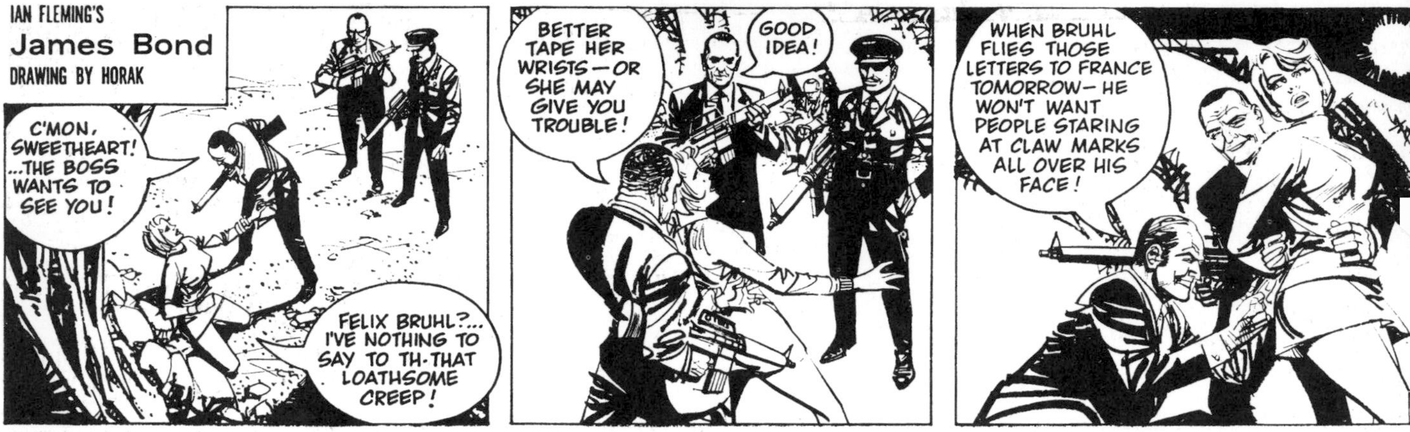
IAN FLEMING'S
James Bond
DRAWING BY HORAK
C'MON, SWEETHEART! ...THE BOSS WANTS TO SEE YOU!
FELIX BRUHL?... I'VE NOTHING TO SAY TO TH-THAT LOATHSOME CREEP!
BETTER TAPE HER WRISTS—OR SHE MAY GIVE YOU TROUBLE!
GOOD IDEA!
WHEN BRUHL FLIES THOSE LETTERS TO FRANCE TOMORROW—HE WON'T WANT PEOPLE STARING AT CLAW MARKS ALL OVER HIS FACE!
1479

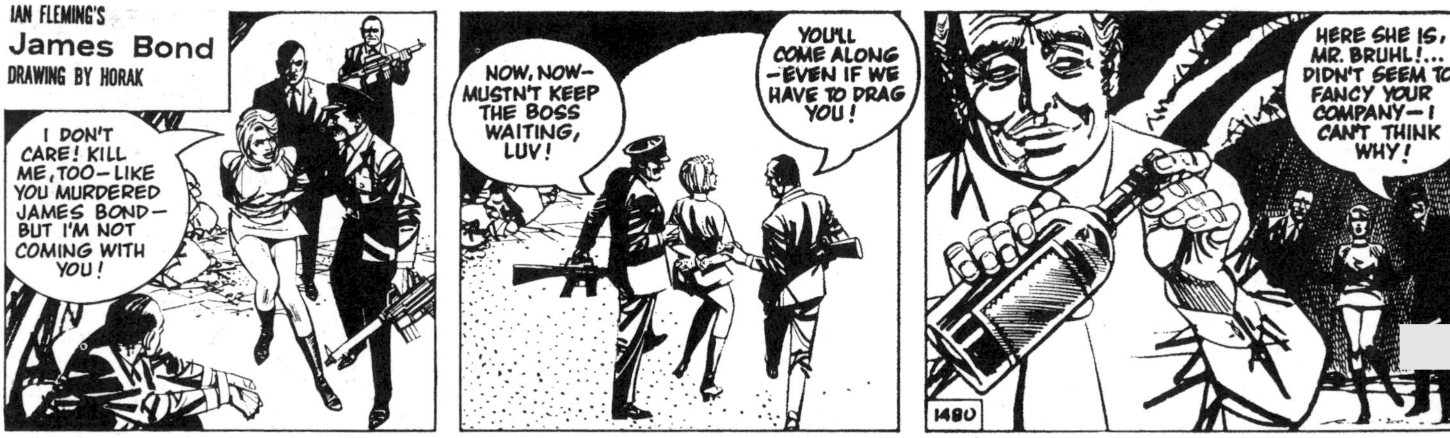
IAN FLEMING'S
James Bond
DRAWING BY HORAK
I DON'T CARE! KILL ME, TOO—LIKE YOU MURDERED JAMES BOND—BUT I'M NOT COMING WITH YOU!
NOW, NOW—MUSTN'T KEEP THE BOSS WAITING, LUV!
YOU'LL COME ALONG —EVEN IF WE HAVE TO DRAG YOU!
HERE SHE IS, MR. BRUHL!... DIDN'T SEEM TO FANCY YOUR COMPANY—I CAN'T THINK WHY!
1480

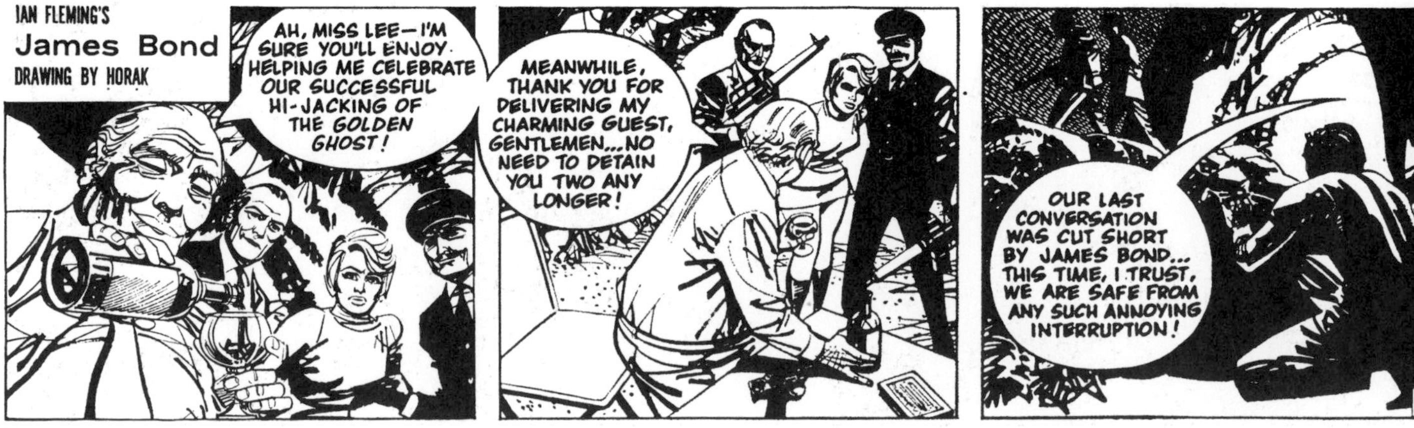
IAN FLEMING'S
James Bond
DRAWING BY HORAK
AH, MISS LEE—I'M SURE YOU'LL ENJOY HELPING ME CELEBRATE OUR SUCCESSFUL HI-JACKING OF THE GOLDEN GHOST!
MEANWHILE, THANK YOU FOR DELIVERING MY CHARMING GUEST, GENTLEMEN... NO NEED TO DETAIN YOU TWO ANY LONGER!
OUR LAST CONVERSATION WAS CUT SHORT BY JAMES BOND... THIS TIME, I TRUST, WE ARE SAFE FROM ANY SUCH ANNOYING INTERRUPTION!
1481

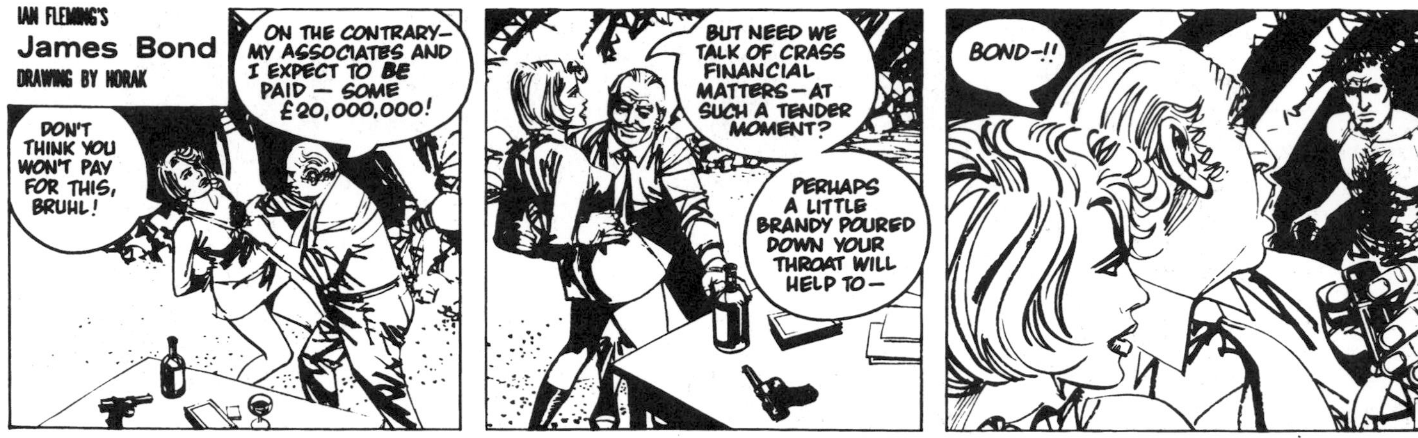
IAN FLEMING'S
James Bond
DRAWING BY HORAK
DON'T THINK YOU WON'T PAY FOR THIS, BRUHL!
ON THE CONTRARY— MY ASSOCIATES AND I EXPECT TO BE PAID — SOME £20,000,000!
BUT NEED WE TALK OF CRASS FINANCIAL MATTERS — AT SUCH A TENDER MOMENT?
PERHAPS A LITTLE BRANDY POURED DOWN YOUR THROAT WILL HELP TO—
BOND—!!
1482

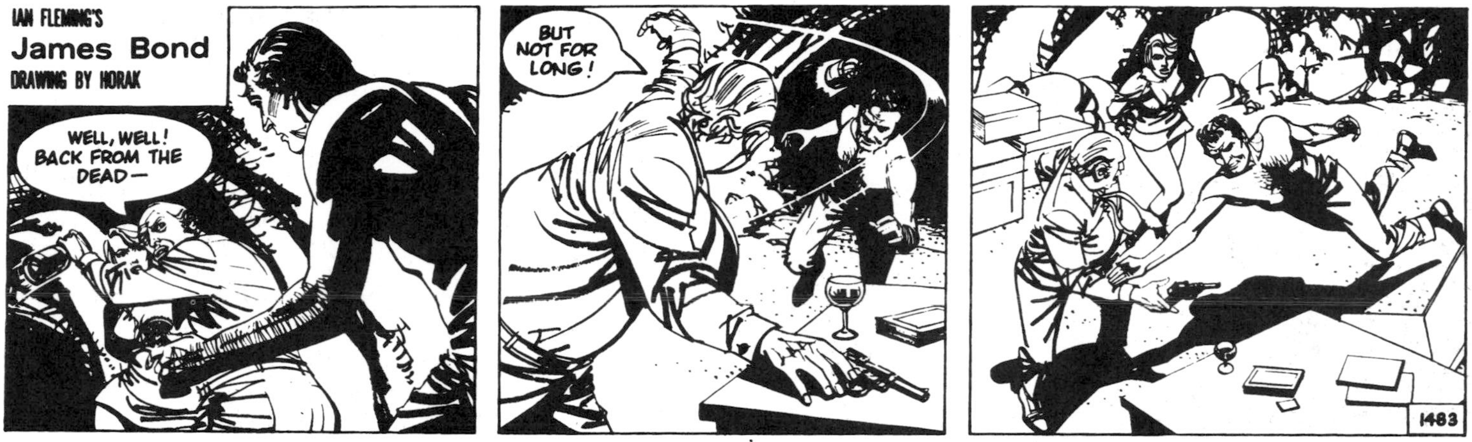
IAN FLEMING'S
James Bond
DRAWING BY HORAK
WELL, WELL! BACK FROM THE DEAD—
BUT NOT FOR LONG!
1483

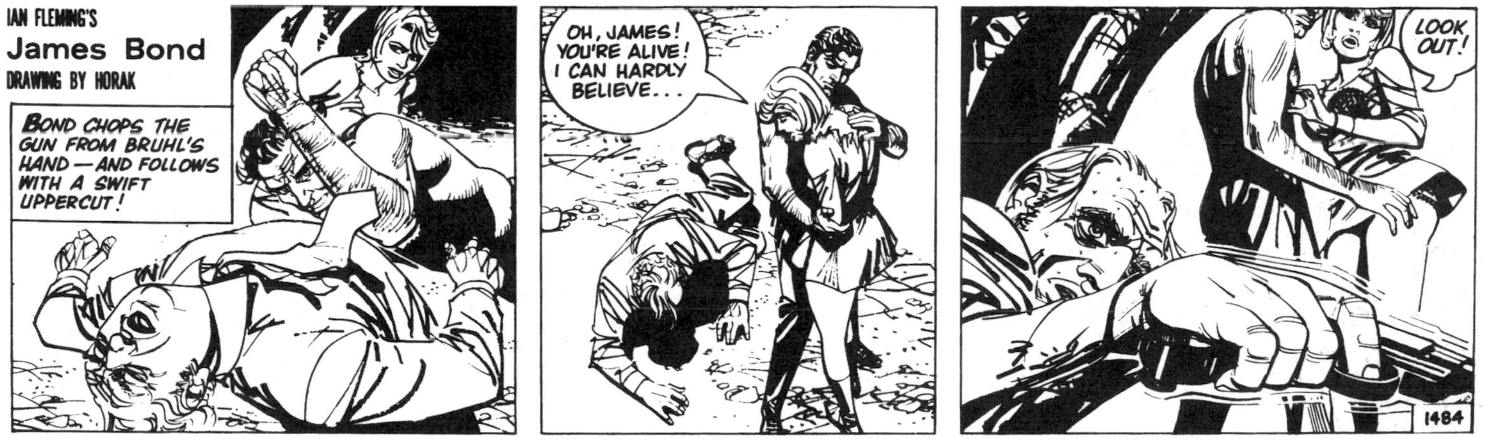
IAN FLEMING'S
James Bond
DRAWING BY HORAK
BOND CHOPS THE GUN FROM BRUHL'S HAND — AND FOLLOWS WITH A SWIFT UPPERCUT!
OH, JAMES! YOU'RE ALIVE! I CAN HARDLY BELIEVE...
LOOK OUT!
1484

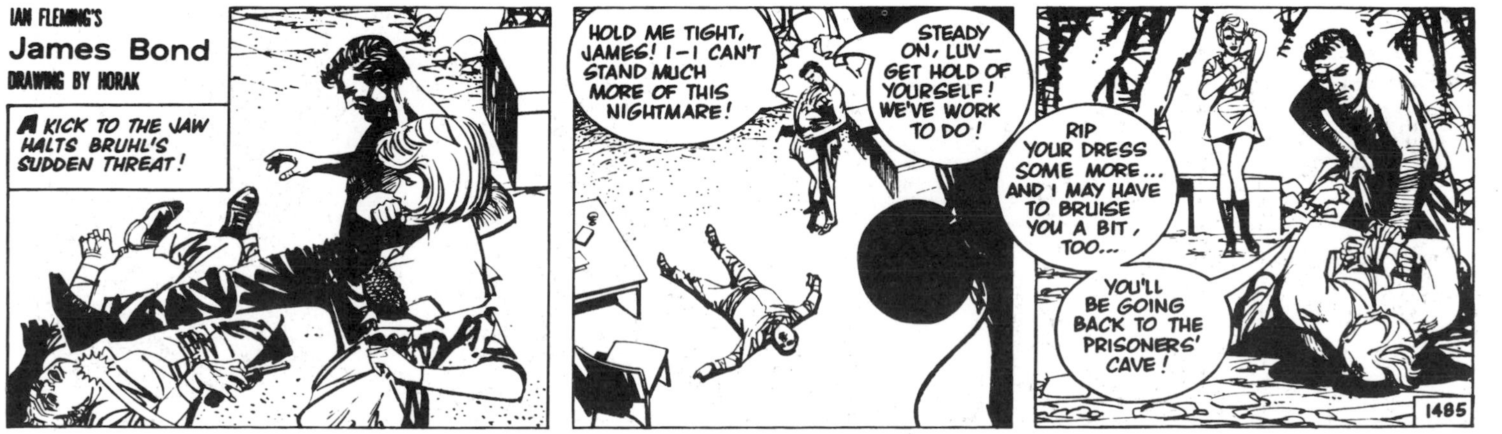
IAN FLEMING'S
James Bond
DRAWING BY HORAK
A KICK TO THE JAW HALTS BRUHL'S SUDDEN THREAT!
HOLD ME TIGHT, JAMES! I—I CAN'T STAND MUCH MORE OF THIS NIGHTMARE!
STEADY ON, LUV— GET HOLD OF YOURSELF! WE'VE WORK TO DO!
RIP YOUR DRESS SOME MORE... AND I MAY HAVE TO BRUISE YOU A BIT, TOO...
YOU'LL BE GOING BACK TO THE PRISONERS' CAVE!
1485

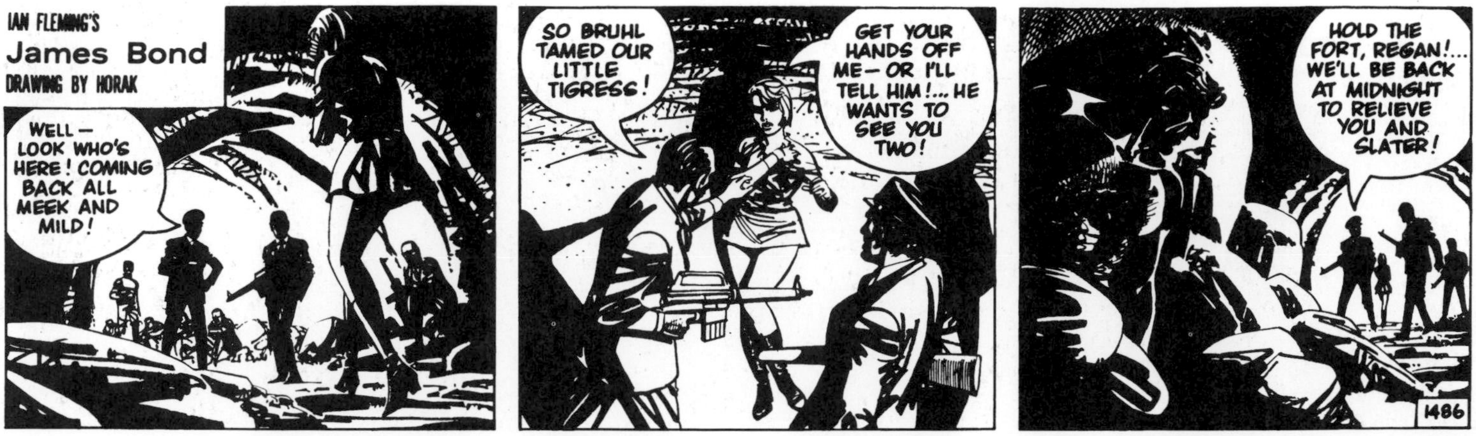
IAN FLEMING'S
James Bond
DRAWING BY HORAK
WELL— LOOK WHO'S HERE! COMING BACK ALL MEEK AND MILD!
SO BRUHL TAMED OUR LITTLE TIGRESS!
GET YOUR HANDS OFF ME—OR I'LL TELL HIM!... HE WANTS TO SEE YOU TWO!
HOLD THE FORT, REGAN!... WE'LL BE BACK AT MIDNIGHT TO RELIEVE YOU AND SLATER!
1486

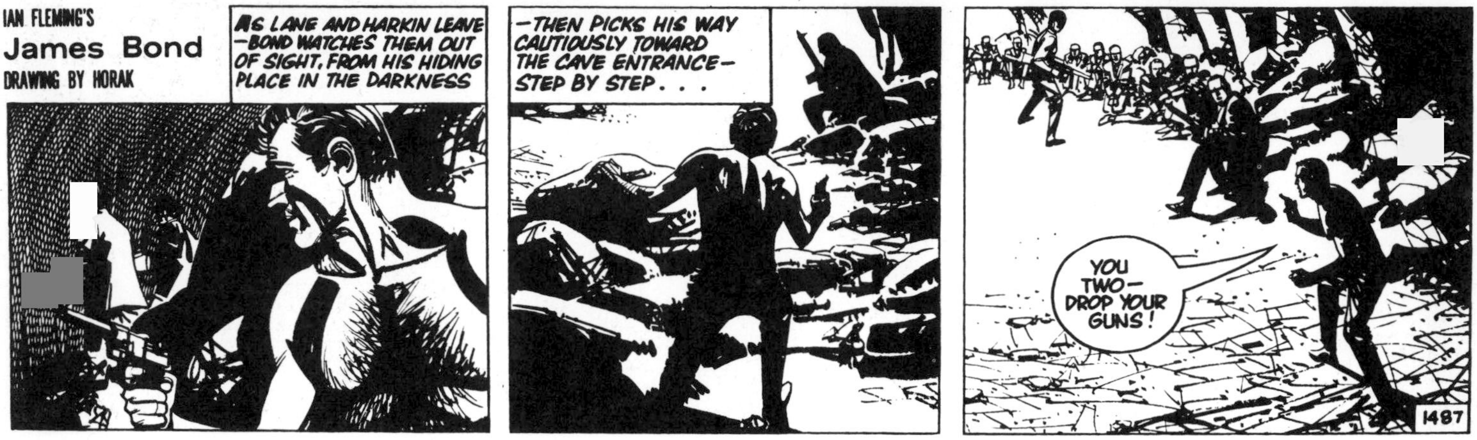
IAN FLEMING'S
James Bond
DRAWING BY HORAK
AS LANE AND HARKIN LEAVE —BOND WATCHES THEM OUT OF SIGHT. FROM HIS HIDING PLACE IN THE DARKNESS
—THEN PICKS HIS WAY CAUTIOUSLY TOWARD THE CAVE ENTRANCE— STEP BY STEP . . .
YOU TWO— DROP YOUR GUNS!
1487

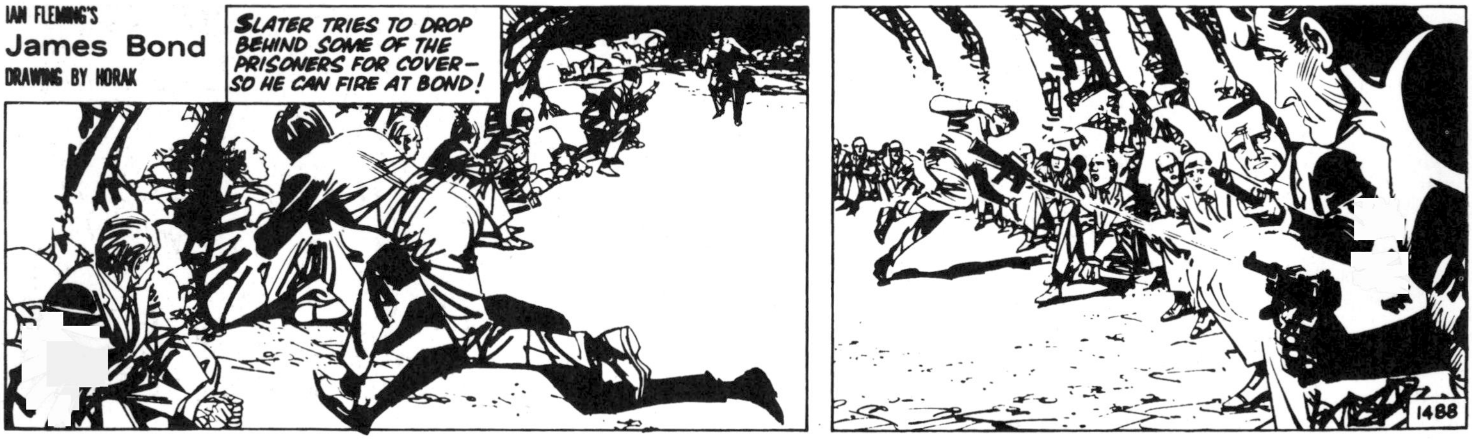
IAN FLEMING'S
James Bond
DRAWING BY HORAK
SLATER TRIES TO DROP BEHIND SOME OF THE PRISONERS FOR COVER— SO HE CAN FIRE AT BOND!
1488

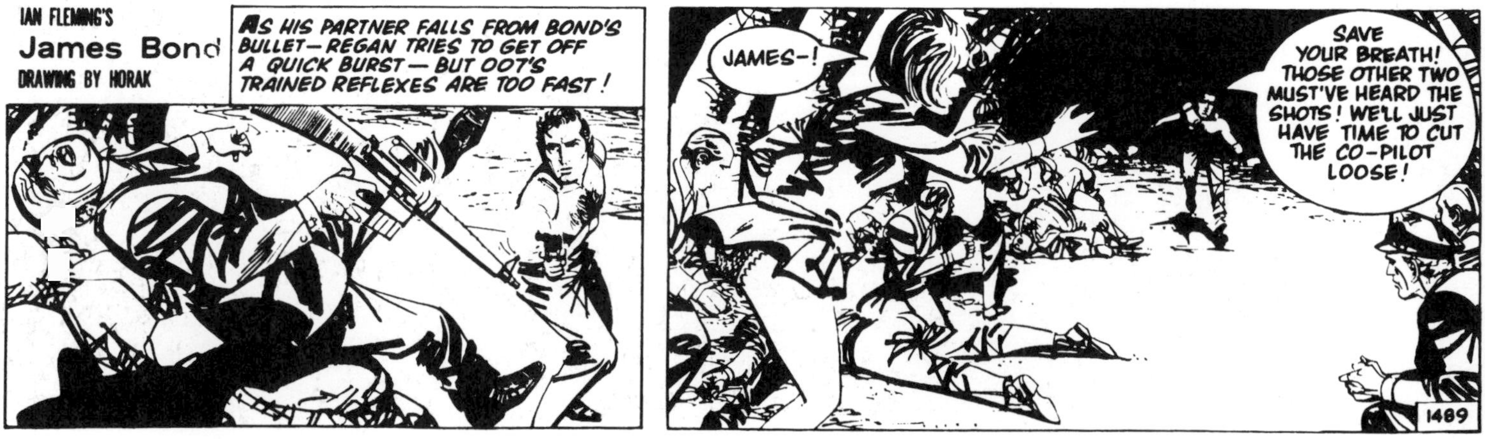
IAN FLEMING'S
James Bond
DRAWING BY HORAK
AS HIS PARTNER FALLS FROM BOND'S BULLET— REGAN TRIES TO GET OFF A QUICK BURST— BUT 007'S TRAINED REFLEXES ARE TOO FAST!
JAMES—!
SAVE YOUR BREATH! THOSE OTHER TWO MUST'VE HEARD THE SHOTS! WE'LL JUST HAVE TIME TO CUT THE CO-PILOT LOOSE!
1489

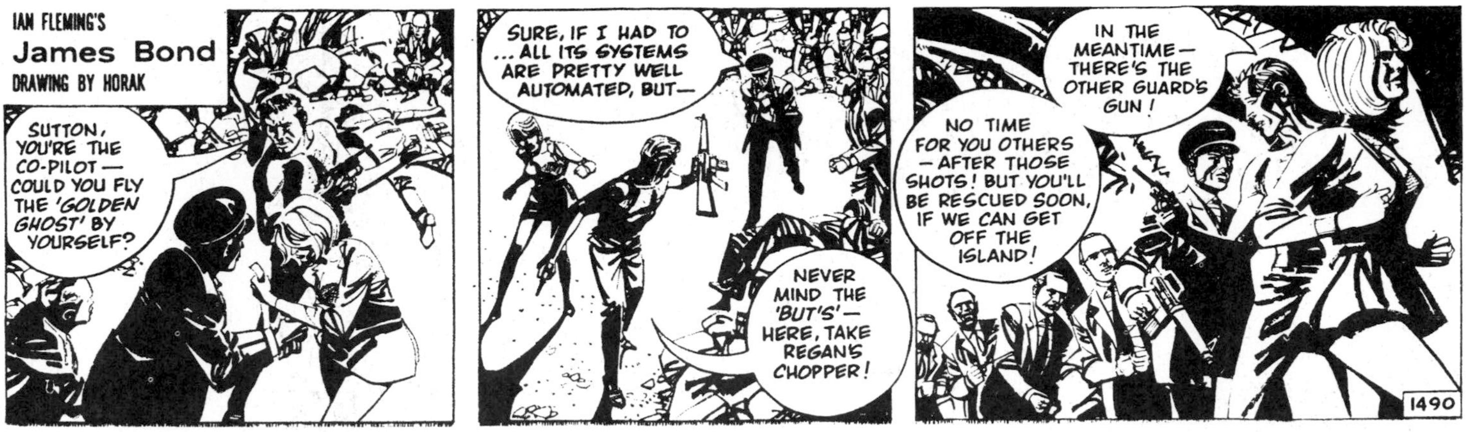
IAN FLEMING'S
James Bond
DRAWING BY HORAK
SUTTON, YOU'RE THE CO-PILOT — COULD YOU FLY THE 'GOLDEN GHOST' BY YOURSELF?
SURE, IF I HAD TO ... ALL ITS SYSTEMS ARE PRETTY WELL AUTOMATED, BUT—
NEVER MIND THE 'BUT'S' — HERE, TAKE REGAN'S CHOPPER!
IN THE MEANTIME — THERE'S THE OTHER GUARD'S GUN!
NO TIME FOR YOU OTHERS — AFTER THOSE SHOTS! BUT YOU'LL BE RESCUED SOON, IF WE CAN GET OFF THE ISLAND!
1490

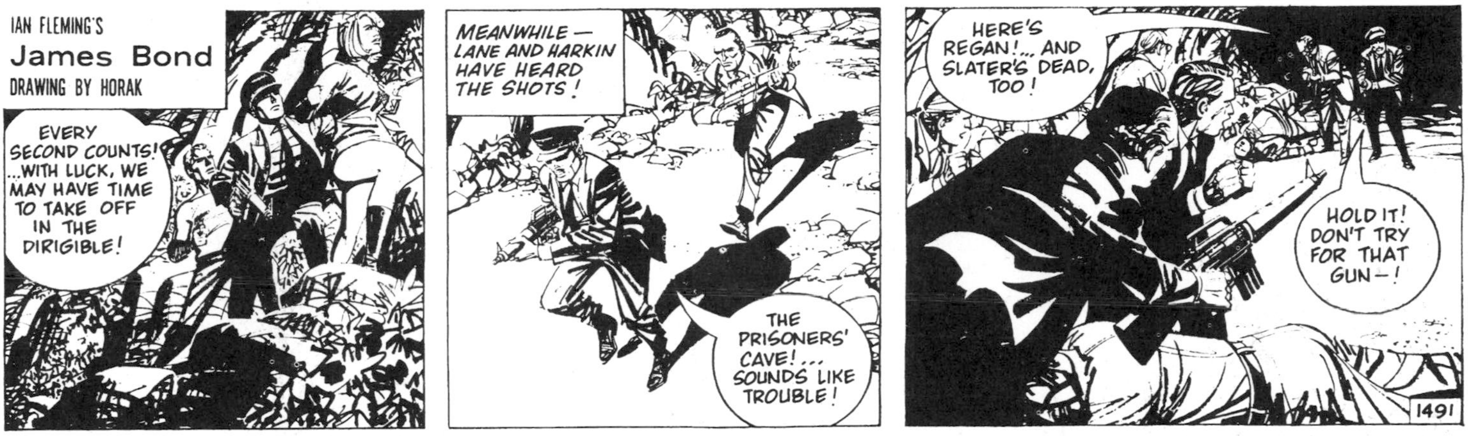
IAN FLEMING'S
James Bond
DRAWING BY HORAK
EVERY SECOND COUNTS! ...WITH LUCK, WE MAY HAVE TIME TO TAKE OFF IN THE DIRIGIBLE!
MEANWHILE — LANE AND HARKIN HAVE HEARD THE SHOTS!
THE PRISONERS' CAVE! ... SOUNDS LIKE TROUBLE!
HERE'S REGAN!... AND SLATER'S DEAD, TOO!
HOLD IT! DON'T TRY FOR THAT GUN—!
1491

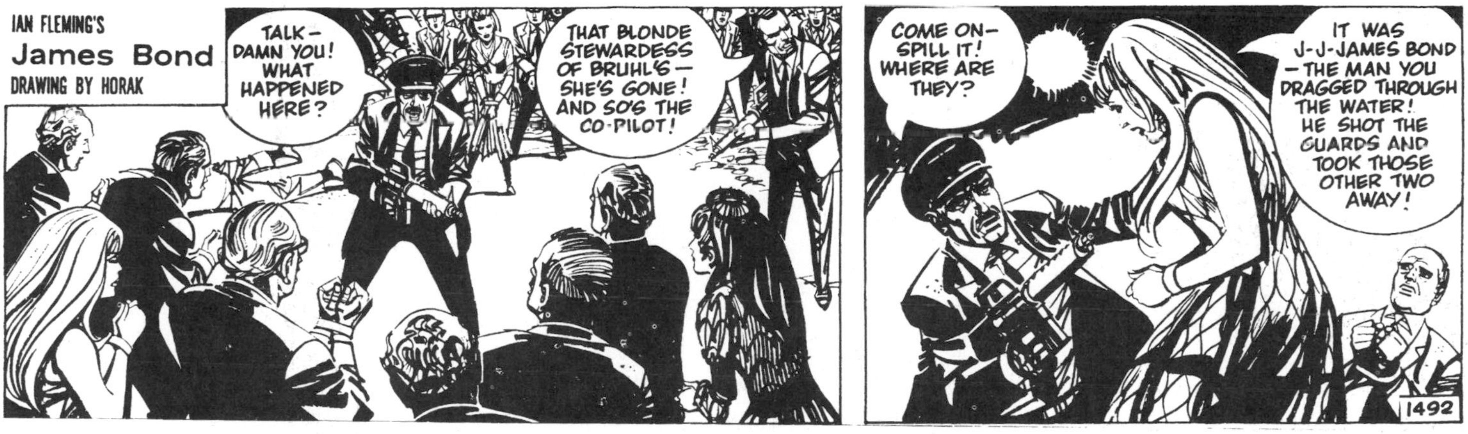
IAN FLEMING'S
James Bond
DRAWING BY HORAK
TALK— DAMN YOU! WHAT HAPPENED HERE?
THAT BLONDE STEWARDESS OF BRUHL'S — SHE'S GONE! AND SO'S THE CO-PILOT!
COME ON— SPILL IT! WHERE ARE THEY?
IT WAS J-J-JAMES BOND — THE MAN YOU DRAGGED THROUGH THE WATER! HE SHOT THE GUARDS AND TOOK THOSE OTHER TWO AWAY!
1492

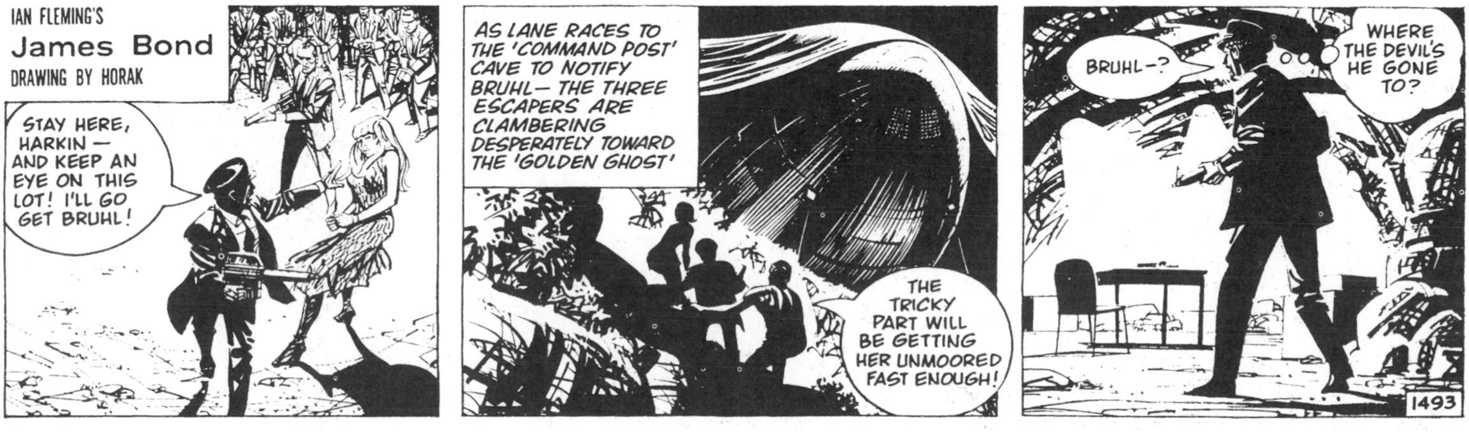
IAN FLEMING'S
James Bond
DRAWING BY HORAK
STAY HERE, HARKIN — AND KEEP AN EYE ON THIS LOT! I'LL GO GET BRUHL!
AS LANE RACES TO THE 'COMMAND POST' CAVE TO NOTIFY BRUHL— THE THREE ESCAPERS ARE CLAMBERING DESPERATELY TOWARD THE 'GOLDEN GHOST'
THE TRICKY PART WILL BE GETTING HER UNMOORED FAST ENOUGH!
BRUHL—?
WHERE THE DEVIL'S HE GONE TO?
1493

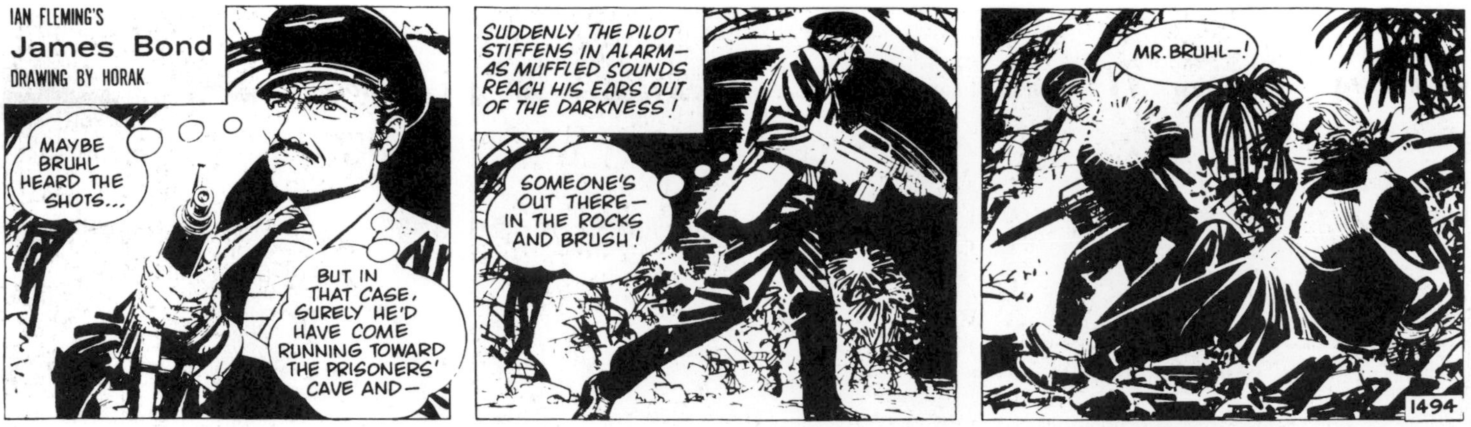
IAN FLEMING'S
James Bond
DRAWING BY HORAK
MAYBE BRUHL HEARD THE SHOTS...
BUT IN THAT CASE, SURELY HE'D HAVE COME RUNNING TOWARD THE PRISONERS' CAVE AND—
SUDDENLY THE PILOT STIFFENS IN ALARM— AS MUFFLED SOUNDS REACH HIS EARS OUT OF THE DARKNESS!
SOMEONE'S OUT THERE— IN THE ROCKS AND BRUSH!
MR. BRUHL—!
1494

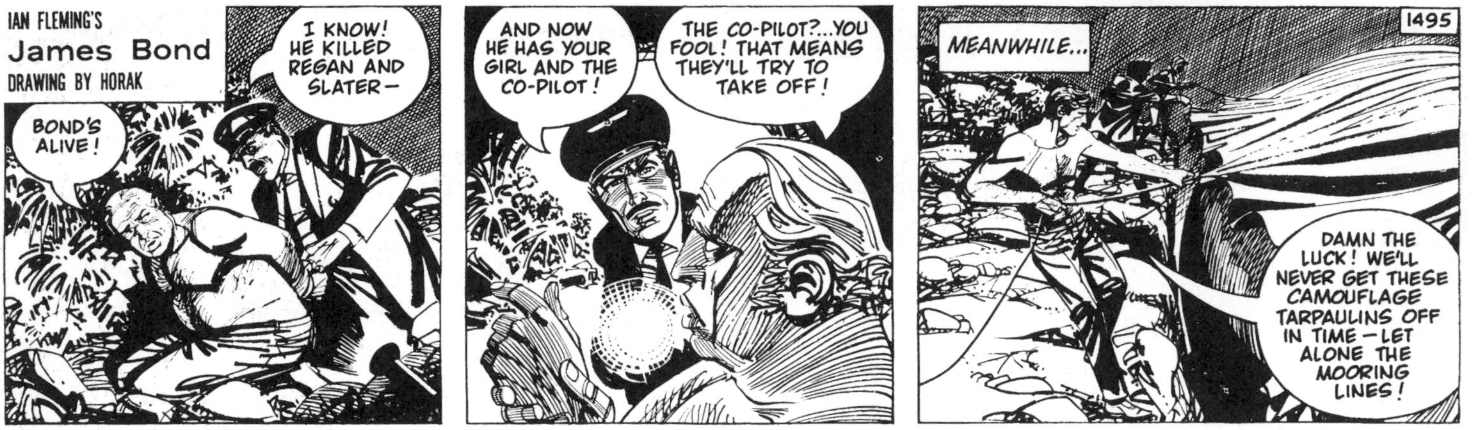
IAN FLEMING'S
James Bond
DRAWING BY HORAK
BOND'S ALIVE!
I KNOW! HE KILLED REGAN AND SLATER—
AND NOW HE HAS YOUR GIRL AND THE CO-PILOT!
THE CO-PILOT?...YOU FOOL! THAT MEANS THEY'LL TRY TO TAKE OFF!
1495
MEANWHILE...
DAMN THE LUCK! WE'LL NEVER GET THESE CAMOUFLAGE TARPAULINS OFF IN TIME—LET ALONE THE MOORING LINES!

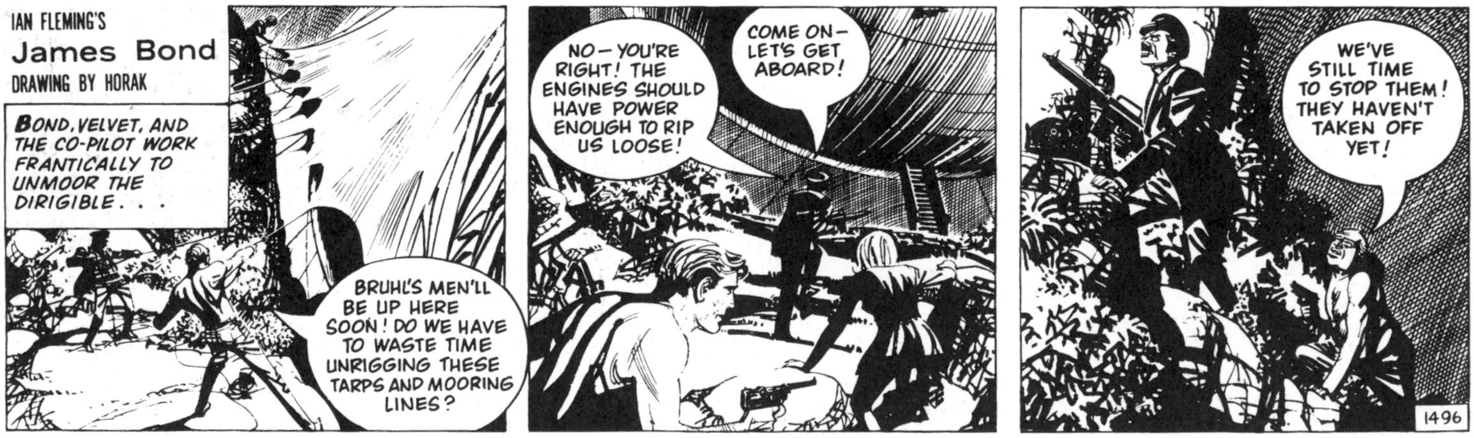
IAN FLEMING'S
James Bond
DRAWING BY HORAK
BOND, VELVET, AND THE CO-PILOT WORK FRANTICALLY TO UNMOOR THE DIRIGIBLE . . .
BRUHL'S MEN'LL BE UP HERE SOON! DO WE HAVE TO WASTE TIME UNRIGGING THESE TARPS AND MOORING LINES?
NO— YOU'RE RIGHT! THE ENGINES SHOULD HAVE POWER ENOUGH TO RIP US LOOSE!
COME ON— LET'S GET ABOARD!
WE'VE STILL TIME TO STOP THEM! THEY HAVEN'T TAKEN OFF YET!
1496

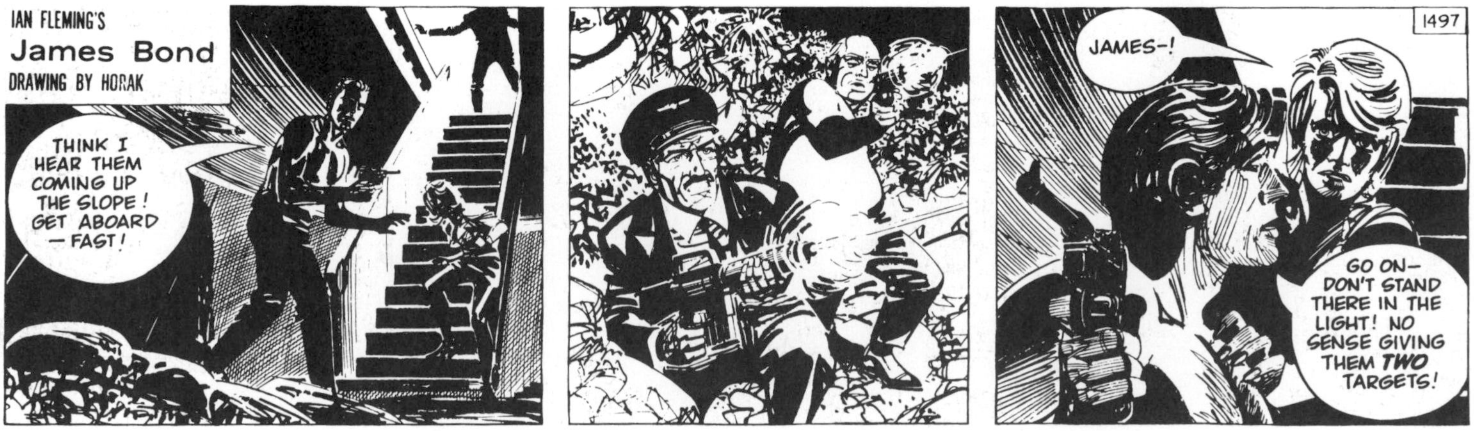
IAN FLEMING'S
James Bond
DRAWING BY HORAK
THINK I HEAR THEM COMING UP THE SLOPE! GET ABOARD —FAST!
1497
JAMES—!
GO ON— DON'T STAND THERE IN THE LIGHT! NO SENSE GIVING THEM TWO TARGETS!

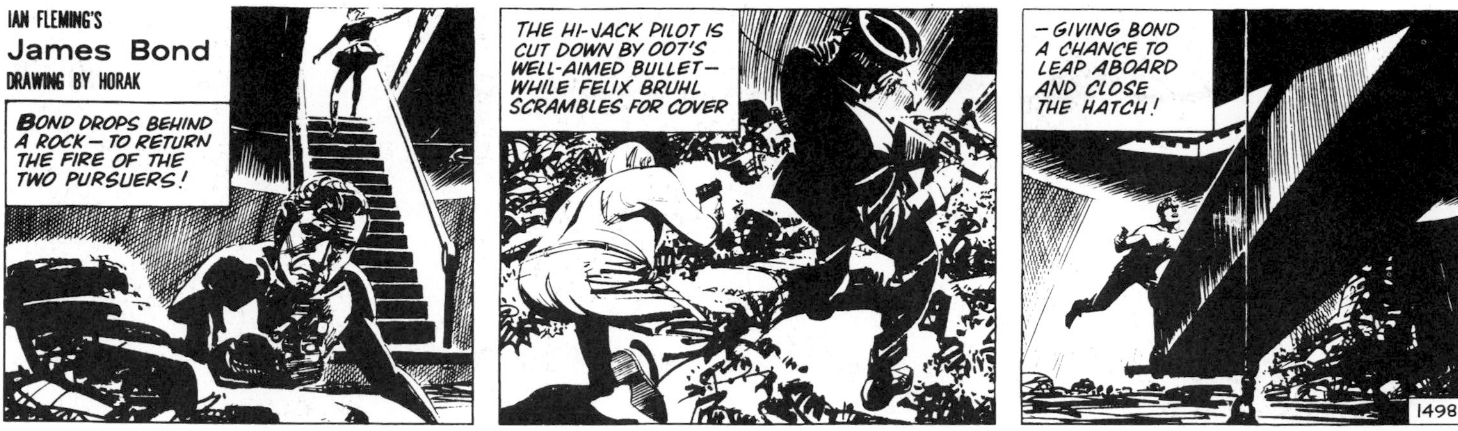
IAN FLEMING'S
James Bond
DRAWING BY HORAK
BOND DROPS BEHIND A ROCK—TO RETURN THE FIRE OF THE TWO PURSUERS!
THE HI-JACK PILOT IS CUT DOWN BY 007'S WELL-AIMED BULLET—WHILE FELIX BRUHL SCRAMBLES FOR COVER
—GIVING BOND A CHANCE TO LEAP ABOARD AND CLOSE THE HATCH!
1498

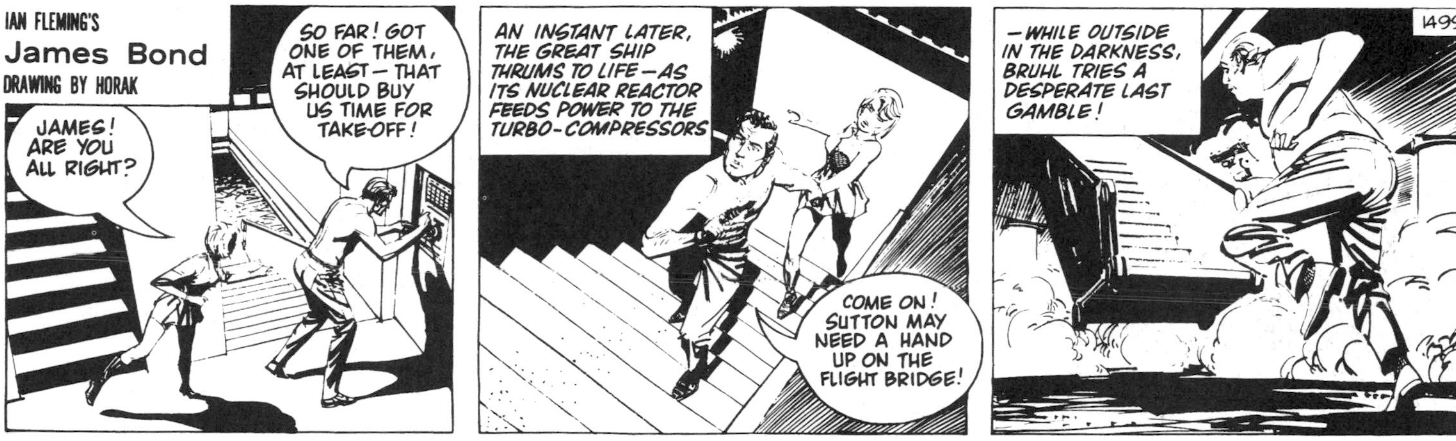
IAN FLEMING'S
James Bond
DRAWING BY HORAK
JAMES! ARE YOU ALL RIGHT?
SO FAR! GOT ONE OF THEM, AT LEAST—THAT SHOULD BUY US TIME FOR TAKE-OFF!
AN INSTANT LATER, THE GREAT SHIP THRUMS TO LIFE—AS ITS NUCLEAR REACTOR FEEDS POWER TO THE TURBO-COMPRESSORS
COME ON! SUTTON MAY NEED A HAND UP ON THE FLIGHT BRIDGE!
1499
—WHILE OUTSIDE IN THE DARKNESS, BRUHL TRIES A DESPERATE LAST GAMBLE!

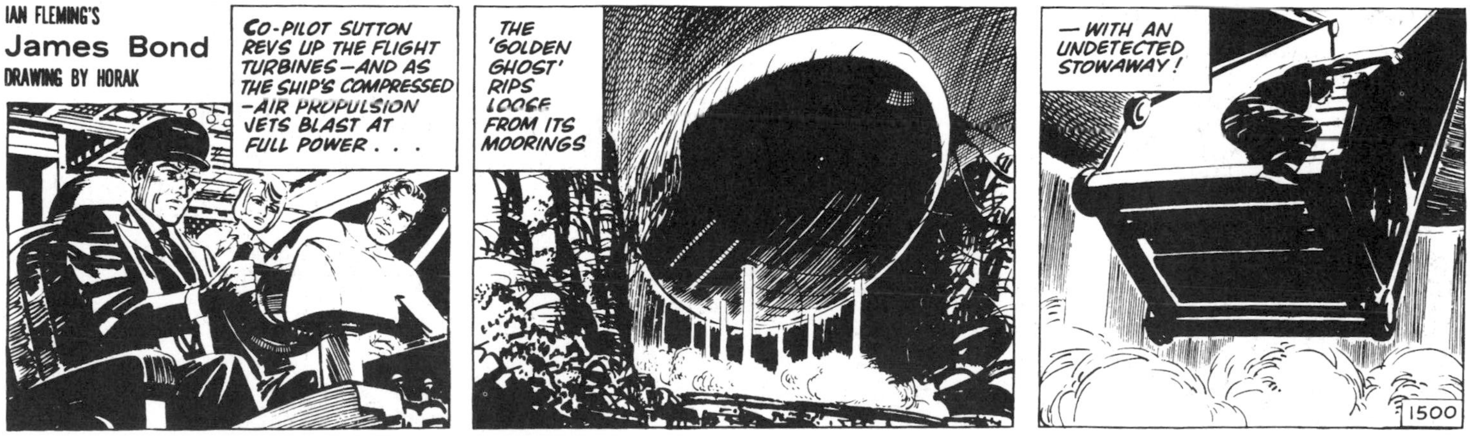
IAN FLEMING'S
James Bond
DRAWING BY HORAK
CO-PILOT SUTTON REVS UP THE FLIGHT TURBINES—AND AS THE SHIP'S COMPRESSED-AIR PROPULSION JETS BLAST AT FULL POWER . . .
THE 'GOLDEN GHOST' RIPS LOOSE FROM ITS MOORINGS
—WITH AN UNDETECTED STOWAWAY!
1500

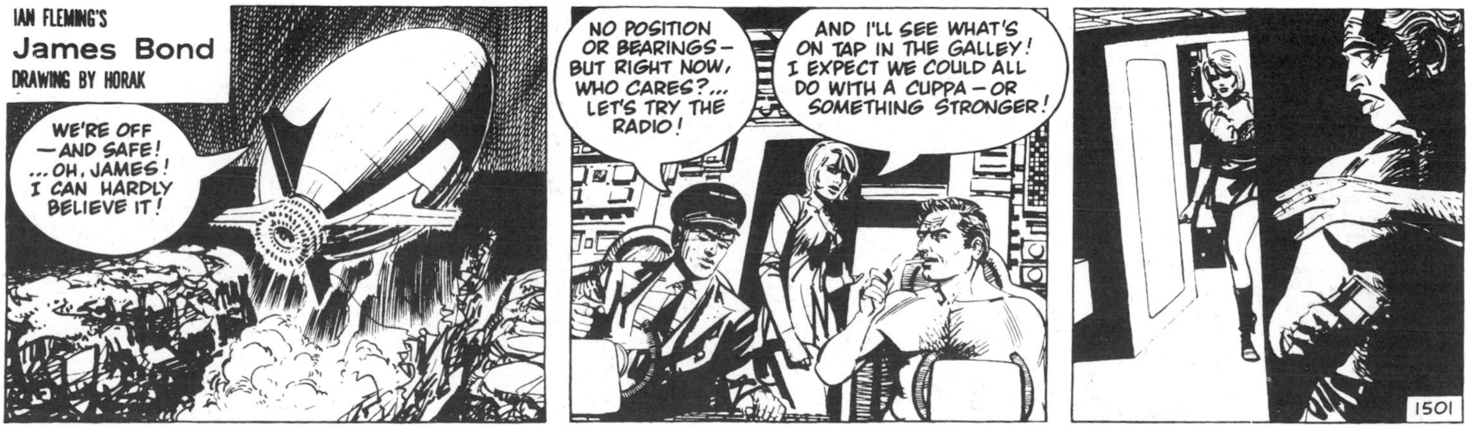
IAN FLEMING'S
James Bond
DRAWING BY HORAK
WE'RE OFF—AND SAFE! ...OH, JAMES! I CAN HARDLY BELIEVE IT!
NO POSITION OR BEARINGS—BUT RIGHT NOW, WHO CARES?... LET'S TRY THE RADIO!
AND I'LL SEE WHAT'S ON TAP IN THE GALLEY! I EXPECT WE COULD ALL DO WITH A CUPPA—OR SOMETHING STRONGER!
1501

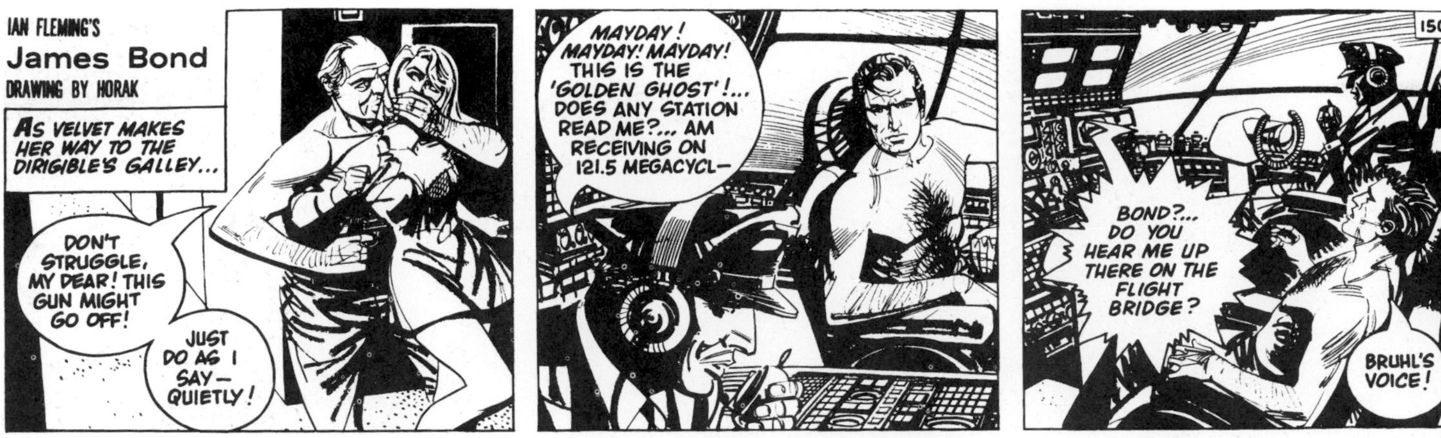
IAN FLEMING'S
James Bond
DRAWING BY HORAK
AS VELVET MAKES HER WAY TO THE DIRIGIBLE'S GALLEY...
DON'T STRUGGLE, MY DEAR! THIS GUN MIGHT GO OFF!
JUST DO AS I SAY— QUIETLY!
MAYDAY! MAYDAY! MAYDAY! THIS IS THE 'GOLDEN GHOST'!... DOES ANY STATION READ ME?... AM RECEIVING ON 121.5 MEGACYCL—
1502
BOND?... DO YOU HEAR ME UP THERE ON THE FLIGHT BRIDGE?
BRUHL'S VOICE!

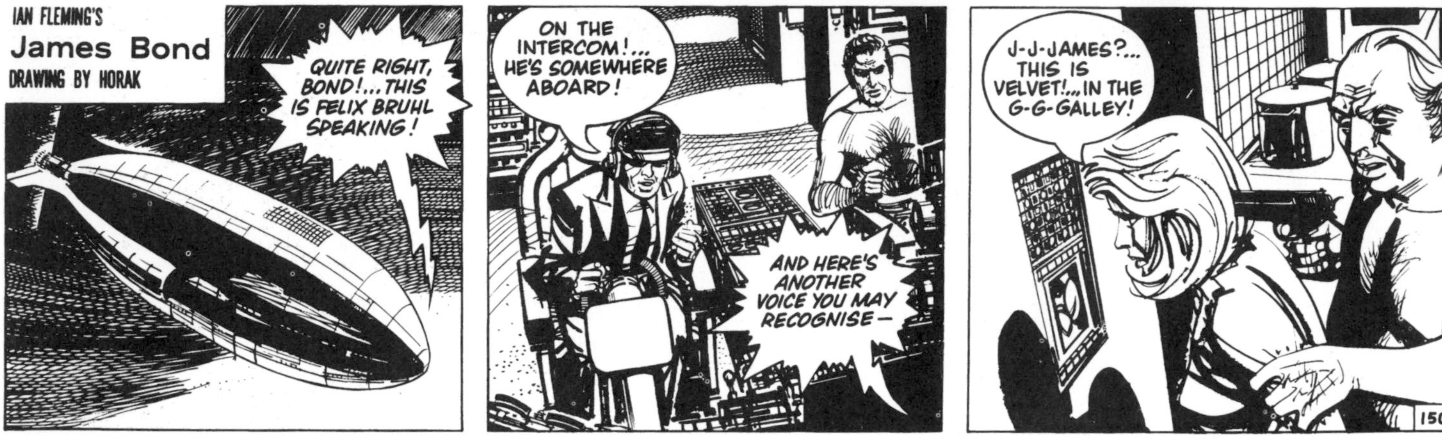
IAN FLEMING'S
James Bond
DRAWING BY HORAK
QUITE RIGHT, BOND!... THIS IS FELIX BRUHL SPEAKING!
ON THE INTERCOM!... HE'S SOMEWHERE ABOARD!
AND HERE'S ANOTHER VOICE YOU MAY RECOGNISE—
J-J-JAMES?... THIS IS VELVET!... IN THE G-G-GALLEY!
1503

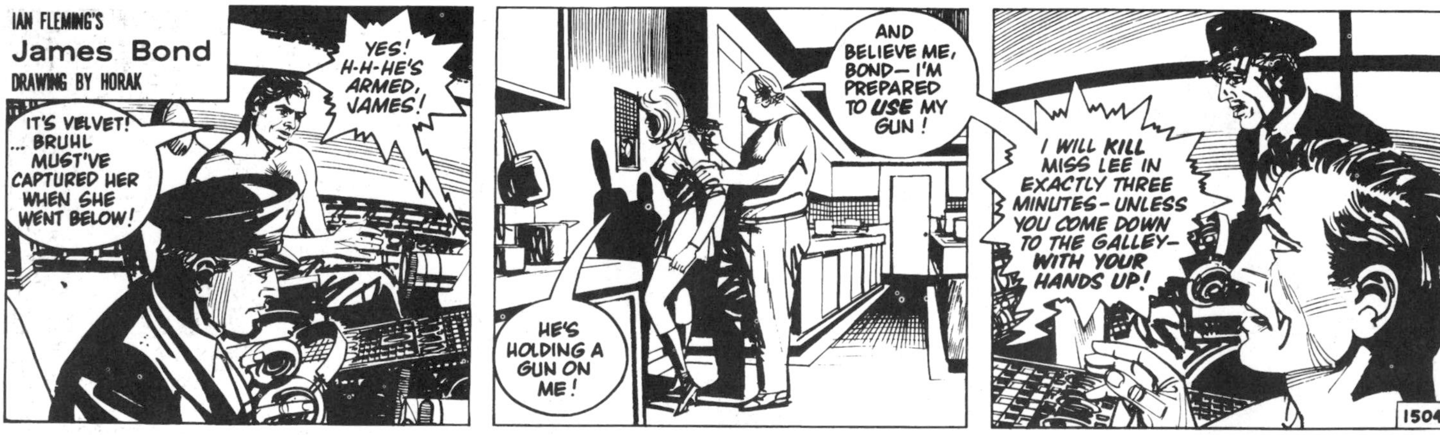
IAN FLEMING'S
James Bond
DRAWING BY HORAK
YES! H-H-HE'S ARMED, JAMES!
IT'S VELVET! ... BRUHL MUST'VE CAPTURED HER WHEN SHE WENT BELOW!
AND BELIEVE ME, BOND— I'M PREPARED TO USE MY GUN!
HE'S HOLDING A GUN ON ME!
I WILL KILL MISS LEE IN EXACTLY THREE MINUTES— UNLESS YOU COME DOWN TO THE GALLEY— WITH YOUR HANDS UP!
1504

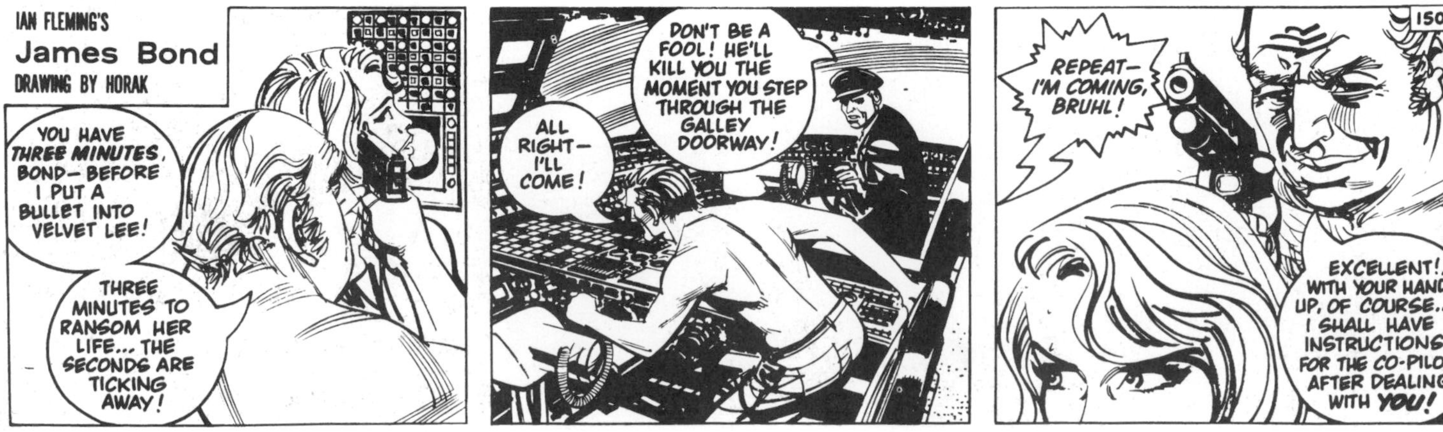
IAN FLEMING'S
James Bond
DRAWING BY HORAK
YOU HAVE THREE MINUTES, BOND— BEFORE I PUT A BULLET INTO VELVET LEE!
THREE MINUTES TO RANSOM HER LIFE... THE SECONDS ARE TICKING AWAY!
DON'T BE A FOOL! HE'LL KILL YOU THE MOMENT YOU STEP THROUGH THE GALLEY DOORWAY!
ALL RIGHT— I'LL COME!
1505
REPEAT— I'M COMING, BRUHL!
EXCELLENT!... WITH YOUR HANDS UP, OF COURSE... I SHALL HAVE INSTRUCTIONS FOR THE CO-PILOT AFTER DEALING WITH YOU!

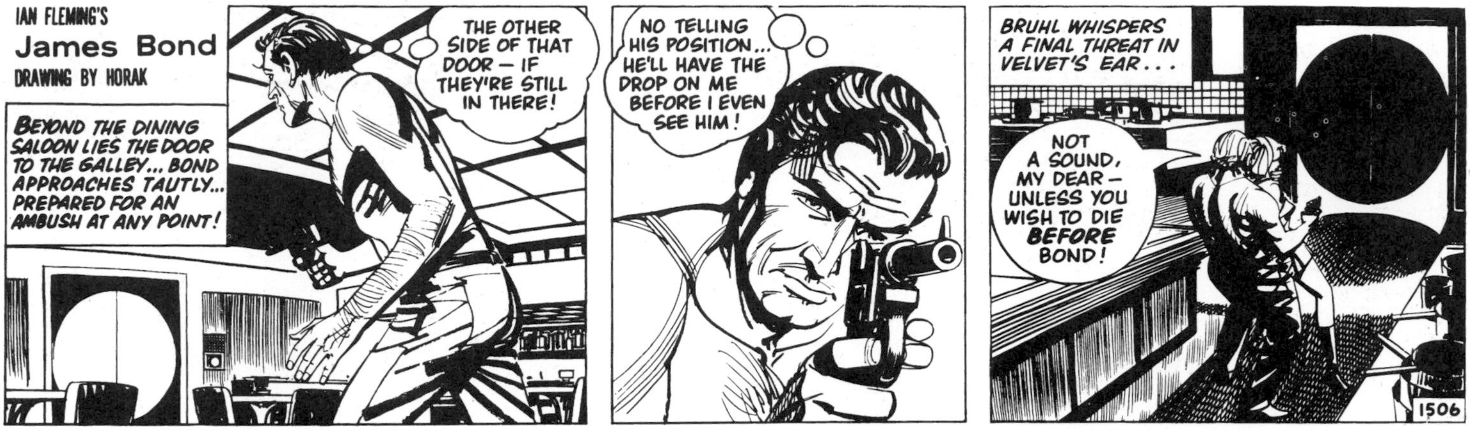
IAN FLEMING'S
James Bond
DRAWING BY HORAK
BEYOND THE DINING SALOON LIES THE DOOR TO THE GALLEY... BOND APPROACHES TAUTLY... PREPARED FOR AN AMBUSH AT ANY POINT!
THE OTHER SIDE OF THAT DOOR — IF THEY'RE STILL IN THERE!
NO TELLING HIS POSITION... HE'LL HAVE THE DROP ON ME BEFORE I EVEN SEE HIM!
BRUHL WHISPERS A FINAL THREAT IN VELVET'S EAR...
NOT A SOUND, MY DEAR — UNLESS YOU WISH TO DIE BEFORE BOND!
1506

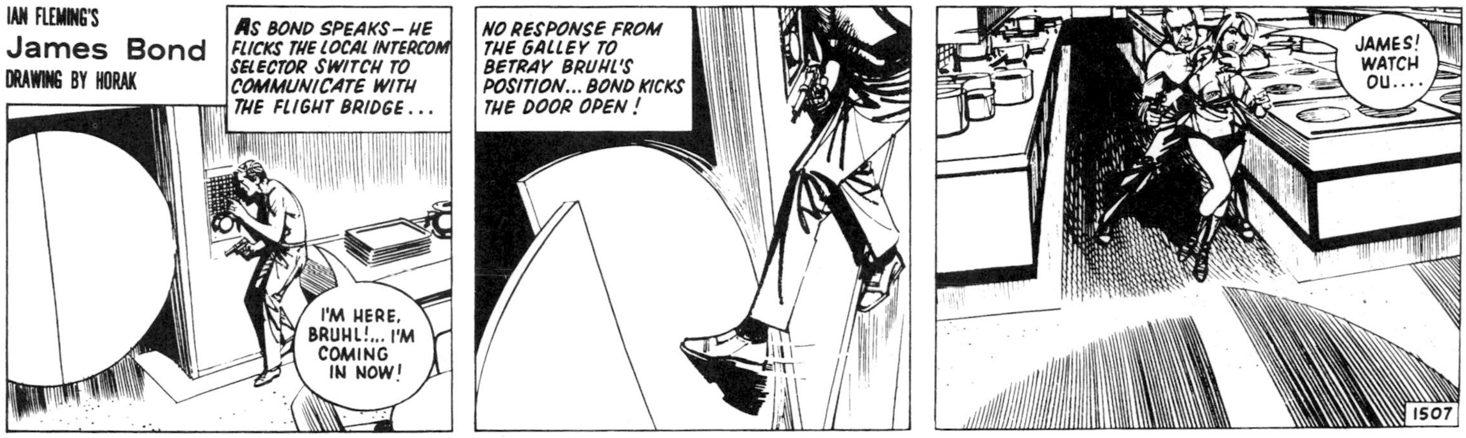
IAN FLEMING'S
James Bond
DRAWING BY HORAK
AS BOND SPEAKS — HE FLICKS THE LOCAL INTERCOM SELECTOR SWITCH TO COMMUNICATE WITH THE FLIGHT BRIDGE...
I'M HERE, BRUHL!... I'M COMING IN NOW!
NO RESPONSE FROM THE GALLEY TO BETRAY BRUHL'S POSITION... BOND KICKS THE DOOR OPEN!
JAMES! WATCH OU....
1507

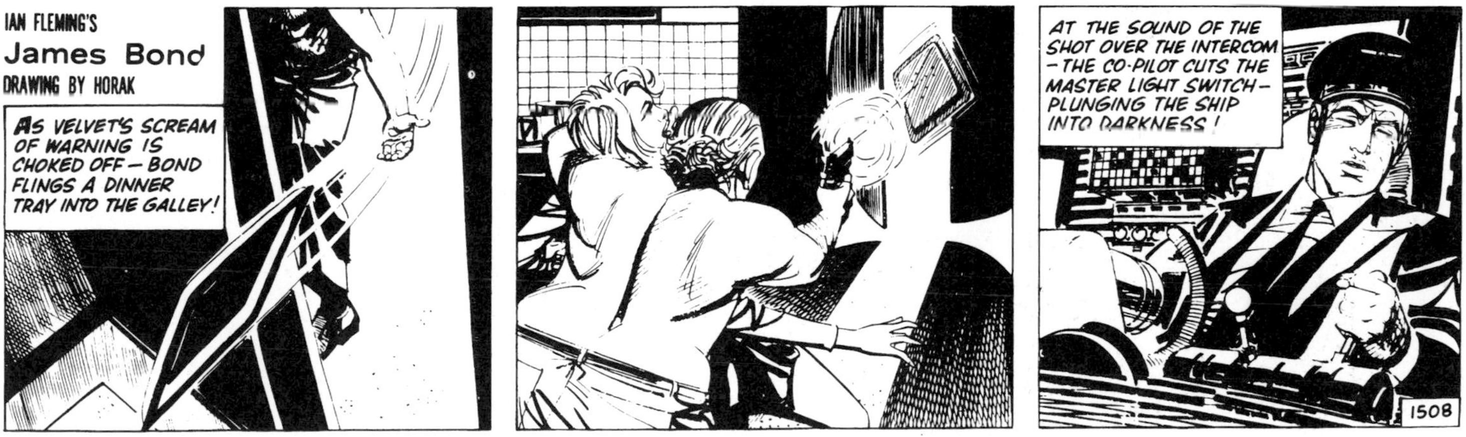
IAN FLEMING'S
James Bond
DRAWING BY HORAK
AS VELVET'S SCREAM OF WARNING IS CHOKED OFF — BOND FLINGS A DINNER TRAY INTO THE GALLEY!
AT THE SOUND OF THE SHOT OVER THE INTERCOM — THE CO-PILOT CUTS THE MASTER LIGHT SWITCH — PLUNGING THE SHIP INTO DARKNESS!
1508

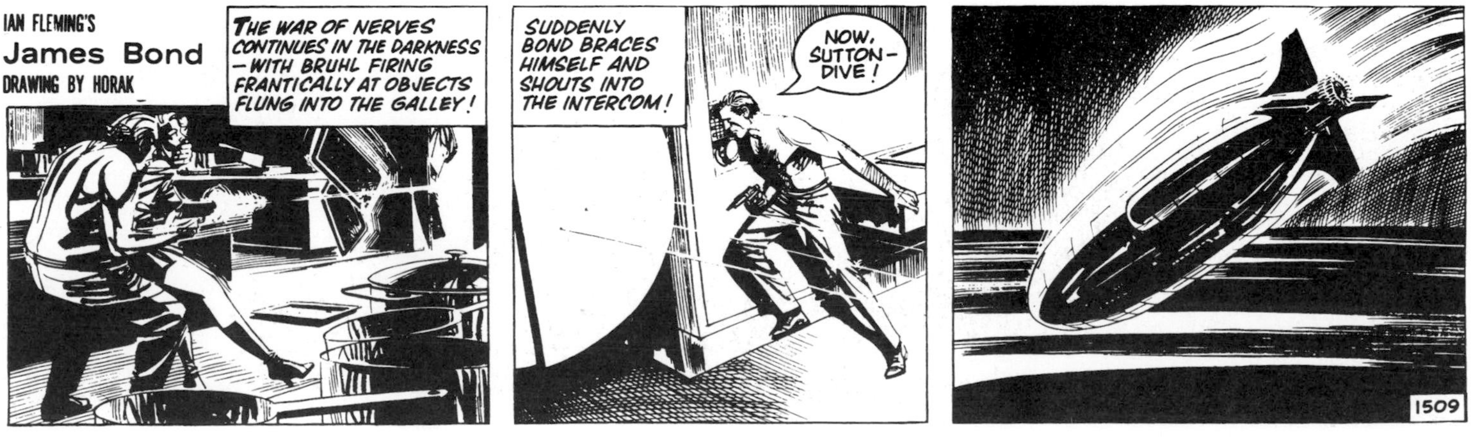
IAN FLEMING'S
James Bond
DRAWING BY HORAK
THE WAR OF NERVES CONTINUES IN THE DARKNESS — WITH BRUHL FIRING FRANTICALLY AT OBJECTS FLUNG INTO THE GALLEY!
SUDDENLY BOND BRACES HIMSELF AND SHOUTS INTO THE INTERCOM!
NOW, SUTTON — DIVE!
1509

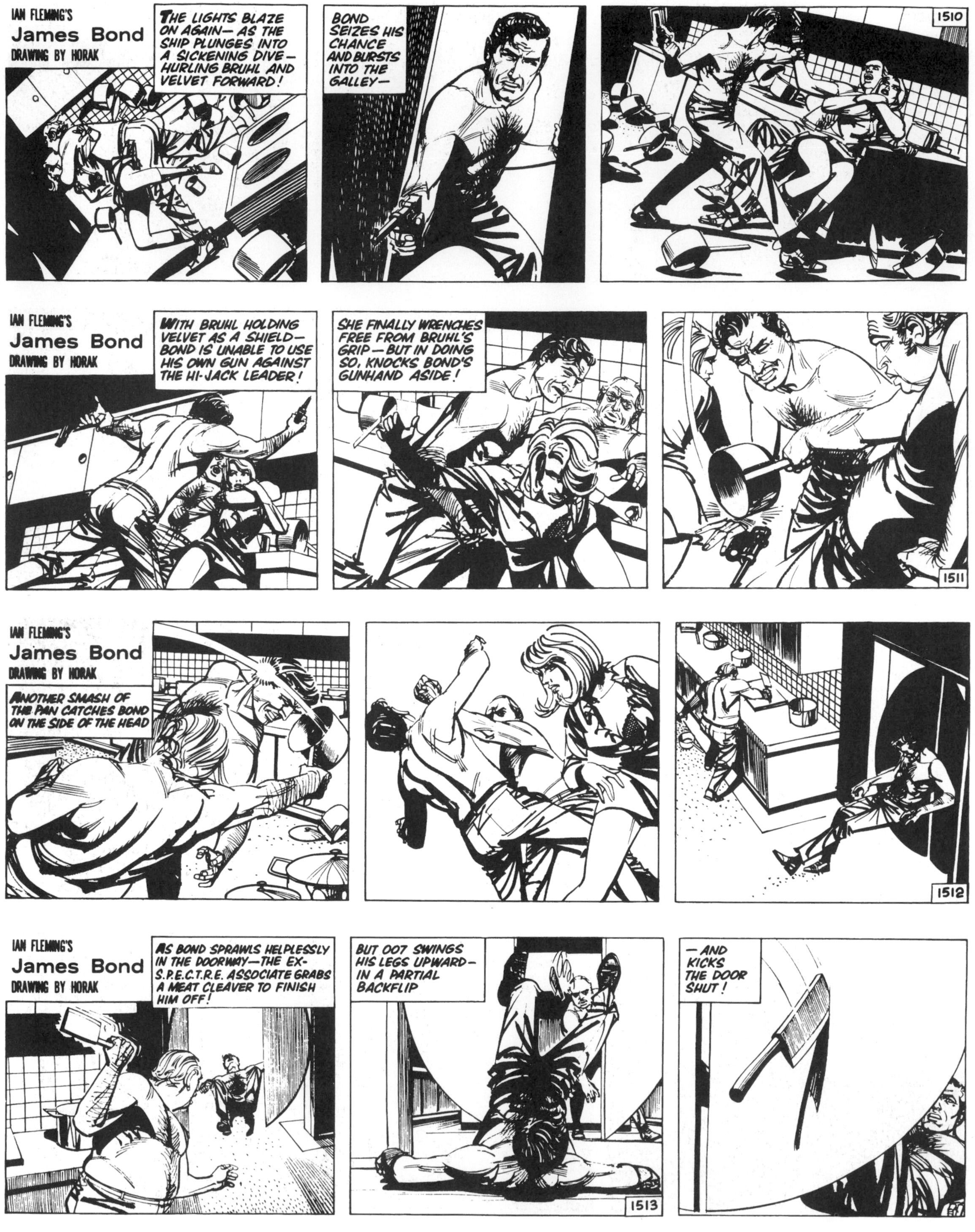
IAN FLEMING'S
James Bond
DRAWING BY HORAK
THE LIGHTS BLAZE ON AGAIN— AS THE SHIP PLUNGES INTO A SICKENING DIVE— HURLING BRUHL AND VELVET FORWARD!
BOND SEIZES HIS CHANCE AND BURSTS INTO THE GALLEY—
1510
IAN FLEMING'S
James Bond
DRAWING BY HORAK
WITH BRUHL HOLDING VELVET AS A SHIELD— BOND IS UNABLE TO USE HIS OWN GUN AGAINST THE HI-JACK LEADER!
SHE FINALLY WRENCHES FREE FROM BRUHL'S GRIP— BUT IN DOING SO, KNOCKS BOND'S GUNHAND ASIDE!
1511
IAN FLEMING'S
James Bond
DRAWING BY HORAK
ANOTHER SMASH OF THE PAN CATCHES BOND ON THE SIDE OF THE HEAD
1512
IAN FLEMING'S
James Bond
DRAWING BY HORAK
AS BOND SPRAWLS HELPLESSLY IN THE DOORWAY— THE EX-S.P.E.C.T.R.E. ASSOCIATE GRABS A MEAT CLEAVER TO FINISH HIM OFF!
BUT 007 SWINGS HIS LEGS UPWARD— IN A PARTIAL BACKFLIP
1513
—AND KICKS THE DOOR SHUT!

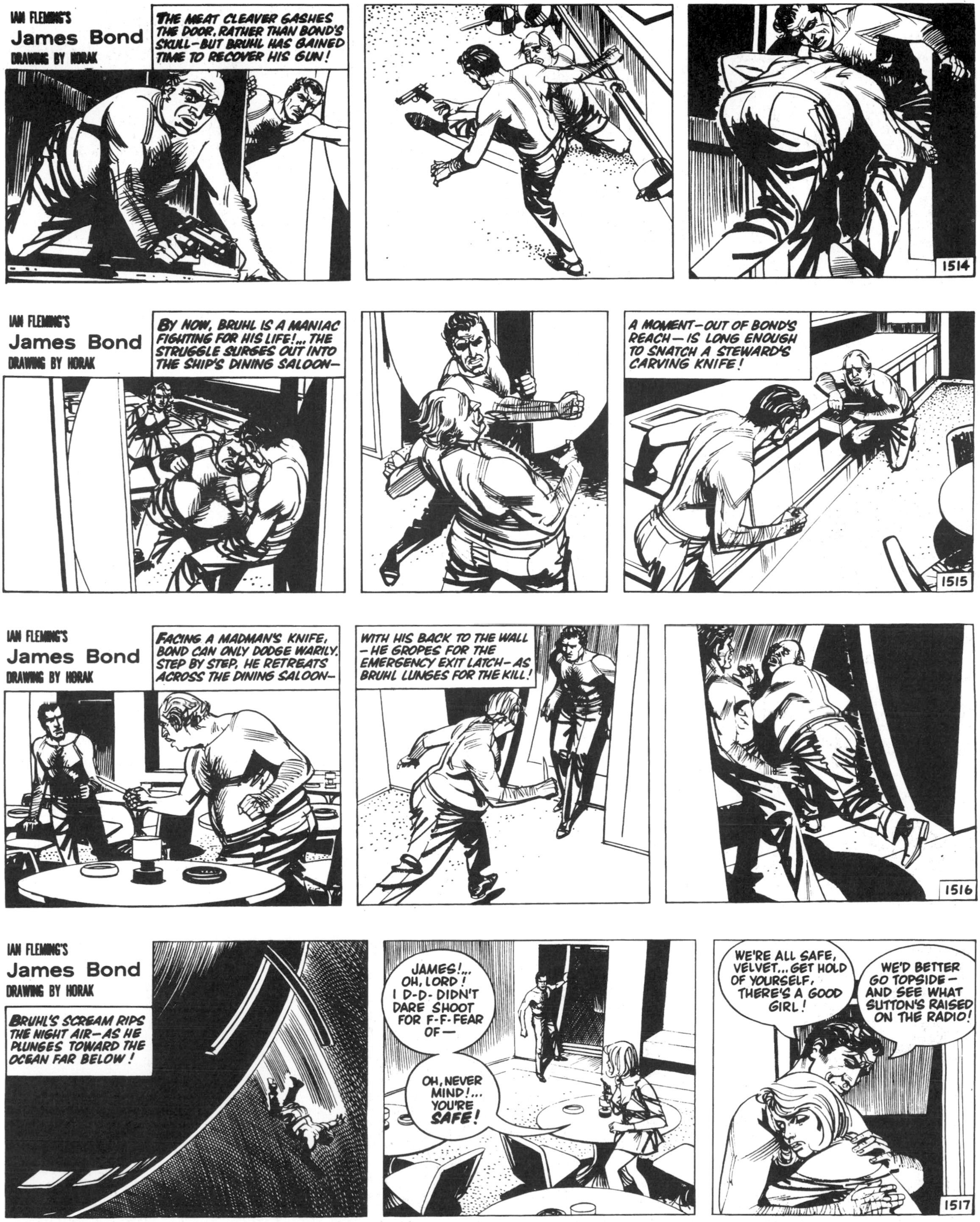
IAN FLEMING'S
James Bond
DRAWING BY HORAK
THE MEAT CLEAVER GASHES THE DOOR, RATHER THAN BOND'S SKULL–BUT BRUHL HAS GAINED TIME TO RECOVER HIS GUN!
1514
IAN FLEMING'S
James Bond
DRAWING BY HORAK
BY NOW, BRUHL IS A MANIAC FIGHTING FOR HIS LIFE!... THE STRUGGLE SURGES OUT INTO THE SHIP'S DINING SALOON–
A MOMENT–OUT OF BOND'S REACH–IS LONG ENOUGH TO SNATCH A STEWARD'S CARVING KNIFE!
1515
IAN FLEMING'S
James Bond
DRAWING BY HORAK
FACING A MADMAN'S KNIFE, BOND CAN ONLY DODGE WARILY. STEP BY STEP, HE RETREATS ACROSS THE DINING SALOON–
WITH HIS BACK TO THE WALL –HE GROPES FOR THE EMERGENCY EXIT LATCH–AS BRUHL LUNGES FOR THE KILL!
1516
IAN FLEMING'S
James Bond
DRAWING BY HORAK
BRUHL'S SCREAM RIPS THE NIGHT AIR–AS HE PLUNGES TOWARD THE OCEAN FAR BELOW!
JAMES!... OH, LORD! I D-D-DIDN'T DARE SHOOT FOR F-F-FEAR OF—
OH, NEVER MIND!... YOU'RE SAFE!
WE'RE ALL SAFE, VELVET... GET HOLD OF YOURSELF, THERE'S A GOOD GIRL!
WE'D BETTER GO TOPSIDE–AND SEE WHAT SUTTON'S RAISED ON THE RADIO!
1517

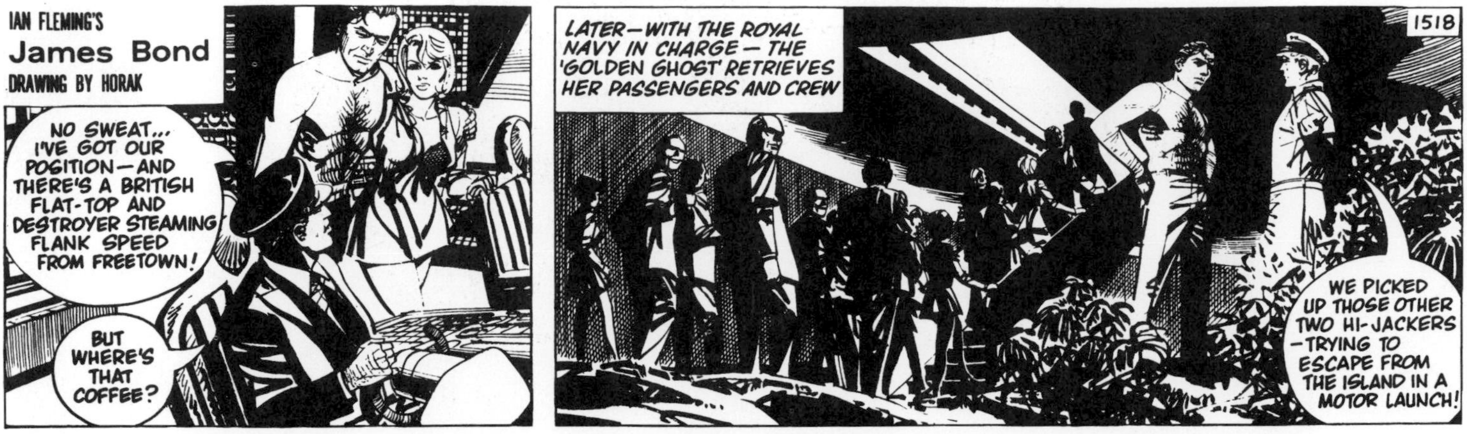
IAN FLEMING'S
James Bond
DRAWING BY HORAK
NO SWEAT... I'VE GOT OUR POSITION—AND THERE'S A BRITISH FLAT-TOP AND DESTROYER STEAMING FLANK SPEED FROM FREETOWN!
BUT WHERE'S THAT COFFEE?
LATER—WITH THE ROYAL NAVY IN CHARGE—THE 'GOLDEN GHOST' RETRIEVES HER PASSENGERS AND CREW
1518
WE PICKED UP THOSE OTHER TWO HI-JACKERS—TRYING TO ESCAPE FROM THE ISLAND IN A MOTOR LAUNCH!

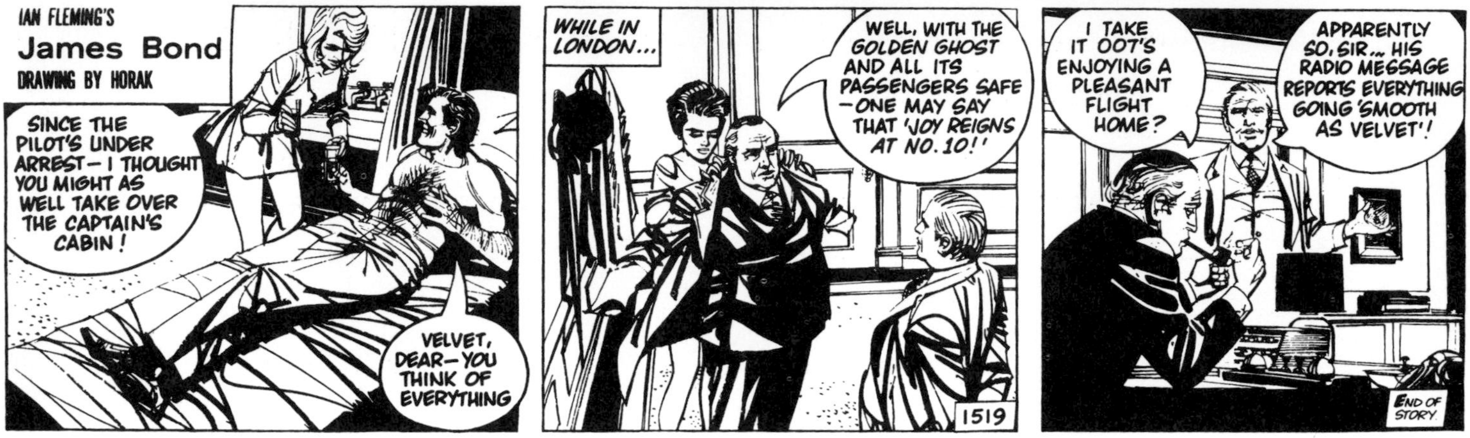
IAN FLEMING'S
James Bond
DRAWING BY HORAK
SINCE THE PILOT'S UNDER ARREST—I THOUGHT YOU MIGHT AS WELL TAKE OVER THE CAPTAIN'S CABIN!
VELVET, DEAR—YOU THINK OF EVERYTHING
WHILE IN LONDON...
WELL, WITH THE GOLDEN GHOST AND ALL ITS PASSENGERS SAFE—ONE MAY SAY THAT 'JOY REIGNS AT NO. 10!'
1519
I TAKE IT OOT'S ENJOYING A PLEASANT FLIGHT HOME?
APPARENTLY SO, SIR... HIS RADIO MESSAGE REPORTS EVERYTHING GOING 'SMOOTH AS VELVET'!
END OF STORY

FEAR FACE

Agent 0013 – Briony Thorne – is introduced in this story, which sees her teaming up with the only man she can trust – 007 – to prove her loyalty to MI6. It is implied that Briony is reinstated into the 00-section at the end of the tale, and may be the only female double-0 in service, based on the all-male meeting of agents earlier in the story. Suzy Kew takes over as Bond's regular female 00 agent sidekick in later adventures.

Writer Jim Lawrence slips up a gear into sci-fi mode in this story, with remote-control robots capable of passing as humans. The 'faceless' automatons are the inspiration for the title of the adventure.

The plot seems to be heavily influenced by an episode of the popular television series *The Avengers*, which aired a couple of years prior to the first publication of this strip. Emma Peel (played by later *Bond* girl Diana Rigg in *On Her Majesty's Secret Service*) and John Steed (played by Patrick Macnee, who would appear later in *A View To A Kill*) go on the hunt for killer robots with blank, expressionless faces.

Inspector Craig best describes the plot during the strip: 'The whole thing is utterly impossible, except in science-fiction yarns.'

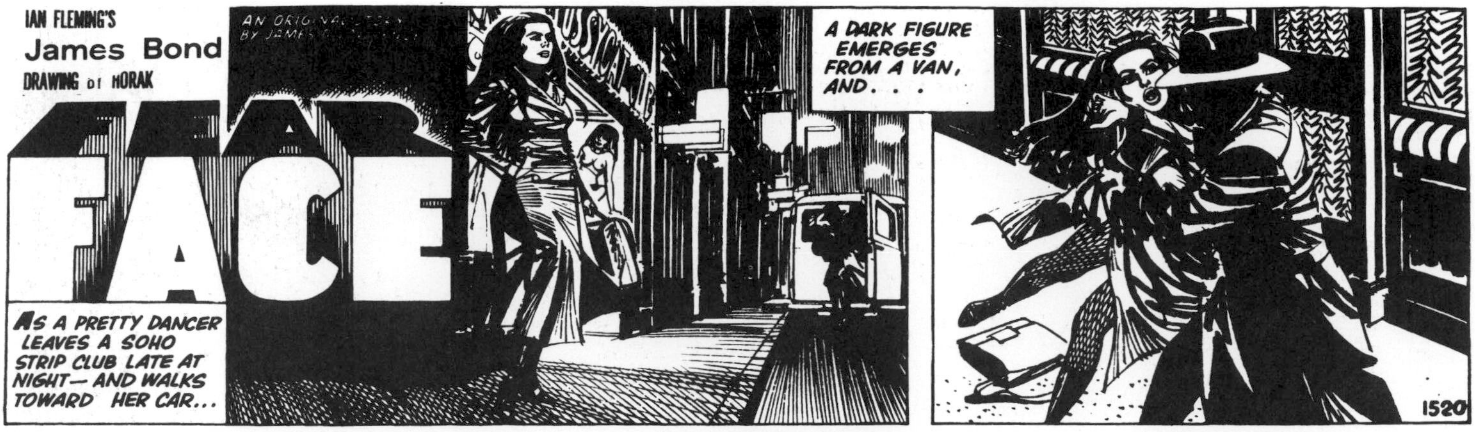
IAN FLEMING'S
James Bond
DRAWING BY HORAK
FEAR FACE
AS A PRETTY DANCER LEAVES A SOHO STRIP CLUB LATE AT NIGHT— AND WALKS TOWARD HER CAR...
A DARK FIGURE EMERGES FROM A VAN, AND . . .
1520

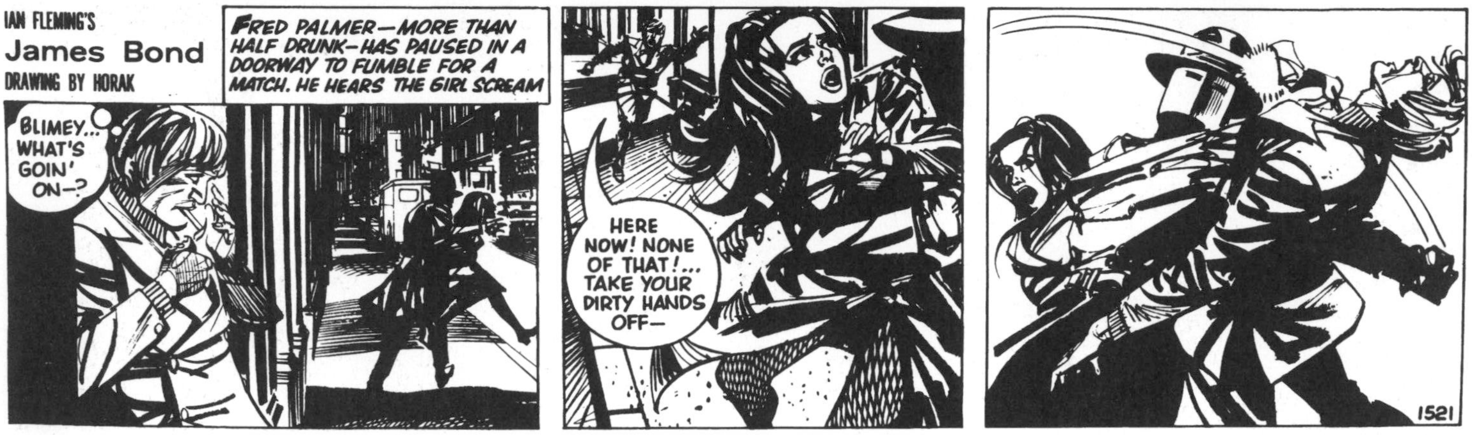
IAN FLEMING'S
James Bond
DRAWING BY HORAK
FRED PALMER—MORE THAN HALF DRUNK—HAS PAUSED IN A DOORWAY TO FUMBLE FOR A MATCH. HE HEARS THE GIRL SCREAM
BLIMEY... WHAT'S GOIN' ON—?
HERE NOW! NONE OF THAT!... TAKE YOUR DIRTY HANDS OFF—
1521

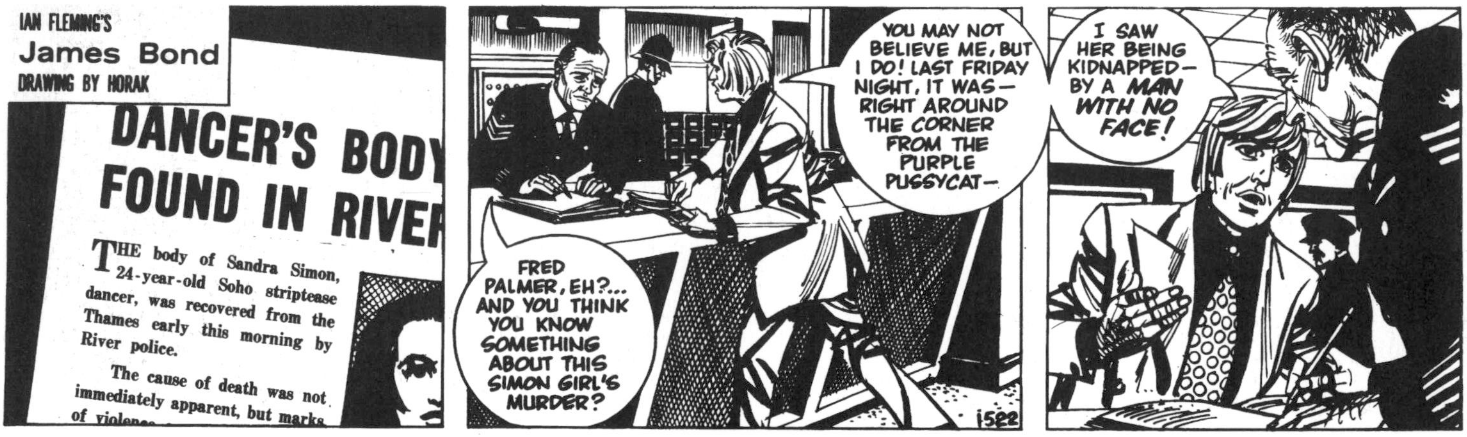
IAN FLEMING'S
James Bond
DRAWING BY HORAK
DANCER'S BODY FOUND IN RIVER
THE body of Sandra Simon, 24-year-old Soho striptease dancer, was recovered from the Thames early this morning by River police.
The cause of death was not immediately apparent, but marks
YOU MAY NOT BELIEVE ME, BUT I DO! LAST FRIDAY NIGHT, IT WAS— RIGHT AROUND THE CORNER FROM THE PURPLE PUSSYCAT—
FRED PALMER, EH?... AND YOU THINK YOU KNOW SOMETHING ABOUT THIS SIMON GIRL'S MURDER?
I SAW HER BEING KIDNAPPED— BY A MAN WITH NO FACE!
1522

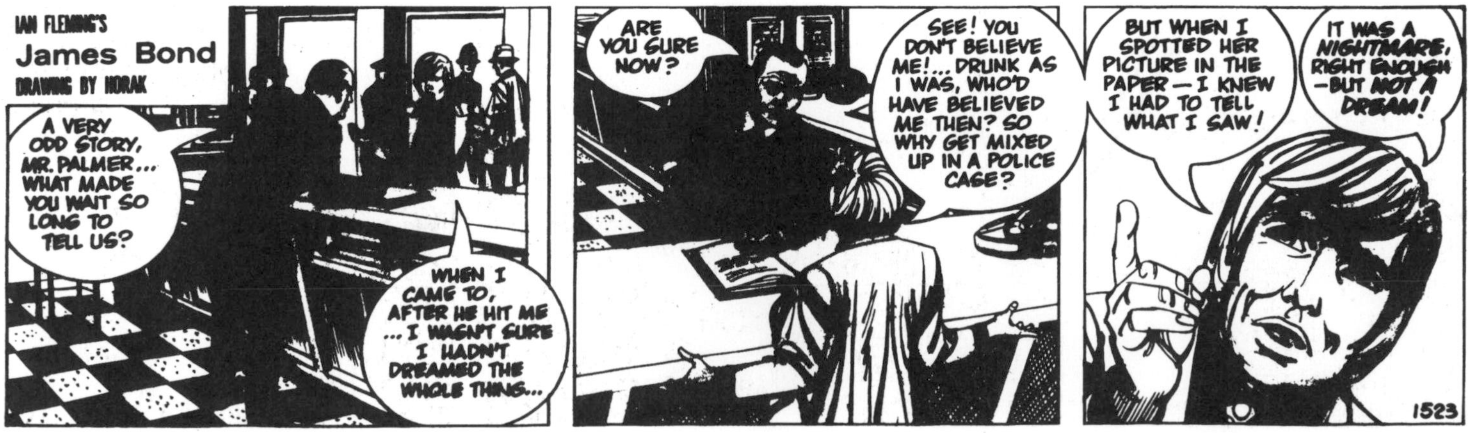
IAN FLEMING'S
James Bond
DRAWING BY HORAK
A VERY ODD STORY, MR. PALMER... WHAT MADE YOU WAIT SO LONG TO TELL US?
WHEN I CAME TO, AFTER HE HIT ME ...I WASN'T SURE I HADN'T DREAMED THE WHOLE THING...
ARE YOU SURE NOW?
SEE! YOU DON'T BELIEVE ME!... DRUNK AS I WAS, WHO'D HAVE BELIEVED ME THEN? SO WHY GET MIXED UP IN A POLICE CASE?
BUT WHEN I SPOTTED HER PICTURE IN THE PAPER — I KNEW I HAD TO TELL WHAT I SAW!
IT WAS A NIGHTMARE, RIGHT ENOUGH —BUT NOT A DREAM!
1523

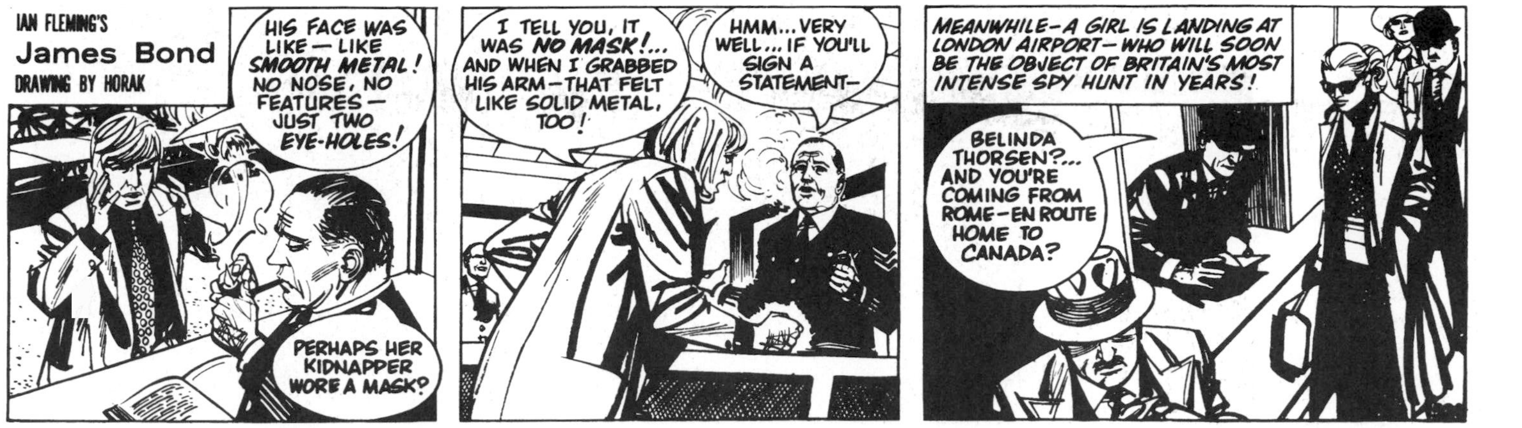
IAN FLEMING'S
James Bond
DRAWING BY HORAK
HIS FACE WAS LIKE — LIKE SMOOTH METAL! NO NOSE, NO FEATURES — JUST TWO EYE-HOLES!
PERHAPS HER KIDNAPPER WORE A MASK?
I TELL YOU, IT WAS NO MASK!... AND WHEN I GRABBED HIS ARM — THAT FELT LIKE SOLID METAL, TOO!
HMM... VERY WELL... IF YOU'LL SIGN A STATEMENT—
MEANWHILE — A GIRL IS LANDING AT LONDON AIRPORT — WHO WILL SOON BE THE OBJECT OF BRITAIN'S MOST INTENSE SPY HUNT IN YEARS!
BELINDA THORSEN?... AND YOU'RE COMING FROM ROME — EN ROUTE HOME TO CANADA?

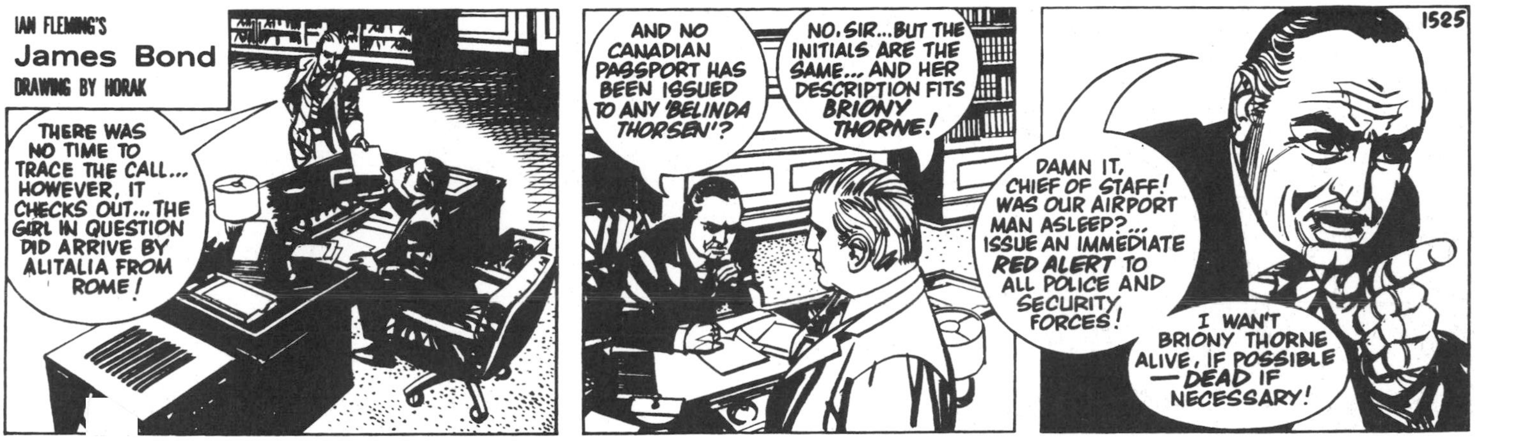
IAN FLEMING'S
James Bond
DRAWING BY HORAK
THERE WAS NO TIME TO TRACE THE CALL... HOWEVER, IT CHECKS OUT... THE GIRL IN QUESTION DID ARRIVE BY ALITALIA FROM ROME!
AND NO CANADIAN PASSPORT HAS BEEN ISSUED TO ANY 'BELINDA THORSEN'?
NO, SIR... BUT THE INITIALS ARE THE SAME... AND HER DESCRIPTION FITS BRIONY THORNE!
1525
DAMN IT, CHIEF OF STAFF! WAS OUR AIRPORT MAN ASLEEP?... ISSUE AN IMMEDIATE RED ALERT TO ALL POLICE AND SECURITY FORCES!
I WAN'T BRIONY THORNE ALIVE, IF POSSIBLE — DEAD IF NECESSARY!

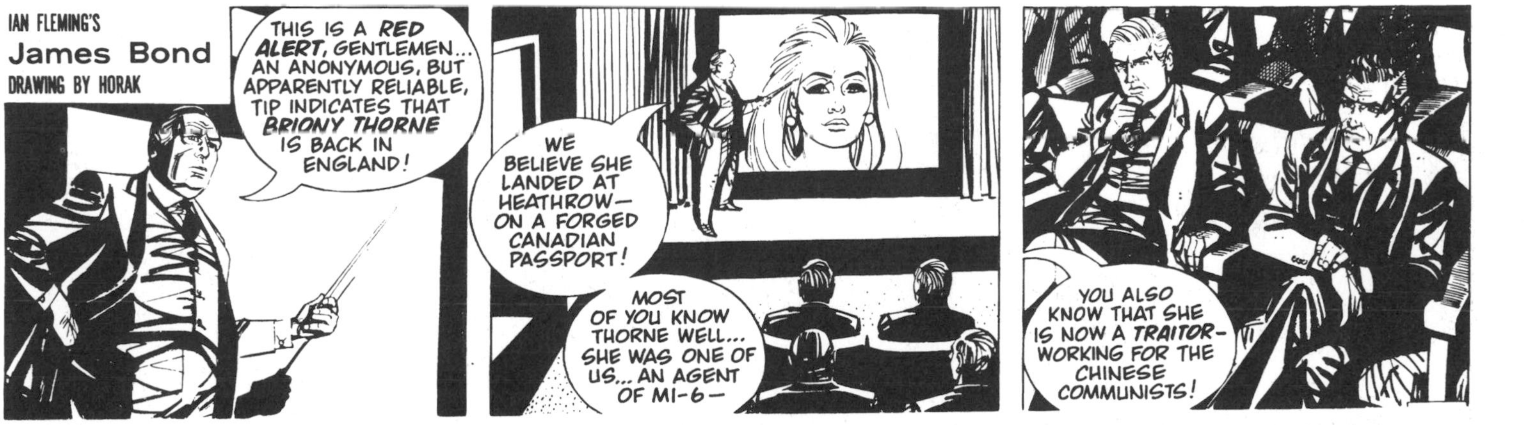
IAN FLEMING'S
James Bond
DRAWING BY HORAK
THIS IS A RED ALERT, GENTLEMEN... AN ANONYMOUS, BUT APPARENTLY RELIABLE, TIP INDICATES THAT BRIONY THORNE IS BACK IN ENGLAND!
WE BELIEVE SHE LANDED AT HEATHROW — ON A FORGED CANADIAN PASSPORT!
MOST OF YOU KNOW THORNE WELL... SHE WAS ONE OF US... AN AGENT OF MI-6 —
YOU ALSO KNOW THAT SHE IS NOW A TRAITOR — WORKING FOR THE CHINESE COMMUNISTS!

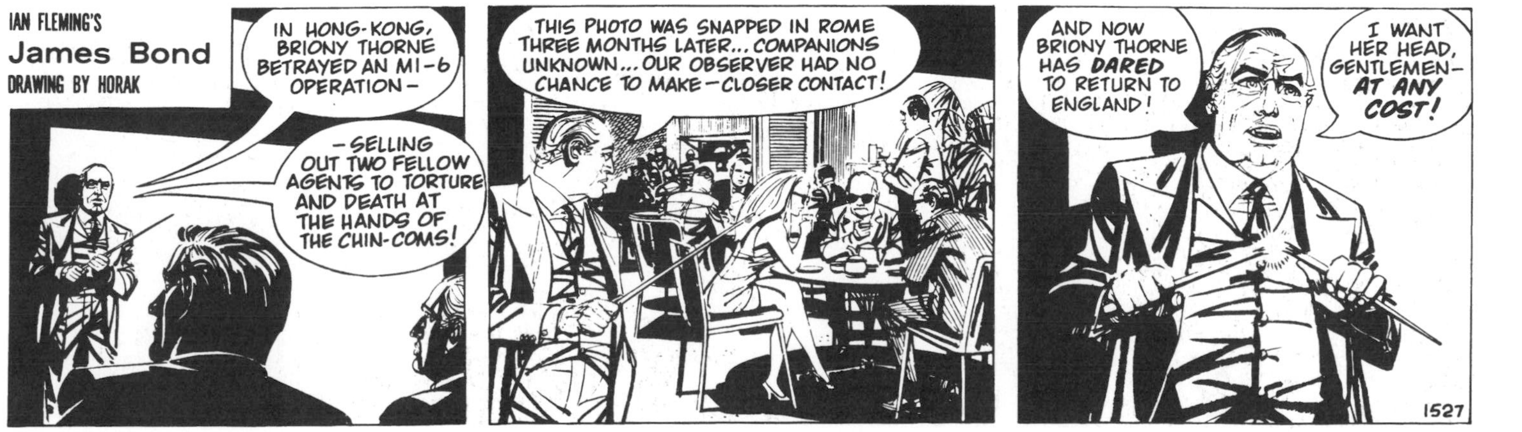
IAN FLEMING'S
James Bond
DRAWING BY HORAK
IN HONG-KONG, BRIONY THORNE BETRAYED AN MI-6 OPERATION —
— SELLING OUT TWO FELLOW AGENTS TO TORTURE AND DEATH AT THE HANDS OF THE CHIN-COMS!
THIS PHOTO WAS SNAPPED IN ROME THREE MONTHS LATER... COMPANIONS UNKNOWN... OUR OBSERVER HAD NO CHANCE TO MAKE — CLOSER CONTACT!
AND NOW BRIONY THORNE HAS DARED TO RETURN TO ENGLAND!
I WANT HER HEAD, GENTLEMEN — AT ANY COST!
1527

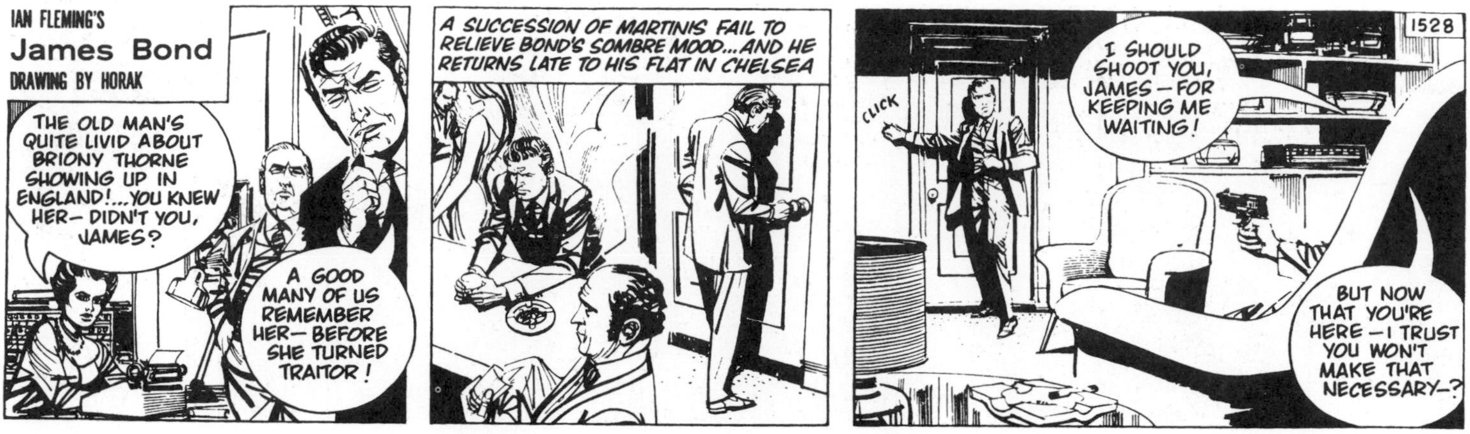
IAN FLEMING'S
James Bond
DRAWING BY HORAK
THE OLD MAN'S QUITE LIVID ABOUT BRIONY THORNE SHOWING UP IN ENGLAND!... YOU KNEW HER– DIDN'T YOU, JAMES?
A GOOD MANY OF US REMEMBER HER– BEFORE SHE TURNED TRAITOR!
A SUCCESSION OF MARTINIS FAIL TO RELIEVE BOND'S SOMBRE MOOD... AND HE RETURNS LATE TO HIS FLAT IN CHELSEA
1528
CLICK
I SHOULD SHOOT YOU, JAMES – FOR KEEPING ME WAITING!
BUT NOW THAT YOU'RE HERE – I TRUST YOU WON'T MAKE THAT NECESSARY–?

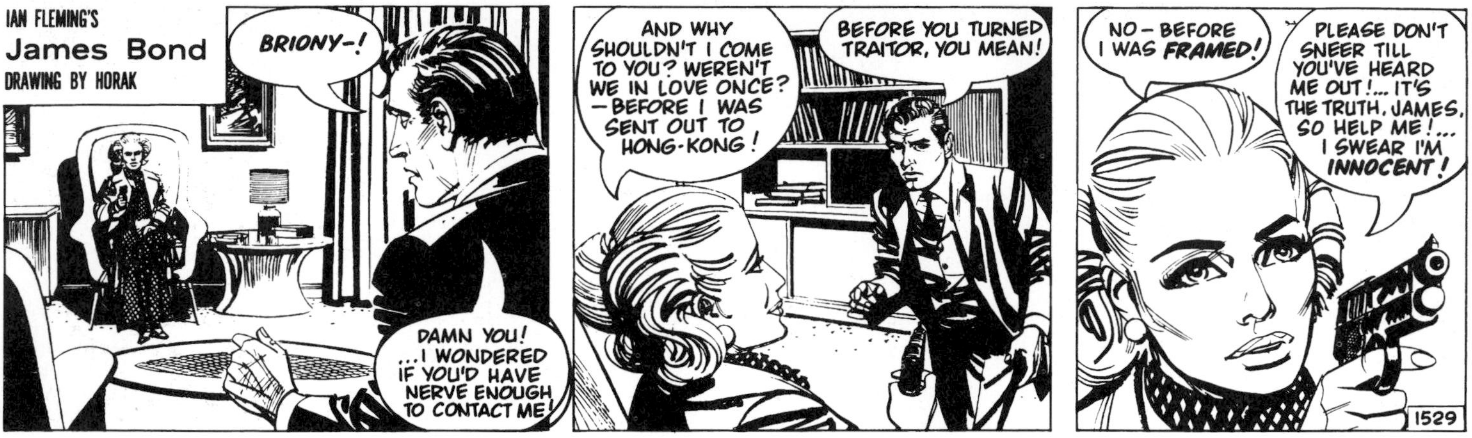
IAN FLEMING'S
James Bond
DRAWING BY HORAK
BRIONY–!
DAMN YOU! ...I WONDERED IF YOU'D HAVE NERVE ENOUGH TO CONTACT ME!
AND WHY SHOULDN'T I COME TO YOU? WEREN'T WE IN LOVE ONCE? – BEFORE I WAS SENT OUT TO HONG-KONG!
BEFORE YOU TURNED TRAITOR, YOU MEAN!
NO – BEFORE I WAS FRAMED!
PLEASE DON'T SNEER TILL YOU'VE HEARD ME OUT!... IT'S THE TRUTH, JAMES, SO HELP ME!... I SWEAR I'M INNOCENT!
1529

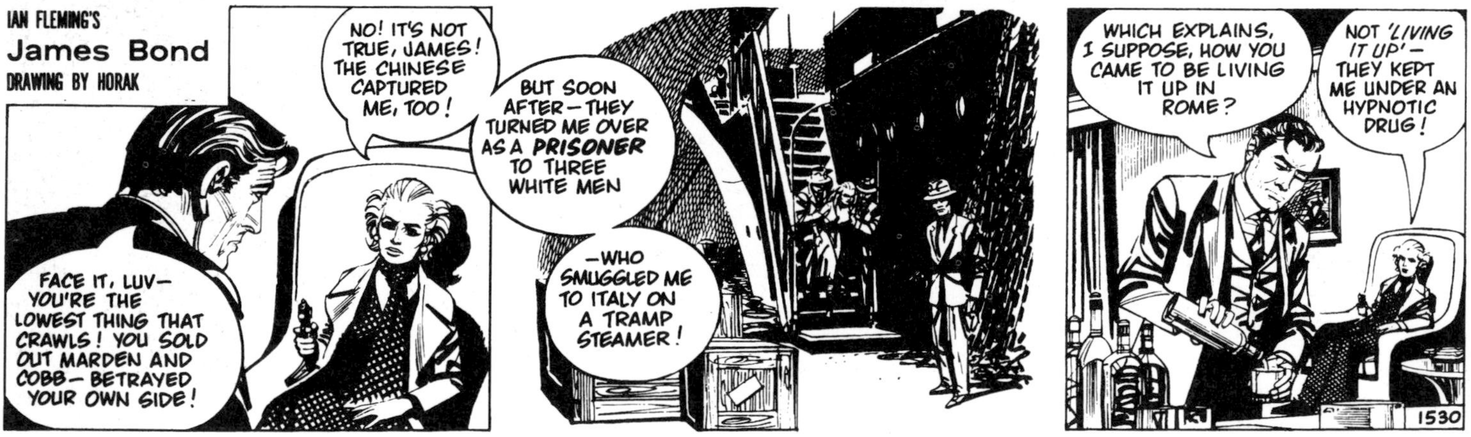
IAN FLEMING'S
James Bond
DRAWING BY HORAK
FACE IT, LUV– YOU'RE THE LOWEST THING THAT CRAWLS! YOU SOLD OUT MARDEN AND COBB– BETRAYED YOUR OWN SIDE!
NO! IT'S NOT TRUE, JAMES! THE CHINESE CAPTURED ME, TOO!
BUT SOON AFTER– THEY TURNED ME OVER AS A PRISONER TO THREE WHITE MEN
–WHO SMUGGLED ME TO ITALY ON A TRAMP STEAMER!
WHICH EXPLAINS, I SUPPOSE, HOW YOU CAME TO BE LIVING IT UP IN ROME?
NOT 'LIVING IT UP' – THEY KEPT ME UNDER AN HYPNOTIC DRUG!
1530

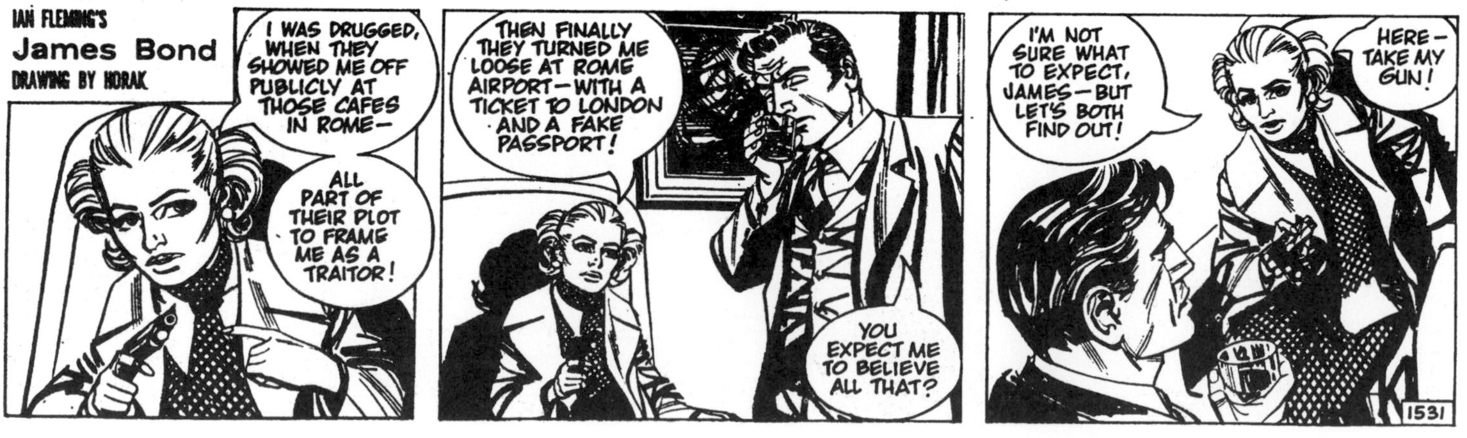
IAN FLEMING'S
James Bond
DRAWING BY HORAK
I WAS DRUGGED, WHEN THEY SHOWED ME OFF PUBLICLY AT THOSE CAFES IN ROME–
ALL PART OF THEIR PLOT TO FRAME ME AS A TRAITOR!
THEN FINALLY THEY TURNED ME LOOSE AT ROME AIRPORT– WITH A TICKET TO LONDON AND A FAKE PASSPORT!
YOU EXPECT ME TO BELIEVE ALL THAT?
I'M NOT SURE WHAT TO EXPECT, JAMES– BUT LET'S BOTH FIND OUT!
HERE– TAKE MY GUN!
1531

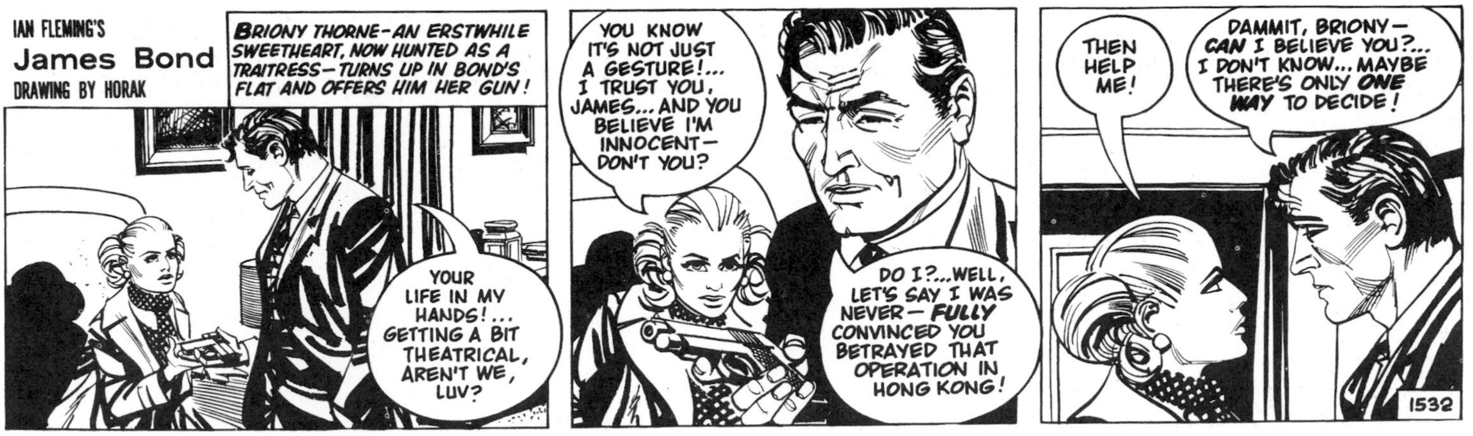
IAN FLEMING'S
James Bond
DRAWING BY HORAK
BRIONY THORNE—AN ERSTWHILE SWEETHEART, NOW HUNTED AS A TRAITRESS—TURNS UP IN BOND'S FLAT AND OFFERS HIM HER GUN!
YOUR LIFE IN MY HANDS!... GETTING A BIT THEATRICAL, AREN'T WE, LUV?
YOU KNOW IT'S NOT JUST A GESTURE!... I TRUST YOU, JAMES... AND YOU BELIEVE I'M INNOCENT—DON'T YOU?
DO I?... WELL, LET'S SAY I WAS NEVER—FULLY CONVINCED YOU BETRAYED THAT OPERATION IN HONG KONG!
THEN HELP ME!
DAMMIT, BRIONY—CAN I BELIEVE YOU?... I DON'T KNOW... MAYBE THERE'S ONLY ONE WAY TO DECIDE!
1532

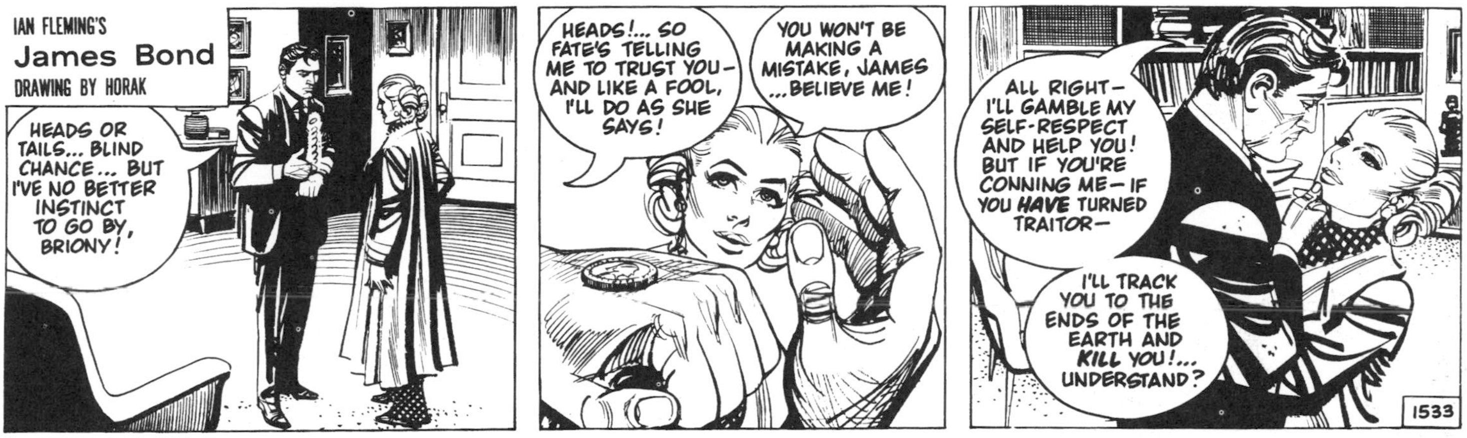
IAN FLEMING'S
James Bond
DRAWING BY HORAK
HEADS OR TAILS... BLIND CHANCE... BUT I'VE NO BETTER INSTINCT TO GO BY, BRIONY!
HEADS!... SO FATE'S TELLING ME TO TRUST YOU—AND LIKE A FOOL, I'LL DO AS SHE SAYS!
YOU WON'T BE MAKING A MISTAKE, JAMES ...BELIEVE ME!
ALL RIGHT—I'LL GAMBLE MY SELF-RESPECT AND HELP YOU! BUT IF YOU'RE CONNING ME—IF YOU HAVE TURNED TRAITOR—
I'LL TRACK YOU TO THE ENDS OF THE EARTH AND KILL YOU!... UNDERSTAND?
1533

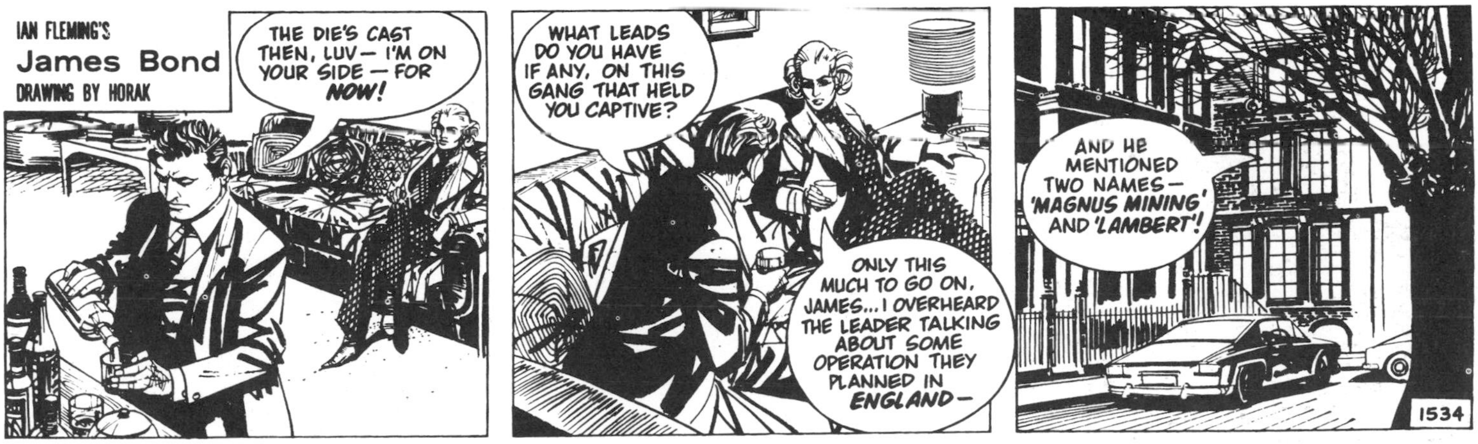
IAN FLEMING'S
James Bond
DRAWING BY HORAK
THE DIE'S CAST THEN, LUV—I'M ON YOUR SIDE—FOR NOW!
WHAT LEADS DO YOU HAVE IF ANY, ON THIS GANG THAT HELD YOU CAPTIVE?
ONLY THIS MUCH TO GO ON, JAMES... I OVERHEARD THE LEADER TALKING ABOUT SOME OPERATION THEY PLANNED IN ENGLAND—
AND HE MENTIONED TWO NAMES—'MAGNUS MINING' AND 'LAMBERT'!
1534

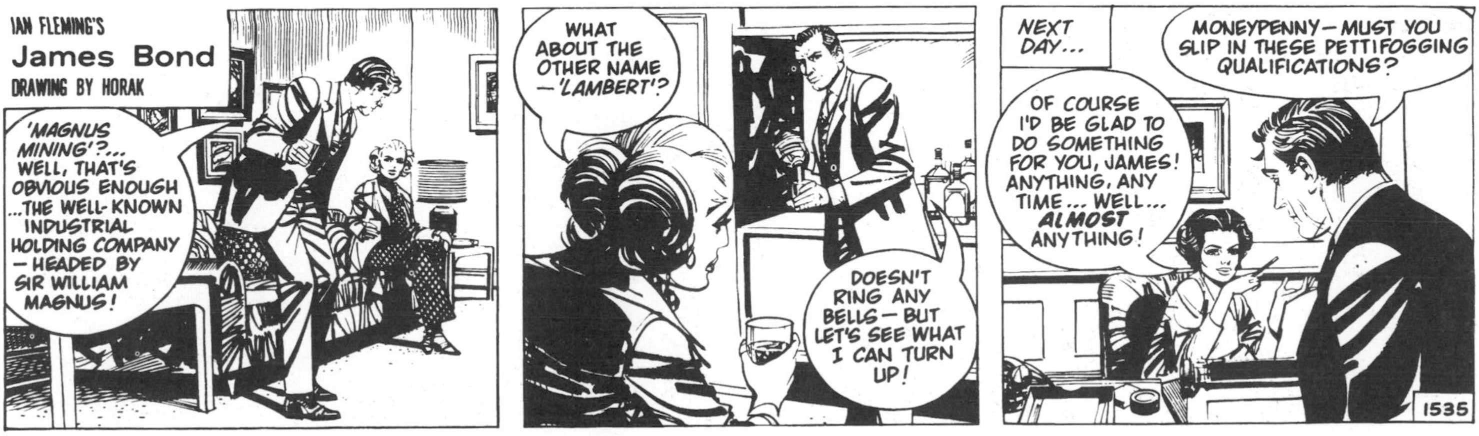
IAN FLEMING'S
James Bond
DRAWING BY HORAK
'MAGNUS MINING'?... WELL, THAT'S OBVIOUS ENOUGH ...THE WELL-KNOWN INDUSTRIAL HOLDING COMPANY —HEADED BY SIR WILLIAM MAGNUS!
WHAT ABOUT THE OTHER NAME —'LAMBERT'?
DOESN'T RING ANY BELLS—BUT LET'S SEE WHAT I CAN TURN UP!
NEXT DAY...
MONEYPENNY—MUST YOU SLIP IN THESE PETTIFOGGING QUALIFICATIONS?
OF COURSE I'D BE GLAD TO DO SOMETHING FOR YOU, JAMES! ANYTHING, ANY TIME... WELL... ALMOST ANYTHING!
1535

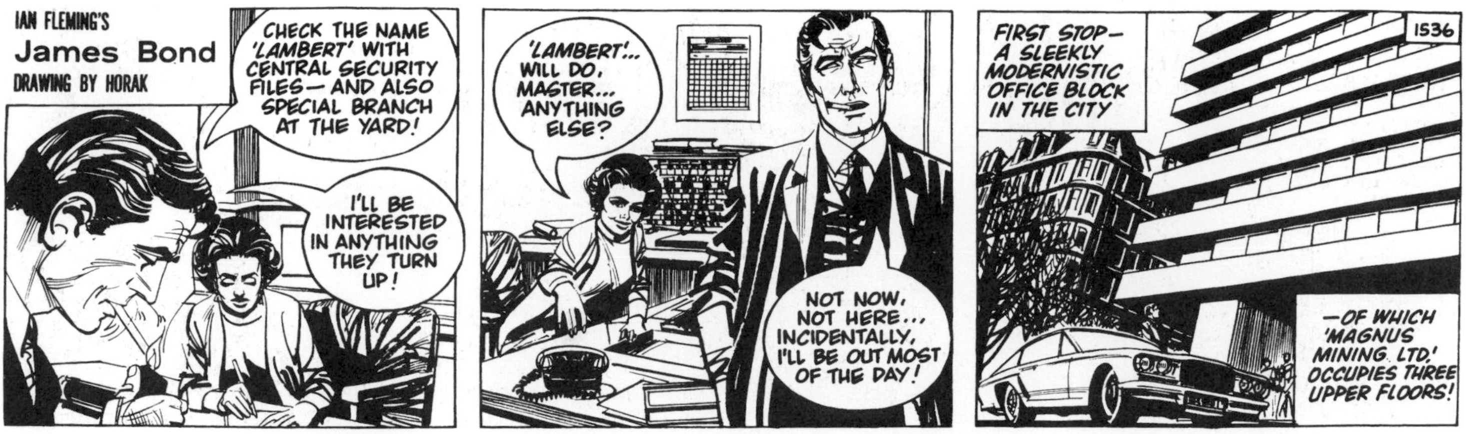
IAN FLEMING'S
James Bond
DRAWING BY HORAK
CHECK THE NAME 'LAMBERT' WITH CENTRAL SECURITY FILES—AND ALSO SPECIAL BRANCH AT THE YARD!
I'LL BE INTERESTED IN ANYTHING THEY TURN UP!
'LAMBERT'... WILL DO, MASTER... ANYTHING ELSE?
NOT NOW, NOT HERE... INCIDENTALLY, I'LL BE OUT MOST OF THE DAY!
1536
FIRST STOP—A SLEEKLY MODERNISTIC OFFICE BLOCK IN THE CITY
—OF WHICH 'MAGNUS MINING LTD.' OCCUPIES THREE UPPER FLOORS!

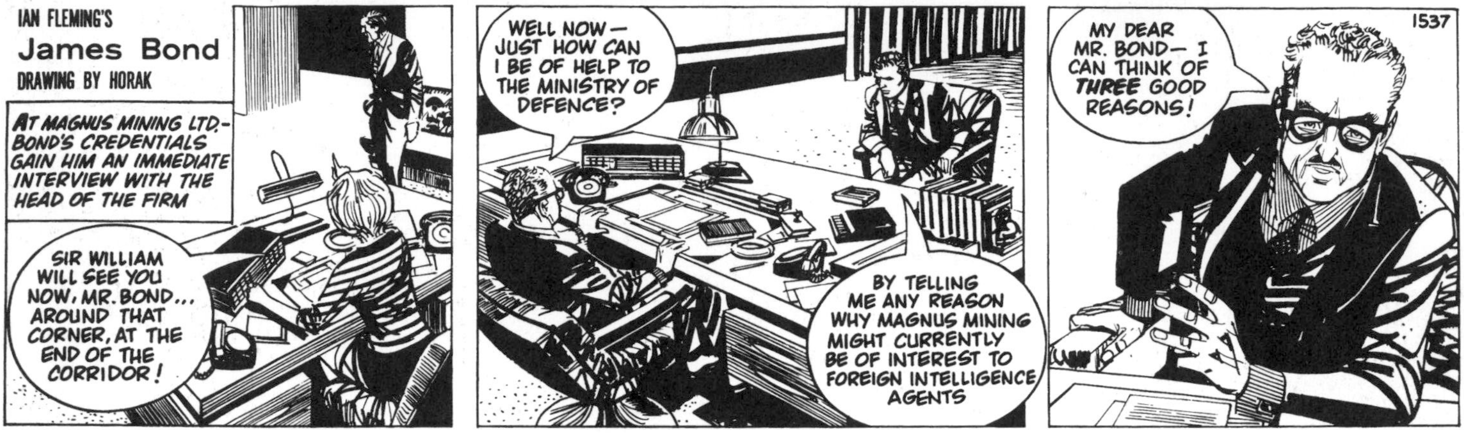
IAN FLEMING'S
James Bond
DRAWING BY HORAK
AT MAGNUS MINING LTD.—BOND'S CREDENTIALS GAIN HIM AN IMMEDIATE INTERVIEW WITH THE HEAD OF THE FIRM
SIR WILLIAM WILL SEE YOU NOW, MR. BOND... AROUND THAT CORNER, AT THE END OF THE CORRIDOR!
WELL NOW—JUST HOW CAN I BE OF HELP TO THE MINISTRY OF DEFENCE?
BY TELLING ME ANY REASON WHY MAGNUS MINING MIGHT CURRENTLY BE OF INTEREST TO FOREIGN INTELLIGENCE AGENTS
1537
MY DEAR MR. BOND—I CAN THINK OF THREE GOOD REASONS!

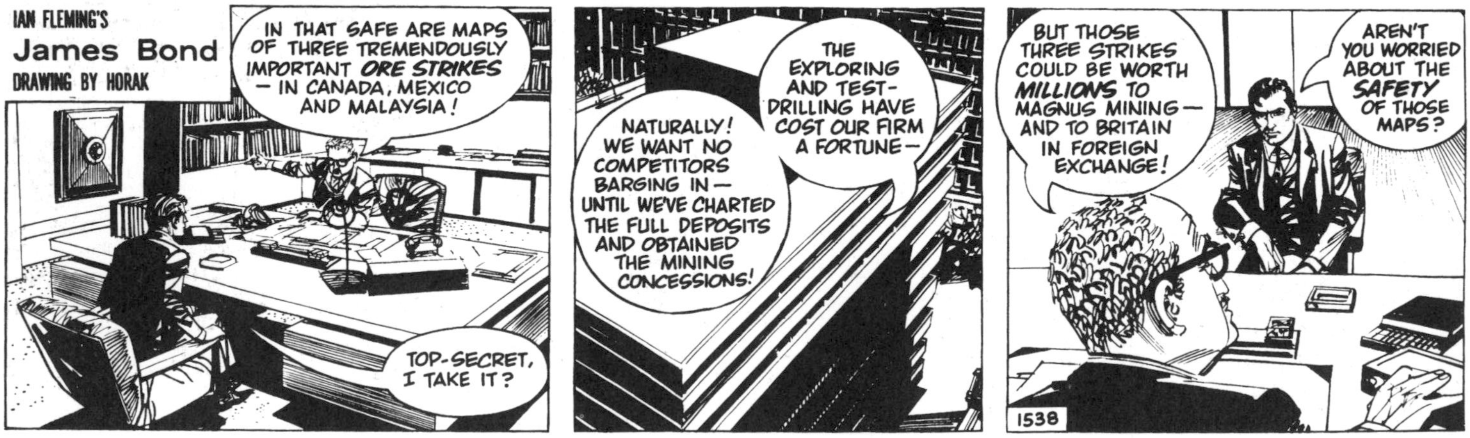
IAN FLEMING'S
James Bond
DRAWING BY HORAK
IN THAT SAFE ARE MAPS OF THREE TREMENDOUSLY IMPORTANT ORE STRIKES—IN CANADA, MEXICO AND MALAYSIA!
TOP-SECRET, I TAKE IT?
THE EXPLORING AND TEST-DRILLING HAVE COST OUR FIRM A FORTUNE—
NATURALLY! WE WANT NO COMPETITORS BARGING IN—UNTIL WE'VE CHARTED THE FULL DEPOSITS AND OBTAINED THE MINING CONCESSIONS!
BUT THOSE THREE STRIKES COULD BE WORTH MILLIONS TO MAGNUS MINING—AND TO BRITAIN IN FOREIGN EXCHANGE!
AREN'T YOU WORRIED ABOUT THE SAFETY OF THOSE MAPS?
1538

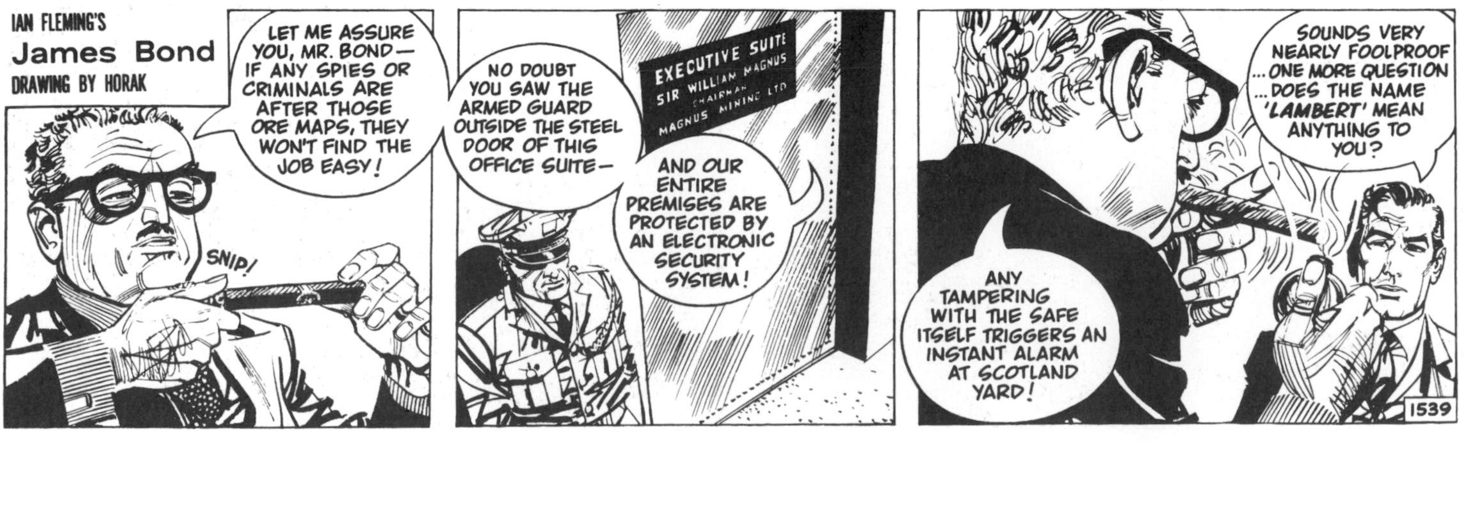
IAN FLEMING'S
James Bond
DRAWING BY HORAK
LET ME ASSURE YOU, MR. BOND—IF ANY SPIES OR CRIMINALS ARE AFTER THOSE ORE MAPS, THEY WON'T FIND THE JOB EASY!
SNIP!
NO DOUBT YOU SAW THE ARMED GUARD OUTSIDE THE STEEL DOOR OF THIS OFFICE SUITE—
EXECUTIVE SUITE
SIR WILLIAM MAGNUS
CHAIRMAN
MAGNUS MINING LTD
AND OUR ENTIRE PREMISES ARE PROTECTED BY AN ELECTRONIC SECURITY SYSTEM!
ANY TAMPERING WITH THE SAFE ITSELF TRIGGERS AN INSTANT ALARM AT SCOTLAND YARD!
SOUNDS VERY NEARLY FOOLPROOF ...ONE MORE QUESTION ...DOES THE NAME 'LAMBERT' MEAN ANYTHING TO YOU?
1539

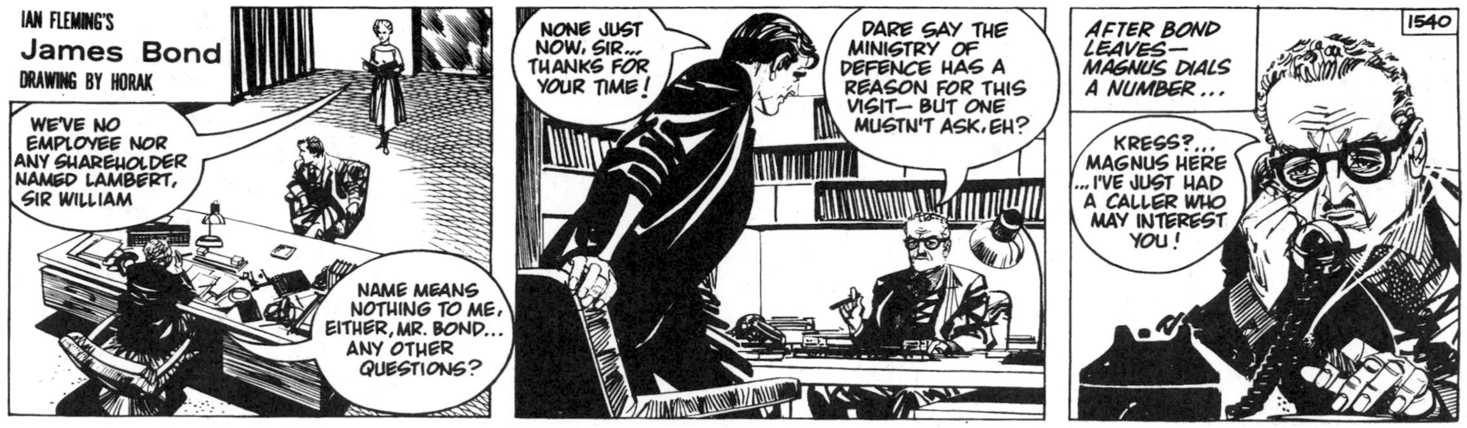
IAN FLEMING'S
James Bond
DRAWING BY HORAK
WE'VE NO EMPLOYEE NOR ANY SHAREHOLDER NAMED LAMBERT, SIR WILLIAM
NAME MEANS NOTHING TO ME, EITHER, MR. BOND... ANY OTHER QUESTIONS?
NONE JUST NOW, SIR... THANKS FOR YOUR TIME!
DARE SAY THE MINISTRY OF DEFENCE HAS A REASON FOR THIS VISIT— BUT ONE MUSTN'T ASK, EH?
1540
AFTER BOND LEAVES— MAGNUS DIALS A NUMBER...
KRESS?... MAGNUS HERE ...I'VE JUST HAD A CALLER WHO MAY INTEREST YOU!

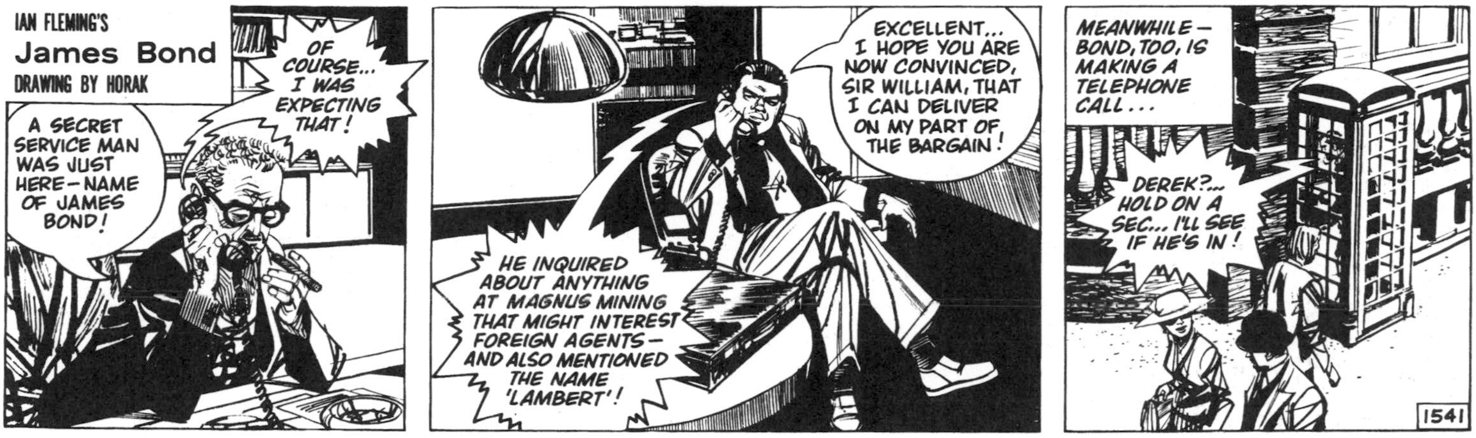
IAN FLEMING'S
James Bond
DRAWING BY HORAK
OF COURSE... I WAS EXPECTING THAT!
A SECRET SERVICE MAN WAS JUST HERE—NAME OF JAMES BOND!
EXCELLENT... I HOPE YOU ARE NOW CONVINCED, SIR WILLIAM, THAT I CAN DELIVER ON MY PART OF THE BARGAIN!
HE INQUIRED ABOUT ANYTHING AT MAGNUS MINING THAT MIGHT INTEREST FOREIGN AGENTS— AND ALSO MENTIONED THE NAME 'LAMBERT'!
MEANWHILE— BOND, TOO, IS MAKING A TELEPHONE CALL...
DEREK?... HOLD ON A SEC... I'LL SEE IF HE'S IN!
1541

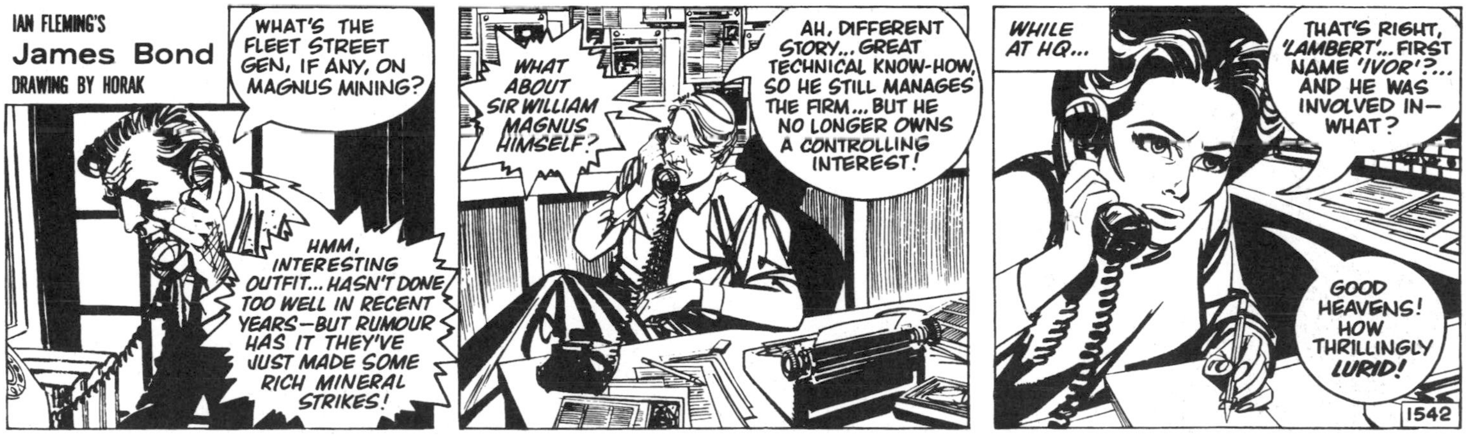
IAN FLEMING'S
James Bond
DRAWING BY HORAK
WHAT'S THE FLEET STREET GEN, IF ANY, ON MAGNUS MINING?
HMM, INTERESTING OUTFIT... HASN'T DONE TOO WELL IN RECENT YEARS—BUT RUMOUR HAS IT THEY'VE JUST MADE SOME RICH MINERAL STRIKES!
WHAT ABOUT SIR WILLIAM MAGNUS HIMSELF?
AH, DIFFERENT STORY... GREAT TECHNICAL KNOW-HOW, SO HE STILL MANAGES THE FIRM... BUT HE NO LONGER OWNS A CONTROLLING INTEREST!
WHILE AT HQ...
THAT'S RIGHT, 'LAMBERT'... FIRST NAME 'IVOR'?... AND HE WAS INVOLVED IN— WHAT?
GOOD HEAVENS! HOW THRILLINGLY LURID!
1542

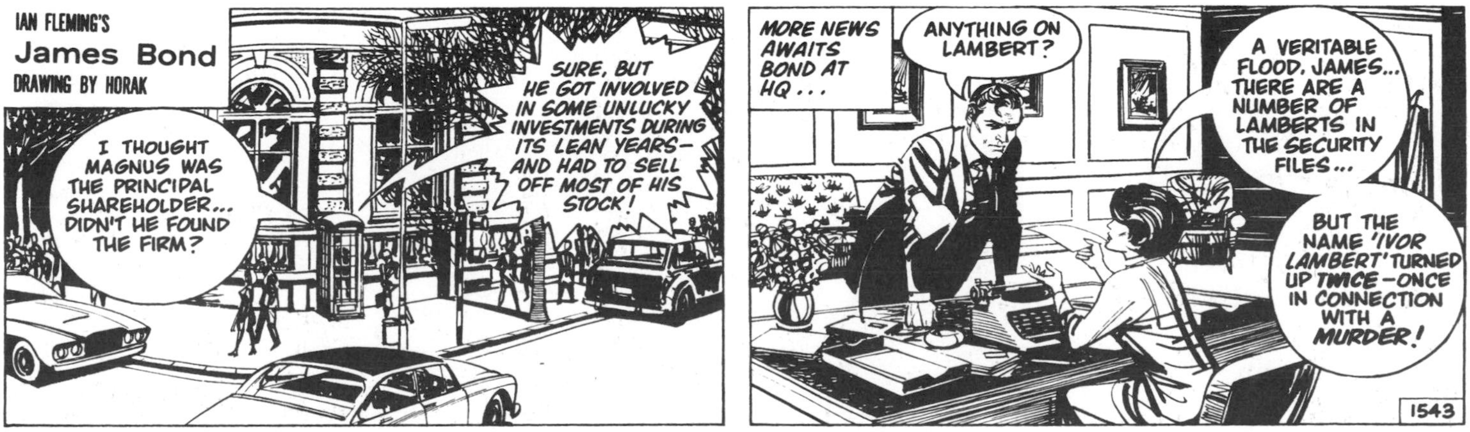
IAN FLEMING'S
James Bond
DRAWING BY HORAK
I THOUGHT MAGNUS WAS THE PRINCIPAL SHAREHOLDER... DIDN'T HE FOUND THE FIRM?
SURE, BUT HE GOT INVOLVED IN SOME UNLUCKY INVESTMENTS DURING ITS LEAN YEARS— AND HAD TO SELL OFF MOST OF HIS STOCK!
MORE NEWS AWAITS BOND AT HQ...
ANYTHING ON LAMBERT?
A VERITABLE FLOOD, JAMES... THERE ARE A NUMBER OF LAMBERTS IN THE SECURITY FILES...
BUT THE NAME 'IVOR LAMBERT' TURNED UP TWICE—ONCE IN CONNECTION WITH A MURDER!
1543

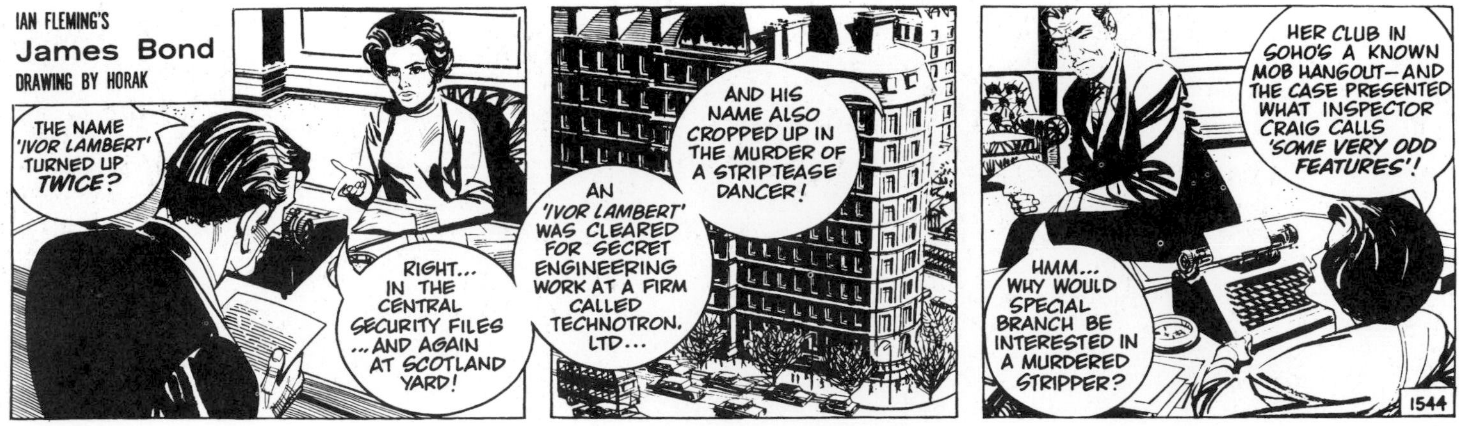
IAN FLEMING'S
James Bond
DRAWING BY HORAK
THE NAME 'IVOR LAMBERT' TURNED UP TWICE?
RIGHT... IN THE CENTRAL SECURITY FILES ...AND AGAIN AT SCOTLAND YARD!
AN 'IVOR LAMBERT' WAS CLEARED FOR SECRET ENGINEERING WORK AT A FIRM CALLED TECHNOTRON, LTD...
AND HIS NAME ALSO CROPPED UP IN THE MURDER OF A STRIPTEASE DANCER!
HER CLUB IN SOHO'S A KNOWN MOB HANGOUT—AND THE CASE PRESENTED WHAT INSPECTOR CRAIG CALLS 'SOME VERY ODD FEATURES'!
HMM... WHY WOULD SPECIAL BRANCH BE INTERESTED IN A MURDERED STRIPPER?
1544

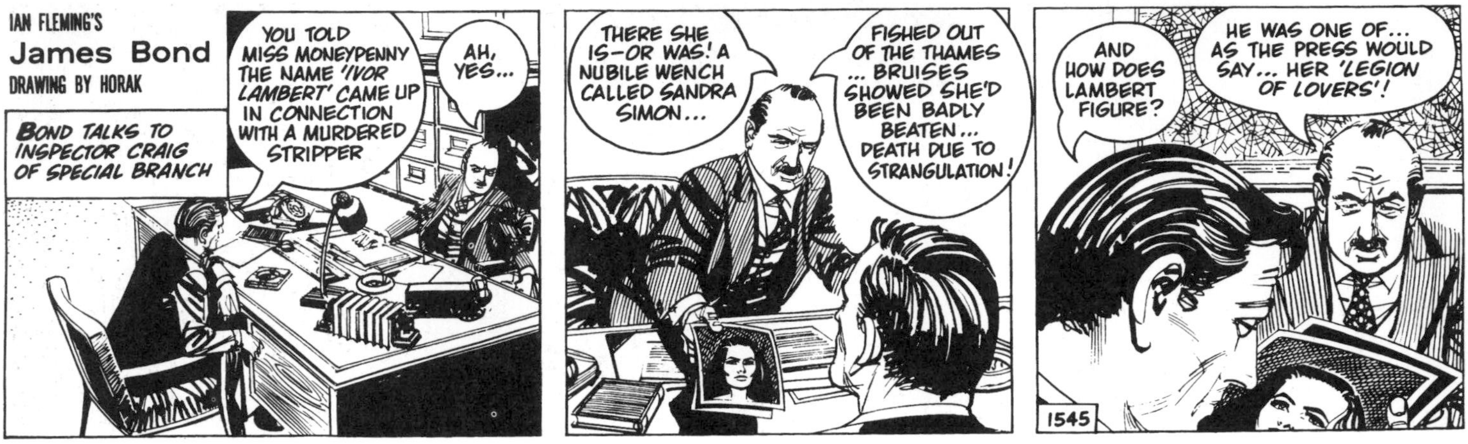
IAN FLEMING'S
James Bond
DRAWING BY HORAK
BOND TALKS TO INSPECTOR CRAIG OF SPECIAL BRANCH
YOU TOLD MISS MONEYPENNY THE NAME 'IVOR LAMBERT' CAME UP IN CONNECTION WITH A MURDERED STRIPPER
AH, YES...
THERE SHE IS—OR WAS! A NUBILE WENCH CALLED SANDRA SIMON...
FISHED OUT OF THE THAMES ... BRUISES SHOWED SHE'D BEEN BADLY BEATEN... DEATH DUE TO STRANGULATION!
AND HOW DOES LAMBERT FIGURE?
HE WAS ONE OF... AS THE PRESS WOULD SAY... HER 'LEGION OF LOVERS'!
1545

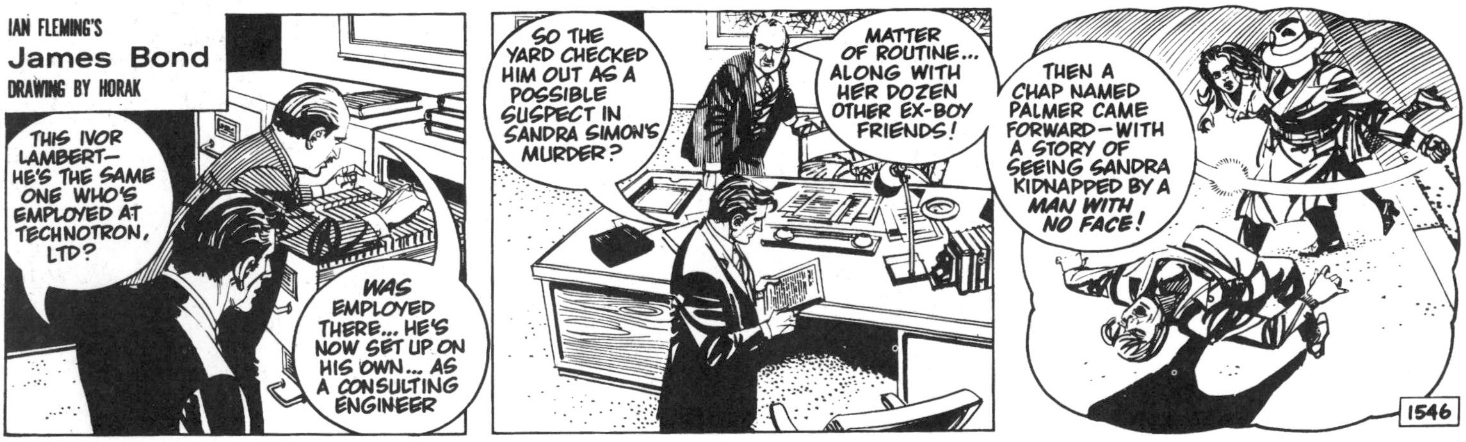
IAN FLEMING'S
James Bond
DRAWING BY HORAK
THIS IVOR LAMBERT—HE'S THE SAME ONE WHO'S EMPLOYED AT TECHNOTRON, LTD?
WAS EMPLOYED THERE... HE'S NOW SET UP ON HIS OWN... AS A CONSULTING ENGINEER
SO THE YARD CHECKED HIM OUT AS A POSSIBLE SUSPECT IN SANDRA SIMON'S MURDER?
MATTER OF ROUTINE... ALONG WITH HER DOZEN OTHER EX-BOY FRIENDS!
THEN A CHAP NAMED PALMER CAME FORWARD—WITH A STORY OF SEEING SANDRA KIDNAPPED BY A MAN WITH NO FACE!
1546

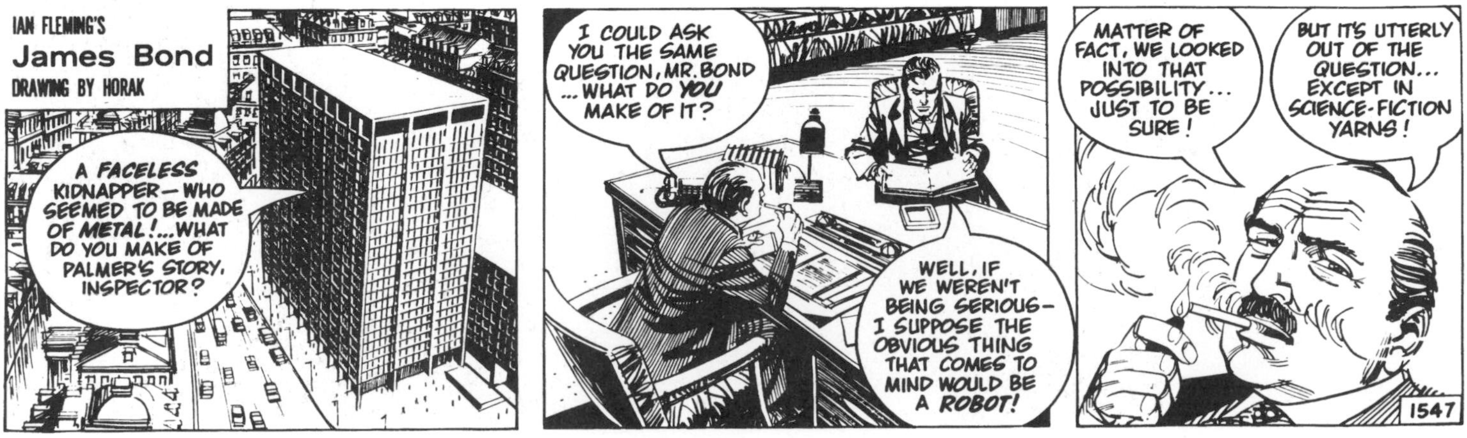
IAN FLEMING'S
James Bond
DRAWING BY HORAK
A FACELESS KIDNAPPER—WHO SEEMED TO BE MADE OF METAL!...WHAT DO YOU MAKE OF PALMER'S STORY, INSPECTOR?
I COULD ASK YOU THE SAME QUESTION, MR. BOND ...WHAT DO YOU MAKE OF IT?
WELL, IF WE WEREN'T BEING SERIOUS—I SUPPOSE THE OBVIOUS THING THAT COMES TO MIND WOULD BE A ROBOT!
MATTER OF FACT, WE LOOKED INTO THAT POSSIBILITY... JUST TO BE SURE!
BUT IT'S UTTERLY OUT OF THE QUESTION... EXCEPT IN SCIENCE-FICTION YARNS!
1547

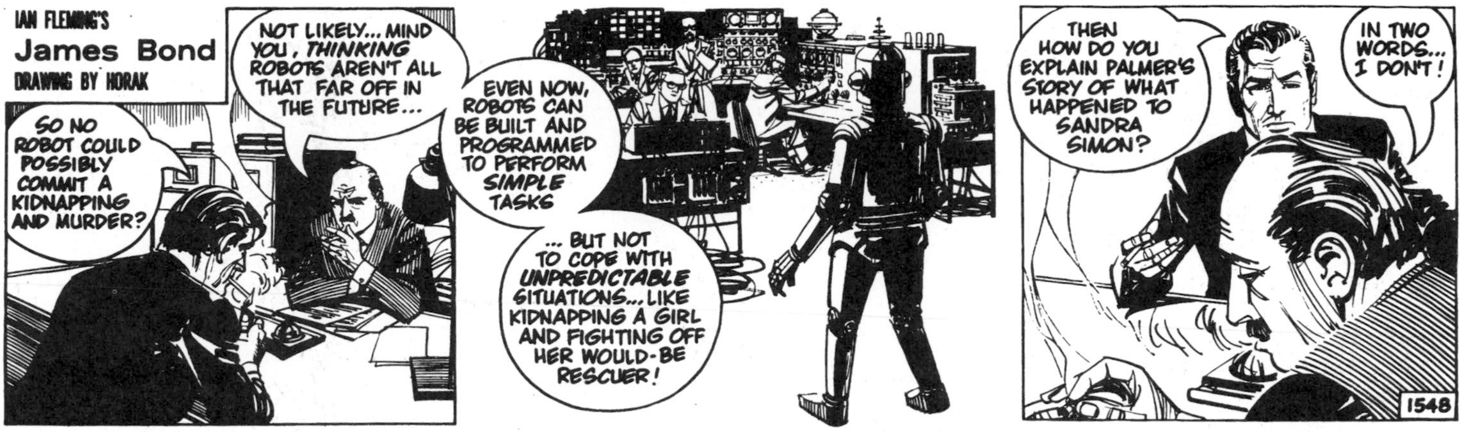
IAN FLEMING'S
James Bond
DRAWING BY HORAK
SO NO ROBOT COULD POSSIBLY COMMIT A KIDNAPPING AND MURDER?
NOT LIKELY... MIND YOU, THINKING ROBOTS AREN'T ALL THAT FAR OFF IN THE FUTURE...
EVEN NOW, ROBOTS CAN BE BUILT AND PROGRAMMED TO PERFORM SIMPLE TASKS
... BUT NOT TO COPE WITH UNPREDICTABLE SITUATIONS... LIKE KIDNAPPING A GIRL AND FIGHTING OFF HER WOULD-BE RESCUER!
THEN HOW DO YOU EXPLAIN PALMER'S STORY OF WHAT HAPPENED TO SANDRA SIMON?
IN TWO WORDS... I DON'T!
1548

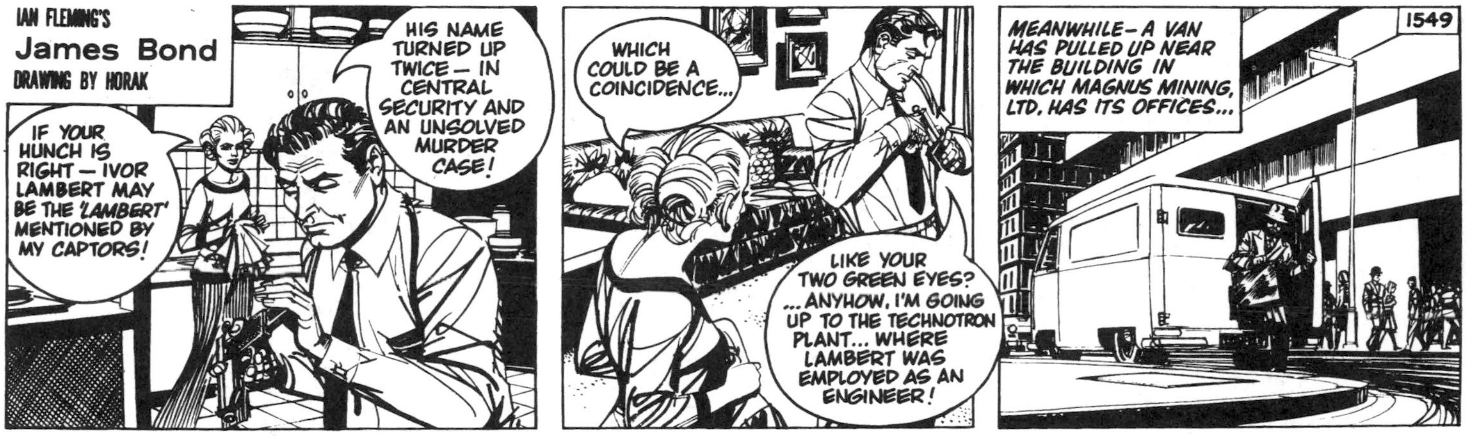
IAN FLEMING'S
James Bond
DRAWING BY HORAK
IF YOUR HUNCH IS RIGHT — IVOR LAMBERT MAY BE THE 'LAMBERT' MENTIONED BY MY CAPTORS!
HIS NAME TURNED UP TWICE — IN CENTRAL SECURITY AND AN UNSOLVED MURDER CASE!
WHICH COULD BE A COINCIDENCE...
LIKE YOUR TWO GREEN EYES? ...ANYHOW, I'M GOING UP TO THE TECHNOTRON PLANT... WHERE LAMBERT WAS EMPLOYED AS AN ENGINEER!
MEANWHILE— A VAN HAS PULLED UP NEAR THE BUILDING IN WHICH MAGNUS MINING, LTD. HAS ITS OFFICES...
1549

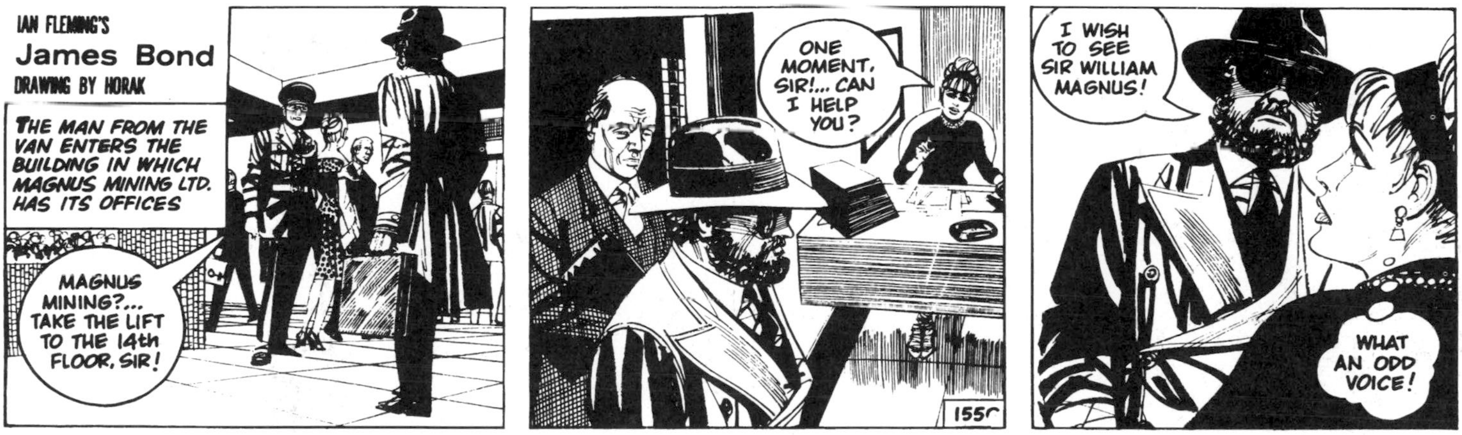
IAN FLEMING'S
James Bond
DRAWING BY HORAK
THE MAN FROM THE VAN ENTERS THE BUILDING IN WHICH MAGNUS MINING LTD. HAS ITS OFFICES
MAGNUS MINING?... TAKE THE LIFT TO THE 14th FLOOR, SIR!
ONE MOMENT, SIR!... CAN I HELP YOU?
1550
I WISH TO SEE SIR WILLIAM MAGNUS!
WHAT AN ODD VOICE!

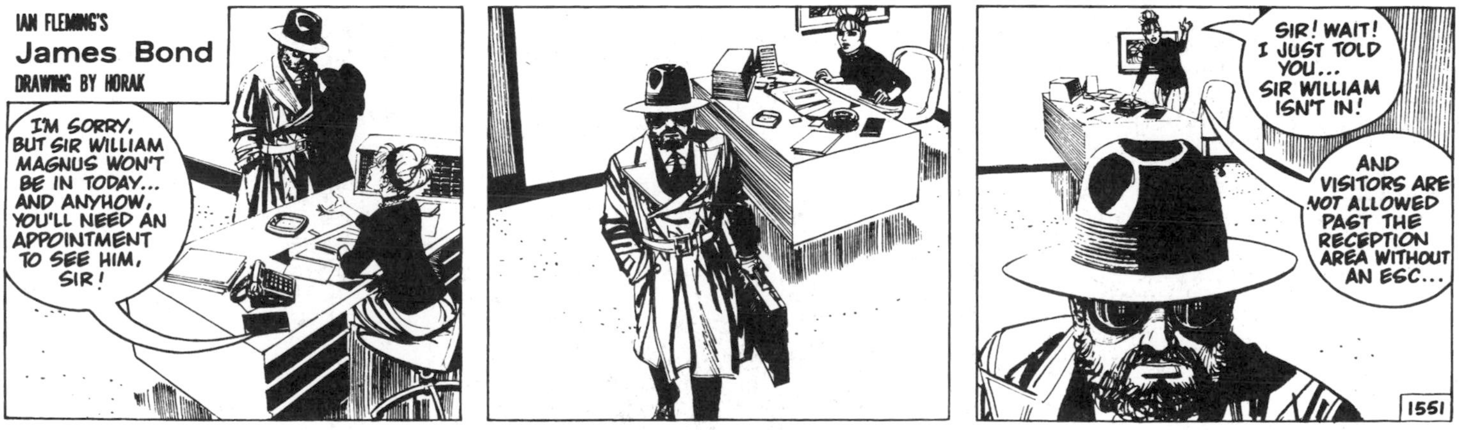
IAN FLEMING'S
James Bond
DRAWING BY HORAK
I'M SORRY, BUT SIR WILLIAM MAGNUS WON'T BE IN TODAY... AND ANYHOW, YOU'LL NEED AN APPOINTMENT TO SEE HIM, SIR!
SIR! WAIT! I JUST TOLD YOU... SIR WILLIAM ISN'T IN!
AND VISITORS ARE NOT ALLOWED PAST THE RECEPTION AREA WITHOUT AN ESC...
1551

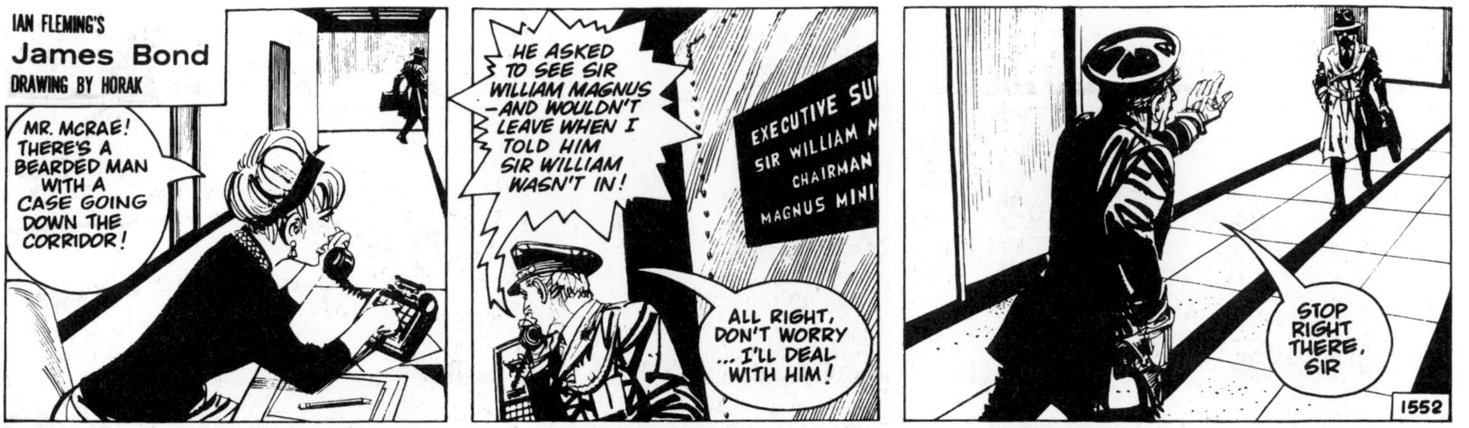
IAN FLEMING'S
James Bond
DRAWING BY HORAK
MR. MCRAE! THERE'S A BEARDED MAN WITH A CASE GOING DOWN THE CORRIDOR!
HE ASKED TO SEE SIR WILLIAM MAGNUS —AND WOULDN'T LEAVE WHEN I TOLD HIM SIR WILLIAM WASN'T IN!
EXECUTIVE SU
SIR WILLIAM M
CHAIRMAN
MAGNUS MINI
ALL RIGHT, DON'T WORRY ... I'LL DEAL WITH HIM!
STOP RIGHT THERE, SIR
1552

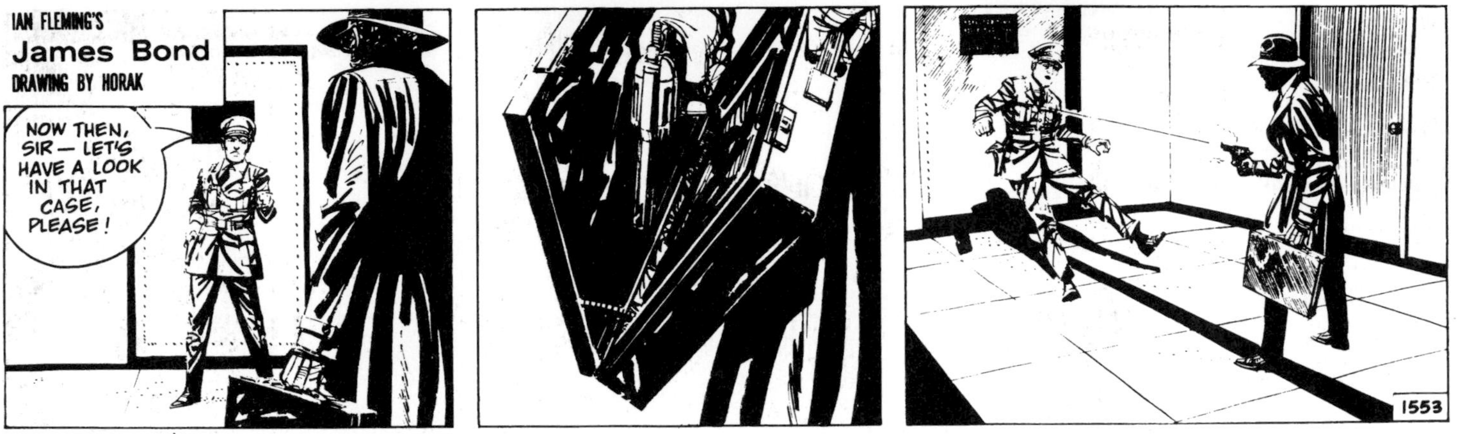
IAN FLEMING'S
James Bond
DRAWING BY HORAK
NOW THEN, SIR — LET'S HAVE A LOOK IN THAT CASE, PLEASE!
1553

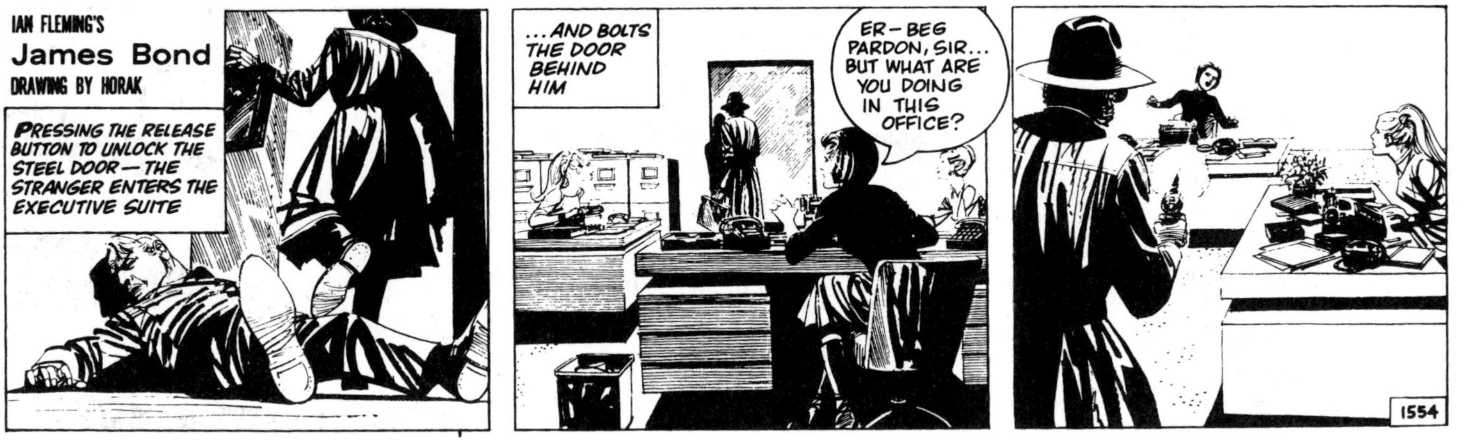
IAN FLEMING'S
James Bond
DRAWING BY HORAK
PRESSING THE RELEASE BUTTON TO UNLOCK THE STEEL DOOR — THE STRANGER ENTERS THE EXECUTIVE SUITE
... AND BOLTS THE DOOR BEHIND HIM
ER — BEG PARDON, SIR... BUT WHAT ARE YOU DOING IN THIS OFFICE?
1554

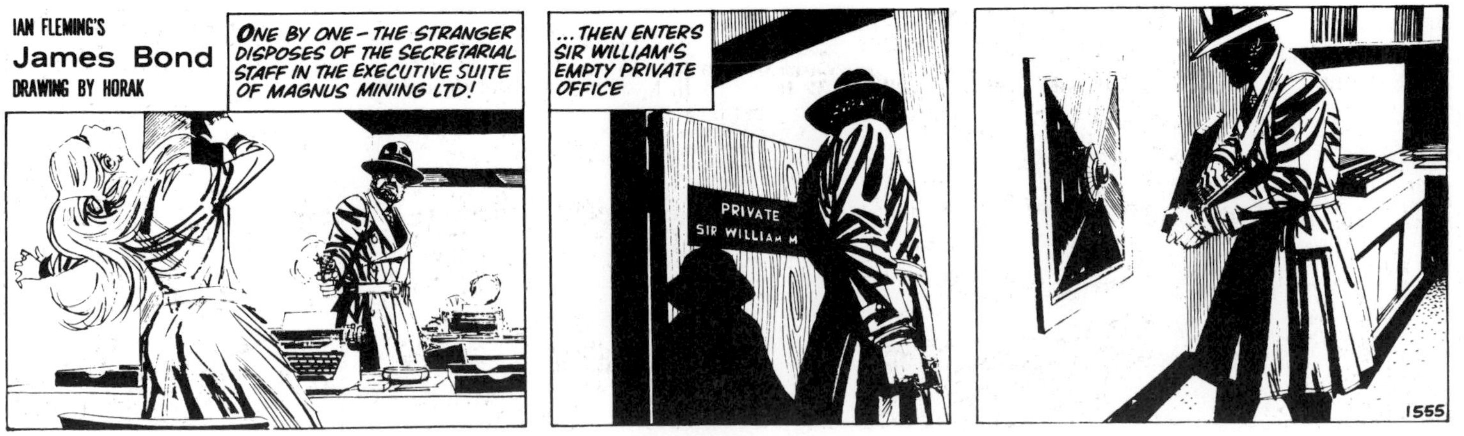
IAN FLEMING'S
James Bond
DRAWING BY HORAK
ONE BY ONE — THE STRANGER DISPOSES OF THE SECRETARIAL STAFF IN THE EXECUTIVE SUITE OF MAGNUS MINING LTD!
... THEN ENTERS SIR WILLIAM'S EMPTY PRIVATE OFFICE
PRIVATE
SIR WILLIAM M
1555

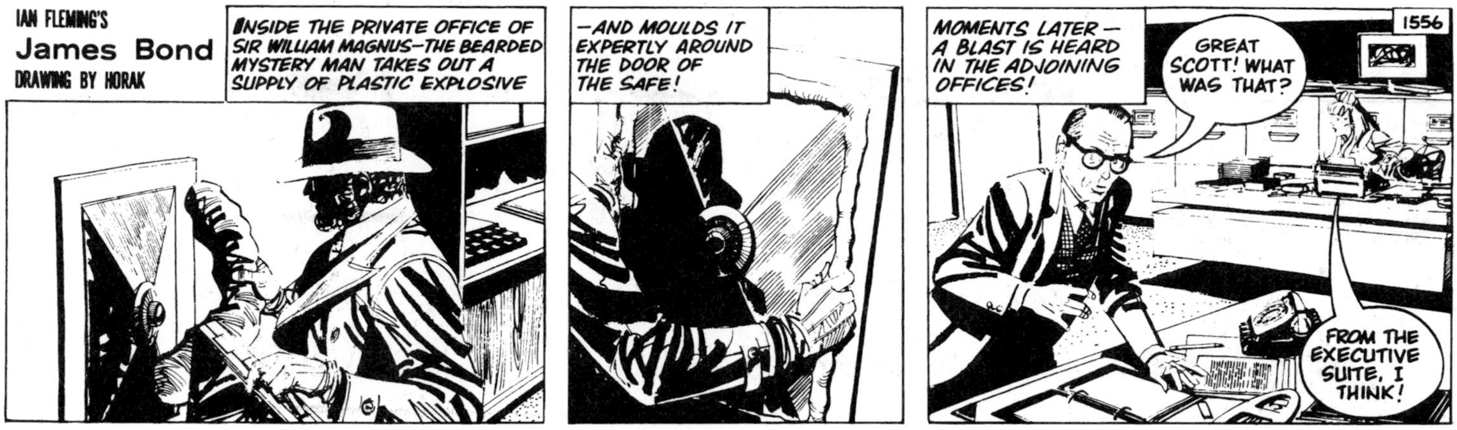

IAN FLEMING'S
James Bond
DRAWING BY HORAK
INSIDE THE PRIVATE OFFICE OF SIR WILLIAM MAGNUS—THE BEARDED MYSTERY MAN TAKES OUT A SUPPLY OF PLASTIC EXPLOSIVE
—AND MOULDS IT EXPERTLY AROUND THE DOOR OF THE SAFE!
MOMENTS LATER—A BLAST IS HEARD IN THE ADJOINING OFFICES!
GREAT SCOTT! WHAT WAS THAT?
FROM THE EXECUTIVE SUITE, I THINK!
1556

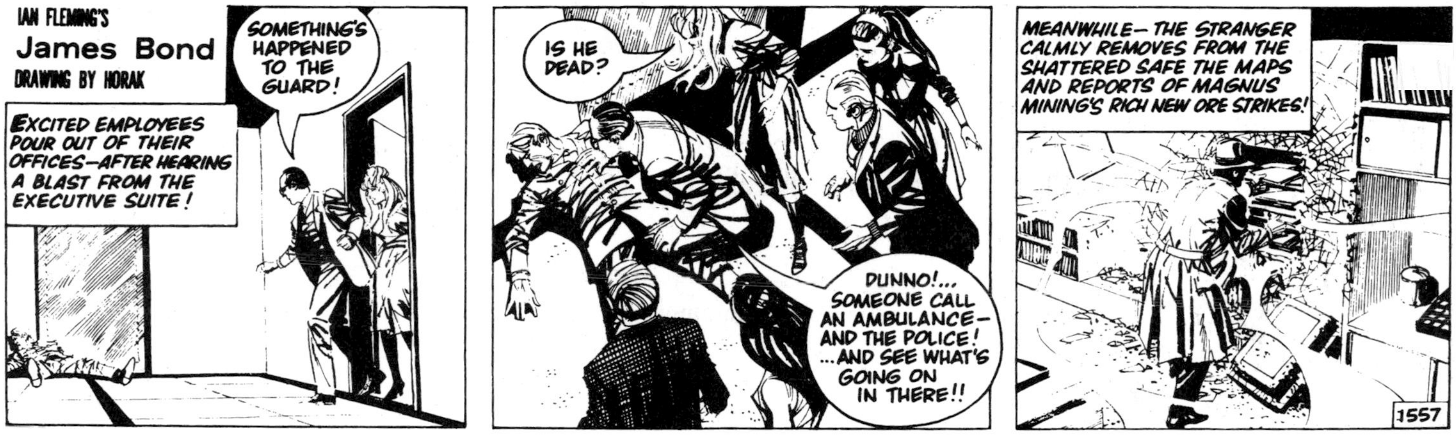

IAN FLEMING'S
James Bond
DRAWING BY HORAK
EXCITED EMPLOYEES POUR OUT OF THEIR OFFICES—AFTER HEARING A BLAST FROM THE EXECUTIVE SUITE!
SOMETHING'S HAPPENED TO THE GUARD!
IS HE DEAD?
DUNNO!... SOMEONE CALL AN AMBULANCE—AND THE POLICE! ...AND SEE WHAT'S GOING ON IN THERE!!
MEANWHILE—THE STRANGER CALMLY REMOVES FROM THE SHATTERED SAFE THE MAPS AND REPORTS OF MAGNUS MINING'S RICH NEW ORE STRIKES!
1557

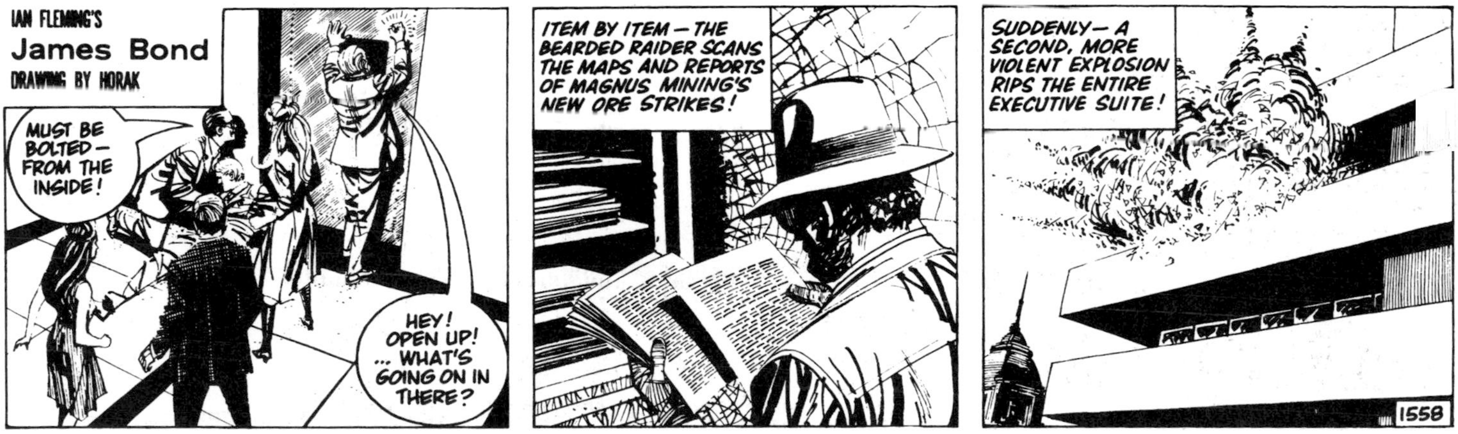

IAN FLEMING'S
James Bond
DRAWING BY HORAK
MUST BE BOLTED—FROM THE INSIDE!
HEY! OPEN UP! ... WHAT'S GOING ON IN THERE?
ITEM BY ITEM—THE BEARDED RAIDER SCANS THE MAPS AND REPORTS OF MAGNUS MINING'S NEW ORE STRIKES!
SUDDENLY—A SECOND, MORE VIOLENT EXPLOSION RIPS THE ENTIRE EXECUTIVE SUITE!
1558

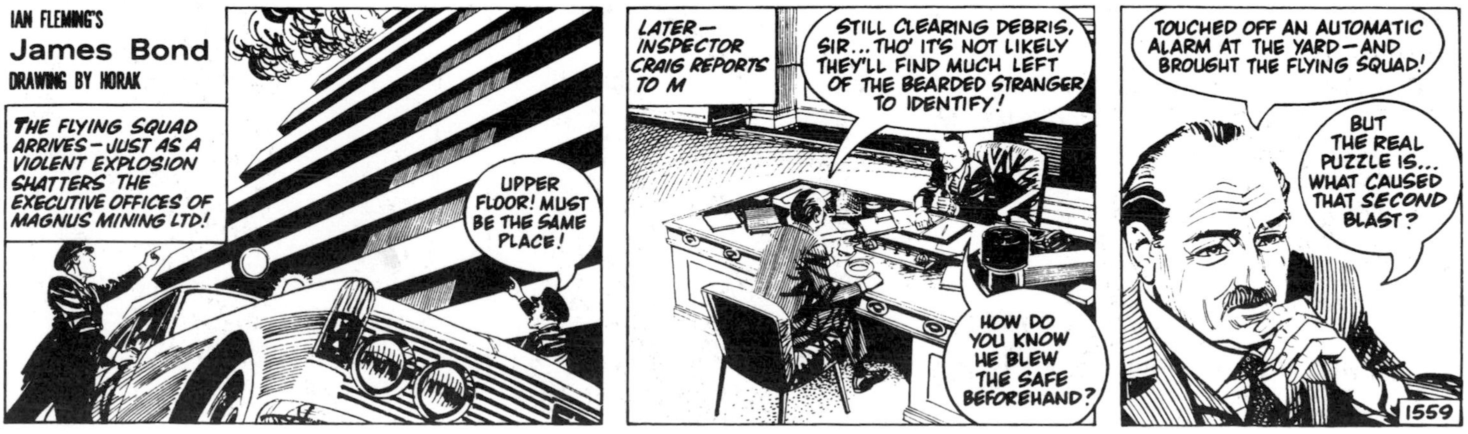

IAN FLEMING'S
James Bond
DRAWING BY HORAK
THE FLYING SQUAD ARRIVES—JUST AS A VIOLENT EXPLOSION SHATTERS THE EXECUTIVE OFFICES OF MAGNUS MINING LTD!
UPPER FLOOR! MUST BE THE SAME PLACE!
LATER—INSPECTOR CRAIG REPORTS TO M
STILL CLEARING DEBRIS, SIR... THO' IT'S NOT LIKELY THEY'LL FIND MUCH LEFT OF THE BEARDED STRANGER TO IDENTIFY!
HOW DO YOU KNOW HE BLEW THE SAFE BEFOREHAND?
TOUCHED OFF AN AUTOMATIC ALARM AT THE YARD—AND BROUGHT THE FLYING SQUAD!
BUT THE REAL PUZZLE IS... WHAT CAUSED THAT SECOND BLAST?
1559

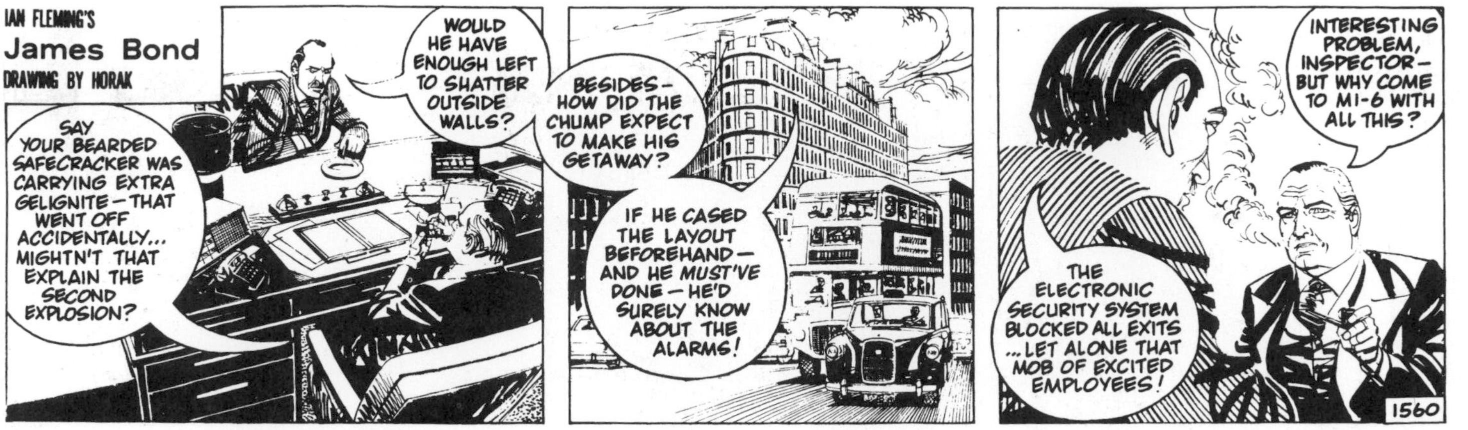
IAN FLEMING'S
James Bond
DRAWING BY HORAK
SAY YOUR BEARDED SAFECRACKER WAS CARRYING EXTRA GELIGNITE—THAT WENT OFF ACCIDENTALLY... MIGHTN'T THAT EXPLAIN THE SECOND EXPLOSION?
WOULD HE HAVE ENOUGH LEFT TO SHATTER OUTSIDE WALLS?
BESIDES—HOW DID THE CHUMP EXPECT TO MAKE HIS GETAWAY?
IF HE CASED THE LAYOUT BEFOREHAND—AND HE MUST'VE DONE—HE'D SURELY KNOW ABOUT THE ALARMS!
INTERESTING PROBLEM, INSPECTOR—BUT WHY COME TO MI-6 WITH ALL THIS?
THE ELECTRONIC SECURITY SYSTEM BLOCKED ALL EXITS ...LET ALONE THAT MOB OF EXCITED EMPLOYEES!
1560

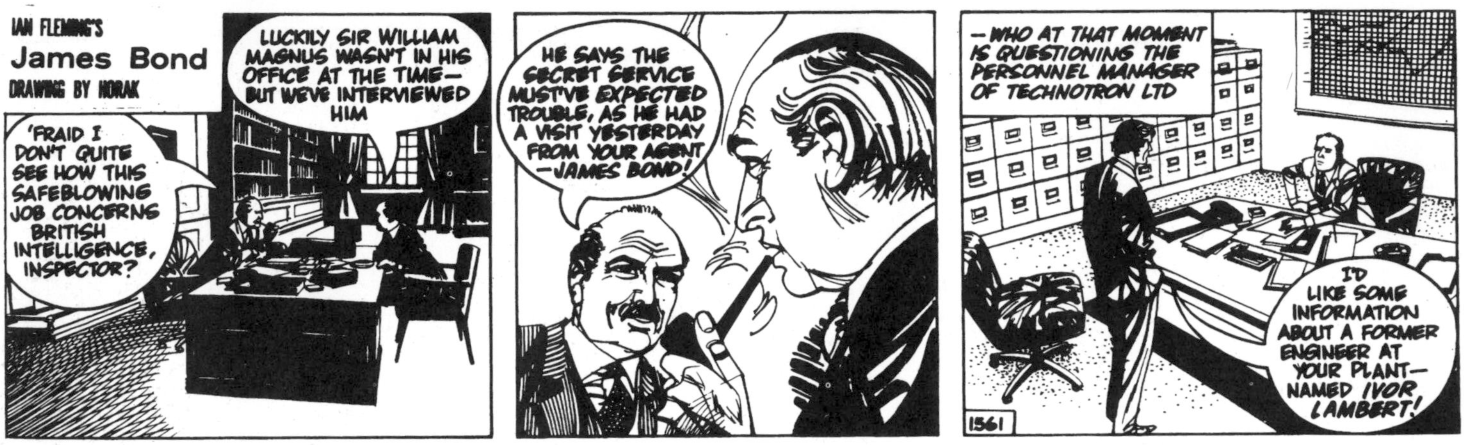
IAN FLEMING'S
James Bond
DRAWING BY HORAK
'FRAID I DON'T QUITE SEE HOW THIS SAFEBLOWING JOB CONCERNS BRITISH INTELLIGENCE, INSPECTOR?
LUCKILY SIR WILLIAM MAGNUS WASN'T IN HIS OFFICE AT THE TIME—BUT WE'VE INTERVIEWED HIM
HE SAYS THE SECRET SERVICE MUST'VE EXPECTED TROUBLE, AS HE HAD A VISIT YESTERDAY FROM YOUR AGENT—JAMES BOND!
1561
—WHO AT THAT MOMENT IS QUESTIONING THE PERSONNEL MANAGER OF TECHNOTRON LTD
I'D LIKE SOME INFORMATION ABOUT A FORMER ENGINEER AT YOUR PLANT—NAMED IVOR LAMBERT!

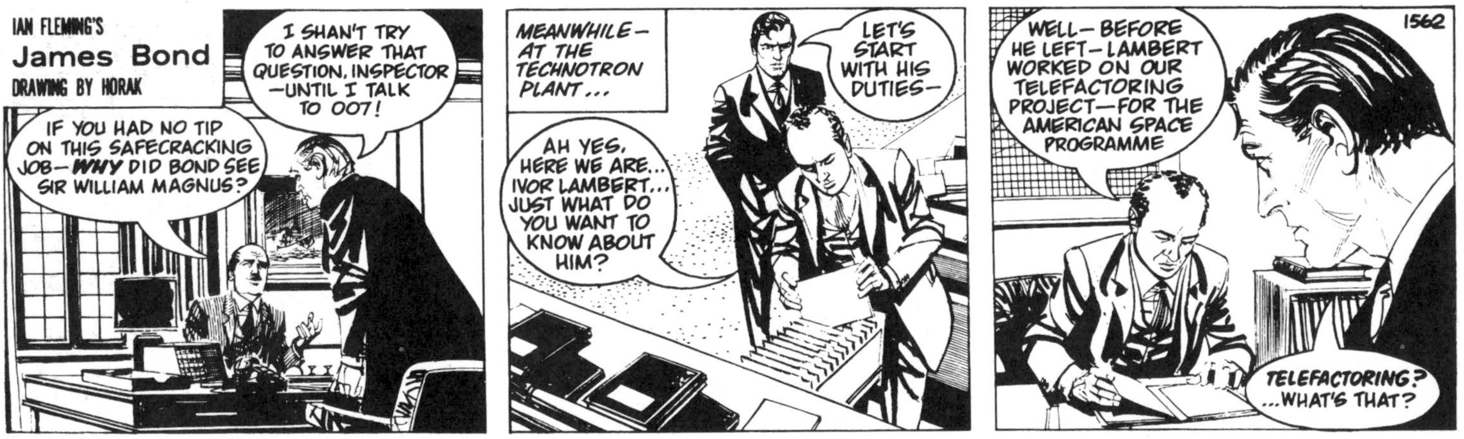
IAN FLEMING'S
James Bond
DRAWING BY HORAK
IF YOU HAD NO TIP ON THIS SAFECRACKING JOB—WHY DID BOND SEE SIR WILLIAM MAGNUS?
I SHAN'T TRY TO ANSWER THAT QUESTION, INSPECTOR—UNTIL I TALK TO 007!
MEANWHILE—AT THE TECHNOTRON PLANT...
LET'S START WITH HIS DUTIES—
AH YES, HERE WE ARE... IVOR LAMBERT... JUST WHAT DO YOU WANT TO KNOW ABOUT HIM?
1562
WELL—BEFORE HE LEFT—LAMBERT WORKED ON OUR TELEFACTORING PROJECT—FOR THE AMERICAN SPACE PROGRAMME
TELEFACTORING? ...WHAT'S THAT?

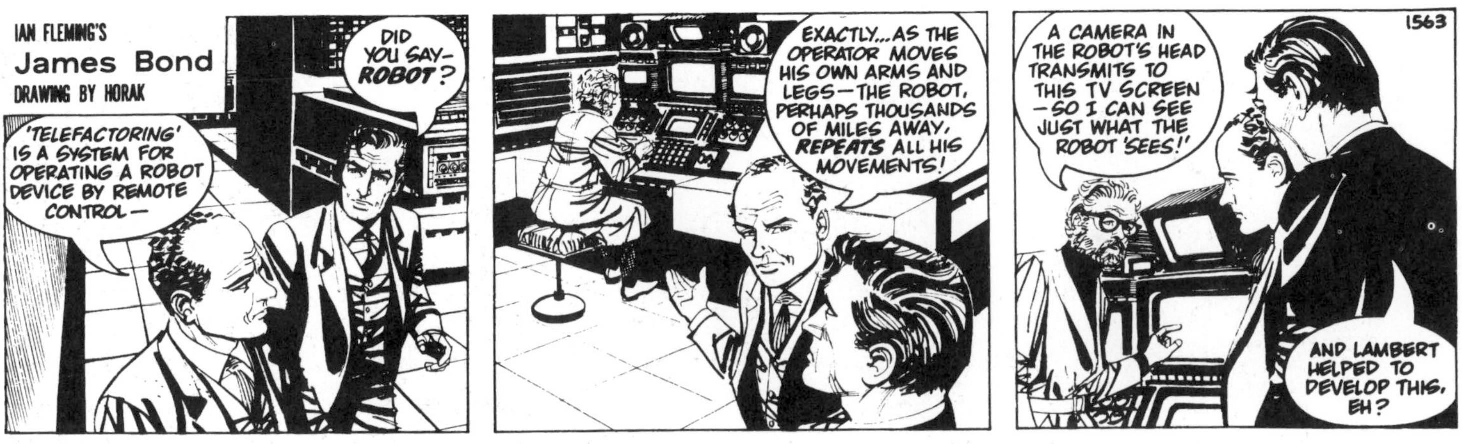
IAN FLEMING'S
James Bond
DRAWING BY HORAK
'TELEFACTORING' IS A SYSTEM FOR OPERATING A ROBOT DEVICE BY REMOTE CONTROL—
DID YOU SAY—ROBOT?
EXACTLY... AS THE OPERATOR MOVES HIS OWN ARMS AND LEGS—THE ROBOT, PERHAPS THOUSANDS OF MILES AWAY, REPEATS ALL HIS MOVEMENTS!
1563
A CAMERA IN THE ROBOT'S HEAD TRANSMITS TO THIS TV SCREEN—SO I CAN SEE JUST WHAT THE ROBOT 'SEES!'
AND LAMBERT HELPED TO DEVELOP THIS, EH?

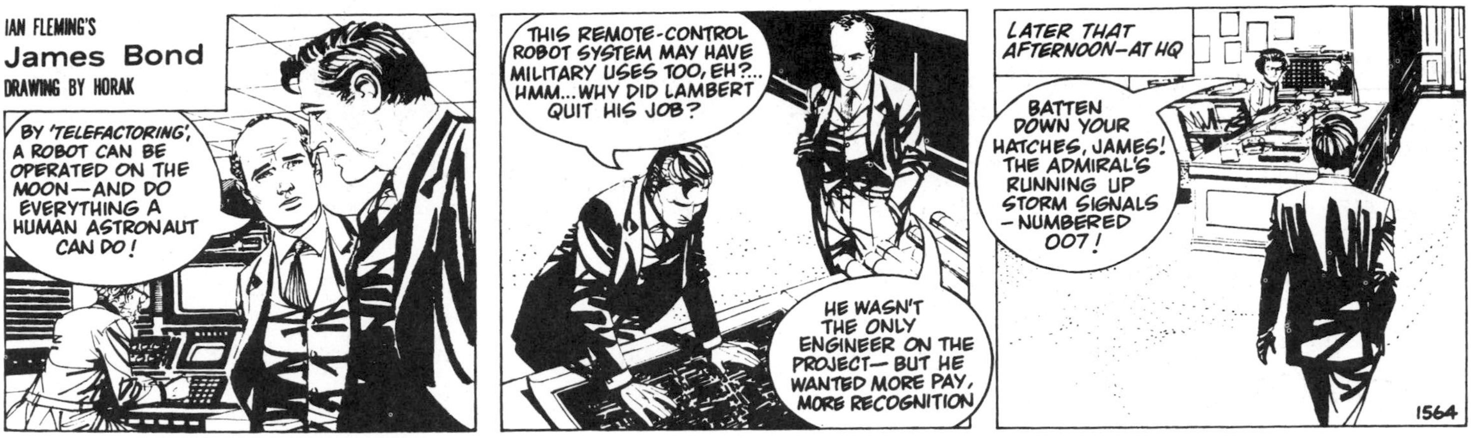
IAN FLEMING'S
James Bond
DRAWING BY HORAK
BY 'TELEFACTORING', A ROBOT CAN BE OPERATED ON THE MOON—AND DO EVERYTHING A HUMAN ASTRONAUT CAN DO!
THIS REMOTE-CONTROL ROBOT SYSTEM MAY HAVE MILITARY USES TOO, EH?... HMM...WHY DID LAMBERT QUIT HIS JOB?
HE WASN'T THE ONLY ENGINEER ON THE PROJECT—BUT HE WANTED MORE PAY, MORE RECOGNITION
LATER THAT AFTERNOON—AT HQ
BATTEN DOWN YOUR HATCHES, JAMES! THE ADMIRAL'S RUNNING UP STORM SIGNALS—NUMBERED 007!
1564

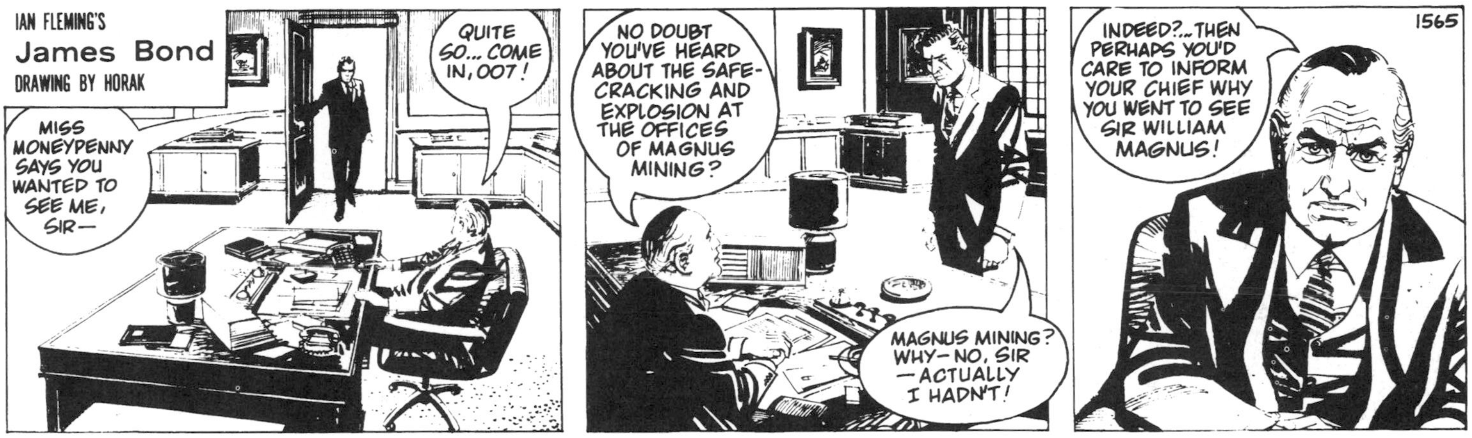
IAN FLEMING'S
James Bond
DRAWING BY HORAK
MISS MONEYPENNY SAYS YOU WANTED TO SEE ME, SIR—
QUITE SO... COME IN, 007!
NO DOUBT YOU'VE HEARD ABOUT THE SAFE-CRACKING AND EXPLOSION AT THE OFFICES OF MAGNUS MINING?
MAGNUS MINING? WHY—NO, SIR—ACTUALLY I HADN'T!
1565
INDEED?...THEN PERHAPS YOU'D CARE TO INFORM YOUR CHIEF WHY YOU WENT TO SEE SIR WILLIAM MAGNUS!

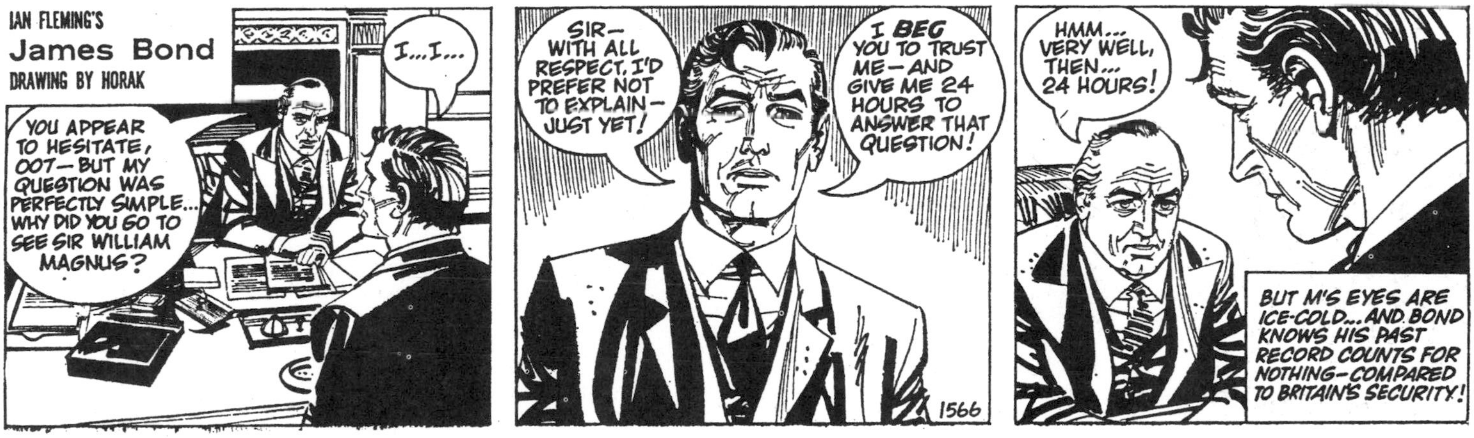
IAN FLEMING'S
James Bond
DRAWING BY HORAK
YOU APPEAR TO HESITATE, 007—BUT MY QUESTION WAS PERFECTLY SIMPLE... WHY DID YOU GO TO SEE SIR WILLIAM MAGNUS?
I...I...
SIR—WITH ALL RESPECT, I'D PREFER NOT TO EXPLAIN—JUST YET!
I BEG YOU TO TRUST ME—AND GIVE ME 24 HOURS TO ANSWER THAT QUESTION!
1566
HMM... VERY WELL, THEN... 24 HOURS!
BUT M'S EYES ARE ICE-COLD... AND BOND KNOWS HIS PAST RECORD COUNTS FOR NOTHING—COMPARED TO BRITAIN'S SECURITY!

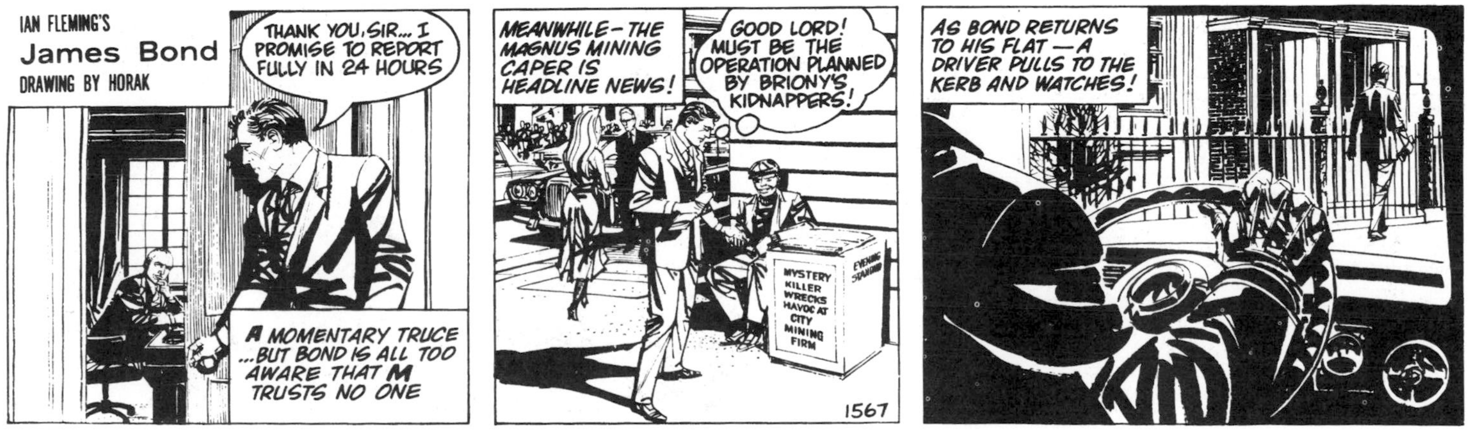
IAN FLEMING'S
James Bond
DRAWING BY HORAK
THANK YOU, SIR... I PROMISE TO REPORT FULLY IN 24 HOURS
A MOMENTARY TRUCE ...BUT BOND IS ALL TOO AWARE THAT M TRUSTS NO ONE
MEANWHILE—THE MAGNUS MINING CAPER IS HEADLINE NEWS!
GOOD LORD! MUST BE THE OPERATION PLANNED BY BRIONY'S KIDNAPPERS!
EVENING STANDARD
MYSTERY KILLER WRECKS HAVOC AT CITY MINING FIRM
1567
AS BOND RETURNS TO HIS FLAT—A DRIVER PULLS TO THE KERB AND WATCHES!

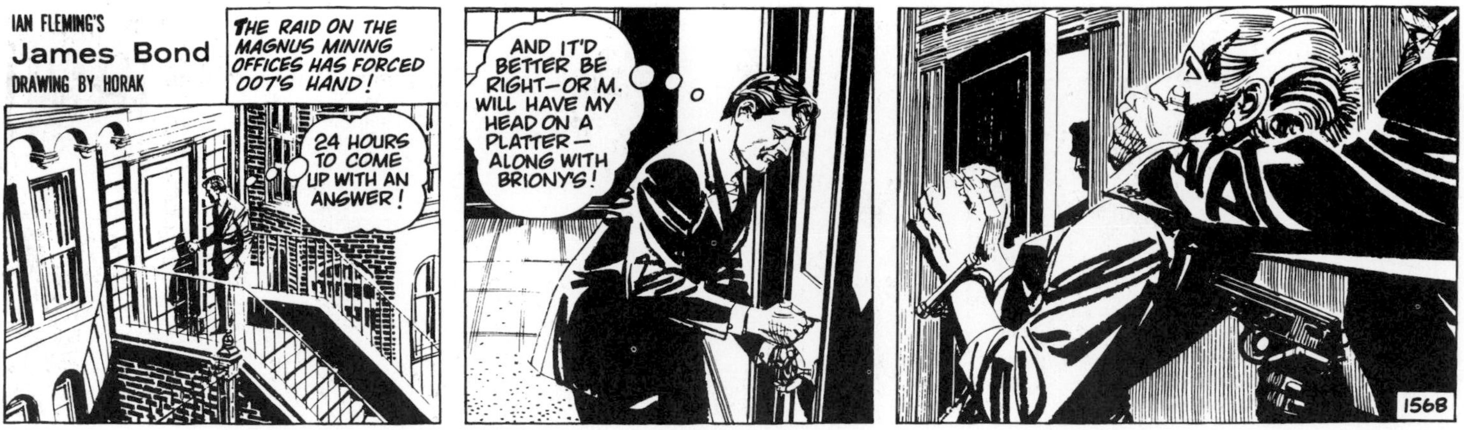
IAN FLEMING'S
James Bond
DRAWING BY HORAK
THE RAID ON THE MAGNUS MINING OFFICES HAS FORCED 007'S HAND!
24 HOURS TO COME UP WITH AN ANSWER!
AND IT'D BETTER BE RIGHT—OR M. WILL HAVE MY HEAD ON A PLATTER—ALONG WITH BRIONY'S!
1568

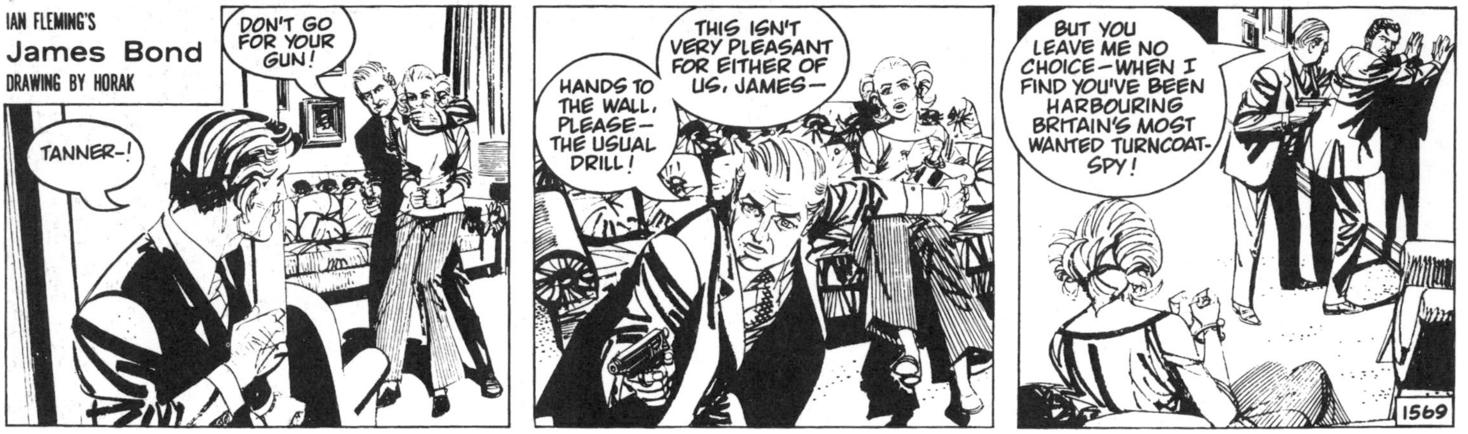
IAN FLEMING'S
James Bond
DRAWING BY HORAK
DON'T GO FOR YOUR GUN!
TANNER—!
THIS ISN'T VERY PLEASANT FOR EITHER OF US, JAMES—
HANDS TO THE WALL, PLEASE—THE USUAL DRILL!
BUT YOU LEAVE ME NO CHOICE—WHEN I FIND YOU'VE BEEN HARBOURING BRITAIN'S MOST WANTED TURNCOAT-SPY!
1569

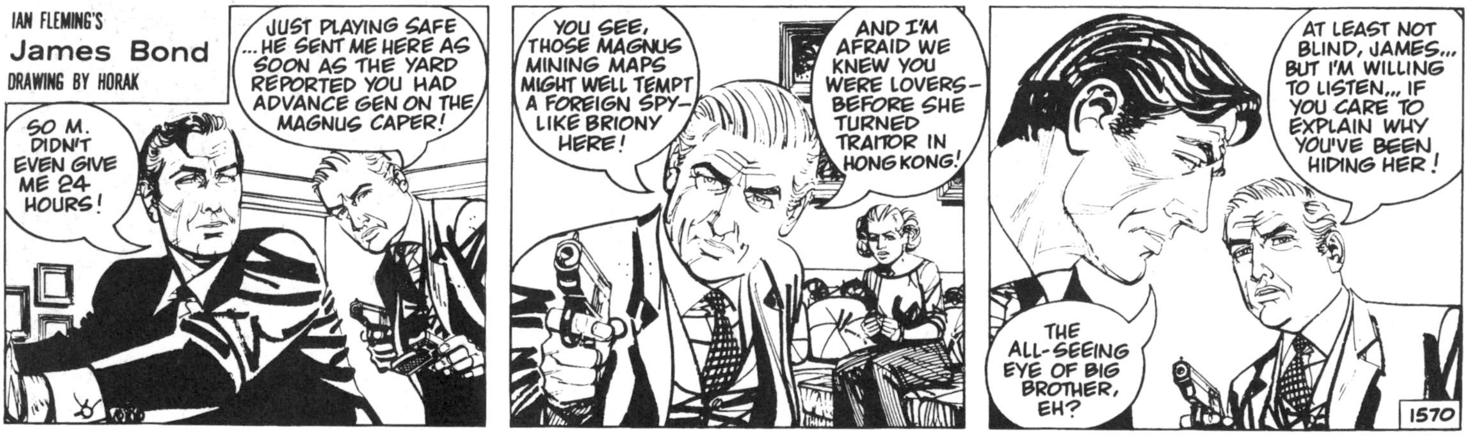
IAN FLEMING'S
James Bond
DRAWING BY HORAK
SO M. DIDN'T EVEN GIVE ME 24 HOURS!
JUST PLAYING SAFE ...HE SENT ME HERE AS SOON AS THE YARD REPORTED YOU HAD ADVANCE GEN ON THE MAGNUS CAPER!
YOU SEE, THOSE MAGNUS MINING MAPS MIGHT WELL TEMPT A FOREIGN SPY—LIKE BRIONY HERE!
AND I'M AFRAID WE KNEW YOU WERE LOVERS—BEFORE SHE TURNED TRAITOR IN HONG KONG!
THE ALL-SEEING EYE OF BIG BROTHER, EH?
AT LEAST NOT BLIND, JAMES... BUT I'M WILLING TO LISTEN... IF YOU CARE TO EXPLAIN WHY YOU'VE BEEN HIDING HER!
1570

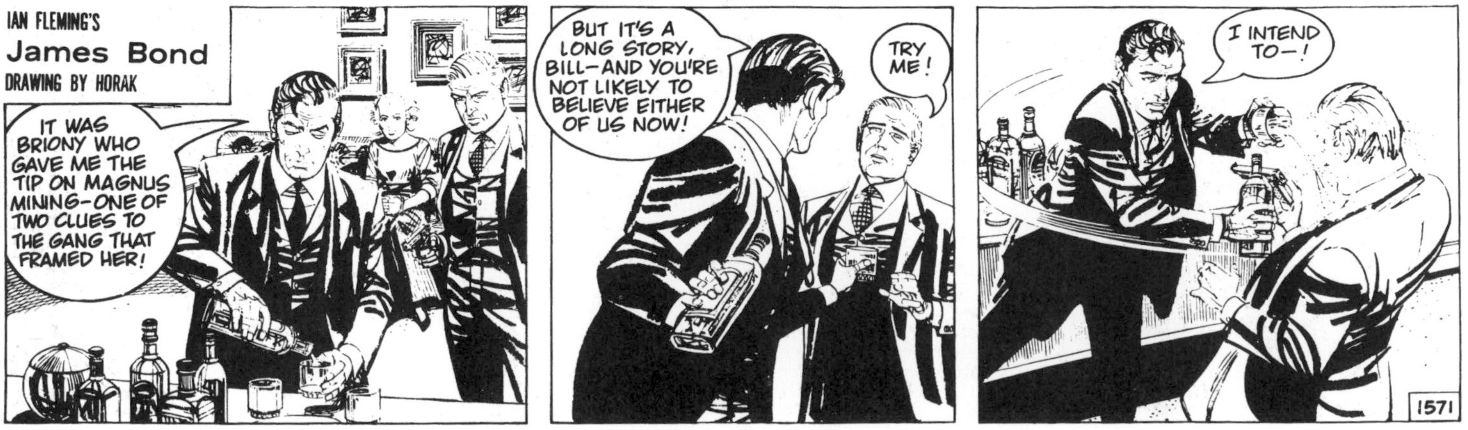
IAN FLEMING'S
James Bond
DRAWING BY HORAK
IT WAS BRIONY WHO GAVE ME THE TIP ON MAGNUS MINING—ONE OF TWO CLUES TO THE GANG THAT FRAMED HER!
BUT IT'S A LONG STORY, BILL—AND YOU'RE NOT LIKELY TO BELIEVE EITHER OF US NOW!
TRY ME!
I INTEND TO—!
1571

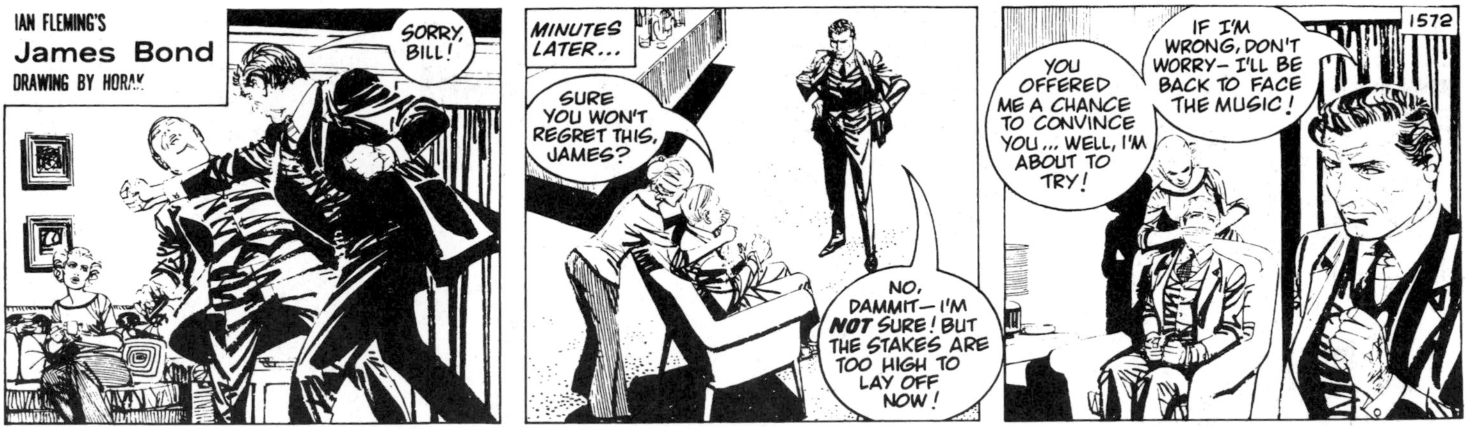
IAN FLEMING'S
James Bond
DRAWING BY HORAK
SORRY, BILL!
MINUTES LATER...
SURE YOU WON'T REGRET THIS, JAMES?
NO, DAMMIT— I'M **NOT** SURE! BUT THE STAKES ARE TOO HIGH TO LAY OFF NOW!
1572
YOU OFFERED ME A CHANCE TO CONVINCE YOU... WELL, I'M ABOUT TO TRY!
IF I'M WRONG, DON'T WORRY– I'LL BE BACK TO FACE THE MUSIC!

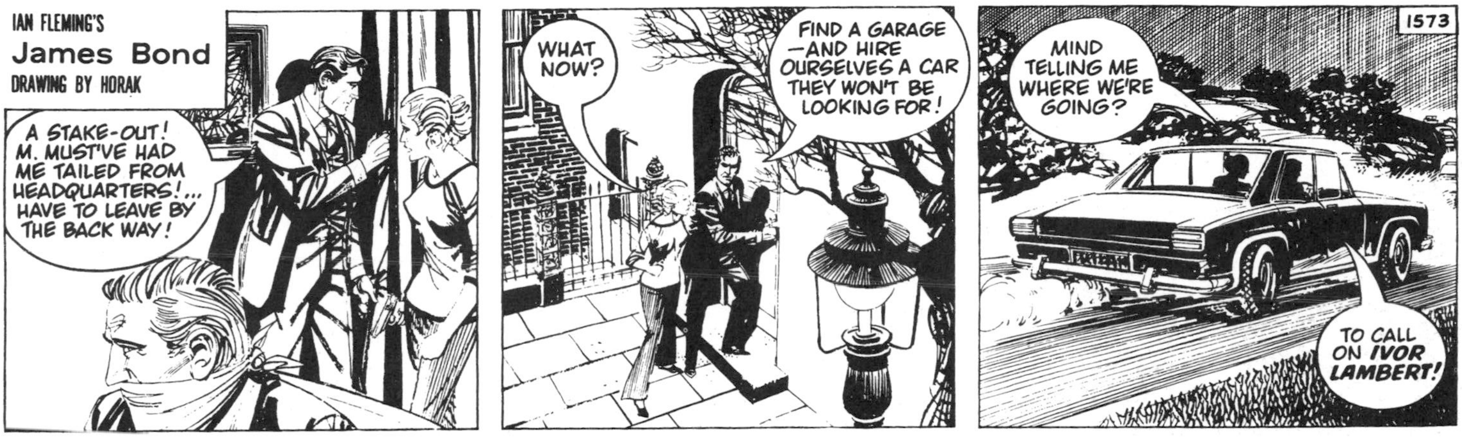
IAN FLEMING'S
James Bond
DRAWING BY HORAK
A STAKE-OUT! M. MUST'VE HAD ME TAILED FROM HEADQUARTERS!... HAVE TO LEAVE BY THE BACK WAY!
WHAT NOW?
FIND A GARAGE —AND HIRE OURSELVES A CAR THEY WON'T BE LOOKING FOR!
1573
MIND TELLING ME WHERE WE'RE GOING?
TO CALL ON ***IVOR LAMBERT!***

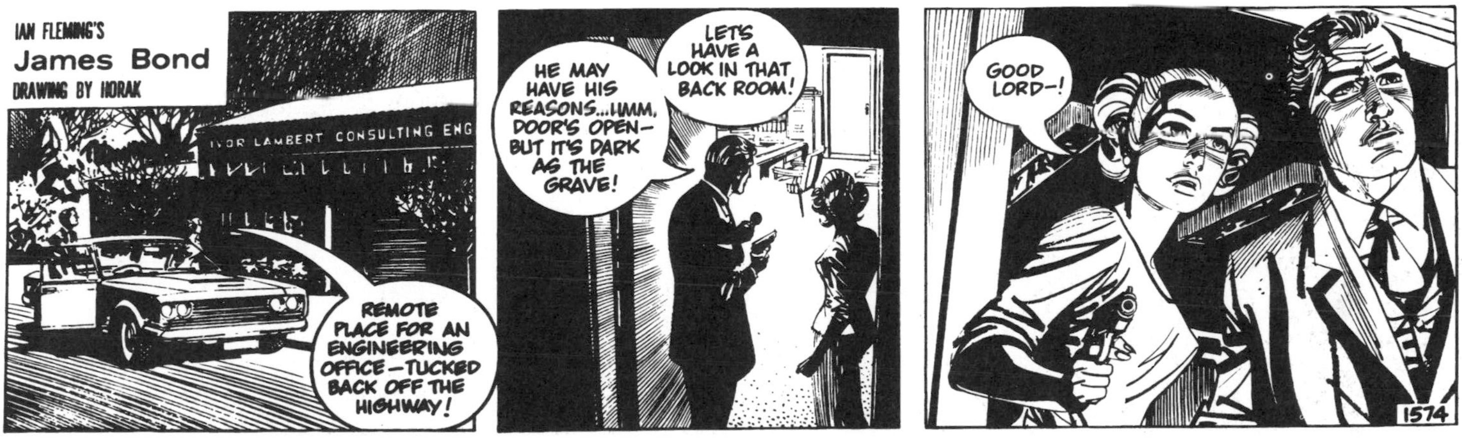
IAN FLEMING'S
James Bond
DRAWING BY HORAK
IVOR LAMBERT CONSULTING ENG
REMOTE PLACE FOR AN ENGINEERING OFFICE—TUCKED BACK OFF THE HIGHWAY!
HE MAY HAVE HIS REASONS...UMM, DOOR'S OPEN- BUT IT'S DARK AS THE GRAVE!
LET'S HAVE A LOOK IN THAT BACK ROOM!
GOOD LORD–!
1574

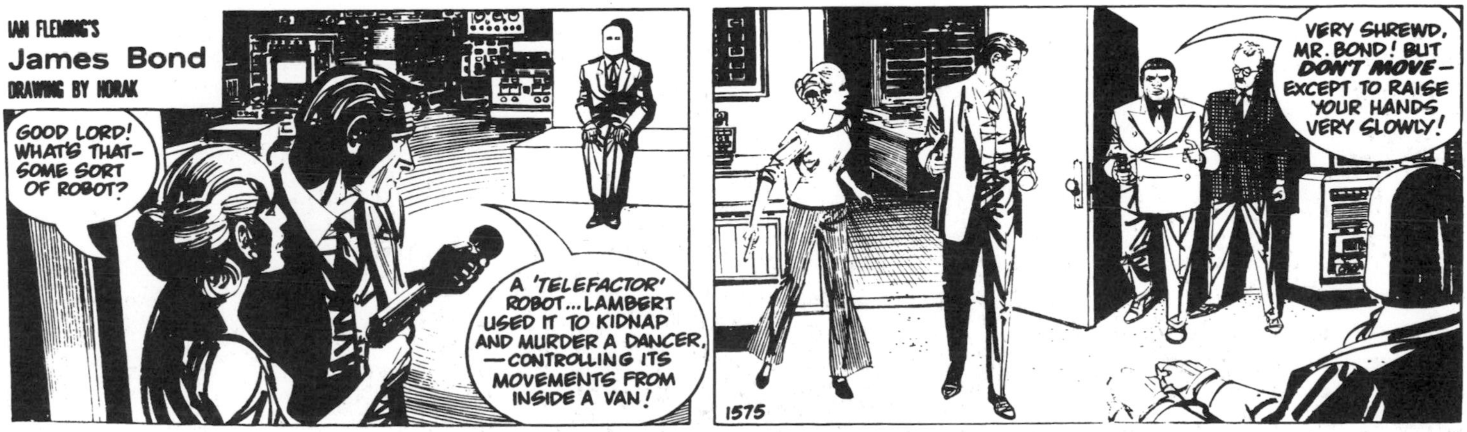
IAN FLEMING'S
James Bond
DRAWING BY HORAK
GOOD LORD! WHAT'S THAT- SOME SORT OF ROBOT?
A *'TELEFACTOR'* ROBOT... LAMBERT USED IT TO KIDNAP AND MURDER A DANCER, —CONTROLLING ITS MOVEMENTS FROM INSIDE A VAN!
1575
VERY SHREWD, MR. BOND! BUT ***DON'T MOVE***— EXCEPT TO RAISE YOUR HANDS VERY SLOWLY!

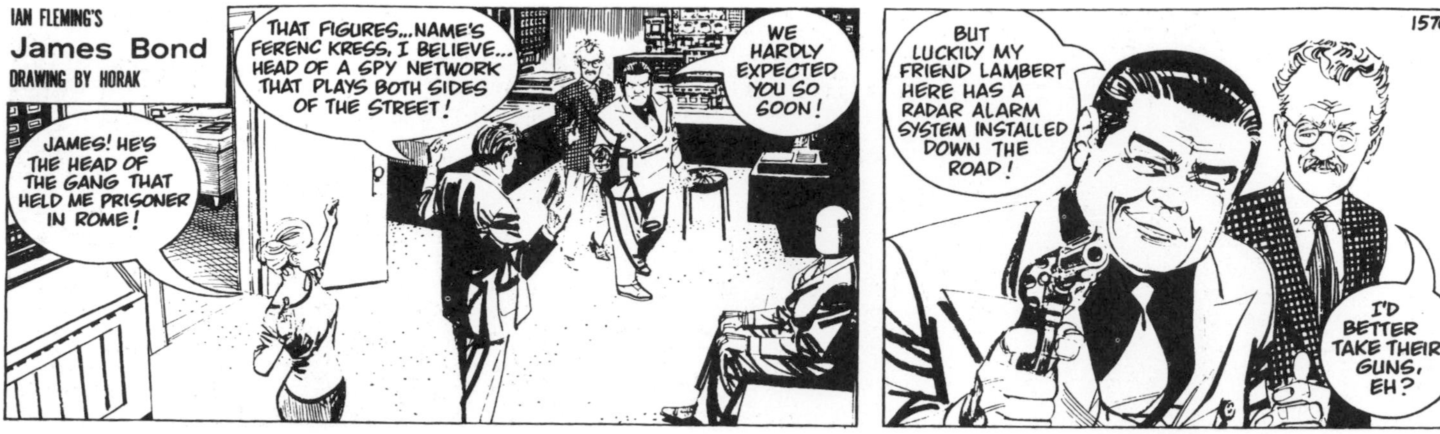
IAN FLEMING'S
James Bond
DRAWING BY HORAK
JAMES! HE'S THE HEAD OF THE GANG THAT HELD ME PRISONER IN ROME!
THAT FIGURES... NAME'S FERENC KRESS, I BELIEVE... HEAD OF A SPY NETWORK THAT PLAYS BOTH SIDES OF THE STREET!
WE HARDLY EXPECTED YOU SO SOON!
1576
BUT LUCKILY MY FRIEND LAMBERT HERE HAS A RADAR ALARM SYSTEM INSTALLED DOWN THE ROAD!
I'D BETTER TAKE THEIR GUNS, EH?

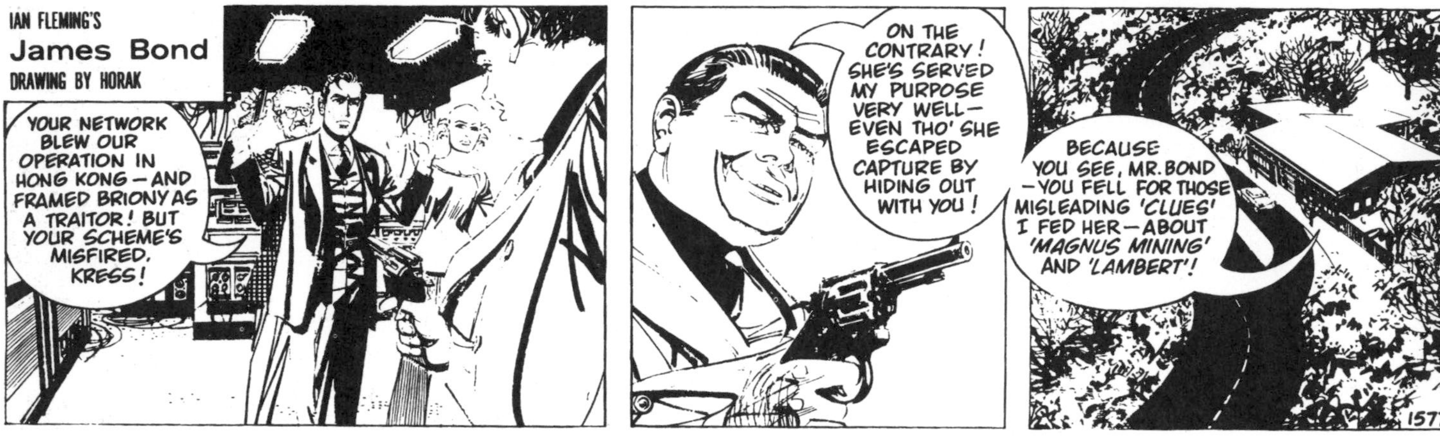
IAN FLEMING'S
James Bond
DRAWING BY HORAK
YOUR NETWORK BLEW OUR OPERATION IN HONG KONG — AND FRAMED BRIONY AS A TRAITOR! BUT YOUR SCHEME'S MISFIRED, KRESS!
ON THE CONTRARY! SHE'S SERVED MY PURPOSE VERY WELL— EVEN THO' SHE ESCAPED CAPTURE BY HIDING OUT WITH YOU!
BECAUSE YOU SEE, MR. BOND — YOU FELL FOR THOSE MISLEADING 'CLUES' I FED HER — ABOUT 'MAGNUS MINING' AND 'LAMBERT'!
1577

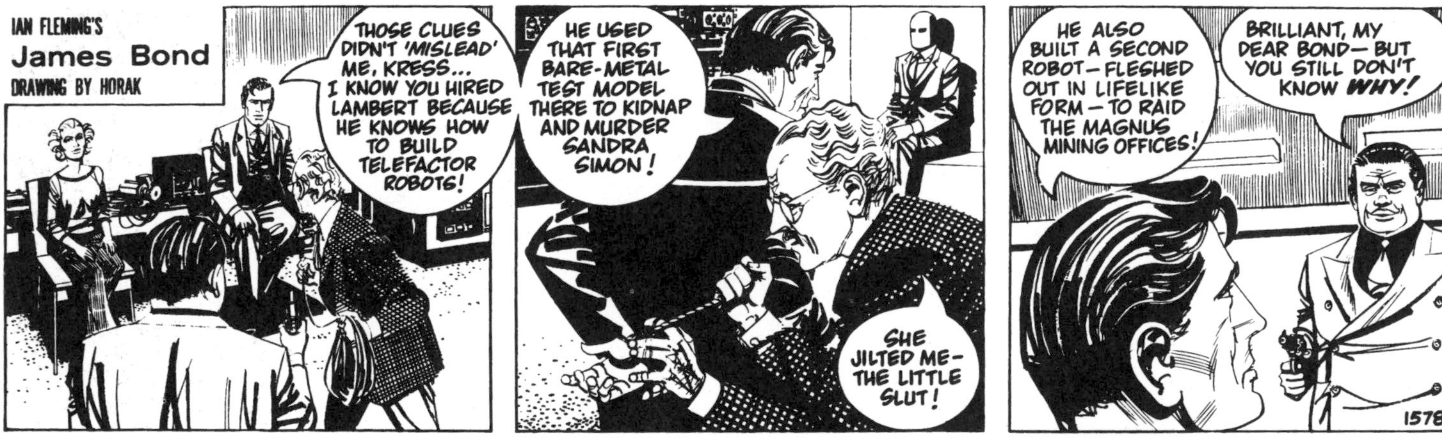
IAN FLEMING'S
James Bond
DRAWING BY HORAK
THOSE CLUES DIDN'T 'MISLEAD' ME, KRESS... I KNOW YOU HIRED LAMBERT BECAUSE HE KNOWS HOW TO BUILD TELEFACTOR ROBOTS!
HE USED THAT FIRST BARE-METAL TEST MODEL THERE TO KIDNAP AND MURDER SANDRA SIMON!
SHE JILTED ME— THE LITTLE SLUT!
HE ALSO BUILT A SECOND ROBOT — FLESHED OUT IN LIFELIKE FORM — TO RAID THE MAGNUS MINING OFFICES!
BRILLIANT, MY DEAR BOND — BUT YOU STILL DON'T KNOW **WHY!**
1578

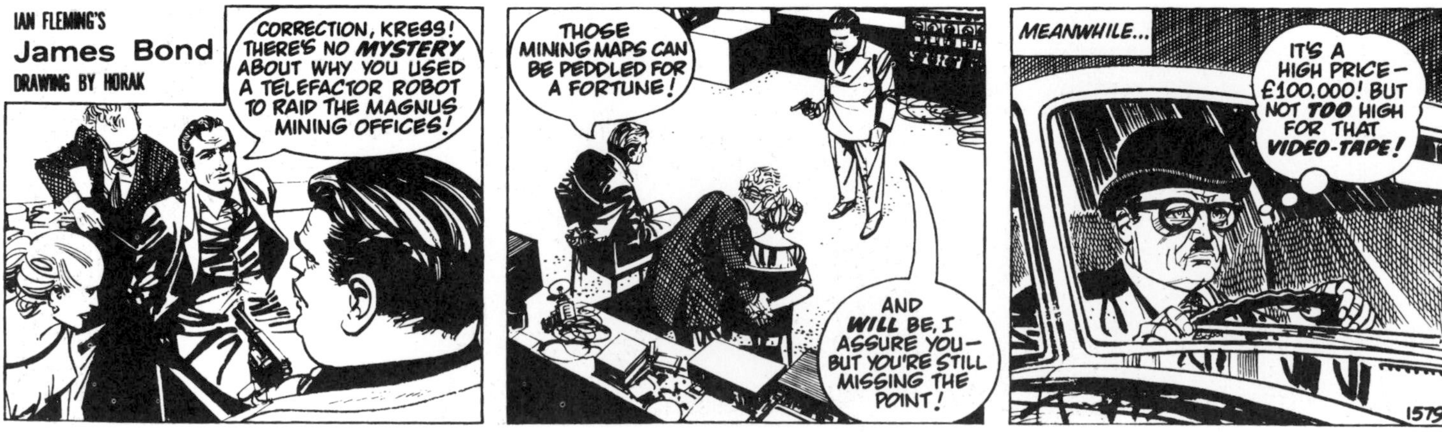
IAN FLEMING'S
James Bond
DRAWING BY HORAK
CORRECTION, KRESS! THERE'S NO **MYSTERY** ABOUT WHY YOU USED A TELEFACTOR ROBOT TO RAID THE MAGNUS MINING OFFICES!
THOSE MINING MAPS CAN BE PEDDLED FOR A FORTUNE!
AND **WILL** BE, I ASSURE YOU— BUT YOU'RE STILL MISSING THE POINT!
MEANWHILE...
IT'S A HIGH PRICE— £100,000! BUT NOT **TOO** HIGH FOR THAT **VIDEO-TAPE!**
1579

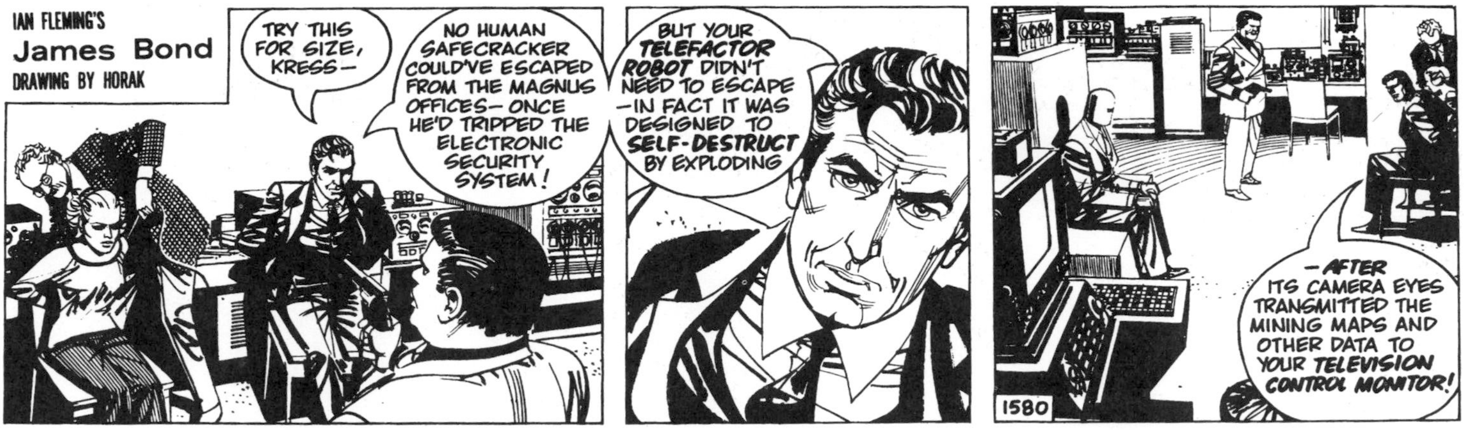
IAN FLEMING'S
James Bond
DRAWING BY HORAK
TRY THIS FOR SIZE, KRESS—
NO HUMAN SAFECRACKER COULD'VE ESCAPED FROM THE MAGNUS OFFICES—ONCE HE'D TRIPPED THE ELECTRONIC SECURITY SYSTEM!
BUT YOUR TELEFACTOR ROBOT DIDN'T NEED TO ESCAPE —IN FACT IT WAS DESIGNED TO SELF-DESTRUCT BY EXPLODING
—AFTER ITS CAMERA EYES TRANSMITTED THE MINING MAPS AND OTHER DATA TO YOUR TELEVISION CONTROL MONITOR!
1580

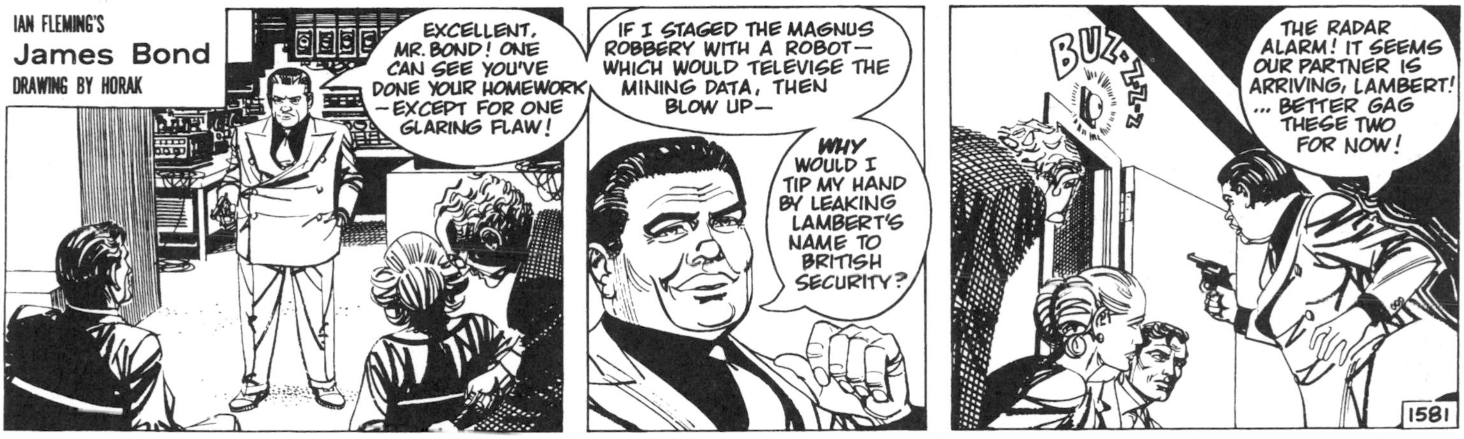
IAN FLEMING'S
James Bond
DRAWING BY HORAK
EXCELLENT, MR. BOND! ONE CAN SEE YOU'VE DONE YOUR HOMEWORK —EXCEPT FOR ONE GLARING FLAW!
IF I STAGED THE MAGNUS ROBBERY WITH A ROBOT— WHICH WOULD TELEVISE THE MINING DATA, THEN BLOW UP—
WHY WOULD I TIP MY HAND BY LEAKING LAMBERT'S NAME TO BRITISH SECURITY?
BUZ-Z-Z-Z
THE RADAR ALARM! IT SEEMS OUR PARTNER IS ARRIVING, LAMBERT! ... BETTER GAG THESE TWO FOR NOW!
1581

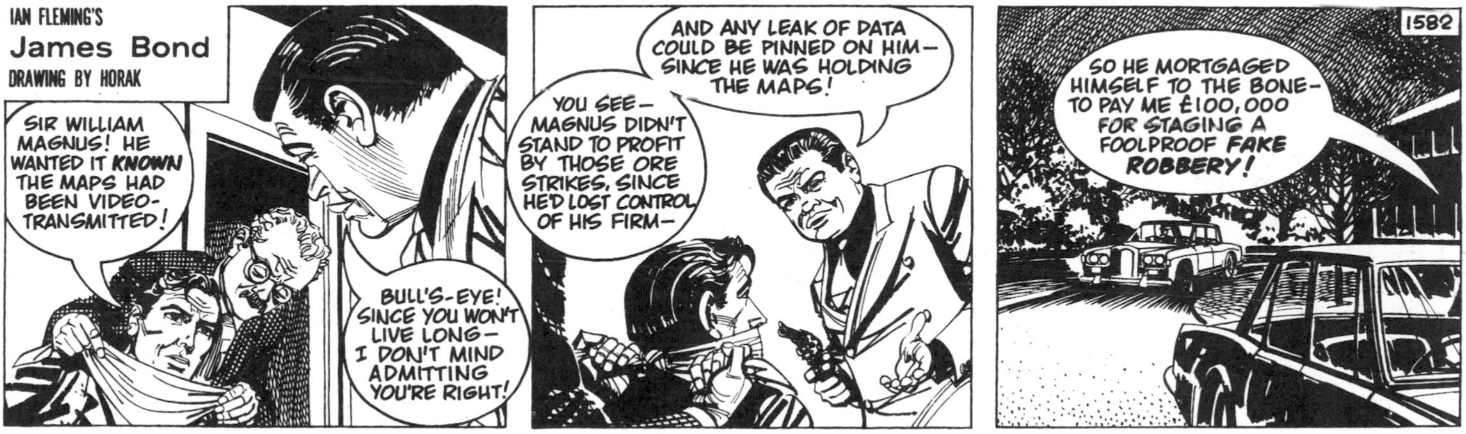
IAN FLEMING'S
James Bond
DRAWING BY HORAK
SIR WILLIAM MAGNUS! HE WANTED IT KNOWN THE MAPS HAD BEEN VIDEO-TRANSMITTED!
BULL'S-EYE! SINCE YOU WON'T LIVE LONG— I DON'T MIND ADMITTING YOU'RE RIGHT!
YOU SEE— MAGNUS DIDN'T STAND TO PROFIT BY THOSE ORE STRIKES, SINCE HE'D LOST CONTROL OF HIS FIRM—
AND ANY LEAK OF DATA COULD BE PINNED ON HIM— SINCE HE WAS HOLDING THE MAPS!
1582
SO HE MORTGAGED HIMSELF TO THE BONE— TO PAY ME £100,000 FOR STAGING A FOOLPROOF FAKE ROBBERY!

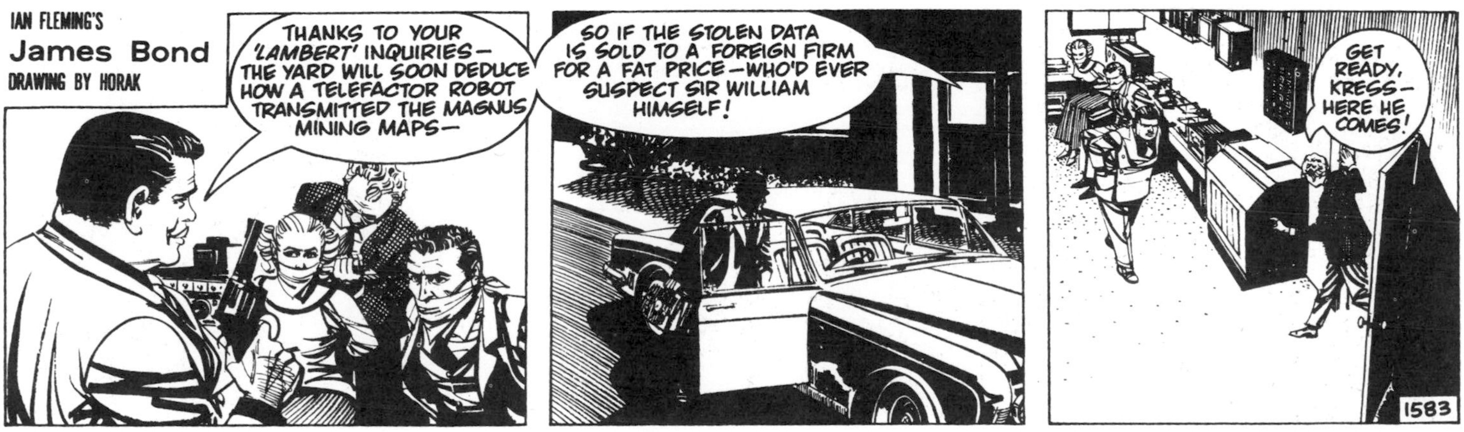
IAN FLEMING'S
James Bond
DRAWING BY HORAK
THANKS TO YOUR 'LAMBERT' INQUIRIES— THE YARD WILL SOON DEDUCE HOW A TELEFACTOR ROBOT TRANSMITTED THE MAGNUS MINING MAPS—
SO IF THE STOLEN DATA IS SOLD TO A FOREIGN FIRM FOR A FAT PRICE—WHO'D EVER SUSPECT SIR WILLIAM HIMSELF!
GET READY, KRESS— HERE HE COMES!
1583

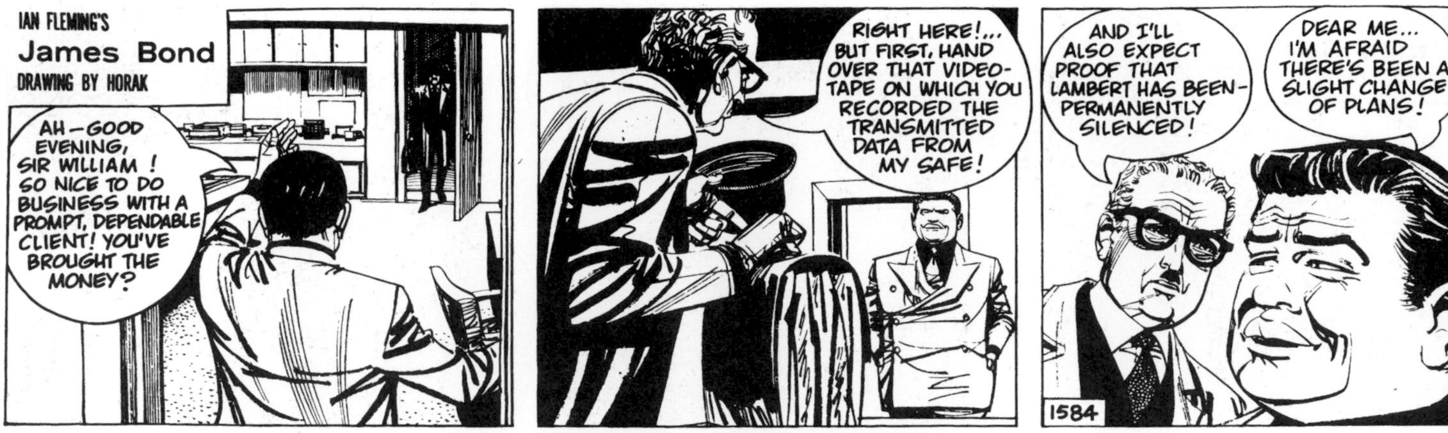
IAN FLEMING'S
James Bond
DRAWING BY HORAK
AH—GOOD EVENING, SIR WILLIAM ! SO NICE TO DO BUSINESS WITH A PROMPT, DEPENDABLE CLIENT! YOU'VE BROUGHT THE MONEY?
RIGHT HERE!... BUT FIRST, HAND OVER THAT VIDEO-TAPE ON WHICH YOU RECORDED THE TRANSMITTED DATA FROM MY SAFE!
AND I'LL ALSO EXPECT PROOF THAT LAMBERT HAS BEEN-PERMANENTLY SILENCED!
DEAR ME... I'M AFRAID THERE'S BEEN A SLIGHT CHANGE OF PLANS!
1584

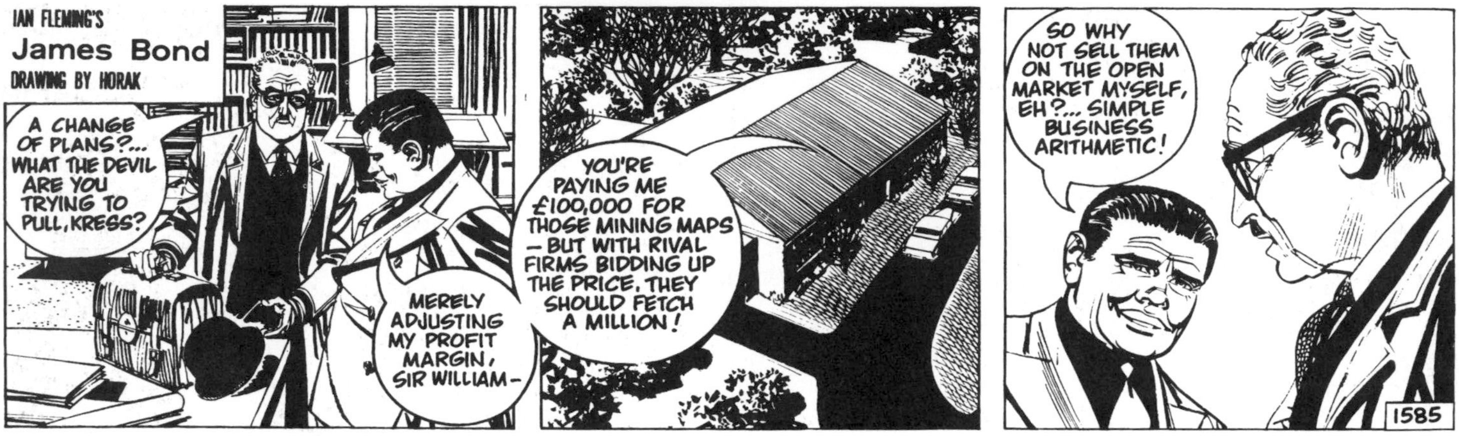
IAN FLEMING'S
James Bond
DRAWING BY HORAK
A CHANGE OF PLANS?... WHAT THE DEVIL ARE YOU TRYING TO PULL, KRESS?
MERELY ADJUSTING MY PROFIT MARGIN, SIR WILLIAM—
YOU'RE PAYING ME £100,000 FOR THOSE MINING MAPS—BUT WITH RIVAL FIRMS BIDDING UP THE PRICE, THEY SHOULD FETCH A MILLION!
SO WHY NOT SELL THEM ON THE OPEN MARKET MYSELF, EH?... SIMPLE BUSINESS ARITHMETIC!
1585

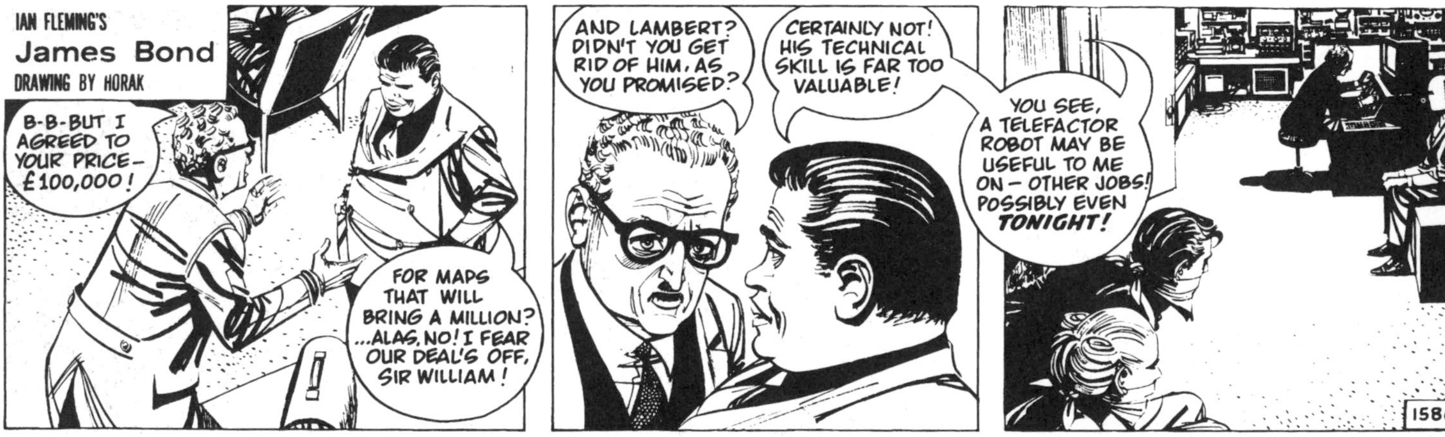
IAN FLEMING'S
James Bond
DRAWING BY HORAK
B-B-BUT I AGREED TO YOUR PRICE—£100,000!
FOR MAPS THAT WILL BRING A MILLION? ...ALAS, NO! I FEAR OUR DEAL'S OFF, SIR WILLIAM!
AND LAMBERT? DIDN'T YOU GET RID OF HIM, AS YOU PROMISED?
CERTAINLY NOT! HIS TECHNICAL SKILL IS FAR TOO VALUABLE!
YOU SEE, A TELEFACTOR ROBOT MAY BE USEFUL TO ME ON—OTHER JOBS! POSSIBLY EVEN TONIGHT!
1586

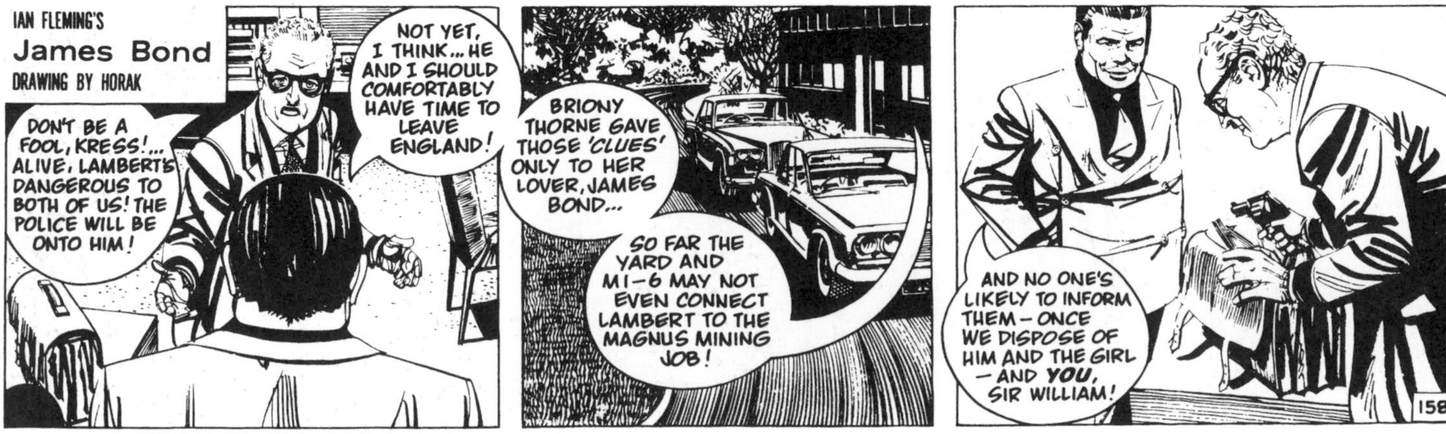
IAN FLEMING'S
James Bond
DRAWING BY HORAK
DON'T BE A FOOL, KRESS!... ALIVE, LAMBERT'S DANGEROUS TO BOTH OF US! THE POLICE WILL BE ONTO HIM!
NOT YET, I THINK... HE AND I SHOULD COMFORTABLY HAVE TIME TO LEAVE ENGLAND!
BRIONY THORNE GAVE THOSE 'CLUES' ONLY TO HER LOVER, JAMES BOND...
SO FAR THE YARD AND MI-6 MAY NOT EVEN CONNECT LAMBERT TO THE MAGNUS MINING JOB!
AND NO ONE'S LIKELY TO INFORM THEM—ONCE WE DISPOSE OF HIM AND THE GIRL—AND YOU, SIR WILLIAM!
1587

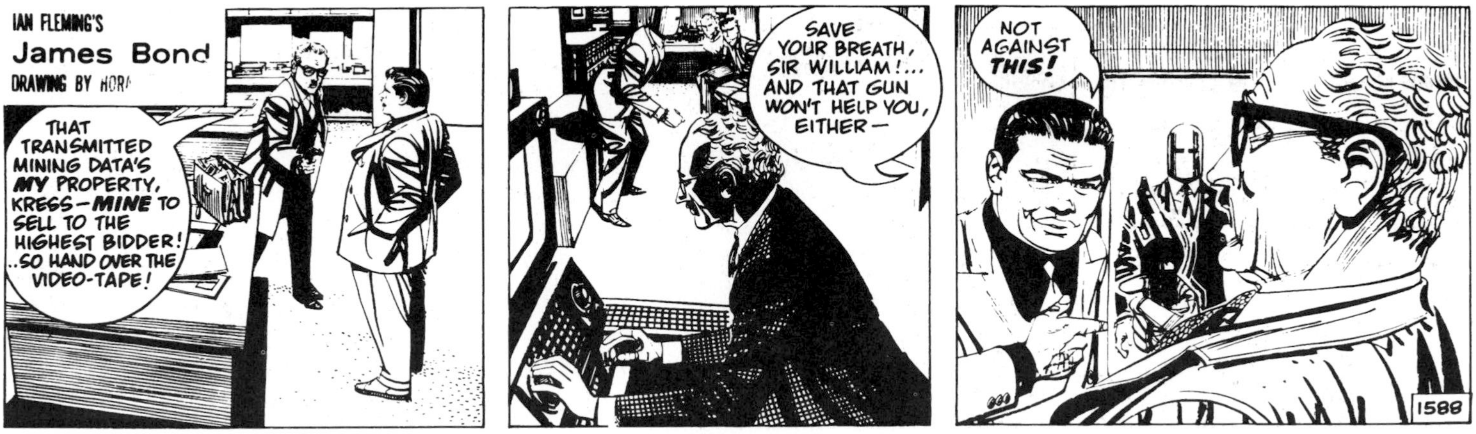
IAN FLEMING'S
James Bond
DRAWING BY HORAK
THAT TRANSMITTED MINING DATA'S **MY** PROPERTY, KRESS—**MINE** TO SELL TO THE HIGHEST BIDDER! ..SO HAND OVER THE VIDEO-TAPE!
SAVE YOUR BREATH, SIR WILLIAM!... AND THAT GUN WON'T HELP YOU, EITHER—
NOT AGAINST **THIS!**
1588

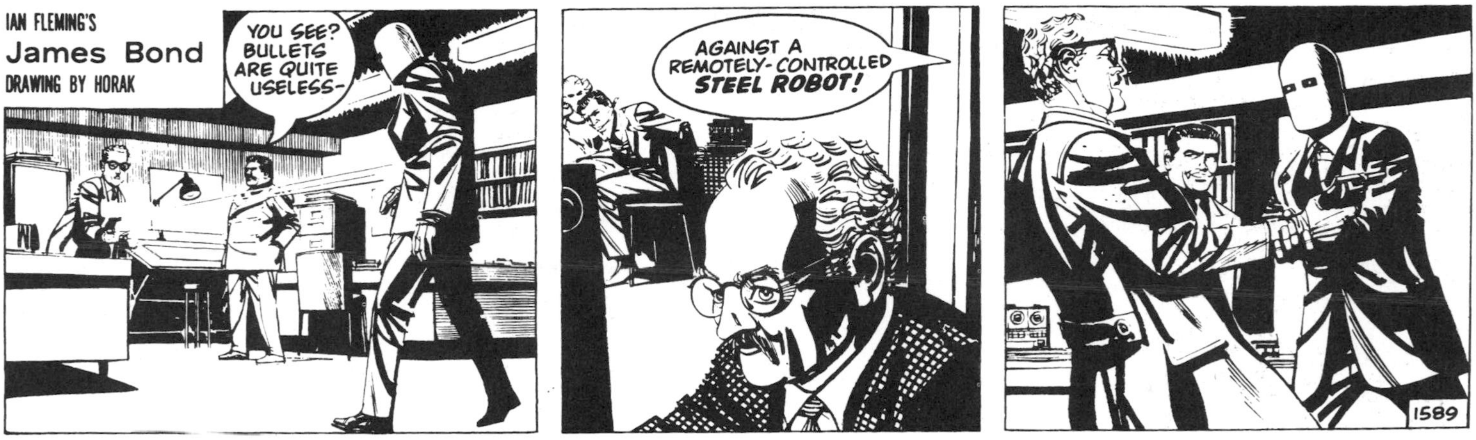
IAN FLEMING'S
James Bond
DRAWING BY HORAK
YOU SEE? BULLETS ARE QUITE USELESS—
AGAINST A REMOTELY-CONTROLLED **STEEL ROBOT!**
1589

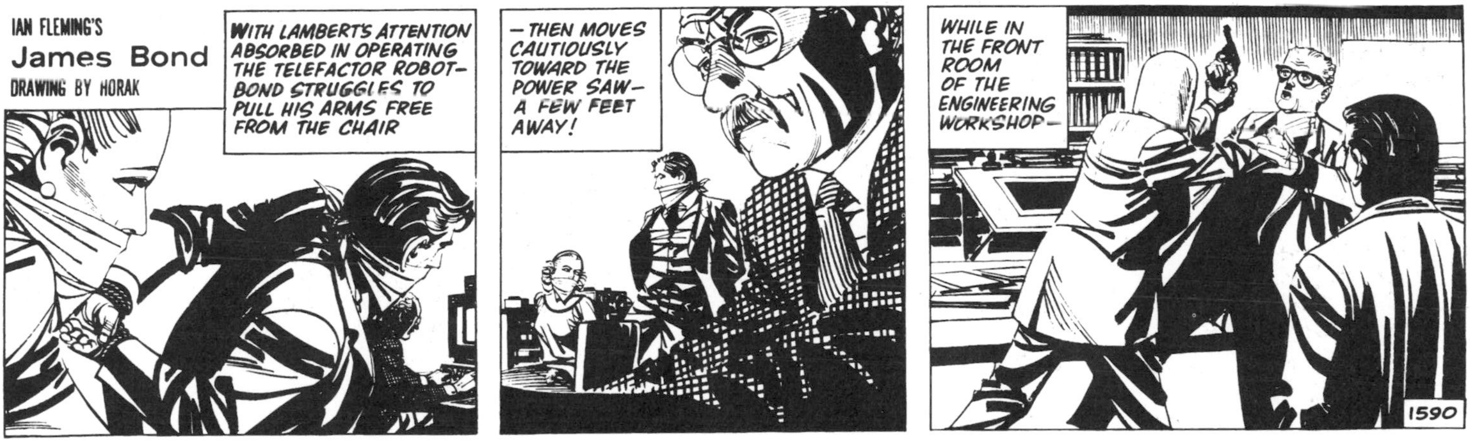
IAN FLEMING'S
James Bond
DRAWING BY HORAK
WITH LAMBERT'S ATTENTION ABSORBED IN OPERATING THE TELEFACTOR ROBOT-BOND STRUGGLES TO PULL HIS ARMS FREE FROM THE CHAIR
—THEN MOVES CAUTIOUSLY TOWARD THE POWER SAW—A FEW FEET AWAY!
WHILE IN THE FRONT ROOM OF THE ENGINEERING WORKSHOP—
1590

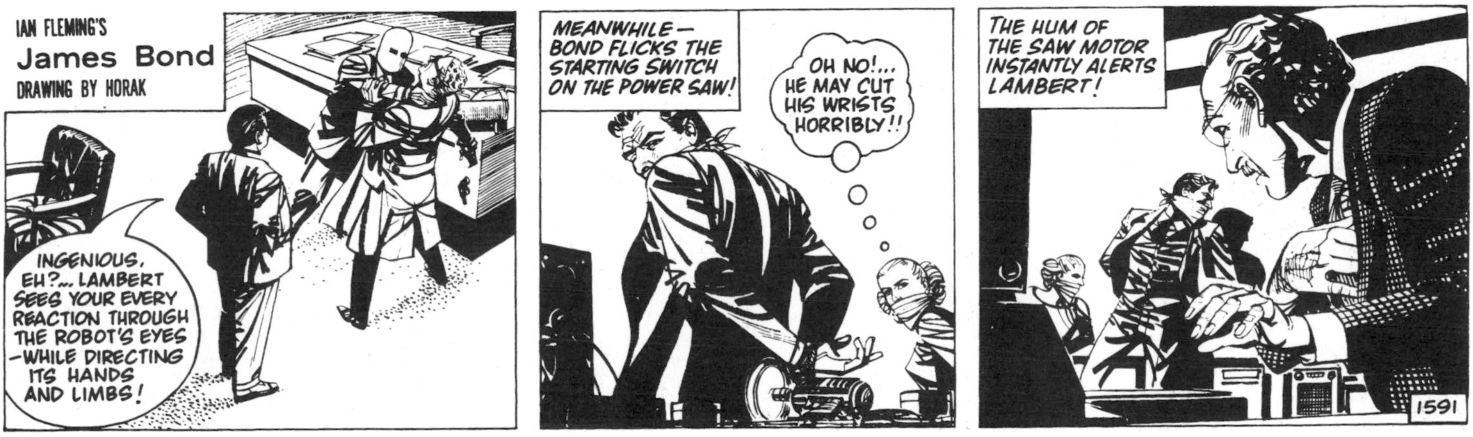
IAN FLEMING'S
James Bond
DRAWING BY HORAK
INGENIOUS, EH?... LAMBERT SEES YOUR EVERY REACTION THROUGH THE ROBOT'S EYES —WHILE DIRECTING ITS HANDS AND LIMBS!
MEANWHILE—BOND FLICKS THE STARTING SWITCH ON THE POWER SAW!
OH NO!... HE MAY CUT HIS WRISTS HORRIBLY!!
THE HUM OF THE SAW MOTOR INSTANTLY ALERTS LAMBERT!
1591

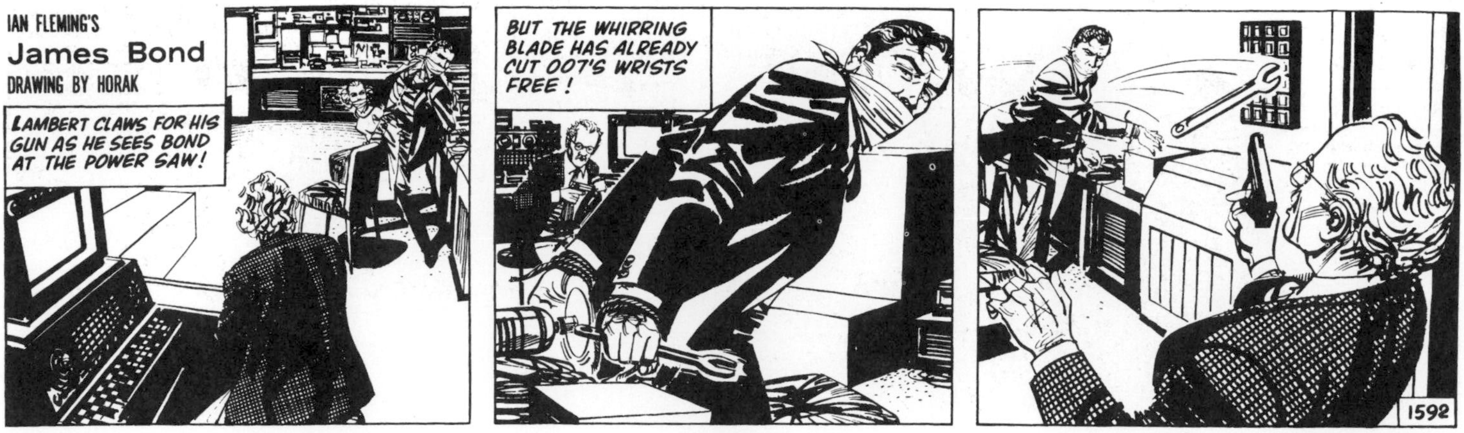
IAN FLEMING'S
James Bond
DRAWING BY HORAK
LAMBERT CLAWS FOR HIS GUN AS HE SEES BOND AT THE POWER SAW!
BUT THE WHIRRING BLADE HAS ALREADY CUT 007'S WRISTS FREE!
1592

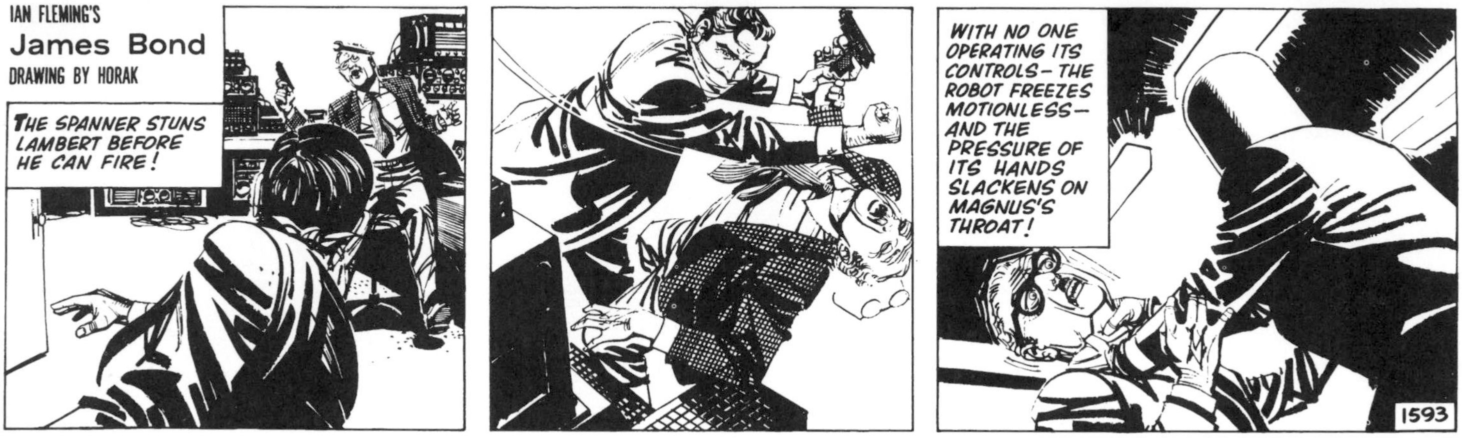
IAN FLEMING'S
James Bond
DRAWING BY HORAK
THE SPANNER STUNS LAMBERT BEFORE HE CAN FIRE!
WITH NO ONE OPERATING ITS CONTROLS–THE ROBOT FREEZES MOTIONLESS–AND THE PRESSURE OF ITS HANDS SLACKENS ON MAGNUS'S THROAT!
1593

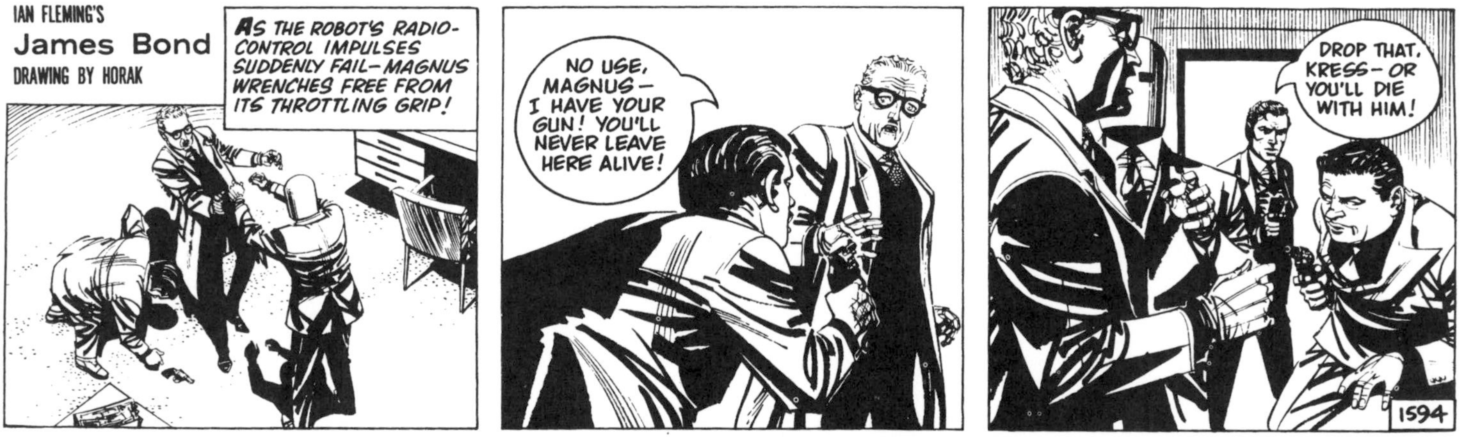
IAN FLEMING'S
James Bond
DRAWING BY HORAK
AS THE ROBOT'S RADIO-CONTROL IMPULSES SUDDENLY FAIL–MAGNUS WRENCHES FREE FROM ITS THROTTLING GRIP!
NO USE, MAGNUS–I HAVE YOUR GUN! YOU'LL NEVER LEAVE HERE ALIVE!
DROP THAT, KRESS–OR YOU'LL DIE WITH HIM!
1594

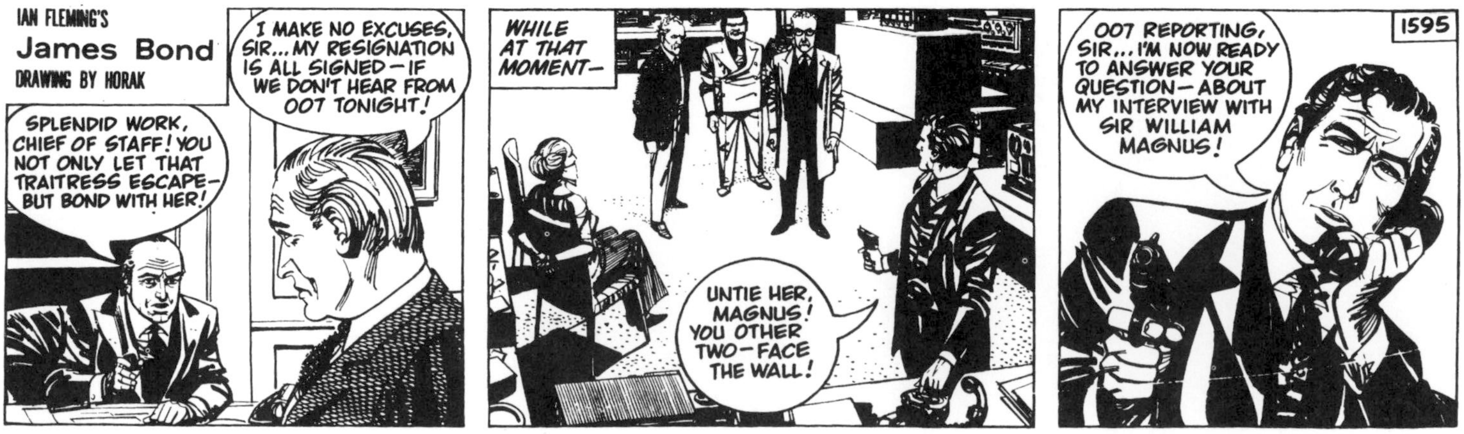
IAN FLEMING'S
James Bond
DRAWING BY HORAK
SPLENDID WORK, CHIEF OF STAFF! YOU NOT ONLY LET THAT TRAITRESS ESCAPE–BUT BOND WITH HER!
I MAKE NO EXCUSES, SIR... MY RESIGNATION IS ALL SIGNED–IF WE DON'T HEAR FROM 007 TONIGHT!
WHILE AT THAT MOMENT–
UNTIE HER, MAGNUS! YOU OTHER TWO–FACE THE WALL!
1595
007 REPORTING, SIR... I'M NOW READY TO ANSWER YOUR QUESTION–ABOUT MY INTERVIEW WITH SIR WILLIAM MAGNUS!

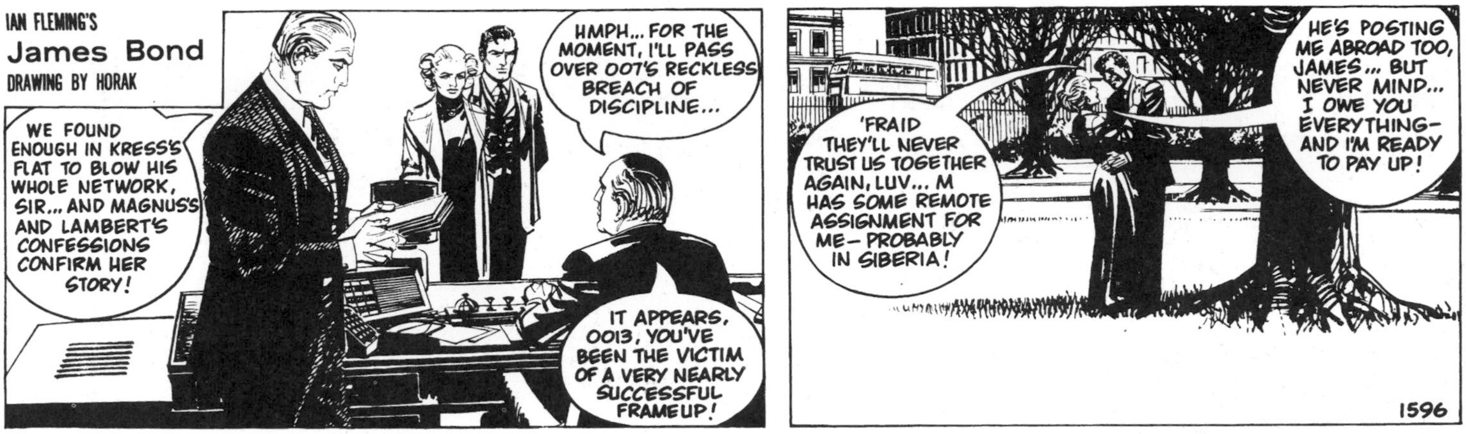
IAN FLEMING'S
James Bond
DRAWING BY HORAK
WE FOUND ENOUGH IN KRESS'S FLAT TO BLOW HIS WHOLE NETWORK, SIR... AND MAGNUS'S AND LAMBERT'S CONFESSIONS CONFIRM HER STORY!
HMPH... FOR THE MOMENT, I'LL PASS OVER 007'S RECKLESS BREACH OF DISCIPLINE...
IT APPEARS, 0013, YOU'VE BEEN THE VICTIM OF A VERY NEARLY SUCCESSFUL FRAMEUP!
'FRAID THEY'LL NEVER TRUST US TOGETHER AGAIN, LUV... M HAS SOME REMOTE ASSIGNMENT FOR ME—PROBABLY IN SIBERIA!
HE'S POSTING ME ABROAD TOO, JAMES... BUT NEVER MIND... I OWE YOU EVERYTHING—AND I'M READY TO PAY UP!
1596

DOUBLE JEOPARDY

Two years before the film *Live And Let Die* opened in theatres, *Double Jeopardy* features an almost identical sequence where Bond infiltrates the enemy's location via a hang glider, a sport that was little known at the time. However, unlike Roger Moore's stunt – for which he underwent extensive training – Bond in the strip also wears water-skis! It is all just 'a simple matter of aerodynamic principles,' according to 007, though.

Upon arriving in Marrakesh, Bond uses the alias of Jeremy Blade, from the London Ornithological Society, a nod to Fleming's inspiration for his character's name.

In an amazing coincidence that ties up distinctly different sub-plots, writer Jim Lawrence joins the two strands of the story together as Bond uncovers a conspiracy to replace world leaders with surgically created doubles.

Continuation author Raymond Benson would later re-visit the concept of body doubles at peace talks in his similarly titled novel, *Doubleshot*, in 2000 – almost thirty years on from the comic strip's first publication.

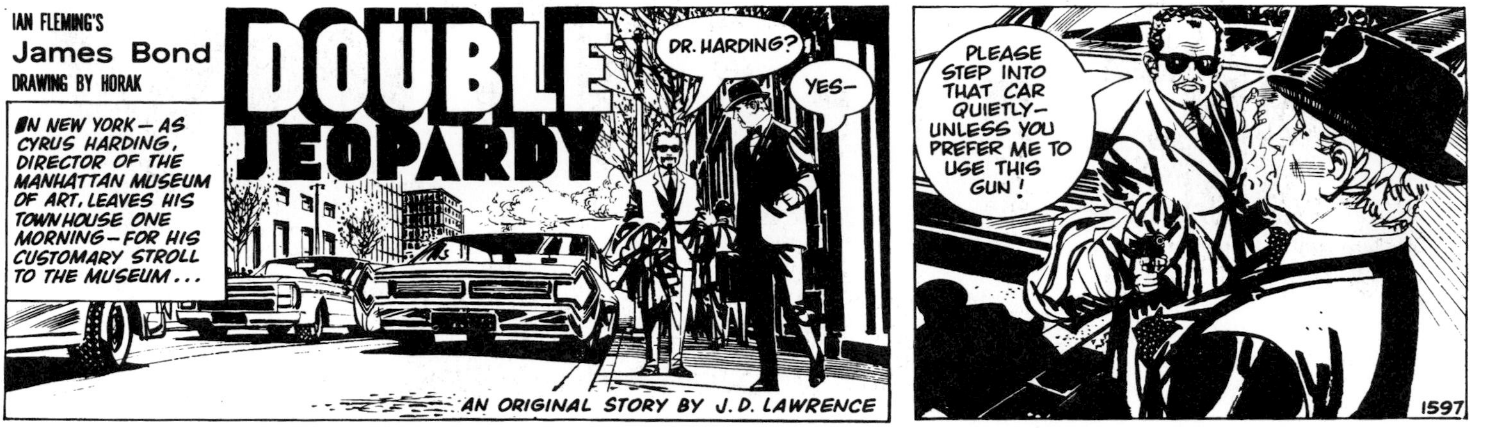
IAN FLEMING'S
James Bond
DRAWING BY HORAK
DOUBLE JEOPARDY
IN NEW YORK — AS CYRUS HARDING, DIRECTOR OF THE MANHATTAN MUSEUM OF ART, LEAVES HIS TOWNHOUSE ONE MORNING — FOR HIS CUSTOMARY STROLL TO THE MUSEUM . . .
DR. HARDING?
YES—
AN ORIGINAL STORY BY J. D. LAWRENCE
PLEASE STEP INTO THAT CAR QUIETLY— UNLESS YOU PREFER ME TO USE THIS GUN!
1597

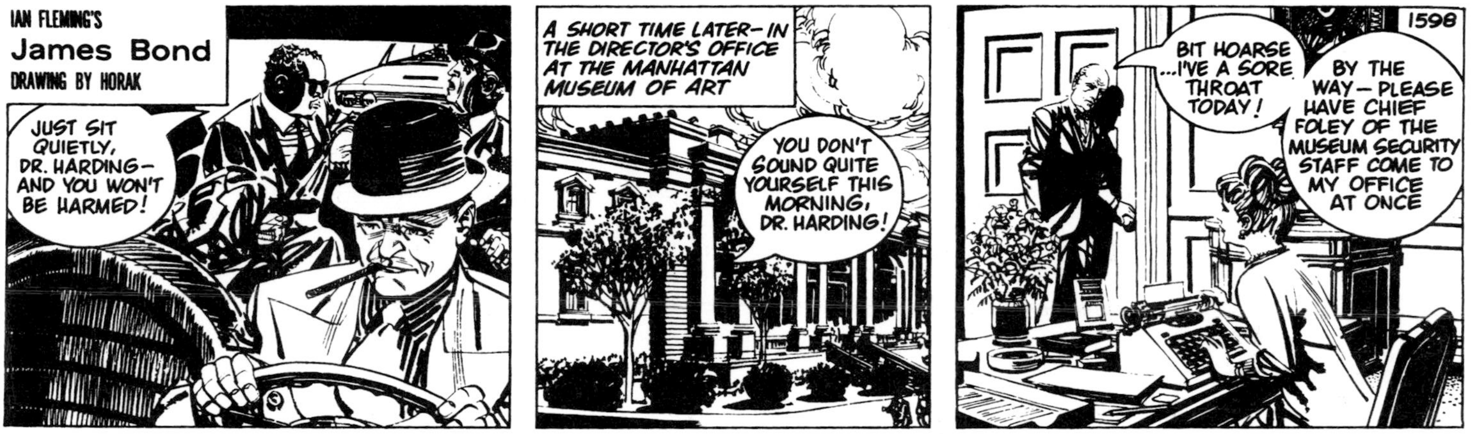
IAN FLEMING'S
James Bond
DRAWING BY HORAK
JUST SIT QUIETLY, DR. HARDING— AND YOU WON'T BE HARMED!
A SHORT TIME LATER— IN THE DIRECTOR'S OFFICE AT THE MANHATTAN MUSEUM OF ART
YOU DON'T SOUND QUITE YOURSELF THIS MORNING, DR. HARDING!
1598
BIT HOARSE ...I'VE A SORE THROAT TODAY!
BY THE WAY— PLEASE HAVE CHIEF FOLEY OF THE MUSEUM SECURITY STAFF COME TO MY OFFICE AT ONCE

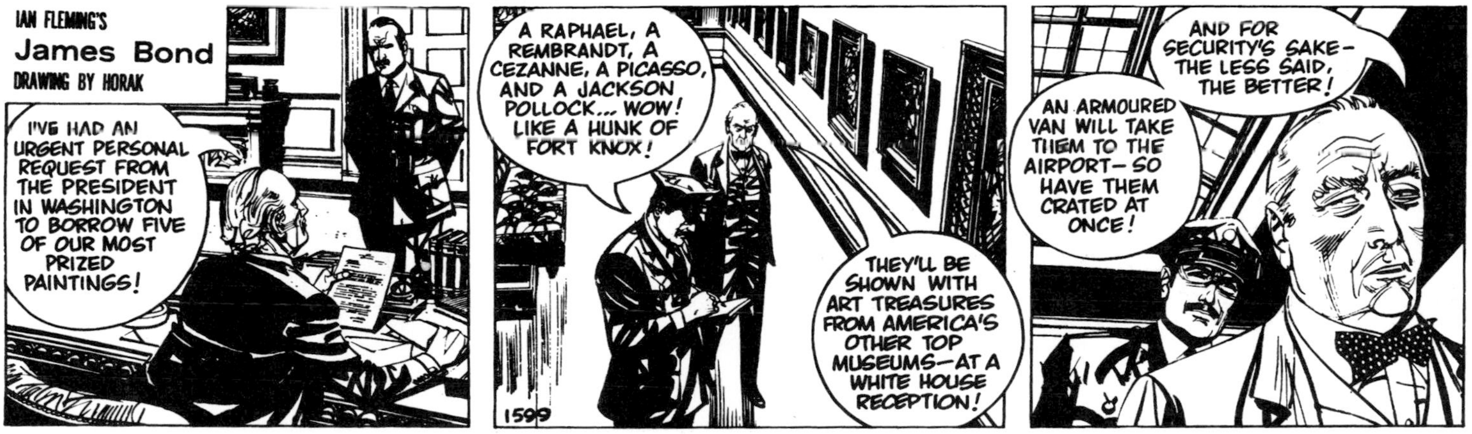
IAN FLEMING'S
James Bond
DRAWING BY HORAK
I'VE HAD AN URGENT PERSONAL REQUEST FROM THE PRESIDENT IN WASHINGTON TO BORROW FIVE OF OUR MOST PRIZED PAINTINGS!
A RAPHAEL, A REMBRANDT, A CEZANNE, A PICASSO, AND A JACKSON POLLOCK... WOW! LIKE A HUNK OF FORT KNOX!
THEY'LL BE SHOWN WITH ART TREASURES FROM AMERICA'S OTHER TOP MUSEUMS—AT A WHITE HOUSE RECEPTION!
1599
AND FOR SECURITY'S SAKE— THE LESS SAID, THE BETTER!
AN ARMOURED VAN WILL TAKE THEM TO THE AIRPORT— SO HAVE THEM CRATED AT ONCE!

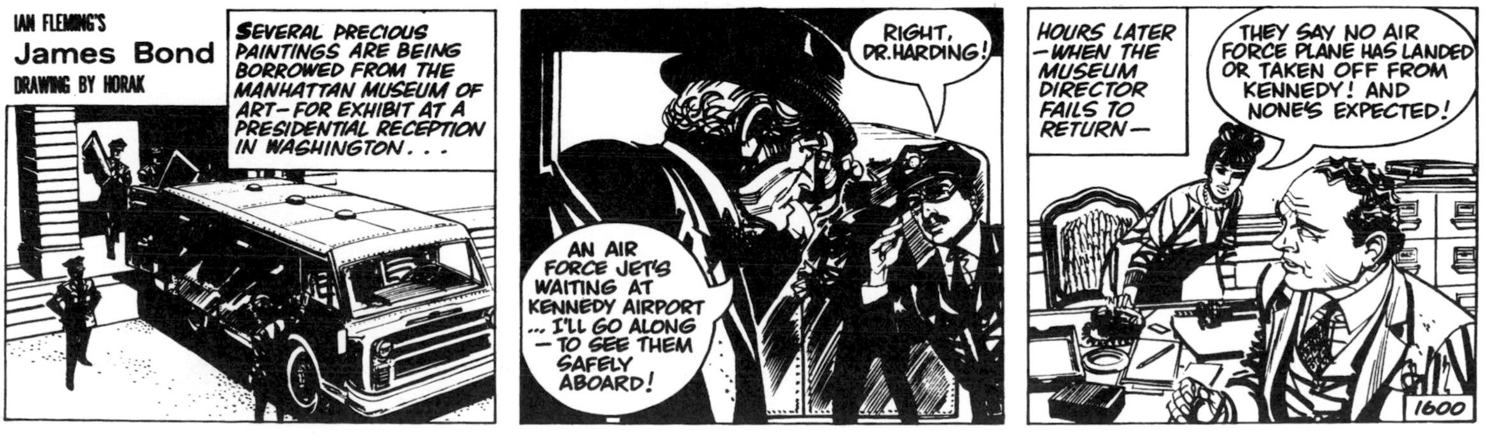
IAN FLEMING'S
James Bond
DRAWING BY HORAK
SEVERAL PRECIOUS PAINTINGS ARE BEING BORROWED FROM THE MANHATTAN MUSEUM OF ART— FOR EXHIBIT AT A PRESIDENTIAL RECEPTION IN WASHINGTON . . .
AN AIR FORCE JET'S WAITING AT KENNEDY AIRPORT ... I'LL GO ALONG — TO SEE THEM SAFELY ABOARD!
RIGHT, DR. HARDING!
HOURS LATER —WHEN THE MUSEUM DIRECTOR FAILS TO RETURN—
THEY SAY NO AIR FORCE PLANE HAS LANDED OR TAKEN OFF FROM KENNEDY! AND NONE'S EXPECTED!
1600

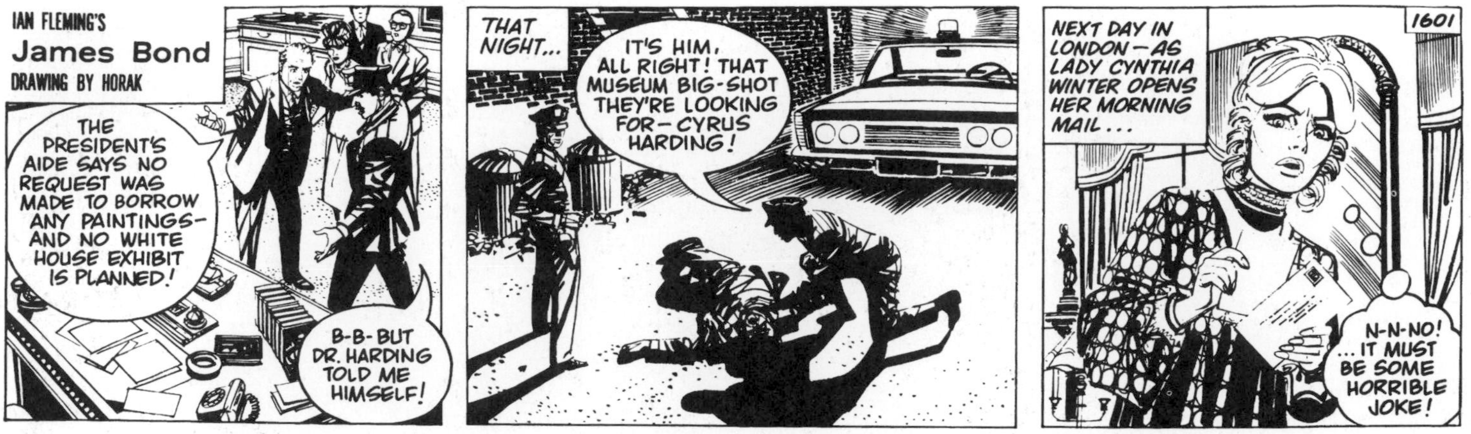
IAN FLEMING'S
James Bond
DRAWING BY HORAK
THE PRESIDENT'S AIDE SAYS NO REQUEST WAS MADE TO BORROW ANY PAINTINGS— AND NO WHITE HOUSE EXHIBIT IS PLANNED!
B-B-BUT DR. HARDING TOLD ME HIMSELF!
THAT NIGHT...
IT'S HIM, ALL RIGHT! THAT MUSEUM BIG-SHOT THEY'RE LOOKING FOR—CYRUS HARDING!
1601
NEXT DAY IN LONDON—AS LADY CYNTHIA WINTER OPENS HER MORNING MAIL...
N-N-NO! ...IT MUST BE SOME HORRIBLE JOKE!

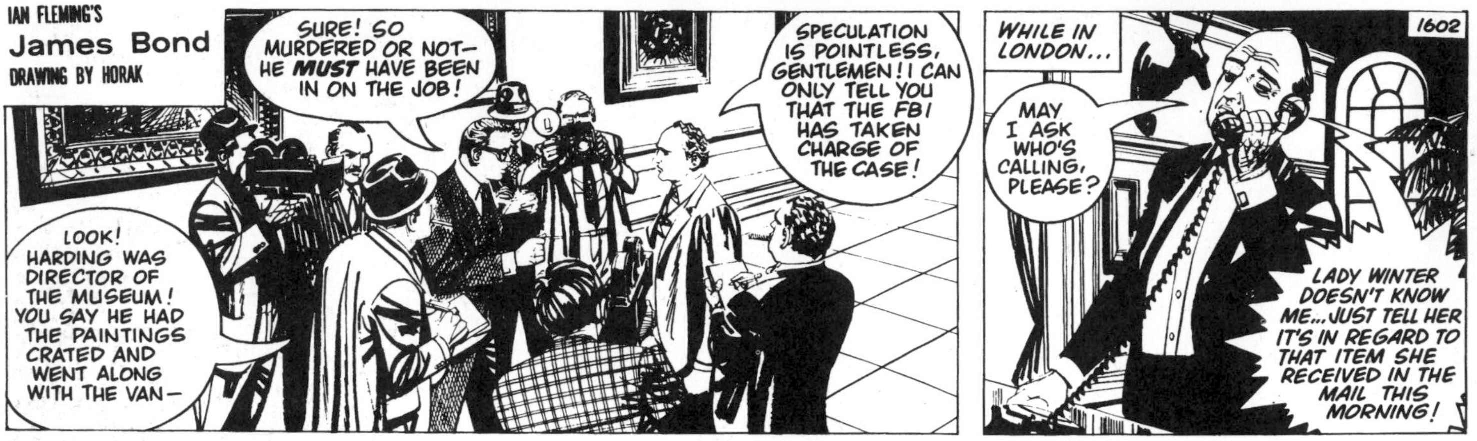
IAN FLEMING'S
James Bond
DRAWING BY HORAK
LOOK! HARDING WAS DIRECTOR OF THE MUSEUM! YOU SAY HE HAD THE PAINTINGS CRATED AND WENT ALONG WITH THE VAN—
SURE! SO MURDERED OR NOT— HE MUST HAVE BEEN IN ON THE JOB!
SPECULATION IS POINTLESS, GENTLEMEN! I CAN ONLY TELL YOU THAT THE FBI HAS TAKEN CHARGE OF THE CASE!
1602
WHILE IN LONDON...
MAY I ASK WHO'S CALLING, PLEASE?
LADY WINTER DOESN'T KNOW ME... JUST TELL HER IT'S IN REGARD TO THAT ITEM SHE RECEIVED IN THE MAIL THIS MORNING!

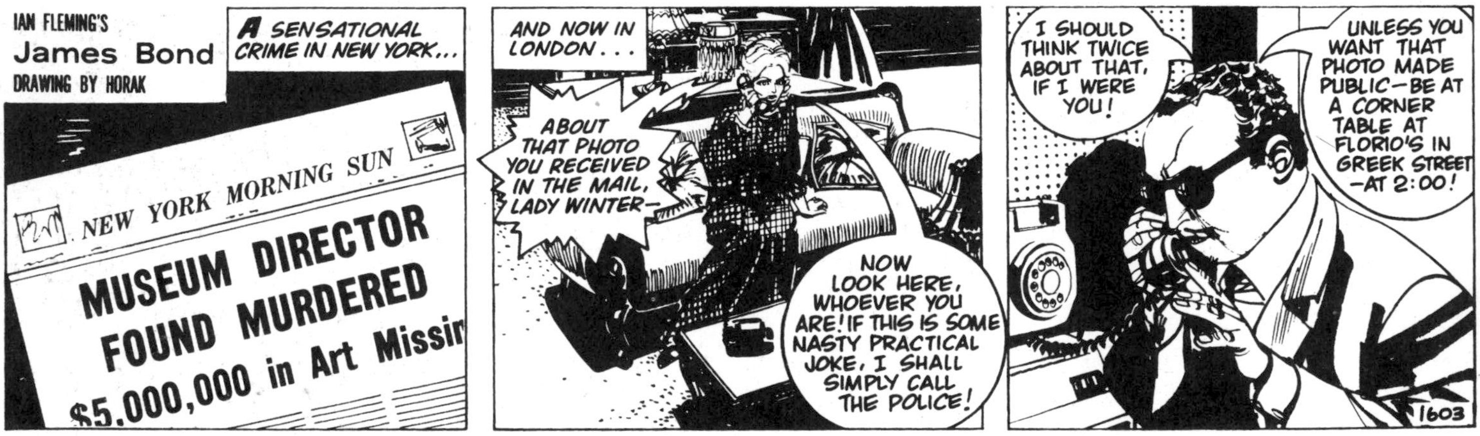
IAN FLEMING'S
James Bond
DRAWING BY HORAK
A SENSATIONAL CRIME IN NEW YORK...
NEW YORK MORNING SUN
MUSEUM DIRECTOR FOUND MURDERED
$5,000,000 in Art Missir
AND NOW IN LONDON...
ABOUT THAT PHOTO YOU RECEIVED IN THE MAIL, LADY WINTER—
NOW LOOK HERE, WHOEVER YOU ARE! IF THIS IS SOME NASTY PRACTICAL JOKE, I SHALL SIMPLY CALL THE POLICE!
I SHOULD THINK TWICE ABOUT THAT, IF I WERE YOU!
UNLESS YOU WANT THAT PHOTO MADE PUBLIC—BE AT A CORNER TABLE AT FLORIO'S IN GREEK STREET —AT 2:00!
1603

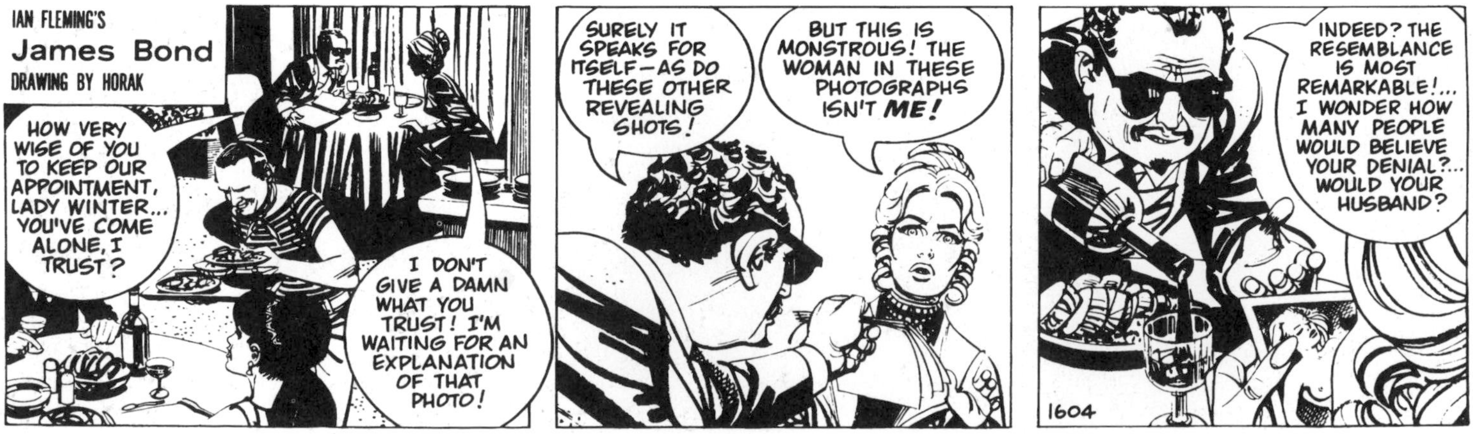
IAN FLEMING'S
James Bond
DRAWING BY HORAK
HOW VERY WISE OF YOU TO KEEP OUR APPOINTMENT, LADY WINTER... YOU'VE COME ALONE, I TRUST?
I DON'T GIVE A DAMN WHAT YOU TRUST! I'M WAITING FOR AN EXPLANATION OF THAT PHOTO!
SURELY IT SPEAKS FOR ITSELF—AS DO THESE OTHER REVEALING SHOTS!
BUT THIS IS MONSTROUS! THE WOMAN IN THESE PHOTOGRAPHS ISN'T ME!
1604
INDEED? THE RESEMBLANCE IS MOST REMARKABLE!... I WONDER HOW MANY PEOPLE WOULD BELIEVE YOUR DENIAL?... WOULD YOUR HUSBAND?

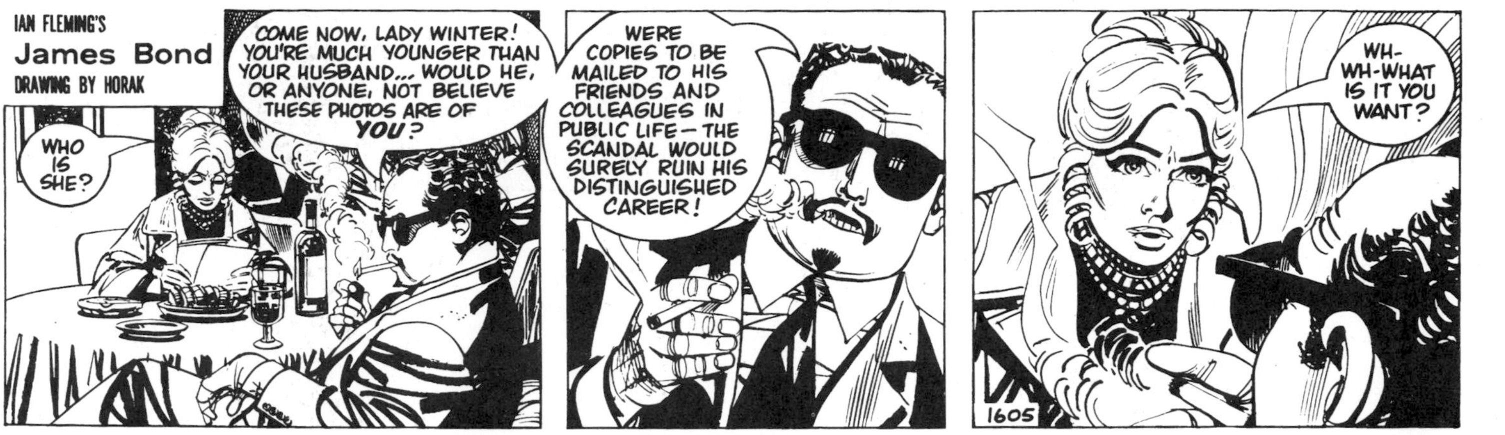
IAN FLEMING'S
James Bond
DRAWING BY HORAK
WHO IS SHE?
COME NOW, LADY WINTER! YOU'RE MUCH YOUNGER THAN YOUR HUSBAND... WOULD HE, OR ANYONE, NOT BELIEVE THESE PHOTOS ARE OF YOU?
WERE COPIES TO BE MAILED TO HIS FRIENDS AND COLLEAGUES IN PUBLIC LIFE — THE SCANDAL WOULD SURELY RUIN HIS DISTINGUISHED CAREER!
WH-WH-WHAT IS IT YOU WANT?
1605

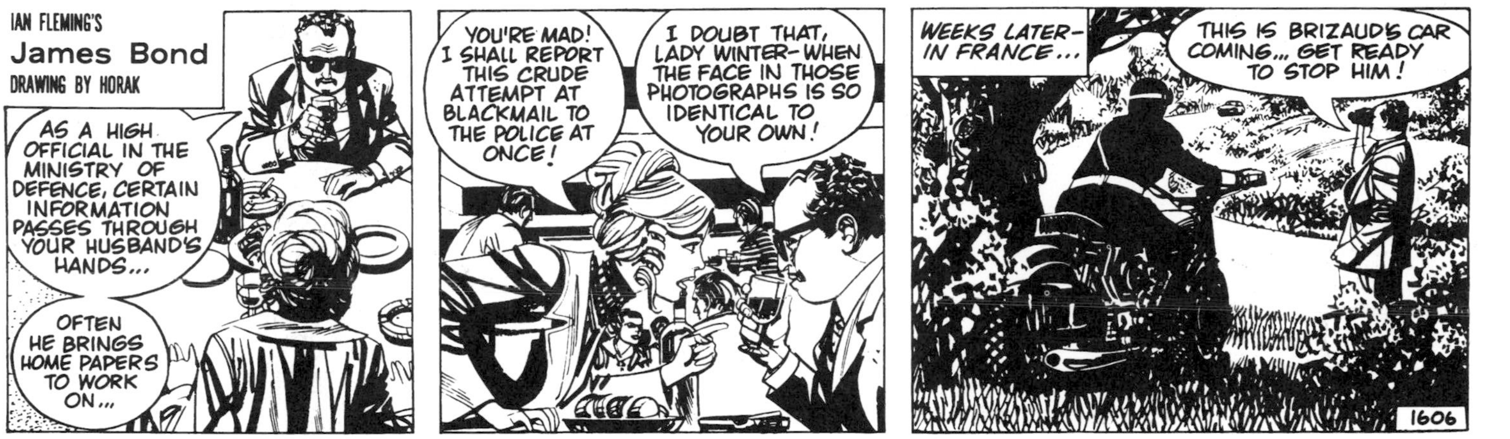
IAN FLEMING'S
James Bond
DRAWING BY HORAK
AS A HIGH OFFICIAL IN THE MINISTRY OF DEFENCE, CERTAIN INFORMATION PASSES THROUGH YOUR HUSBAND'S HANDS...
OFTEN HE BRINGS HOME PAPERS TO WORK ON...
YOU'RE MAD! I SHALL REPORT THIS CRUDE ATTEMPT AT BLACKMAIL TO THE POLICE AT ONCE!
I DOUBT THAT, LADY WINTER — WHEN THE FACE IN THOSE PHOTOGRAPHS IS SO IDENTICAL TO YOUR OWN!
WEEKS LATER — IN FRANCE...
THIS IS BRIZAUD'S CAR COMING... GET READY TO STOP HIM!
1606

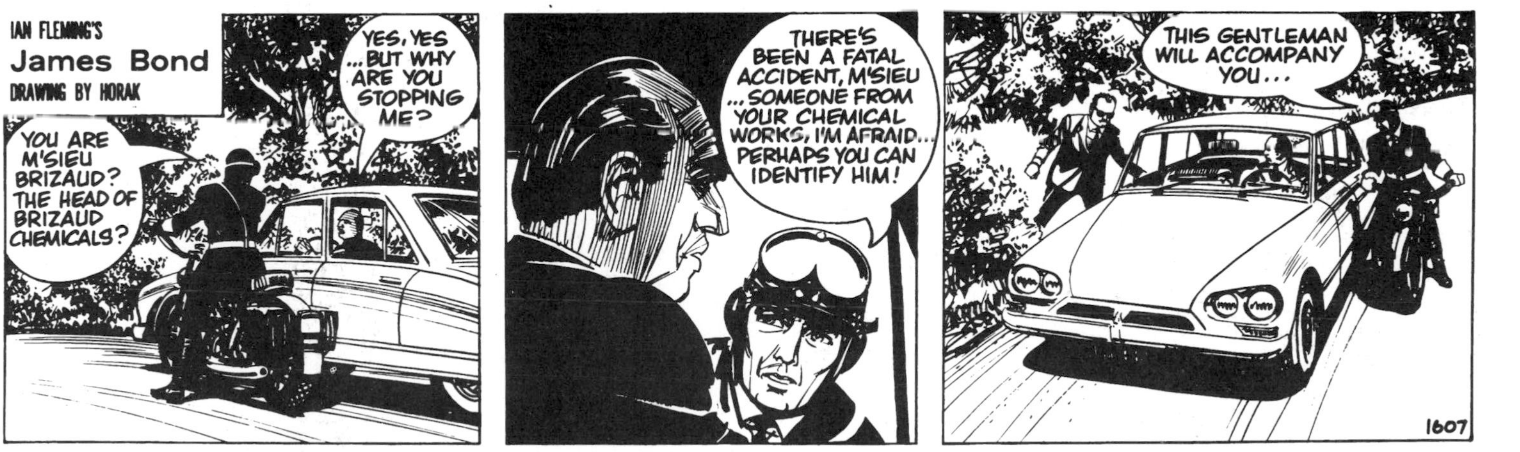
IAN FLEMING'S
James Bond
DRAWING BY HORAK
YOU ARE M'SIEU BRIZAUD? THE HEAD OF BRIZAUD CHEMICALS?
YES, YES ...BUT WHY ARE YOU STOPPING ME?
THERE'S BEEN A FATAL ACCIDENT, M'SIEU ...SOMEONE FROM YOUR CHEMICAL WORKS, I'M AFRAID... PERHAPS YOU CAN IDENTIFY HIM!
THIS GENTLEMAN WILL ACCOMPANY YOU...
1607

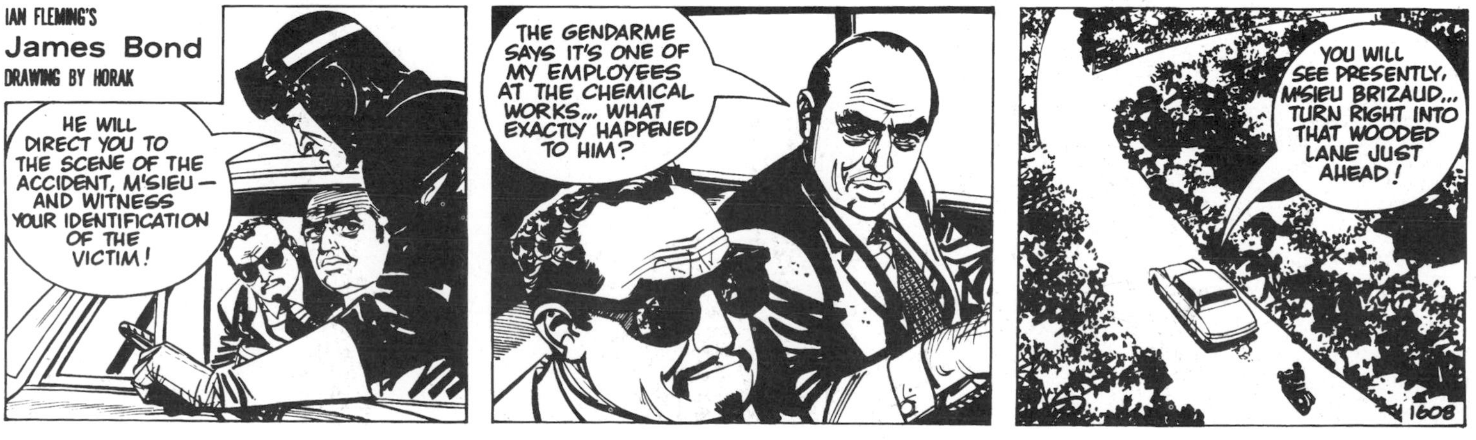
IAN FLEMING'S
James Bond
DRAWING BY HORAK
HE WILL DIRECT YOU TO THE SCENE OF THE ACCIDENT, M'SIEU — AND WITNESS YOUR IDENTIFICATION OF THE VICTIM!
THE GENDARME SAYS IT'S ONE OF MY EMPLOYEES AT THE CHEMICAL WORKS... WHAT EXACTLY HAPPENED TO HIM?
YOU WILL SEE PRESENTLY, M'SIEU BRIZAUD... TURN RIGHT INTO THAT WOODED LANE JUST AHEAD!
1608

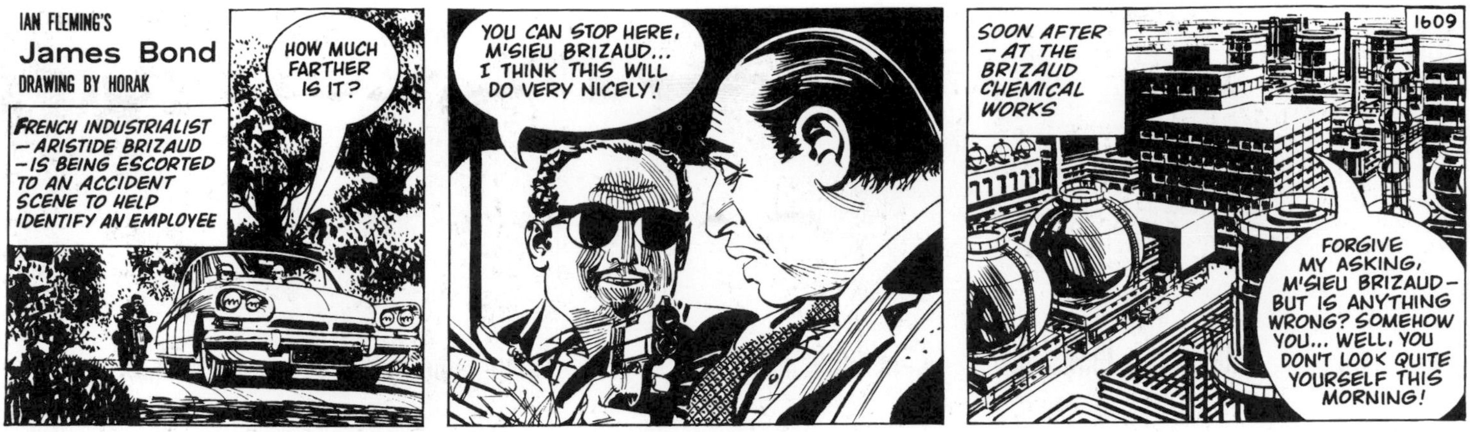
IAN FLEMING'S
James Bond
DRAWING BY HORAK
FRENCH INDUSTRIALIST —ARISTIDE BRIZAUD —IS BEING ESCORTED TO AN ACCIDENT SCENE TO HELP IDENTIFY AN EMPLOYEE
HOW MUCH FARTHER IS IT?
YOU CAN STOP HERE, M'SIEU BRIZAUD... I THINK THIS WILL DO VERY NICELY!
SOON AFTER —AT THE BRIZAUD CHEMICAL WORKS
1609
FORGIVE MY ASKING, M'SIEU BRIZAUD— BUT IS ANYTHING WRONG? SOMEHOW YOU... WELL, YOU DON'T LOOK QUITE YOURSELF THIS MORNING!

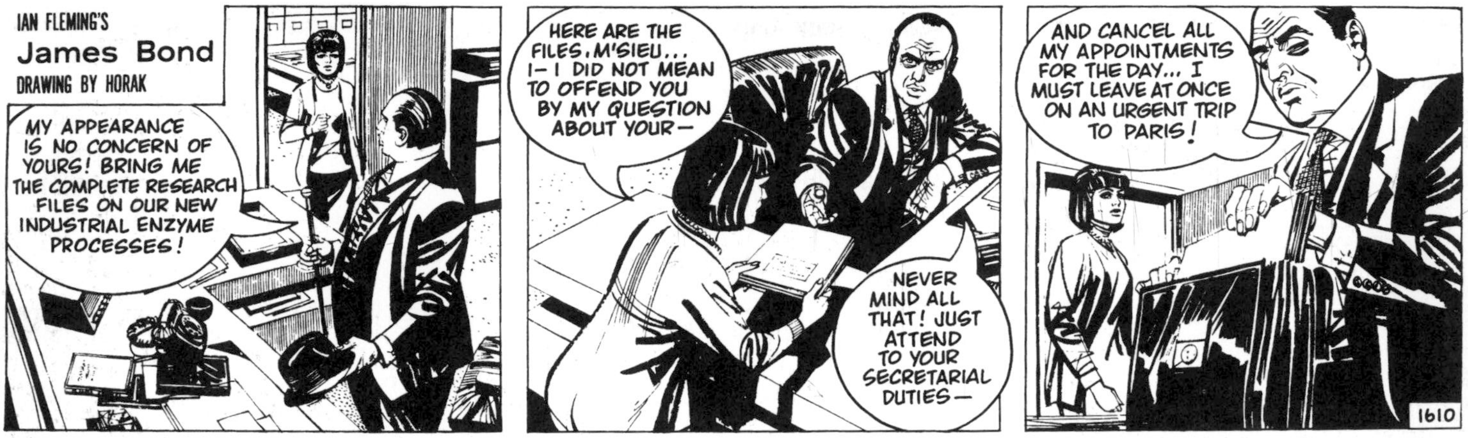
IAN FLEMING'S
James Bond
DRAWING BY HORAK
MY APPEARANCE IS NO CONCERN OF YOURS! BRING ME THE COMPLETE RESEARCH FILES ON OUR NEW INDUSTRIAL ENZYME PROCESSES!
HERE ARE THE FILES, M'SIEU... I— I DID NOT MEAN TO OFFEND YOU BY MY QUESTION ABOUT YOUR—
NEVER MIND ALL THAT! JUST ATTEND TO YOUR SECRETARIAL DUTIES—
AND CANCEL ALL MY APPOINTMENTS FOR THE DAY... I MUST LEAVE AT ONCE ON AN URGENT TRIP TO PARIS!
1610

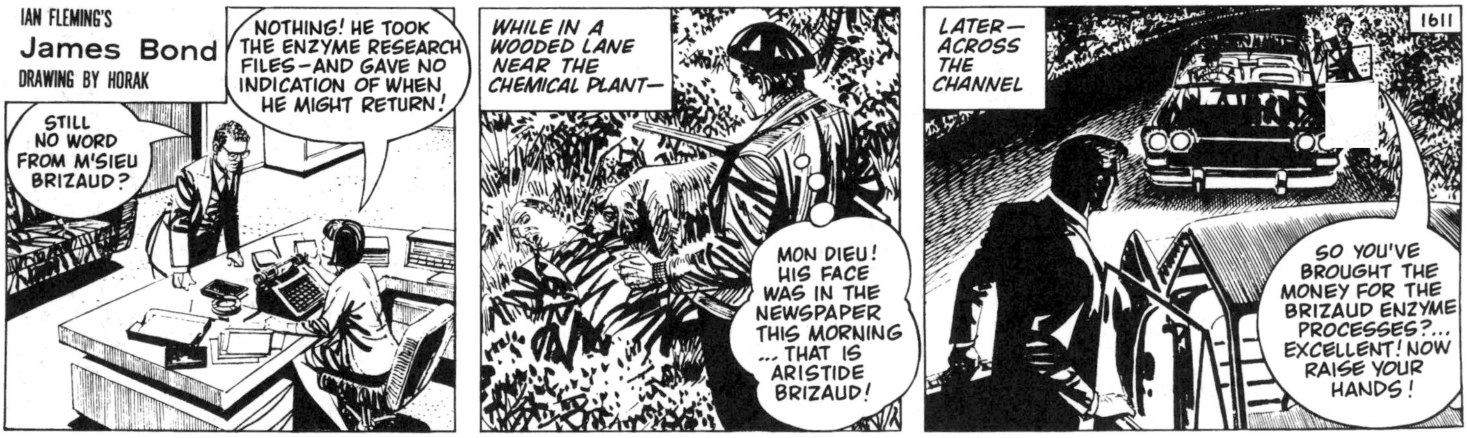
IAN FLEMING'S
James Bond
DRAWING BY HORAK
STILL NO WORD FROM M'SIEU BRIZAUD?
NOTHING! HE TOOK THE ENZYME RESEARCH FILES—AND GAVE NO INDICATION OF WHEN HE MIGHT RETURN!
WHILE IN A WOODED LANE NEAR THE CHEMICAL PLANT—
MON DIEU! HIS FACE WAS IN THE NEWSPAPER THIS MORNING ... THAT IS ARISTIDE BRIZAUD!
LATER— ACROSS THE CHANNEL
1611
SO YOU'VE BROUGHT THE MONEY FOR THE BRIZAUD ENZYME PROCESSES?... EXCELLENT! NOW RAISE YOUR HANDS!

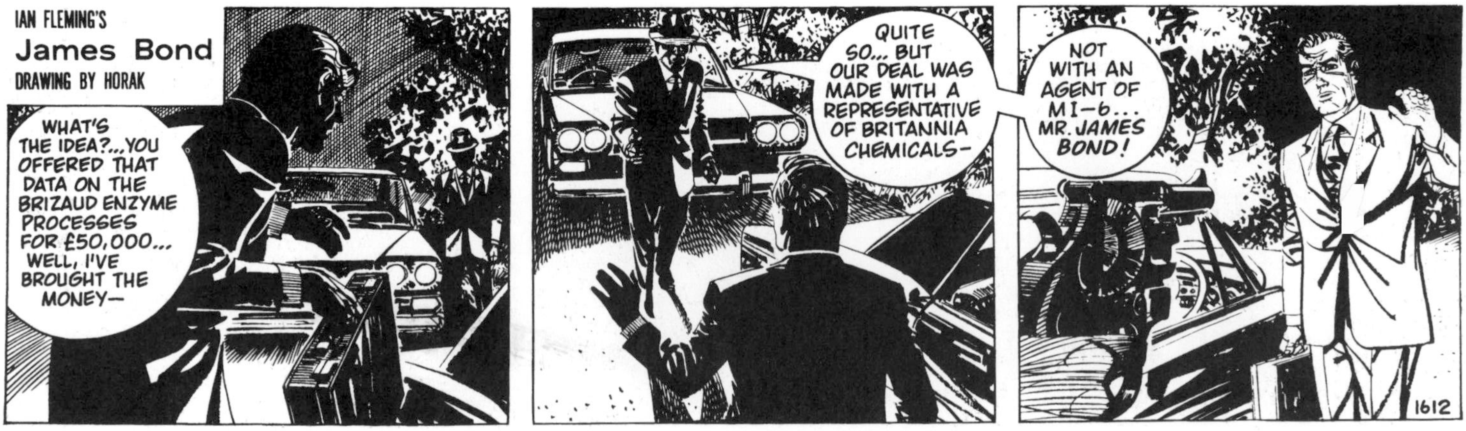
IAN FLEMING'S
James Bond
DRAWING BY HORAK
WHAT'S THE IDEA?... YOU OFFERED THAT DATA ON THE BRIZAUD ENZYME PROCESSES FOR £50,000... WELL, I'VE BROUGHT THE MONEY—
QUITE SO... BUT OUR DEAL WAS MADE WITH A REPRESENTATIVE OF BRITANNIA CHEMICALS—
NOT WITH AN AGENT OF MI-6... MR. JAMES BOND!
1612

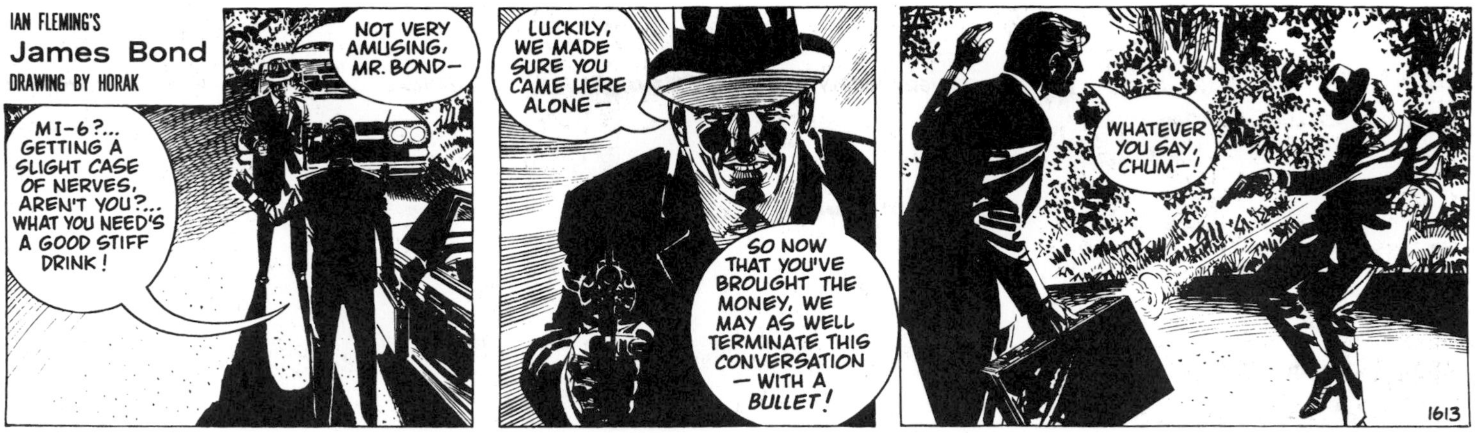
IAN FLEMING'S
James Bond
DRAWING BY HORAK
NOT VERY AMUSING, MR. BOND—
MI-6?... GETTING A SLIGHT CASE OF NERVES, AREN'T YOU?... WHAT YOU NEED'S A GOOD STIFF DRINK!
LUCKILY, WE MADE SURE YOU CAME HERE ALONE—
SO NOW THAT YOU'VE BROUGHT THE MONEY, WE MAY AS WELL TERMINATE THIS CONVERSATION —WITH A BULLET!
WHATEVER YOU SAY, CHUM—!
1613

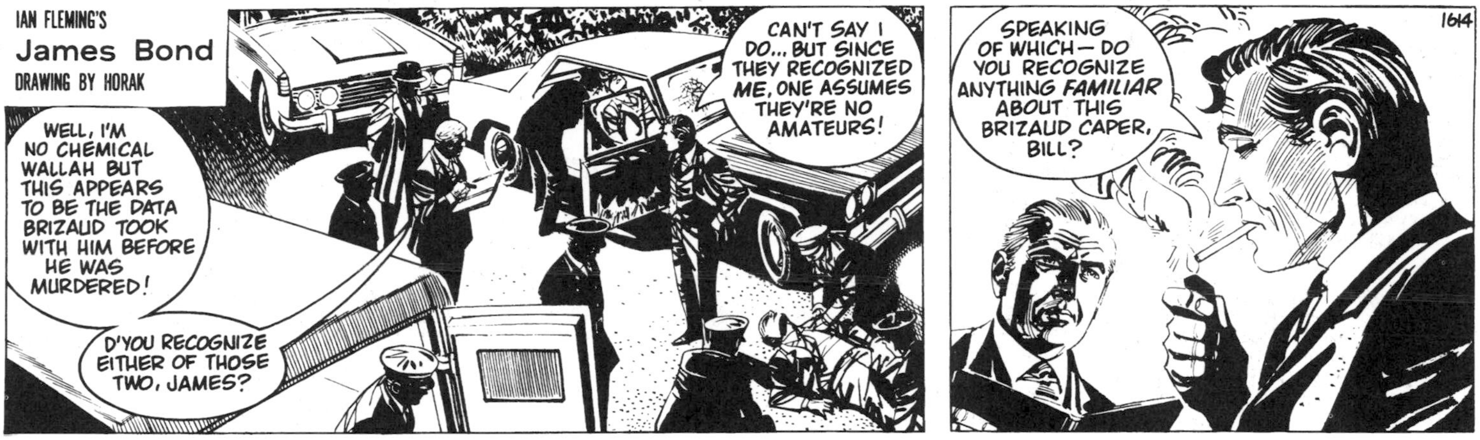
IAN FLEMING'S
James Bond
DRAWING BY HORAK
WELL, I'M NO CHEMICAL WALLAH BUT THIS APPEARS TO BE THE DATA BRIZAUD TOOK WITH HIM BEFORE HE WAS MURDERED!
D'YOU RECOGNIZE EITHER OF THOSE TWO, JAMES?
CAN'T SAY I DO... BUT SINCE THEY RECOGNIZED ME, ONE ASSUMES THEY'RE NO AMATEURS!
1614
SPEAKING OF WHICH—DO YOU RECOGNIZE ANYTHING FAMILIAR ABOUT THIS BRIZAUD CAPER, BILL?

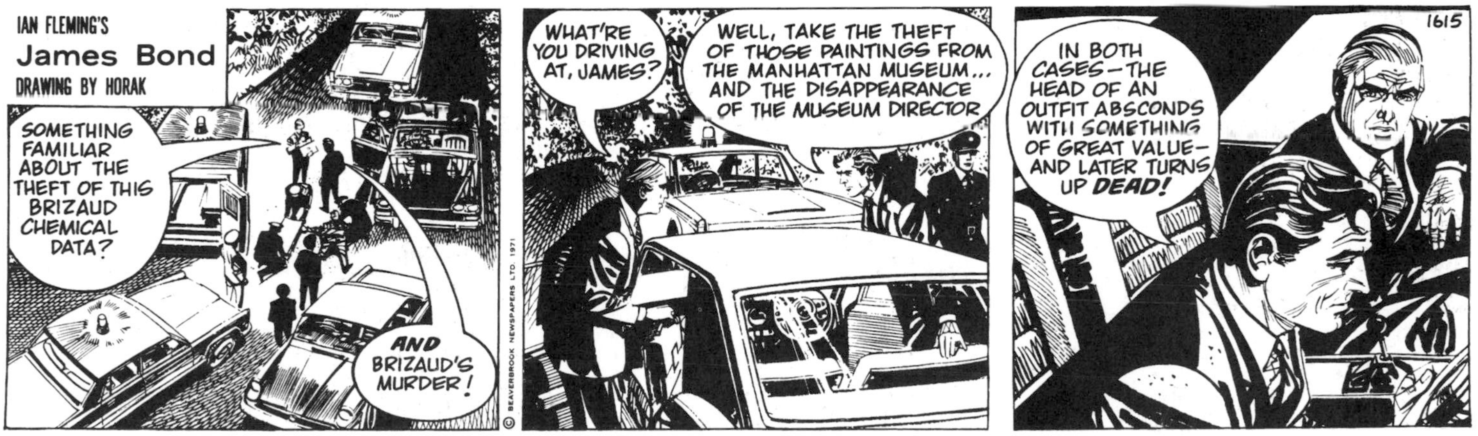
IAN FLEMING'S
James Bond
DRAWING BY HORAK
SOMETHING FAMILIAR ABOUT THE THEFT OF THIS BRIZAUD CHEMICAL DATA?
AND BRIZAUD'S MURDER!
© BEAVERBROOK NEWSPAPERS LTD. 1971
WHAT'RE YOU DRIVING AT, JAMES?
WELL, TAKE THE THEFT OF THOSE PAINTINGS FROM THE MANHATTAN MUSEUM... AND THE DISAPPEARANCE OF THE MUSEUM DIRECTOR
1615
IN BOTH CASES—THE HEAD OF AN OUTFIT ABSCONDS WITH SOMETHING OF GREAT VALUE—AND LATER TURNS UP DEAD!

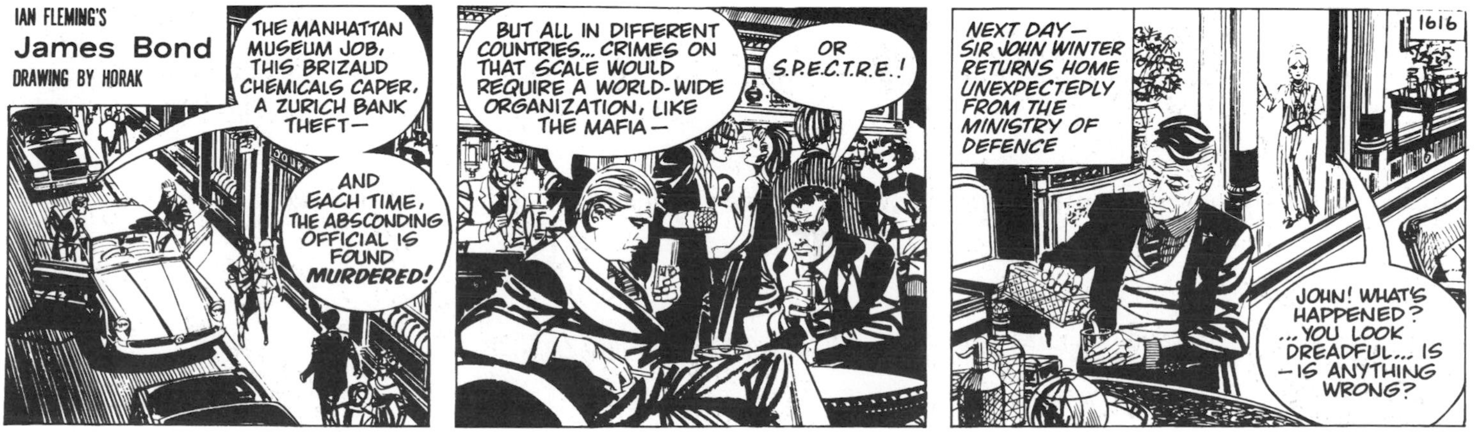
IAN FLEMING'S
James Bond
DRAWING BY HORAK
THE MANHATTAN MUSEUM JOB, THIS BRIZAUD CHEMICALS CAPER, A ZURICH BANK THEFT—
AND EACH TIME, THE ABSCONDING OFFICIAL IS FOUND MURDERED!
BUT ALL IN DIFFERENT COUNTRIES... CRIMES ON THAT SCALE WOULD REQUIRE A WORLD-WIDE ORGANIZATION, LIKE THE MAFIA—
OR S.P.E.C.T.R.E.!
NEXT DAY—SIR JOHN WINTER RETURNS HOME UNEXPECTEDLY FROM THE MINISTRY OF DEFENCE
1616
JOHN! WHAT'S HAPPENED? ...YOU LOOK DREADFUL... IS —IS ANYTHING WRONG?

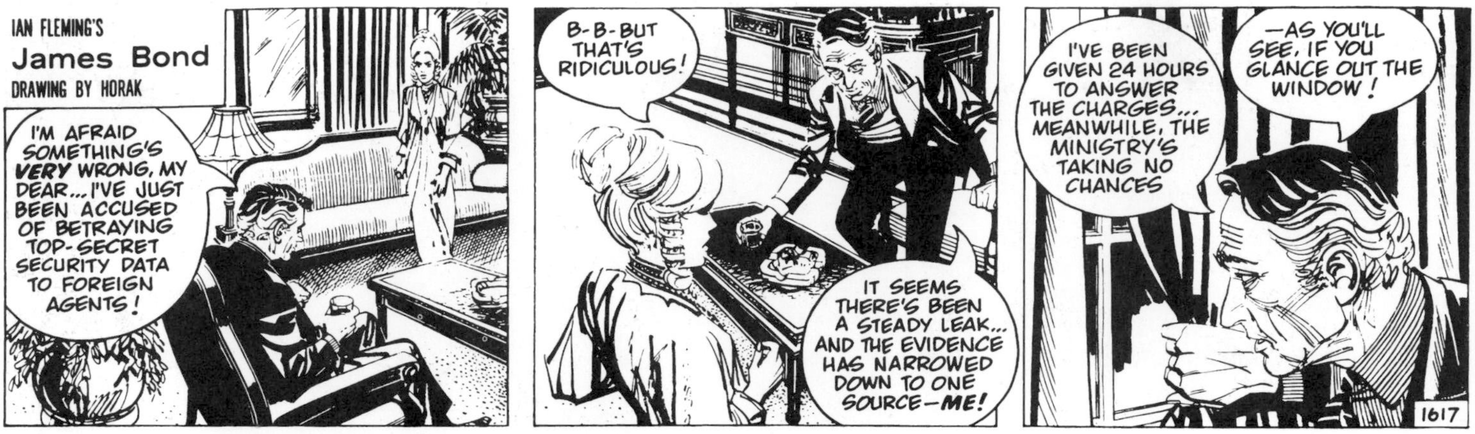
IAN FLEMING'S
James Bond
DRAWING BY HORAK
I'M AFRAID SOMETHING'S **VERY** WRONG, MY DEAR... I'VE JUST BEEN ACCUSED OF BETRAYING TOP-SECRET SECURITY DATA TO FOREIGN AGENTS!
B-B-BUT THAT'S RIDICULOUS!
IT SEEMS THERE'S BEEN A STEADY LEAK... AND THE EVIDENCE HAS NARROWED DOWN TO ONE SOURCE—**ME!**
I'VE BEEN GIVEN 24 HOURS TO ANSWER THE CHARGES... MEANWHILE, THE MINISTRY'S TAKING NO CHANCES
—AS YOU'LL SEE, IF YOU GLANCE OUT THE WINDOW!
1617

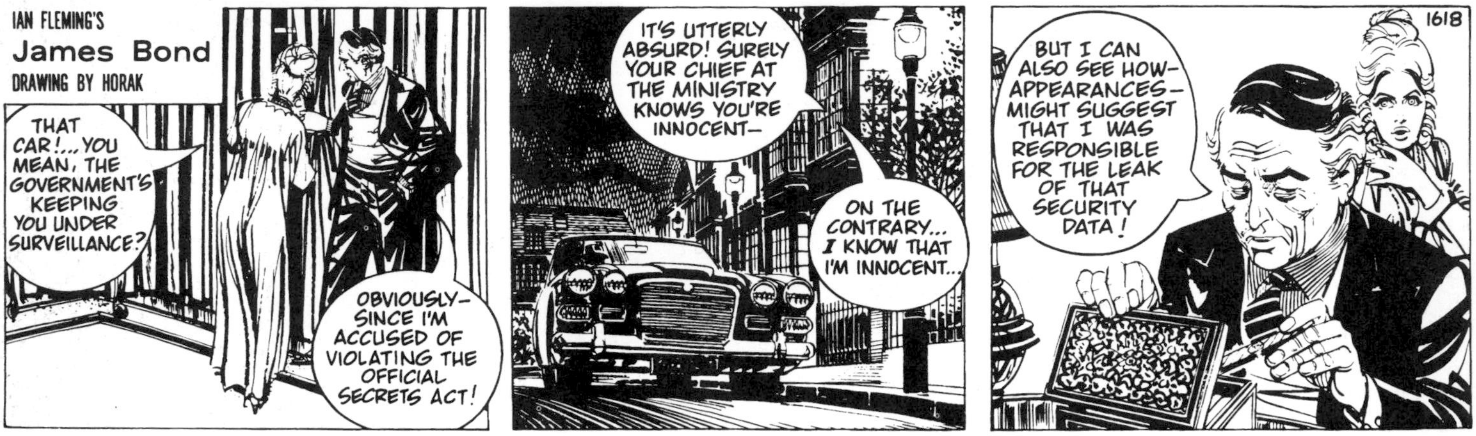
IAN FLEMING'S
James Bond
DRAWING BY HORAK
THAT CAR!... YOU MEAN, THE GOVERNMENT'S KEEPING YOU UNDER SURVEILLANCE?
OBVIOUSLY—SINCE I'M ACCUSED OF VIOLATING THE OFFICIAL SECRETS ACT!
IT'S UTTERLY ABSURD! SURELY YOUR CHIEF AT THE MINISTRY KNOWS YOU'RE INNOCENT—
ON THE CONTRARY... ***I*** KNOW THAT I'M INNOCENT...
1618
BUT I CAN ALSO SEE HOW—APPEARANCES—MIGHT SUGGEST THAT I WAS RESPONSIBLE FOR THE LEAK OF THAT SECURITY DATA!

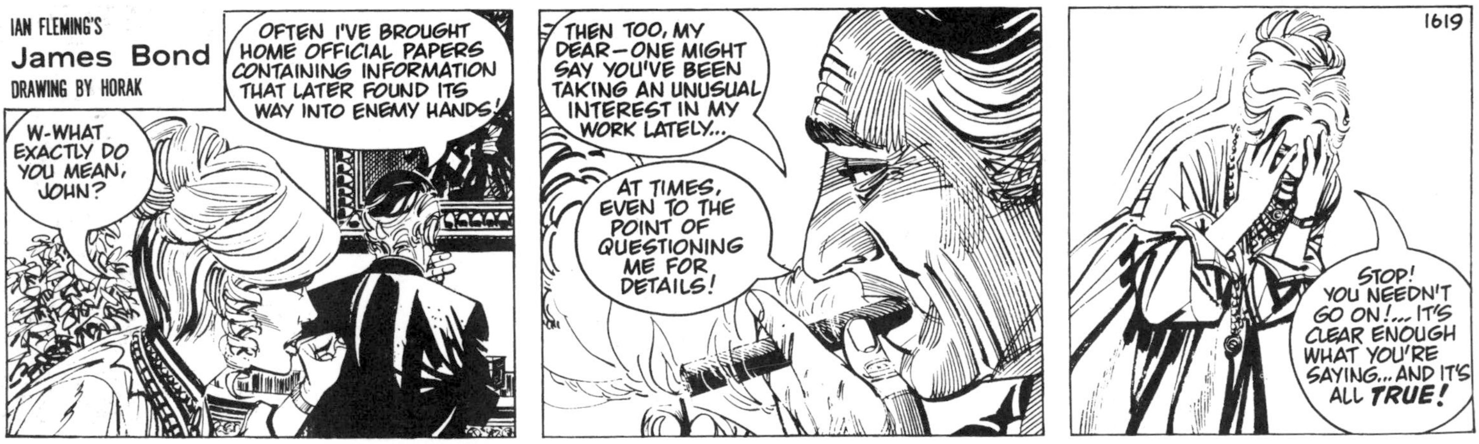
IAN FLEMING'S
James Bond
DRAWING BY HORAK
W-WHAT EXACTLY DO YOU MEAN, JOHN?
OFTEN I'VE BROUGHT HOME OFFICIAL PAPERS CONTAINING INFORMATION THAT LATER FOUND ITS WAY INTO ENEMY HANDS!
THEN TOO, MY DEAR—ONE MIGHT SAY YOU'VE BEEN TAKING AN UNUSUAL INTEREST IN MY WORK LATELY...
AT TIMES, EVEN TO THE POINT OF QUESTIONING ME FOR DETAILS!
1619
STOP! YOU NEEDN'T GO ON!... IT'S CLEAR ENOUGH WHAT YOU'RE SAYING... AND IT'S ALL **TRUE!**

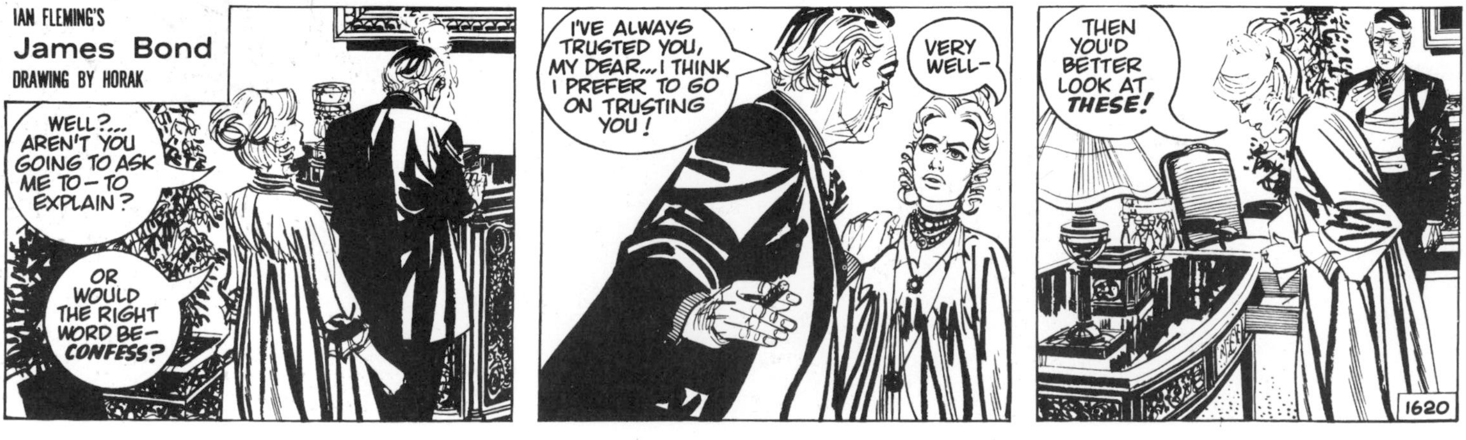
IAN FLEMING'S
James Bond
DRAWING BY HORAK
WELL?... AREN'T YOU GOING TO ASK ME TO—TO EXPLAIN?
OR WOULD THE RIGHT WORD BE—**CONFESS?**
I'VE ALWAYS TRUSTED YOU, MY DEAR... I THINK I PREFER TO GO ON TRUSTING YOU!
VERY WELL—
THEN YOU'D BETTER LOOK AT **THESE!**
1620

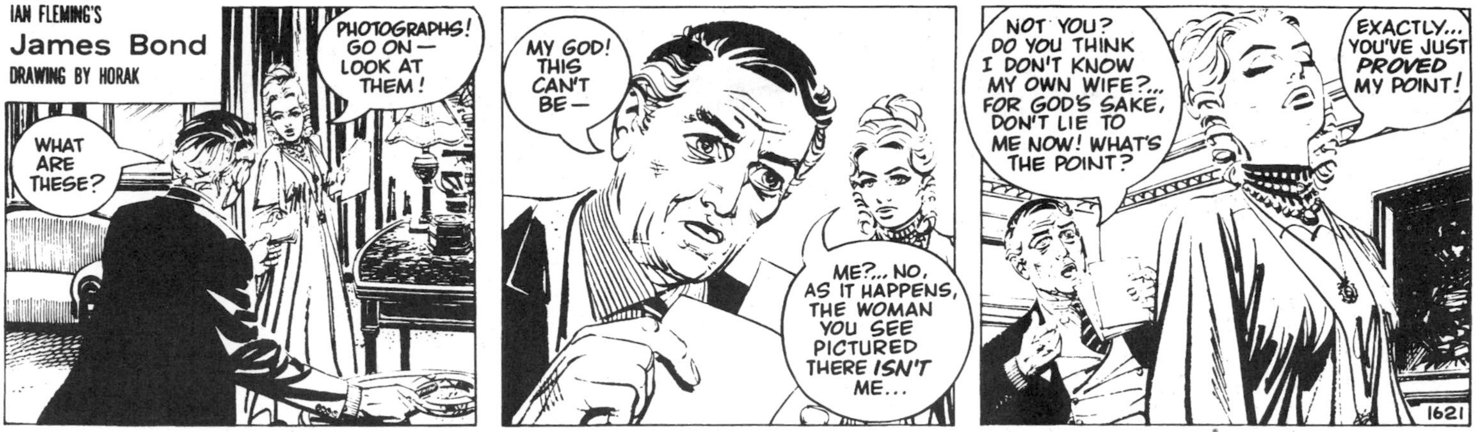
IAN FLEMING'S
James Bond
DRAWING BY HORAK
PHOTOGRAPHS! GO ON— LOOK AT THEM!
WHAT ARE THESE?
MY GOD! THIS CAN'T BE—
ME?... NO, AS IT HAPPENS, THE WOMAN YOU SEE PICTURED THERE ISN'T ME...
NOT YOU? DO YOU THINK I DON'T KNOW MY OWN WIFE?... FOR GOD'S SAKE, DON'T LIE TO ME NOW! WHAT'S THE POINT?
EXACTLY... YOU'VE JUST PROVED MY POINT!
1621

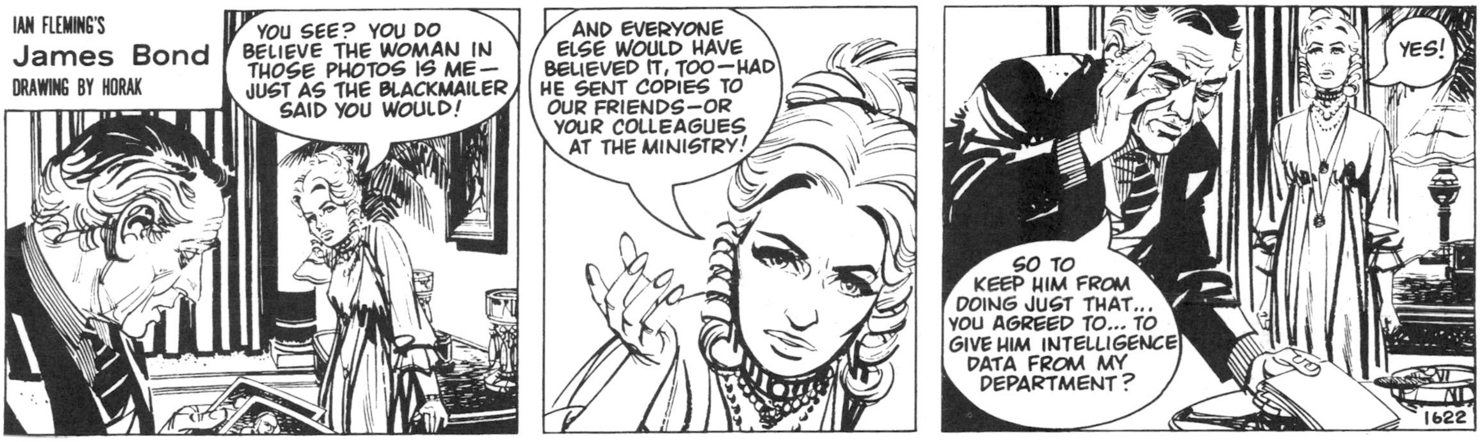
IAN FLEMING'S
James Bond
DRAWING BY HORAK
YOU SEE? YOU DO BELIEVE THE WOMAN IN THOSE PHOTOS IS ME— JUST AS THE BLACKMAILER SAID YOU WOULD!
AND EVERYONE ELSE WOULD HAVE BELIEVED IT, TOO—HAD HE SENT COPIES TO OUR FRIENDS—OR YOUR COLLEAGUES AT THE MINISTRY!
YES!
SO TO KEEP HIM FROM DOING JUST THAT... YOU AGREED TO... TO GIVE HIM INTELLIGENCE DATA FROM MY DEPARTMENT?
1622

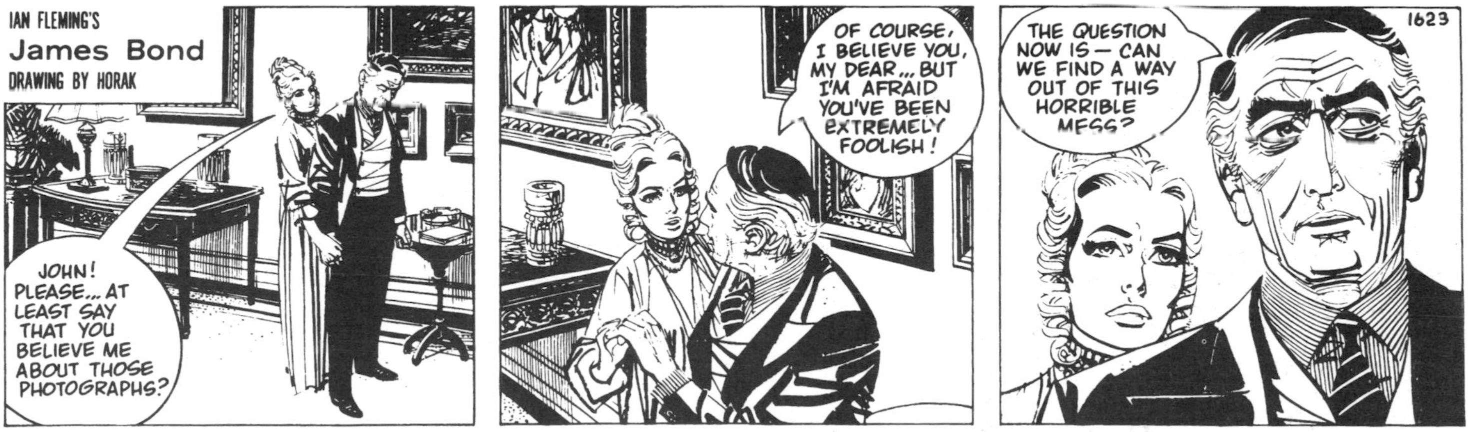
IAN FLEMING'S
James Bond
DRAWING BY HORAK
JOHN! PLEASE... AT LEAST SAY THAT YOU BELIEVE ME ABOUT THOSE PHOTOGRAPHS?
OF COURSE, I BELIEVE YOU, MY DEAR... BUT I'M AFRAID YOU'VE BEEN EXTREMELY FOOLISH!
1623
THE QUESTION NOW IS— CAN WE FIND A WAY OUT OF THIS HORRIBLE MESS?

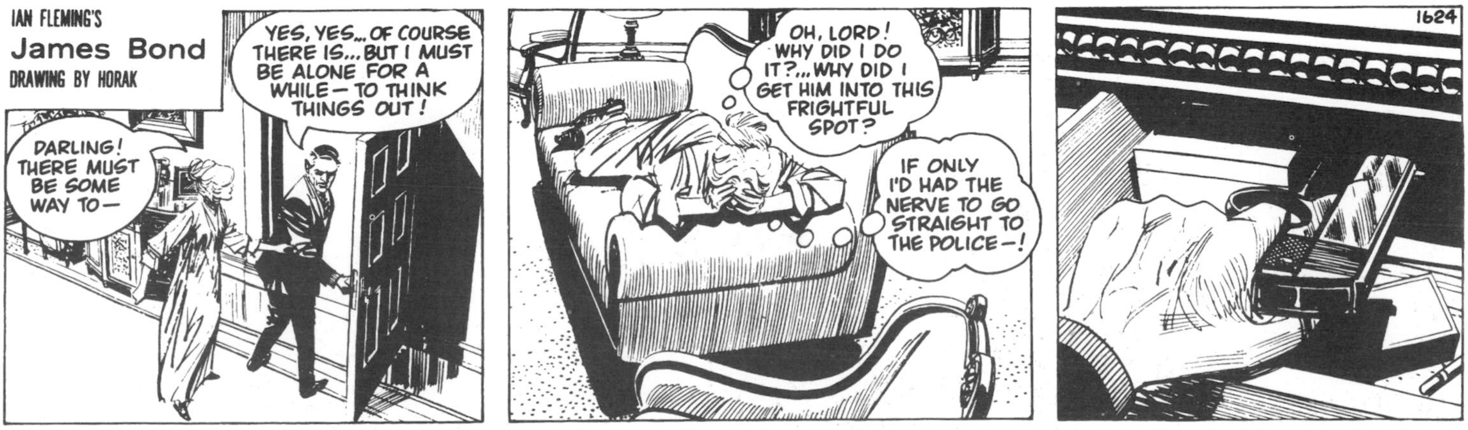
IAN FLEMING'S
James Bond
DRAWING BY HORAK
YES, YES... OF COURSE THERE IS... BUT I MUST BE ALONE FOR A WHILE— TO THINK THINGS OUT!
DARLING! THERE MUST BE SOME WAY TO—
OH, LORD! WHY DID I DO IT?... WHY DID I GET HIM INTO THIS FRIGHTFUL SPOT?
IF ONLY I'D HAD THE NERVE TO GO STRAIGHT TO THE POLICE—!
1624

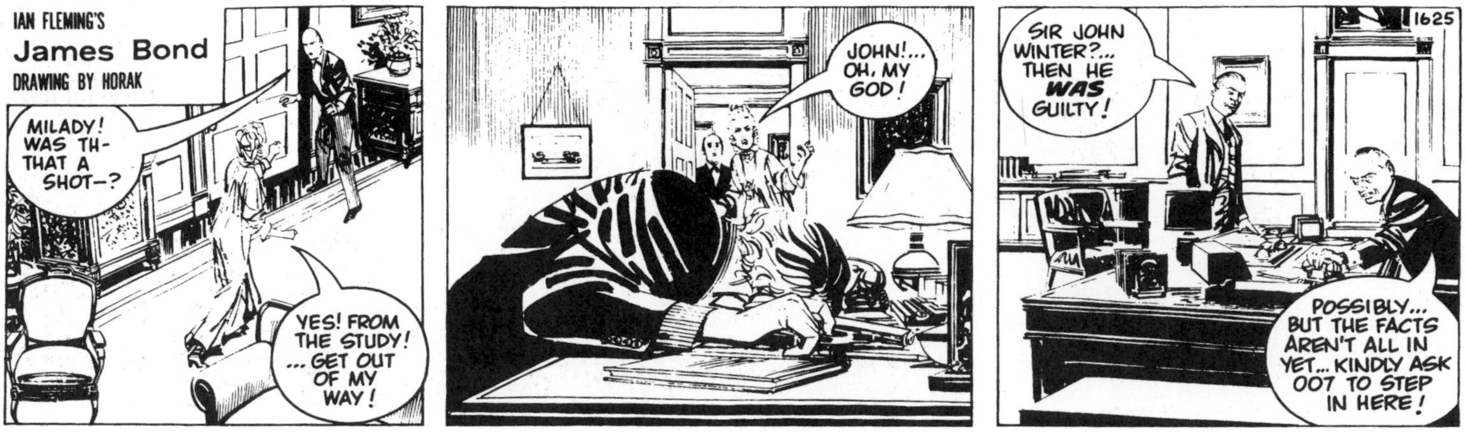
IAN FLEMING'S
James Bond
DRAWING BY HORAK
MILADY! WAS TH- THAT A SHOT–?
YES! FROM THE STUDY! ...GET OUT OF MY WAY!
JOHN!... OH, MY GOD!
1625
SIR JOHN WINTER?... THEN HE WAS GUILTY!
POSSIBLY... BUT THE FACTS AREN'T ALL IN YET... KINDLY ASK 007 TO STEP IN HERE!

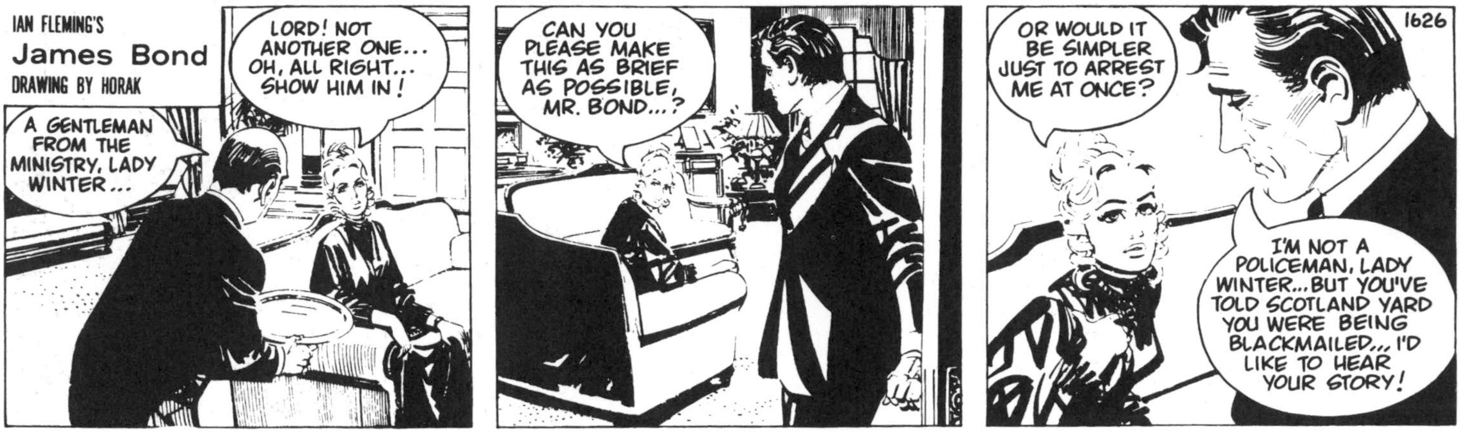
IAN FLEMING'S
James Bond
DRAWING BY HORAK
A GENTLEMAN FROM THE MINISTRY, LADY WINTER...
LORD! NOT ANOTHER ONE... OH, ALL RIGHT... SHOW HIM IN!
CAN YOU PLEASE MAKE THIS AS BRIEF AS POSSIBLE, MR. BOND...?
1626
OR WOULD IT BE SIMPLER JUST TO ARREST ME AT ONCE?
I'M NOT A POLICEMAN, LADY WINTER... BUT YOU'VE TOLD SCOTLAND YARD YOU WERE BEING BLACKMAILED... I'D LIKE TO HEAR YOUR STORY!

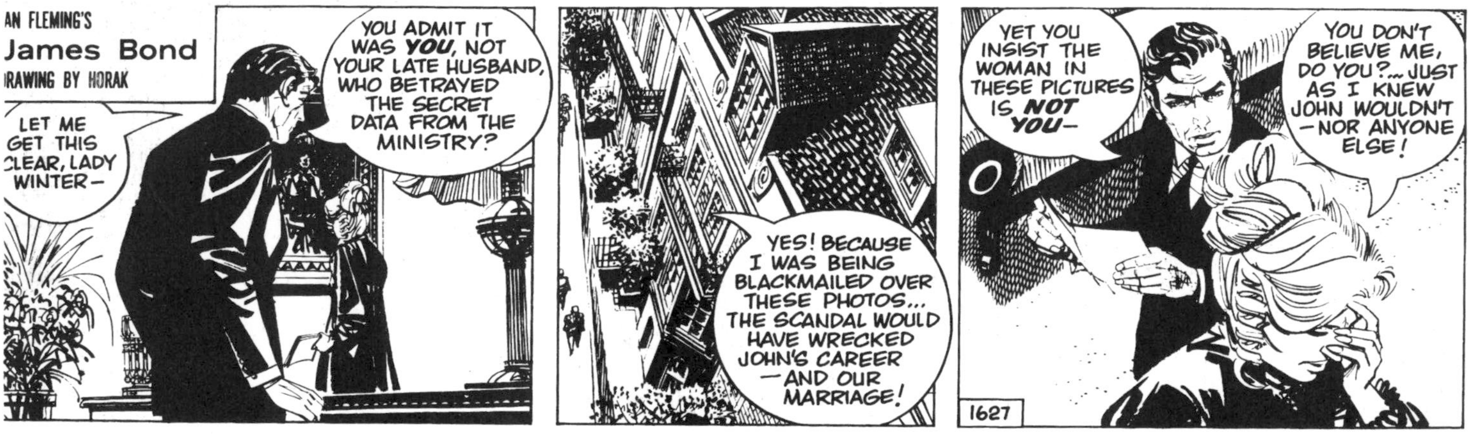
IAN FLEMING'S
James Bond
DRAWING BY HORAK
LET ME GET THIS CLEAR, LADY WINTER–
YOU ADMIT IT WAS YOU, NOT YOUR LATE HUSBAND, WHO BETRAYED THE SECRET DATA FROM THE MINISTRY?
YES! BECAUSE I WAS BEING BLACKMAILED OVER THESE PHOTOS... THE SCANDAL WOULD HAVE WRECKED JOHN'S CAREER —AND OUR MARRIAGE!
1627
YET YOU INSIST THE WOMAN IN THESE PICTURES IS NOT YOU–
YOU DON'T BELIEVE ME, DO YOU?... JUST AS I KNEW JOHN WOULDN'T —NOR ANYONE ELSE!

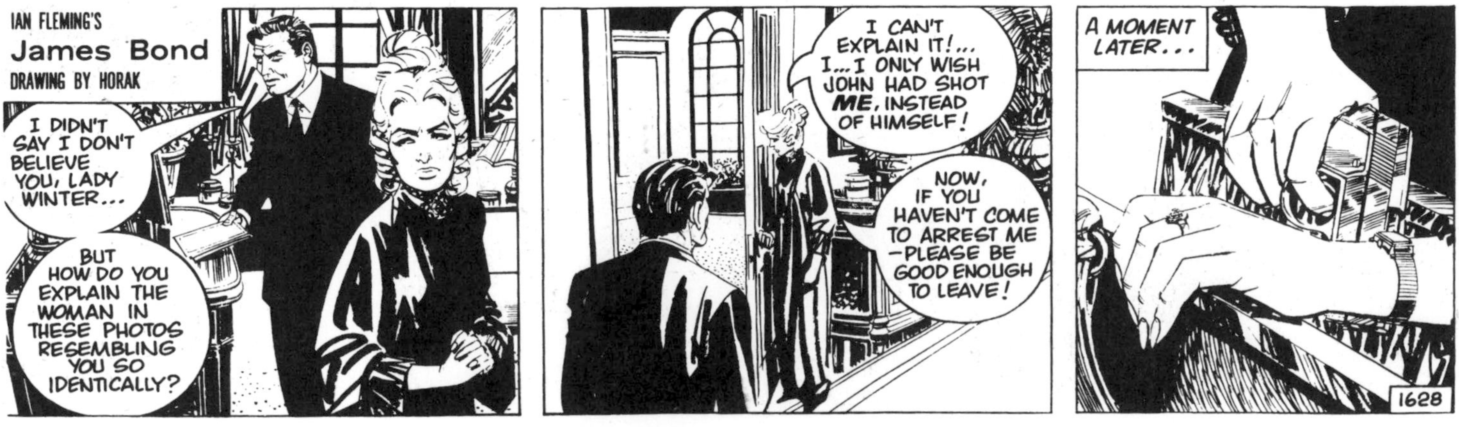
IAN FLEMING'S
James Bond
DRAWING BY HORAK
I DIDN'T SAY I DON'T BELIEVE YOU, LADY WINTER...
BUT HOW DO YOU EXPLAIN THE WOMAN IN THESE PHOTOS RESEMBLING YOU SO IDENTICALLY?
I CAN'T EXPLAIN IT!... I... I ONLY WISH JOHN HAD SHOT ME, INSTEAD OF HIMSELF!
NOW, IF YOU HAVEN'T COME TO ARREST ME —PLEASE BE GOOD ENOUGH TO LEAVE!
A MOMENT LATER...
1628

These pages have been produced from the best available original materials.

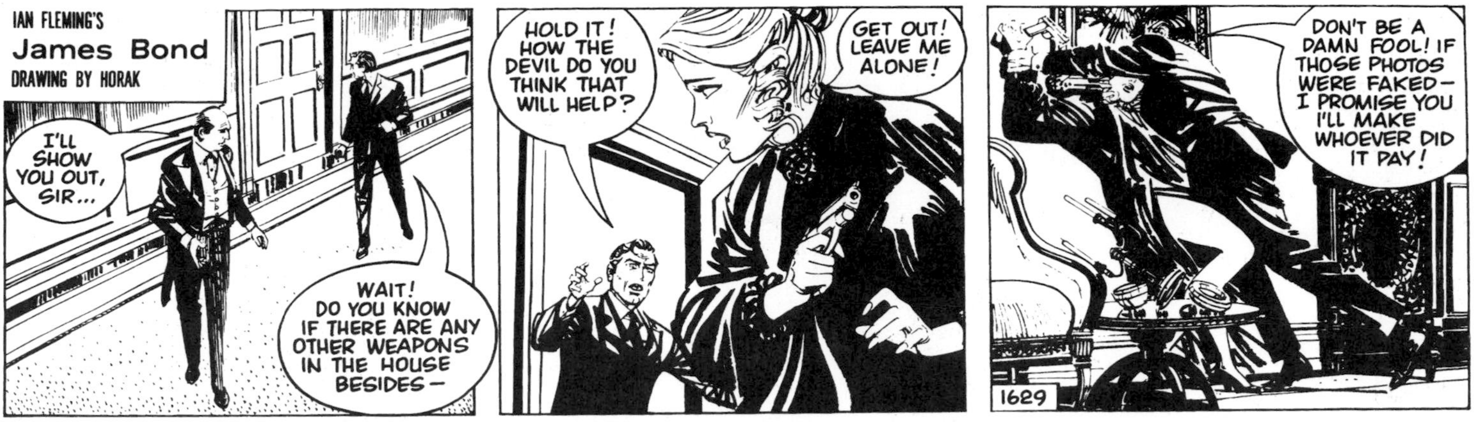
IAN FLEMING'S
James Bond
DRAWING BY HORAK
I'LL SHOW YOU OUT, SIR...
WAIT! DO YOU KNOW IF THERE ARE ANY OTHER WEAPONS IN THE HOUSE BESIDES—
HOLD IT! HOW THE DEVIL DO YOU THINK THAT WILL HELP?
GET OUT! LEAVE ME ALONE!
DON'T BE A DAMN FOOL! IF THOSE PHOTOS WERE FAKED— I PROMISE YOU I'LL MAKE WHOEVER DID IT PAY!
1629

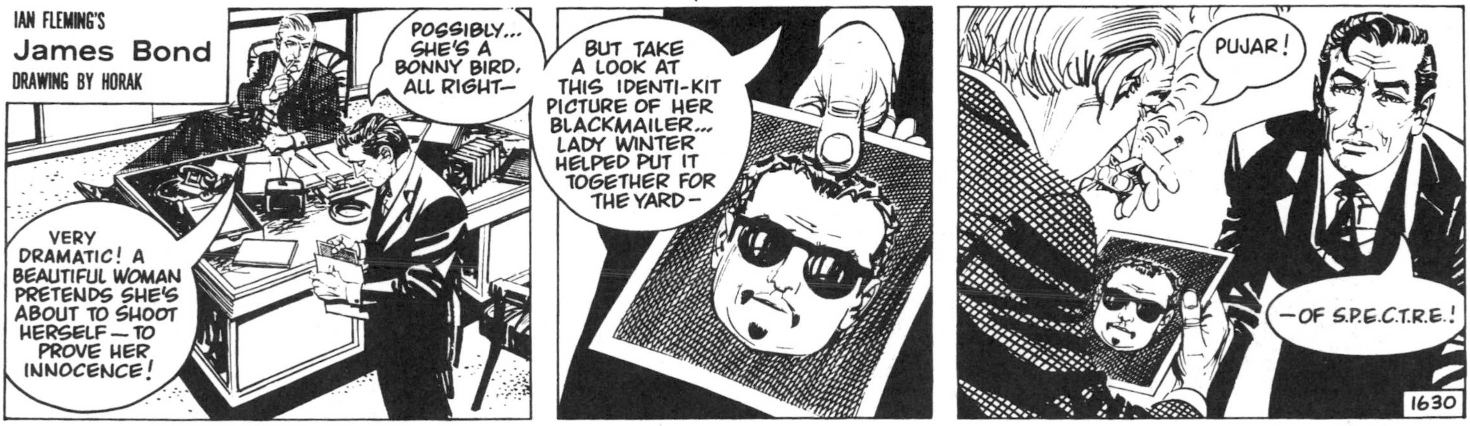
IAN FLEMING'S
James Bond
DRAWING BY HORAK
POSSIBLY... SHE'S A BONNY BIRD, ALL RIGHT—
VERY DRAMATIC! A BEAUTIFUL WOMAN PRETENDS SHE'S ABOUT TO SHOOT HERSELF—TO PROVE HER INNOCENCE!
BUT TAKE A LOOK AT THIS IDENTI-KIT PICTURE OF HER BLACKMAILER... LADY WINTER HELPED PUT IT TOGETHER FOR THE YARD—
PUJAR!
—OF S.P.E.C.T.R.E.!
1630

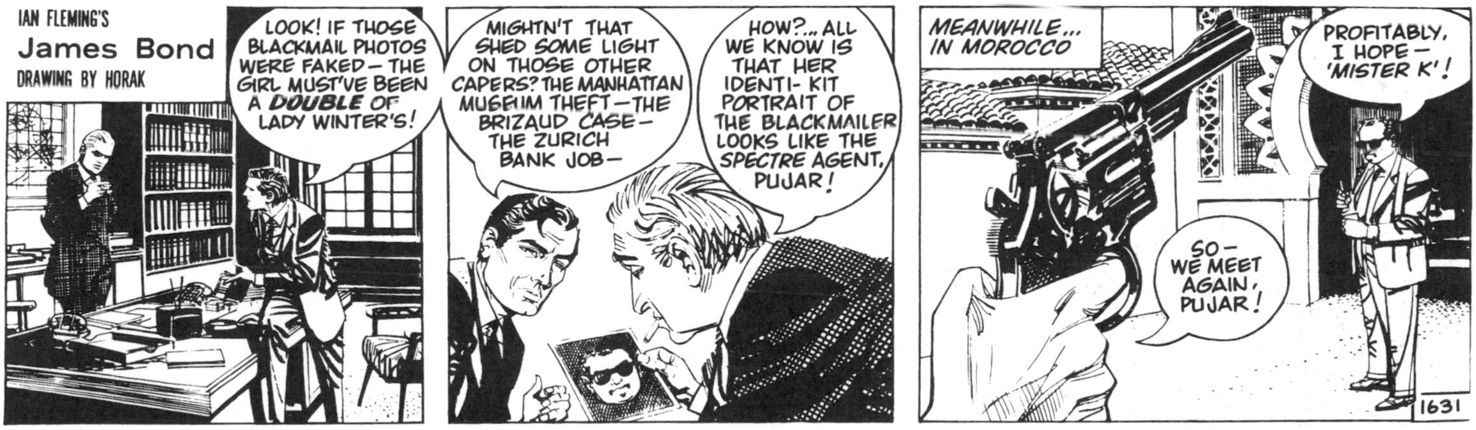
IAN FLEMING'S
James Bond
DRAWING BY HORAK
LOOK! IF THOSE BLACKMAIL PHOTOS WERE FAKED—THE GIRL MUST'VE BEEN A DOUBLE OF LADY WINTER'S!
MIGHTN'T THAT SHED SOME LIGHT ON THOSE OTHER CAPERS? THE MANHATTAN MUSEUM THEFT—THE BRIZAUD CASE—THE ZURICH BANK JOB—
HOW?... ALL WE KNOW IS THAT HER IDENTI-KIT PORTRAIT OF THE BLACKMAILER LOOKS LIKE THE SPECTRE AGENT, PUJAR!
MEANWHILE... IN MOROCCO
PROFITABLY, I HOPE—'MISTER K'!
SO—WE MEET AGAIN, PUJAR!
1631

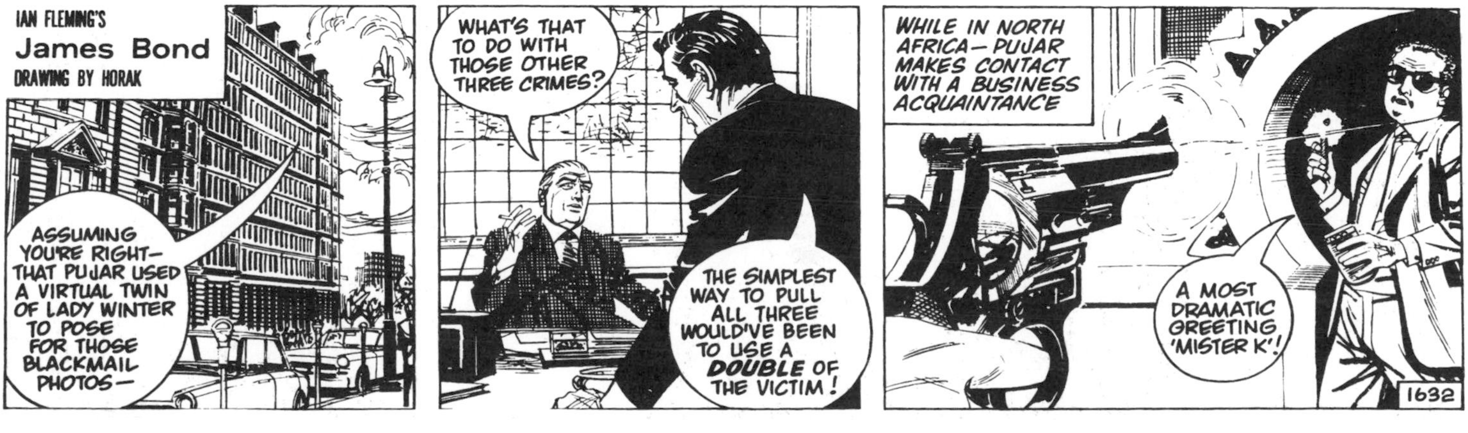
IAN FLEMING'S
James Bond
DRAWING BY HORAK
ASSUMING YOU'RE RIGHT—THAT PUJAR USED A VIRTUAL TWIN OF LADY WINTER TO POSE FOR THOSE BLACKMAIL PHOTOS—
WHAT'S THAT TO DO WITH THOSE OTHER THREE CRIMES?
THE SIMPLEST WAY TO PULL ALL THREE WOULD'VE BEEN TO USE A DOUBLE OF THE VICTIM!
WHILE IN NORTH AFRICA—PUJAR MAKES CONTACT WITH A BUSINESS ACQUAINTANCE
A MOST DRAMATIC GREETING, 'MISTER K'!
1632

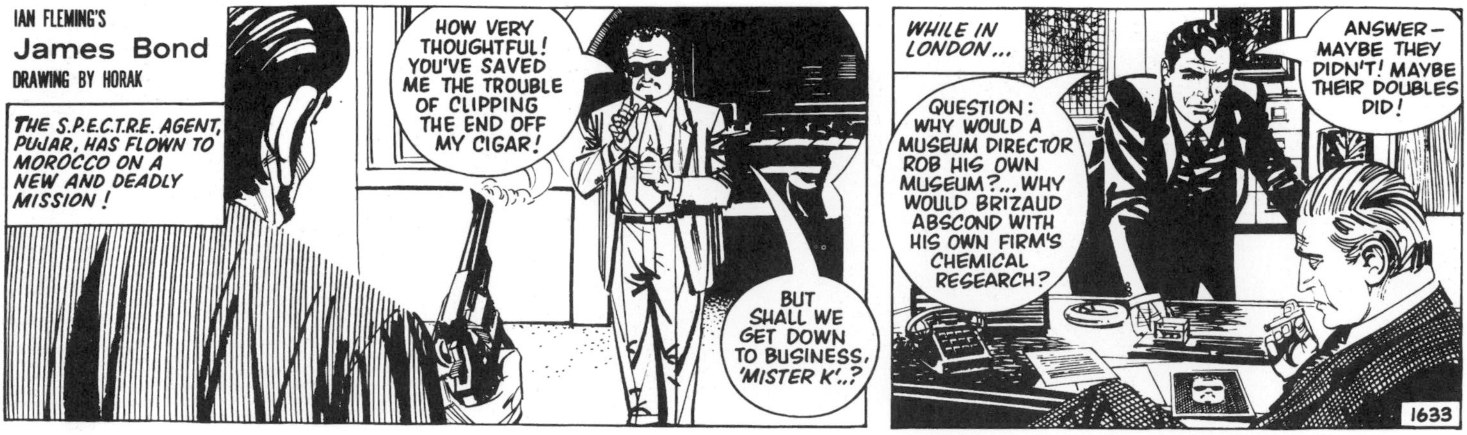
IAN FLEMING'S
James Bond
DRAWING BY HORAK
THE S.P.E.C.T.R.E. AGENT, PUJAR, HAS FLOWN TO MOROCCO ON A NEW AND DEADLY MISSION!
HOW VERY THOUGHTFUL! YOU'VE SAVED ME THE TROUBLE OF CLIPPING THE END OFF MY CIGAR!
BUT SHALL WE GET DOWN TO BUSINESS, 'MISTER K'..?
WHILE IN LONDON...
QUESTION: WHY WOULD A MUSEUM DIRECTOR ROB HIS OWN MUSEUM?... WHY WOULD BRIZAUD ABSCOND WITH HIS OWN FIRM'S CHEMICAL RESEARCH?
ANSWER – MAYBE THEY DIDN'T! MAYBE THEIR DOUBLES DID!
1633

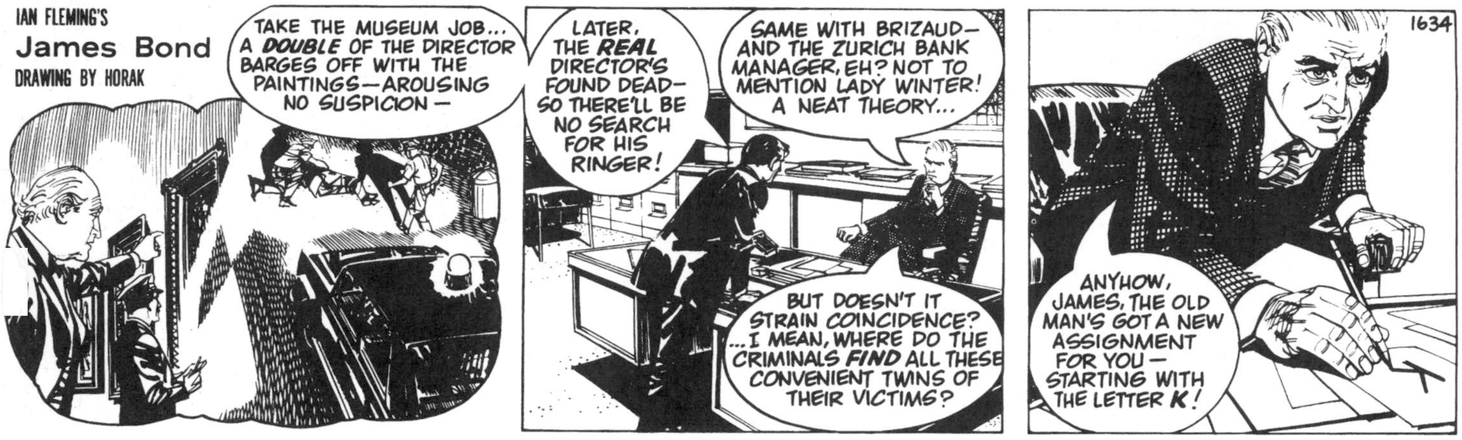
IAN FLEMING'S
James Bond
DRAWING BY HORAK
TAKE THE MUSEUM JOB... A DOUBLE OF THE DIRECTOR BARGES OFF WITH THE PAINTINGS—AROUSING NO SUSPICION—
LATER, THE REAL DIRECTOR'S FOUND DEAD-SO THERE'LL BE NO SEARCH FOR HIS RINGER!
SAME WITH BRIZAUD-AND THE ZURICH BANK MANAGER, EH? NOT TO MENTION LADY WINTER! A NEAT THEORY...
BUT DOESN'T IT STRAIN COINCIDENCE? ...I MEAN, WHERE DO THE CRIMINALS FIND ALL THESE CONVENIENT TWINS OF THEIR VICTIMS?
1634
ANYHOW, JAMES, THE OLD MAN'S GOT A NEW ASSIGNMENT FOR YOU – STARTING WITH THE LETTER K!

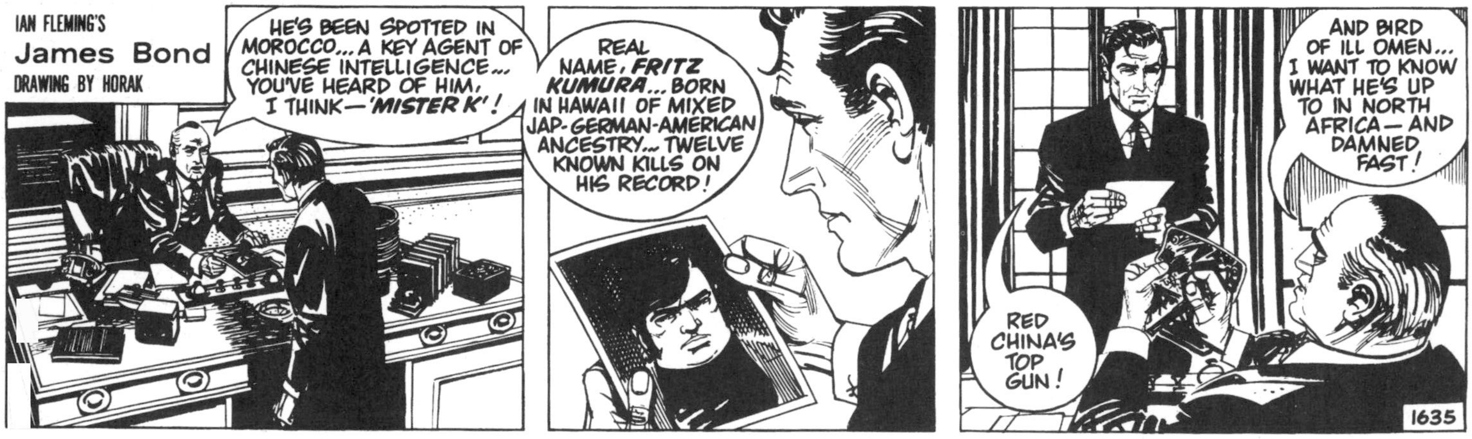
IAN FLEMING'S
James Bond
DRAWING BY HORAK
HE'S BEEN SPOTTED IN MOROCCO... A KEY AGENT OF CHINESE INTELLIGENCE... YOU'VE HEARD OF HIM, I THINK—'MISTER K'!
REAL NAME, FRITZ KUMURA... BORN IN HAWAII OF MIXED JAP-GERMAN-AMERICAN ANCESTRY... TWELVE KNOWN KILLS ON HIS RECORD!
RED CHINA'S TOP GUN!
AND BIRD OF ILL OMEN... I WANT TO KNOW WHAT HE'S UP TO IN NORTH AFRICA—AND DAMNED FAST!
1635

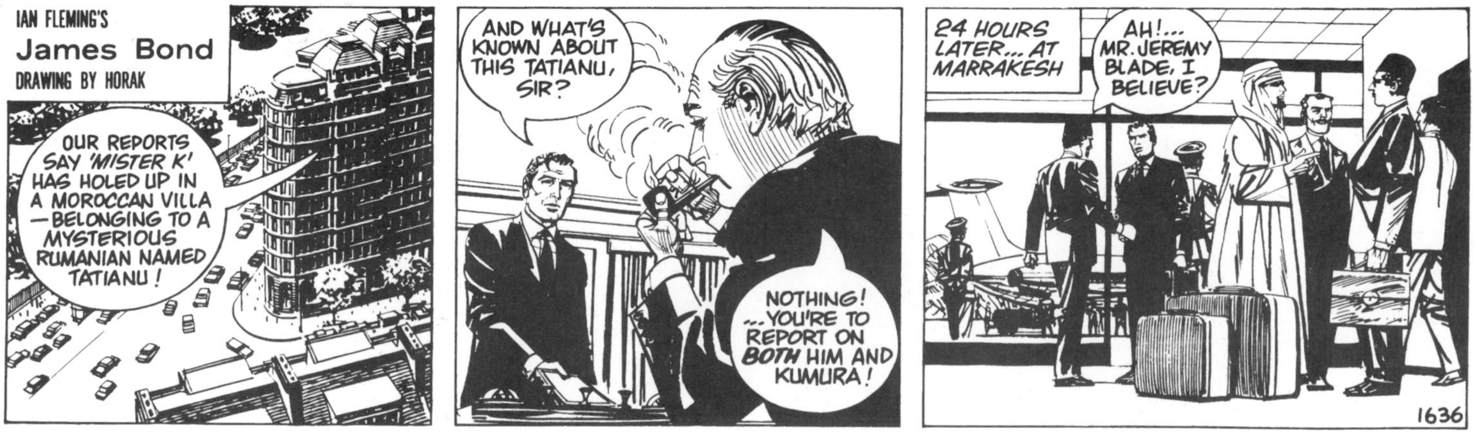
IAN FLEMING'S
James Bond
DRAWING BY HORAK
OUR REPORTS SAY 'MISTER K' HAS HOLED UP IN A MOROCCAN VILLA—BELONGING TO A MYSTERIOUS RUMANIAN NAMED TATIANU!
AND WHAT'S KNOWN ABOUT THIS TATIANU, SIR?
NOTHING! ...YOU'RE TO REPORT ON BOTH HIM AND KUMURA!
24 HOURS LATER... AT MARRAKESH
AH!... MR. JEREMY BLADE, I BELIEVE?
1636

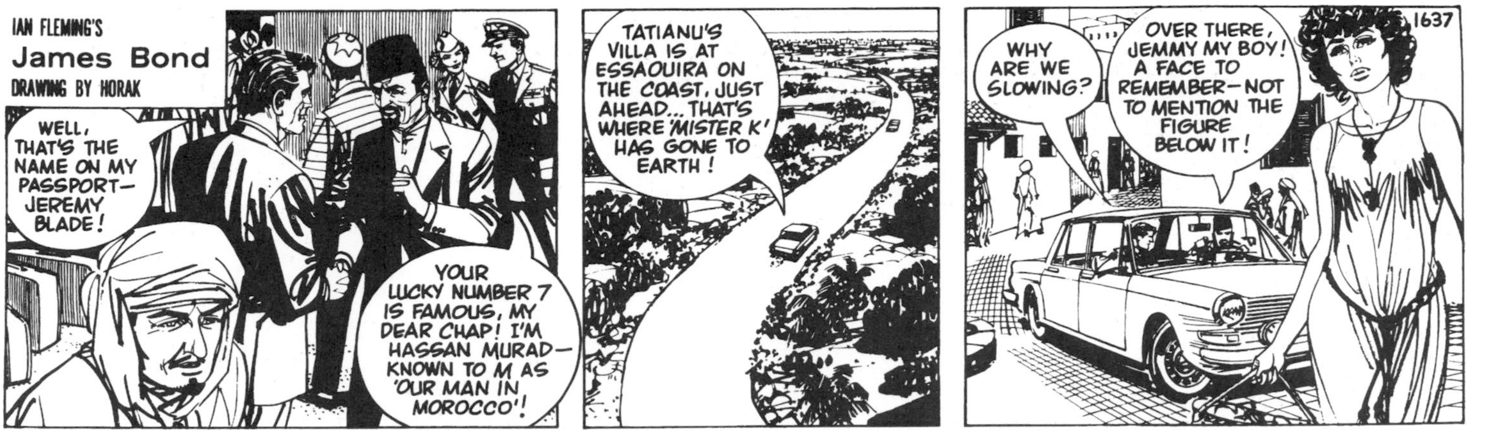
IAN FLEMING'S
James Bond
DRAWING BY HORAK
WELL, THAT'S THE NAME ON MY PASSPORT—JEREMY BLADE!
YOUR LUCKY NUMBER 7 IS FAMOUS, MY DEAR CHAP! I'M HASSAN MURAD—KNOWN TO M AS 'OUR MAN IN MOROCCO'!
TATIANU'S VILLA IS AT ESSAOUIRA ON THE COAST, JUST AHEAD... THAT'S WHERE 'MISTER K' HAS GONE TO EARTH!
1637
WHY ARE WE SLOWING?
OVER THERE, JEMMY MY BOY! A FACE TO REMEMBER—NOT TO MENTION THE FIGURE BELOW IT!

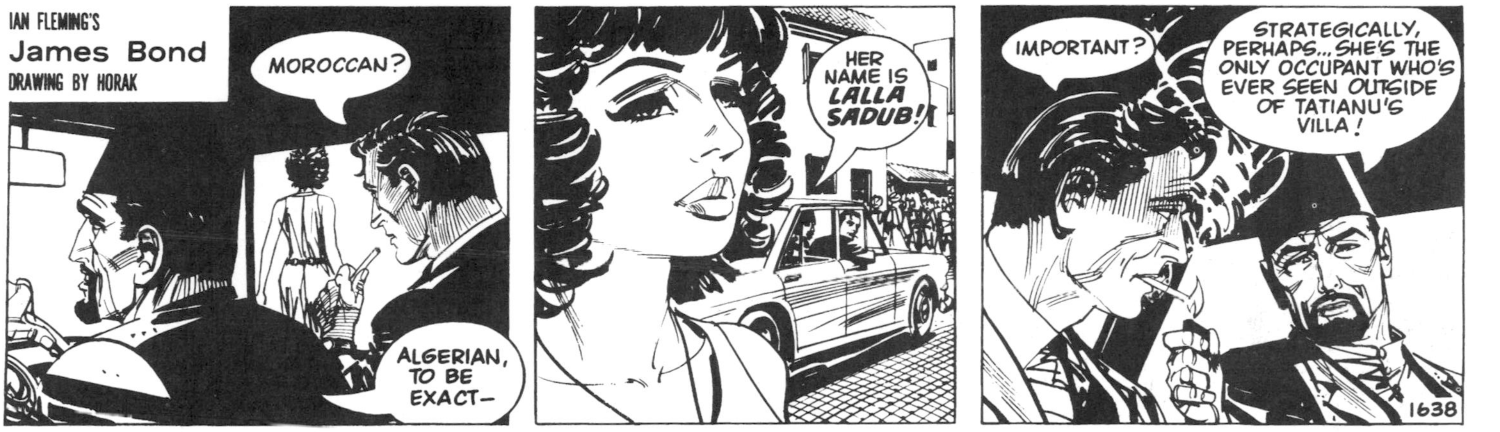
IAN FLEMING'S
James Bond
DRAWING BY HORAK
MOROCCAN?
ALGERIAN, TO BE EXACT—
HER NAME IS LALLA SADUB!
IMPORTANT?
STRATEGICALLY, PERHAPS... SHE'S THE ONLY OCCUPANT WHO'S EVER SEEN OUTSIDE OF TATIANU'S VILLA!
1638

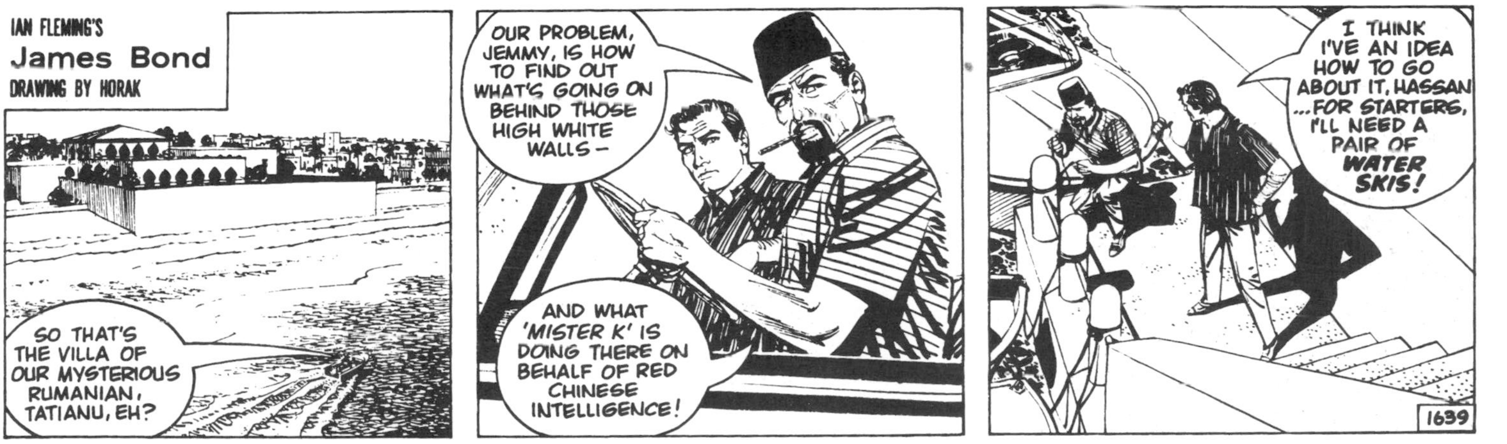
IAN FLEMING'S
James Bond
DRAWING BY HORAK
SO THAT'S THE VILLA OF OUR MYSTERIOUS RUMANIAN, TATIANU, EH?
OUR PROBLEM, JEMMY, IS HOW TO FIND OUT WHAT'S GOING ON BEHIND THOSE HIGH WHITE WALLS—
AND WHAT 'MISTER K' IS DOING THERE ON BEHALF OF RED CHINESE INTELLIGENCE!
I THINK I'VE AN IDEA HOW TO GO ABOUT IT, HASSAN ...FOR STARTERS, I'LL NEED A PAIR OF WATER SKIS!
1639

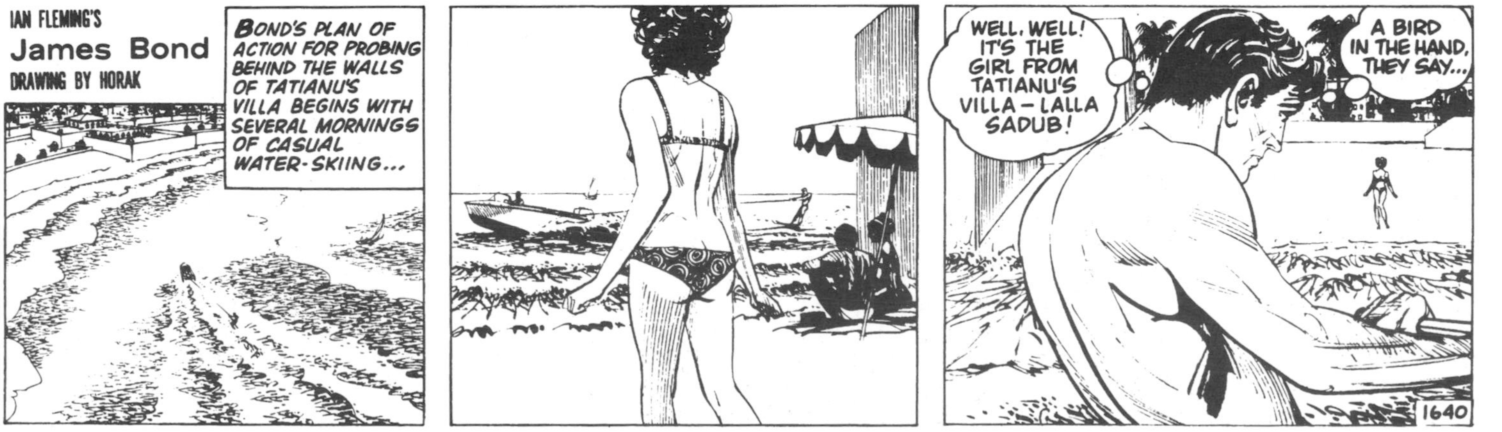
IAN FLEMING'S
James Bond
DRAWING BY HORAK
BOND'S PLAN OF ACTION FOR PROBING BEHIND THE WALLS OF TATIANU'S VILLA BEGINS WITH SEVERAL MORNINGS OF CASUAL WATER-SKIING...
WELL, WELL! IT'S THE GIRL FROM TATIANU'S VILLA—LALLA SADUB!
A BIRD IN THE HAND, THEY SAY...
1640

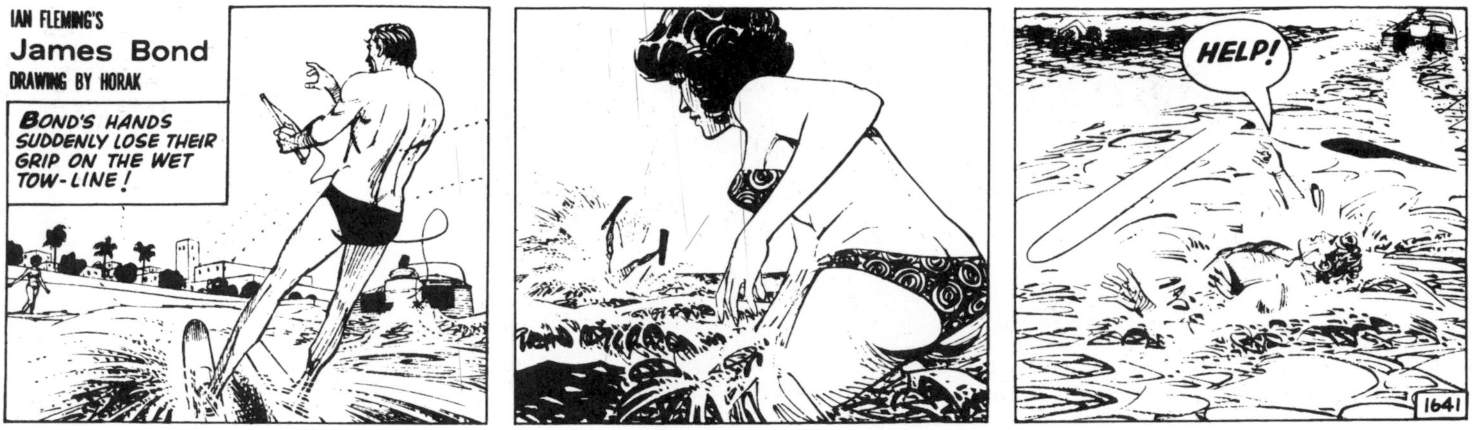
IAN FLEMING'S
James Bond
DRAWING BY HORAK
BOND'S HANDS SUDDENLY LOSE THEIR GRIP ON THE WET TOW-LINE!
HELP!
1641

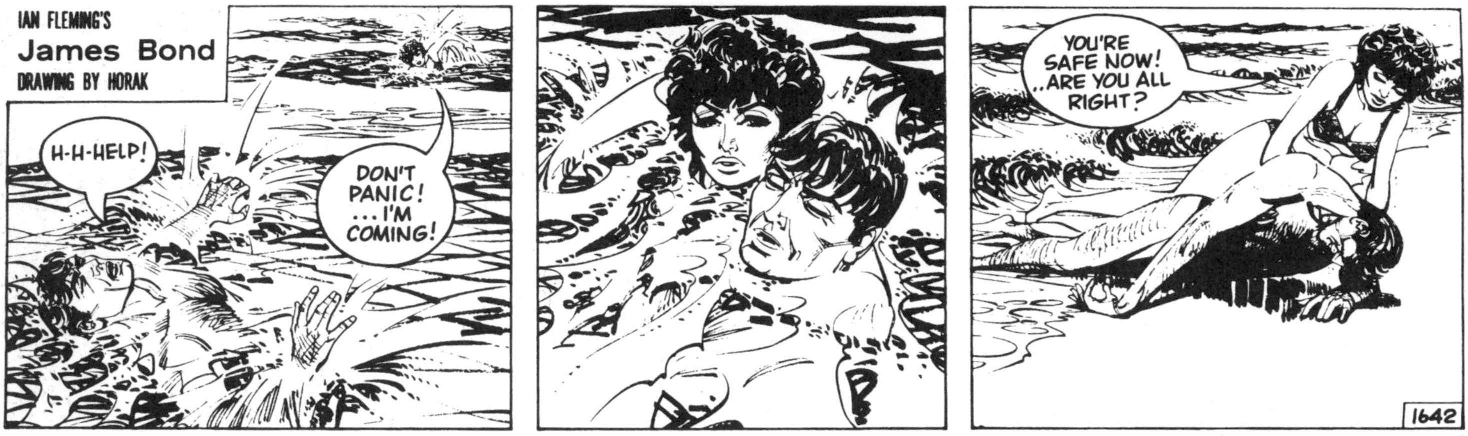
IAN FLEMING'S
James Bond
DRAWING BY HORAK
H-H-HELP!
DON'T PANIC! ...I'M COMING!
YOU'RE SAFE NOW! ..ARE YOU ALL RIGHT?
1642

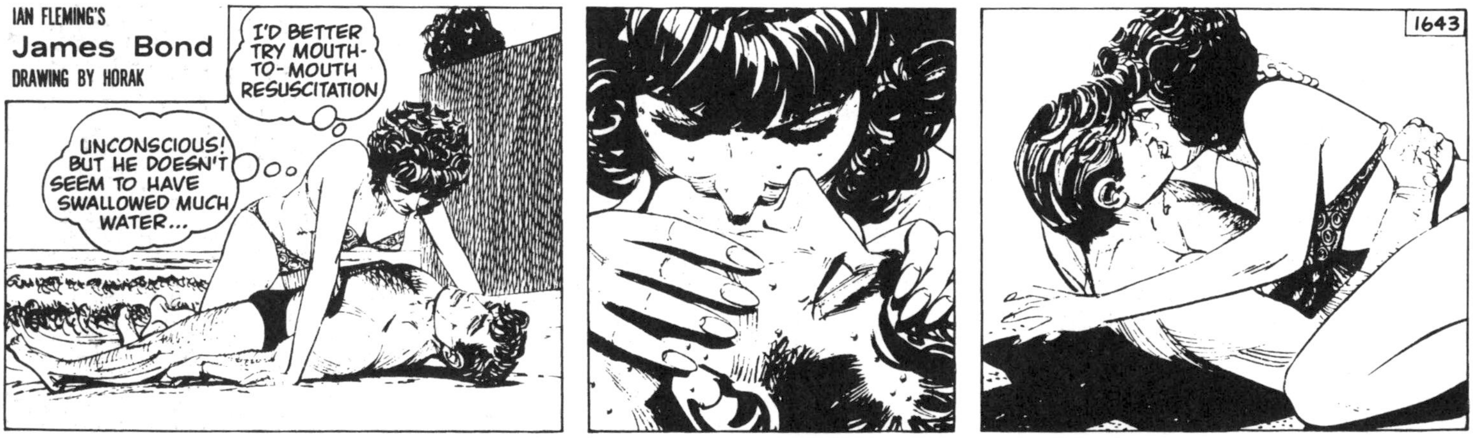
IAN FLEMING'S
James Bond
DRAWING BY HORAK
I'D BETTER TRY MOUTH-TO-MOUTH RESUSCITATION
UNCONSCIOUS! BUT HE DOESN'T SEEM TO HAVE SWALLOWED MUCH WATER...
1643

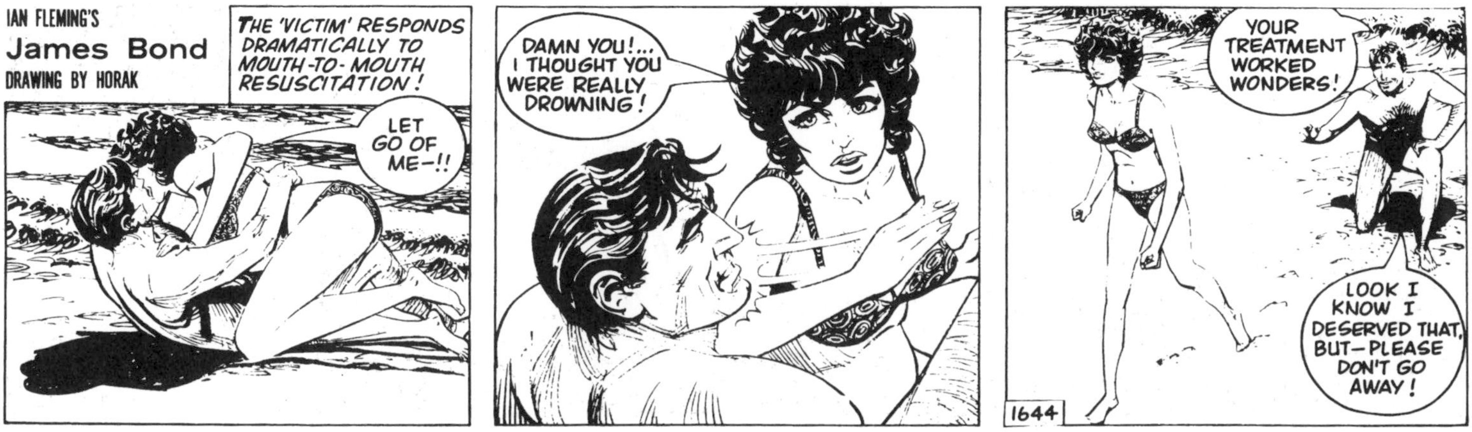
IAN FLEMING'S
James Bond
DRAWING BY HORAK
THE 'VICTIM' RESPONDS DRAMATICALLY TO MOUTH-TO-MOUTH RESUSCITATION!
LET GO OF ME-!!
DAMN YOU!... I THOUGHT YOU WERE REALLY DROWNING!
YOUR TREATMENT WORKED WONDERS!
LOOK I KNOW I DESERVED THAT, BUT-PLEASE DON'T GO AWAY!
1644

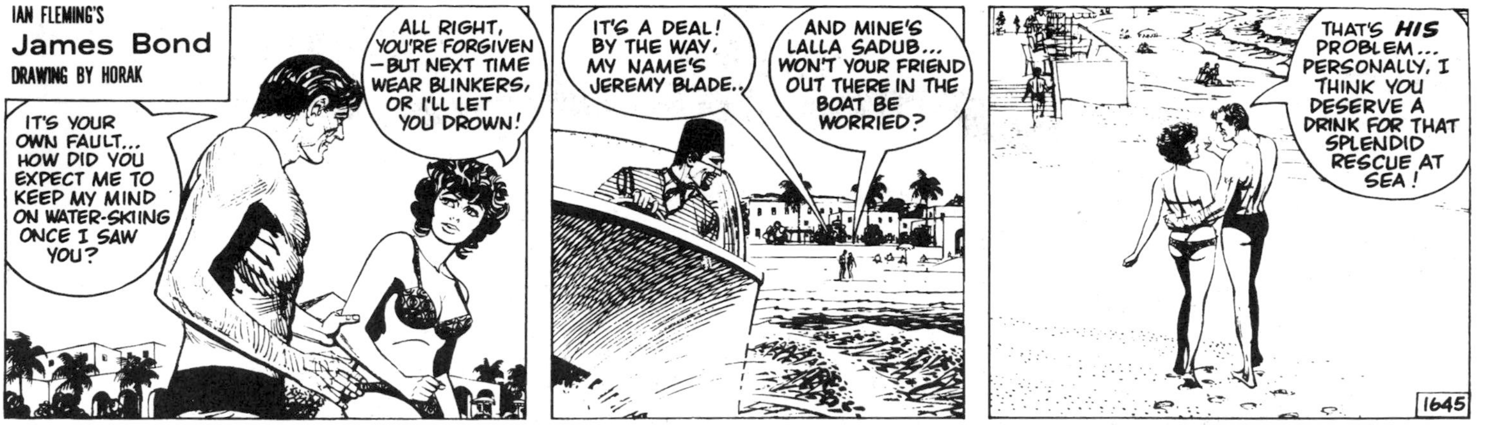
IAN FLEMING'S
James Bond
DRAWING BY HORAK
IT'S YOUR OWN FAULT... HOW DID YOU EXPECT ME TO KEEP MY MIND ON WATER-SKIING ONCE I SAW YOU?
ALL RIGHT, YOU'RE FORGIVEN —BUT NEXT TIME WEAR BLINKERS, OR I'LL LET YOU DROWN!
IT'S A DEAL! BY THE WAY, MY NAME'S JEREMY BLADE..
AND MINE'S LALLA SADUB... WON'T YOUR FRIEND OUT THERE IN THE BOAT BE WORRIED?
THAT'S HIS PROBLEM... PERSONALLY, I THINK YOU DESERVE A DRINK FOR THAT SPLENDID RESCUE AT SEA!
1645

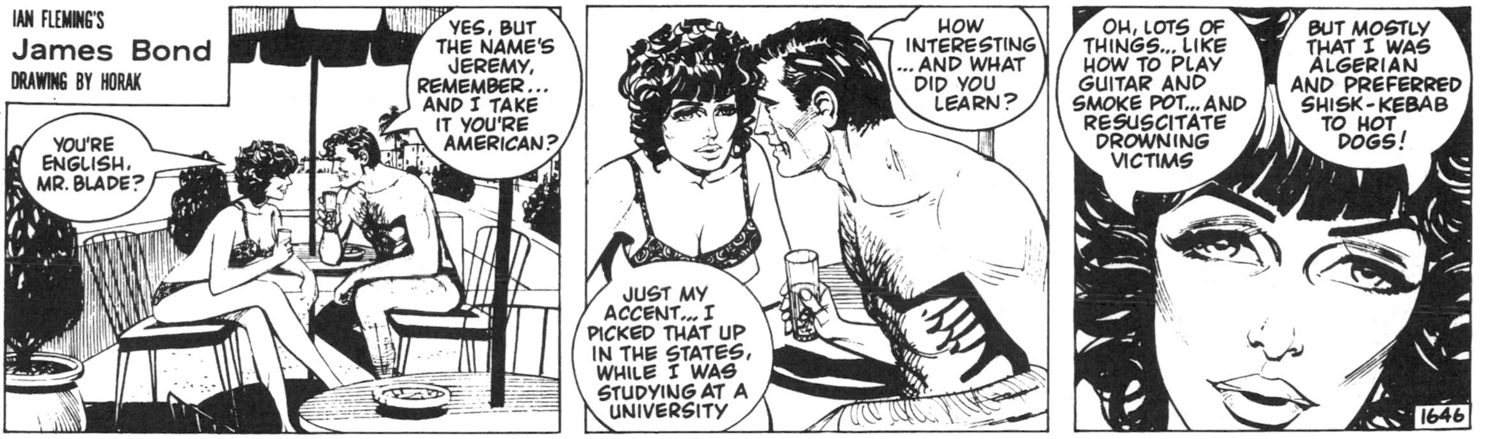
IAN FLEMING'S
James Bond
DRAWING BY HORAK
YOU'RE ENGLISH, MR. BLADE?
YES, BUT THE NAME'S JEREMY, REMEMBER... AND I TAKE IT YOU'RE AMERICAN?
JUST MY ACCENT... I PICKED THAT UP IN THE STATES, WHILE I WAS STUDYING AT A UNIVERSITY
HOW INTERESTING ...AND WHAT DID YOU LEARN?
OH, LOTS OF THINGS... LIKE HOW TO PLAY GUITAR AND SMOKE POT... AND RESUSCITATE DROWNING VICTIMS
BUT MOSTLY THAT I WAS ALGERIAN AND PREFERRED SHISK-KEBAB TO HOT DOGS!
1646

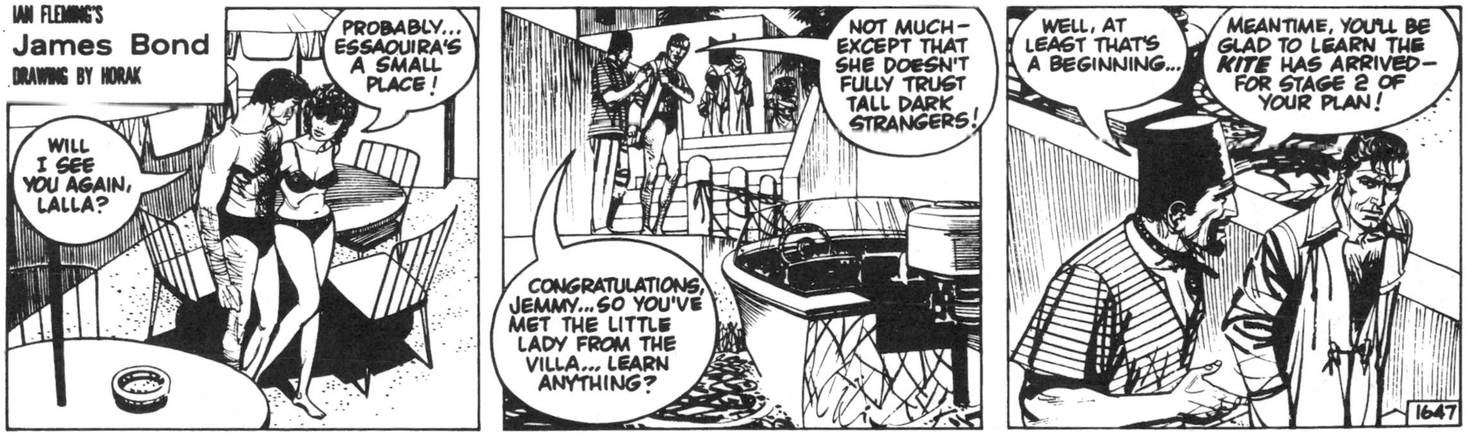
IAN FLEMING'S
James Bond
DRAWING BY HORAK
WILL I SEE YOU AGAIN, LALLA?
PROBABLY... ESSAQUIRA'S A SMALL PLACE!
CONGRATULATIONS, JEMMY... SO YOU'VE MET THE LITTLE LADY FROM THE VILLA... LEARN ANYTHING?
NOT MUCH— EXCEPT THAT SHE DOESN'T FULLY TRUST TALL DARK STRANGERS!
WELL, AT LEAST THAT'S A BEGINNING...
MEANTIME, YOU'LL BE GLAD TO LEARN THE KITE HAS ARRIVED— FOR STAGE 2 OF YOUR PLAN!
1647

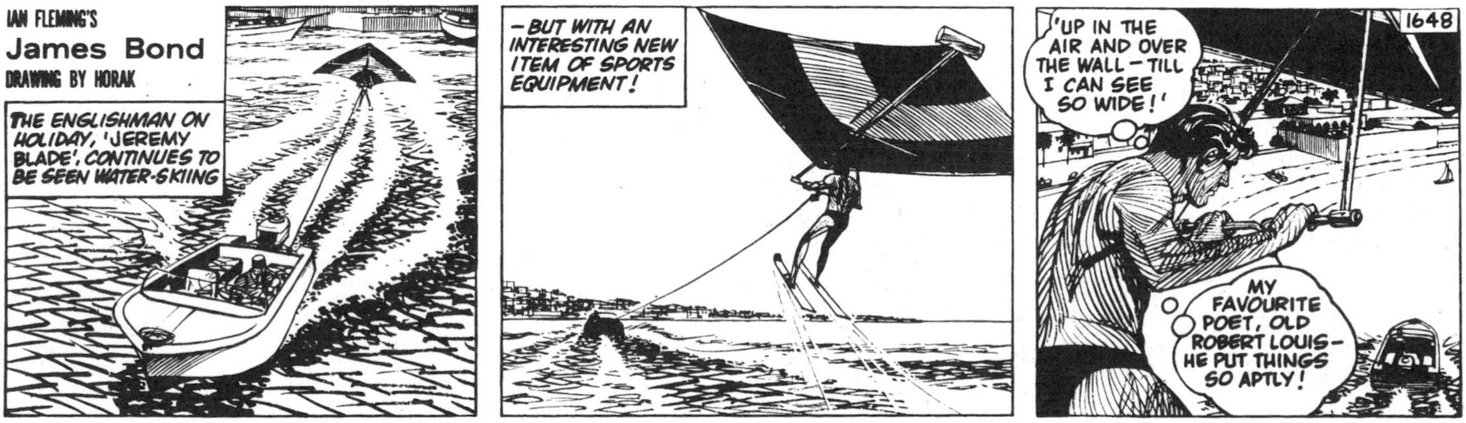
IAN FLEMING'S
James Bond
DRAWING BY HORAK
THE ENGLISHMAN ON HOLIDAY, 'JEREMY BLADE', CONTINUES TO BE SEEN WATER-SKIING
—BUT WITH AN INTERESTING NEW ITEM OF SPORTS EQUIPMENT!
1648
'UP IN THE AIR AND OVER THE WALL — TILL I CAN SEE SO WIDE!'
MY FAVOURITE POET, OLD ROBERT LOUIS— HE PUT THINGS SO APTLY!

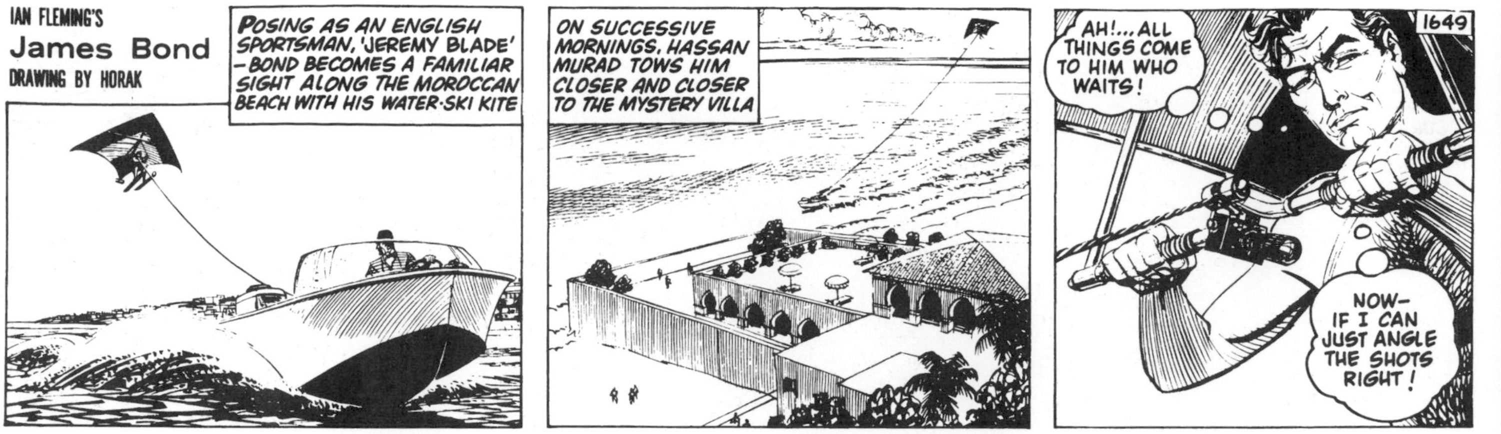
IAN FLEMING'S
James Bond
DRAWING BY HORAK
POSING AS AN ENGLISH SPORTSMAN, 'JEREMY BLADE' —BOND BECOMES A FAMILIAR SIGHT ALONG THE MOROCCAN BEACH WITH HIS WATER-SKI KITE
ON SUCCESSIVE MORNINGS, HASSAN MURAD TOWS HIM CLOSER AND CLOSER TO THE MYSTERY VILLA
1649
AH!... ALL THINGS COME TO HIM WHO WAITS!
NOW— IF I CAN JUST ANGLE THE SHOTS RIGHT!

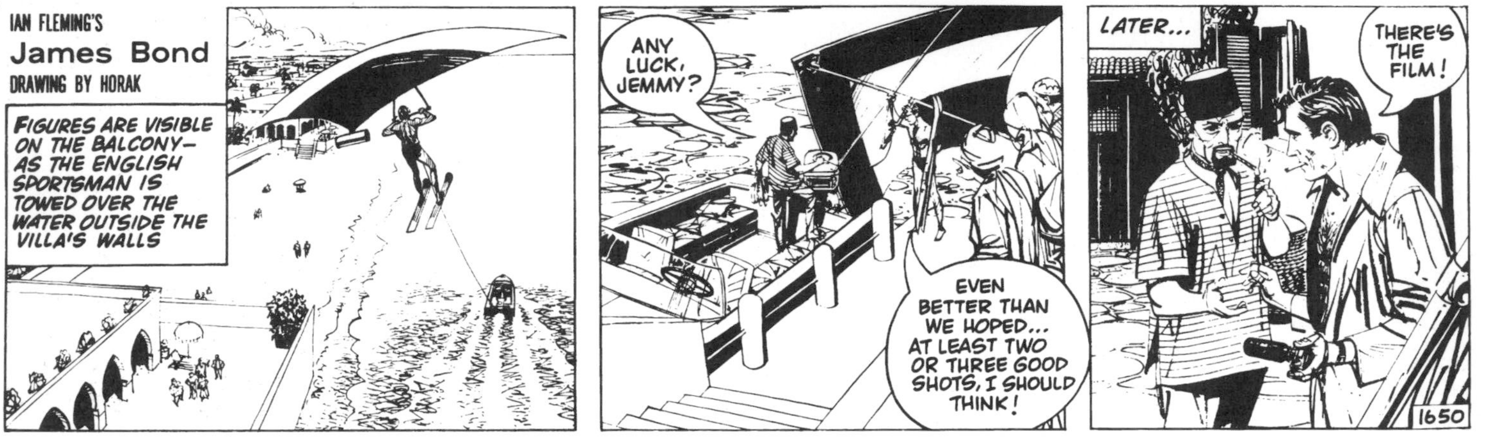
IAN FLEMING'S
James Bond
DRAWING BY HORAK
FIGURES ARE VISIBLE ON THE BALCONY— AS THE ENGLISH SPORTSMAN IS TOWED OVER THE WATER OUTSIDE THE VILLA'S WALLS
ANY LUCK, JEMMY?
EVEN BETTER THAN WE HOPED... AT LEAST TWO OR THREE GOOD SHOTS, I SHOULD THINK!
LATER...
THERE'S THE FILM!
1650

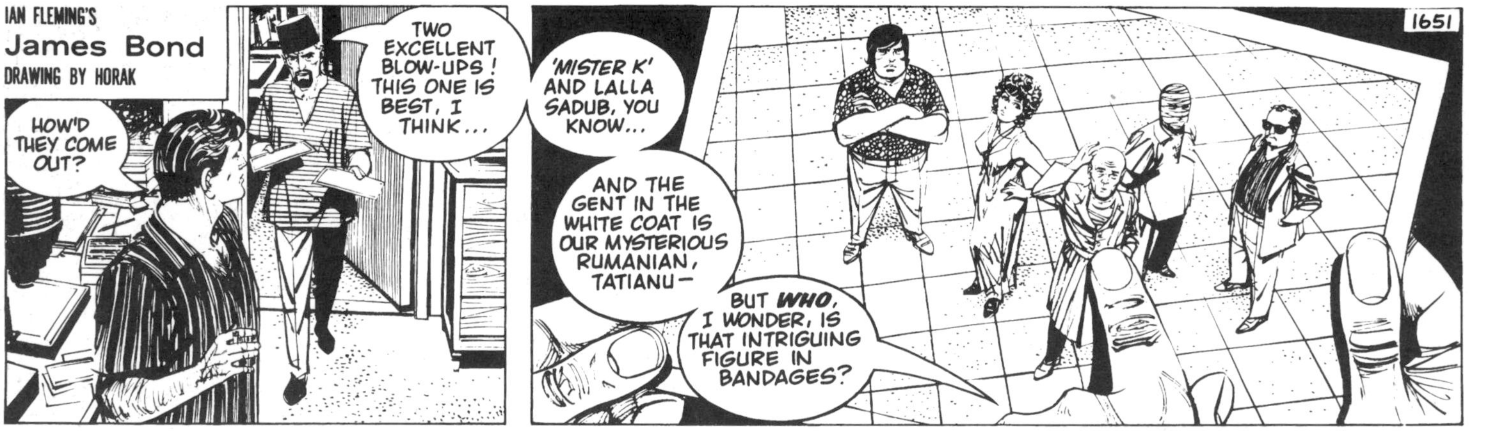
IAN FLEMING'S
James Bond
DRAWING BY HORAK
HOW'D THEY COME OUT?
TWO EXCELLENT BLOW-UPS! THIS ONE IS BEST, I THINK...
1651
'MISTER K' AND LALLA SADUB, YOU KNOW...
AND THE GENT IN THE WHITE COAT IS OUR MYSTERIOUS RUMANIAN, TATIANU—
BUT WHO, I WONDER, IS THAT INTRIGUING FIGURE IN BANDAGES?

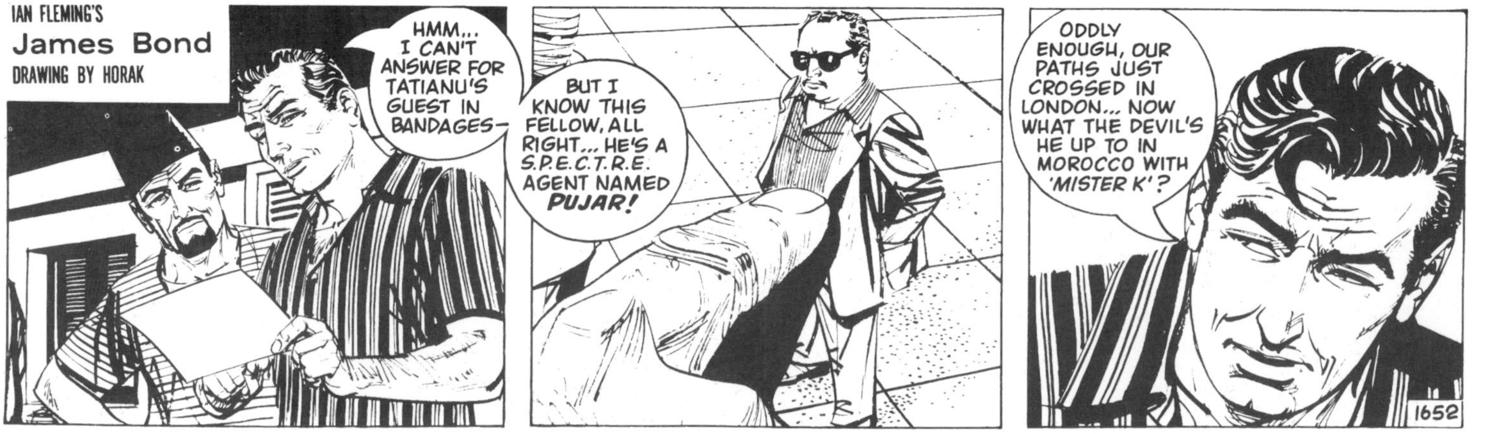
IAN FLEMING'S
James Bond
DRAWING BY HORAK
HMM... I CAN'T ANSWER FOR TATIANU'S GUEST IN BANDAGES—
BUT I KNOW THIS FELLOW, ALL RIGHT... HE'S A S.P.E.C.T.R.E. AGENT NAMED PUJAR!
ODDLY ENOUGH, OUR PATHS JUST CROSSED IN LONDON... NOW WHAT THE DEVIL'S HE UP TO IN MOROCCO WITH 'MISTER K'?
1652

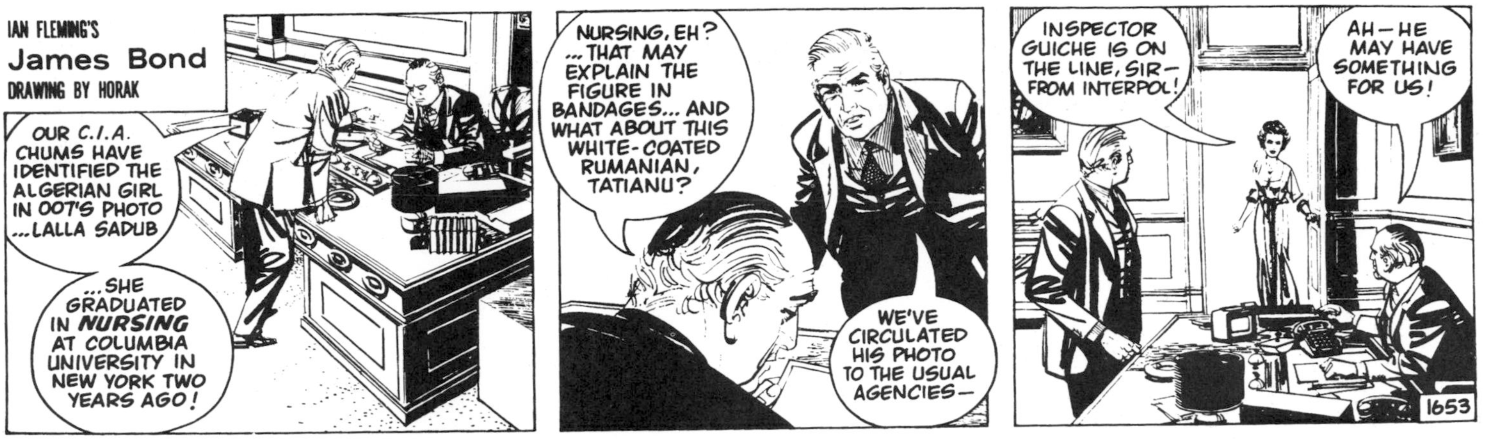
IAN FLEMING'S
James Bond
DRAWING BY HORAK
OUR C.I.A. CHUMS HAVE IDENTIFIED THE ALGERIAN GIRL IN 007'S PHOTO ...LALLA SADUB
...SHE GRADUATED IN NURSING AT COLUMBIA UNIVERSITY IN NEW YORK TWO YEARS AGO!
NURSING, EH? ...THAT MAY EXPLAIN THE FIGURE IN BANDAGES... AND WHAT ABOUT THIS WHITE-COATED RUMANIAN, TATIANU?
WE'VE CIRCULATED HIS PHOTO TO THE USUAL AGENCIES—
INSPECTOR GUICHE IS ON THE LINE, SIR—FROM INTERPOL!
AH—HE MAY HAVE SOMETHING FOR US!
1653

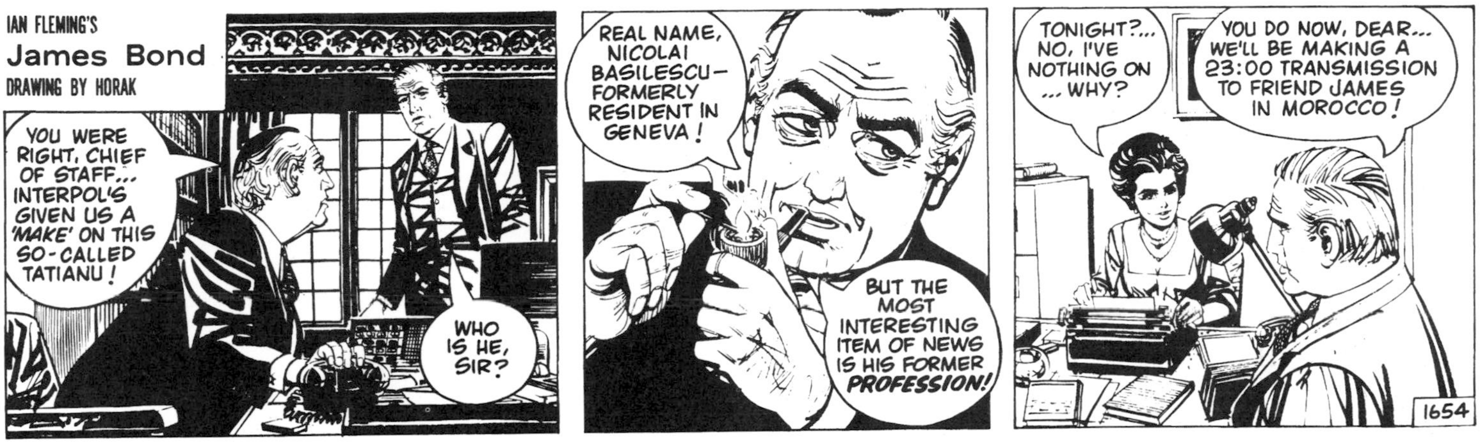
IAN FLEMING'S
James Bond
DRAWING BY HORAK
YOU WERE RIGHT, CHIEF OF STAFF... INTERPOL'S GIVEN US A 'MAKE' ON THIS SO-CALLED TATIANU!
WHO IS HE, SIR?
REAL NAME, NICOLAI BASILESCU—FORMERLY RESIDENT IN GENEVA!
BUT THE MOST INTERESTING ITEM OF NEWS IS HIS FORMER PROFESSION!
TONIGHT?... NO, I'VE NOTHING ON ... WHY?
YOU DO NOW, DEAR... WE'LL BE MAKING A 23:00 TRANSMISSION TO FRIEND JAMES IN MOROCCO!
1654

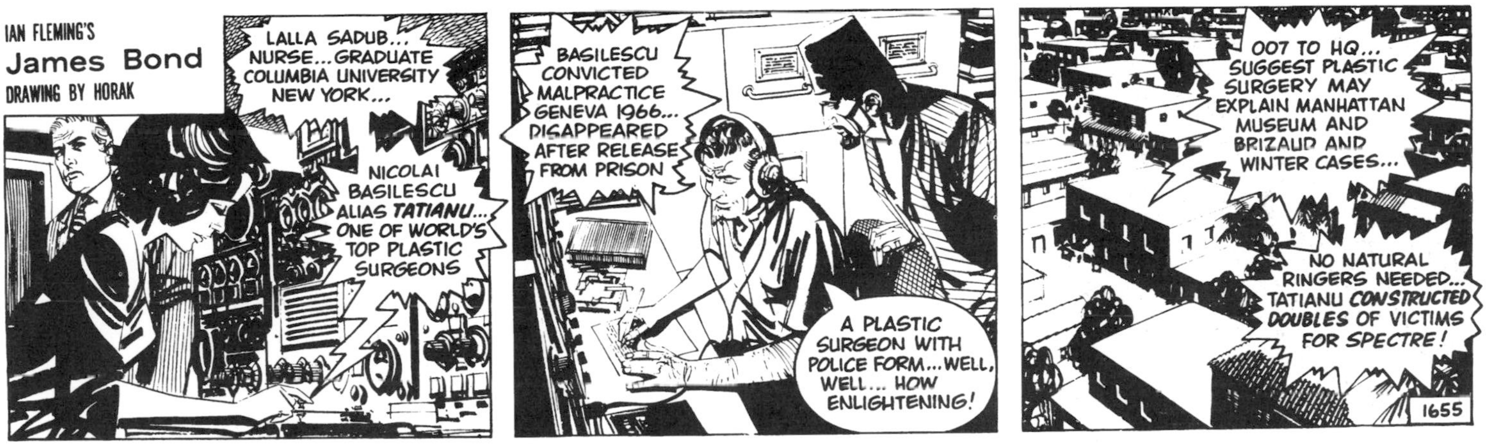
IAN FLEMING'S
James Bond
DRAWING BY HORAK
LALLA SADUB... NURSE... GRADUATE COLUMBIA UNIVERSITY NEW YORK...
NICOLAI BASILESCU ALIAS TATIANU... ONE OF WORLD'S TOP PLASTIC SURGEONS
BASILESCU CONVICTED MALPRACTICE GENEVA 1966... DISAPPEARED AFTER RELEASE FROM PRISON
A PLASTIC SURGEON WITH POLICE FORM... WELL, WELL... HOW ENLIGHTENING!
007 TO HQ... SUGGEST PLASTIC SURGERY MAY EXPLAIN MANHATTAN MUSEUM AND BRIZAUD AND WINTER CASES...
NO NATURAL RINGERS NEEDED... TATIANU CONSTRUCTED DOUBLES OF VICTIMS FOR SPECTRE!
1655

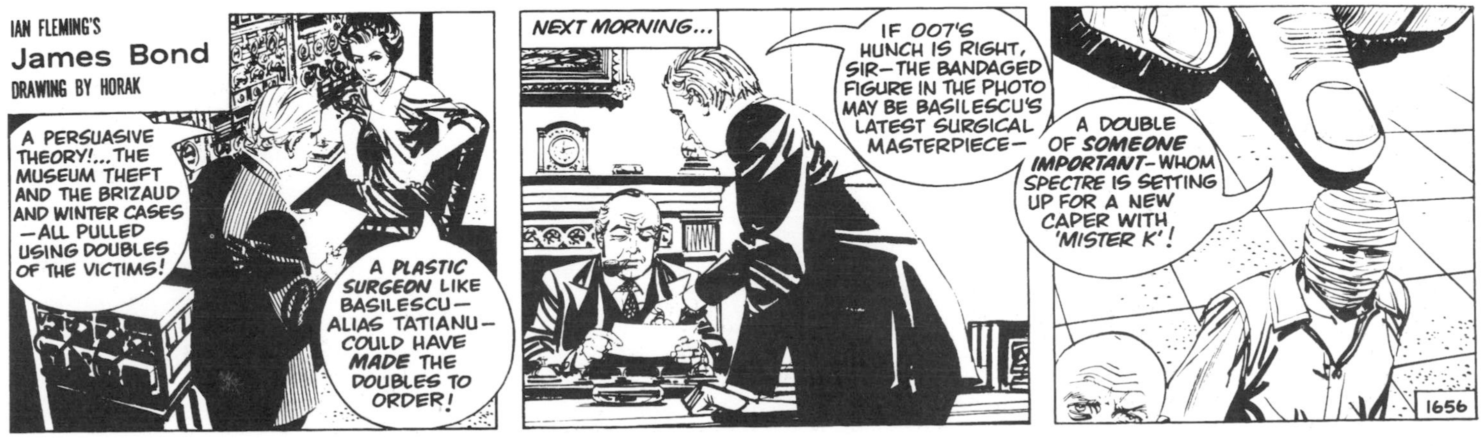
IAN FLEMING'S
James Bond
DRAWING BY HORAK
A PERSUASIVE THEORY!... THE MUSEUM THEFT AND THE BRIZAUD AND WINTER CASES —ALL PULLED USING DOUBLES OF THE VICTIMS!
A PLASTIC SURGEON LIKE BASILESCU—ALIAS TATIANU—COULD HAVE MADE THE DOUBLES TO ORDER!
NEXT MORNING...
IF 007'S HUNCH IS RIGHT, SIR—THE BANDAGED FIGURE IN THE PHOTO MAY BE BASILESCU'S LATEST SURGICAL MASTERPIECE—
A DOUBLE OF SOMEONE IMPORTANT—WHOM SPECTRE IS SETTING UP FOR A NEW CAPER WITH 'MISTER K'!
1656

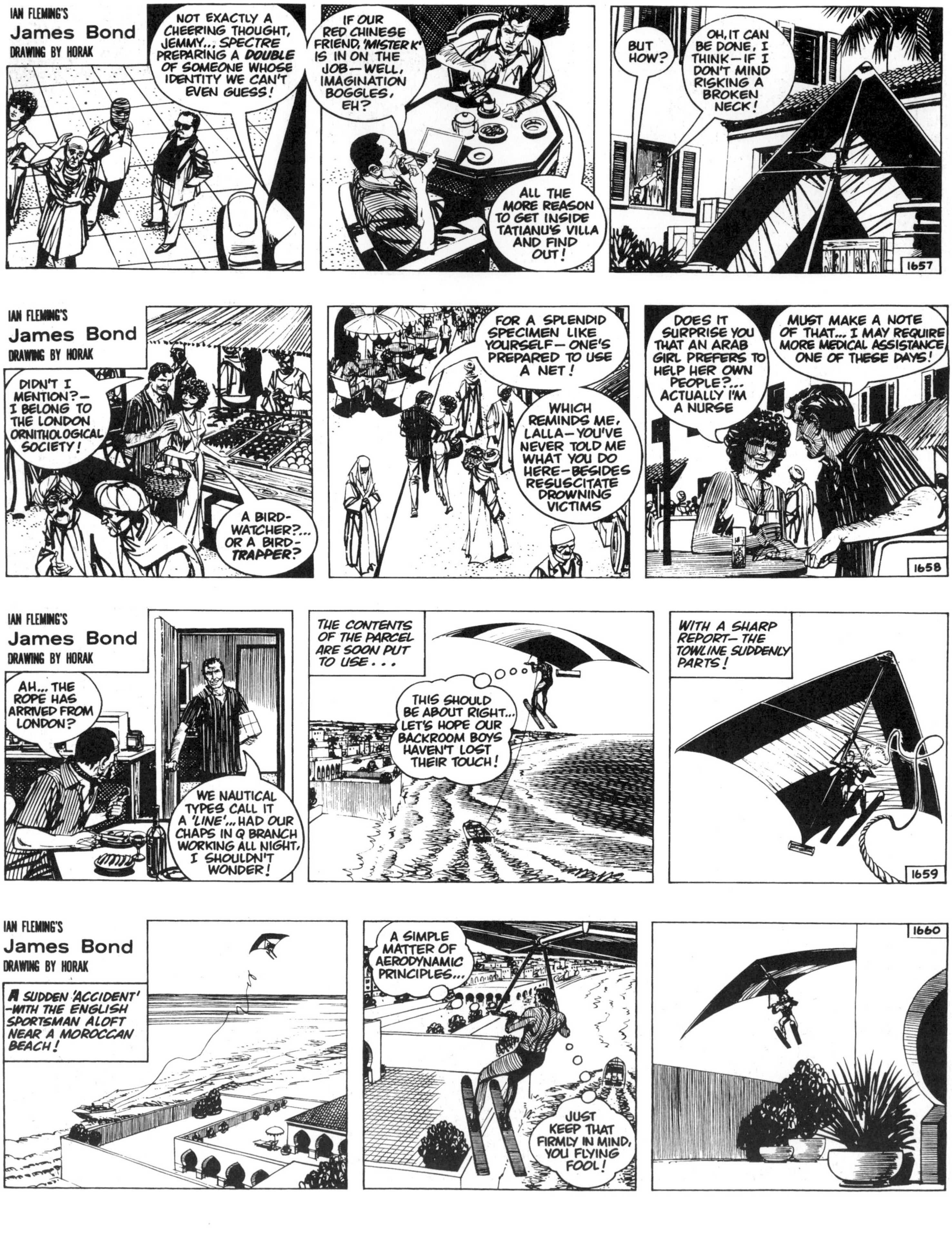
IAN FLEMING'S
James Bond
DRAWING BY HORAK
NOT EXACTLY A CHEERING THOUGHT, JEMMY... SPECTRE PREPARING A DOUBLE OF SOMEONE WHOSE IDENTITY WE CAN'T EVEN GUESS!
IF OUR RED CHINESE FRIEND, 'MISTER K' IS IN ON THE JOB—WELL, IMAGINATION BOGGLES, EH?
ALL THE MORE REASON TO GET INSIDE TATIANU'S VILLA AND FIND OUT!
BUT HOW?
OH, IT CAN BE DONE, I THINK—IF I DON'T MIND RISKING A BROKEN NECK!
1657
IAN FLEMING'S
James Bond
DRAWING BY HORAK
DIDN'T I MENTION?— I BELONG TO THE LONDON ORNITHOLOGICAL SOCIETY!
A BIRD-WATCHER?... OR A BIRD-TRAPPER?
FOR A SPLENDID SPECIMEN LIKE YOURSELF—ONE'S PREPARED TO USE A NET!
WHICH REMINDS ME, LALLA—YOU'VE NEVER TOLD ME WHAT YOU DO HERE—BESIDES RESUSCITATE DROWNING VICTIMS
DOES IT SURPRISE YOU THAT AN ARAB GIRL PREFERS TO HELP HER OWN PEOPLE?... ACTUALLY I'M A NURSE
MUST MAKE A NOTE OF THAT... I MAY REQUIRE MORE MEDICAL ASSISTANCE ONE OF THESE DAYS!
1658
IAN FLEMING'S
James Bond
DRAWING BY HORAK
AH... THE ROPE HAS ARRIVED FROM LONDON?
WE NAUTICAL TYPES CALL IT A 'LINE'... HAD OUR CHAPS IN Q BRANCH WORKING ALL NIGHT, I SHOULDN'T WONDER!
THE CONTENTS OF THE PARCEL ARE SOON PUT TO USE . . .
THIS SHOULD BE ABOUT RIGHT... LET'S HOPE OUR BACKROOM BOYS HAVEN'T LOST THEIR TOUCH!
WITH A SHARP REPORT—THE TOWLINE SUDDENLY PARTS!
1659
IAN FLEMING'S
James Bond
DRAWING BY HORAK
A SUDDEN 'ACCIDENT' —WITH THE ENGLISH SPORTSMAN ALOFT NEAR A MOROCCAN BEACH!
A SIMPLE MATTER OF AERODYNAMIC PRINCIPLES...
JUST KEEP THAT FIRMLY IN MIND, YOU FLYING FOOL!
1660

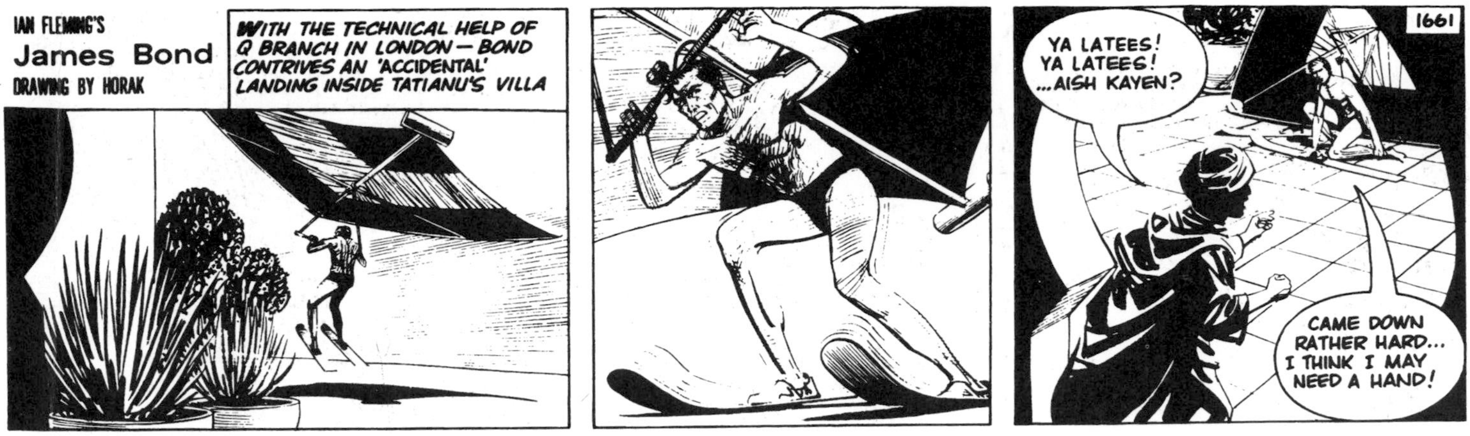
IAN FLEMING'S
James Bond
DRAWING BY HORAK
WITH THE TECHNICAL HELP OF Q BRANCH IN LONDON — BOND CONTRIVES AN 'ACCIDENTAL' LANDING INSIDE TATIANU'S VILLA
1661
YA LATEES! YA LATEES! ...AISH KAYEN?
CAME DOWN RATHER HARD... I THINK I MAY NEED A HAND!

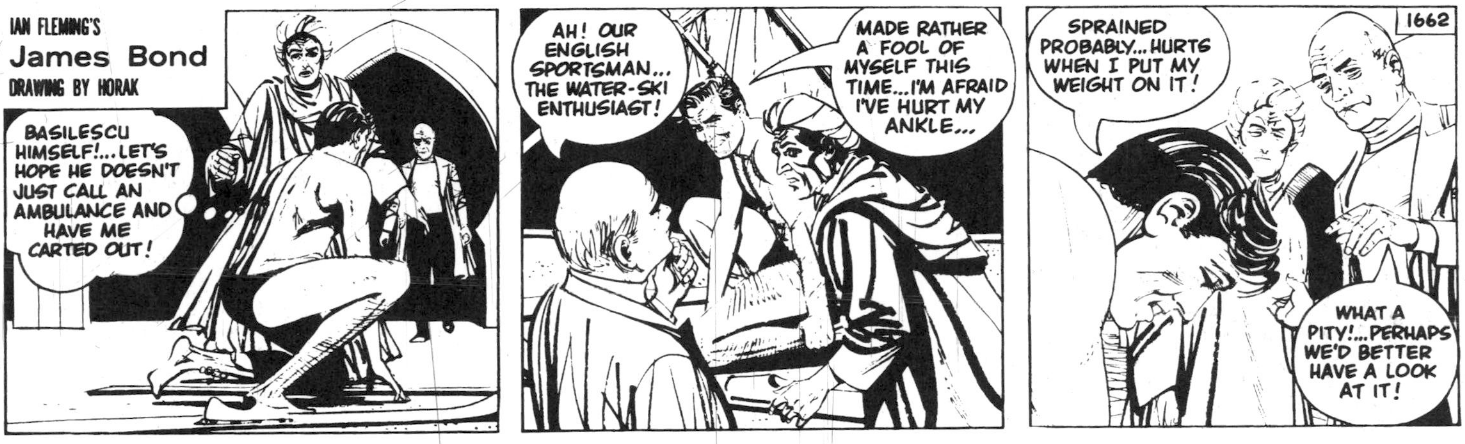
IAN FLEMING'S
James Bond
DRAWING BY HORAK
BASILESCU HIMSELF!...LET'S HOPE HE DOESN'T JUST CALL AN AMBULANCE AND HAVE ME CARTED OUT!
AH! OUR ENGLISH SPORTSMAN... THE WATER-SKI ENTHUSIAST!
MADE RATHER A FOOL OF MYSELF THIS TIME...I'M AFRAID I'VE HURT MY ANKLE...
1662
SPRAINED PROBABLY...HURTS WHEN I PUT MY WEIGHT ON IT!
WHAT A PITY!...PERHAPS WE'D BETTER HAVE A LOOK AT IT!

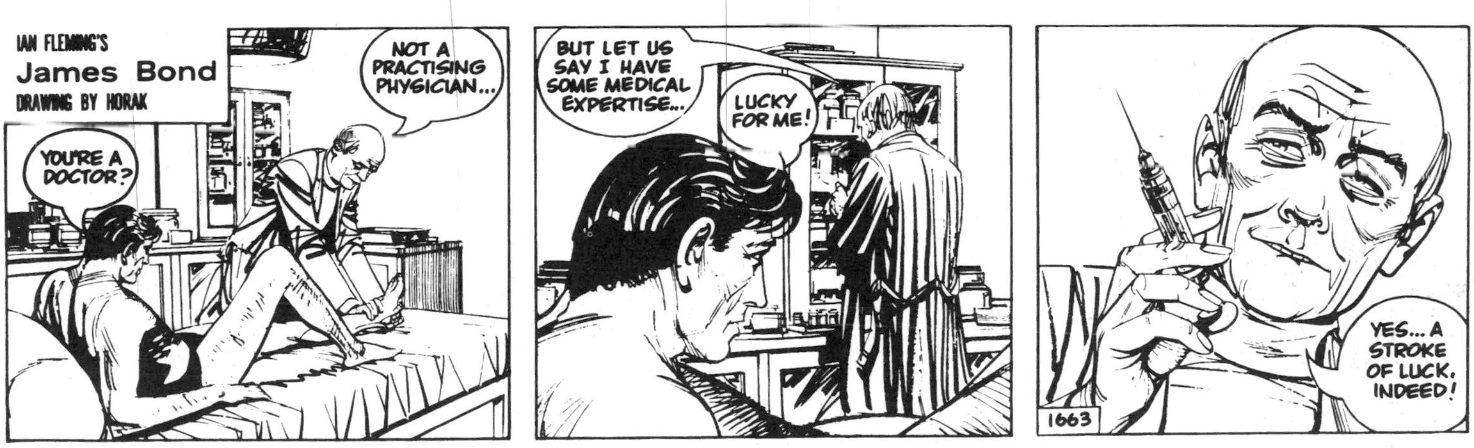
IAN FLEMING'S
James Bond
DRAWING BY HORAK
YOU'RE A DOCTOR?
NOT A PRACTISING PHYSICIAN...
BUT LET US SAY I HAVE SOME MEDICAL EXPERTISE...
LUCKY FOR ME!
YES... A STROKE OF LUCK, INDEED!
1663

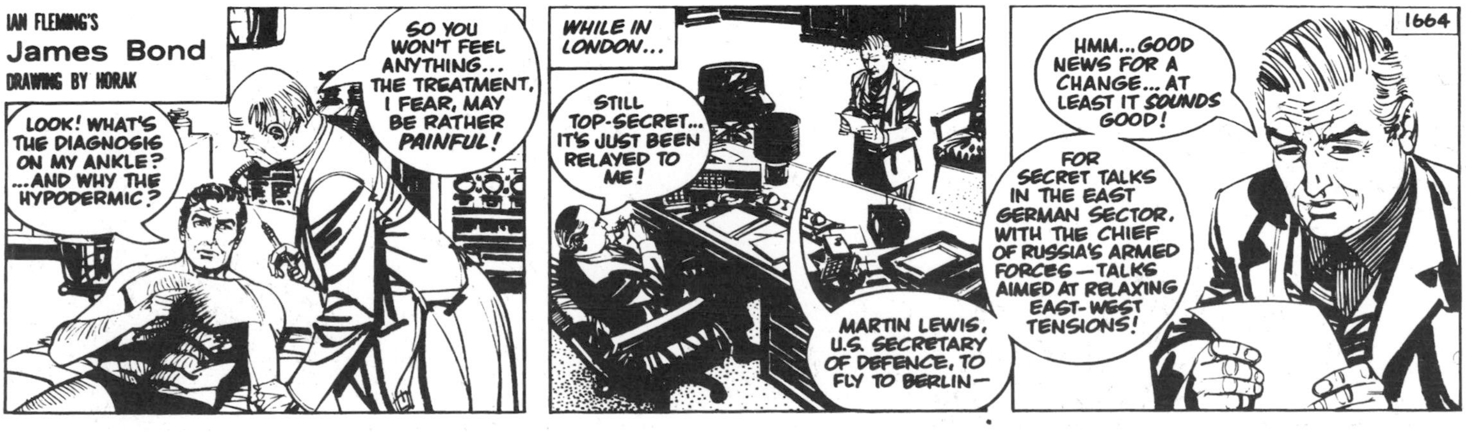
IAN FLEMING'S
James Bond
DRAWING BY HORAK
LOOK! WHAT'S THE DIAGNOSIS ON MY ANKLE? ...AND WHY THE HYPODERMIC?
SO YOU WON'T FEEL ANYTHING... THE TREATMENT, I FEAR, MAY BE RATHER PAINFUL!
WHILE IN LONDON...
STILL TOP-SECRET... IT'S JUST BEEN RELAYED TO ME!
MARTIN LEWIS, U.S. SECRETARY OF DEFENCE, TO FLY TO BERLIN—
1664
HMM...GOOD NEWS FOR A CHANGE... AT LEAST IT SOUNDS GOOD!
FOR SECRET TALKS IN THE EAST GERMAN SECTOR, WITH THE CHIEF OF RUSSIA'S ARMED FORCES — TALKS AIMED AT RELAXING EAST-WEST TENSIONS!

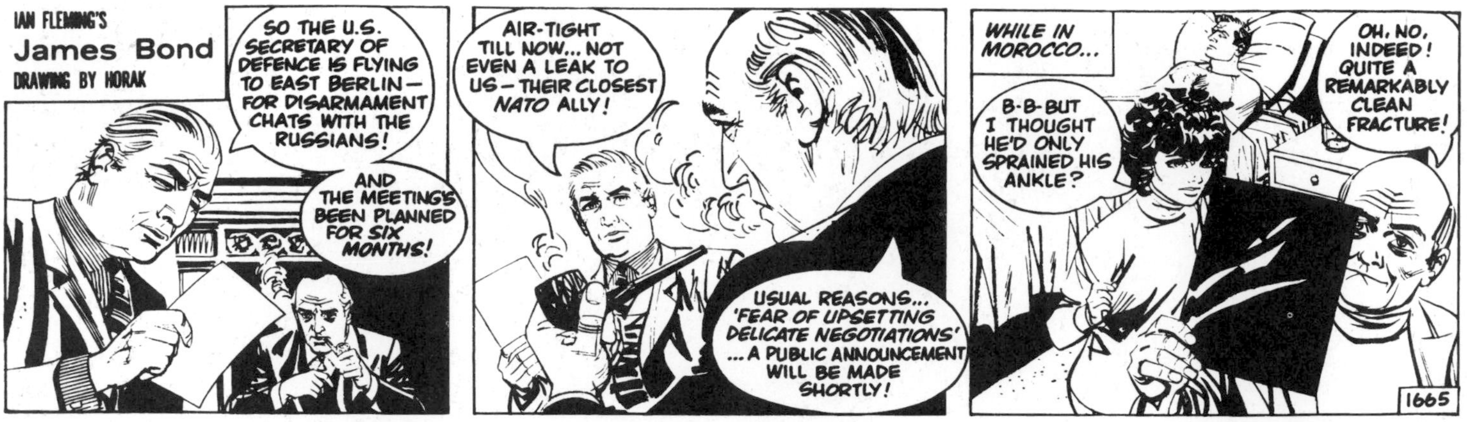
IAN FLEMING'S
James Bond
DRAWING BY HORAK
SO THE U.S. SECRETARY OF DEFENCE IS FLYING TO EAST BERLIN—FOR DISARMAMENT CHATS WITH THE RUSSIANS!
AND THE MEETING'S BEEN PLANNED FOR SIX MONTHS!
AIR-TIGHT TILL NOW... NOT EVEN A LEAK TO US—THEIR CLOSEST NATO ALLY!
USUAL REASONS... 'FEAR OF UPSETTING DELICATE NEGOTIATIONS' ... A PUBLIC ANNOUNCEMENT WILL BE MADE SHORTLY!
WHILE IN MOROCCO...
B-B-BUT I THOUGHT HE'D ONLY SPRAINED HIS ANKLE?
OH, NO, INDEED! QUITE A REMARKABLY CLEAN FRACTURE!
1665

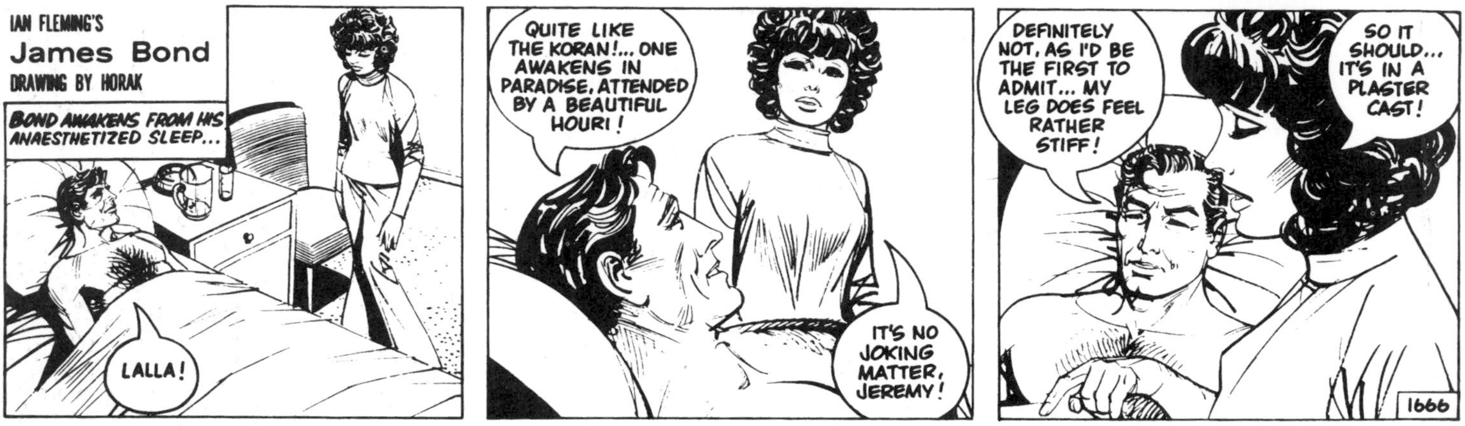
IAN FLEMING'S
James Bond
DRAWING BY HORAK
BOND AWAKENS FROM HIS ANAESTHETIZED SLEEP...
LALLA!
QUITE LIKE THE KORAN!... ONE AWAKENS IN PARADISE, ATTENDED BY A BEAUTIFUL HOURI!
IT'S NO JOKING MATTER, JEREMY!
DEFINITELY NOT, AS I'D BE THE FIRST TO ADMIT... MY LEG DOES FEEL RATHER STIFF!
SO IT SHOULD... IT'S IN A PLASTER CAST!
1666

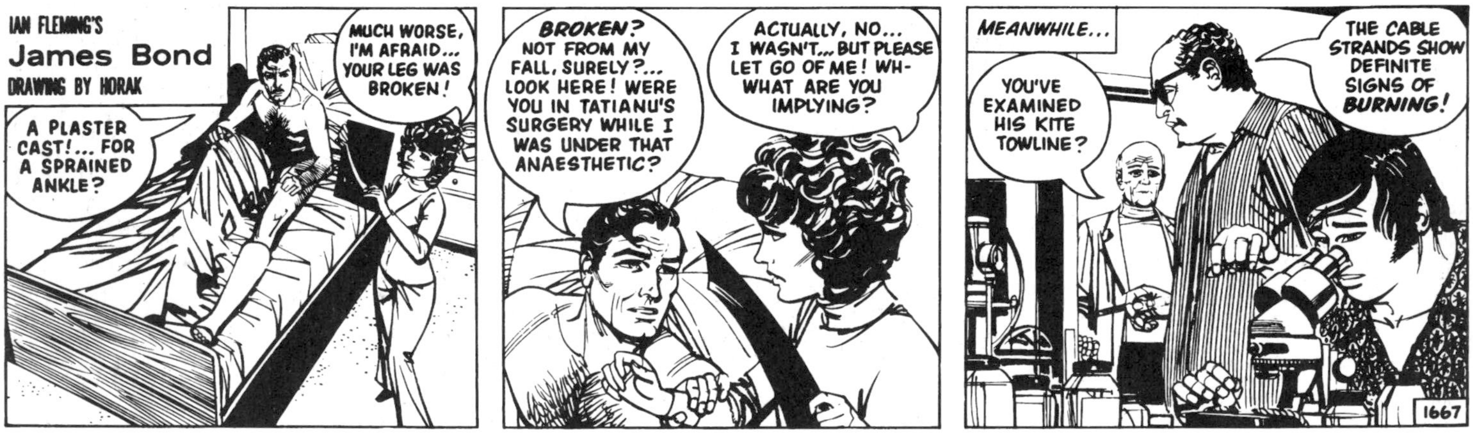
IAN FLEMING'S
James Bond
DRAWING BY HORAK
A PLASTER CAST!... FOR A SPRAINED ANKLE?
MUCH WORSE, I'M AFRAID... YOUR LEG WAS BROKEN!
BROKEN? NOT FROM MY FALL, SURELY?... LOOK HERE! WERE YOU IN TATIANU'S SURGERY WHILE I WAS UNDER THAT ANAESTHETIC?
ACTUALLY, NO... I WASN'T... BUT PLEASE LET GO OF ME! WH-WHAT ARE YOU IMPLYING?
MEANWHILE...
YOU'VE EXAMINED HIS KITE TOWLINE?
THE CABLE STRANDS SHOW DEFINITE SIGNS OF BURNING!
1667

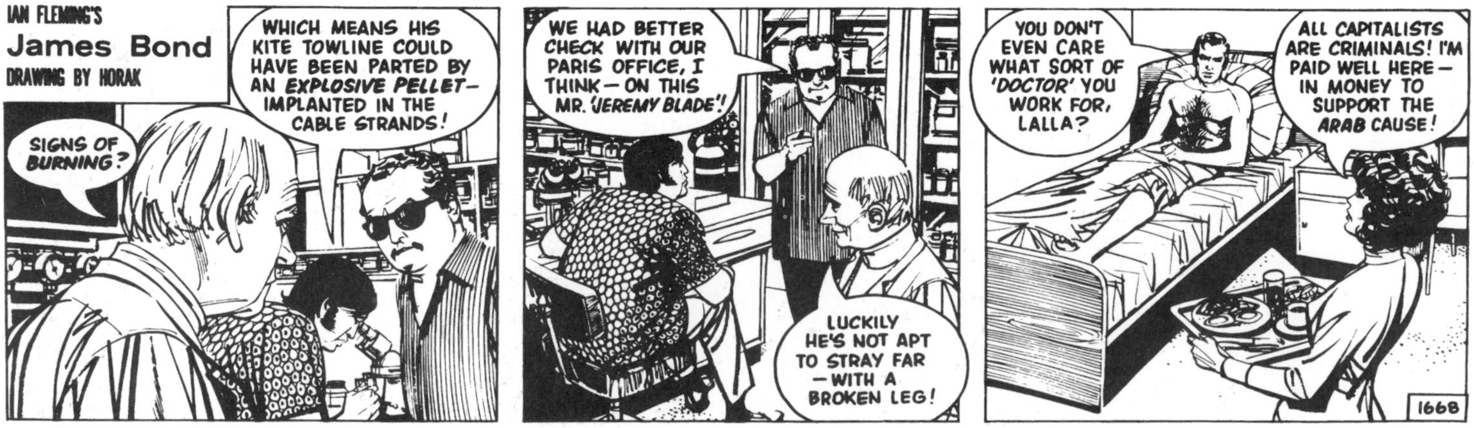
IAN FLEMING'S
James Bond
DRAWING BY HORAK
SIGNS OF BURNING?
WHICH MEANS HIS KITE TOWLINE COULD HAVE BEEN PARTED BY AN EXPLOSIVE PELLET—IMPLANTED IN THE CABLE STRANDS!
WE HAD BETTER CHECK WITH OUR PARIS OFFICE, I THINK—ON THIS MR. 'JEREMY BLADE'!
LUCKILY HE'S NOT APT TO STRAY FAR—WITH A BROKEN LEG!
YOU DON'T EVEN CARE WHAT SORT OF 'DOCTOR' YOU WORK FOR, LALLA?
ALL CAPITALISTS ARE CRIMINALS! I'M PAID WELL HERE—IN MONEY TO SUPPORT THE ARAB CAUSE!
1668

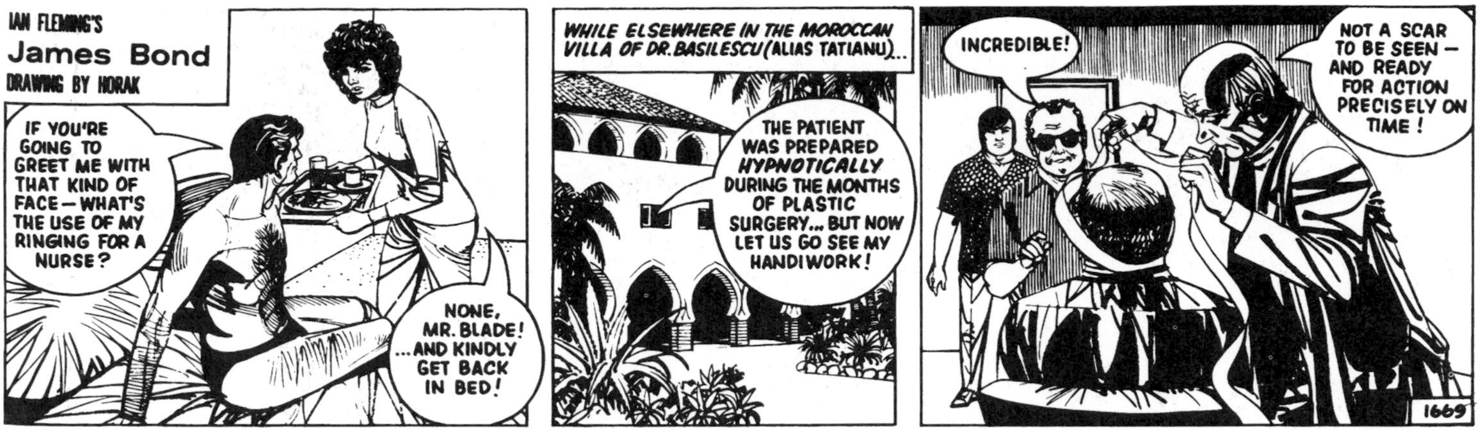
IAN FLEMING'S
James Bond
DRAWING BY HORAK
IF YOU'RE GOING TO GREET ME WITH THAT KIND OF FACE—WHAT'S THE USE OF MY RINGING FOR A NURSE?
NONE, MR. BLADE! ...AND KINDLY GET BACK IN BED!
WHILE ELSEWHERE IN THE MOROCCAN VILLA OF DR. BASILESCU (ALIAS TATIANU)...
THE PATIENT WAS PREPARED HYPNOTICALLY DURING THE MONTHS OF PLASTIC SURGERY... BUT NOW LET US GO SEE MY HANDIWORK!
INCREDIBLE!
NOT A SCAR TO BE SEEN — AND READY FOR ACTION PRECISELY ON TIME!
1669

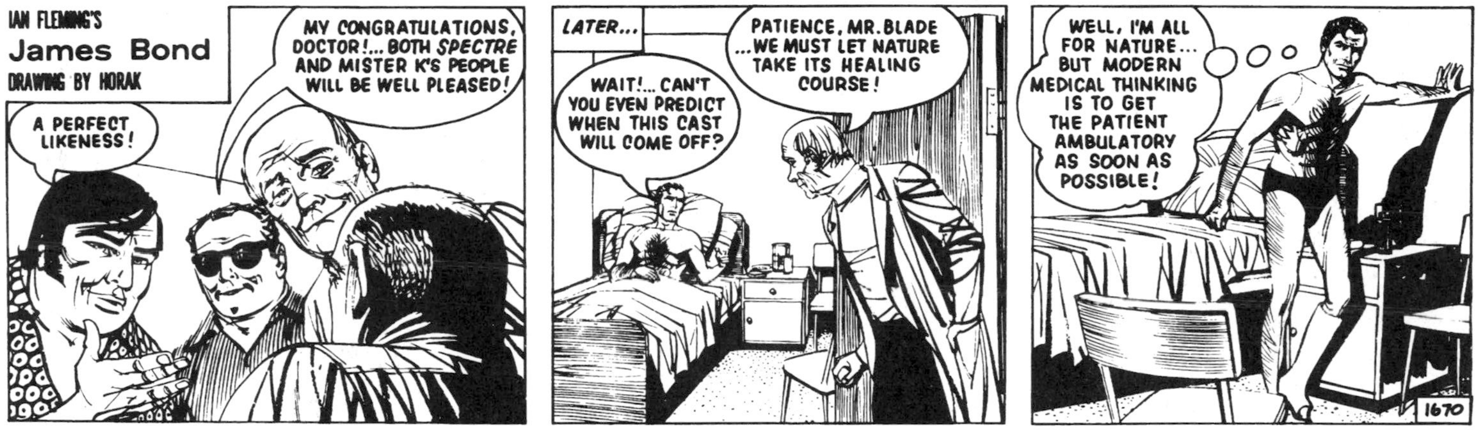
IAN FLEMING'S
James Bond
DRAWING BY HORAK
A PERFECT LIKENESS!
MY CONGRATULATIONS, DOCTOR!... BOTH SPECTRE AND MISTER K'S PEOPLE WILL BE WELL PLEASED!
LATER...
WAIT!... CAN'T YOU EVEN PREDICT WHEN THIS CAST WILL COME OFF?
PATIENCE, MR. BLADE ...WE MUST LET NATURE TAKE ITS HEALING COURSE!
WELL, I'M ALL FOR NATURE... BUT MODERN MEDICAL THINKING IS TO GET THE PATIENT AMBULATORY AS SOON AS POSSIBLE!
1670

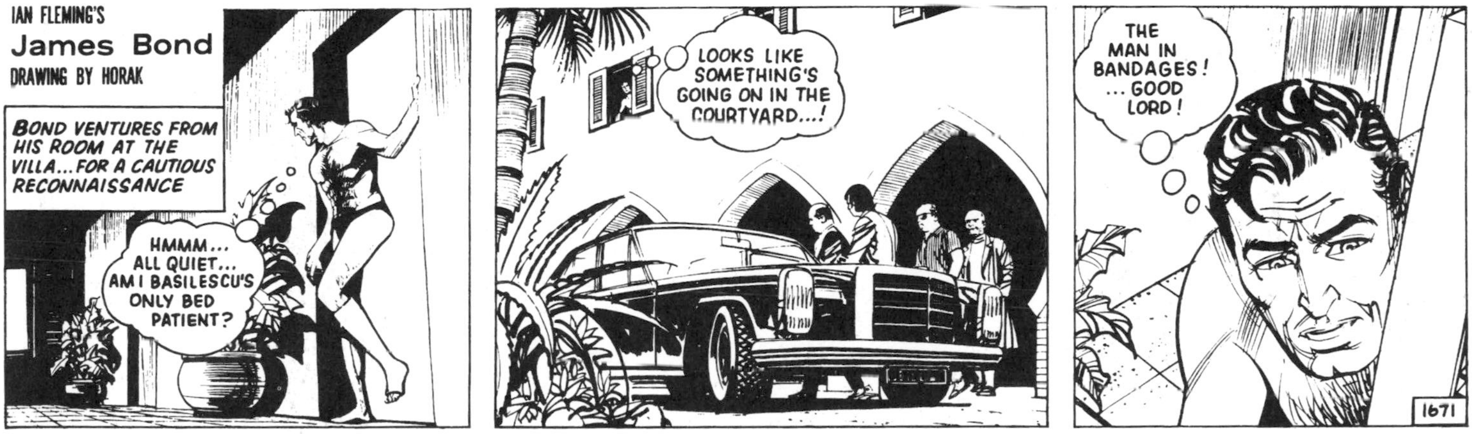
IAN FLEMING'S
James Bond
DRAWING BY HORAK
BOND VENTURES FROM HIS ROOM AT THE VILLA... FOR A CAUTIOUS RECONNAISSANCE
HMMM... ALL QUIET... AM I BASILESCU'S ONLY BED PATIENT?
LOOKS LIKE SOMETHING'S GOING ON IN THE COURTYARD...!
THE MAN IN BANDAGES! ... GOOD LORD!
1671

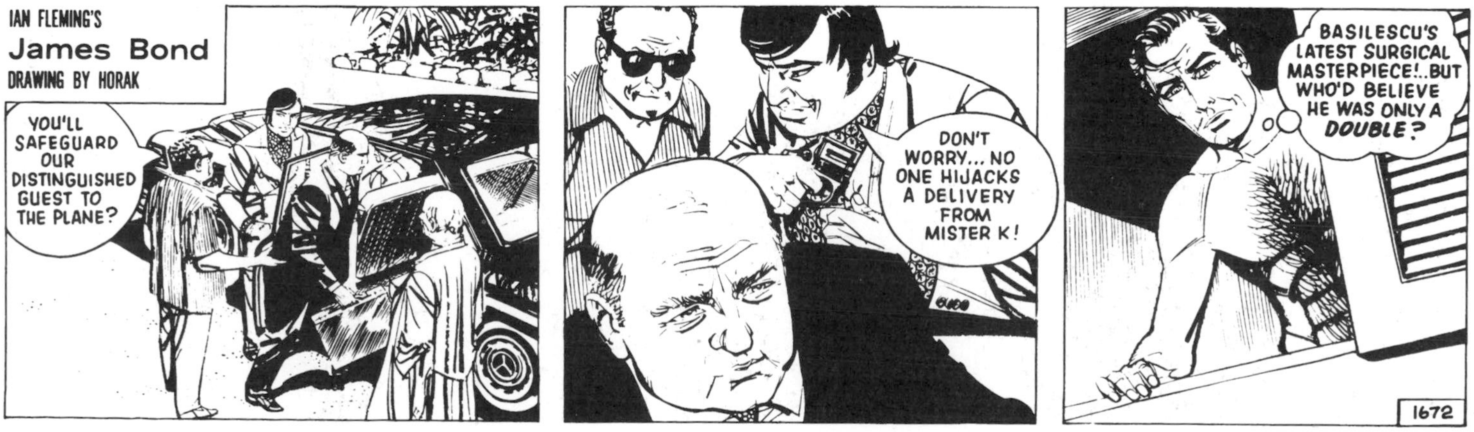
IAN FLEMING'S
James Bond
DRAWING BY HORAK
YOU'LL SAFEGUARD OUR DISTINGUISHED GUEST TO THE PLANE?
DON'T WORRY... NO ONE HIJACKS A DELIVERY FROM MISTER K!
BASILESCU'S LATEST SURGICAL MASTERPIECE!..BUT WHO'D BELIEVE HE WAS ONLY A DOUBLE?
1672

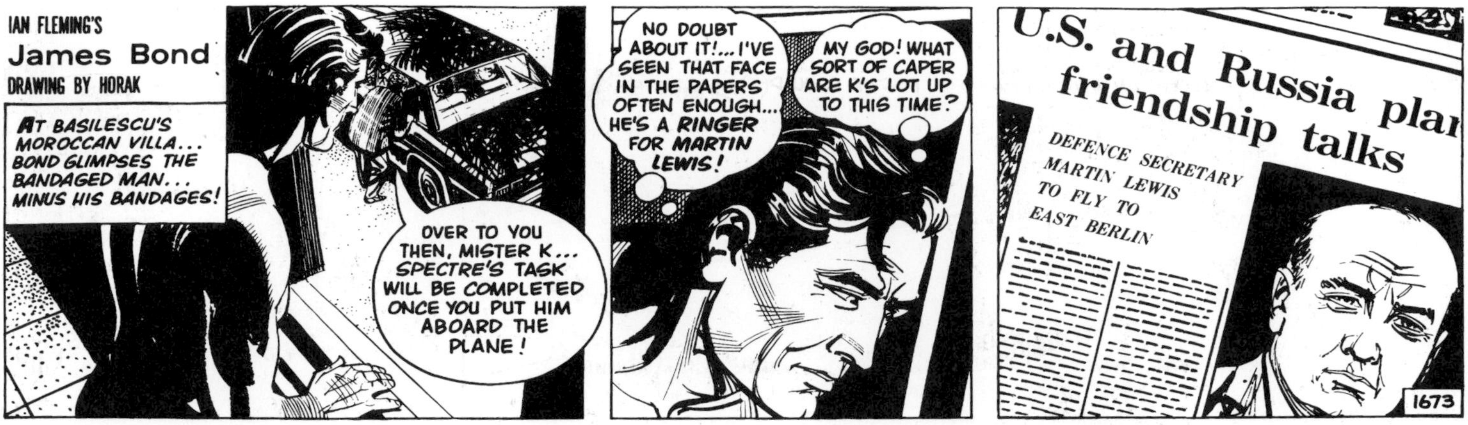
IAN FLEMING'S
James Bond
DRAWING BY HORAK
AT BASILESCU'S MOROCCAN VILLA... BOND GLIMPSES THE BANDAGED MAN... MINUS HIS BANDAGES!
OVER TO YOU THEN, MISTER K... SPECTRE'S TASK WILL BE COMPLETED ONCE YOU PUT HIM ABOARD THE PLANE!
NO DOUBT ABOUT IT!... I'VE SEEN THAT FACE IN THE PAPERS OFTEN ENOUGH... HE'S A RINGER FOR MARTIN LEWIS!
MY GOD! WHAT SORT OF CAPER ARE K'S LOT UP TO THIS TIME?
U.S. and Russia plan friendship talks
DEFENCE SECRETARY MARTIN LEWIS TO FLY TO EAST BERLIN
1673

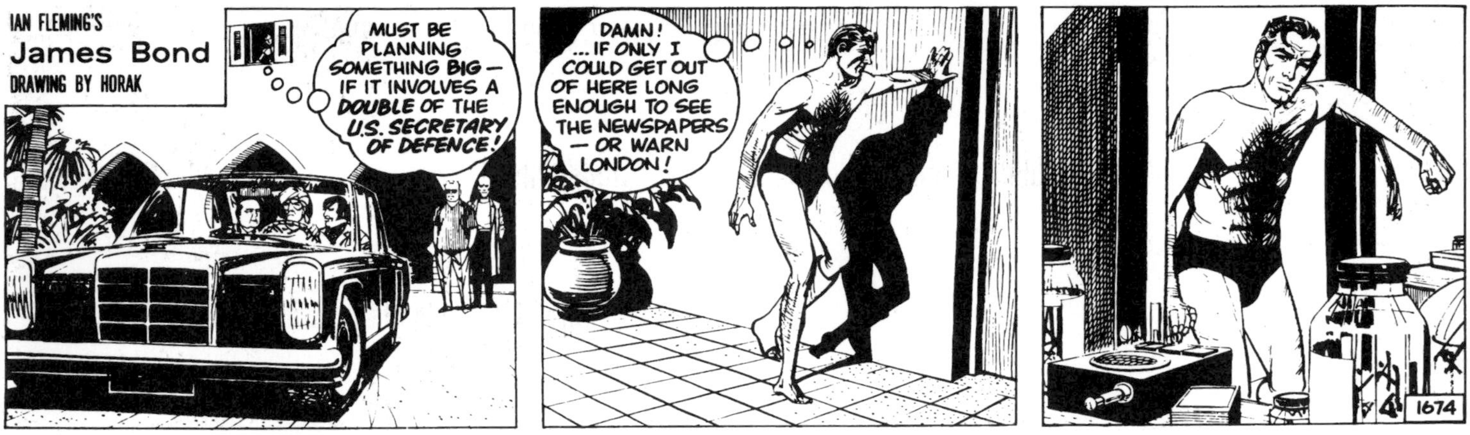
IAN FLEMING'S
James Bond
DRAWING BY HORAK
MUST BE PLANNING SOMETHING BIG — IF IT INVOLVES A DOUBLE OF THE U.S. SECRETARY OF DEFENCE!
DAMN! ...IF ONLY I COULD GET OUT OF HERE LONG ENOUGH TO SEE THE NEWSPAPERS — OR WARN LONDON!
1674

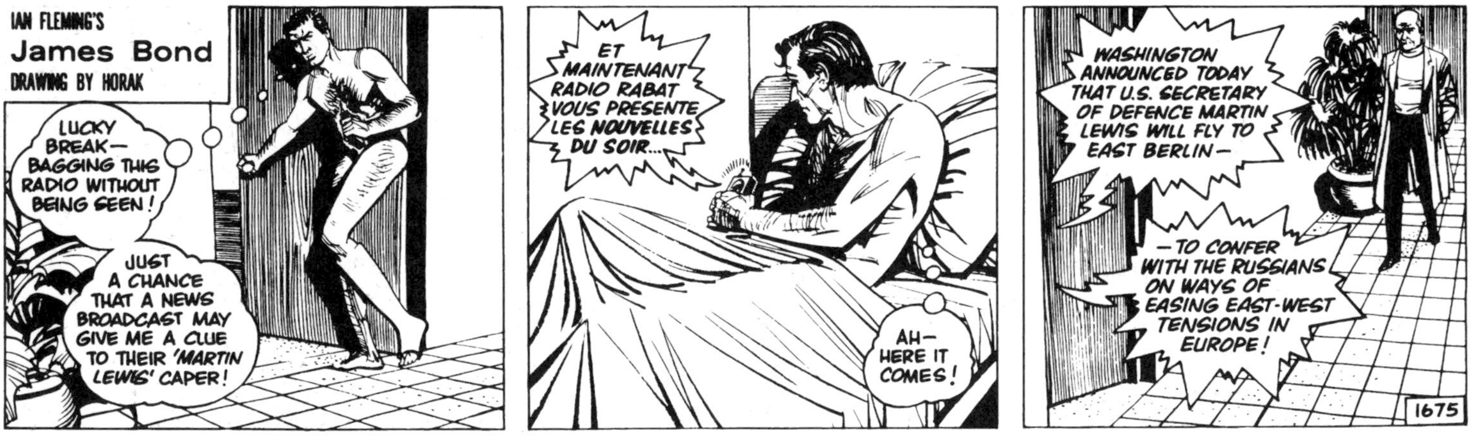
IAN FLEMING'S
James Bond
DRAWING BY HORAK
LUCKY BREAK— BAGGING THIS RADIO WITHOUT BEING SEEN!
JUST A CHANCE THAT A NEWS BROADCAST MAY GIVE ME A CLUE TO THEIR 'MARTIN LEWIS' CAPER!
ET MAINTENANT RADIO RABAT VOUS PRESENTE LES NOUVELLES DU SOIR...
AH— HERE IT COMES!
WASHINGTON ANNOUNCED TODAY THAT U.S. SECRETARY OF DEFENCE MARTIN LEWIS WILL FLY TO EAST BERLIN—
—TO CONFER WITH THE RUSSIANS ON WAYS OF EASING EAST-WEST TENSIONS IN EUROPE!
1675

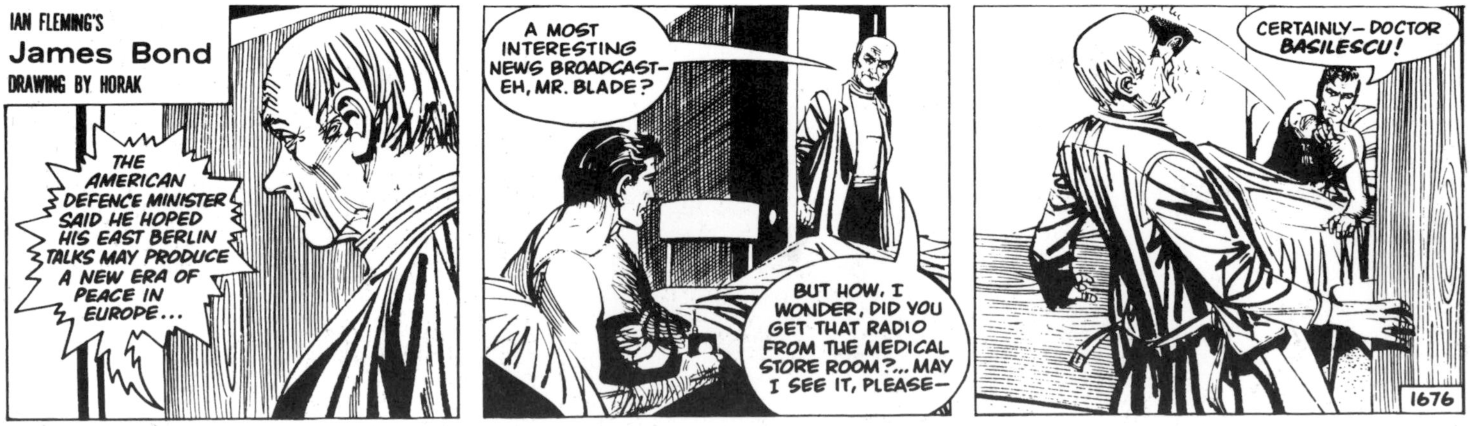
IAN FLEMING'S
James Bond
DRAWING BY HORAK
THE AMERICAN DEFENCE MINISTER SAID HE HOPED HIS EAST BERLIN TALKS MAY PRODUCE A NEW ERA OF PEACE IN EUROPE...
A MOST INTERESTING NEWS BROADCAST— EH, MR. BLADE?
BUT HOW, I WONDER, DID YOU GET THAT RADIO FROM THE MEDICAL STORE ROOM?... MAY I SEE IT, PLEASE—
CERTAINLY— DOCTOR BASILESCU!
1676

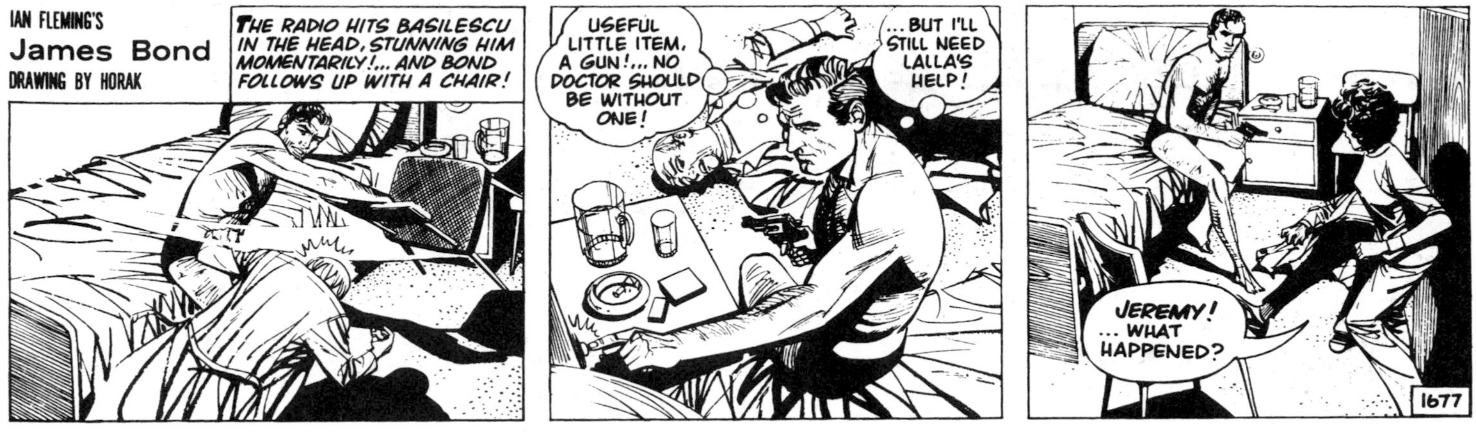
IAN FLEMING'S
James Bond
DRAWING BY HORAK
THE RADIO HITS BASILESCU IN THE HEAD, STUNNING HIM MOMENTARILY!... AND BOND FOLLOWS UP WITH A CHAIR!
USEFUL LITTLE ITEM, A GUN!... NO DOCTOR SHOULD BE WITHOUT ONE!
... BUT I'LL STILL NEED LALLA'S HELP!
JEREMY! ... WHAT HAPPENED?
1677

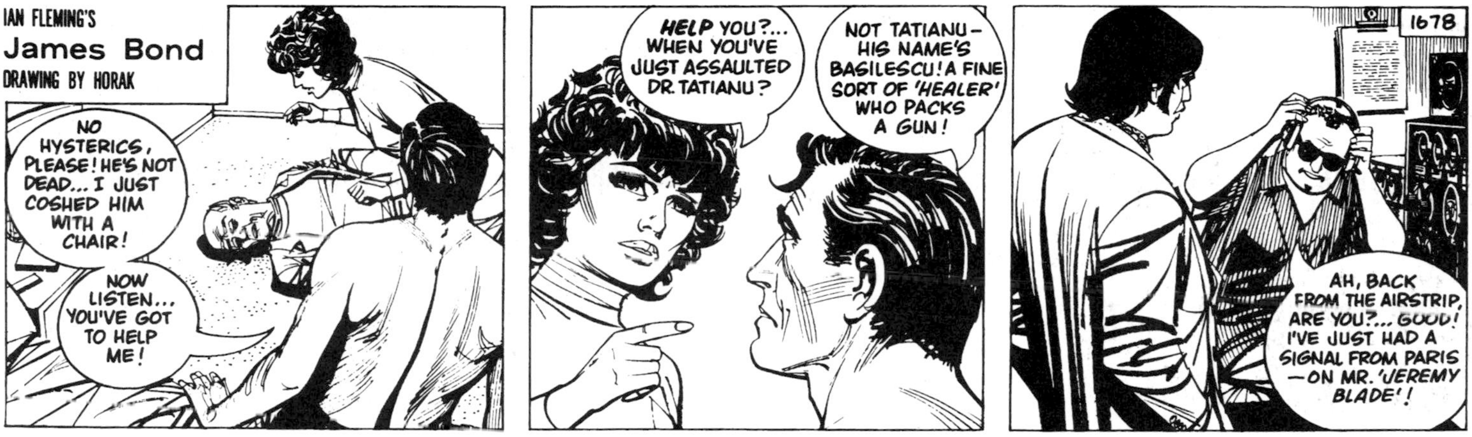
IAN FLEMING'S
James Bond
DRAWING BY HORAK
NO HYSTERICS, PLEASE! HE'S NOT DEAD... I JUST COSHED HIM WITH A CHAIR!
NOW LISTEN... YOU'VE GOT TO HELP ME!
HELP YOU?... WHEN YOU'VE JUST ASSAULTED DR. TATIANU?
NOT TATIANU—HIS NAME'S BASILESCU! A FINE SORT OF 'HEALER' WHO PACKS A GUN!
1678
AH, BACK FROM THE AIRSTRIP, ARE YOU?... GOOD! I'VE JUST HAD A SIGNAL FROM PARIS —ON MR. 'JEREMY BLADE'!

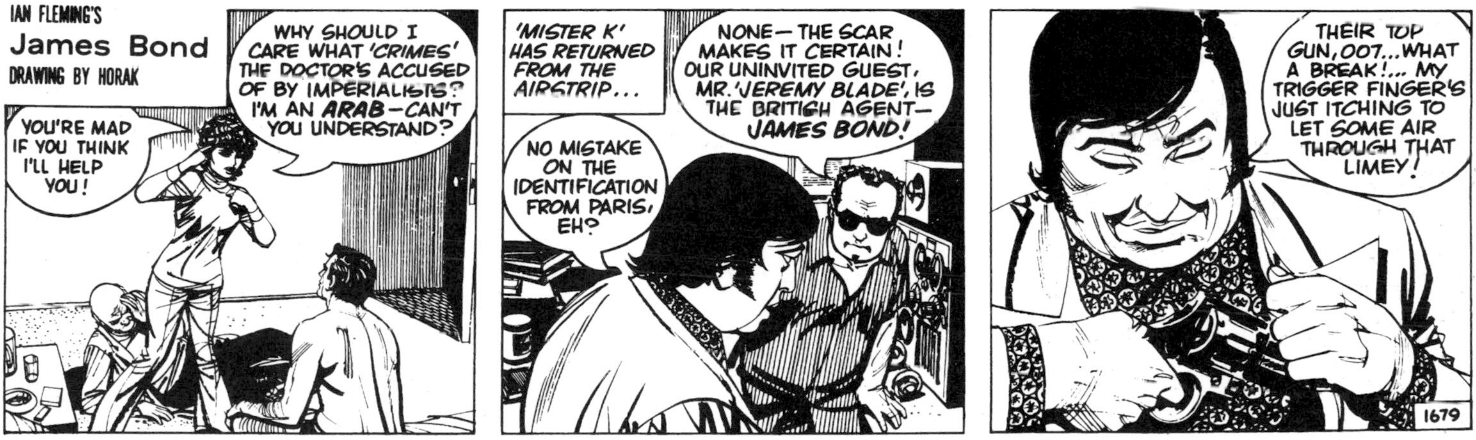
IAN FLEMING'S
James Bond
DRAWING BY HORAK
YOU'RE MAD IF YOU THINK I'LL HELP YOU!
WHY SHOULD I CARE WHAT 'CRIMES' THE DOCTOR'S ACCUSED OF BY IMPERIALISTS? I'M AN ARAB—CAN'T YOU UNDERSTAND?
'MISTER K' HAS RETURNED FROM THE AIRSTRIP...
NO MISTAKE ON THE IDENTIFICATION FROM PARIS, EH?
NONE—THE SCAR MAKES IT CERTAIN! OUR UNINVITED GUEST, MR. 'JEREMY BLADE', IS THE BRITISH AGENT—JAMES BOND!
THEIR TOP GUN, 007... WHAT A BREAK!... MY TRIGGER FINGER'S JUST ITCHING TO LET SOME AIR THROUGH THAT LIMEY!
1679

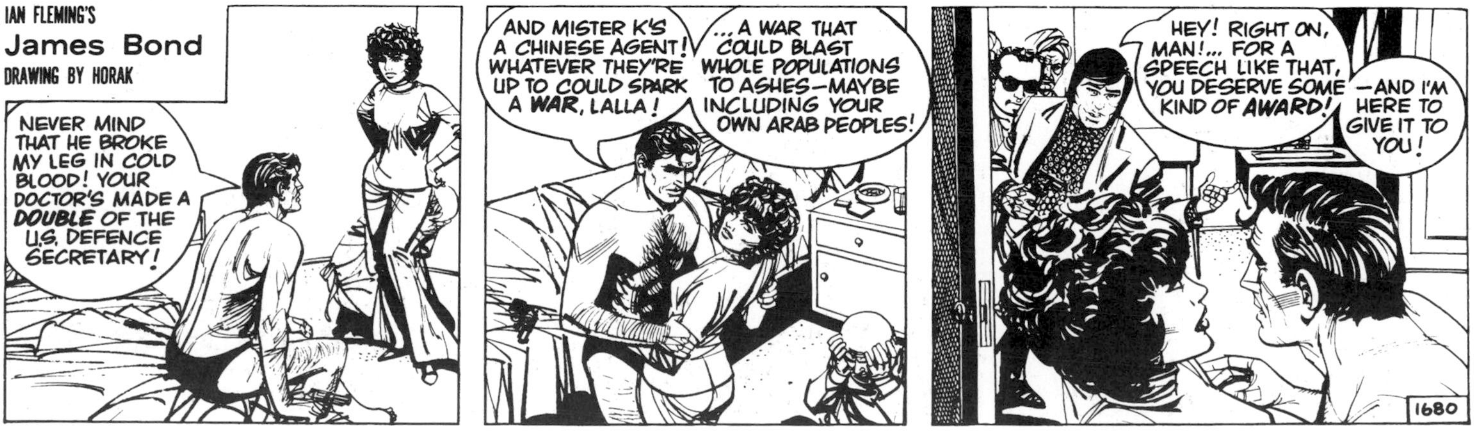
IAN FLEMING'S
James Bond
DRAWING BY HORAK
NEVER MIND THAT HE BROKE MY LEG IN COLD BLOOD! YOUR DOCTOR'S MADE A DOUBLE OF THE U.S. DEFENCE SECRETARY!
AND MISTER K'S A CHINESE AGENT! WHATEVER THEY'RE UP TO COULD SPARK A WAR, LALLA!
... A WAR THAT COULD BLAST WHOLE POPULATIONS TO ASHES—MAYBE INCLUDING YOUR OWN ARAB PEOPLES!
HEY! RIGHT ON, MAN!... FOR A SPEECH LIKE THAT, YOU DESERVE SOME KIND OF AWARD!
—AND I'M HERE TO GIVE IT TO YOU!
1680

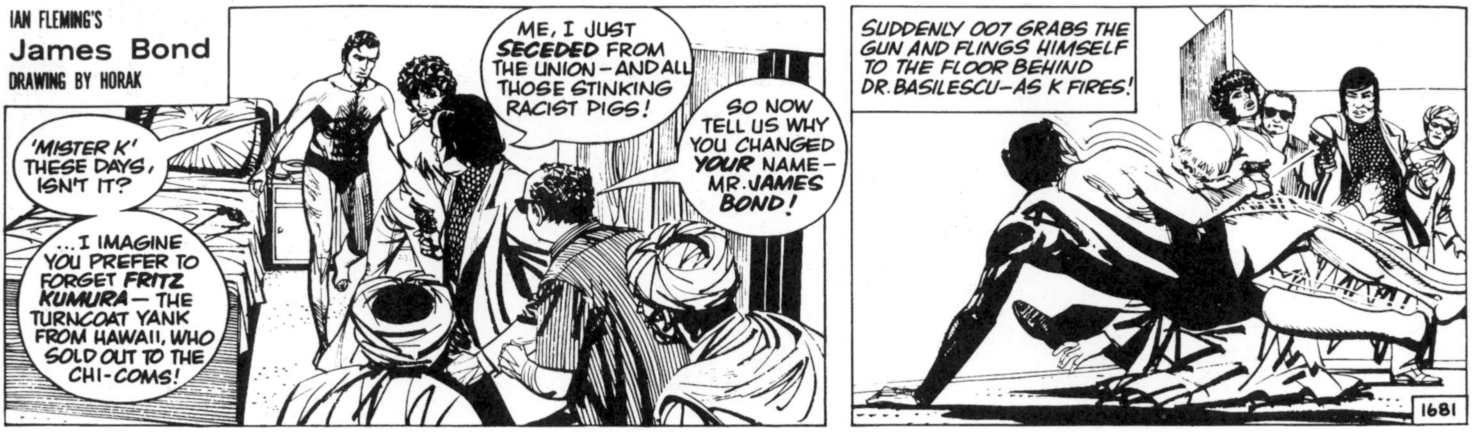
IAN FLEMING'S
James Bond
DRAWING BY HORAK
'MISTER K' THESE DAYS, ISN'T IT?
...I IMAGINE YOU PREFER TO FORGET FRITZ KUMURA — THE TURNCOAT YANK FROM HAWAII, WHO SOLD OUT TO THE CHI-COMS!
ME, I JUST SECEDED FROM THE UNION — AND ALL THOSE STINKING RACIST PIGS!
SO NOW TELL US WHY YOU CHANGED YOUR NAME — MR. JAMES BOND!
SUDDENLY 007 GRABS THE GUN AND FLINGS HIMSELF TO THE FLOOR BEHIND DR. BASILESCU — AS K FIRES!
1681

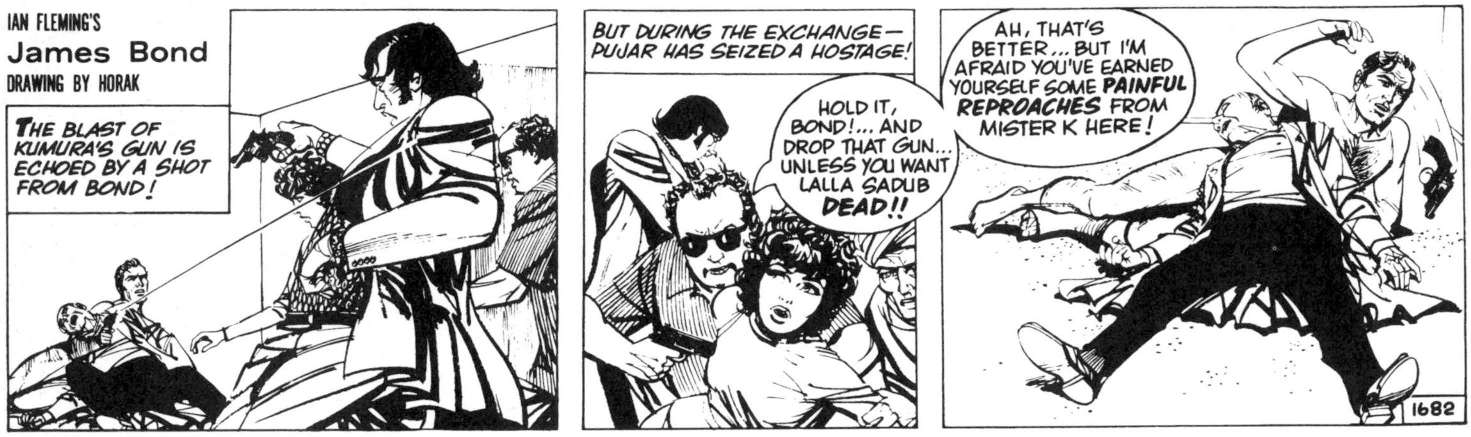
IAN FLEMING'S
James Bond
DRAWING BY HORAK
THE BLAST OF KUMURA'S GUN IS ECHOED BY A SHOT FROM BOND!
BUT DURING THE EXCHANGE — PUJAR HAS SEIZED A HOSTAGE!
HOLD IT, BOND!... AND DROP THAT GUN... UNLESS YOU WANT LALLA SADUB DEAD!!
AH, THAT'S BETTER... BUT I'M AFRAID YOU'VE EARNED YOURSELF SOME PAINFUL REPROACHES FROM MISTER K HERE!
1682

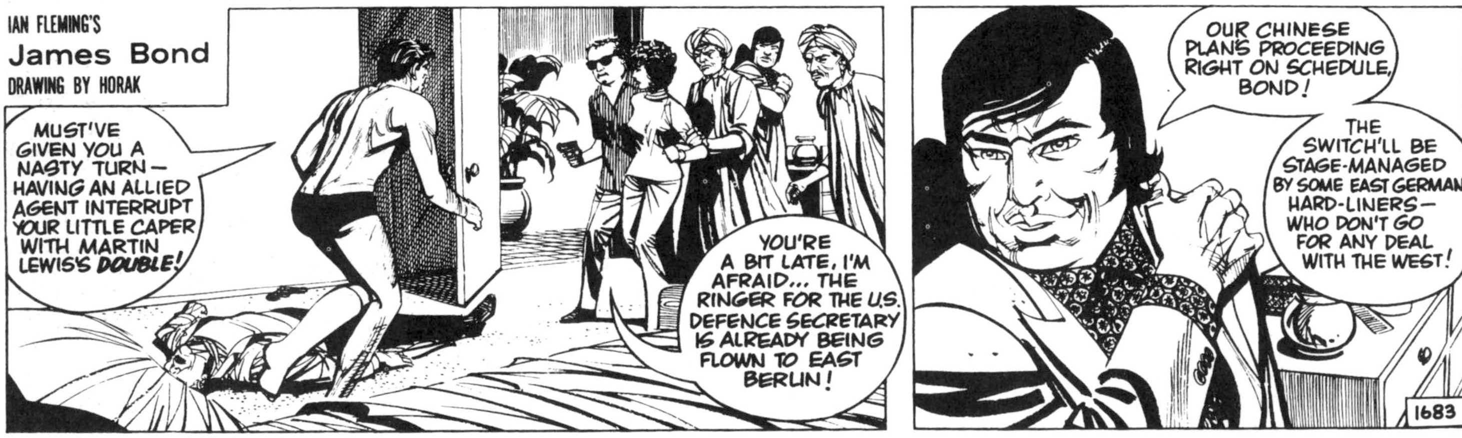
IAN FLEMING'S
James Bond
DRAWING BY HORAK
MUST'VE GIVEN YOU A NASTY TURN — HAVING AN ALLIED AGENT INTERRUPT YOUR LITTLE CAPER WITH MARTIN LEWIS'S DOUBLE!
YOU'RE A BIT LATE, I'M AFRAID... THE RINGER FOR THE U.S. DEFENCE SECRETARY IS ALREADY BEING FLOWN TO EAST BERLIN!
OUR CHINESE PLAN'S PROCEEDING RIGHT ON SCHEDULE, BOND!
THE SWITCH'LL BE STAGE-MANAGED BY SOME EAST GERMAN HARD-LINERS — WHO DON'T GO FOR ANY DEAL WITH THE WEST!
1683

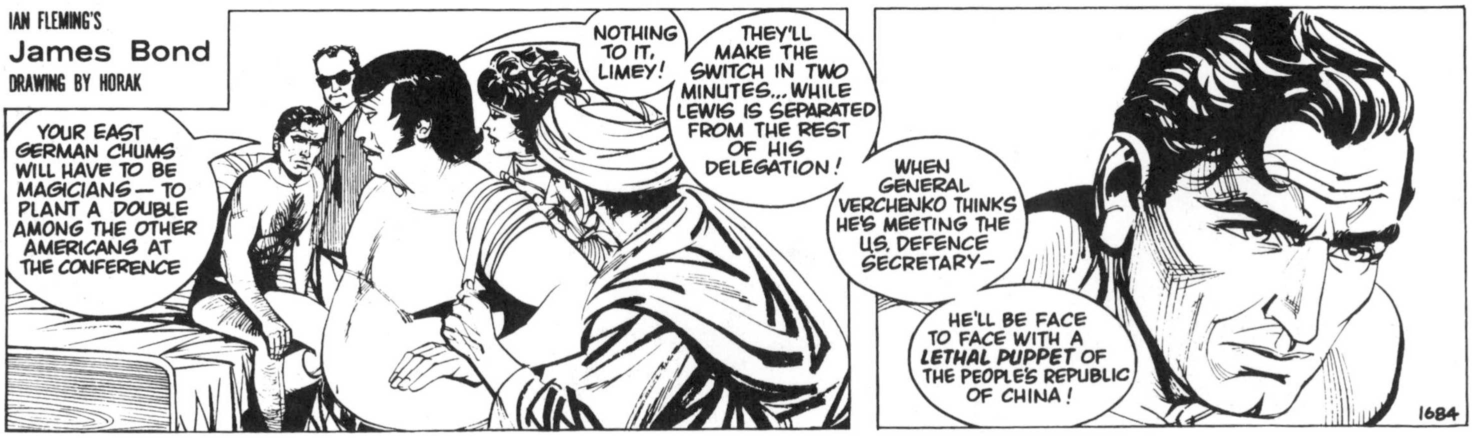
IAN FLEMING'S
James Bond
DRAWING BY HORAK
YOUR EAST GERMAN CHUMS WILL HAVE TO BE MAGICIANS — TO PLANT A DOUBLE AMONG THE OTHER AMERICANS AT THE CONFERENCE
NOTHING TO IT, LIMEY!
THEY'LL MAKE THE SWITCH IN TWO MINUTES... WHILE LEWIS IS SEPARATED FROM THE REST OF HIS DELEGATION!
WHEN GENERAL VERCHENKO THINKS HE'S MEETING THE U.S. DEFENCE SECRETARY —
HE'LL BE FACE TO FACE WITH A LETHAL PUPPET OF THE PEOPLE'S REPUBLIC OF CHINA!
1684

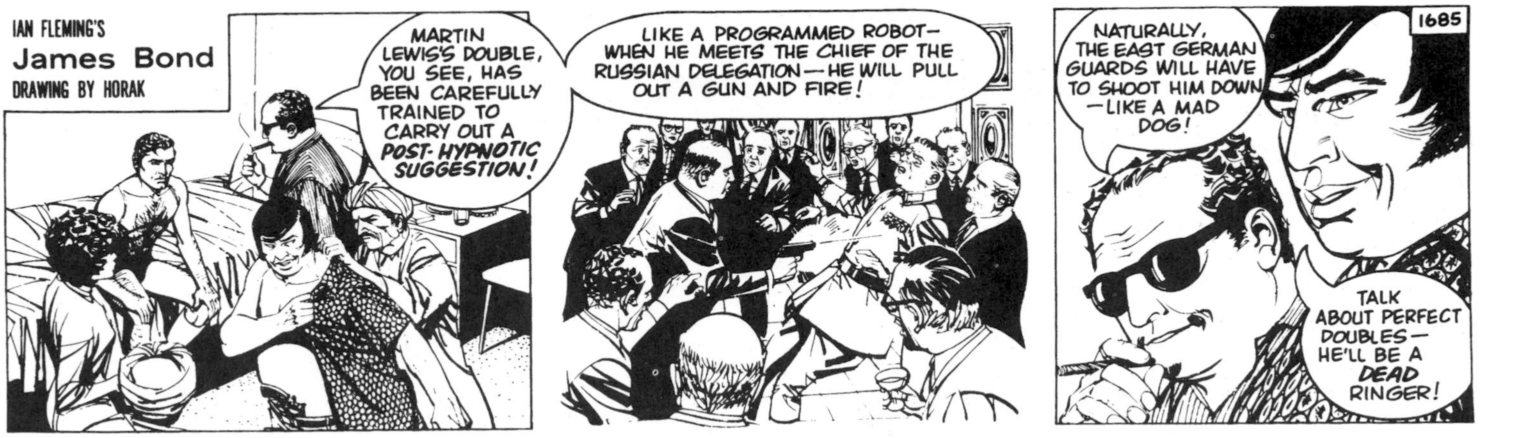
IAN FLEMING'S
James Bond
DRAWING BY HORAK
MARTIN LEWIS'S DOUBLE, YOU SEE, HAS BEEN CAREFULLY TRAINED TO CARRY OUT A POST-HYPNOTIC SUGGESTION!
LIKE A PROGRAMMED ROBOT— WHEN HE MEETS THE CHIEF OF THE RUSSIAN DELEGATION—HE WILL PULL OUT A GUN AND FIRE!
1685
NATURALLY, THE EAST GERMAN GUARDS WILL HAVE TO SHOOT HIM DOWN —LIKE A MAD DOG!
TALK ABOUT PERFECT DOUBLES— HE'LL BE A DEAD RINGER!

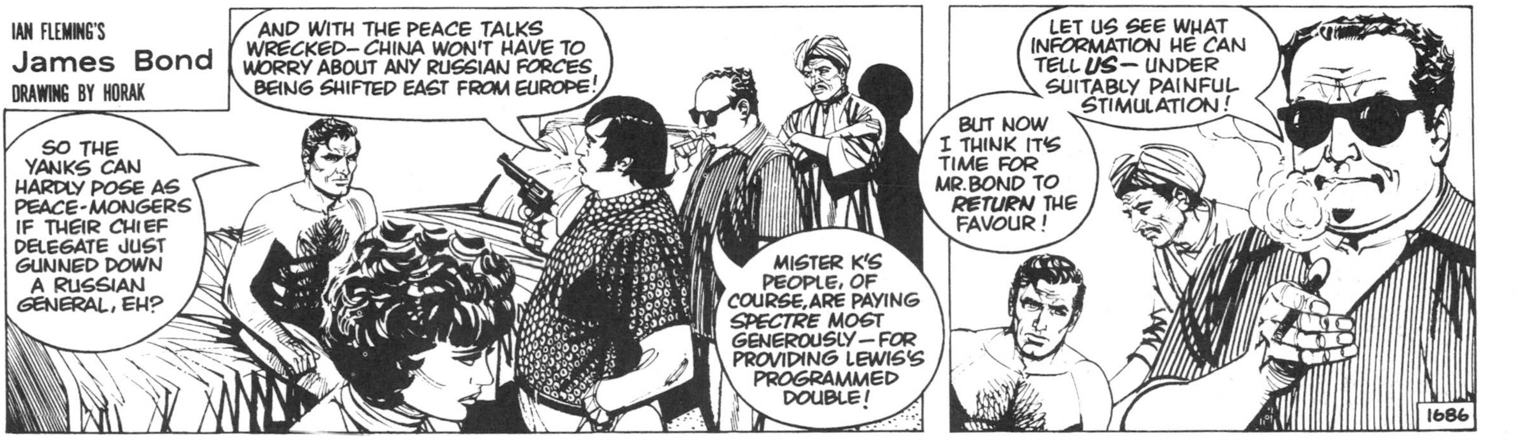
IAN FLEMING'S
James Bond
DRAWING BY HORAK
AND WITH THE PEACE TALKS WRECKED—CHINA WON'T HAVE TO WORRY ABOUT ANY RUSSIAN FORCES BEING SHIFTED EAST FROM EUROPE!
SO THE YANKS CAN HARDLY POSE AS PEACE-MONGERS IF THEIR CHIEF DELEGATE JUST GUNNED DOWN A RUSSIAN GENERAL, EH?
MISTER K'S PEOPLE, OF COURSE, ARE PAYING SPECTRE MOST GENEROUSLY—FOR PROVIDING LEWIS'S PROGRAMMED DOUBLE!
LET US SEE WHAT INFORMATION HE CAN TELL US— UNDER SUITABLY PAINFUL STIMULATION!
BUT NOW I THINK IT'S TIME FOR MR. BOND TO RETURN THE FAVOUR!
1686

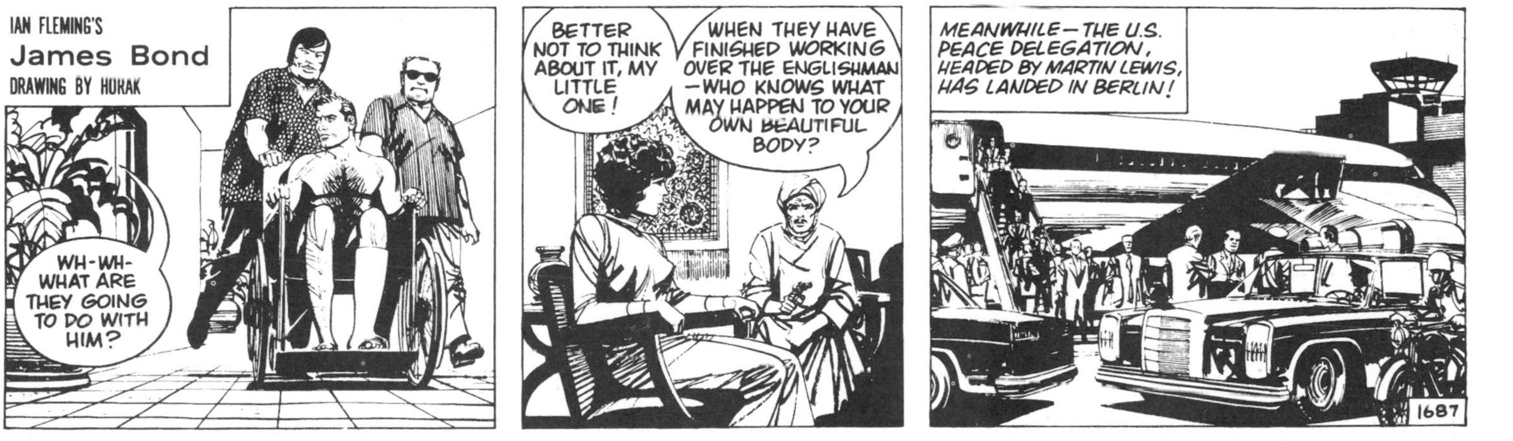
IAN FLEMING'S
James Bond
DRAWING BY HORAK
WH-WH- WHAT ARE THEY GOING TO DO WITH HIM?
BETTER NOT TO THINK ABOUT IT, MY LITTLE ONE!
WHEN THEY HAVE FINISHED WORKING OVER THE ENGLISHMAN —WHO KNOWS WHAT MAY HAPPEN TO YOUR OWN BEAUTIFUL BODY?
MEANWHILE—THE U.S. PEACE DELEGATION, HEADED BY MARTIN LEWIS, HAS LANDED IN BERLIN!
1687

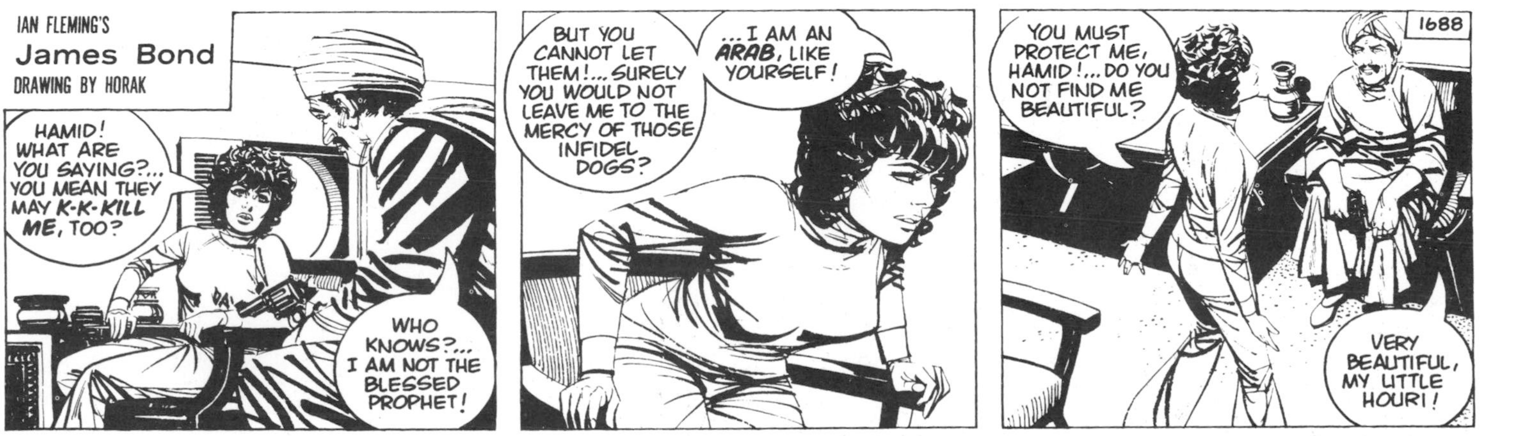
IAN FLEMING'S
James Bond
DRAWING BY HORAK
HAMID! WHAT ARE YOU SAYING?... YOU MEAN THEY MAY K-K-KILL ME, TOO?
WHO KNOWS?... I AM NOT THE BLESSED PROPHET!
BUT YOU CANNOT LET THEM!... SURELY YOU WOULD NOT LEAVE ME TO THE MERCY OF THOSE INFIDEL DOGS?
... I AM AN ARAB, LIKE YOURSELF!
1688
YOU MUST PROTECT ME, HAMID!... DO YOU NOT FIND ME BEAUTIFUL?
VERY BEAUTIFUL, MY LITTLE HOURI!

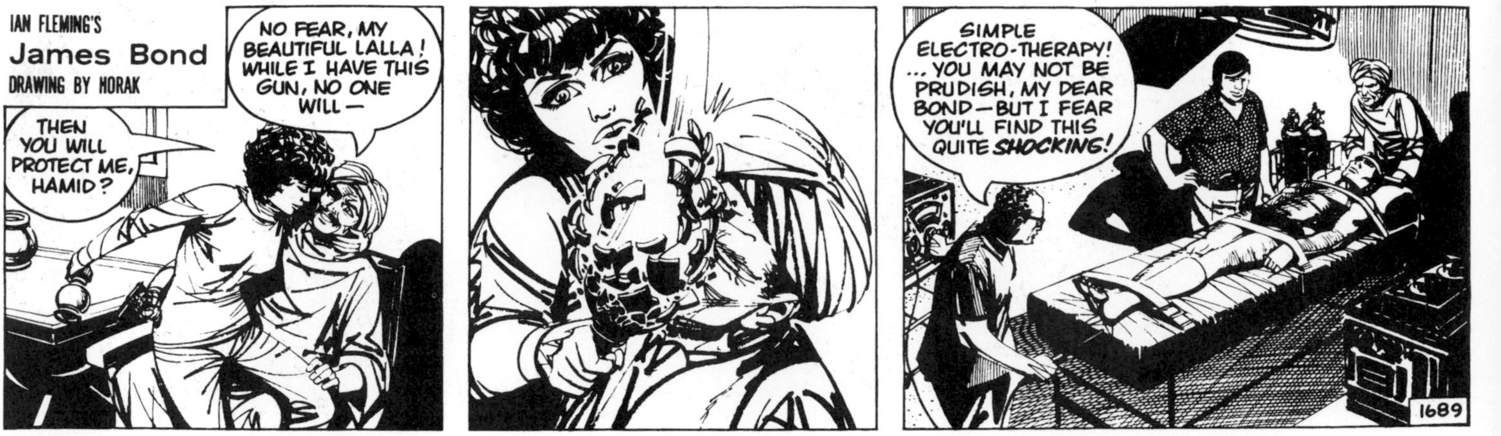

IAN FLEMING'S
James Bond
DRAWING BY HORAK
THEN YOU WILL PROTECT ME, HAMID?
NO FEAR, MY BEAUTIFUL LALLA! WHILE I HAVE THIS GUN, NO ONE WILL —
SIMPLE ELECTRO-THERAPY! ... YOU MAY NOT BE PRUDISH, MY DEAR BOND — BUT I FEAR YOU'LL FIND THIS QUITE SHOCKING!
1689

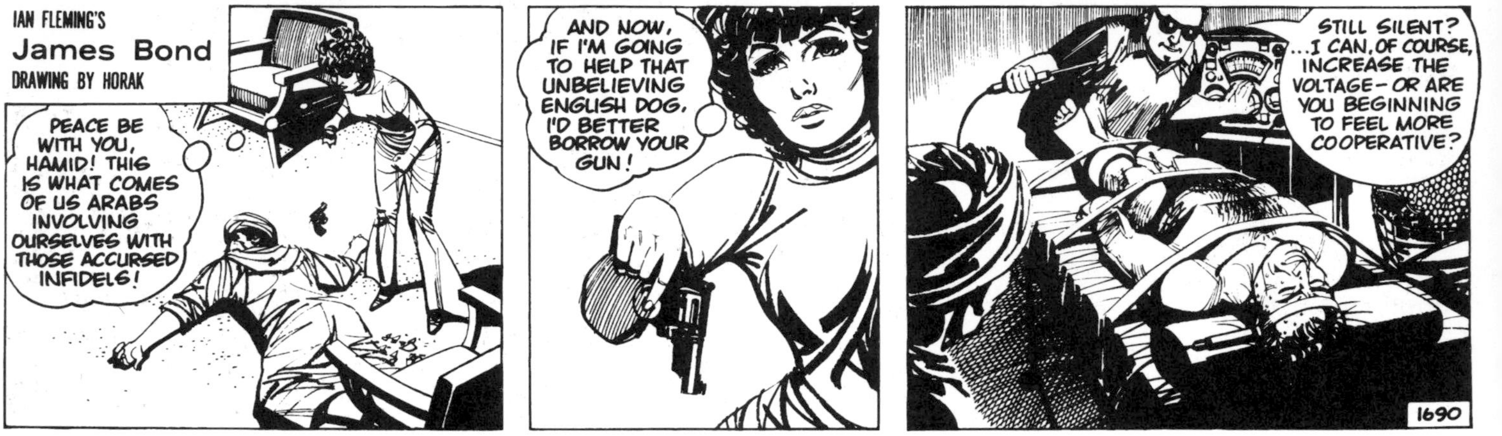

IAN FLEMING'S
James Bond
DRAWING BY HORAK
PEACE BE WITH YOU, HAMID! THIS IS WHAT COMES OF US ARABS INVOLVING OURSELVES WITH THOSE ACCURSED INFIDELS!
AND NOW, IF I'M GOING TO HELP THAT UNBELIEVING ENGLISH DOG, I'D BETTER BORROW YOUR GUN!
STILL SILENT? ...I CAN, OF COURSE, INCREASE THE VOLTAGE — OR ARE YOU BEGINNING TO FEEL MORE COOPERATIVE?
1690

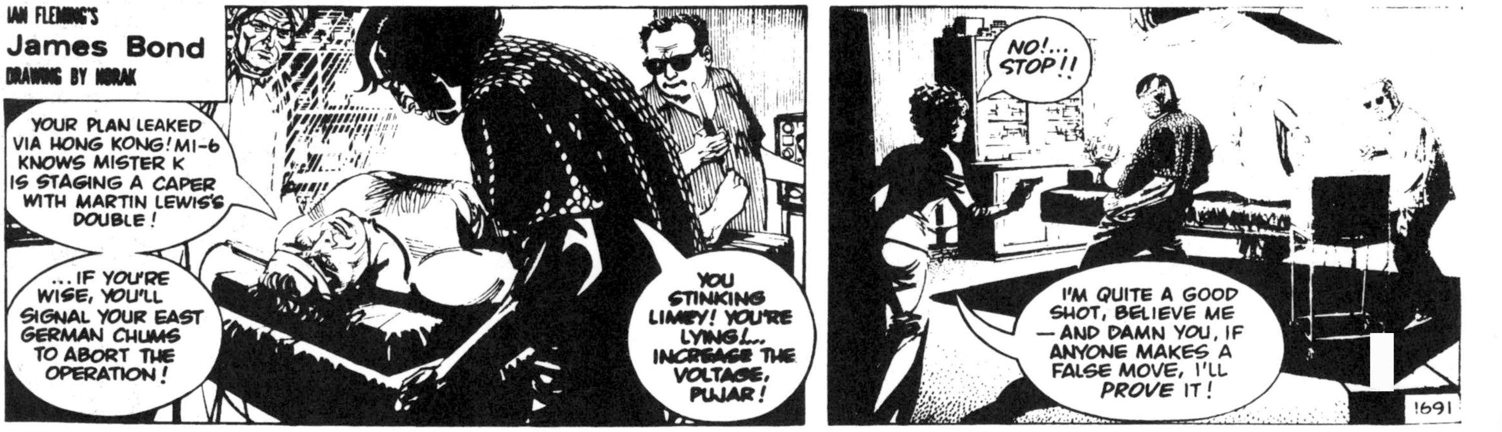

IAN FLEMING'S
James Bond
DRAWING BY HORAK
YOUR PLAN LEAKED VIA HONG KONG! MI-6 KNOWS MISTER K IS STAGING A CAPER WITH MARTIN LEWIS'S DOUBLE!
... IF YOU'RE WISE, YOU'LL SIGNAL YOUR EAST GERMAN CHUMS TO ABORT THE OPERATION!
YOU STINKING LIMEY! YOU'RE LYING!... INCREASE THE VOLTAGE, PUJAR!
NO!... STOP!!
I'M QUITE A GOOD SHOT, BELIEVE ME — AND DAMN YOU, IF ANYONE MAKES A FALSE MOVE, I'LL PROVE IT!
1691

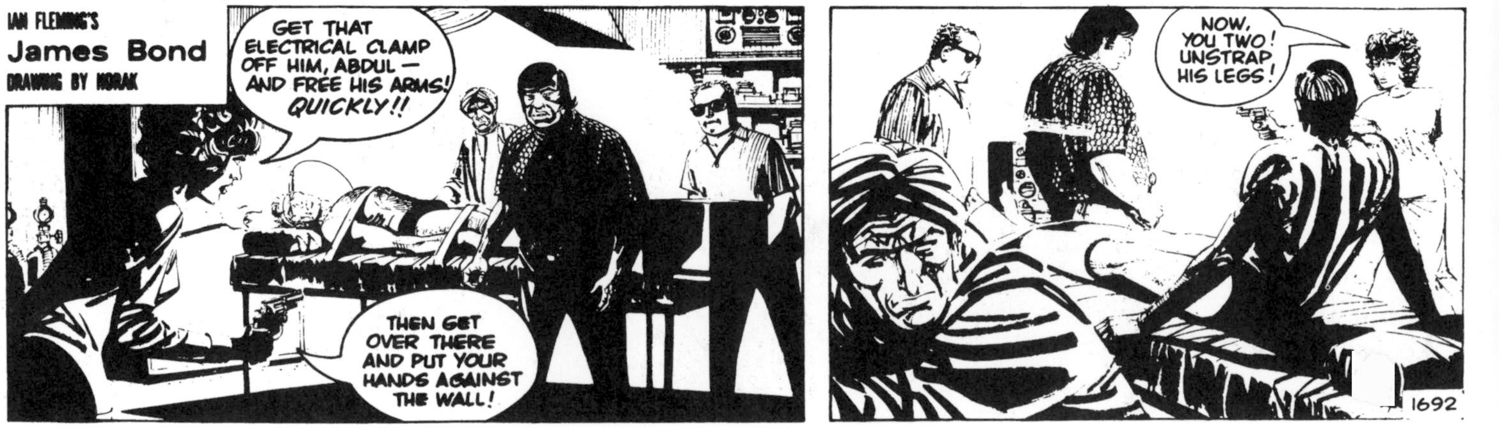

IAN FLEMING'S
James Bond
DRAWING BY HORAK
GET THAT ELECTRICAL CLAMP OFF HIM, ABDUL — AND FREE HIS ARMS! QUICKLY!!
THEN GET OVER THERE AND PUT YOUR HANDS AGAINST THE WALL!
NOW, YOU TWO! UNSTRAP HIS LEGS!
1692

These pages have been produced from the best available original materials.

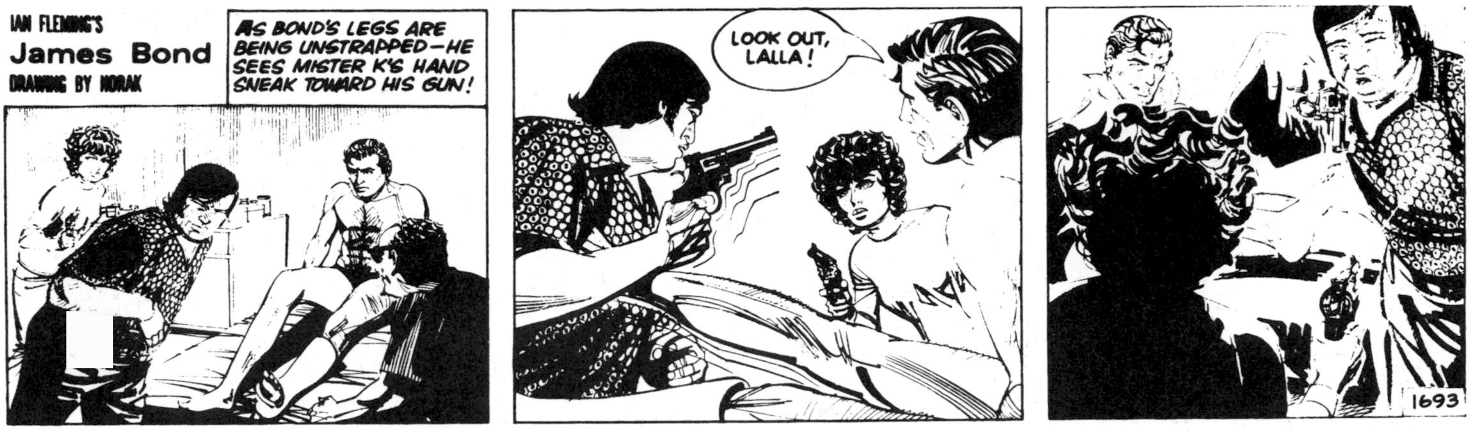
IAN FLEMING'S
James Bond
DRAWING BY NORAK
AS BOND'S LEGS ARE BEING UNSTRAPPED—HE SEES MISTER K'S HAND SNEAK TOWARD HIS GUN!
LOOK OUT, LALLA!
1693

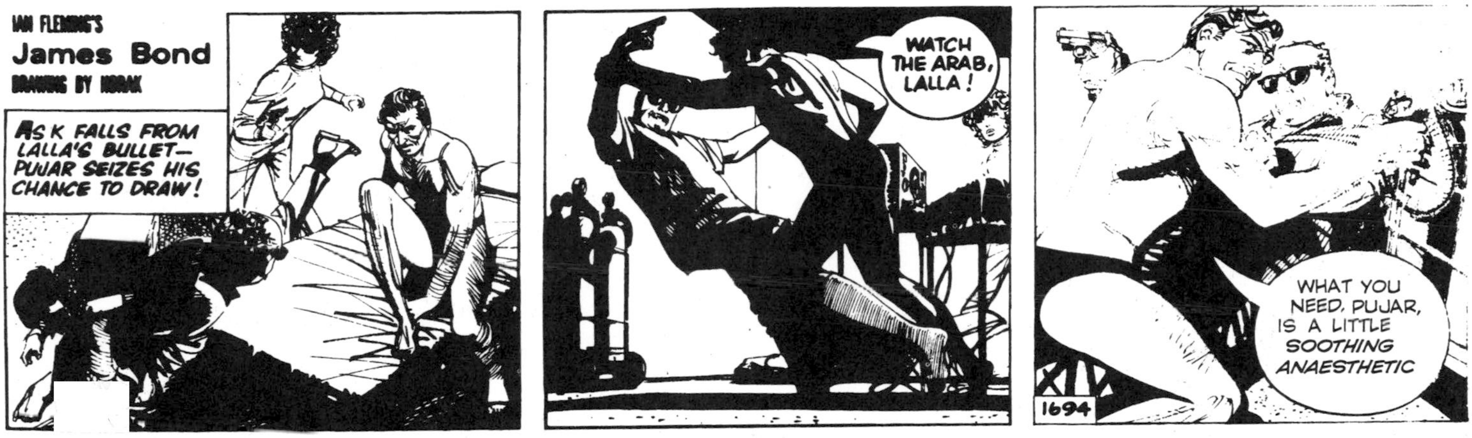
IAN FLEMING'S
James Bond
DRAWING BY NORAK
AS K FALLS FROM LALLA'S BULLET—PUJAR SEIZES HIS CHANCE TO DRAW!
WATCH THE ARAB, LALLA!
WHAT YOU NEED, PUJAR, IS A LITTLE SOOTHING ANAESTHETIC
1694

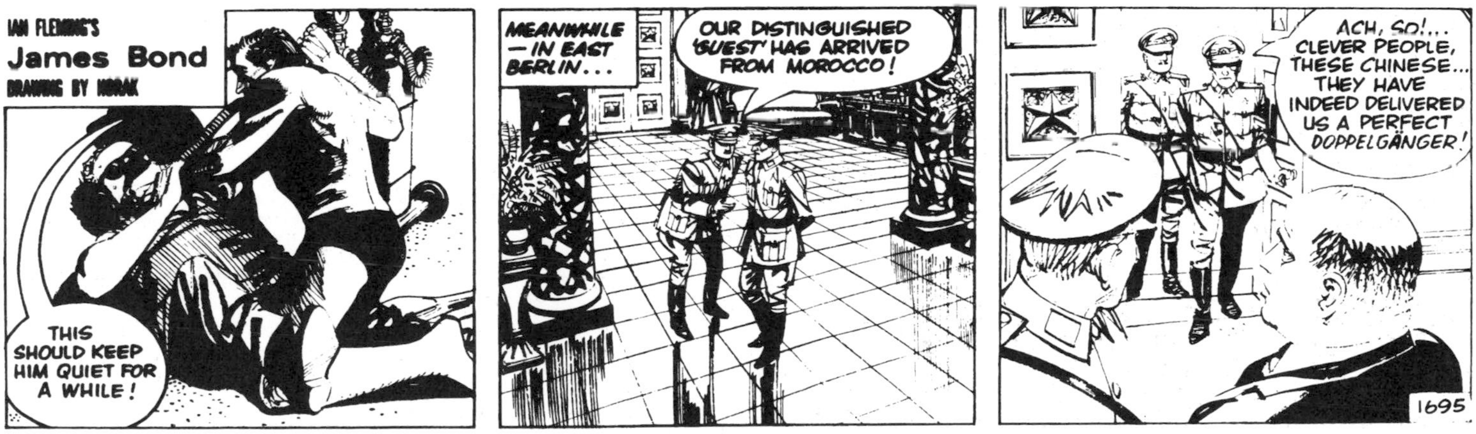
IAN FLEMING'S
James Bond
DRAWING BY NORAK
THIS SHOULD KEEP HIM QUIET FOR A WHILE!
MEANWHILE —IN EAST BERLIN...
OUR DISTINGUISHED 'GUEST' HAS ARRIVED FROM MOROCCO!
ACH, SO!... CLEVER PEOPLE, THESE CHINESE... THEY HAVE INDEED DELIVERED US A PERFECT DOPPELGÄNGER!
1695

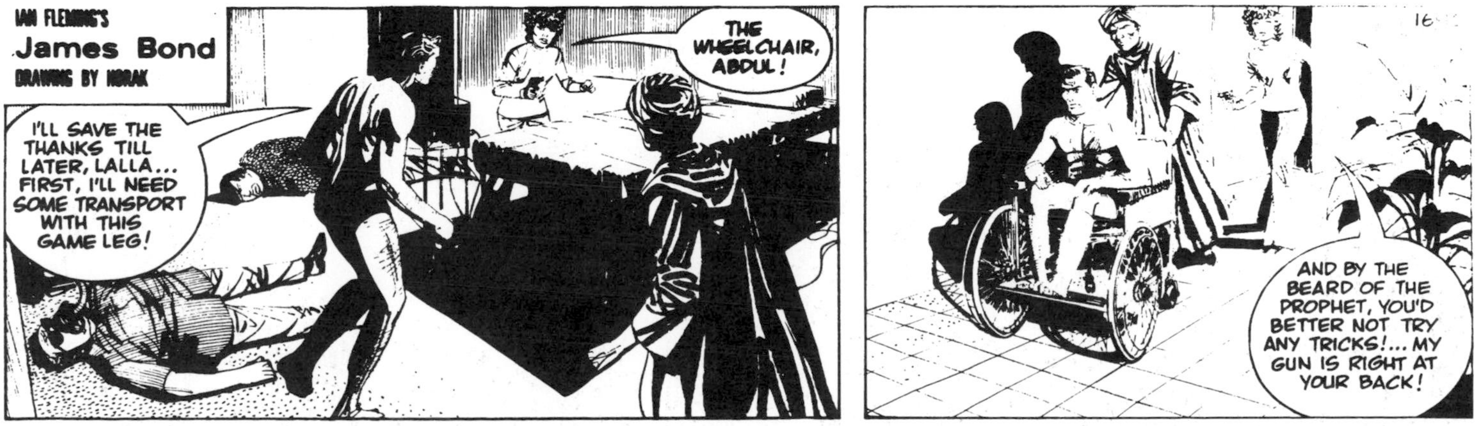
IAN FLEMING'S
James Bond
DRAWING BY NORAK
I'LL SAVE THE THANKS TILL LATER, LALLA... FIRST, I'LL NEED SOME TRANSPORT WITH THIS GAME LEG!
THE WHEELCHAIR, ABDUL!
AND BY THE BEARD OF THE PROPHET, YOU'D BETTER NOT TRY ANY TRICKS!... MY GUN IS RIGHT AT YOUR BACK!

These pages have been produced from the best available original materials.

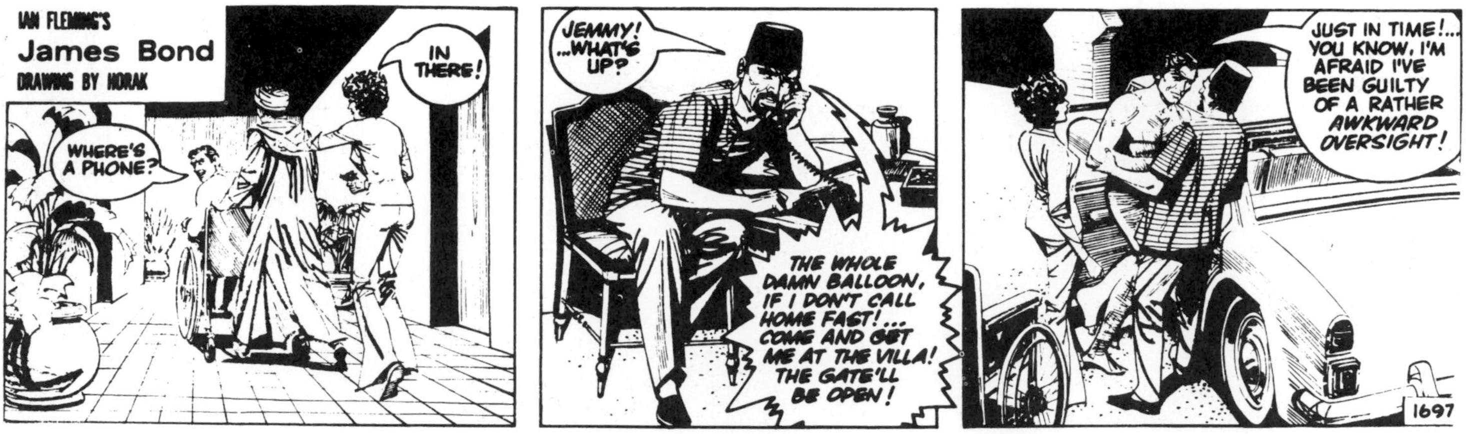
IAN FLEMING'S
James Bond
DRAWING BY HORAK
IN THERE!
WHERE'S A PHONE?
JEMMY! ...WHAT'S UP?
THE WHOLE DAMN BALLOON, IF I DON'T CALL HOME FAST!... COME AND GET ME AT THE VILLA! THE GATE'LL BE OPEN!
JUST IN TIME!... YOU KNOW, I'M AFRAID I'VE BEEN GUILTY OF A RATHER AWKWARD OVERSIGHT!
1697

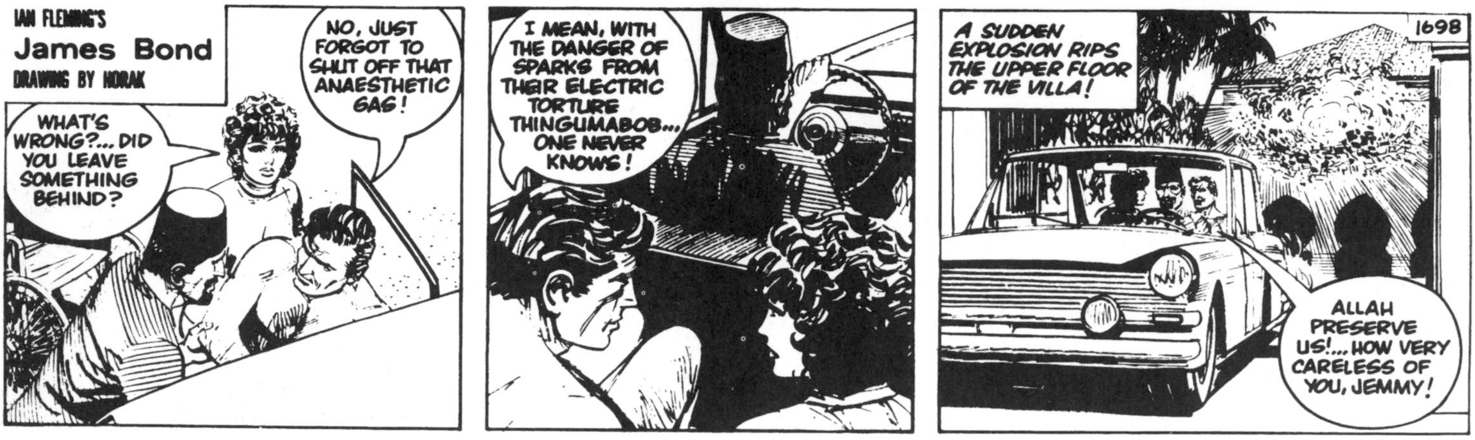
IAN FLEMING'S
James Bond
DRAWING BY HORAK
NO, JUST FORGOT TO SHUT OFF THAT ANAESTHETIC GAS!
WHAT'S WRONG?... DID YOU LEAVE SOMETHING BEHIND?
I MEAN, WITH THE DANGER OF SPARKS FROM THEIR ELECTRIC TORTURE THINGUMABOB... ONE NEVER KNOWS!
A SUDDEN EXPLOSION RIPS THE UPPER FLOOR OF THE VILLA!
1698
ALLAH PRESERVE US!... HOW VERY CARELESS OF YOU, JEMMY!

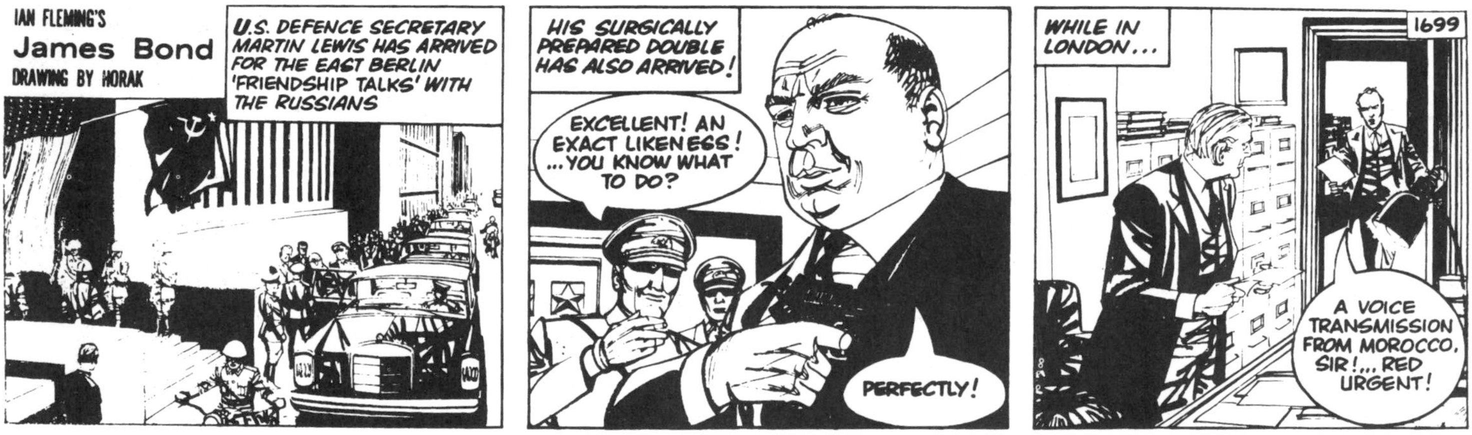
IAN FLEMING'S
James Bond
DRAWING BY HORAK
U.S. DEFENCE SECRETARY MARTIN LEWIS HAS ARRIVED FOR THE EAST BERLIN 'FRIENDSHIP TALKS' WITH THE RUSSIANS
HIS SURGICALLY PREPARED DOUBLE HAS ALSO ARRIVED!
EXCELLENT! AN EXACT LIKENESS! ...YOU KNOW WHAT TO DO?
PERFECTLY!
WHILE IN LONDON...
1699
A VOICE TRANSMISSION FROM MOROCCO, SIR!... RED URGENT!

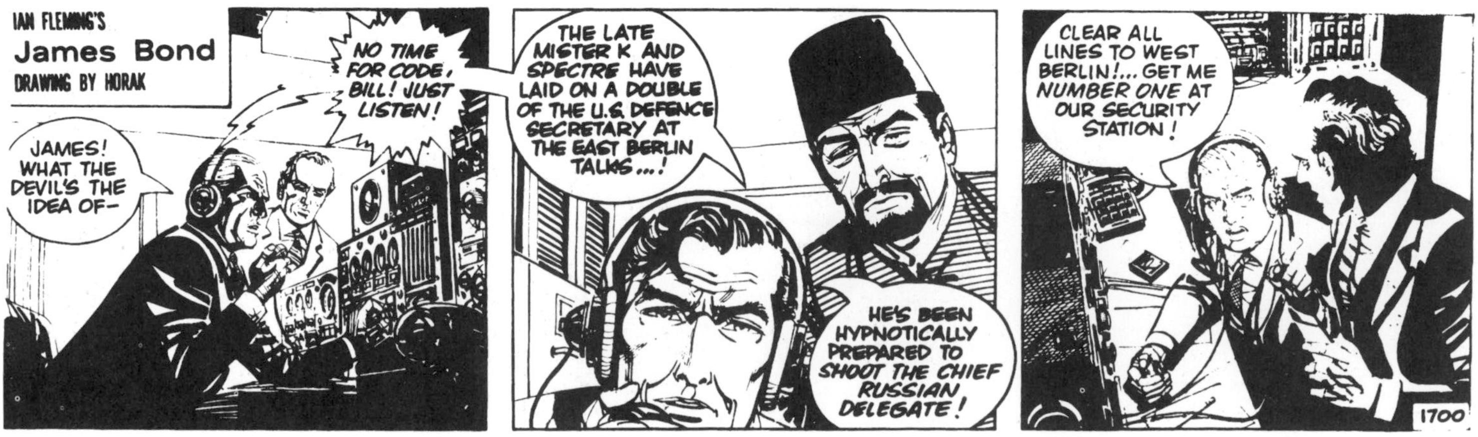
IAN FLEMING'S
James Bond
DRAWING BY HORAK
NO TIME FOR CODE, BILL! JUST LISTEN!
JAMES! WHAT THE DEVIL'S THE IDEA OF-
THE LATE MISTER K AND SPECTRE HAVE LAID ON A DOUBLE OF THE U.S. DEFENCE SECRETARY AT THE EAST BERLIN TALKS...!
HE'S BEEN HYPNOTICALLY PREPARED TO SHOOT THE CHIEF RUSSIAN DELEGATE!
CLEAR ALL LINES TO WEST BERLIN!... GET ME NUMBER ONE AT OUR SECURITY STATION!
1700

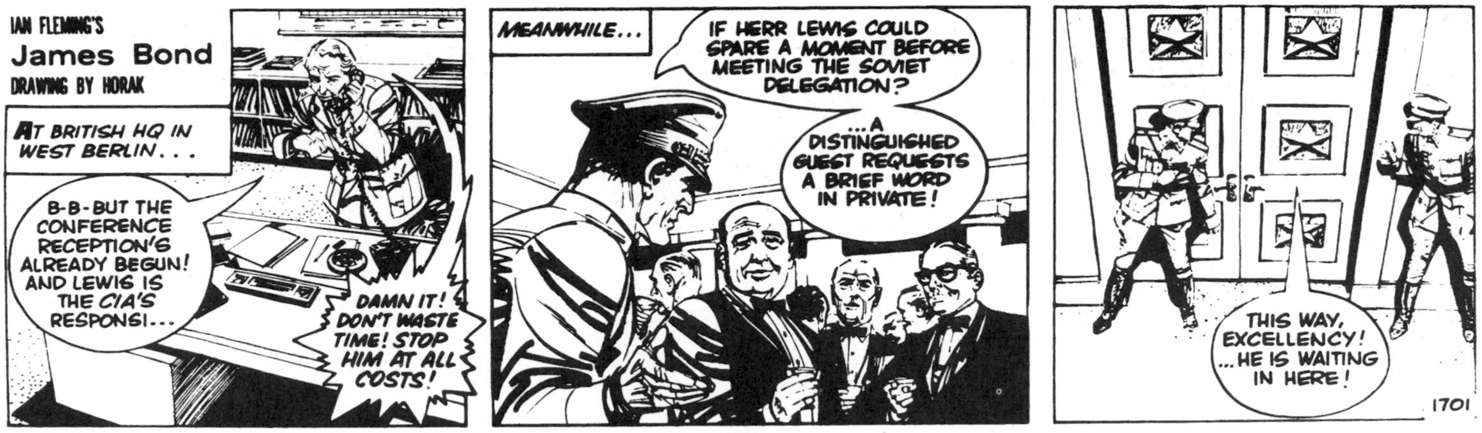
IAN FLEMING'S
James Bond
DRAWING BY HORAK
AT BRITISH HQ IN WEST BERLIN . . .
B-B-BUT THE CONFERENCE RECEPTION'S ALREADY BEGUN! AND LEWIS IS THE CIA'S RESPONSI...
DAMN IT! DON'T WASTE TIME! STOP HIM AT ALL COSTS!
MEANWHILE...
IF HERR LEWIS COULD SPARE A MOMENT BEFORE MEETING THE SOVIET DELEGATION?
...A DISTINGUISHED GUEST REQUESTS A BRIEF WORD IN PRIVATE!
THIS WAY, EXCELLENCY! ...HE IS WAITING IN HERE!
1701

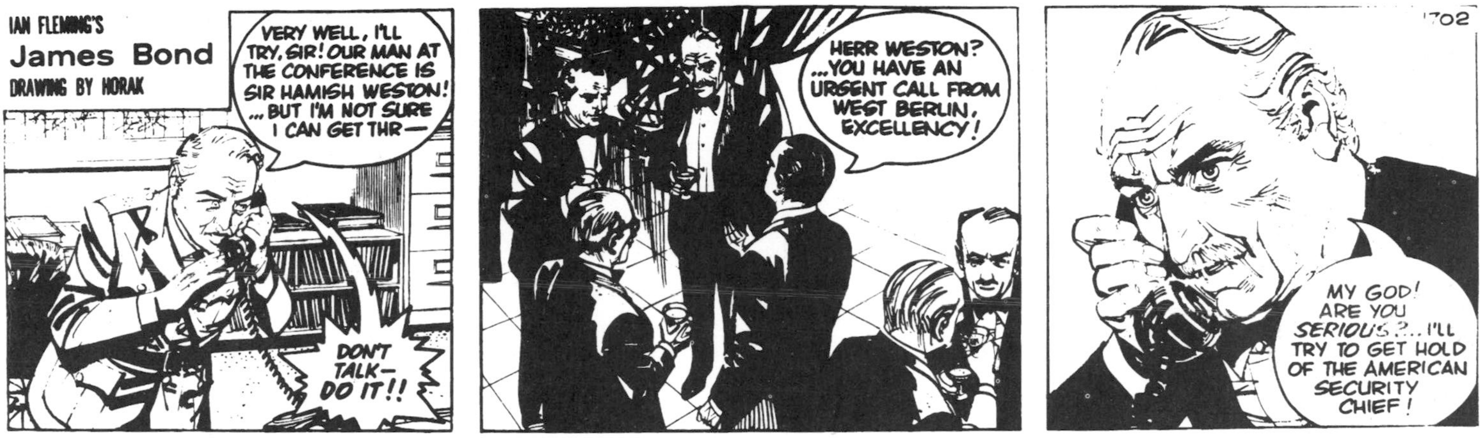
IAN FLEMING'S
James Bond
DRAWING BY HORAK
VERY WELL, I'LL TRY, SIR! OUR MAN AT THE CONFERENCE IS SIR HAMISH WESTON! ...BUT I'M NOT SURE I CAN GET THR—
DON'T TALK—DO IT!!
HERR WESTON? ...YOU HAVE AN URGENT CALL FROM WEST BERLIN, EXCELLENCY!
1702
MY GOD! ARE YOU SERIOUS?...I'LL TRY TO GET HOLD OF THE AMERICAN SECURITY CHIEF!

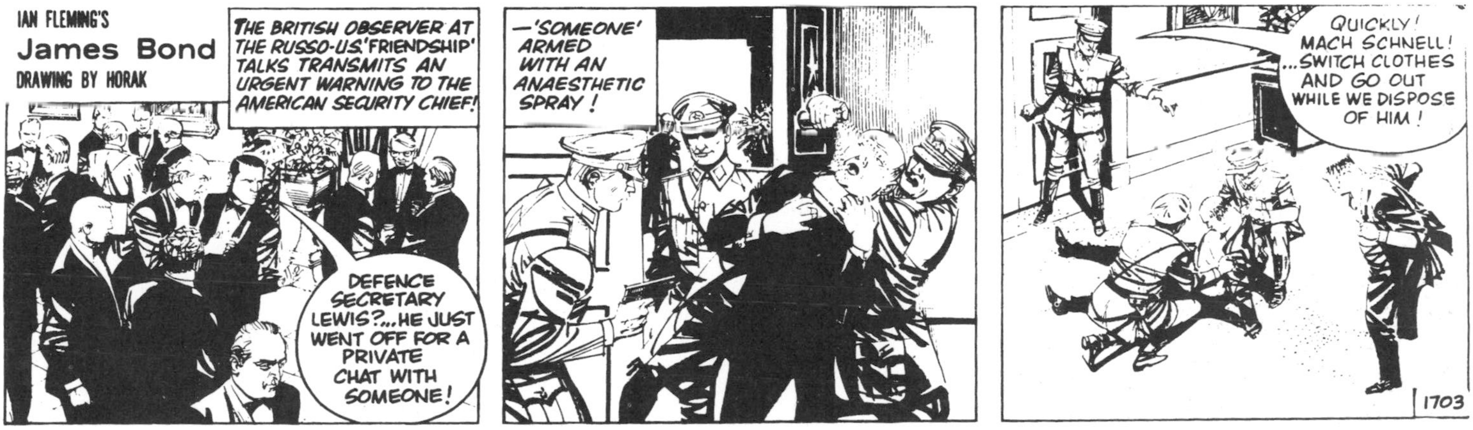
IAN FLEMING'S
James Bond
DRAWING BY HORAK
THE BRITISH OBSERVER AT THE RUSSO-U.S.'FRIENDSHIP' TALKS TRANSMITS AN URGENT WARNING TO THE AMERICAN SECURITY CHIEF!
DEFENCE SECRETARY LEWIS?...HE JUST WENT OFF FOR A PRIVATE CHAT WITH SOMEONE!
—'SOMEONE' ARMED WITH AN ANAESTHETIC SPRAY!
QUICKLY! MACH SCHNELL! ...SWITCH CLOTHES AND GO OUT WHILE WE DISPOSE OF HIM!
1703

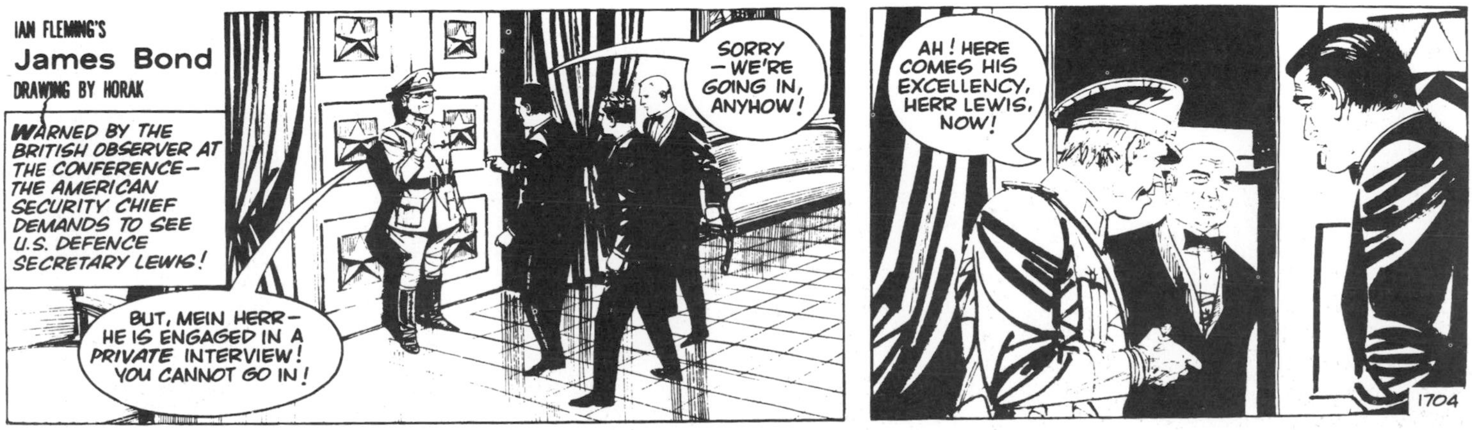
IAN FLEMING'S
James Bond
DRAWING BY HORAK
WARNED BY THE BRITISH OBSERVER AT THE CONFERENCE—THE AMERICAN SECURITY CHIEF DEMANDS TO SEE U.S. DEFENCE SECRETARY LEWIS!
BUT, MEIN HERR—HE IS ENGAGED IN A PRIVATE INTERVIEW! YOU CANNOT GO IN!
SORRY—WE'RE GOING IN, ANYHOW!
AH! HERE COMES HIS EXCELLENCY, HERR LEWIS, NOW!
1704

These pages have been produced from the best available original materials.

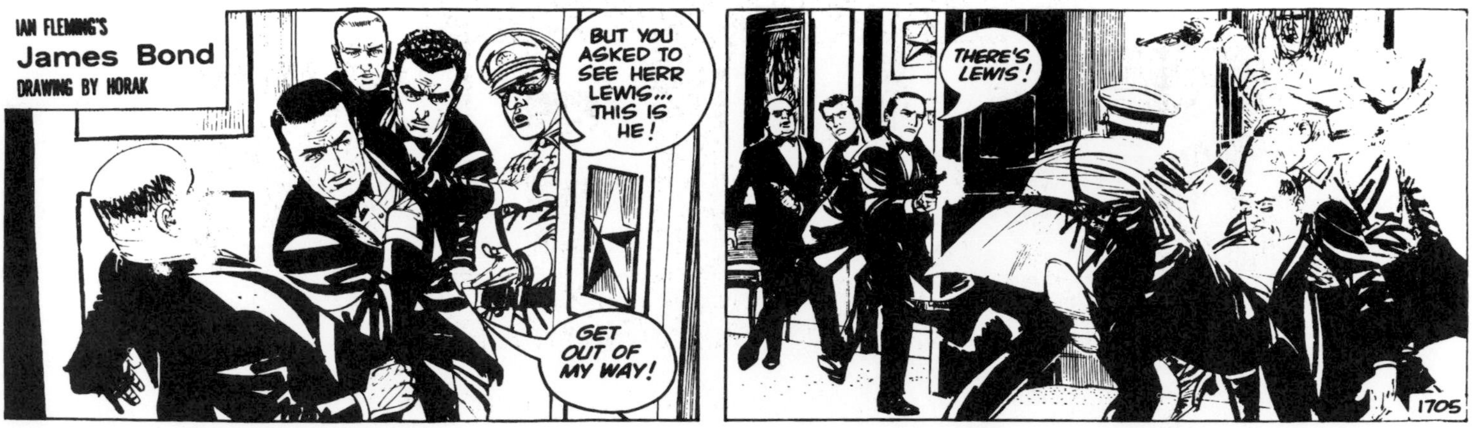
IAN FLEMING'S
James Bond
DRAWING BY HORAK
BUT YOU ASKED TO SEE HERR LEWIS... THIS IS HE!
GET OUT OF MY WAY!
THERE'S LEWIS!
1705

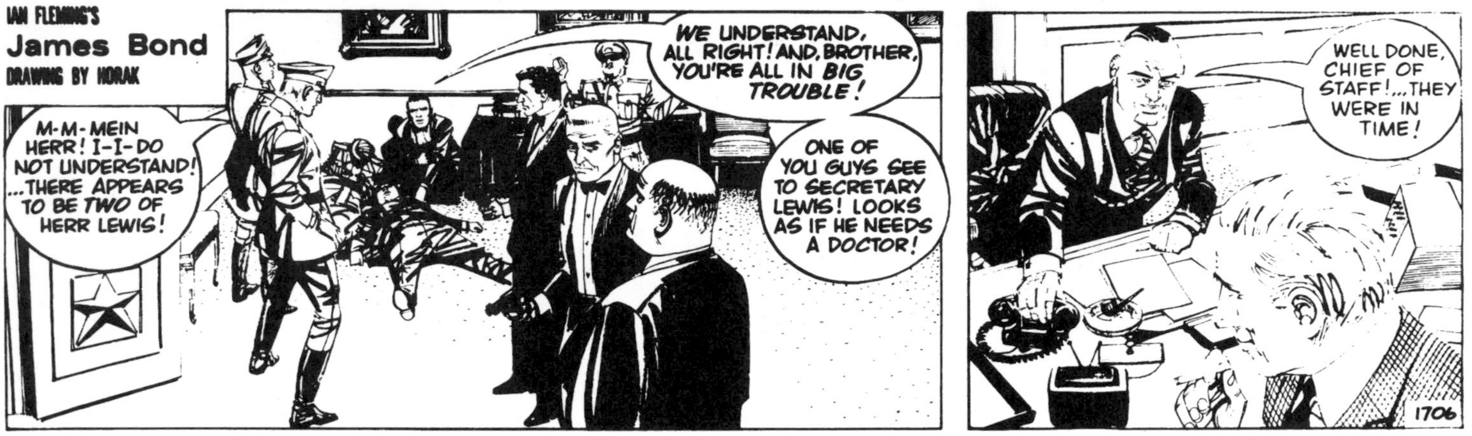
IAN FLEMING'S
James Bond
DRAWING BY HORAK
M-M-MEIN HERR! I-I-DO NOT UNDERSTAND! ...THERE APPEARS TO BE TWO OF HERR LEWIS!
WE UNDERSTAND, ALL RIGHT! AND, BROTHER, YOU'RE ALL IN BIG TROUBLE!
ONE OF YOU GUYS SEE TO SECRETARY LEWIS! LOOKS AS IF HE NEEDS A DOCTOR!
WELL DONE, CHIEF OF STAFF!... THEY WERE IN TIME!
1706

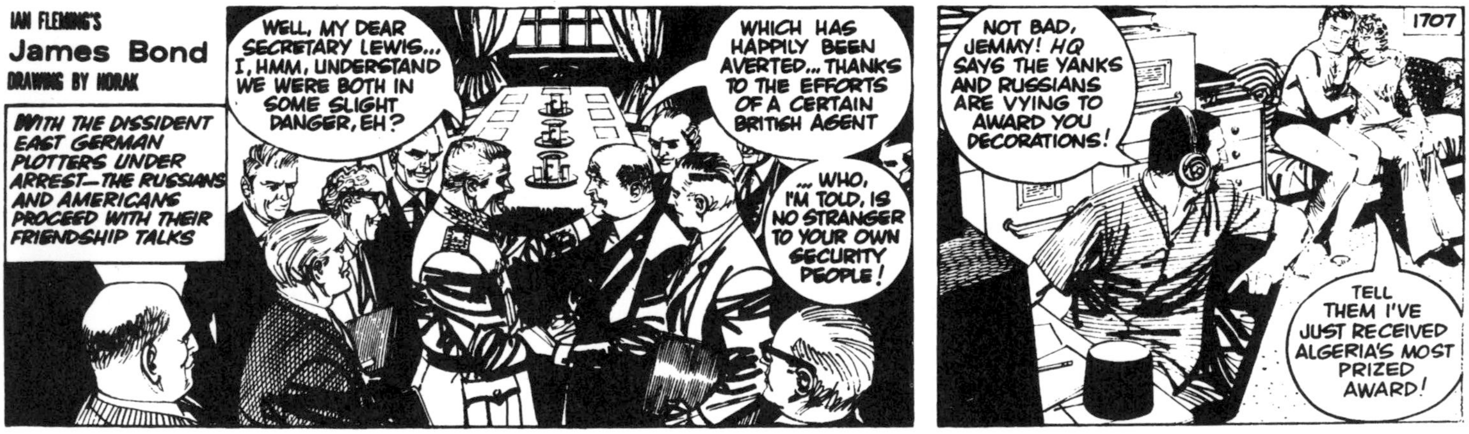
IAN FLEMING'S
James Bond
DRAWING BY HORAK
WITH THE DISSIDENT EAST GERMAN PLOTTERS UNDER ARREST—THE RUSSIANS AND AMERICANS PROCEED WITH THEIR FRIENDSHIP TALKS
WELL, MY DEAR SECRETARY LEWIS... I, HMM, UNDERSTAND WE WERE BOTH IN SOME SLIGHT DANGER, EH?
WHICH HAS HAPPILY BEEN AVERTED... THANKS TO THE EFFORTS OF A CERTAIN BRITISH AGENT
... WHO, I'M TOLD, IS NO STRANGER TO YOUR OWN SECURITY PEOPLE!
1707
NOT BAD, JEMMY! HQ SAYS THE YANKS AND RUSSIANS ARE VYING TO AWARD YOU DECORATIONS!
TELL THEM I'VE JUST RECEIVED ALGERIA'S MOST PRIZED AWARD!

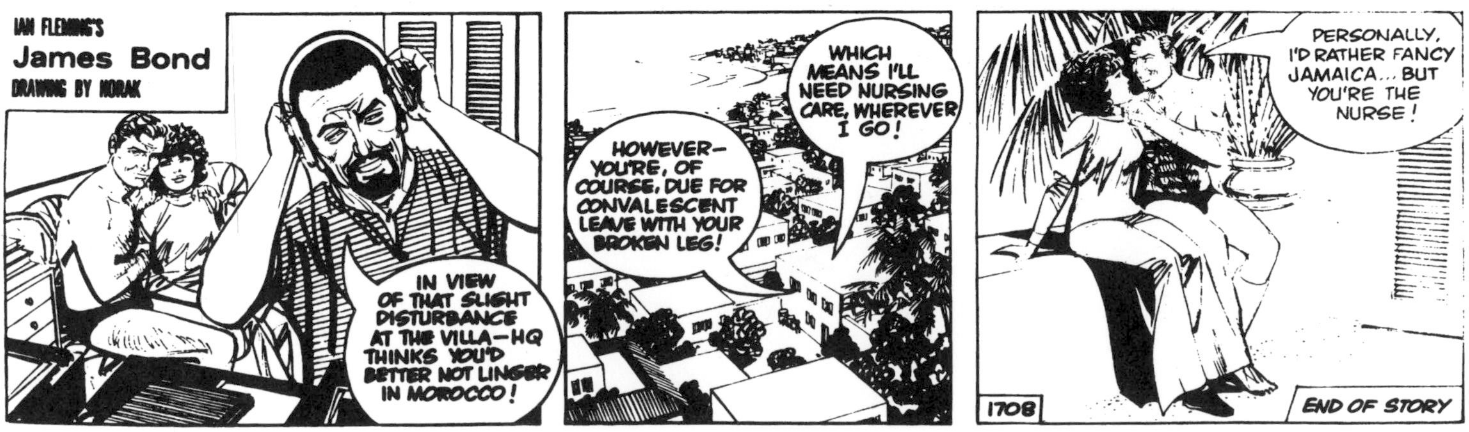
IAN FLEMING'S
James Bond
DRAWING BY HORAK
IN VIEW OF THAT SLIGHT DISTURBANCE AT THE VILLA—HQ THINKS YOU'D BETTER NOT LINGER IN MOROCCO!
HOWEVER—YOU'RE, OF COURSE, DUE FOR CONVALESCENT LEAVE WITH YOUR BROKEN LEG!
WHICH MEANS I'LL NEED NURSING CARE, WHEREVER I GO!
PERSONALLY, I'D RATHER FANCY JAMAICA... BUT YOU'RE THE NURSE!
1708
END OF STORY

These pages have been produced from the best available original materials.

STAR FIRE

To many *Bond* fans, Jim Lawrence's plot may seem simple compared to the previous comic strip outings. The style and placement of some characters does not gel well in the opening panels, but as the story arc develops, everything starts to fall into place. Although some of the sequences do warrant fast-paced action and vivid panels, Horak leaves out just enough for readers to imagine the finer points beyond the illustrations.

The visual style of *Star Fire* certainly has the look and feel of the Connery era. One-liners are written as if they were made for the infamous Scot to utter, and Horak's illustrations of the action sequences are reminiscent of his rough-and-ready fighting style.

Plot twists abound as *Star Fire* reaches its conclusion, with Lawrence playing up the S.P.E.C.T.R.E. infighting that was first hinted at in *The Golden Ghost*. Madame Spectra also gets a name check, but *Star Fire* is the last comic strip to feature the organisation until *Doomcrack*, published ten years later.

Despite the lack of a love interest for 007, *Star Fire* proves that *James Bond* adventures can still be exciting with a straight-forward espionage plot.

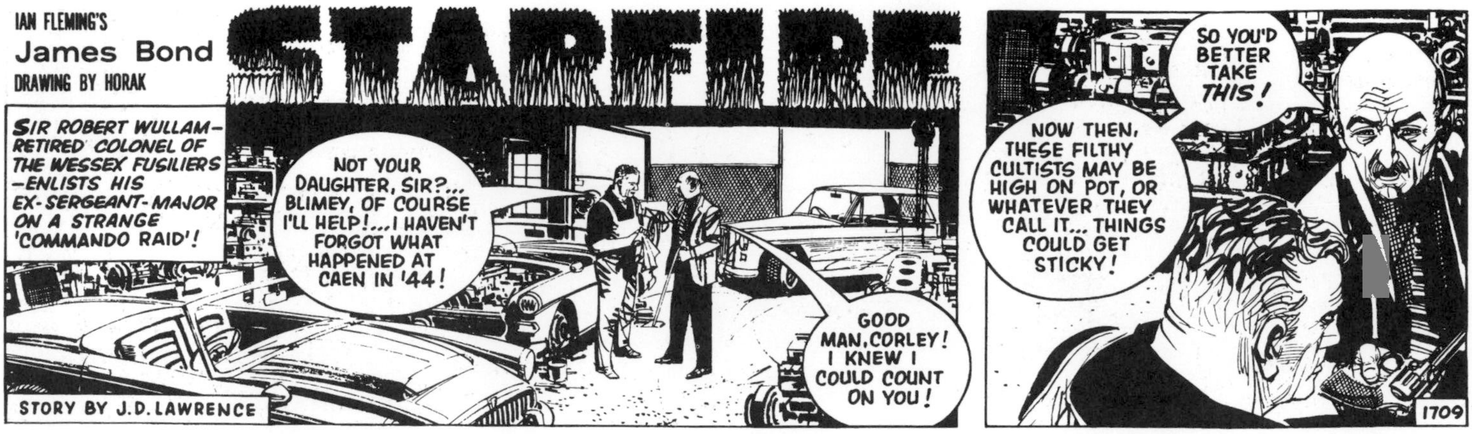
IAN FLEMING'S
James Bond
DRAWING BY HORAK
STARFIRE
SIR ROBERT WULLAM—RETIRED COLONEL OF THE WESSEX FUSILIERS—ENLISTS HIS EX-SERGEANT-MAJOR ON A STRANGE 'COMMANDO RAID'!
NOT YOUR DAUGHTER, SIR?... BLIMEY, OF COURSE I'LL HELP!... I HAVEN'T FORGOT WHAT HAPPENED AT CAEN IN '44!
GOOD MAN, CORLEY! I KNEW I COULD COUNT ON YOU!
STORY BY J.D. LAWRENCE
NOW THEN, THESE FILTHY CULTISTS MAY BE HIGH ON POT, OR WHATEVER THEY CALL IT... THINGS COULD GET STICKY!
SO YOU'D BETTER TAKE THIS!
1709

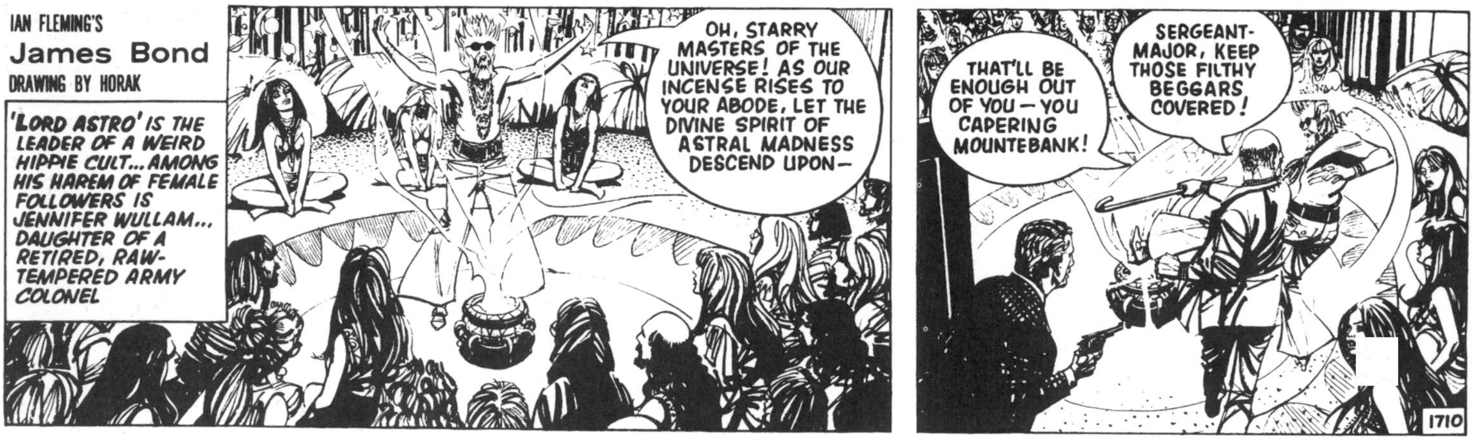
IAN FLEMING'S
James Bond
DRAWING BY HORAK
'LORD ASTRO' IS THE LEADER OF A WEIRD HIPPIE CULT... AMONG HIS HAREM OF FEMALE FOLLOWERS IS JENNIFER WULLAM... DAUGHTER OF A RETIRED, RAW-TEMPERED ARMY COLONEL
OH, STARRY MASTERS OF THE UNIVERSE! AS OUR INCENSE RISES TO YOUR ABODE, LET THE DIVINE SPIRIT OF ASTRAL MADNESS DESCEND UPON—
THAT'LL BE ENOUGH OUT OF YOU—YOU CAPERING MOUNTEBANK!
SERGEANT-MAJOR, KEEP THOSE FILTHY BEGGARS COVERED!
1710

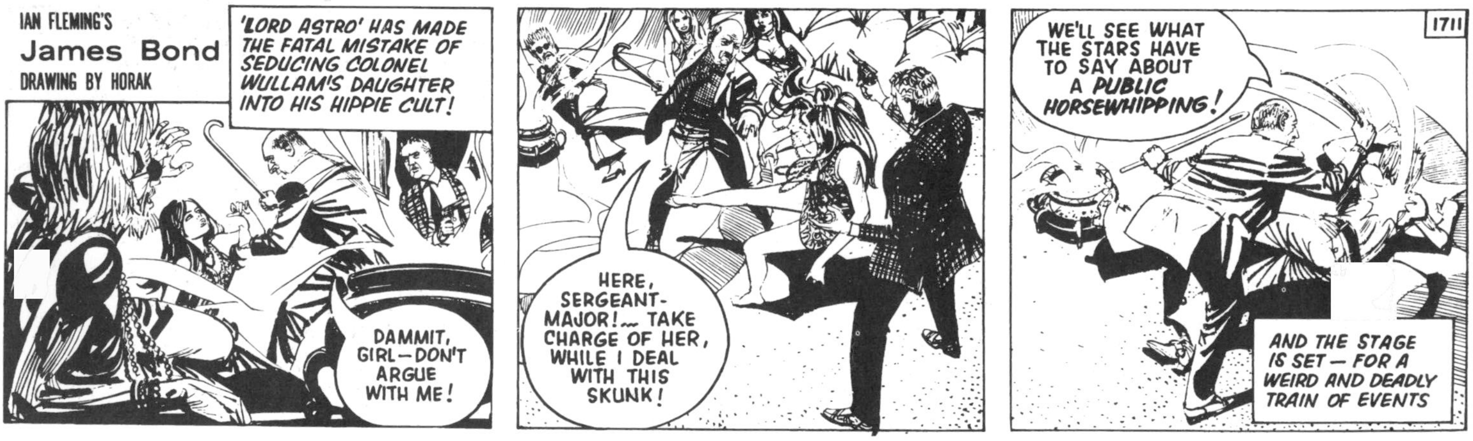
IAN FLEMING'S
James Bond
DRAWING BY HORAK
'LORD ASTRO' HAS MADE THE FATAL MISTAKE OF SEDUCING COLONEL WULLAM'S DAUGHTER INTO HIS HIPPIE CULT!
DAMMIT, GIRL—DON'T ARGUE WITH ME!
HERE, SERGEANT-MAJOR!... TAKE CHARGE OF HER, WHILE I DEAL WITH THIS SKUNK!
1711
WE'LL SEE WHAT THE STARS HAVE TO SAY ABOUT A PUBLIC HORSEWHIPPING!
AND THE STAGE IS SET—FOR A WEIRD AND DEADLY TRAIN OF EVENTS

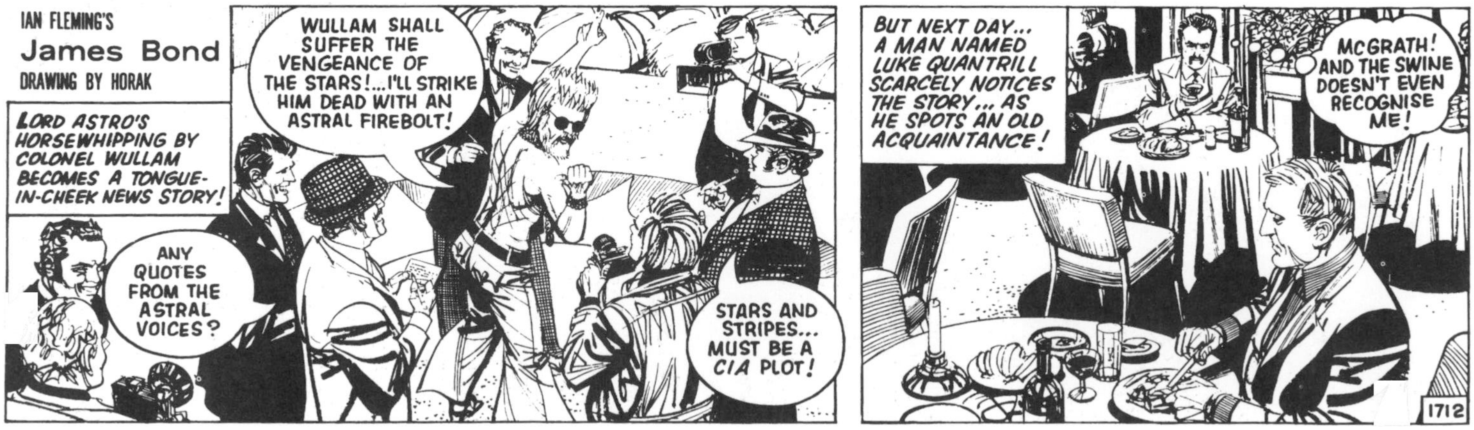
IAN FLEMING'S
James Bond
DRAWING BY HORAK
LORD ASTRO'S HORSEWHIPPING BY COLONEL WULLAM BECOMES A TONGUE-IN-CHEEK NEWS STORY!
ANY QUOTES FROM THE ASTRAL VOICES?
WULLAM SHALL SUFFER THE VENGEANCE OF THE STARS!... I'LL STRIKE HIM DEAD WITH AN ASTRAL FIREBOLT!
STARS AND STRIPES... MUST BE A CIA PLOT!
BUT NEXT DAY... A MAN NAMED LUKE QUANTRILL SCARCELY NOTICES THE STORY... AS HE SPOTS AN OLD ACQUAINTANCE!
MCGRATH! AND THE SWINE DOESN'T EVEN RECOGNISE ME!
1712

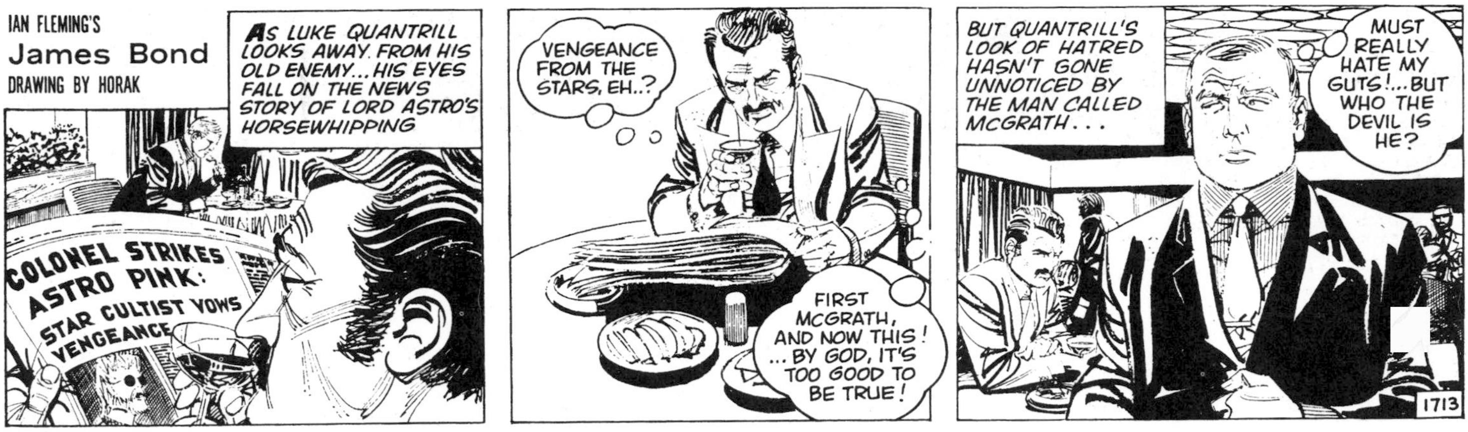
IAN FLEMING'S
James Bond
DRAWING BY HORAK
AS LUKE QUANTRILL LOOKS AWAY FROM HIS OLD ENEMY... HIS EYES FALL ON THE NEWS STORY OF LORD ASTRO'S HORSEWHIPPING
COLONEL STRIKES ASTRO PINK:
STAR CULTIST VOWS VENGEANCE
VENGEANCE FROM THE STARS, EH..?
FIRST McGRATH, AND NOW THIS! ... BY GOD, IT'S TOO GOOD TO BE TRUE!
BUT QUANTRILL'S LOOK OF HATRED HASN'T GONE UNNOTICED BY THE MAN CALLED McGRATH...
MUST REALLY HATE MY GUTS!... BUT WHO THE DEVIL IS HE?
1713

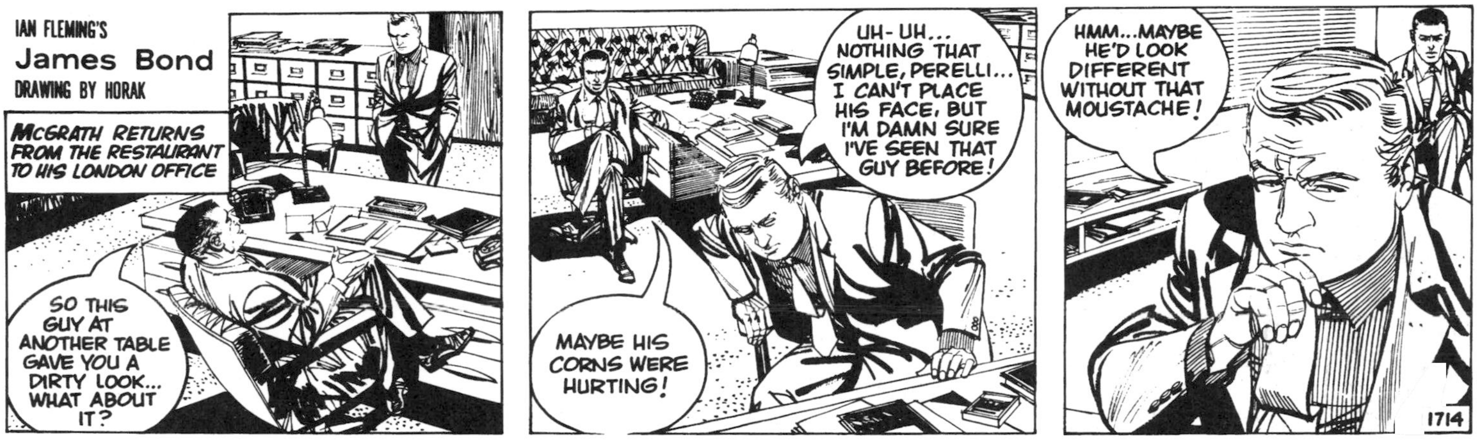
IAN FLEMING'S
James Bond
DRAWING BY HORAK
McGRATH RETURNS FROM THE RESTAURANT TO HIS LONDON OFFICE
SO THIS GUY AT ANOTHER TABLE GAVE YOU A DIRTY LOOK... WHAT ABOUT IT?
UH-UH... NOTHING THAT SIMPLE, PERELLI... I CAN'T PLACE HIS FACE, BUT I'M DAMN SURE I'VE SEEN THAT GUY BEFORE!
MAYBE HIS CORNS WERE HURTING!
HMM... MAYBE HE'D LOOK DIFFERENT WITHOUT THAT MOUSTACHE!
1714

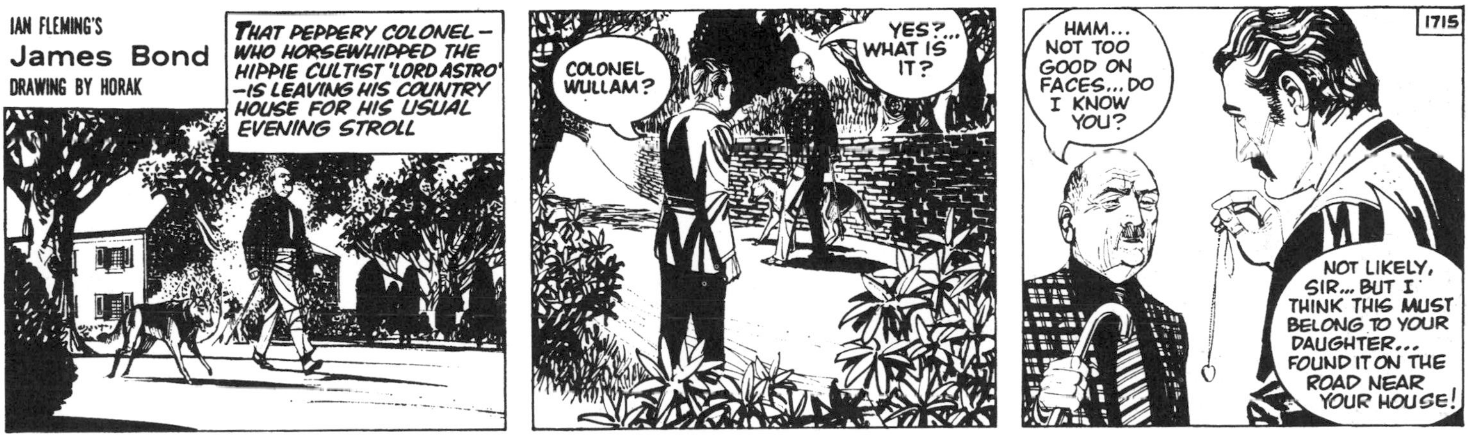
IAN FLEMING'S
James Bond
DRAWING BY HORAK
THAT PEPPERY COLONEL — WHO HORSEWHIPPED THE HIPPIE CULTIST 'LORD ASTRO' — IS LEAVING HIS COUNTRY HOUSE FOR HIS USUAL EVENING STROLL
COLONEL WULLAM?
YES?... WHAT IS IT?
1715
HMM... NOT TOO GOOD ON FACES... DO I KNOW YOU?
NOT LIKELY, SIR... BUT I THINK THIS MUST BELONG TO YOUR DAUGHTER... FOUND IT ON THE ROAD NEAR YOUR HOUSE!

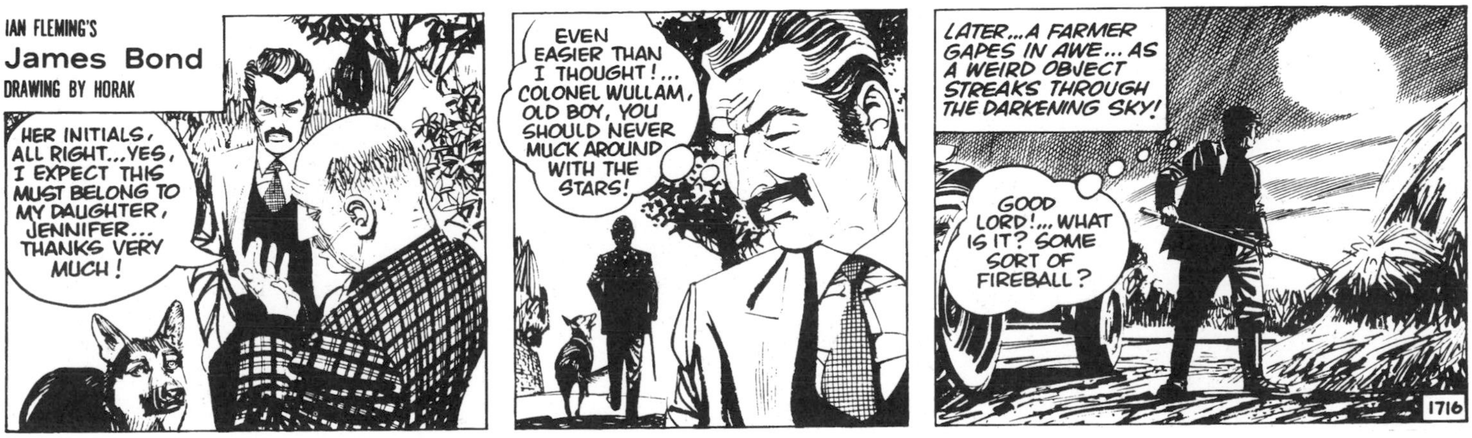
IAN FLEMING'S
James Bond
DRAWING BY HORAK
HER INITIALS, ALL RIGHT... YES, I EXPECT THIS MUST BELONG TO MY DAUGHTER, JENNIFER... THANKS VERY MUCH!
EVEN EASIER THAN I THOUGHT!... COLONEL WULLAM, OLD BOY, YOU SHOULD NEVER MUCK AROUND WITH THE STARS!
LATER... A FARMER GAPES IN AWE... AS A WEIRD OBJECT STREAKS THROUGH THE DARKENING SKY!
GOOD LORD!... WHAT IS IT? SOME SORT OF FIREBALL?
1716

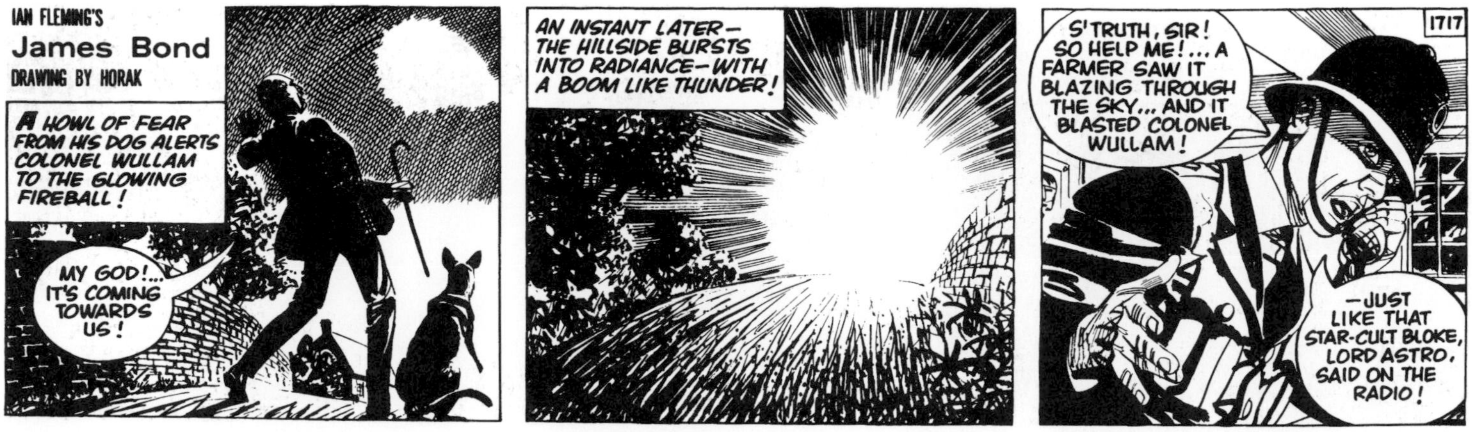
IAN FLEMING'S
James Bond
DRAWING BY HORAK
A HOWL OF FEAR FROM HIS DOG ALERTS COLONEL WULLAM TO THE GLOWING FIREBALL!
MY GOD!... IT'S COMING TOWARDS US!
AN INSTANT LATER— THE HILLSIDE BURSTS INTO RADIANCE—WITH A BOOM LIKE THUNDER!
1717
S'TRUTH, SIR! SO HELP ME!... A FARMER SAW IT BLAZING THROUGH THE SKY... AND IT BLASTED COLONEL WULLAM!
—JUST LIKE THAT STAR-CULT BLOKE, LORD ASTRO, SAID ON THE RADIO!

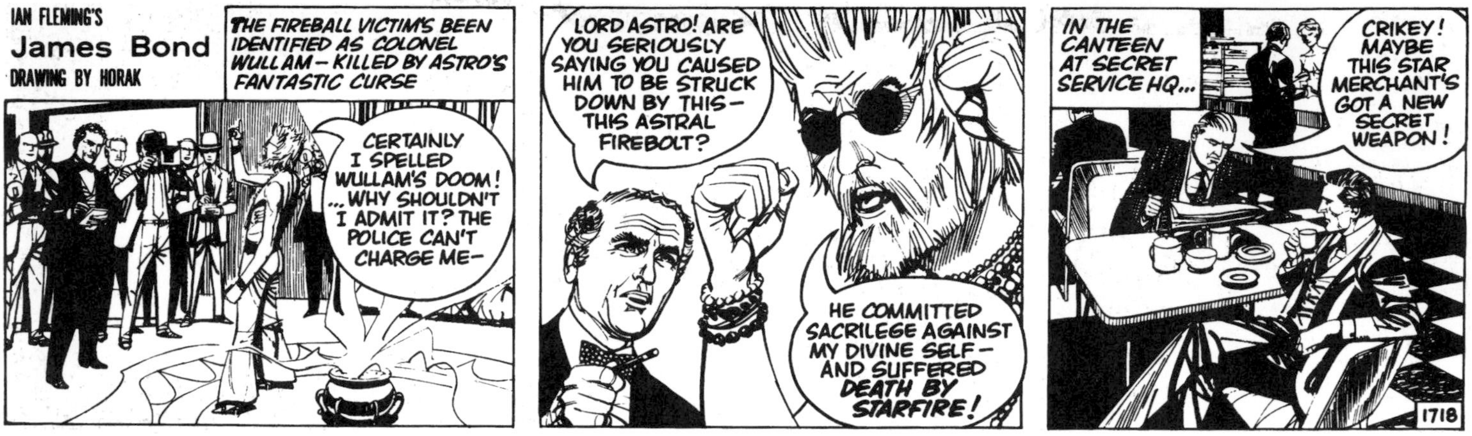
IAN FLEMING'S
James Bond
DRAWING BY HORAK
THE FIREBALL VICTIM'S BEEN IDENTIFIED AS COLONEL WULLAM—KILLED BY ASTRO'S FANTASTIC CURSE
CERTAINLY I SPELLED WULLAM'S DOOM! ...WHY SHOULDN'T I ADMIT IT? THE POLICE CAN'T CHARGE ME—
LORD ASTRO! ARE YOU SERIOUSLY SAYING YOU CAUSED HIM TO BE STRUCK DOWN BY THIS— THIS ASTRAL FIREBOLT?
HE COMMITTED SACRILEGE AGAINST MY DIVINE SELF— AND SUFFERED DEATH BY STARFIRE!
IN THE CANTEEN AT SECRET SERVICE HQ...
CRIKEY! MAYBE THIS STAR MERCHANT'S GOT A NEW SECRET WEAPON!
1718

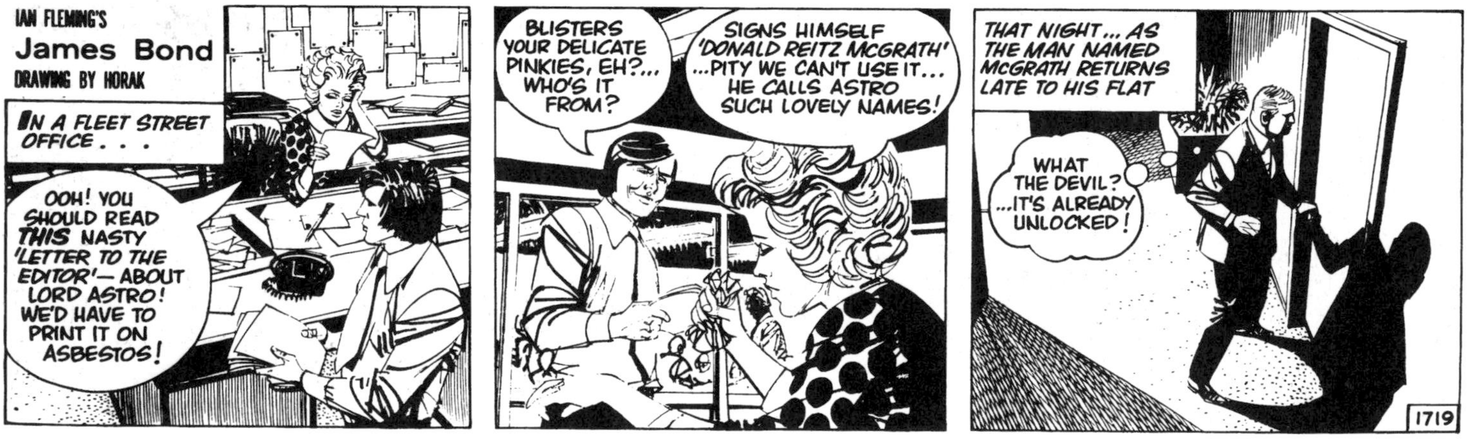
IAN FLEMING'S
James Bond
DRAWING BY HORAK
IN A FLEET STREET OFFICE . . .
OOH! YOU SHOULD READ THIS NASTY 'LETTER TO THE EDITOR'— ABOUT LORD ASTRO! WE'D HAVE TO PRINT IT ON ASBESTOS!
BLISTERS YOUR DELICATE PINKIES, EH?... WHO'S IT FROM?
SIGNS HIMSELF 'DONALD REITZ MCGRATH' ...PITY WE CAN'T USE IT... HE CALLS ASTRO SUCH LOVELY NAMES!
THAT NIGHT... AS THE MAN NAMED MCGRATH RETURNS LATE TO HIS FLAT
WHAT THE DEVIL? ...IT'S ALREADY UNLOCKED!
1719

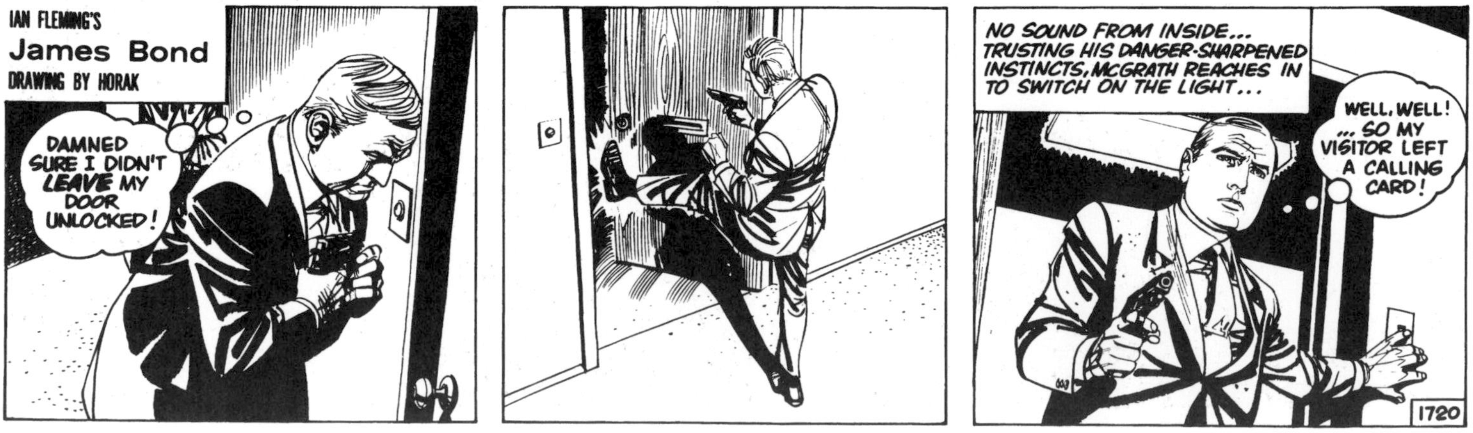
IAN FLEMING'S
James Bond
DRAWING BY HORAK
DAMNED SURE I DIDN'T LEAVE MY DOOR UNLOCKED!
NO SOUND FROM INSIDE... TRUSTING HIS DANGER-SHARPENED INSTINCTS, MCGRATH REACHES IN TO SWITCH ON THE LIGHT...
WELL, WELL! ... SO MY VISITOR LEFT A CALLING CARD!
1720

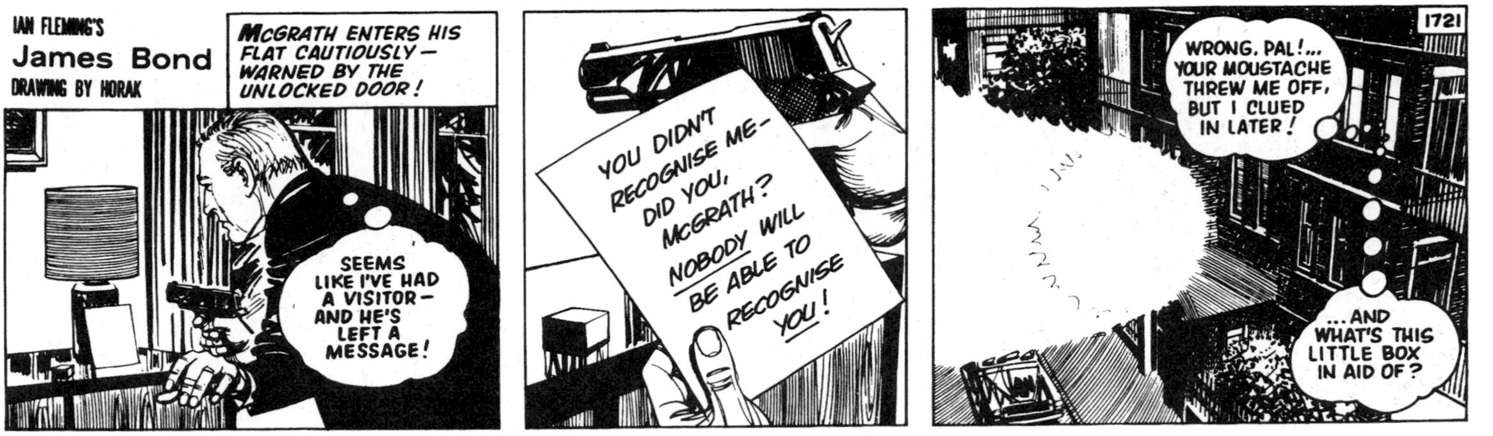
IAN FLEMING'S
James Bond
DRAWING BY HORAK
McGRATH ENTERS HIS FLAT CAUTIOUSLY — WARNED BY THE UNLOCKED DOOR!
SEEMS LIKE I'VE HAD A VISITOR — AND HE'S LEFT A MESSAGE!
YOU DIDN'T RECOGNISE ME — DID YOU, McGRATH? NOBODY WILL BE ABLE TO RECOGNISE YOU!
1721
WRONG, PAL!... YOUR MOUSTACHE THREW ME OFF, BUT I CLUED IN LATER!
...AND WHAT'S THIS LITTLE BOX IN AID OF?

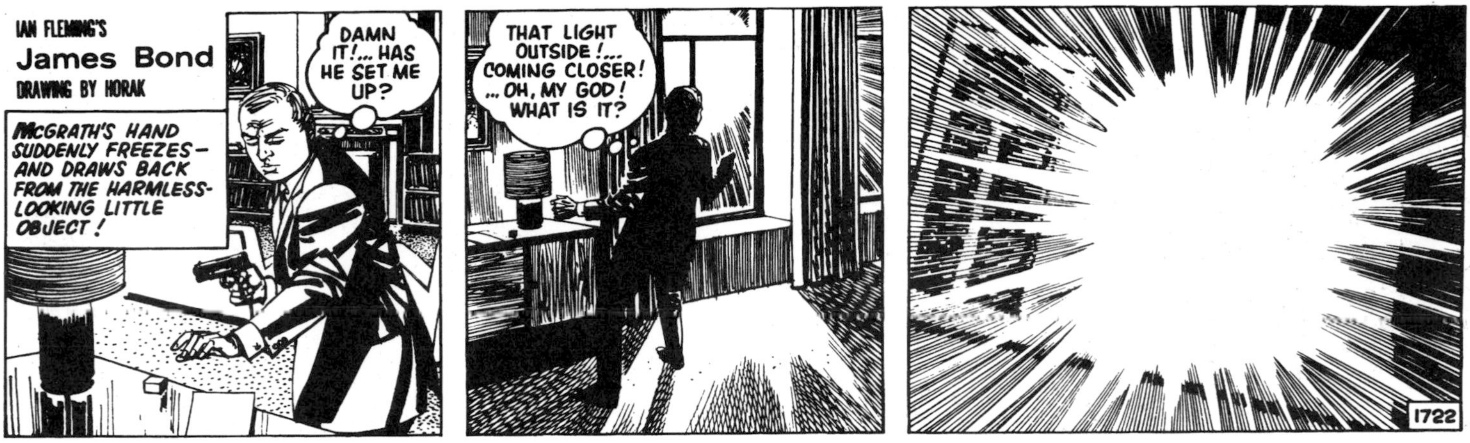
IAN FLEMING'S
James Bond
DRAWING BY HORAK
McGRATH'S HAND SUDDENLY FREEZES — AND DRAWS BACK FROM THE HARMLESS-LOOKING LITTLE OBJECT!
DAMN IT!... HAS HE SET ME UP?
THAT LIGHT OUTSIDE!... COMING CLOSER! ...OH, MY GOD! WHAT IS IT?
1722

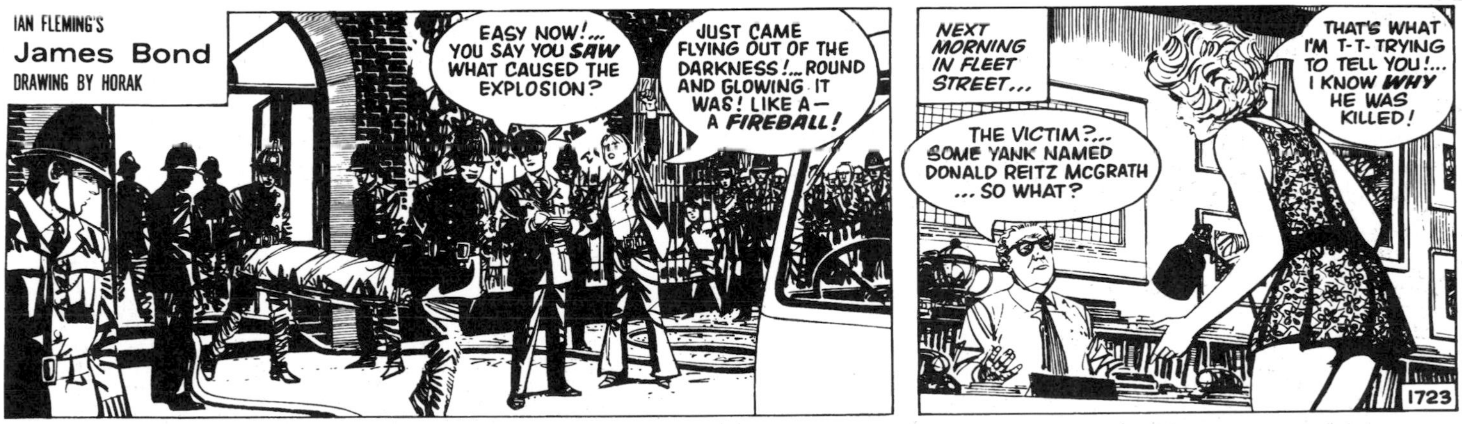
IAN FLEMING'S
James Bond
DRAWING BY HORAK
EASY NOW!... YOU SAY YOU **SAW** WHAT CAUSED THE EXPLOSION?
JUST CAME FLYING OUT OF THE DARKNESS!... ROUND AND GLOWING IT WAS! LIKE A — A **FIREBALL!**
NEXT MORNING IN FLEET STREET...
THE VICTIM?... SOME YANK NAMED DONALD REITZ McGRATH ... SO WHAT?
THAT'S WHAT I'M T-T-TRYING TO TELL YOU!... I KNOW **WHY** HE WAS KILLED!
1723

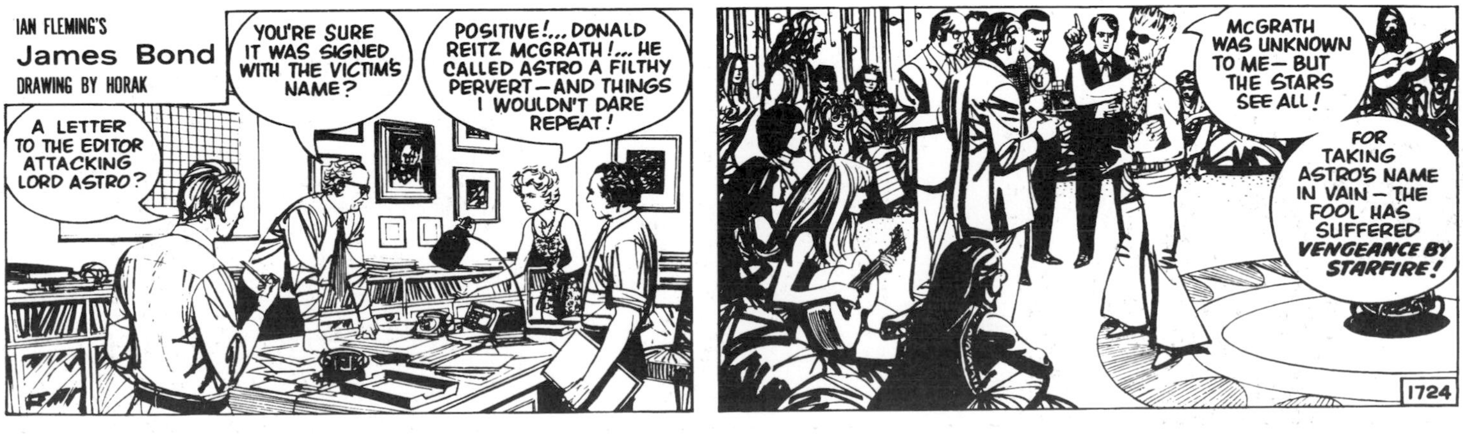
IAN FLEMING'S
James Bond
DRAWING BY HORAK
A LETTER TO THE EDITOR ATTACKING LORD ASTRO?
YOU'RE SURE IT WAS SIGNED WITH THE VICTIM'S NAME?
POSITIVE!... DONALD REITZ McGRATH!... HE CALLED ASTRO A FILTHY PERVERT — AND THINGS I WOULDN'T DARE REPEAT!
McGRATH WAS UNKNOWN TO ME — BUT THE STARS SEE ALL!
FOR TAKING ASTRO'S NAME IN VAIN — THE FOOL HAS SUFFERED **VENGEANCE BY STARFIRE!**
1724

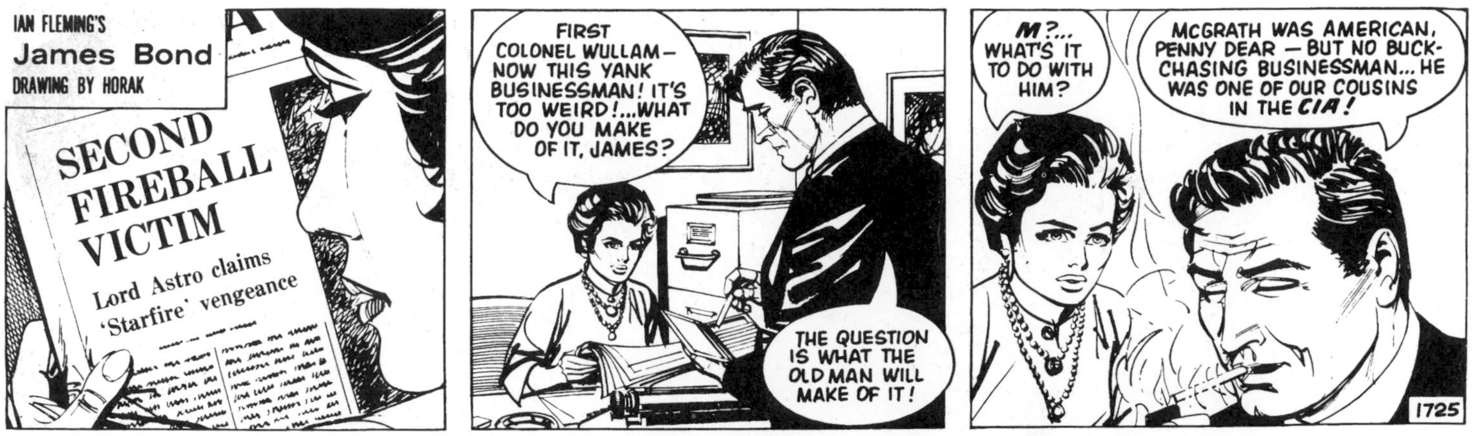
IAN FLEMING'S
James Bond
DRAWING BY HORAK
SECOND FIREBALL VICTIM
Lord Astro claims 'Starfire' vengeance
FIRST COLONEL WULLAM— NOW THIS YANK BUSINESSMAN! IT'S TOO WEIRD!...WHAT DO YOU MAKE OF IT, JAMES?
THE QUESTION IS WHAT THE OLD MAN WILL MAKE OF IT!
M?... WHAT'S IT TO DO WITH HIM?
McGRATH WAS AMERICAN, PENNY DEAR — BUT NO BUCK-CHASING BUSINESSMAN... HE WAS ONE OF OUR COUSINS IN THE CIA!
1725

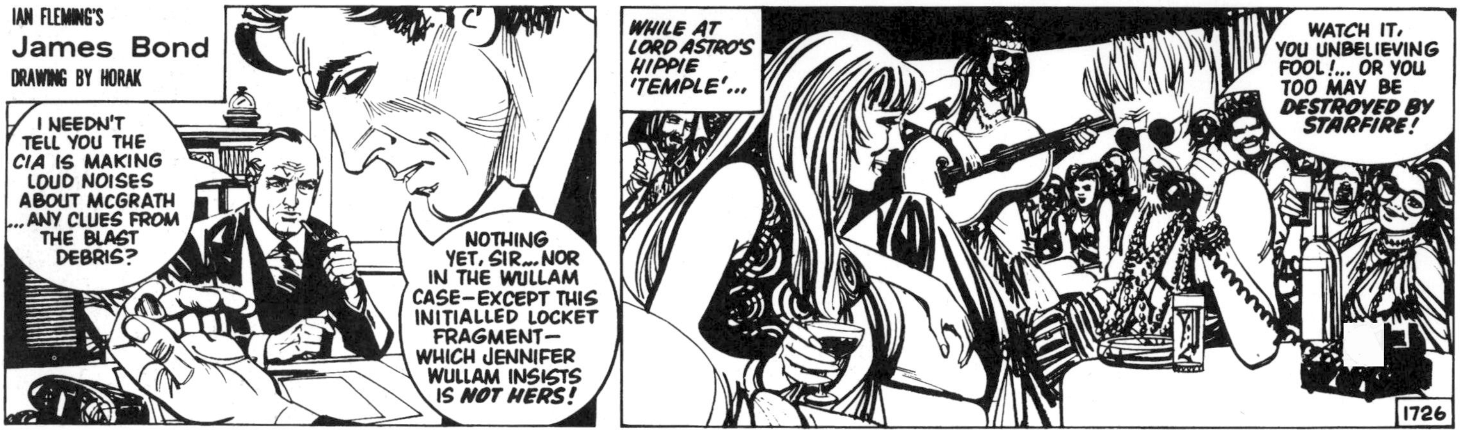
IAN FLEMING'S
James Bond
DRAWING BY HORAK
I NEEDN'T TELL YOU THE CIA IS MAKING LOUD NOISES ABOUT McGRATH ...ANY CLUES FROM THE BLAST DEBRIS?
NOTHING YET, SIR... NOR IN THE WULLAM CASE—EXCEPT THIS INITIALLED LOCKET FRAGMENT— WHICH JENNIFER WULLAM INSISTS IS NOT HERS!
WHILE AT LORD ASTRO'S HIPPIE 'TEMPLE'...
WATCH IT, YOU UNBELIEVING FOOL!... OR YOU TOO MAY BE DESTROYED BY STARFIRE!
1726

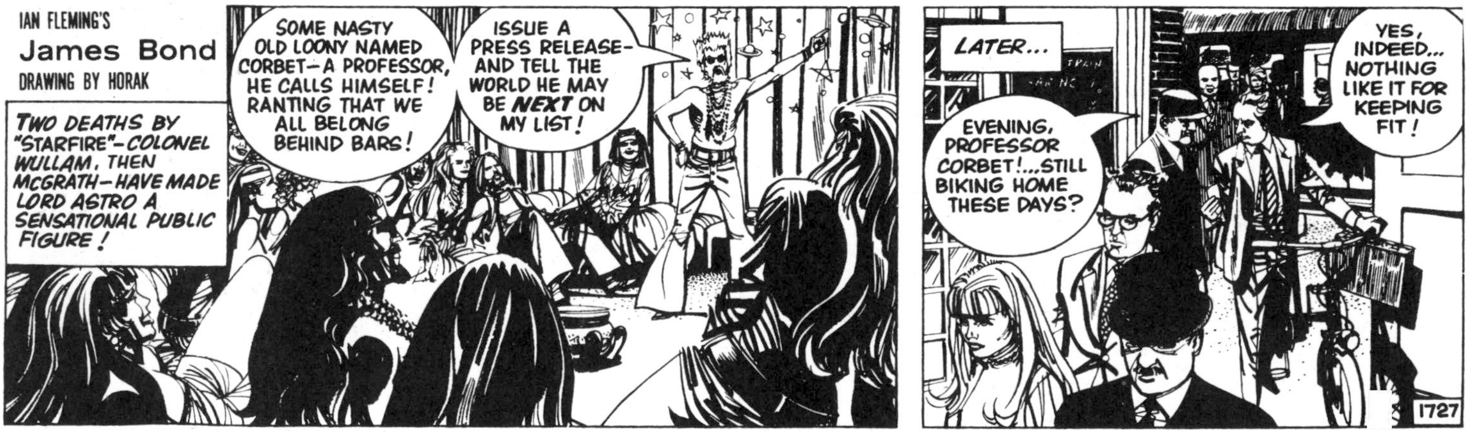
IAN FLEMING'S
James Bond
DRAWING BY HORAK
TWO DEATHS BY "STARFIRE"—COLONEL WULLAM, THEN McGRATH—HAVE MADE LORD ASTRO A SENSATIONAL PUBLIC FIGURE!
SOME NASTY OLD LOONY NAMED CORBET—A PROFESSOR, HE CALLS HIMSELF! RANTING THAT WE ALL BELONG BEHIND BARS!
ISSUE A PRESS RELEASE— AND TELL THE WORLD HE MAY BE NEXT ON MY LIST!
LATER...
EVENING, PROFESSOR CORBET!... STILL BIKING HOME THESE DAYS?
YES, INDEED... NOTHING LIKE IT FOR KEEPING FIT!
1727

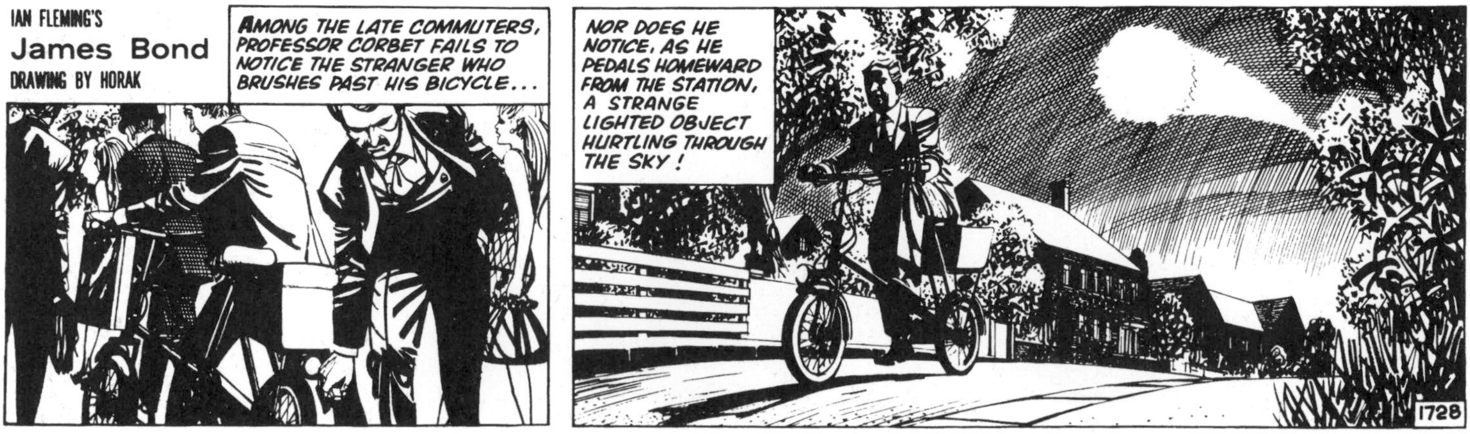
IAN FLEMING'S
James Bond
DRAWING BY HORAK
AMONG THE LATE COMMUTERS, PROFESSOR CORBET FAILS TO NOTICE THE STRANGER WHO BRUSHES PAST HIS BICYCLE...
NOR DOES HE NOTICE, AS HE PEDALS HOMEWARD FROM THE STATION, A STRANGE LIGHTED OBJECT HURTLING THROUGH THE SKY!
1728

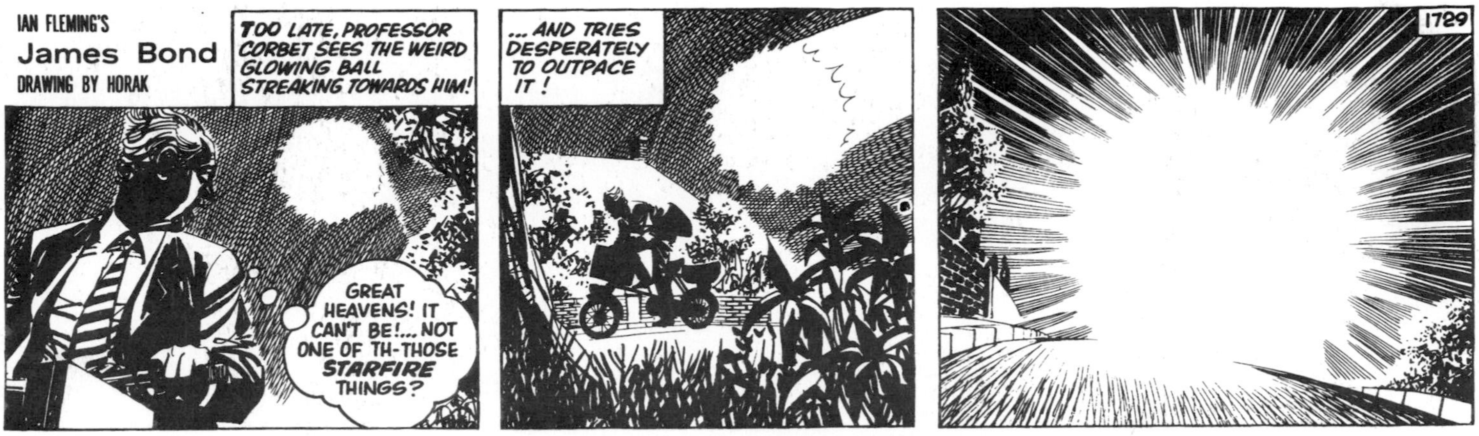
IAN FLEMING'S
James Bond
DRAWING BY HORAK
TOO LATE, PROFESSOR CORBET SEES THE WEIRD GLOWING BALL STREAKING TOWARDS HIM!
GREAT HEAVENS! IT CAN'T BE!... NOT ONE OF TH-THOSE STARFIRE THINGS?
... AND TRIES DESPERATELY TO OUTPACE IT!
1729

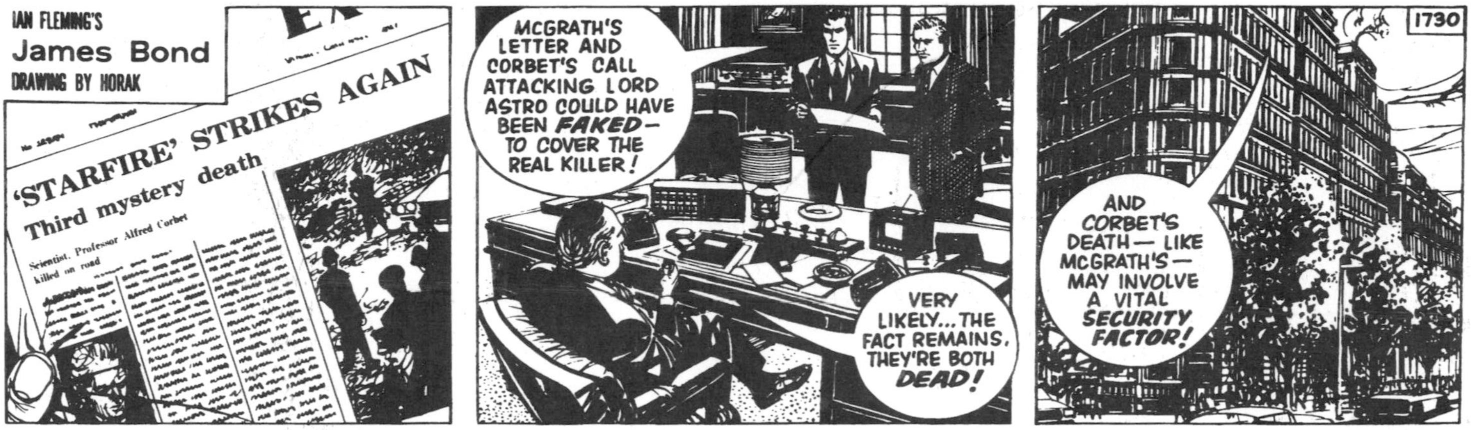
IAN FLEMING'S
James Bond
DRAWING BY HORAK
'STARFIRE' STRIKES AGAIN
'STARFIRE'
Third mystery death
Scientist, Professor Alfred Corbet killed on road
MCGRATH'S LETTER AND CORBET'S CALL ATTACKING LORD ASTRO COULD HAVE BEEN FAKED— TO COVER THE REAL KILLER!
VERY LIKELY... THE FACT REMAINS, THEY'RE BOTH DEAD!
1730
AND CORBET'S DEATH— LIKE MCGRATH'S— MAY INVOLVE A VITAL SECURITY FACTOR!

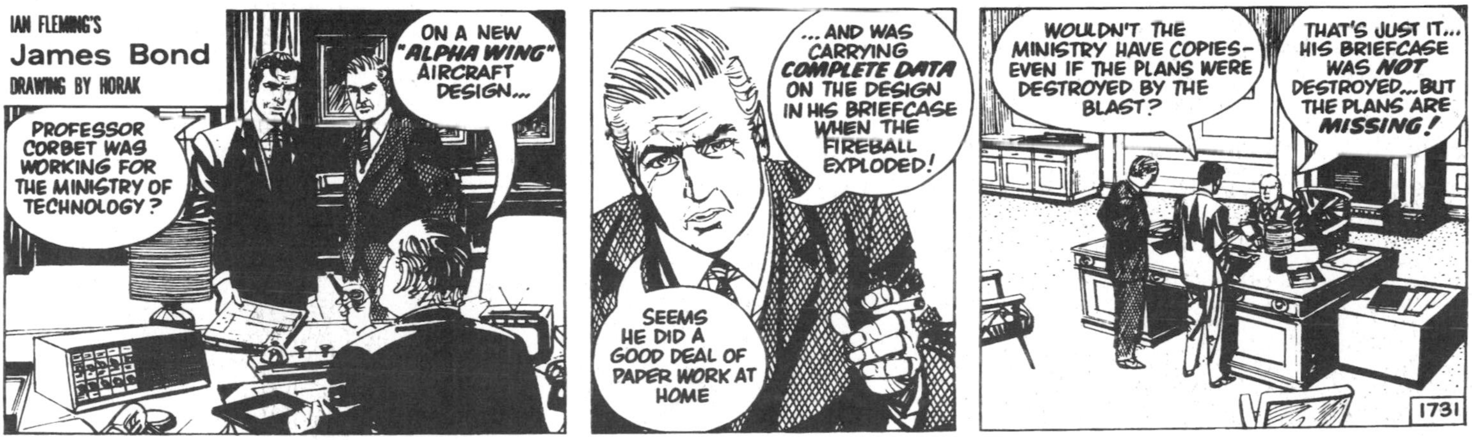
IAN FLEMING'S
James Bond
DRAWING BY HORAK
PROFESSOR CORBET WAS WORKING FOR THE MINISTRY OF TECHNOLOGY?
ON A NEW "ALPHA WING" AIRCRAFT DESIGN...
... AND WAS CARRYING COMPLETE DATA ON THE DESIGN IN HIS BRIEFCASE WHEN THE FIREBALL EXPLODED!
SEEMS HE DID A GOOD DEAL OF PAPER WORK AT HOME
WOULDN'T THE MINISTRY HAVE COPIES— EVEN IF THE PLANS WERE DESTROYED BY THE BLAST?
THAT'S JUST IT... HIS BRIEFCASE WAS NOT DESTROYED... BUT THE PLANS ARE MISSING!
1731

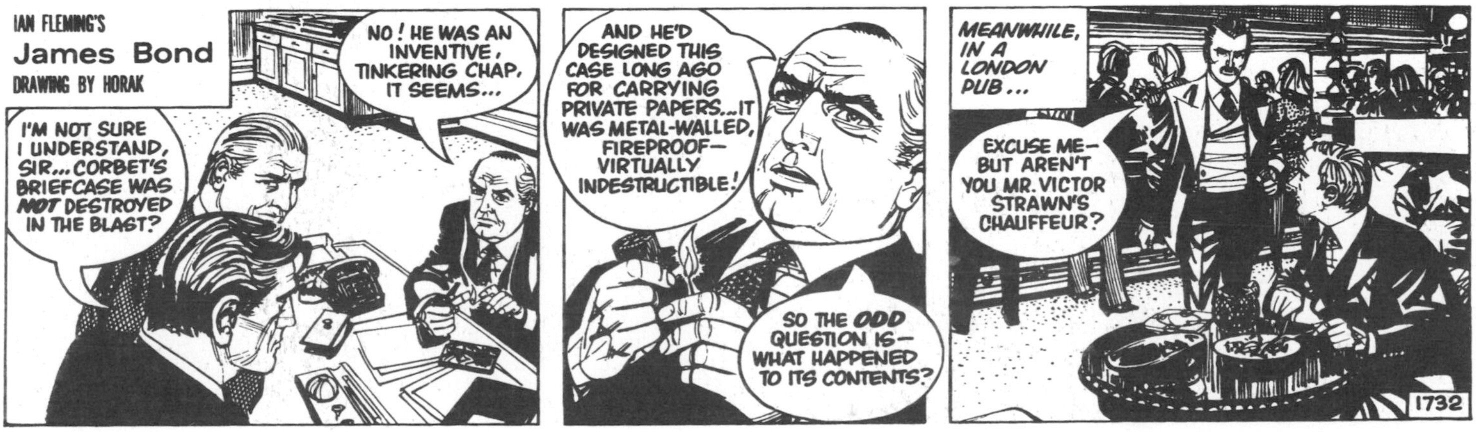
IAN FLEMING'S
James Bond
DRAWING BY HORAK
I'M NOT SURE I UNDERSTAND, SIR... CORBET'S BRIEFCASE WAS NOT DESTROYED IN THE BLAST?
NO! HE WAS AN INVENTIVE, TINKERING CHAP, IT SEEMS...
AND HE'D DESIGNED THIS CASE LONG AGO FOR CARRYING PRIVATE PAPERS... IT WAS METAL-WALLED, FIREPROOF— VIRTUALLY INDESTRUCTIBLE!
SO THE ODD QUESTION IS— WHAT HAPPENED TO ITS CONTENTS?
MEANWHILE, IN A LONDON PUB...
EXCUSE ME— BUT AREN'T YOU MR. VICTOR STRAWN'S CHAUFFEUR?
1732

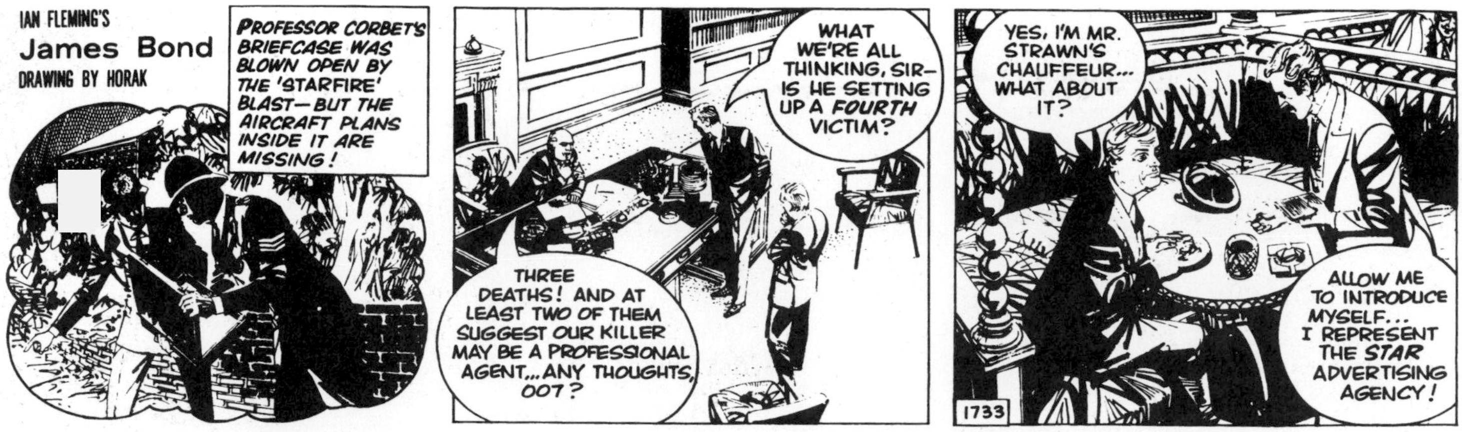
IAN FLEMING'S
James Bond
DRAWING BY HORAK
PROFESSOR CORBET'S BRIEFCASE WAS BLOWN OPEN BY THE 'STARFIRE' BLAST—BUT THE AIRCRAFT PLANS INSIDE IT ARE MISSING!
THREE DEATHS! AND AT LEAST TWO OF THEM SUGGEST OUR KILLER MAY BE A PROFESSIONAL AGENT... ANY THOUGHTS, 007?
WHAT WE'RE ALL THINKING, SIR—IS HE SETTING UP A FOURTH VICTIM?
YES, I'M MR. STRAWN'S CHAUFFEUR... WHAT ABOUT IT?
ALLOW ME TO INTRODUCE MYSELF... I REPRESENT THE STAR ADVERTISING AGENCY!
1733

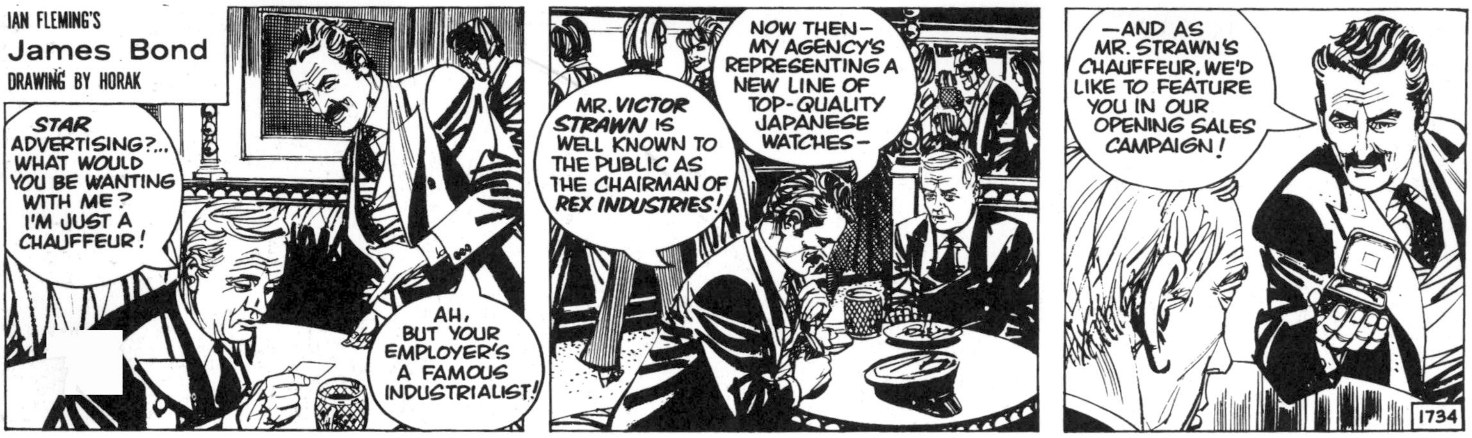
IAN FLEMING'S
James Bond
DRAWING BY HORAK
STAR ADVERTISING?... WHAT WOULD YOU BE WANTING WITH ME? I'M JUST A CHAUFFEUR!
AH, BUT YOUR EMPLOYER'S A FAMOUS INDUSTRIALIST!
MR. VICTOR STRAWN IS WELL KNOWN TO THE PUBLIC AS THE CHAIRMAN OF REX INDUSTRIES!
NOW THEN—MY AGENCY'S REPRESENTING A NEW LINE OF TOP-QUALITY JAPANESE WATCHES—
—AND AS MR. STRAWN'S CHAUFFEUR, WE'D LIKE TO FEATURE YOU IN OUR OPENING SALES CAMPAIGN!
1734

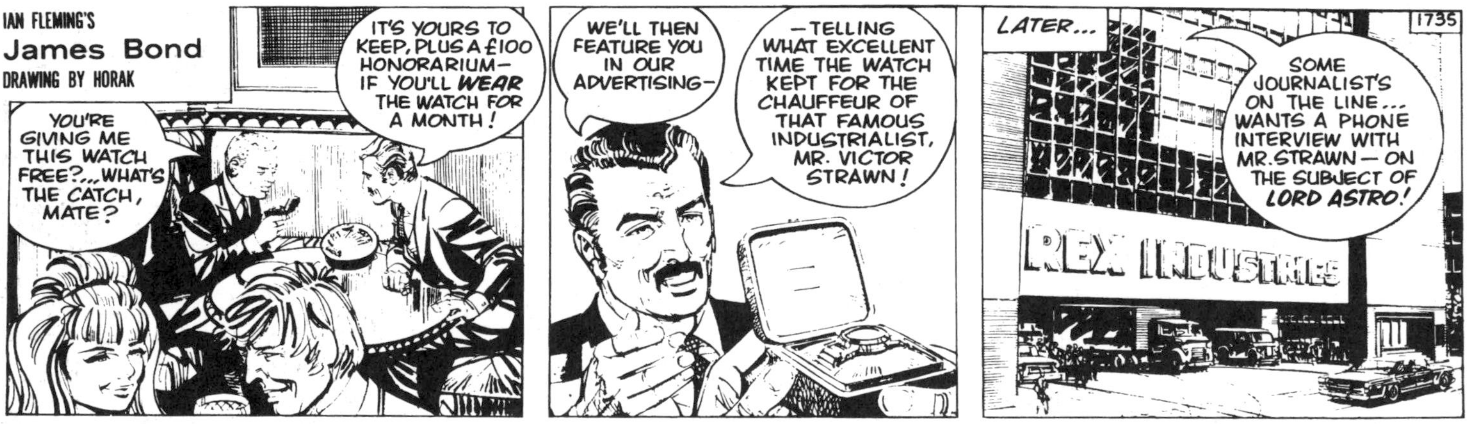
IAN FLEMING'S
James Bond
DRAWING BY HORAK
YOU'RE GIVING ME THIS WATCH FREE?... WHAT'S THE CATCH, MATE?
IT'S YOURS TO KEEP, PLUS A £100 HONORARIUM—IF YOU'LL WEAR THE WATCH FOR A MONTH!
WE'LL THEN FEATURE YOU IN OUR ADVERTISING—
—TELLING WHAT EXCELLENT TIME THE WATCH KEPT FOR THE CHAUFFEUR OF THAT FAMOUS INDUSTRIALIST, MR. VICTOR STRAWN!
LATER...
1735
SOME JOURNALIST'S ON THE LINE... WANTS A PHONE INTERVIEW WITH MR. STRAWN—ON THE SUBJECT OF LORD ASTRO!
REX INDUSTRIES

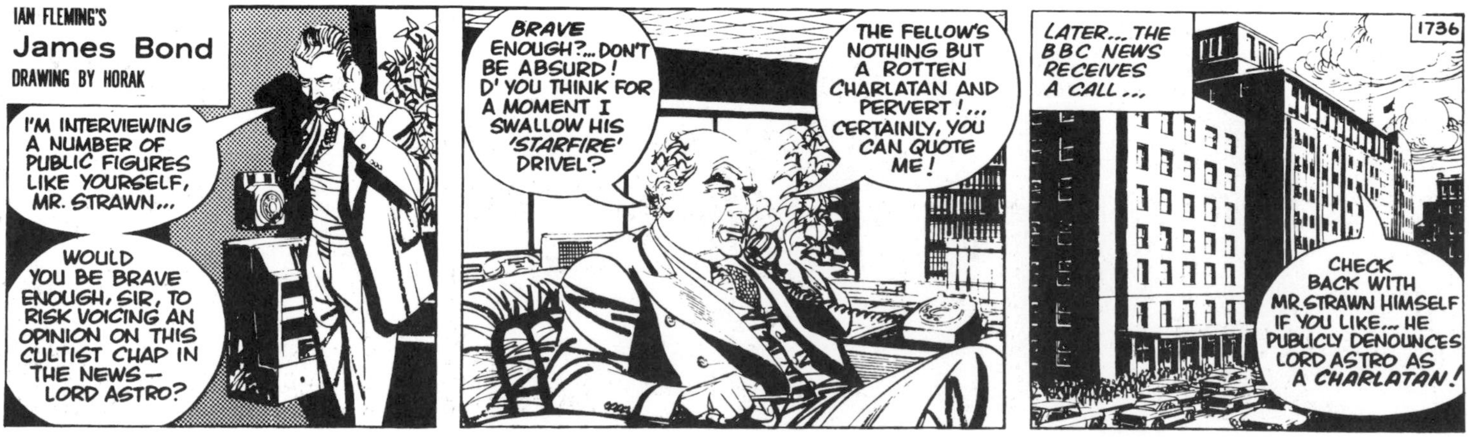
IAN FLEMING'S
James Bond
DRAWING BY HORAK
I'M INTERVIEWING A NUMBER OF PUBLIC FIGURES LIKE YOURSELF, MR. STRAWN...
WOULD YOU BE BRAVE ENOUGH, SIR, TO RISK VOICING AN OPINION ON THIS CULTIST CHAP IN THE NEWS—LORD ASTRO?
BRAVE ENOUGH?... DON'T BE ABSURD! D' YOU THINK FOR A MOMENT I SWALLOW HIS 'STARFIRE' DRIVEL?
THE FELLOW'S NOTHING BUT A ROTTEN CHARLATAN AND PERVERT!... CERTAINLY, YOU CAN QUOTE ME!
LATER... THE BBC NEWS RECEIVES A CALL...
1736
CHECK BACK WITH MR. STRAWN HIMSELF IF YOU LIKE... HE PUBLICLY DENOUNCES LORD ASTRO AS A CHARLATAN!

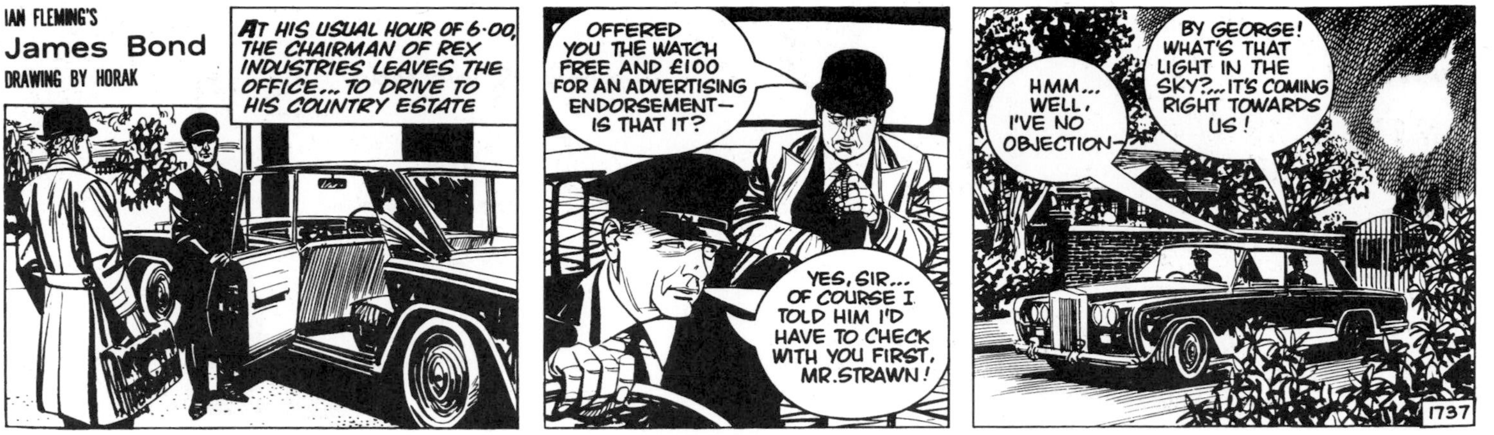
IAN FLEMING'S
James Bond
DRAWING BY HORAK
AT HIS USUAL HOUR OF 6.00, THE CHAIRMAN OF REX INDUSTRIES LEAVES THE OFFICE... TO DRIVE TO HIS COUNTRY ESTATE
OFFERED YOU THE WATCH FREE AND £100 FOR AN ADVERTISING ENDORSEMENT— IS THAT IT?
YES, SIR... OF COURSE I TOLD HIM I'D HAVE TO CHECK WITH YOU FIRST, MR. STRAWN!
HMM... WELL, I'VE NO OBJECTION—
BY GEORGE! WHAT'S THAT LIGHT IN THE SKY?... IT'S COMING RIGHT TOWARDS US!
1737

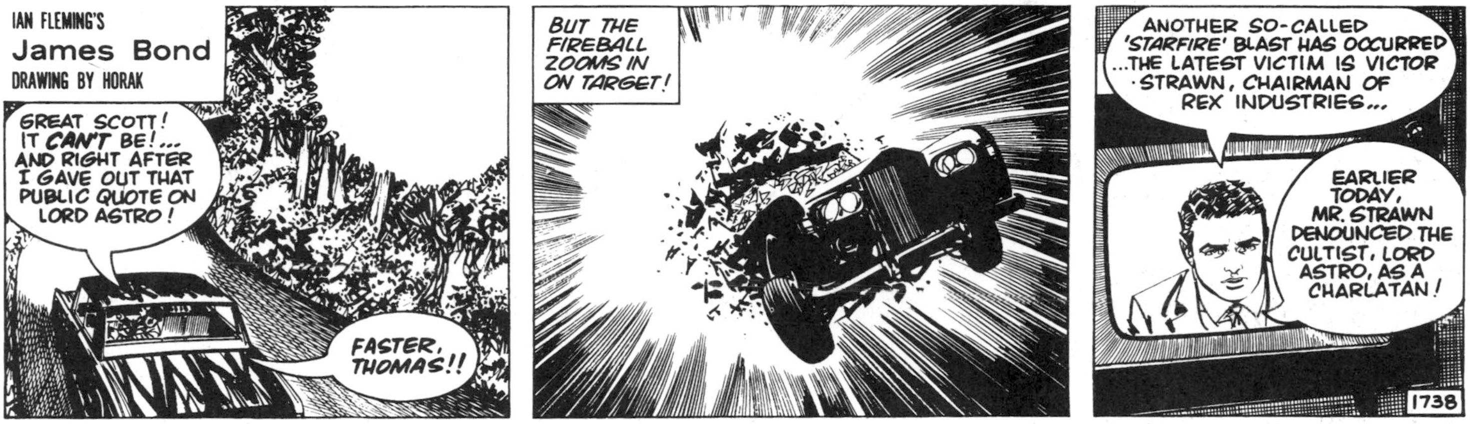
IAN FLEMING'S
James Bond
DRAWING BY HORAK
GREAT SCOTT! IT CAN'T BE!... AND RIGHT AFTER I GAVE OUT THAT PUBLIC QUOTE ON LORD ASTRO!
FASTER, THOMAS!!
BUT THE FIREBALL ZOOMS IN ON TARGET!
ANOTHER SO-CALLED 'STARFIRE' BLAST HAS OCCURRED ...THE LATEST VICTIM IS VICTOR STRAWN, CHAIRMAN OF REX INDUSTRIES...
EARLIER TODAY, MR. STRAWN DENOUNCED THE CULTIST, LORD ASTRO, AS A CHARLATAN!
1738

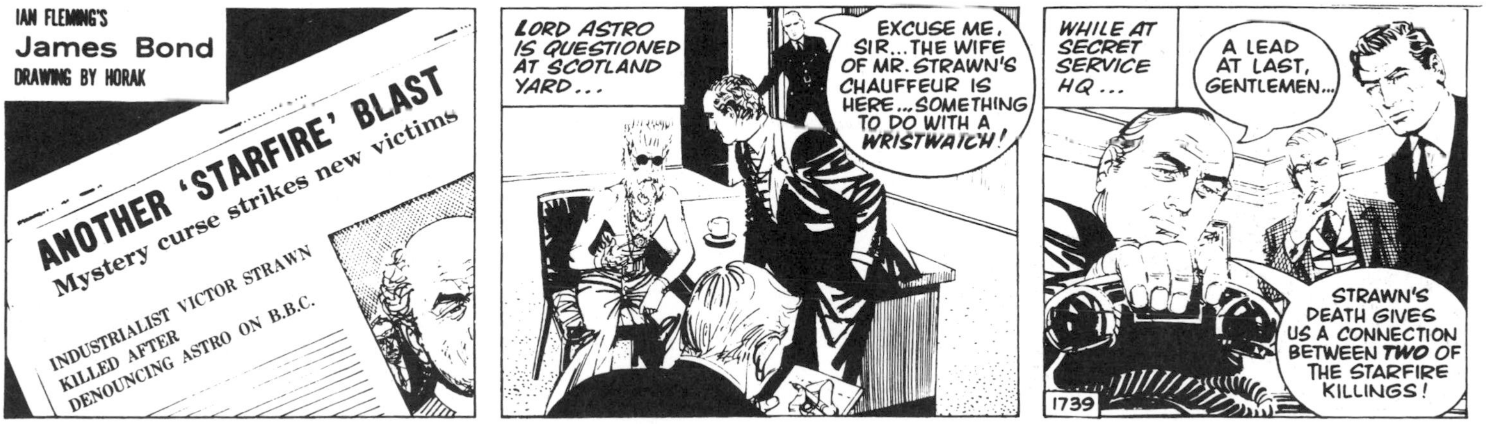
IAN FLEMING'S
James Bond
DRAWING BY HORAK
ANOTHER 'STARFIRE' BLAST
Mystery curse strikes new victims
INDUSTRIALIST VICTOR STRAWN KILLED AFTER DENOUNCING ASTRO ON B.B.C.
LORD ASTRO IS QUESTIONED AT SCOTLAND YARD...
EXCUSE ME, SIR... THE WIFE OF MR. STRAWN'S CHAUFFEUR IS HERE... SOMETHING TO DO WITH A WRISTWATCH!
WHILE AT SECRET SERVICE HQ...
A LEAD AT LAST, GENTLEMEN...
STRAWN'S DEATH GIVES US A CONNECTION BETWEEN TWO OF THE STARFIRE KILLINGS!
1739

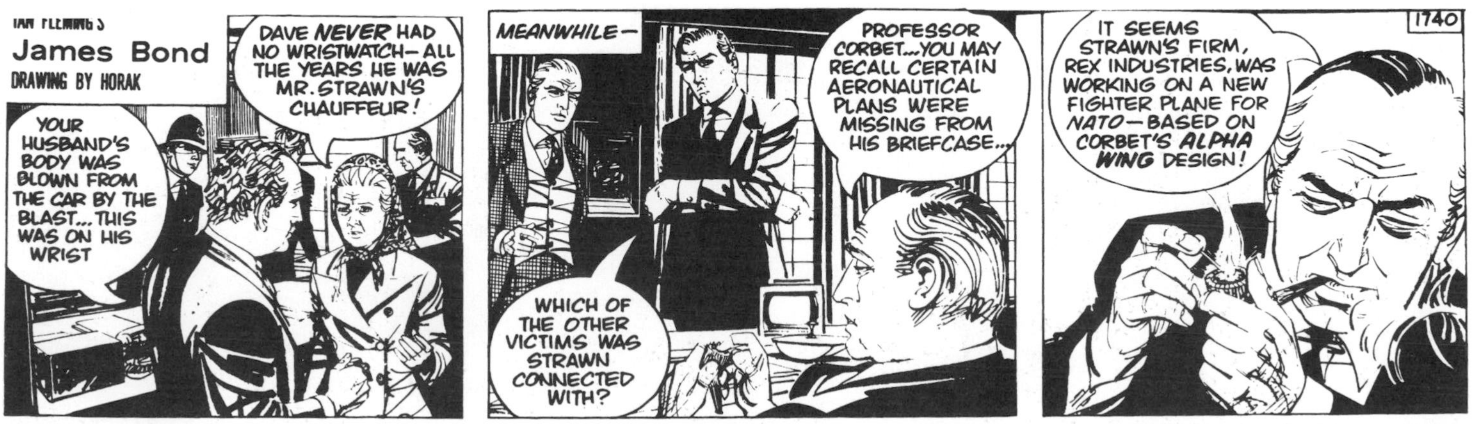
James Bond
DRAWING BY HORAK
YOUR HUSBAND'S BODY WAS BLOWN FROM THE CAR BY THE BLAST... THIS WAS ON HIS WRIST
DAVE NEVER HAD NO WRISTWATCH— ALL THE YEARS HE WAS MR. STRAWN'S CHAUFFEUR!
MEANWHILE—
PROFESSOR CORBET... YOU MAY RECALL CERTAIN AERONAUTICAL PLANS WERE MISSING FROM HIS BRIEFCASE...
WHICH OF THE OTHER VICTIMS WAS STRAWN CONNECTED WITH?
1740
IT SEEMS STRAWN'S FIRM, REX INDUSTRIES, WAS WORKING ON A NEW FIGHTER PLANE FOR NATO— BASED ON CORBET'S ALPHA WING DESIGN!

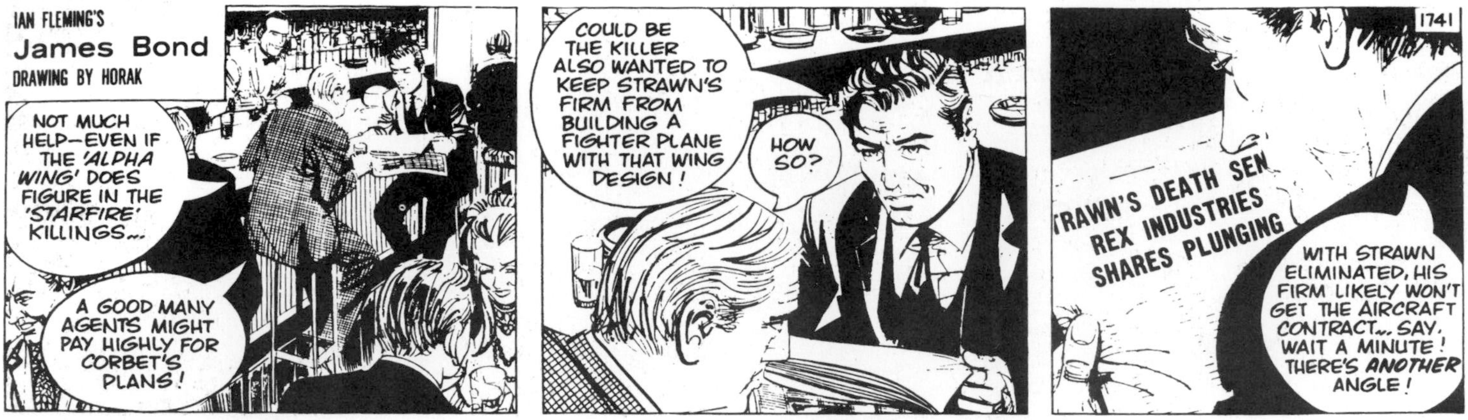
IAN FLEMING'S
James Bond
DRAWING BY HORAK
NOT MUCH HELP—EVEN IF THE 'ALPHA WING' DOES FIGURE IN THE 'STARFIRE' KILLINGS...
A GOOD MANY AGENTS MIGHT PAY HIGHLY FOR CORBET'S PLANS!
COULD BE THE KILLER ALSO WANTED TO KEEP STRAWN'S FIRM FROM BUILDING A FIGHTER PLANE WITH THAT WING DESIGN!
HOW SO?
1741
TRAWN'S DEATH SEN
REX INDUSTRIES
SHARES PLUNGING
WITH STRAWN ELIMINATED, HIS FIRM LIKELY WON'T GET THE AIRCRAFT CONTRACT... SAY, WAIT A MINUTE! THERE'S ANOTHER ANGLE!

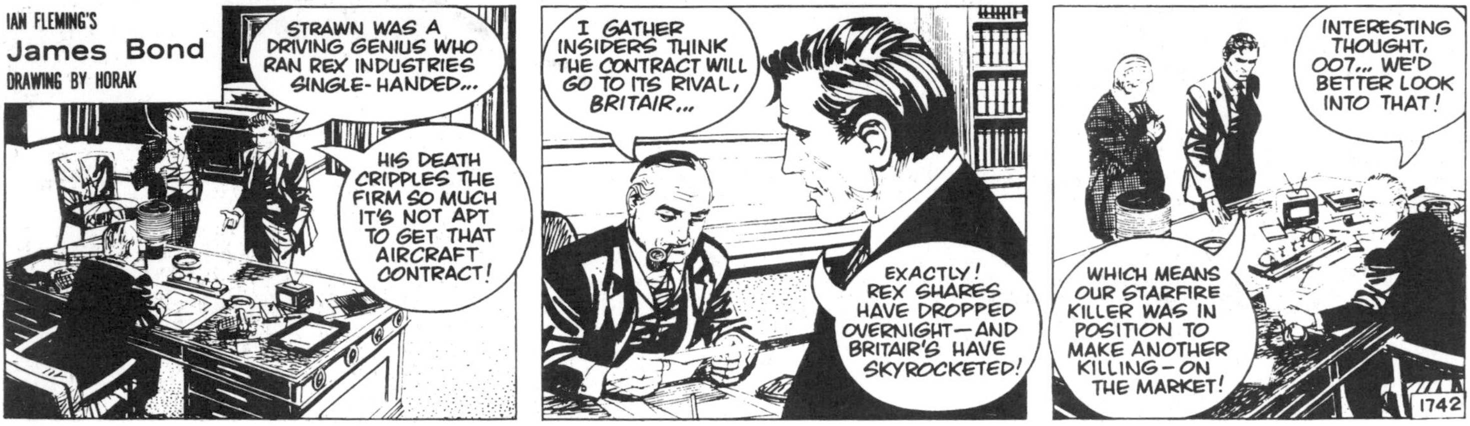
IAN FLEMING'S
James Bond
DRAWING BY HORAK
STRAWN WAS A DRIVING GENIUS WHO RAN REX INDUSTRIES SINGLE-HANDED...
HIS DEATH CRIPPLES THE FIRM SO MUCH IT'S NOT APT TO GET THAT AIRCRAFT CONTRACT!
I GATHER INSIDERS THINK THE CONTRACT WILL GO TO ITS RIVAL, BRITAIR...
EXACTLY! REX SHARES HAVE DROPPED OVERNIGHT—AND BRITAIR'S HAVE SKYROCKETED!
INTERESTING THOUGHT, 007... WE'D BETTER LOOK INTO THAT!
WHICH MEANS OUR STARFIRE KILLER WAS IN POSITION TO MAKE ANOTHER KILLING—ON THE MARKET!
1742

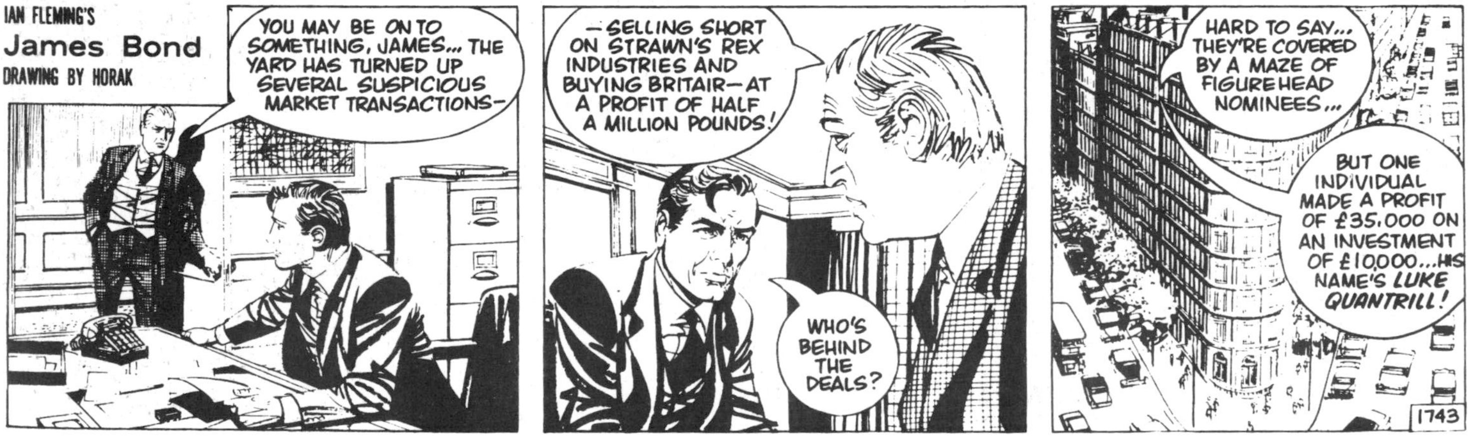
IAN FLEMING'S
James Bond
DRAWING BY HORAK
YOU MAY BE ON TO SOMETHING, JAMES... THE YARD HAS TURNED UP SEVERAL SUSPICIOUS MARKET TRANSACTIONS—
—SELLING SHORT ON STRAWN'S REX INDUSTRIES AND BUYING BRITAIR—AT A PROFIT OF HALF A MILLION POUNDS!
WHO'S BEHIND THE DEALS?
HARD TO SAY... THEY'RE COVERED BY A MAZE OF FIGUREHEAD NOMINEES...
BUT ONE INDIVIDUAL MADE A PROFIT OF £35,000 ON AN INVESTMENT OF £10,000... HIS NAME'S LUKE QUANTRILL!
1743

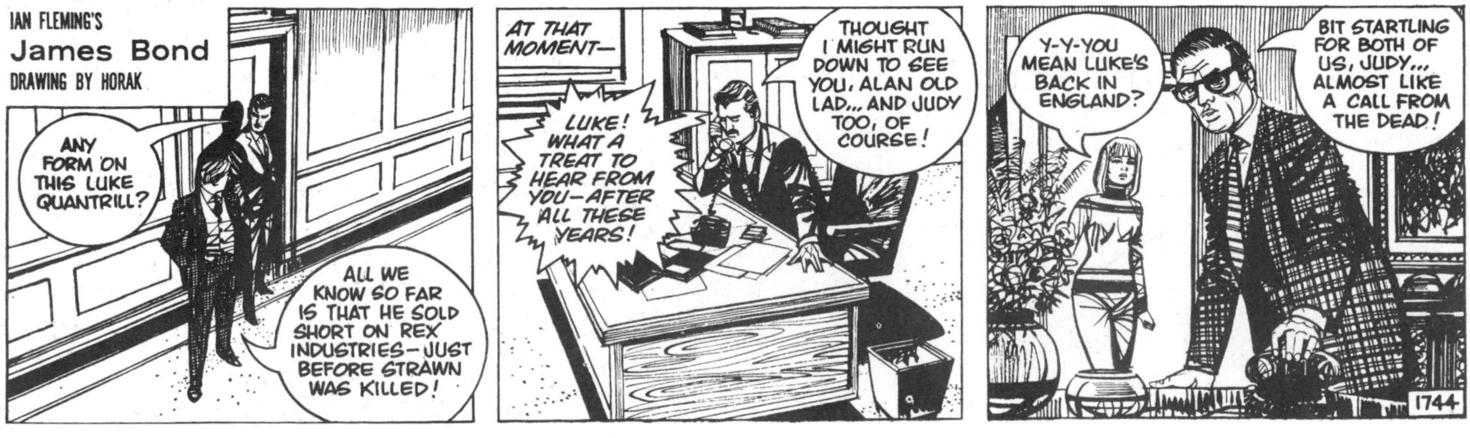
IAN FLEMING'S
James Bond
DRAWING BY HORAK
ANY FORM ON THIS LUKE QUANTRILL?
ALL WE KNOW SO FAR IS THAT HE SOLD SHORT ON REX INDUSTRIES—JUST BEFORE STRAWN WAS KILLED!
AT THAT MOMENT—
LUKE! WHAT A TREAT TO HEAR FROM YOU—AFTER ALL THESE YEARS!
THOUGHT I MIGHT RUN DOWN TO SEE YOU, ALAN OLD LAD... AND JUDY TOO, OF COURSE!
Y-Y-YOU MEAN LUKE'S BACK IN ENGLAND?
BIT STARTLING FOR BOTH OF US, JUDY... ALMOST LIKE A CALL FROM THE DEAD!
1744

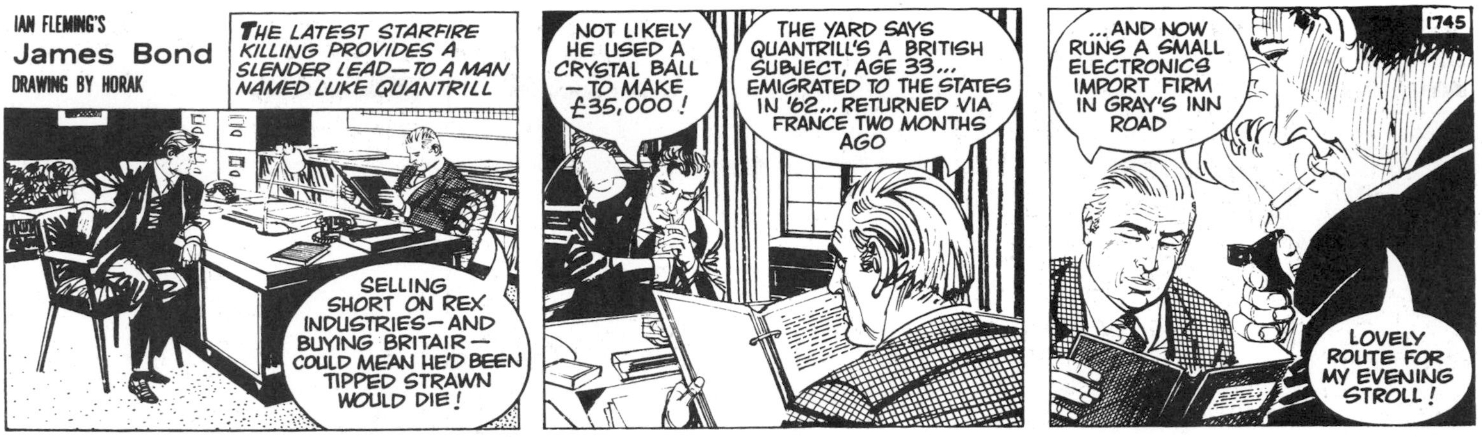
IAN FLEMING'S
James Bond
DRAWING BY HORAK
THE LATEST STARFIRE KILLING PROVIDES A SLENDER LEAD—TO A MAN NAMED LUKE QUANTRILL
SELLING SHORT ON REX INDUSTRIES—AND BUYING BRITAIR—COULD MEAN HE'D BEEN TIPPED STRAWN WOULD DIE!
NOT LIKELY HE USED A CRYSTAL BALL —TO MAKE £35,000!
THE YARD SAYS QUANTRILL'S A BRITISH SUBJECT, AGE 33... EMIGRATED TO THE STATES IN '62... RETURNED VIA FRANCE TWO MONTHS AGO
...AND NOW RUNS A SMALL ELECTRONICS IMPORT FIRM IN GRAY'S INN ROAD
LOVELY ROUTE FOR MY EVENING STROLL!
1745

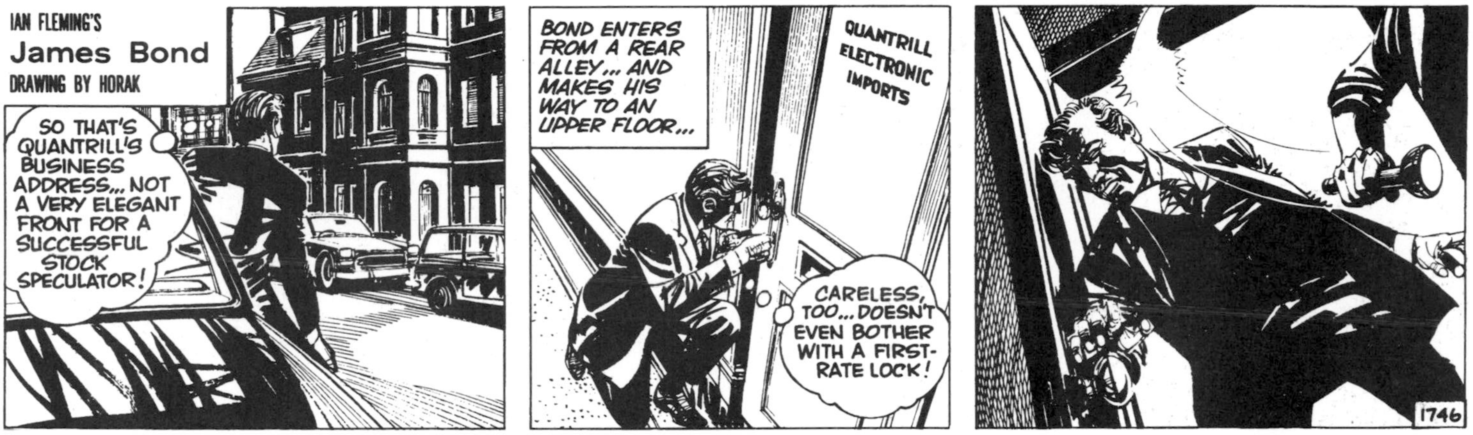
IAN FLEMING'S
James Bond
DRAWING BY HORAK
SO THAT'S QUANTRILL'S BUSINESS ADDRESS... NOT A VERY ELEGANT FRONT FOR A SUCCESSFUL STOCK SPECULATOR!
BOND ENTERS FROM A REAR ALLEY... AND MAKES HIS WAY TO AN UPPER FLOOR...
QUANTRILL ELECTRONIC IMPORTS
CARELESS, TOO... DOESN'T EVEN BOTHER WITH A FIRST-RATE LOCK!
1746

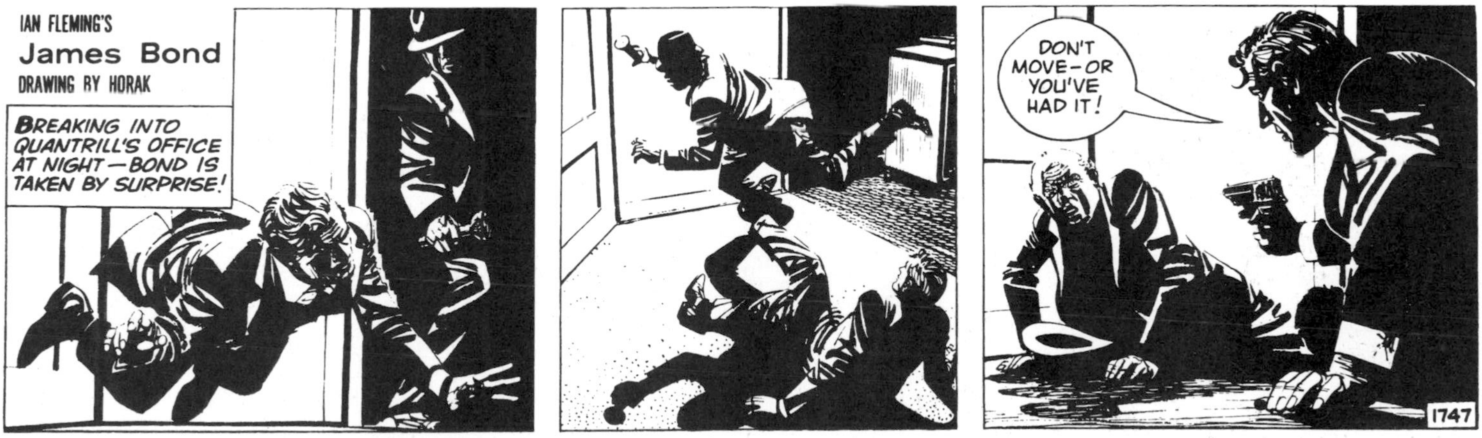
IAN FLEMING'S
James Bond
DRAWING BY HORAK
BREAKING INTO QUANTRILL'S OFFICE AT NIGHT—BOND IS TAKEN BY SURPRISE!
DON'T MOVE—OR YOU'VE HAD IT!
1747

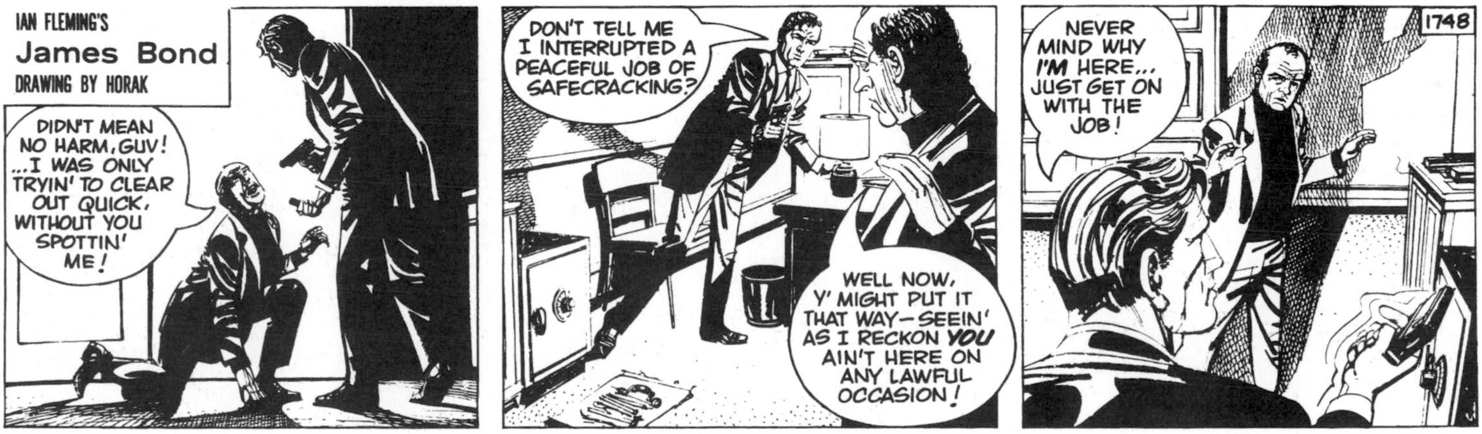
IAN FLEMING'S
James Bond
DRAWING BY HORAK
DIDN'T MEAN NO HARM, GUV! ...I WAS ONLY TRYIN' TO CLEAR OUT QUICK, WITHOUT YOU SPOTTIN' ME!
DON'T TELL ME I INTERRUPTED A PEACEFUL JOB OF SAFECRACKING?
WELL NOW, Y' MIGHT PUT IT THAT WAY—SEEIN' AS I RECKON YOU AIN'T HERE ON ANY LAWFUL OCCASION!
1748
NEVER MIND WHY I'M HERE... JUST GET ON WITH THE JOB!

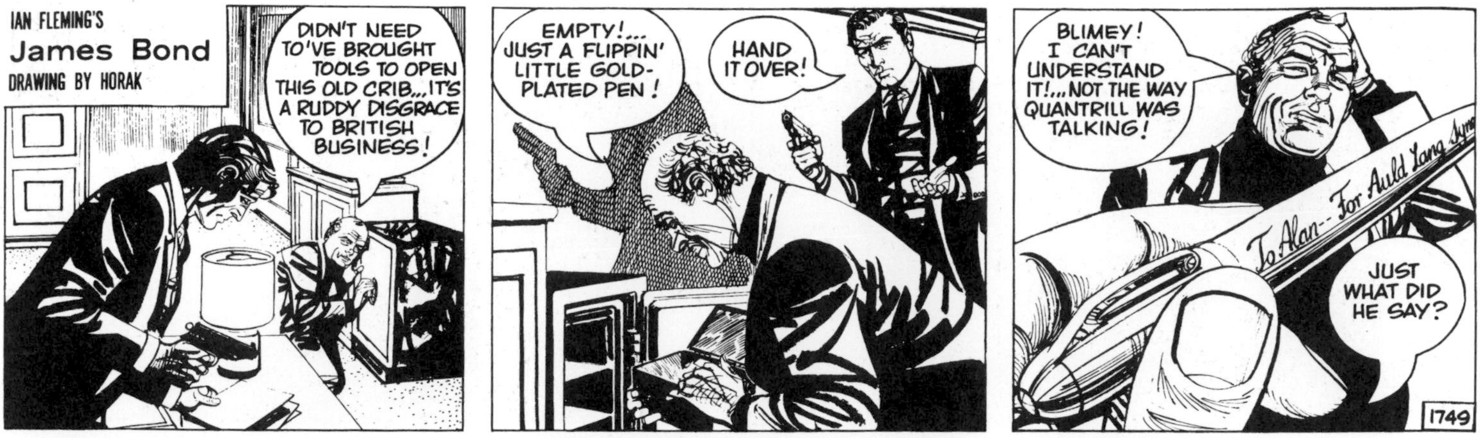
IAN FLEMING'S
James Bond
DRAWING BY HORAK
DIDN'T NEED TO'VE BROUGHT TOOLS TO OPEN THIS OLD CRIB...IT'S A RUDDY DISGRACE TO BRITISH BUSINESS!
EMPTY!... JUST A FLIPPIN' LITTLE GOLD-PLATED PEN!
HAND IT OVER!
BLIMEY! I CAN'T UNDERSTAND IT!...NOT THE WAY QUANTRILL WAS TALKING!
To Alan-- For Auld Lang Syne
JUST WHAT DID HE SAY?
1749

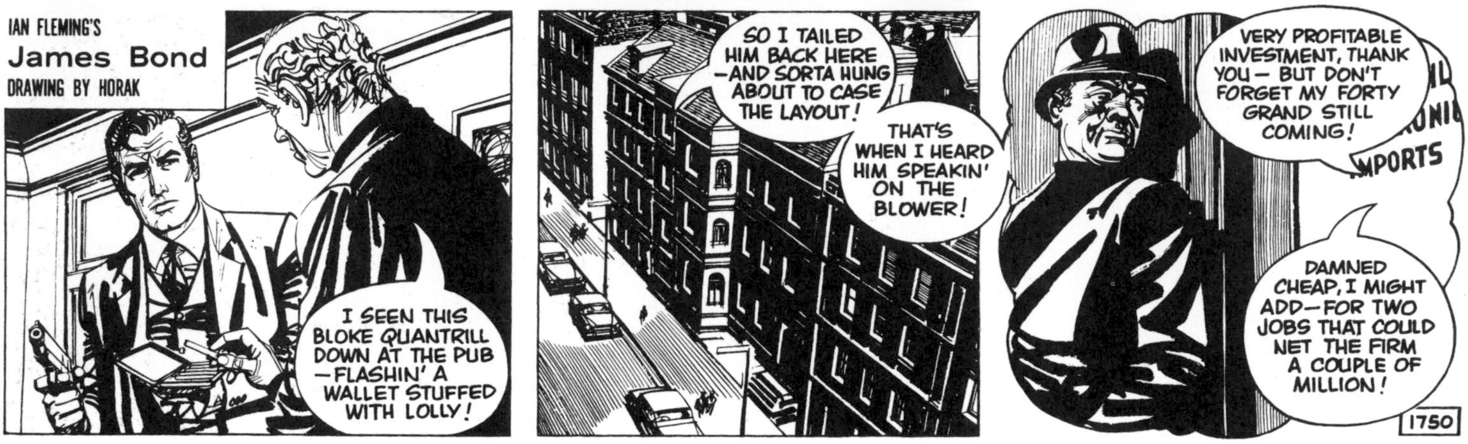
IAN FLEMING'S
James Bond
DRAWING BY HORAK
I SEEN THIS BLOKE QUANTRILL DOWN AT THE PUB —FLASHIN' A WALLET STUFFED WITH LOLLY!
SO I TAILED HIM BACK HERE —AND SORTA HUNG ABOUT TO CASE THE LAYOUT!
THAT'S WHEN I HEARD HIM SPEAKIN' ON THE BLOWER!
VERY PROFITABLE INVESTMENT, THANK YOU— BUT DON'T FORGET MY FORTY GRAND STILL COMING!
DAMNED CHEAP, I MIGHT ADD—FOR TWO JOBS THAT COULD NET THE FIRM A COUPLE OF MILLION!
1750

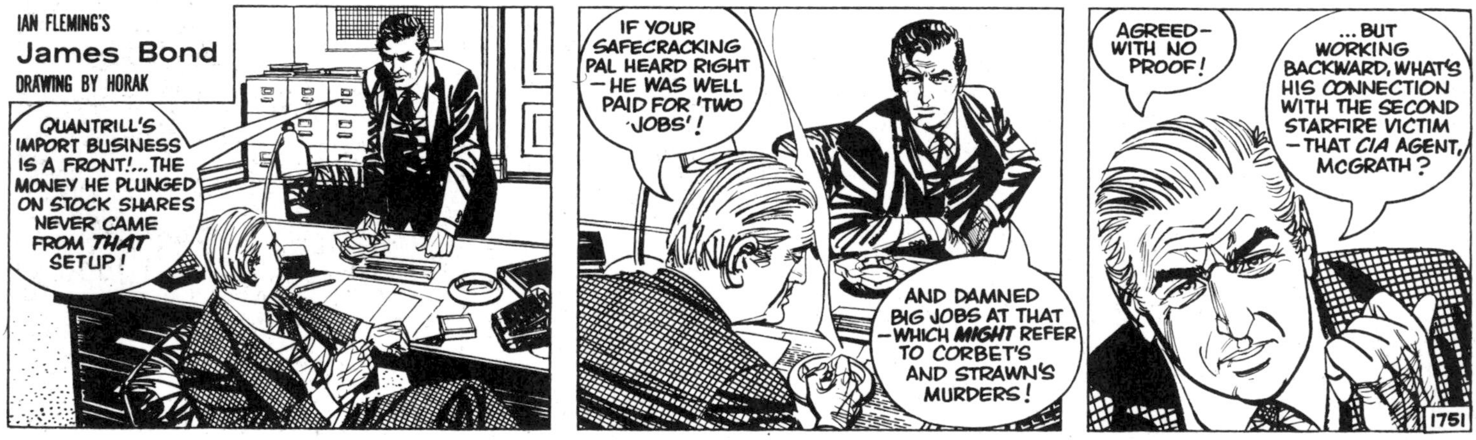
IAN FLEMING'S
James Bond
DRAWING BY HORAK
QUANTRILL'S IMPORT BUSINESS IS A FRONT!...THE MONEY HE PLUNGED ON STOCK SHARES NEVER CAME FROM THAT SETUP!
IF YOUR SAFECRACKING PAL HEARD RIGHT —HE WAS WELL PAID FOR 'TWO JOBS'!
AND DAMNED BIG JOBS AT THAT —WHICH MIGHT REFER TO CORBET'S AND STRAWN'S MURDERS!
AGREED— WITH NO PROOF!
...BUT WORKING BACKWARD, WHAT'S HIS CONNECTION WITH THE SECOND STARFIRE VICTIM —THAT CIA AGENT, MCGRATH?
1751

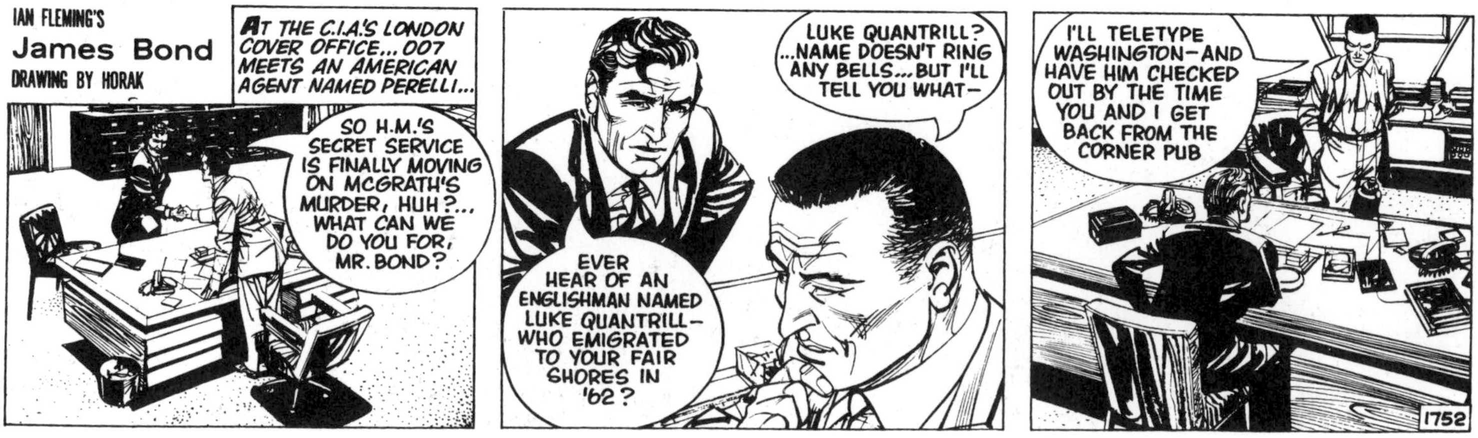
IAN FLEMING'S
James Bond
DRAWING BY HORAK
AT THE C.I.A.'S LONDON COVER OFFICE... 007 MEETS AN AMERICAN AGENT NAMED PERELLI...
SO H.M.'S SECRET SERVICE IS FINALLY MOVING ON MCGRATH'S MURDER, HUH?... WHAT CAN WE DO YOU FOR, MR. BOND?
EVER HEAR OF AN ENGLISHMAN NAMED LUKE QUANTRILL— WHO EMIGRATED TO YOUR FAIR SHORES IN '62?
LUKE QUANTRILL? ...NAME DOESN'T RING ANY BELLS... BUT I'LL TELL YOU WHAT—
I'LL TELETYPE WASHINGTON—AND HAVE HIM CHECKED OUT BY THE TIME YOU AND I GET BACK FROM THE CORNER PUB
1752

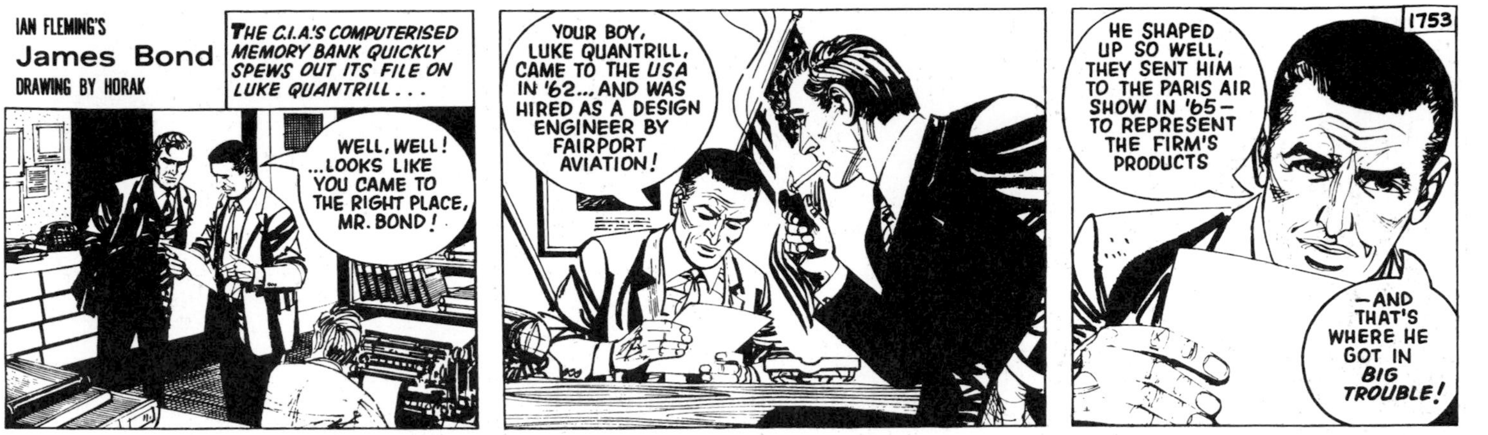
IAN FLEMING'S
James Bond
DRAWING BY HORAK
THE C.I.A.'S COMPUTERISED MEMORY BANK QUICKLY SPEWS OUT ITS FILE ON LUKE QUANTRILL . . .
WELL, WELL! ...LOOKS LIKE YOU CAME TO THE RIGHT PLACE, MR. BOND!
YOUR BOY, LUKE QUANTRILL, CAME TO THE USA IN '62... AND WAS HIRED AS A DESIGN ENGINEER BY FAIRPORT AVIATION!
1753
HE SHAPED UP SO WELL, THEY SENT HIM TO THE PARIS AIR SHOW IN '65 — TO REPRESENT THE FIRM'S PRODUCTS
—AND THAT'S WHERE HE GOT IN BIG TROUBLE!

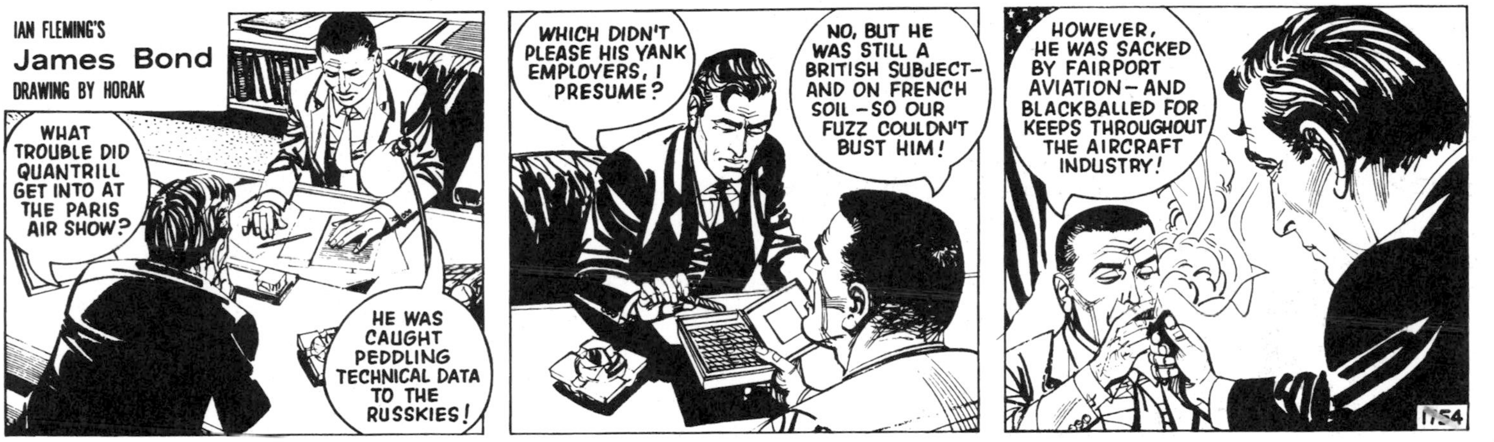
IAN FLEMING'S
James Bond
DRAWING BY HORAK
WHAT TROUBLE DID QUANTRILL GET INTO AT THE PARIS AIR SHOW?
HE WAS CAUGHT PEDDLING TECHNICAL DATA TO THE RUSSKIES!
WHICH DIDN'T PLEASE HIS YANK EMPLOYERS, I PRESUME?
NO, BUT HE WAS STILL A BRITISH SUBJECT— AND ON FRENCH SOIL — SO OUR FUZZ COULDN'T BUST HIM!
HOWEVER, HE WAS SACKED BY FAIRPORT AVIATION — AND BLACKBALLED FOR KEEPS THROUGHOUT THE AIRCRAFT INDUSTRY!
1754

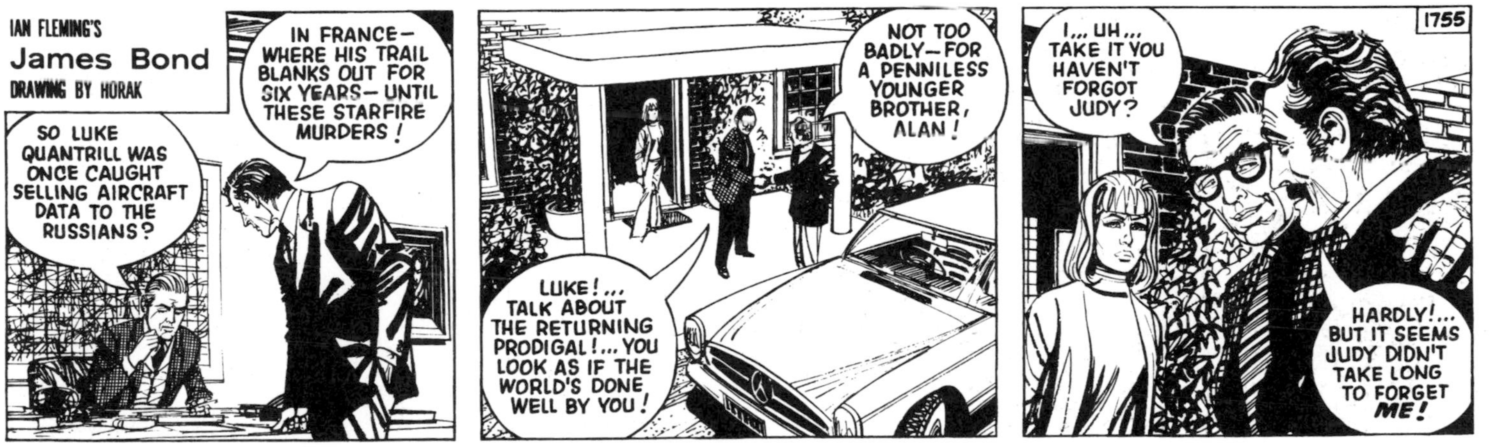
IAN FLEMING'S
James Bond
DRAWING BY HORAK
SO LUKE QUANTRILL WAS ONCE CAUGHT SELLING AIRCRAFT DATA TO THE RUSSIANS?
IN FRANCE— WHERE HIS TRAIL BLANKS OUT FOR SIX YEARS— UNTIL THESE STARFIRE MURDERS!
LUKE!... TALK ABOUT THE RETURNING PRODIGAL!... YOU LOOK AS IF THE WORLD'S DONE WELL BY YOU!
NOT TOO BADLY— FOR A PENNILESS YOUNGER BROTHER, ALAN!
1755
I... UH... TAKE IT YOU HAVEN'T FORGOT JUDY?
HARDLY!... BUT IT SEEMS JUDY DIDN'T TAKE LONG TO FORGET ME!

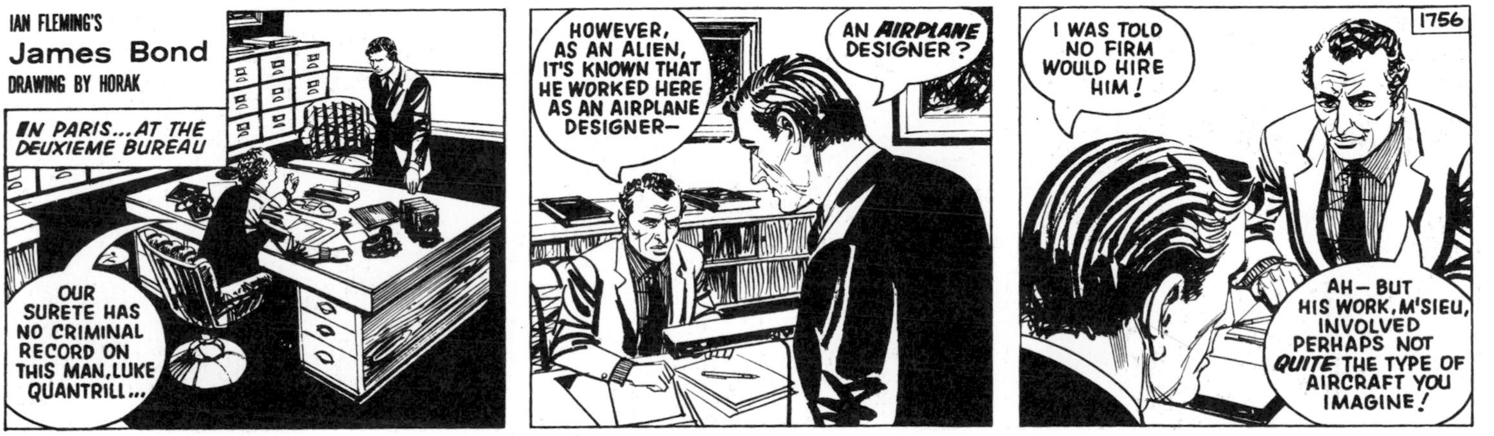
IAN FLEMING'S
James Bond
DRAWING BY HORAK
IN PARIS... AT THE DEUXIEME BUREAU
OUR SURETE HAS NO CRIMINAL RECORD ON THIS MAN, LUKE QUANTRILL...
HOWEVER, AS AN ALIEN, IT'S KNOWN THAT HE WORKED HERE AS AN AIRPLANE DESIGNER—
AN AIRPLANE DESIGNER?
1756
I WAS TOLD NO FIRM WOULD HIRE HIM!
AH— BUT HIS WORK, M'SIEU, INVOLVED PERHAPS NOT QUITE THE TYPE OF AIRCRAFT YOU IMAGINE!

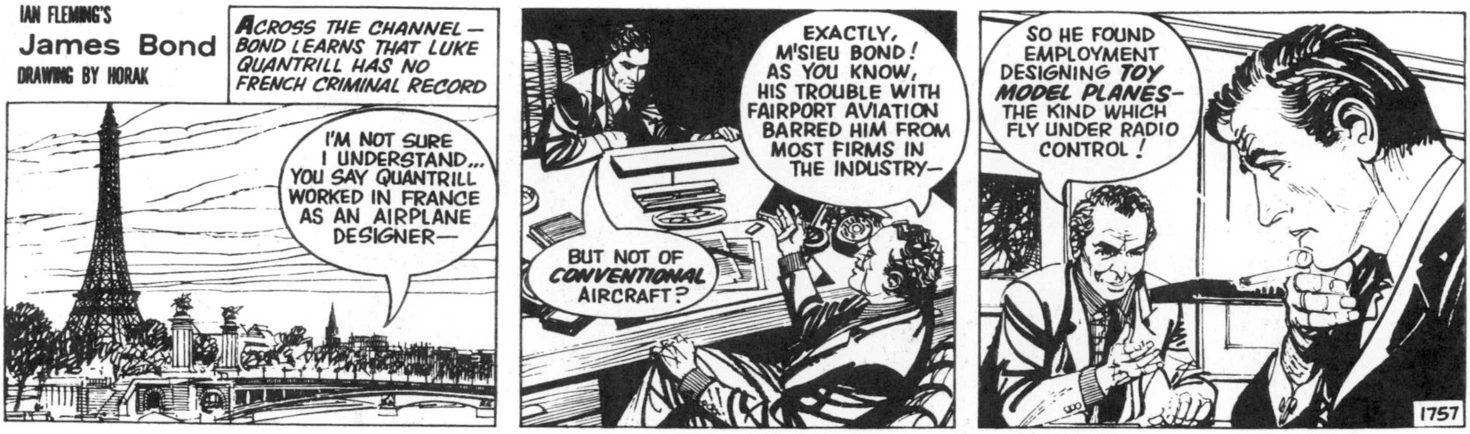
IAN FLEMING'S
James Bond
DRAWING BY HORAK
ACROSS THE CHANNEL—BOND LEARNS THAT LUKE QUANTRILL HAS NO FRENCH CRIMINAL RECORD
I'M NOT SURE I UNDERSTAND... YOU SAY QUANTRILL WORKED IN FRANCE AS AN AIRPLANE DESIGNER—
EXACTLY, M'SIEU BOND! AS YOU KNOW, HIS TROUBLE WITH FAIRPORT AVIATION BARRED HIM FROM MOST FIRMS IN THE INDUSTRY—
BUT NOT OF CONVENTIONAL AIRCRAFT?
SO HE FOUND EMPLOYMENT DESIGNING TOY MODEL PLANES—THE KIND WHICH FLY UNDER RADIO CONTROL!
1757

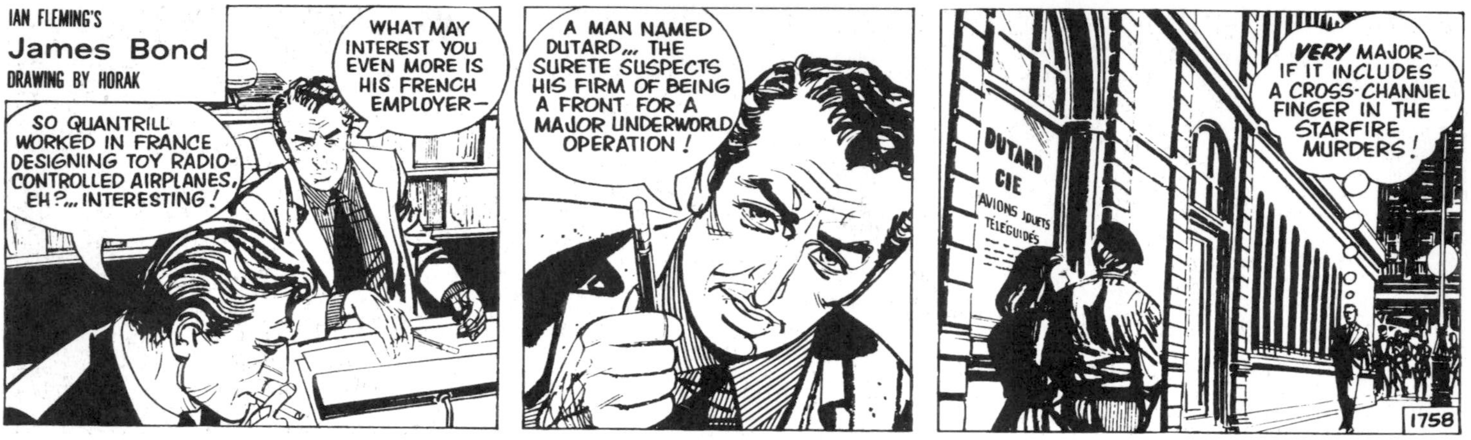
IAN FLEMING'S
James Bond
DRAWING BY HORAK
SO QUANTRILL WORKED IN FRANCE DESIGNING TOY RADIO-CONTROLLED AIRPLANES, EH?... INTERESTING!
WHAT MAY INTEREST YOU EVEN MORE IS HIS FRENCH EMPLOYER—
A MAN NAMED DUTARD... THE SURETE SUSPECTS HIS FIRM OF BEING A FRONT FOR A MAJOR UNDERWORLD OPERATION!
DUTARD CIE
AVIONS JOUETS TÉLÉGUIDÉS
VERY MAJOR—IF IT INCLUDES A CROSS-CHANNEL FINGER IN THE STARFIRE MURDERS!
1758

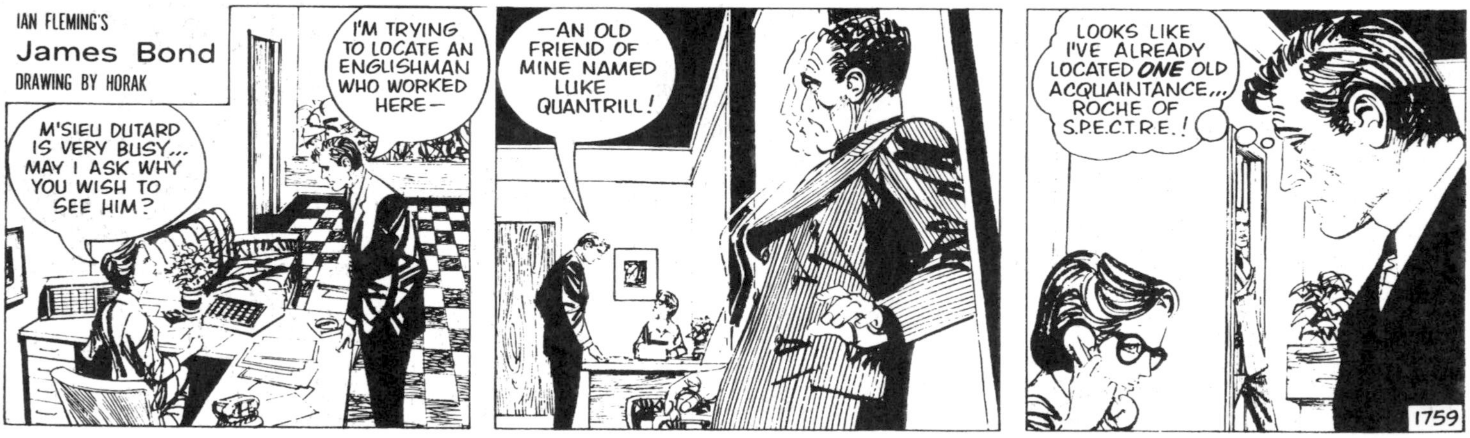
IAN FLEMING'S
James Bond
DRAWING BY HORAK
M'SIEU DUTARD IS VERY BUSY... MAY I ASK WHY YOU WISH TO SEE HIM?
I'M TRYING TO LOCATE AN ENGLISHMAN WHO WORKED HERE—
—AN OLD FRIEND OF MINE NAMED LUKE QUANTRILL!
LOOKS LIKE I'VE ALREADY LOCATED ONE OLD ACQUAINTANCE... ROCHE OF S.P.E.C.T.R.E.!
1759

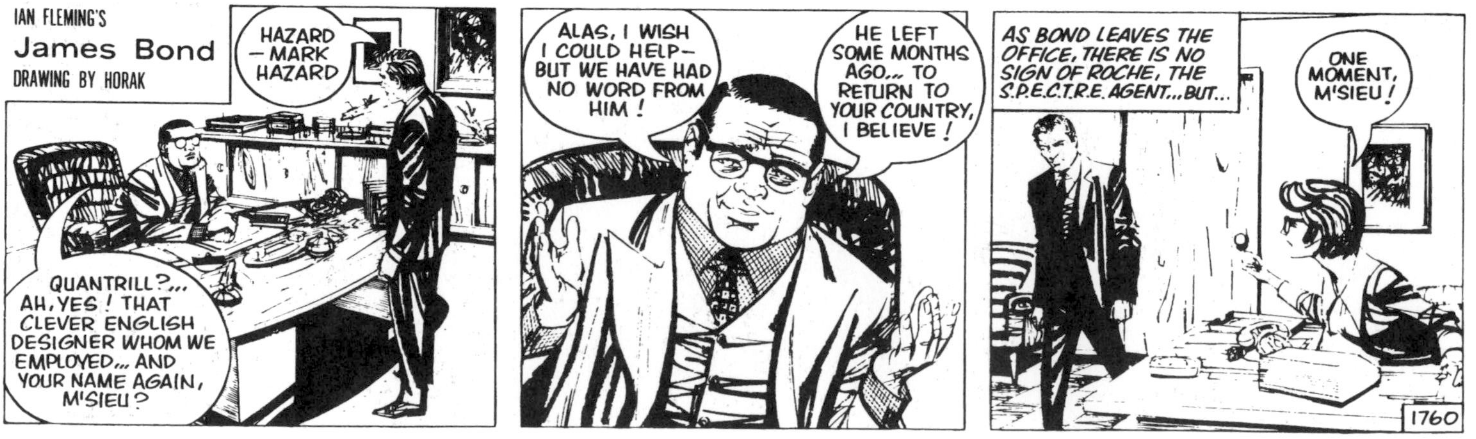
IAN FLEMING'S
James Bond
DRAWING BY HORAK
QUANTRILL?... AH, YES! THAT CLEVER ENGLISH DESIGNER WHOM WE EMPLOYED... AND YOUR NAME AGAIN, M'SIEU?
HAZARD—MARK HAZARD
ALAS, I WISH I COULD HELP—BUT WE HAVE HAD NO WORD FROM HIM!
HE LEFT SOME MONTHS AGO... TO RETURN TO YOUR COUNTRY, I BELIEVE!
AS BOND LEAVES THE OFFICE, THERE IS NO SIGN OF ROCHE, THE S.P.E.C.T.R.E. AGENT... BUT...
ONE MOMENT, M'SIEU!
1760

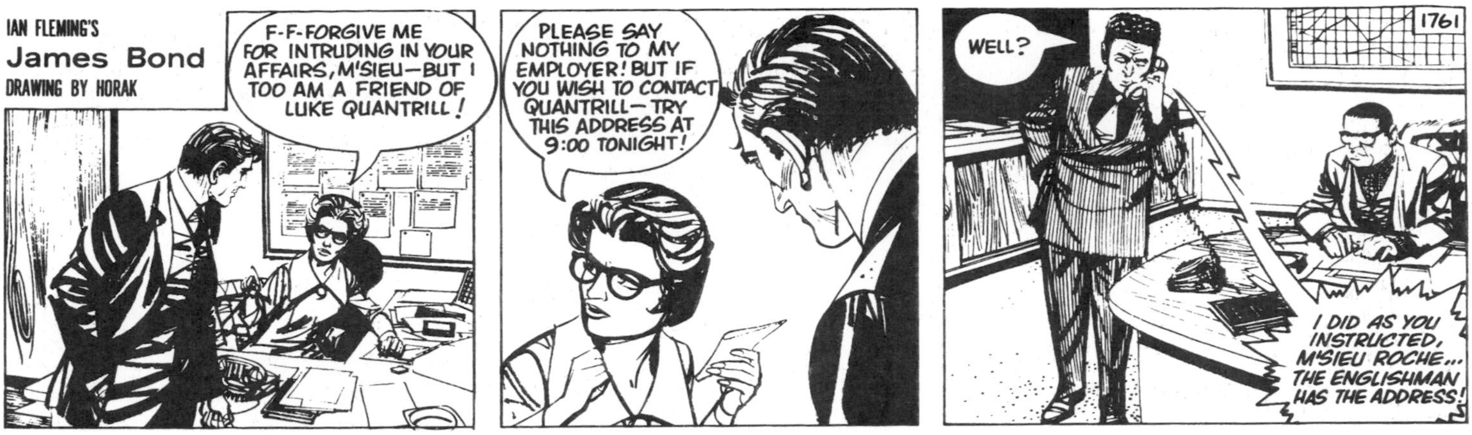
IAN FLEMING'S
James Bond
DRAWING BY HORAK
F-F-FORGIVE ME FOR INTRUDING IN YOUR AFFAIRS, M'SIEU—BUT I TOO AM A FRIEND OF LUKE QUANTRILL!
PLEASE SAY NOTHING TO MY EMPLOYER! BUT IF YOU WISH TO CONTACT QUANTRILL—TRY THIS ADDRESS AT 9:00 TONIGHT!
1761
WELL?
I DID AS YOU INSTRUCTED, M'SIEU ROCHE... THE ENGLISHMAN HAS THE ADDRESS!

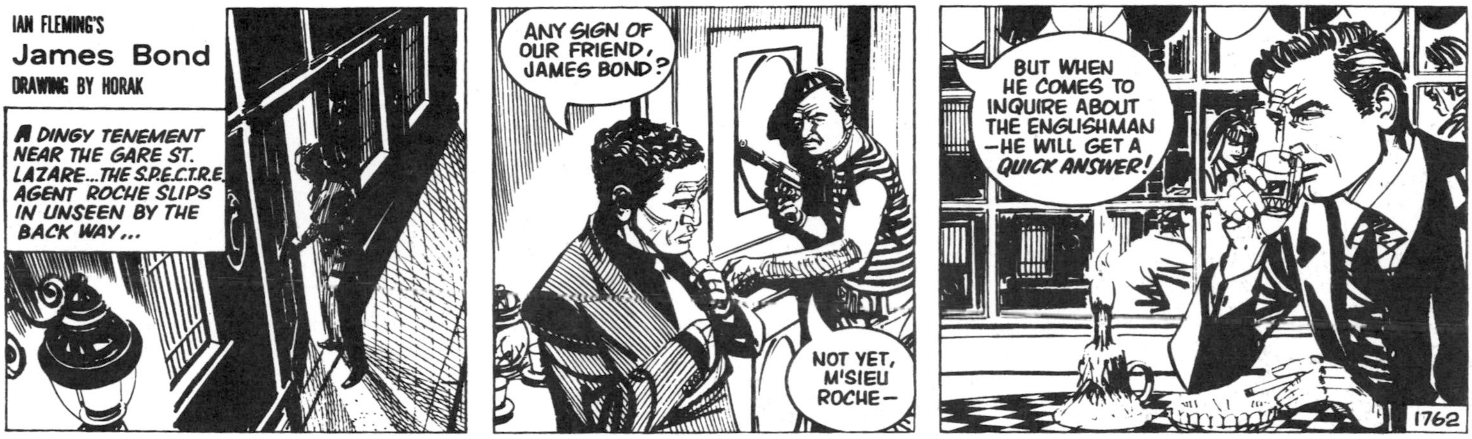
IAN FLEMING'S
James Bond
DRAWING BY HORAK
A DINGY TENEMENT NEAR THE GARE ST. LAZARE...THE S.P.E.C.T.R.E. AGENT ROCHE SLIPS IN UNSEEN BY THE BACK WAY...
ANY SIGN OF OUR FRIEND, JAMES BOND?
NOT YET, M'SIEU ROCHE—
BUT WHEN HE COMES TO INQUIRE ABOUT THE ENGLISHMAN—HE WILL GET A QUICK ANSWER!
1762

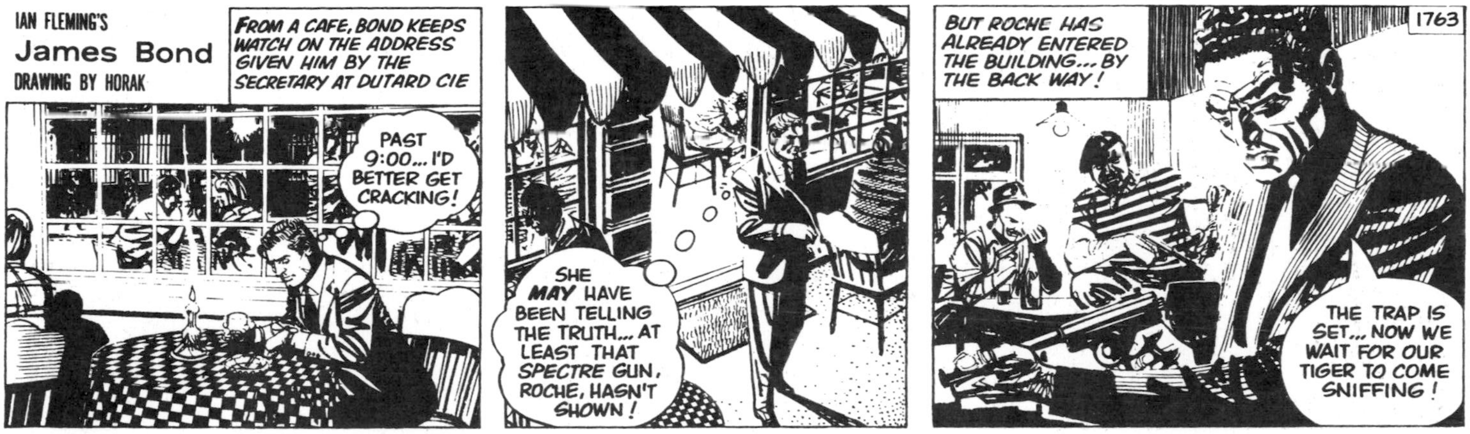
IAN FLEMING'S
James Bond
DRAWING BY HORAK
FROM A CAFE, BOND KEEPS WATCH ON THE ADDRESS GIVEN HIM BY THE SECRETARY AT DUTARD CIE
PAST 9:00... I'D BETTER GET CRACKING!
SHE MAY HAVE BEEN TELLING THE TRUTH... AT LEAST THAT SPECTRE GUN, ROCHE, HASN'T SHOWN!
1763
BUT ROCHE HAS ALREADY ENTERED THE BUILDING... BY THE BACK WAY!
THE TRAP IS SET... NOW WE WAIT FOR OUR TIGER TO COME SNIFFING!

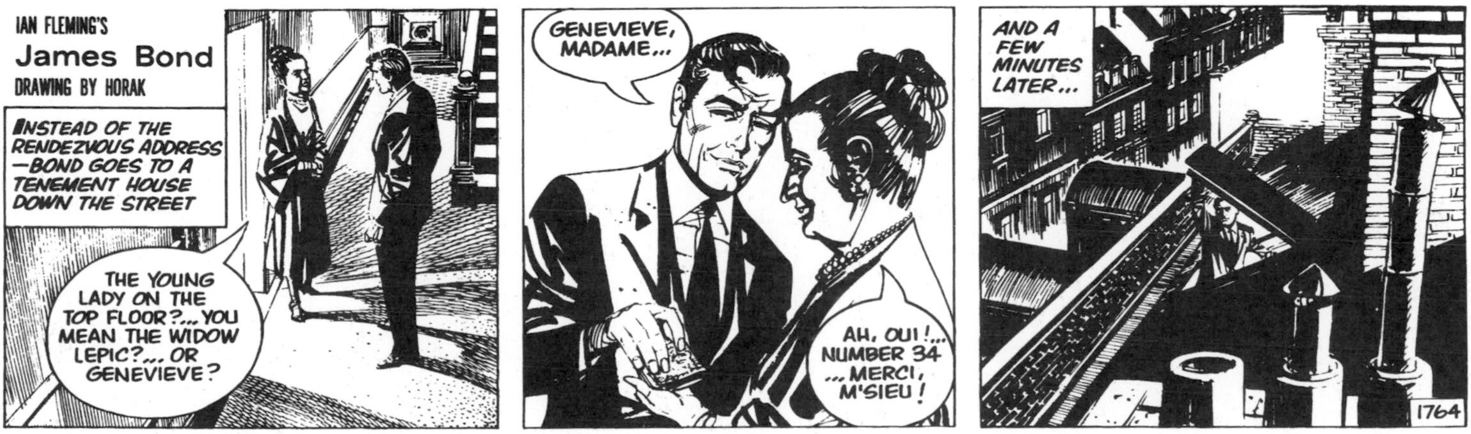
IAN FLEMING'S
James Bond
DRAWING BY HORAK
INSTEAD OF THE RENDEZVOUS ADDRESS—BOND GOES TO A TENEMENT HOUSE DOWN THE STREET
THE YOUNG LADY ON THE TOP FLOOR?... YOU MEAN THE WIDOW LEPIC?... OR GENEVIEVE?
GENEVIEVE, MADAME...
AH, OUI!... NUMBER 34 ...MERCI, M'SIEU!
AND A FEW MINUTES LATER...
1764

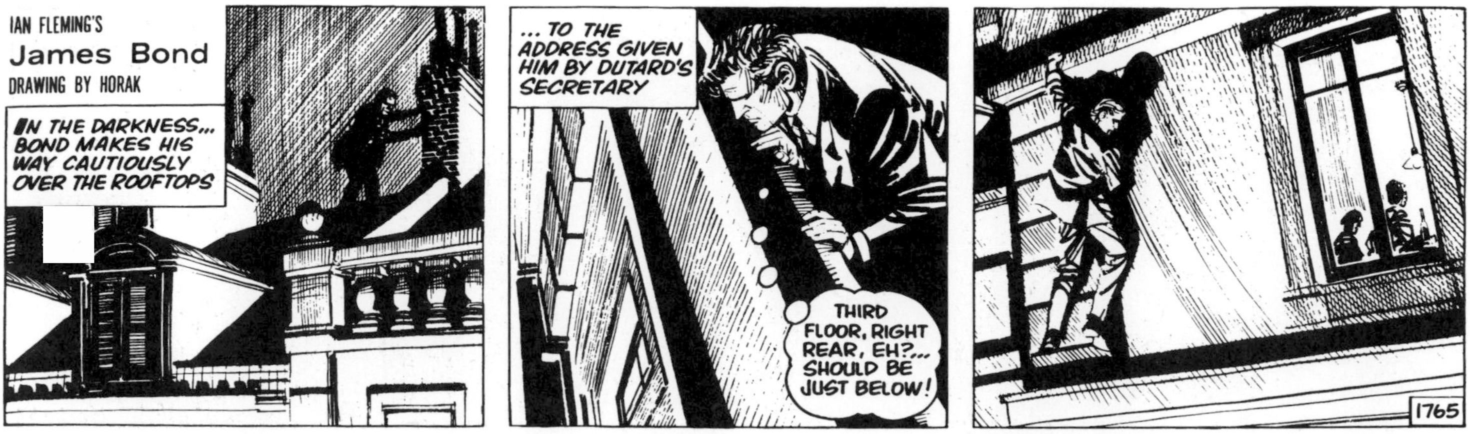
IAN FLEMING'S
James Bond
DRAWING BY HORAK
IN THE DARKNESS... BOND MAKES HIS WAY CAUTIOUSLY OVER THE ROOFTOPS
...TO THE ADDRESS GIVEN HIM BY DUTARD'S SECRETARY
THIRD FLOOR, RIGHT REAR, EH?... SHOULD BE JUST BELOW!
1765

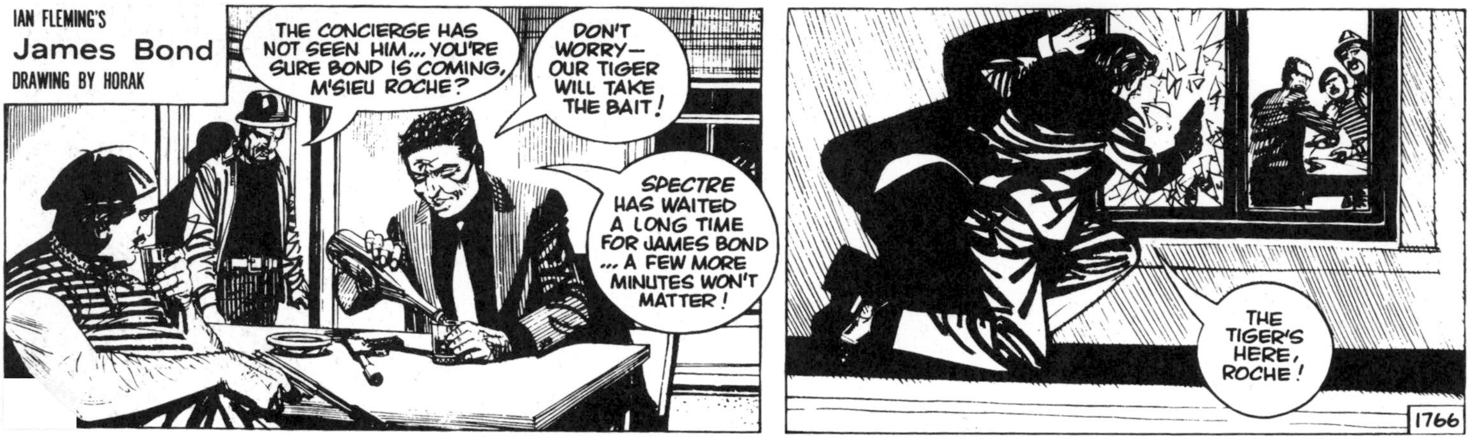
IAN FLEMING'S
James Bond
DRAWING BY HORAK
THE CONCIERGE HAS NOT SEEN HIM... YOU'RE SURE BOND IS COMING, M'SIEU ROCHE?
DON'T WORRY— OUR TIGER WILL TAKE THE BAIT!
SPECTRE HAS WAITED A LONG TIME FOR JAMES BOND ... A FEW MORE MINUTES WON'T MATTER!
THE TIGER'S HERE, ROCHE!
1766

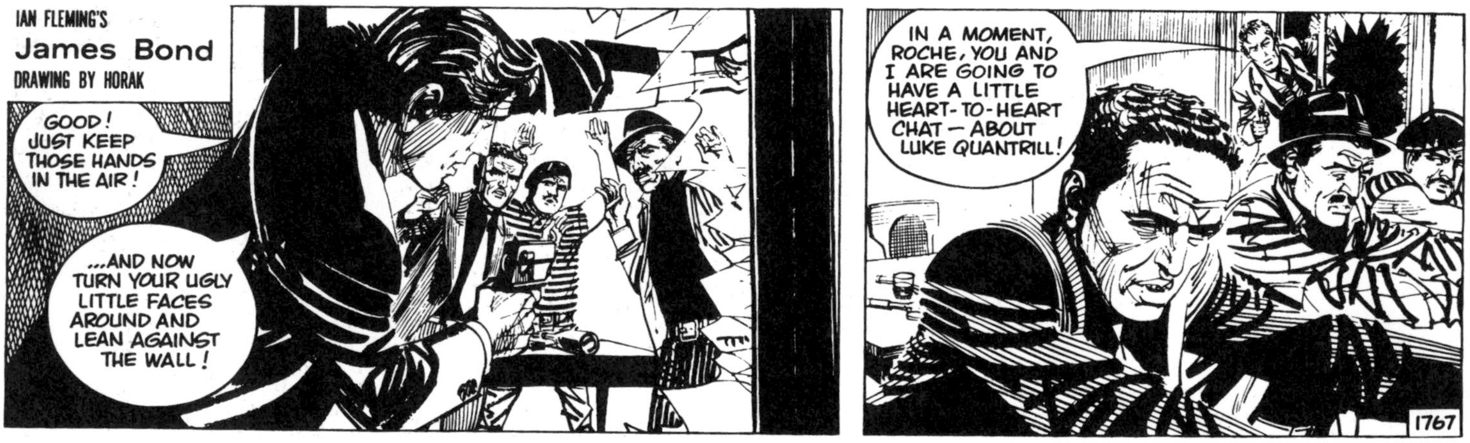
IAN FLEMING'S
James Bond
DRAWING BY HORAK
GOOD! JUST KEEP THOSE HANDS IN THE AIR!
...AND NOW TURN YOUR UGLY LITTLE FACES AROUND AND LEAN AGAINST THE WALL!
IN A MOMENT, ROCHE, YOU AND I ARE GOING TO HAVE A LITTLE HEART-TO-HEART CHAT — ABOUT LUKE QUANTRILL!
1767

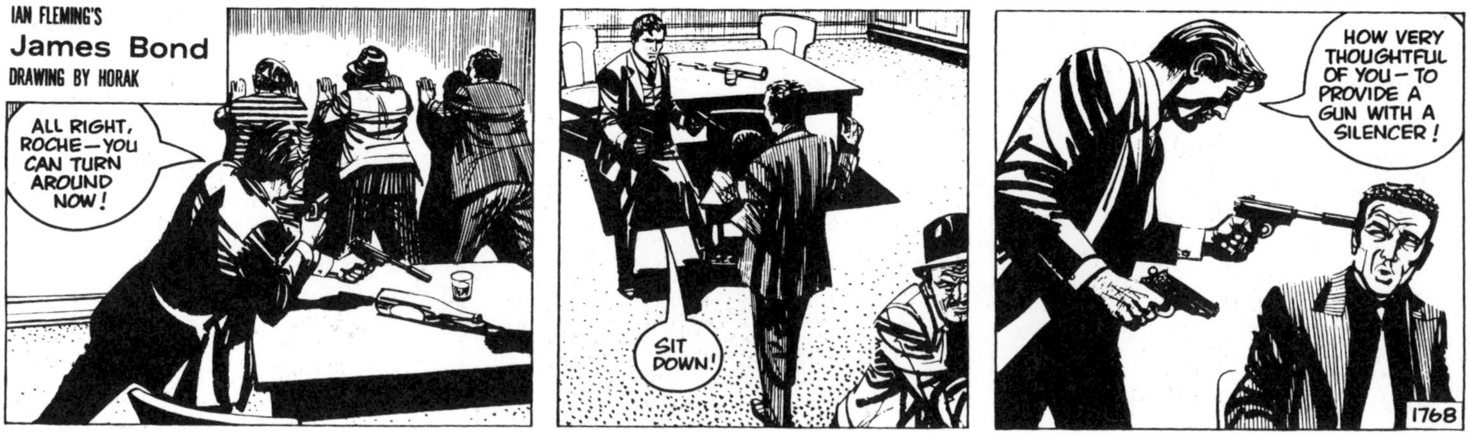
IAN FLEMING'S
James Bond
DRAWING BY HORAK
ALL RIGHT, ROCHE—YOU CAN TURN AROUND NOW!
SIT DOWN!
HOW VERY THOUGHTFUL OF YOU—TO PROVIDE A GUN WITH A SILENCER!
1768

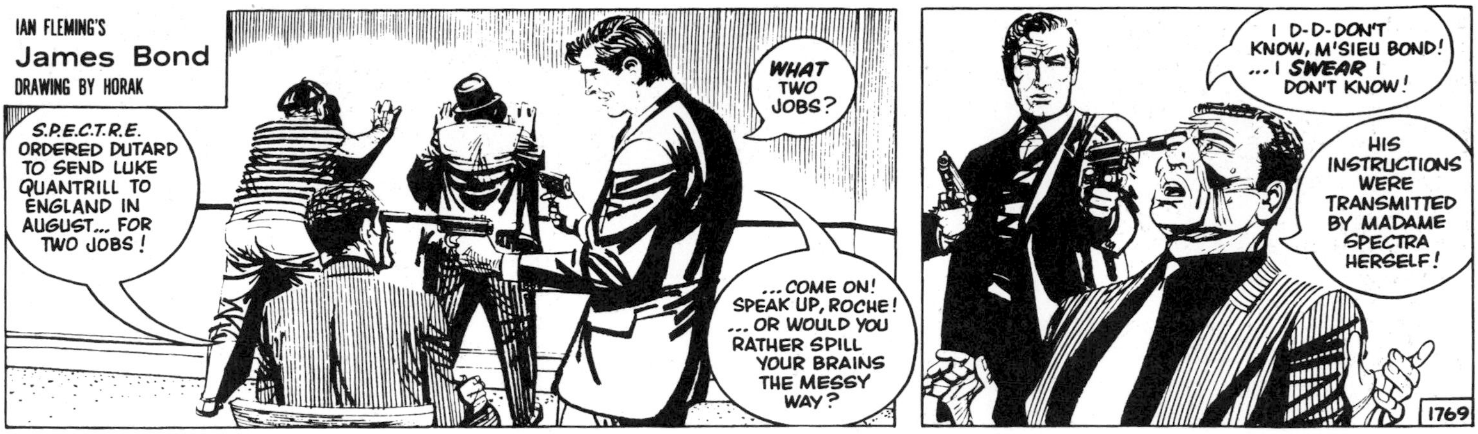
IAN FLEMING'S
James Bond
DRAWING BY HORAK
S.P.E.C.T.R.E. ORDERED DUTARD TO SEND LUKE QUANTRILL TO ENGLAND IN AUGUST... FOR TWO JOBS!
WHAT TWO JOBS?
...COME ON! SPEAK UP, ROCHE! ...OR WOULD YOU RATHER SPILL YOUR BRAINS THE MESSY WAY?
I D-D-DON'T KNOW, M'SIEU BOND! ...I SWEAR! DON'T KNOW!
HIS INSTRUCTIONS WERE TRANSMITTED BY MADAME SPECTRA HERSELF!
1769

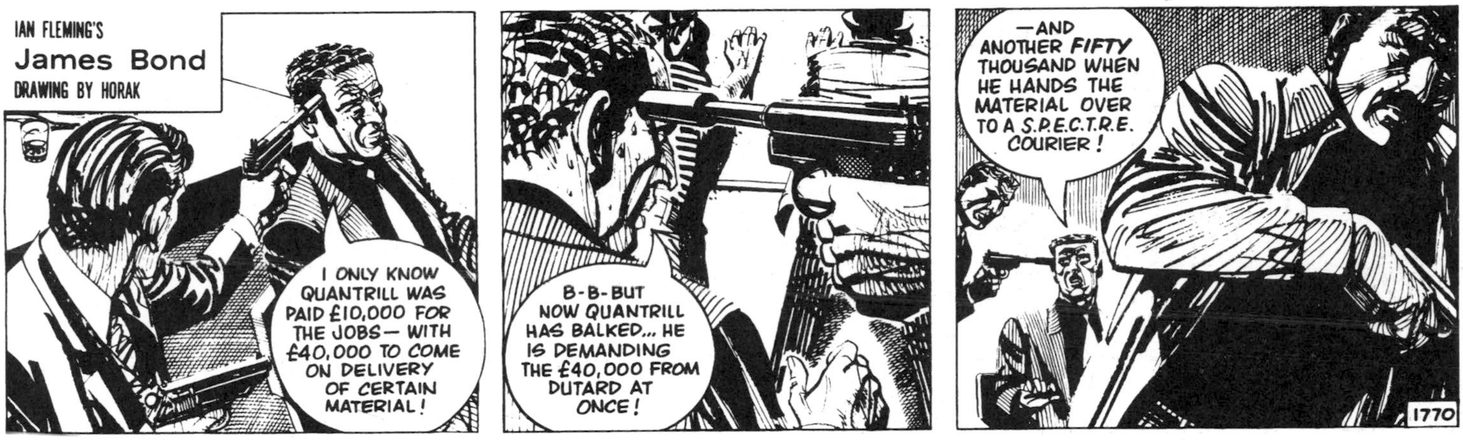
IAN FLEMING'S
James Bond
DRAWING BY HORAK
I ONLY KNOW QUANTRILL WAS PAID £10,000 FOR THE JOBS— WITH £40,000 TO COME ON DELIVERY OF CERTAIN MATERIAL!
B-B-BUT NOW QUANTRILL HAS BALKED... HE IS DEMANDING THE £40,000 FROM DUTARD AT ONCE!
—AND ANOTHER FIFTY THOUSAND WHEN HE HANDS THE MATERIAL OVER TO A S.P.E.C.T.R.E. COURIER!
1770

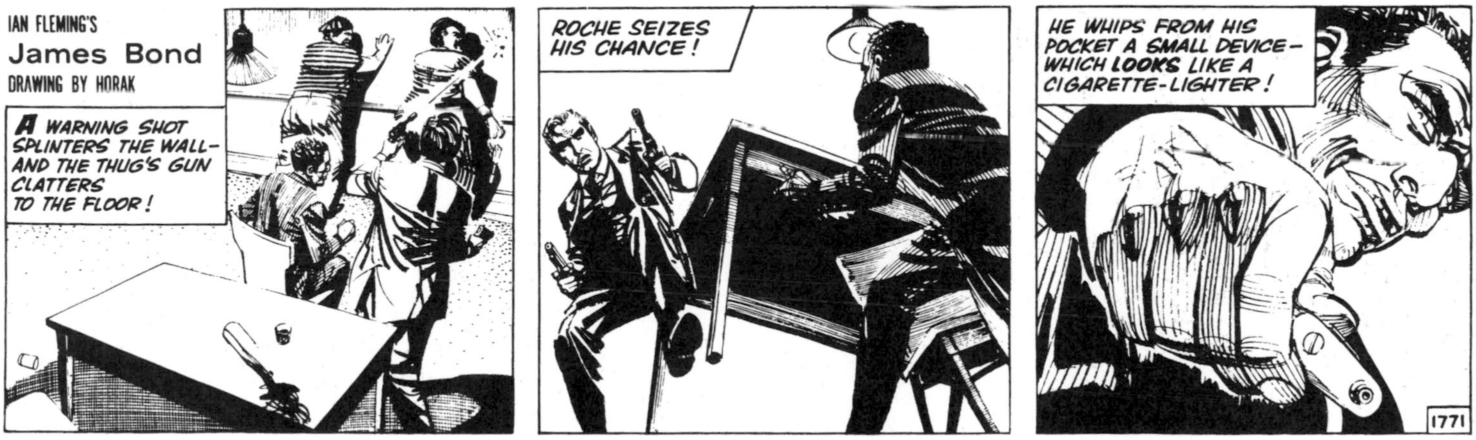
IAN FLEMING'S
James Bond
DRAWING BY HORAK
A WARNING SHOT SPLINTERS THE WALL— AND THE THUG'S GUN CLATTERS TO THE FLOOR!
ROCHE SEIZES HIS CHANCE!
HE WHIPS FROM HIS POCKET A SMALL DEVICE— WHICH LOOKS LIKE A CIGARETTE-LIGHTER!
1771

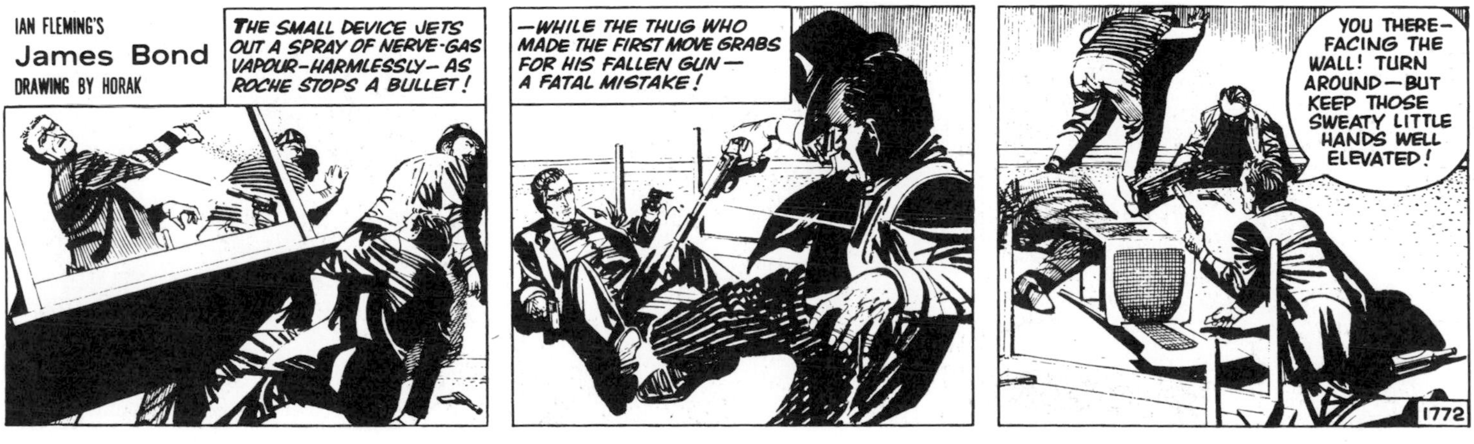
IAN FLEMING'S
James Bond
DRAWING BY HORAK
THE SMALL DEVICE JETS OUT A SPRAY OF NERVE-GAS VAPOUR—HARMLESSLY— AS ROCHE STOPS A BULLET!
—WHILE THE THUG WHO MADE THE FIRST MOVE GRABS FOR HIS FALLEN GUN — A FATAL MISTAKE!
YOU THERE— FACING THE WALL! TURN AROUND—BUT KEEP THOSE SWEATY LITTLE HANDS WELL ELEVATED!
1772

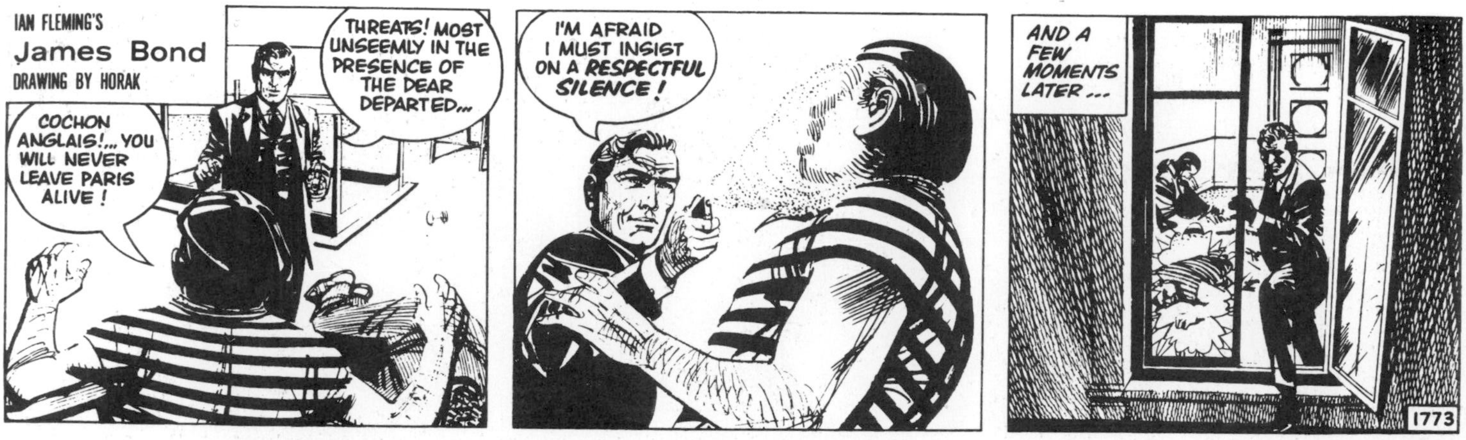
IAN FLEMING'S
James Bond
DRAWING BY HORAK
COCHON ANGLAIS!... YOU WILL NEVER LEAVE PARIS ALIVE!
THREATS! MOST UNSEEMLY IN THE PRESENCE OF THE DEAR DEPARTED...
I'M AFRAID I MUST INSIST ON A RESPECTFUL SILENCE!
AND A FEW MOMENTS LATER ...
1773

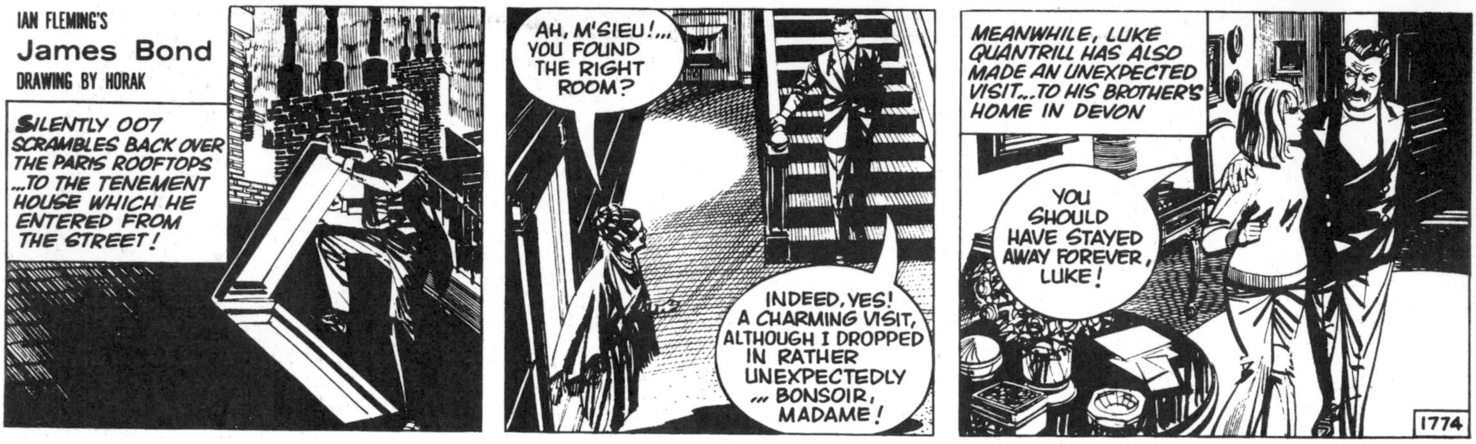
IAN FLEMING'S
James Bond
DRAWING BY HORAK
SILENTLY 007 SCRAMBLES BACK OVER THE PARIS ROOFTOPS ...TO THE TENEMENT HOUSE WHICH HE ENTERED FROM THE STREET!
AH, M'SIEU!... YOU FOUND THE RIGHT ROOM?
INDEED, YES! A CHARMING VISIT, ALTHOUGH I DROPPED IN RATHER UNEXPECTEDLY ... BONSOIR, MADAME!
MEANWHILE, LUKE QUANTRILL HAS ALSO MADE AN UNEXPECTED VISIT...TO HIS BROTHER'S HOME IN DEVON
YOU SHOULD HAVE STAYED AWAY FOREVER, LUKE!
1774

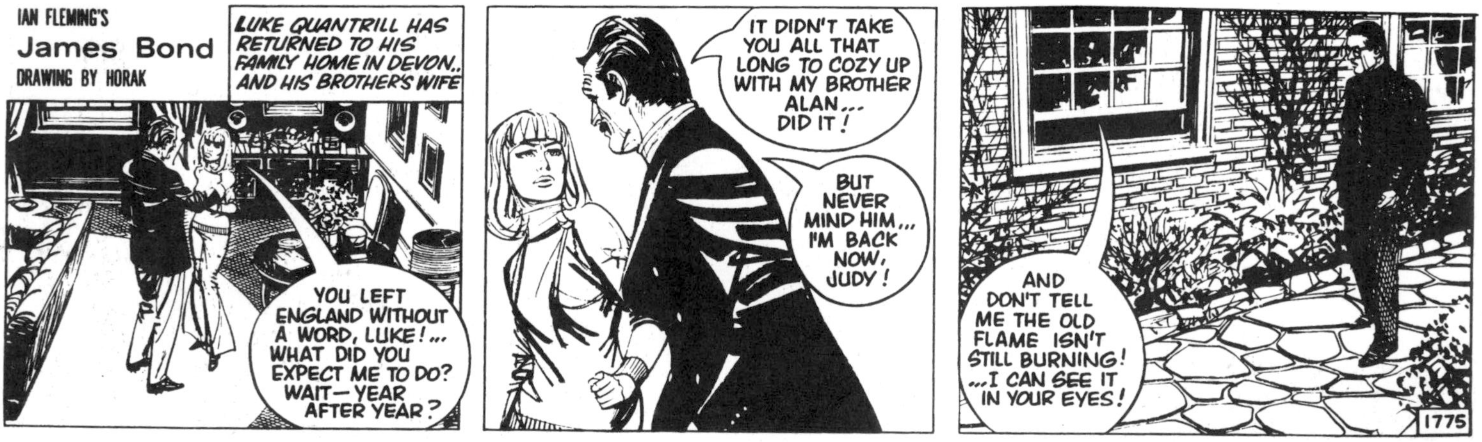
IAN FLEMING'S
James Bond
DRAWING BY HORAK
LUKE QUANTRILL HAS RETURNED TO HIS FAMILY HOME IN DEVON.. AND HIS BROTHER'S WIFE
YOU LEFT ENGLAND WITHOUT A WORD, LUKE!... WHAT DID YOU EXPECT ME TO DO? WAIT—YEAR AFTER YEAR?
IT DIDN'T TAKE YOU ALL THAT LONG TO COZY UP WITH MY BROTHER ALAN... DID IT!
BUT NEVER MIND HIM... I'M BACK NOW, JUDY!
AND DON'T TELL ME THE OLD FLAME ISN'T STILL BURNING! ...I CAN SEE IT IN YOUR EYES!
1775

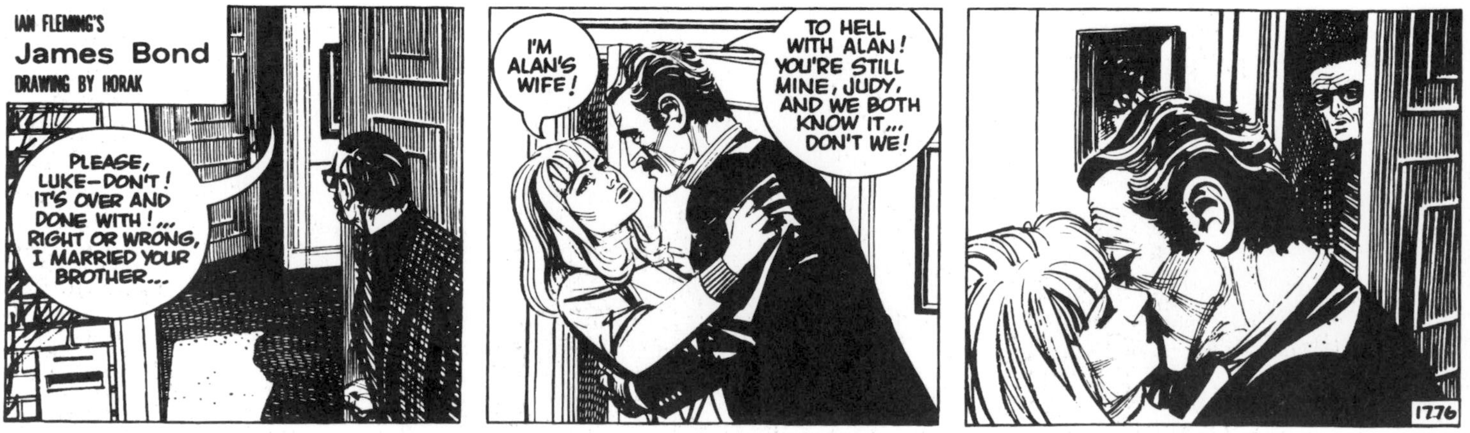
IAN FLEMING'S
James Bond
DRAWING BY HORAK
PLEASE, LUKE—DON'T! IT'S OVER AND DONE WITH!... RIGHT OR WRONG, I MARRIED YOUR BROTHER...
I'M ALAN'S WIFE!
TO HELL WITH ALAN! YOU'RE STILL MINE, JUDY, AND WE BOTH KNOW IT... DON'T WE!
1776

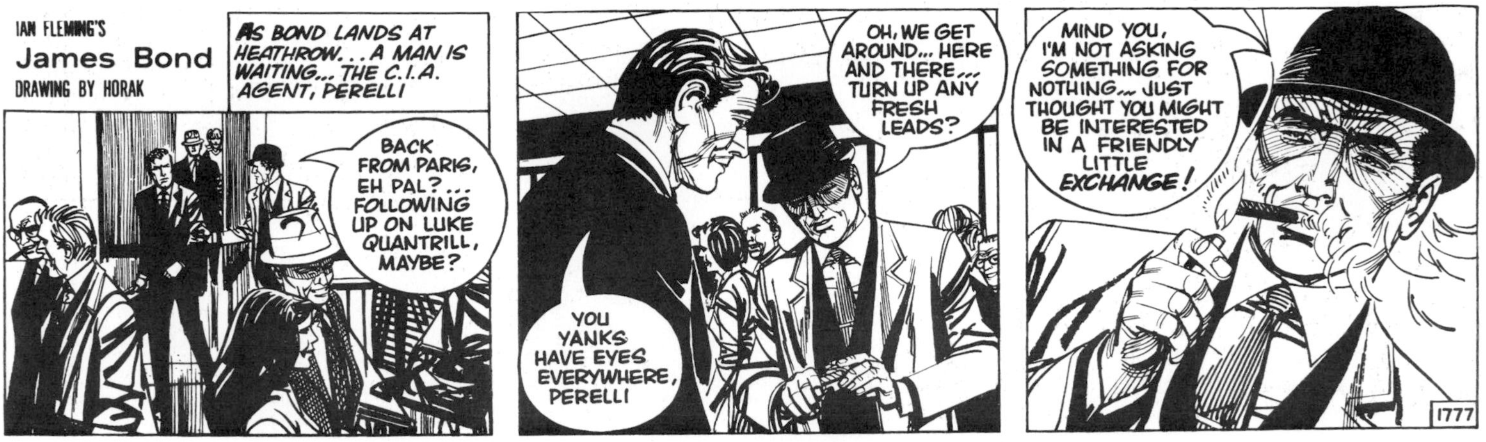
IAN FLEMING'S
James Bond
DRAWING BY HORAK
AS BOND LANDS AT HEATHROW... A MAN IS WAITING... THE C.I.A. AGENT, PERELLI
BACK FROM PARIS, EH PAL?... FOLLOWING UP ON LUKE QUANTRILL, MAYBE?
YOU YANKS HAVE EYES EVERYWHERE, PERELLI
OH, WE GET AROUND... HERE AND THERE... TURN UP ANY FRESH LEADS?
MIND YOU, I'M NOT ASKING SOMETHING FOR NOTHING... JUST THOUGHT YOU MIGHT BE INTERESTED IN A FRIENDLY LITTLE EXCHANGE!
1777

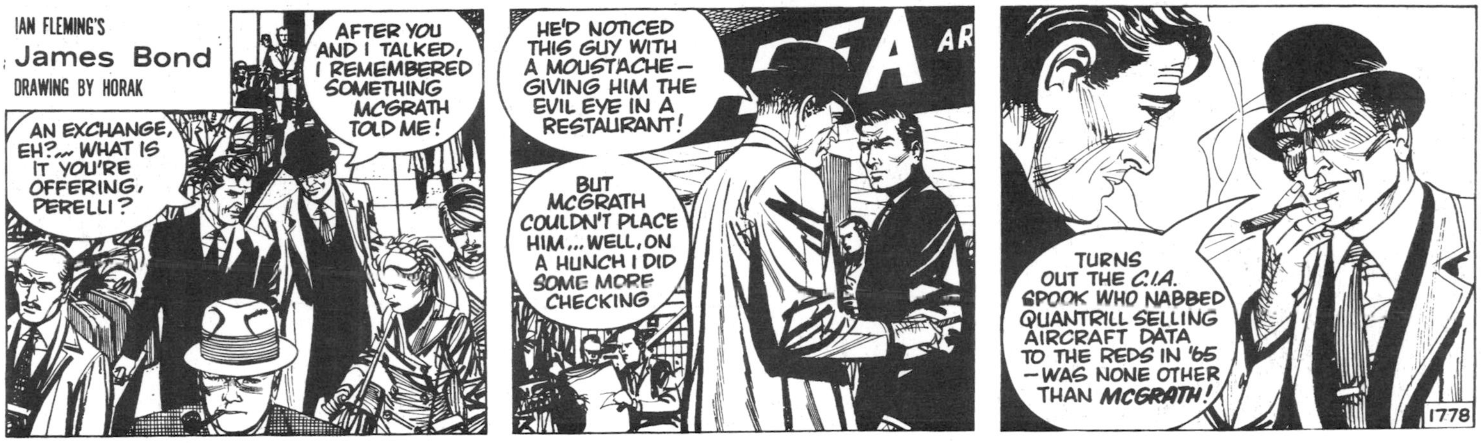
IAN FLEMING'S
James Bond
DRAWING BY HORAK
AN EXCHANGE, EH?... WHAT IS IT YOU'RE OFFERING, PERELLI?
AFTER YOU AND I TALKED, I REMEMBERED SOMETHING MCGRATH TOLD ME!
HE'D NOTICED THIS GUY WITH A MOUSTACHE—GIVING HIM THE EVIL EYE IN A RESTAURANT!
BUT MCGRATH COULDN'T PLACE HIM... WELL, ON A HUNCH I DID SOME MORE CHECKING
TURNS OUT THE C.I.A. SPOOK WHO NABBED QUANTRILL SELLING AIRCRAFT DATA TO THE REDS IN '65—WAS NONE OTHER THAN MCGRATH!
1778

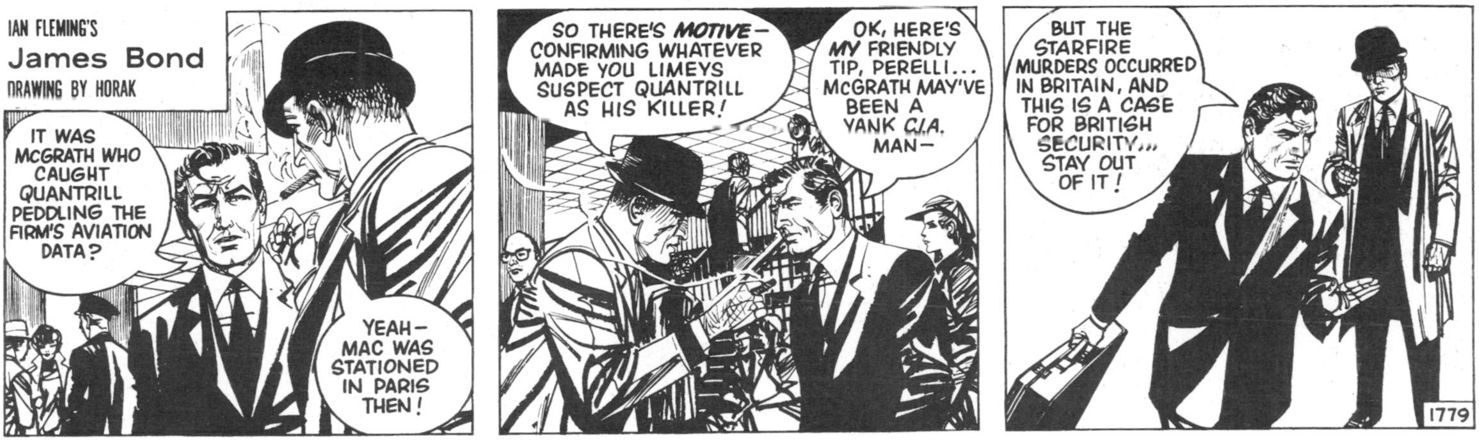
IAN FLEMING'S
James Bond
DRAWING BY HORAK
IT WAS MCGRATH WHO CAUGHT QUANTRILL PEDDLING THE FIRM'S AVIATION DATA?
YEAH—MAC WAS STATIONED IN PARIS THEN!
SO THERE'S MOTIVE—CONFIRMING WHATEVER MADE YOU LIMEYS SUSPECT QUANTRILL AS HIS KILLER!
OK, HERE'S MY FRIENDLY TIP, PERELLI... MCGRATH MAY'VE BEEN A YANK C.I.A. MAN—
BUT THE STARFIRE MURDERS OCCURRED IN BRITAIN, AND THIS IS A CASE FOR BRITISH SECURITY... STAY OUT OF IT!
1779

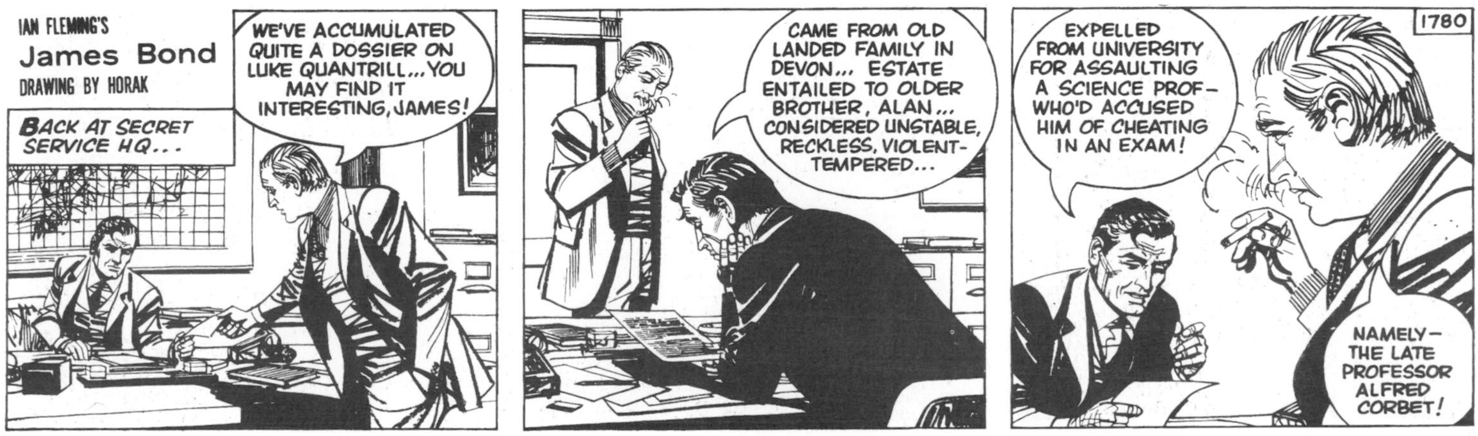
IAN FLEMING'S
James Bond
DRAWING BY HORAK
BACK AT SECRET SERVICE HQ...
WE'VE ACCUMULATED QUITE A DOSSIER ON LUKE QUANTRILL... YOU MAY FIND IT INTERESTING, JAMES!
CAME FROM OLD LANDED FAMILY IN DEVON... ESTATE ENTAILED TO OLDER BROTHER, ALAN... CONSIDERED UNSTABLE, RECKLESS, VIOLENT-TEMPERED...
1780
EXPELLED FROM UNIVERSITY FOR ASSAULTING A SCIENCE PROF—WHO'D ACCUSED HIM OF CHEATING IN AN EXAM!
NAMELY—THE LATE PROFESSOR ALFRED CORBET!

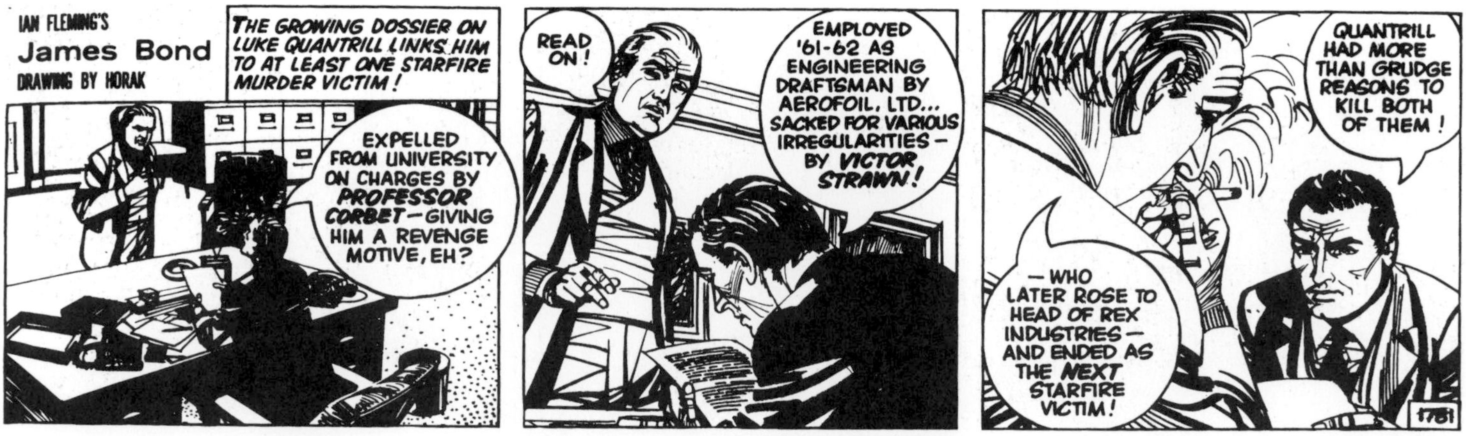
IAN FLEMING'S
James Bond
DRAWING BY HORAK
THE GROWING DOSSIER ON LUKE QUANTRILL LINKS HIM TO AT LEAST ONE STARFIRE MURDER VICTIM!
EXPELLED FROM UNIVERSITY ON CHARGES BY PROFESSOR CORBET—GIVING HIM A REVENGE MOTIVE, EH?
READ ON!
EMPLOYED '61-62 AS ENGINEERING DRAFTSMAN BY AEROFOIL, LTD... SACKED FOR VARIOUS IRREGULARITIES—BY VICTOR STRAWN!
QUANTRILL HAD MORE THAN GRUDGE REASONS TO KILL BOTH OF THEM!
—WHO LATER ROSE TO HEAD OF REX INDUSTRIES—AND ENDED AS THE NEXT STARFIRE VICTIM!
1781

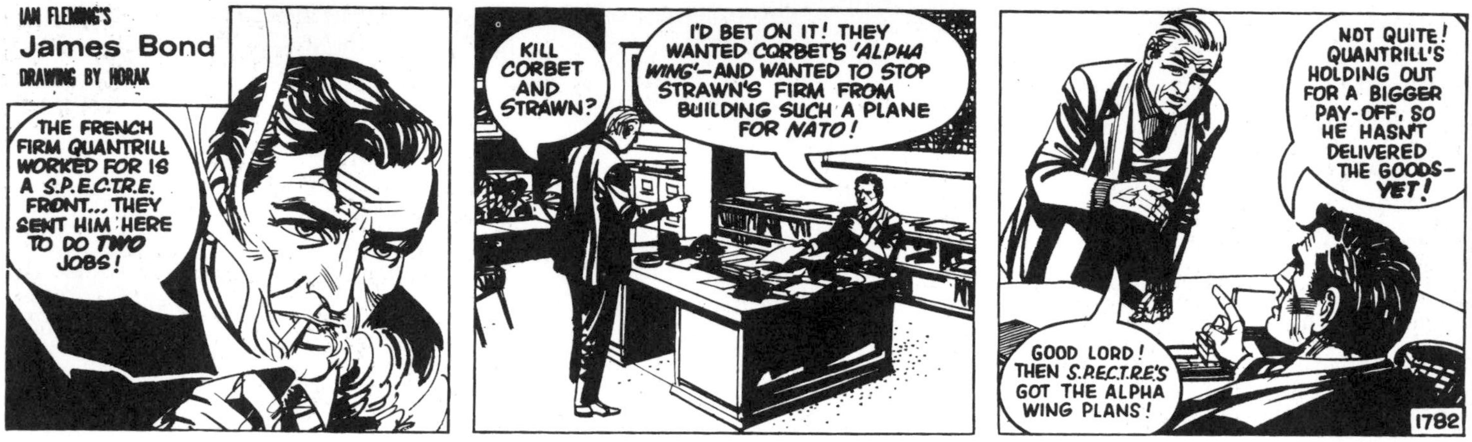
IAN FLEMING'S
James Bond
DRAWING BY HORAK
THE FRENCH FIRM QUANTRILL WORKED FOR IS A S.P.E.C.T.R.E. FRONT... THEY SENT HIM HERE TO DO TWO JOBS!
KILL CORBET AND STRAWN?
I'D BET ON IT! THEY WANTED CORBET'S 'ALPHA WING'—AND WANTED TO STOP STRAWN'S FIRM FROM BUILDING SUCH A PLANE FOR NATO!
NOT QUITE! QUANTRILL'S HOLDING OUT FOR A BIGGER PAY-OFF, SO HE HASN'T DELIVERED THE GOODS—YET!
GOOD LORD! THEN S.P.E.C.T.R.E'S GOT THE ALPHA WING PLANS!
1782

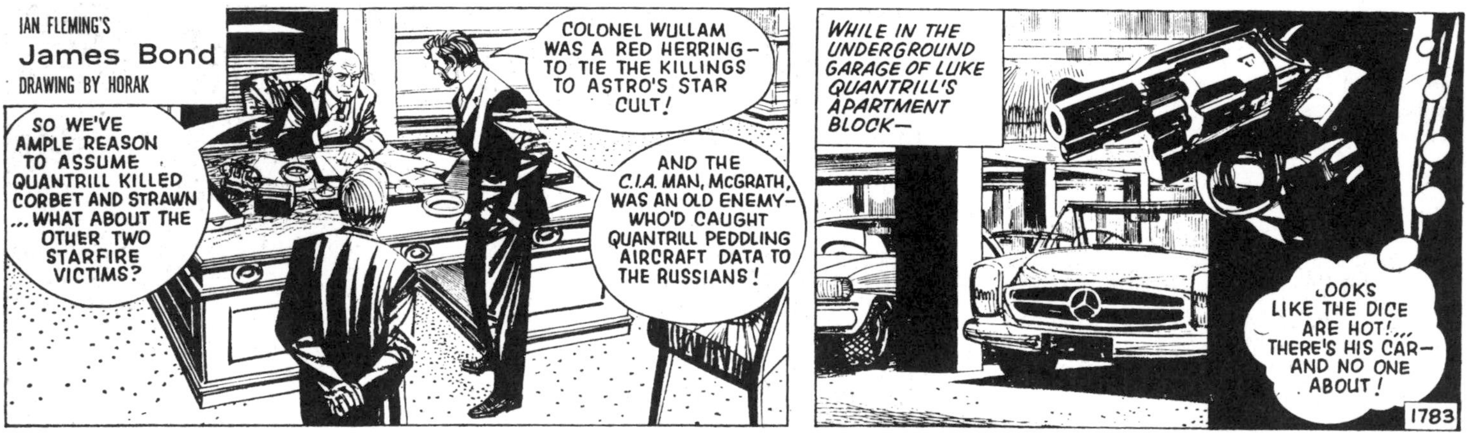
IAN FLEMING'S
James Bond
DRAWING BY HORAK
SO WE'VE AMPLE REASON TO ASSUME QUANTRILL KILLED CORBET AND STRAWN ... WHAT ABOUT THE OTHER TWO STARFIRE VICTIMS?
COLONEL WULLAM WAS A RED HERRING—TO TIE THE KILLINGS TO ASTRO'S STAR CULT!
AND THE C.I.A. MAN, McGRATH, WAS AN OLD ENEMY—WHO'D CAUGHT QUANTRILL PEDDLING AIRCRAFT DATA TO THE RUSSIANS!
WHILE IN THE UNDERGROUND GARAGE OF LUKE QUANTRILL'S APARTMENT BLOCK—
LOOKS LIKE THE DICE ARE HOT!... THERE'S HIS CAR—AND NO ONE ABOUT!
1783

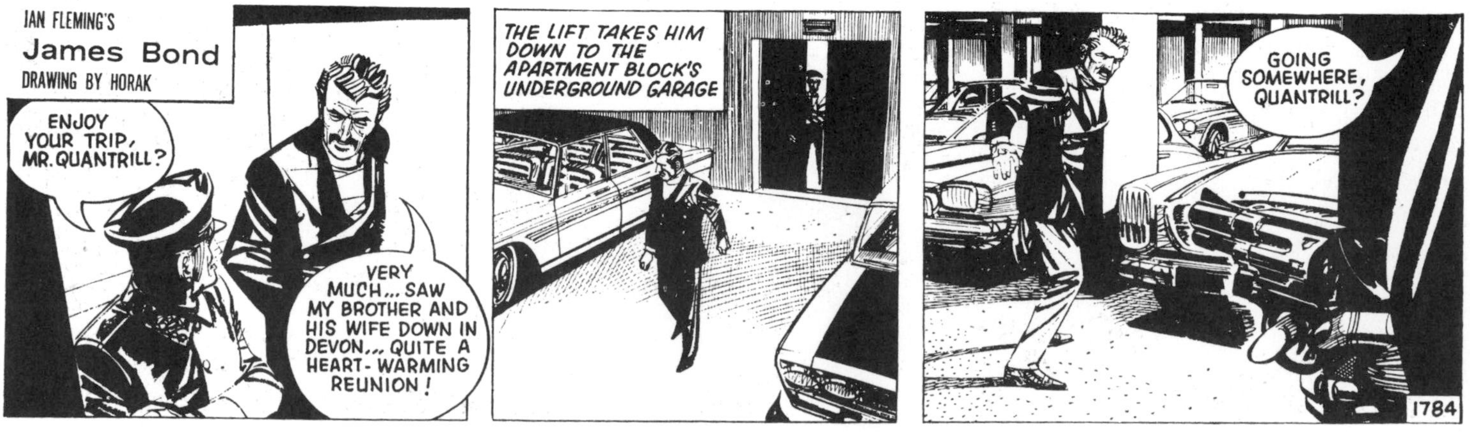
IAN FLEMING'S
James Bond
DRAWING BY HORAK
ENJOY YOUR TRIP, MR. QUANTRILL?
VERY MUCH... SAW MY BROTHER AND HIS WIFE DOWN IN DEVON... QUITE A HEART-WARMING REUNION!
THE LIFT TAKES HIM DOWN TO THE APARTMENT BLOCK'S UNDERGROUND GARAGE
GOING SOMEWHERE, QUANTRILL?
1784

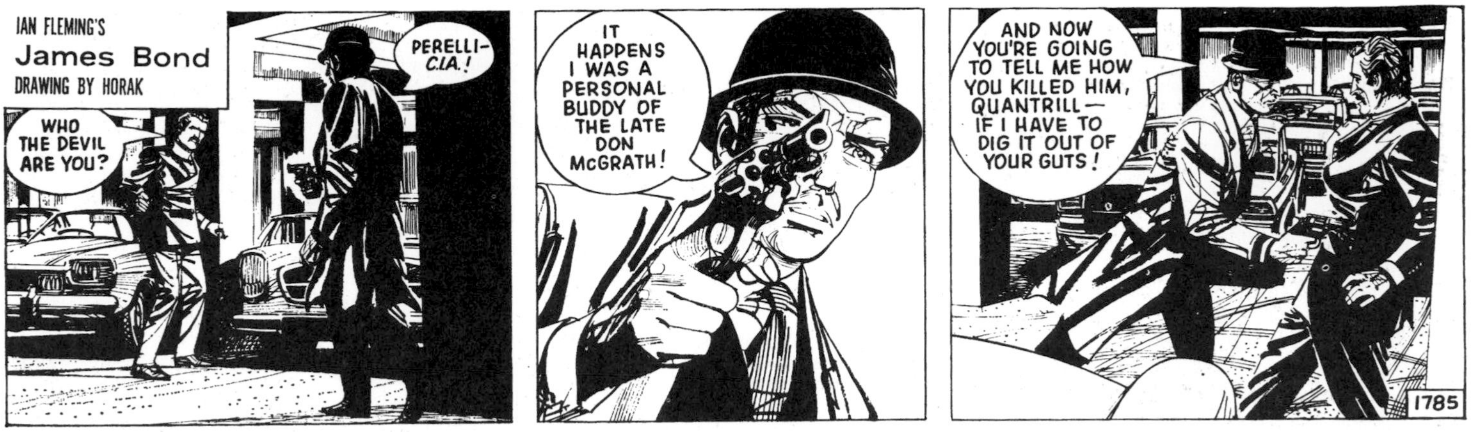
IAN FLEMING'S
James Bond
DRAWING BY HORAK
WHO THE DEVIL ARE YOU?
PERELLI– C.I.A.!
IT HAPPENS I WAS A PERSONAL BUDDY OF THE LATE DON McGRATH!
AND NOW YOU'RE GOING TO TELL ME HOW YOU KILLED HIM, QUANTRILL– IF I HAVE TO DIG IT OUT OF YOUR GUTS!
1785

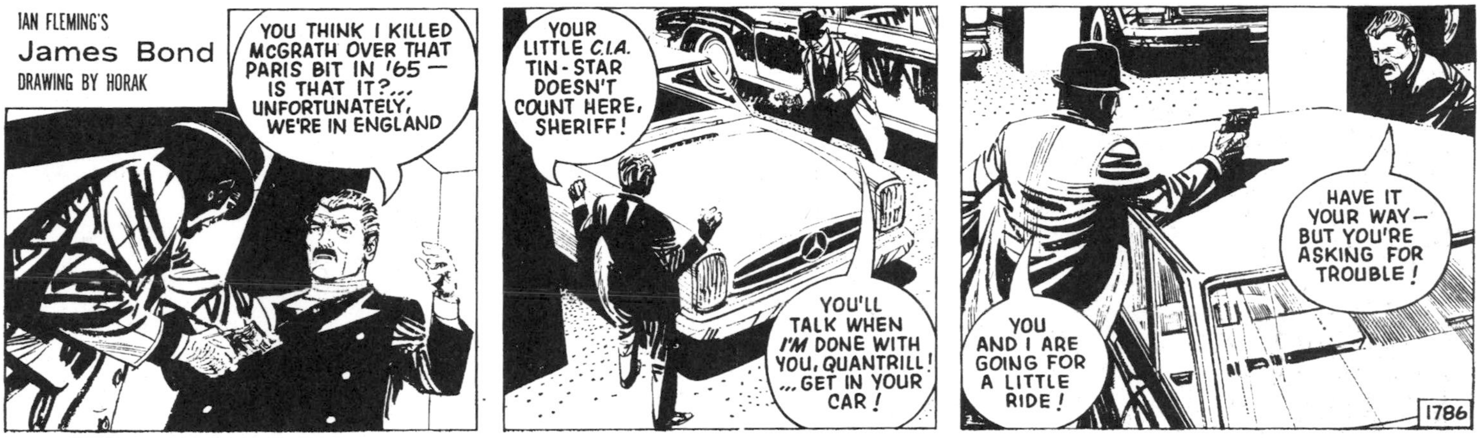
IAN FLEMING'S
James Bond
DRAWING BY HORAK
YOU THINK I KILLED McGRATH OVER THAT PARIS BIT IN '65– IS THAT IT?... UNFORTUNATELY, WE'RE IN ENGLAND
YOUR LITTLE C.I.A. TIN-STAR DOESN'T COUNT HERE, SHERIFF!
YOU'LL TALK WHEN I'M DONE WITH YOU, QUANTRILL! ... GET IN YOUR CAR!
HAVE IT YOUR WAY– BUT YOU'RE ASKING FOR TROUBLE!
YOU AND I ARE GOING FOR A LITTLE RIDE!
1786

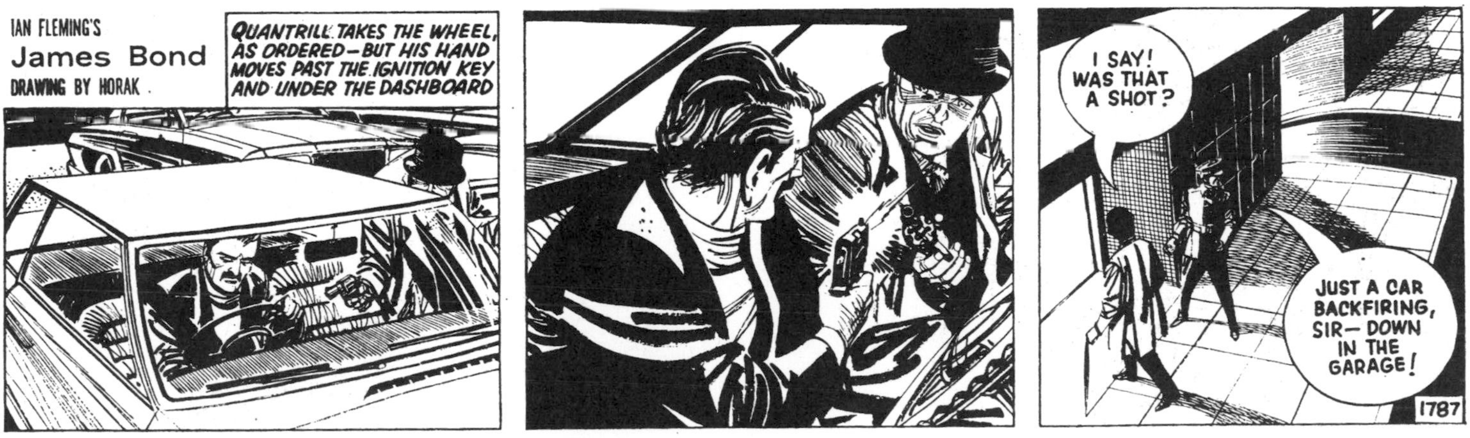
IAN FLEMING'S
James Bond
DRAWING BY HORAK
QUANTRILL TAKES THE WHEEL, AS ORDERED– BUT HIS HAND MOVES PAST THE IGNITION KEY AND UNDER THE DASHBOARD
I SAY! WAS THAT A SHOT?
JUST A CAR BACKFIRING, SIR– DOWN IN THE GARAGE!
1787

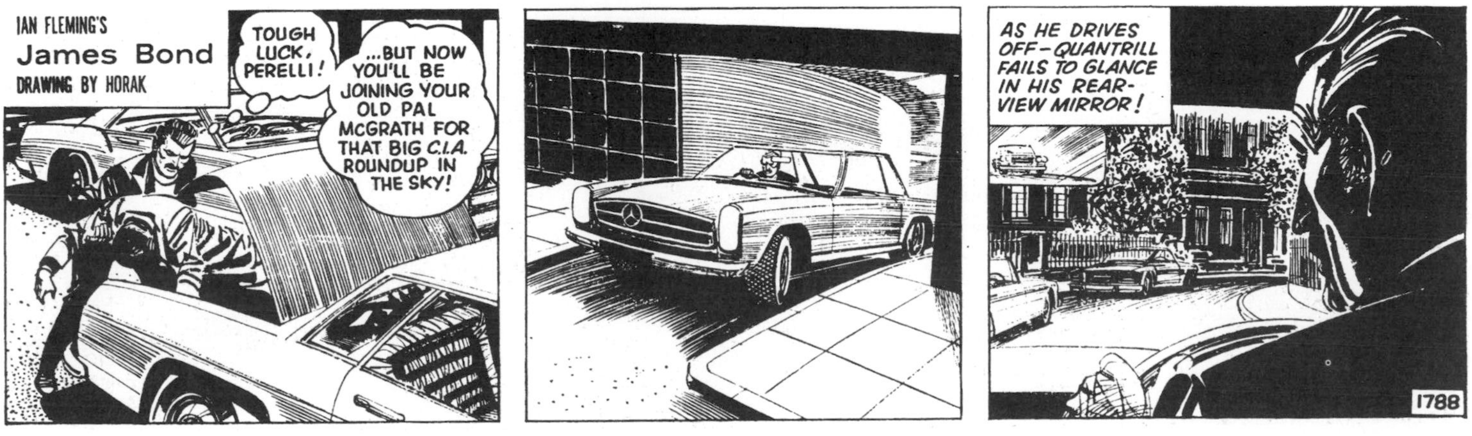
IAN FLEMING'S
James Bond
DRAWING BY HORAK
TOUGH LUCK, PERELLI!
...BUT NOW YOU'LL BE JOINING YOUR OLD PAL McGRATH FOR THAT BIG C.I.A. ROUNDUP IN THE SKY!
AS HE DRIVES OFF– QUANTRILL FAILS TO GLANCE IN HIS REAR-VIEW MIRROR!
1788

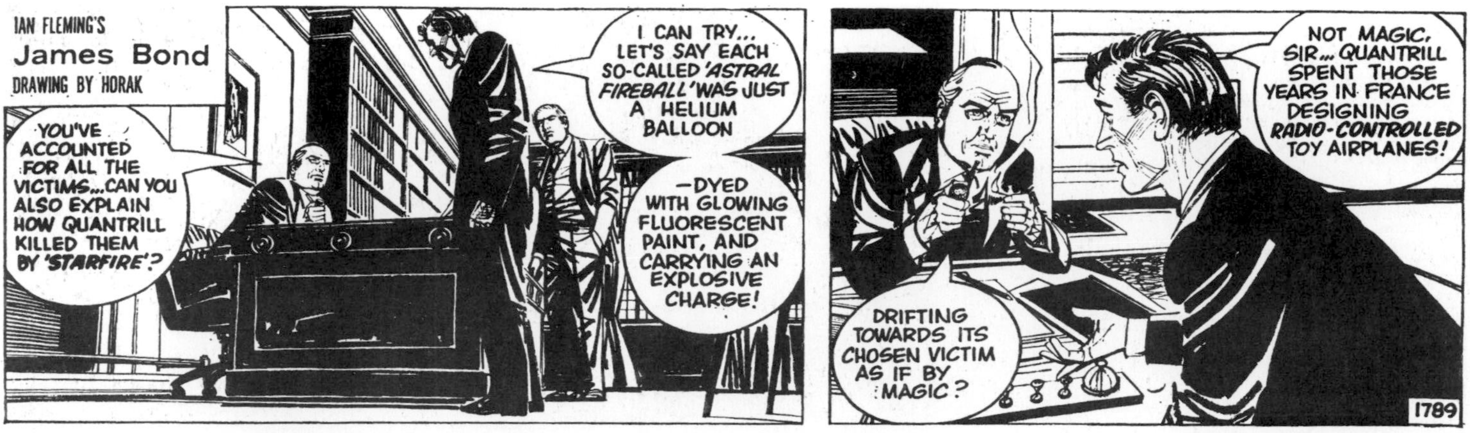
IAN FLEMING'S
James Bond
DRAWING BY HORAK
YOU'VE ACCOUNTED FOR ALL THE VICTIMS...CAN YOU ALSO EXPLAIN HOW QUANTRILL KILLED THEM BY 'STARFIRE'?
I CAN TRY... LET'S SAY EACH SO-CALLED 'ASTRAL FIREBALL' WAS JUST A HELIUM BALLOON
—DYED WITH GLOWING FLUORESCENT PAINT, AND CARRYING AN EXPLOSIVE CHARGE!
DRIFTING TOWARDS ITS CHOSEN VICTIM AS IF BY MAGIC?
NOT MAGIC, SIR... QUANTRILL SPENT THOSE YEARS IN FRANCE DESIGNING RADIO-CONTROLLED TOY AIRPLANES!
1789

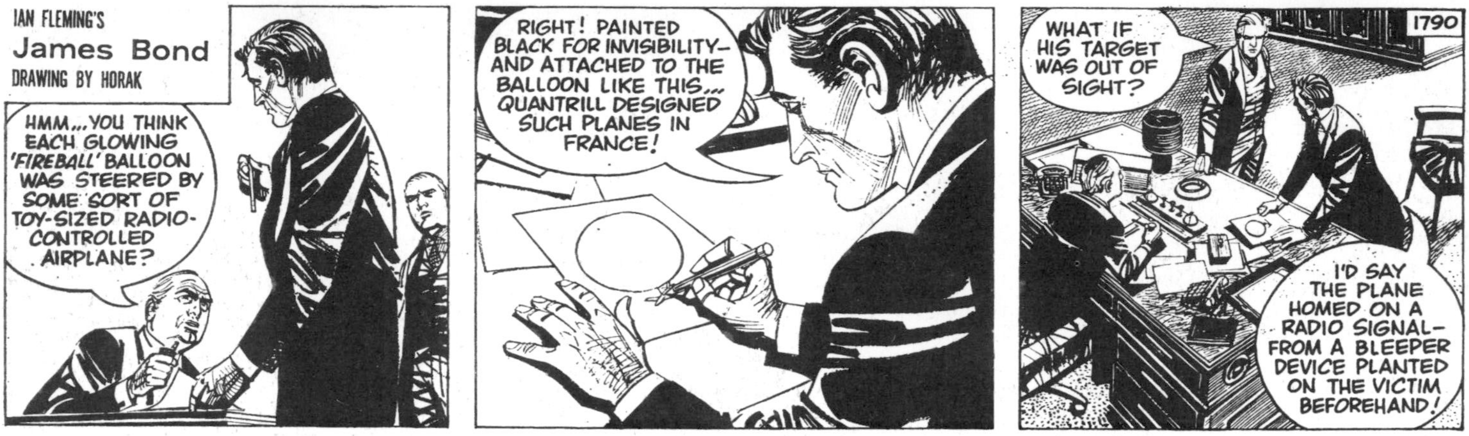
IAN FLEMING'S
James Bond
DRAWING BY HORAK
HMM... YOU THINK EACH GLOWING 'FIREBALL' BALLOON WAS STEERED BY SOME SORT OF TOY-SIZED RADIO-CONTROLLED AIRPLANE?
RIGHT! PAINTED BLACK FOR INVISIBILITY— AND ATTACHED TO THE BALLOON LIKE THIS... QUANTRILL DESIGNED SUCH PLANES IN FRANCE!
1790
WHAT IF HIS TARGET WAS OUT OF SIGHT?
I'D SAY THE PLANE HOMED ON A RADIO SIGNAL— FROM A BLEEPER DEVICE PLANTED ON THE VICTIM BEFOREHAND!

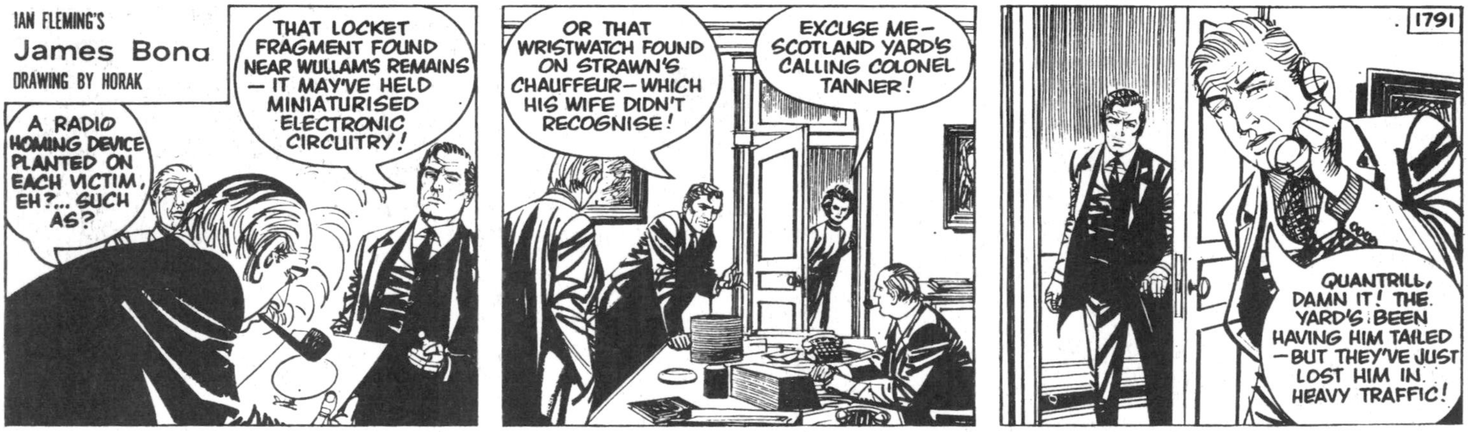
IAN FLEMING'S
James Bond
DRAWING BY HORAK
A RADIO HOMING DEVICE PLANTED ON EACH VICTIM, EH?... SUCH AS?
THAT LOCKET FRAGMENT FOUND NEAR WULLAM'S REMAINS —IT MAY'VE HELD MINIATURISED ELECTRONIC CIRCUITRY!
OR THAT WRISTWATCH FOUND ON STRAWN'S CHAUFFEUR—WHICH HIS WIFE DIDN'T RECOGNISE!
EXCUSE ME— SCOTLAND YARD'S CALLING COLONEL TANNER!
1791
QUANTRILL, DAMN IT! THE YARD'S BEEN HAVING HIM TAILED —BUT THEY'VE JUST LOST HIM IN HEAVY TRAFFIC!

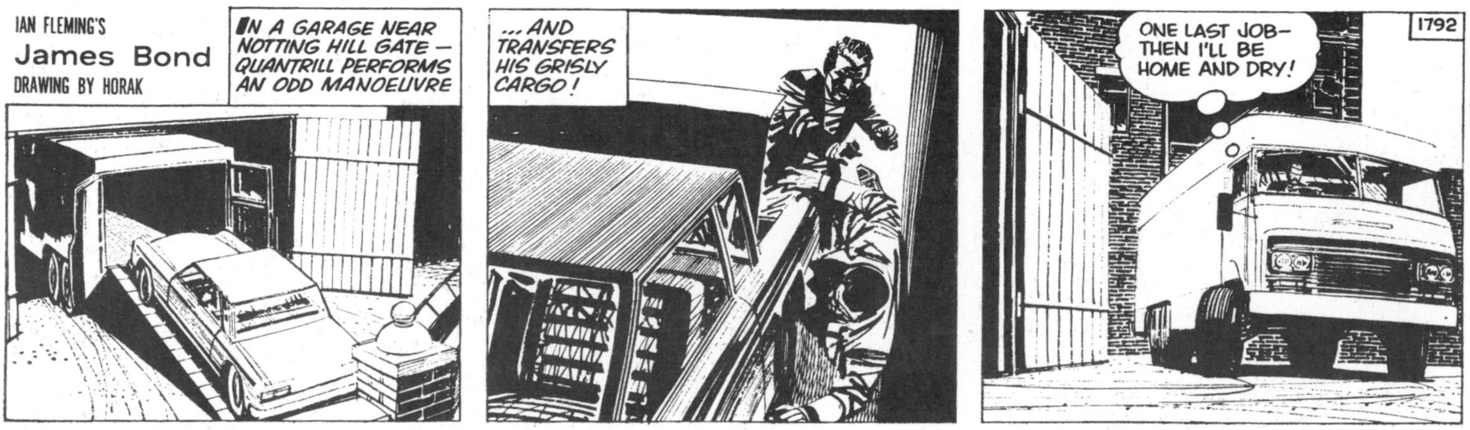
IAN FLEMING'S
James Bond
DRAWING BY HORAK
IN A GARAGE NEAR NOTTING HILL GATE— QUANTRILL PERFORMS AN ODD MANOEUVRE
...AND TRANSFERS HIS GRISLY CARGO!
ONE LAST JOB— THEN I'LL BE HOME AND DRY!
1792

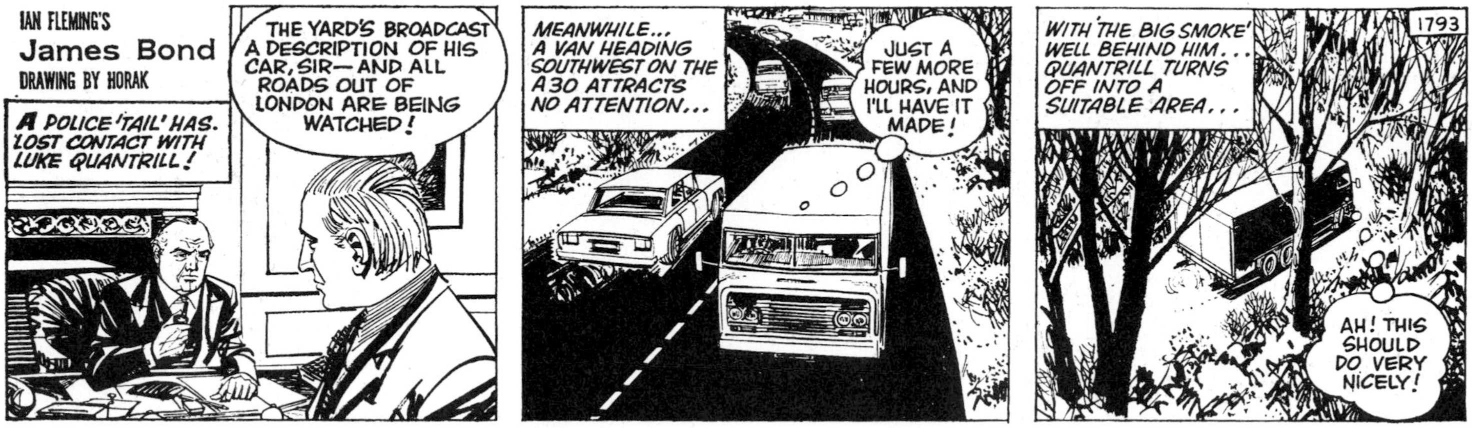
IAN FLEMING'S
James Bond
DRAWING BY HORAK
A POLICE 'TAIL' HAS LOST CONTACT WITH LUKE QUANTRILL!
THE YARD'S BROADCAST A DESCRIPTION OF HIS CAR, SIR— AND ALL ROADS OUT OF LONDON ARE BEING WATCHED!
MEANWHILE... A VAN HEADING SOUTHWEST ON THE A30 ATTRACTS NO ATTENTION...
JUST A FEW MORE HOURS, AND I'LL HAVE IT MADE!
1793
WITH 'THE BIG SMOKE' WELL BEHIND HIM... QUANTRILL TURNS OFF INTO A SUITABLE AREA...
AH! THIS SHOULD DO VERY NICELY!

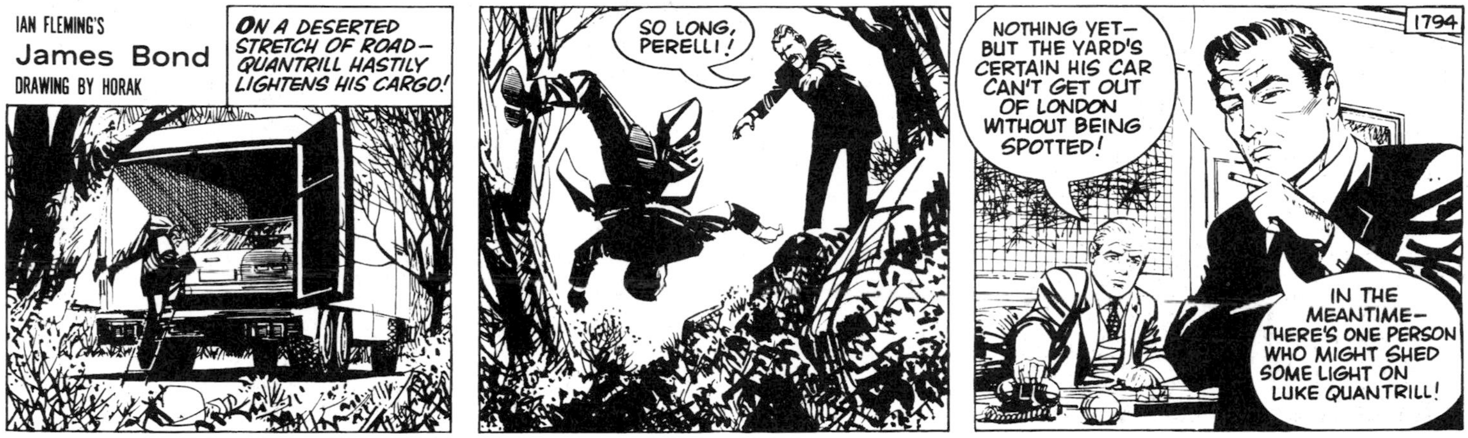
IAN FLEMING'S
James Bond
DRAWING BY HORAK
ON A DESERTED STRETCH OF ROAD— QUANTRILL HASTILY LIGHTENS HIS CARGO!
SO LONG, PERELLI!
1794
NOTHING YET— BUT THE YARD'S CERTAIN HIS CAR CAN'T GET OUT OF LONDON WITHOUT BEING SPOTTED!
IN THE MEANTIME— THERE'S ONE PERSON WHO MIGHT SHED SOME LIGHT ON LUKE QUANTRILL!

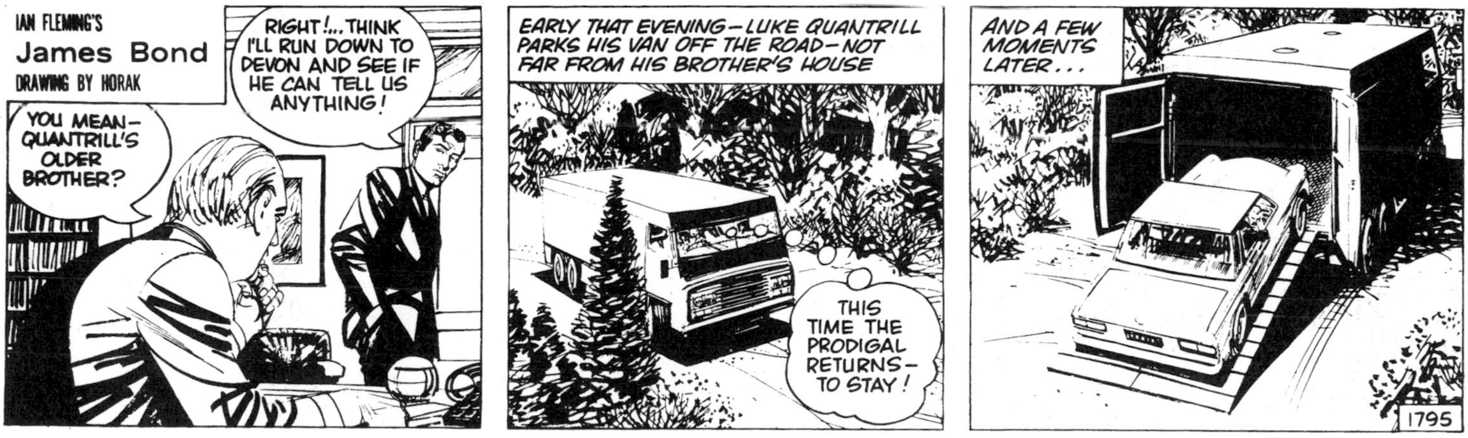
IAN FLEMING'S
James Bond
DRAWING BY HORAK
RIGHT!... THINK I'LL RUN DOWN TO DEVON AND SEE IF HE CAN TELL US ANYTHING!
YOU MEAN— QUANTRILL'S OLDER BROTHER?
EARLY THAT EVENING— LUKE QUANTRILL PARKS HIS VAN OFF THE ROAD— NOT FAR FROM HIS BROTHER'S HOUSE
THIS TIME THE PRODIGAL RETURNS— TO STAY!
AND A FEW MOMENTS LATER...
1795

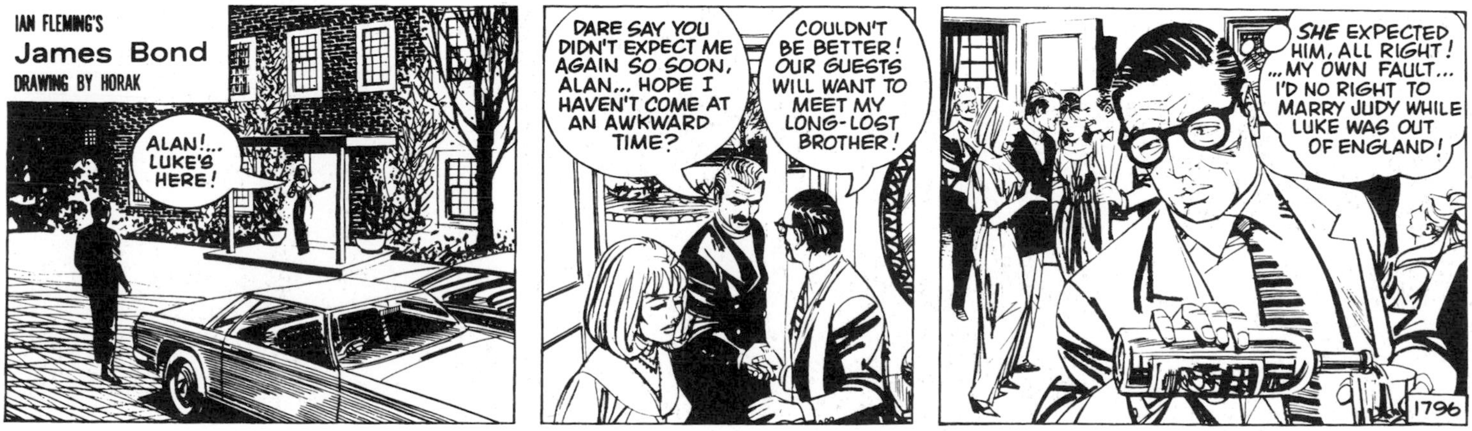
IAN FLEMING'S
James Bond
DRAWING BY HORAK
ALAN!... LUKE'S HERE!
DARE SAY YOU DIDN'T EXPECT ME AGAIN SO SOON, ALAN... HOPE I HAVEN'T COME AT AN AWKWARD TIME?
COULDN'T BE BETTER! OUR GUESTS WILL WANT TO MEET MY LONG-LOST BROTHER!
SHE EXPECTED HIM, ALL RIGHT! ...MY OWN FAULT... I'D NO RIGHT TO MARRY JUDY WHILE LUKE WAS OUT OF ENGLAND!
1796

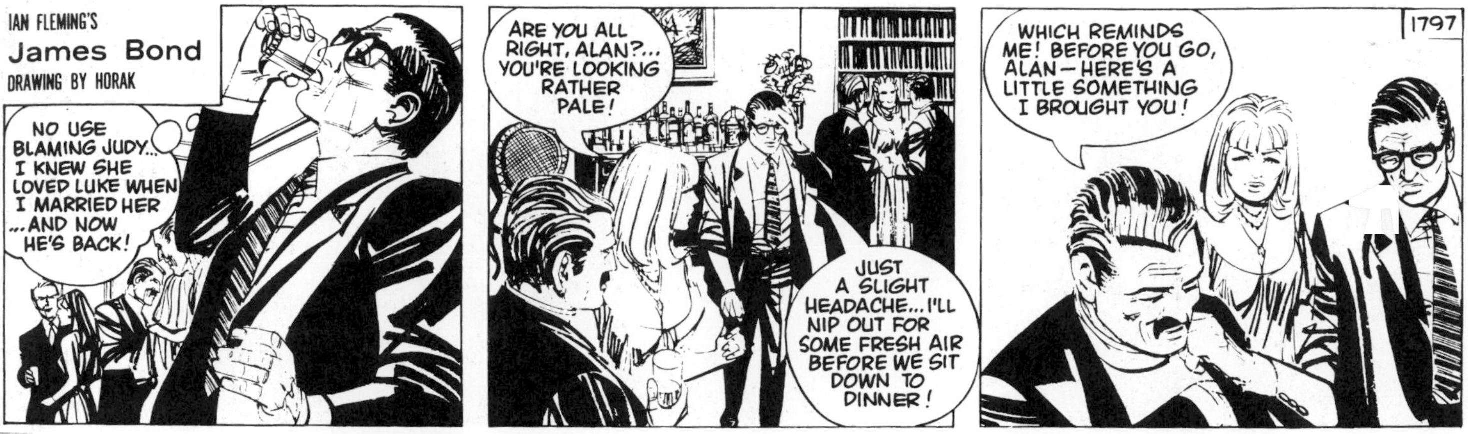
IAN FLEMING'S
James Bond
DRAWING BY HORAK
NO USE BLAMING JUDY... I KNEW SHE LOVED LUKE WHEN I MARRIED HER ...AND NOW HE'S BACK!
ARE YOU ALL RIGHT, ALAN?... YOU'RE LOOKING RATHER PALE!
JUST A SLIGHT HEADACHE... I'LL NIP OUT FOR SOME FRESH AIR BEFORE WE SIT DOWN TO DINNER!
1797
WHICH REMINDS ME! BEFORE YOU GO, ALAN—HERE'S A LITTLE SOMETHING I BROUGHT YOU!

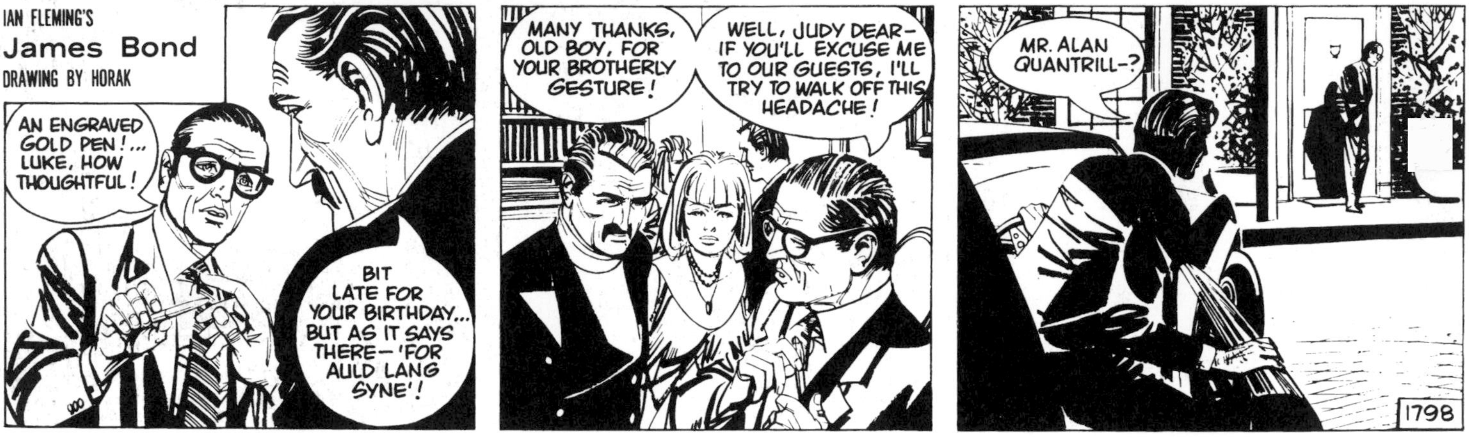
IAN FLEMING'S
James Bond
DRAWING BY HORAK
AN ENGRAVED GOLD PEN!... LUKE, HOW THOUGHTFUL!
BIT LATE FOR YOUR BIRTHDAY... BUT AS IT SAYS THERE—'FOR AULD LANG SYNE'!
MANY THANKS, OLD BOY, FOR YOUR BROTHERLY GESTURE!
WELL, JUDY DEAR—IF YOU'LL EXCUSE ME TO OUR GUESTS, I'LL TRY TO WALK OFF THIS HEADACHE!
MR. ALAN QUANTRILL-?
1798

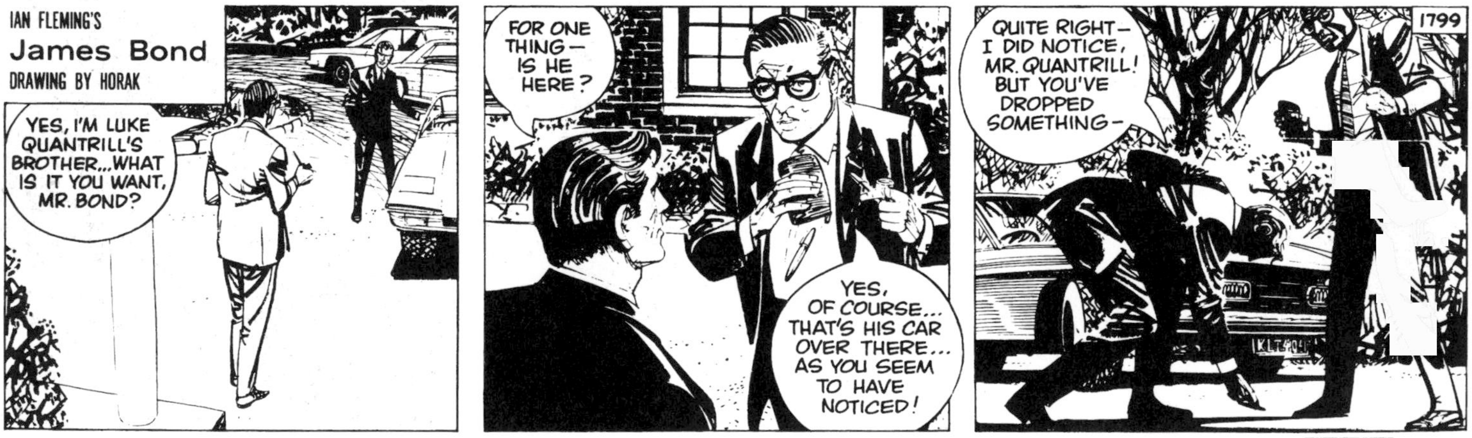
IAN FLEMING'S
James Bond
DRAWING BY HORAK
YES, I'M LUKE QUANTRILL'S BROTHER... WHAT IS IT YOU WANT, MR. BOND?
FOR ONE THING—IS HE HERE?
YES, OF COURSE... THAT'S HIS CAR OVER THERE... AS YOU SEEM TO HAVE NOTICED!
1799
QUITE RIGHT—I DID NOTICE, MR. QUANTRILL! BUT YOU'VE DROPPED SOMETHING—

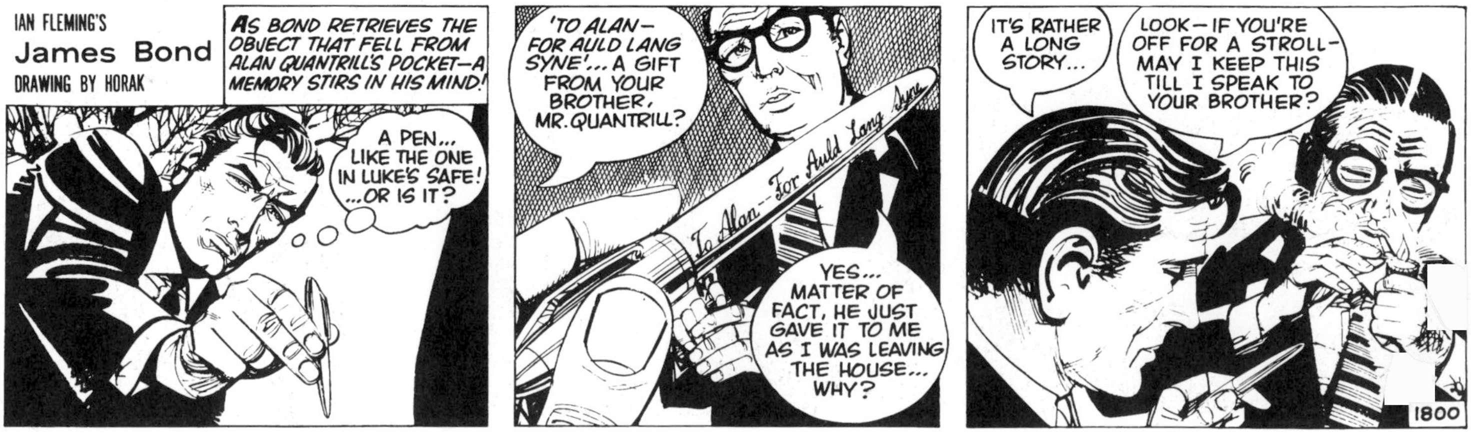
IAN FLEMING'S
James Bond
DRAWING BY HORAK
AS BOND RETRIEVES THE OBJECT THAT FELL FROM ALAN QUANTRILL'S POCKET—A MEMORY STIRS IN HIS MIND!
A PEN... LIKE THE ONE IN LUKE'S SAFE! ...OR IS IT?
'TO ALAN—FOR AULD LANG SYNE'... A GIFT FROM YOUR BROTHER, MR. QUANTRILL?
To Alan—For Auld Lang Syne
YES... MATTER OF FACT, HE JUST GAVE IT TO ME AS I WAS LEAVING THE HOUSE... WHY?
IT'S RATHER A LONG STORY...
LOOK—IF YOU'RE OFF FOR A STROLL—MAY I KEEP THIS TILL I SPEAK TO YOUR BROTHER?
1800

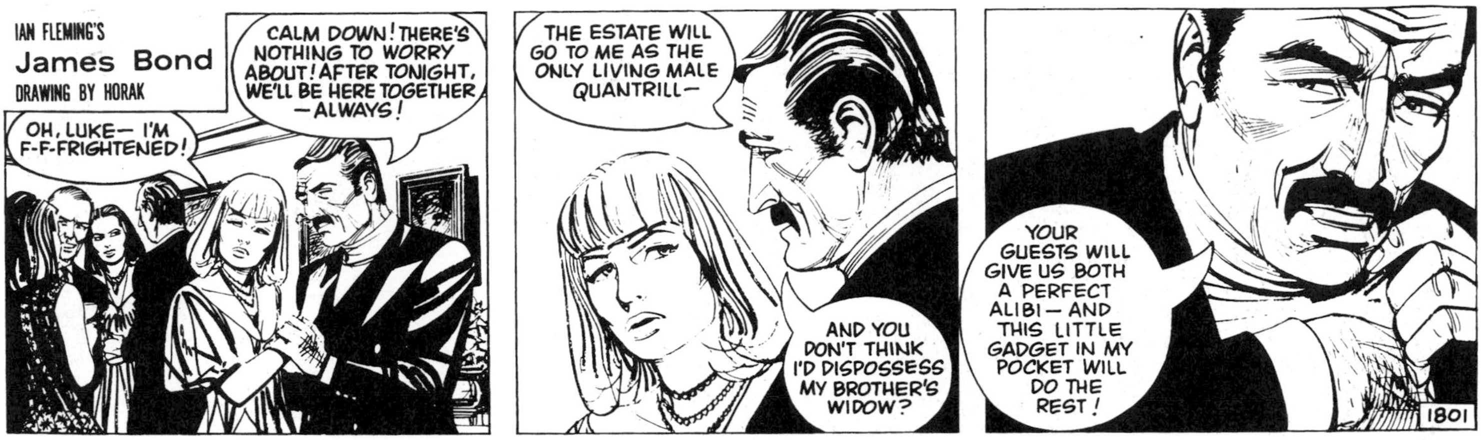
IAN FLEMING'S
James Bond
DRAWING BY HORAK
OH, LUKE— I'M F-F-FRIGHTENED!
CALM DOWN! THERE'S NOTHING TO WORRY ABOUT! AFTER TONIGHT, WE'LL BE HERE TOGETHER —ALWAYS!
THE ESTATE WILL GO TO ME AS THE ONLY LIVING MALE QUANTRILL—
AND YOU DON'T THINK I'D DISPOSSESS MY BROTHER'S WIDOW?
YOUR GUESTS WILL GIVE US BOTH A PERFECT ALIBI — AND THIS LITTLE GADGET IN MY POCKET WILL DO THE REST!
1801

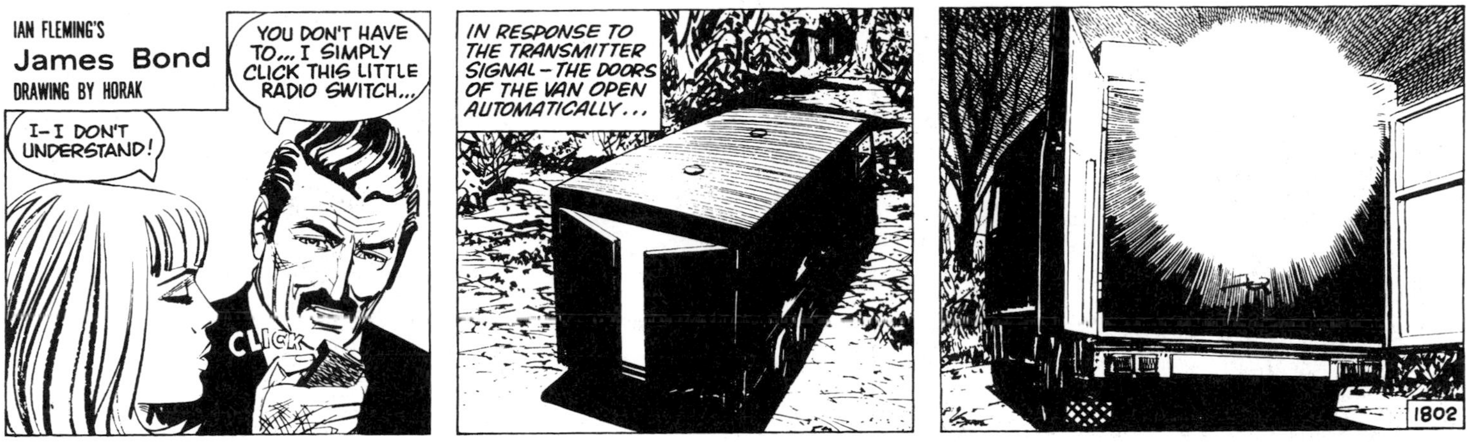
IAN FLEMING'S
James Bond
DRAWING BY HORAK
I-I DON'T UNDERSTAND!
YOU DON'T HAVE TO... I SIMPLY CLICK THIS LITTLE RADIO SWITCH...
CLICK
IN RESPONSE TO THE TRANSMITTER SIGNAL — THE DOORS OF THE VAN OPEN AUTOMATICALLY...
1802

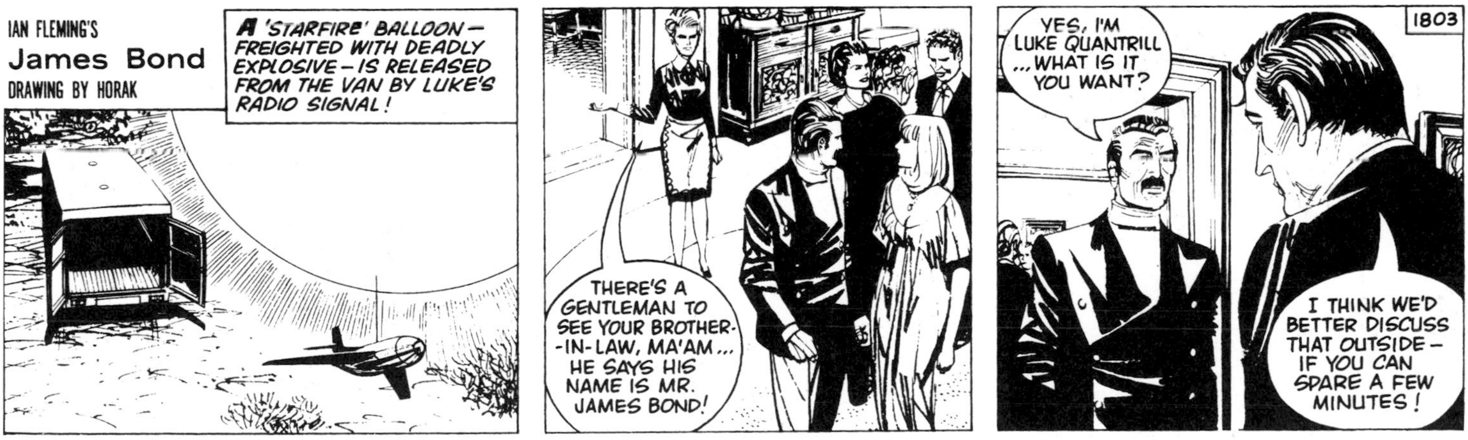
IAN FLEMING'S
James Bond
DRAWING BY HORAK
A 'STARFIRE' BALLOON — FREIGHTED WITH DEADLY EXPLOSIVE — IS RELEASED FROM THE VAN BY LUKE'S RADIO SIGNAL!
THERE'S A GENTLEMAN TO SEE YOUR BROTHER-IN-LAW, MA'AM... HE SAYS HIS NAME IS MR. JAMES BOND!
YES, I'M LUKE QUANTRILL ...WHAT IS IT YOU WANT?
I THINK WE'D BETTER DISCUSS THAT OUTSIDE — IF YOU CAN SPARE A FEW MINUTES!
1803

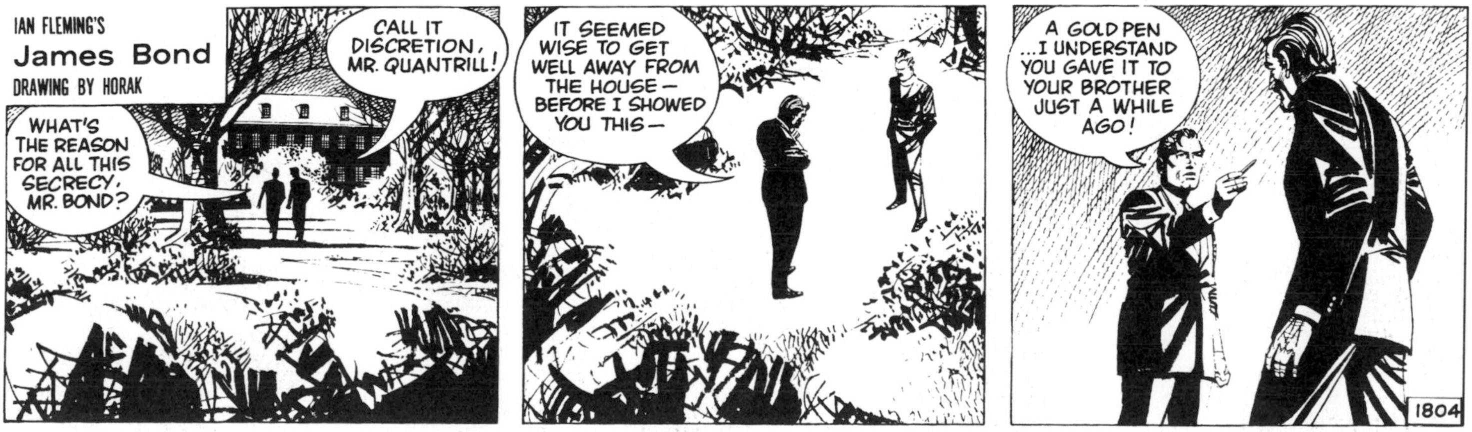
IAN FLEMING'S
James Bond
DRAWING BY HORAK
WHAT'S THE REASON FOR ALL THIS SECRECY, MR. BOND?
CALL IT DISCRETION, MR. QUANTRILL!
IT SEEMED WISE TO GET WELL AWAY FROM THE HOUSE — BEFORE I SHOWED YOU THIS—
A GOLD PEN ...I UNDERSTAND YOU GAVE IT TO YOUR BROTHER JUST A WHILE AGO!
1804

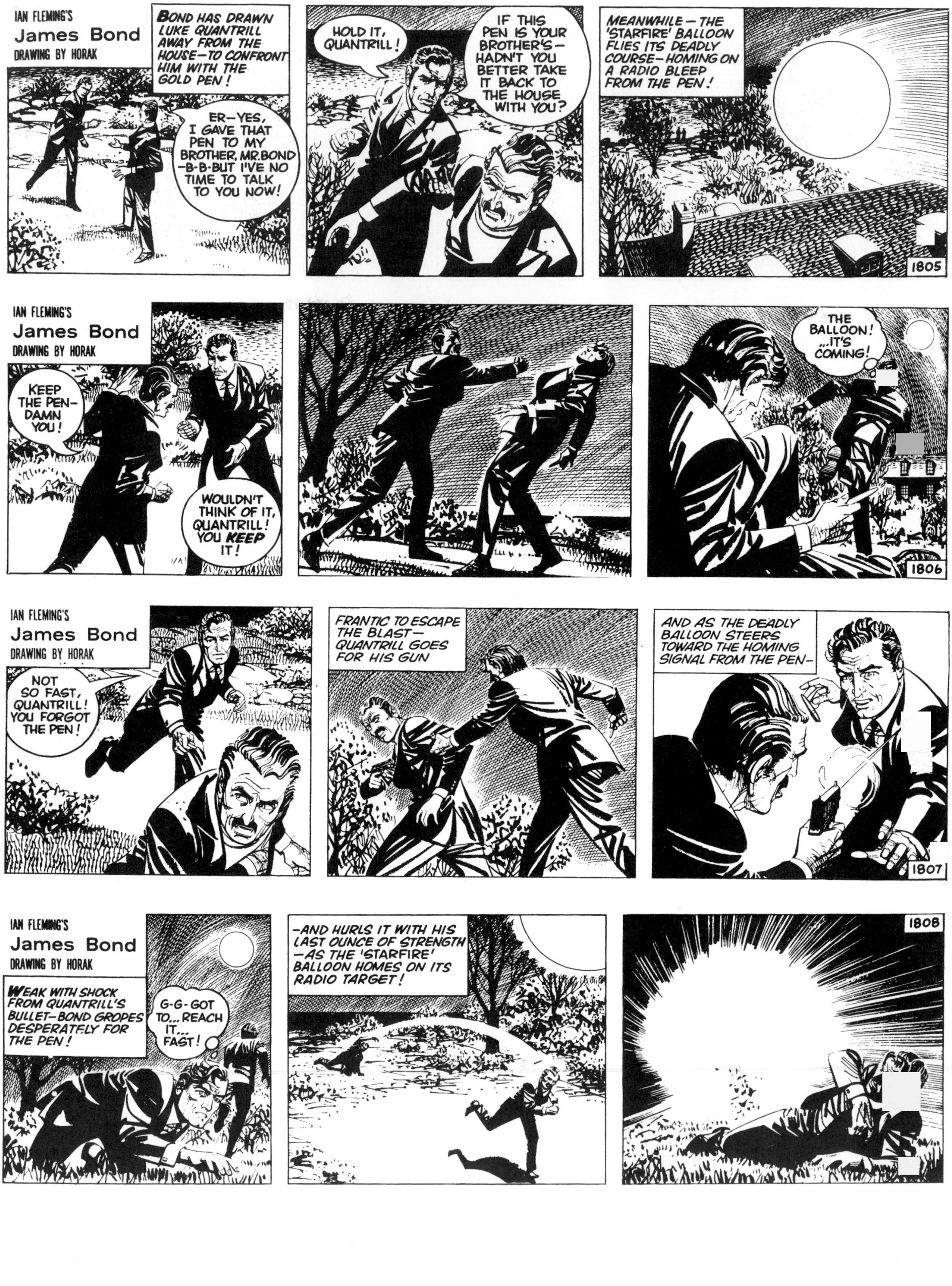
IAN FLEMING'S
James Bond
DRAWING BY HORAK
BOND HAS DRAWN LUKE QUANTRILL AWAY FROM THE HOUSE—TO CONFRONT HIM WITH THE GOLD PEN!
ER—YES, I GAVE THAT PEN TO MY BROTHER, MR. BOND —B-B-BUT I'VE NO TIME TO TALK TO YOU NOW!
HOLD IT, QUANTRILL!
IF THIS PEN IS YOUR BROTHER'S—HADN'T YOU BETTER TAKE IT BACK TO THE HOUSE WITH YOU?
MEANWHILE—THE 'STARFIRE' BALLOON FLIES ITS DEADLY COURSE—HOMING ON A RADIO BLEEP FROM THE PEN!
1805
IAN FLEMING'S
James Bond
DRAWING BY HORAK
KEEP THE PEN—DAMN YOU!
WOULDN'T THINK OF IT, QUANTRILL! YOU KEEP IT!
THE BALLOON! ...IT'S COMING!
1806
IAN FLEMING'S
James Bond
DRAWING BY HORAK
NOT SO FAST, QUANTRILL! YOU FORGOT THE PEN!
FRANTIC TO ESCAPE THE BLAST—QUANTRILL GOES FOR HIS GUN
AND AS THE DEADLY BALLOON STEERS TOWARD THE HOMING SIGNAL FROM THE PEN—
1807
IAN FLEMING'S
James Bond
DRAWING BY HORAK
WEAK WITH SHOCK FROM QUANTRILL'S BULLET—BOND GROPES DESPERATELY FOR THE PEN!
G-G-GOT TO... REACH IT... FAST!
—AND HURLS IT WITH HIS LAST OUNCE OF STRENGTH—AS THE 'STARFIRE' BALLOON HOMES ON ITS RADIO TARGET!
1808

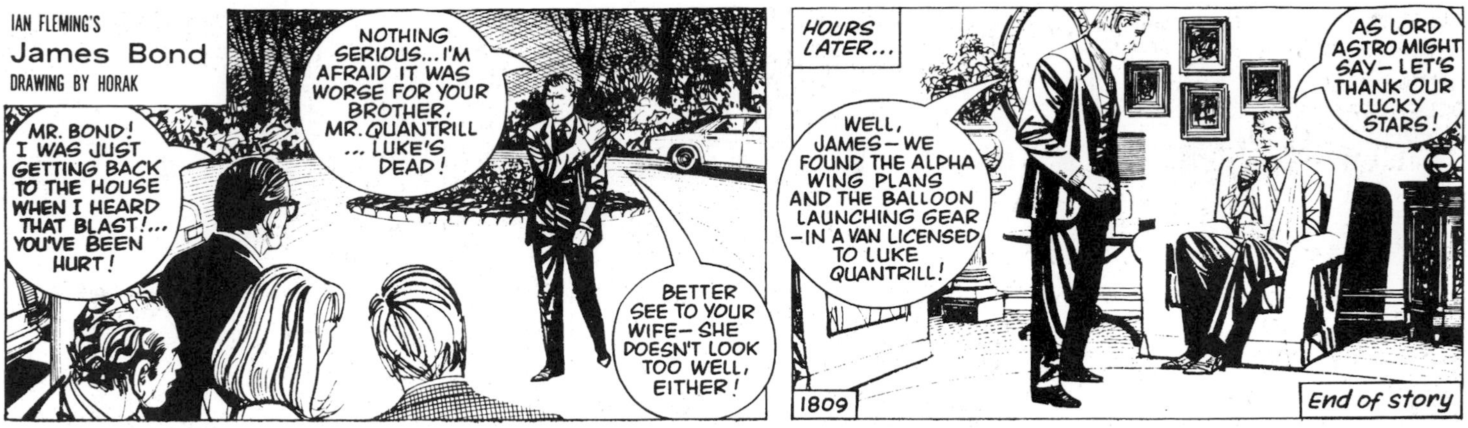
IAN FLEMING'S
James Bond
DRAWING BY HORAK
MR. BOND! I WAS JUST GETTING BACK TO THE HOUSE WHEN I HEARD THAT BLAST!... YOU'VE BEEN HURT!
NOTHING SERIOUS...I'M AFRAID IT WAS WORSE FOR YOUR BROTHER, MR. QUANTRILL ... LUKE'S DEAD!
BETTER SEE TO YOUR WIFE– SHE DOESN'T LOOK TOO WELL, EITHER!
HOURS LATER...
WELL, JAMES– WE FOUND THE ALPHA WING PLANS AND THE BALLOON LAUNCHING GEAR –IN A VAN LICENSED TO LUKE QUANTRILL!
AS LORD ASTRO MIGHT SAY– LET'S THANK OUR LUCKY STARS!
1809
End of story

THE COMPLETE
JAMES BOND
SYNDICATED NEWSPAPER CHECKLIST

The following is a complete checklist of *James Bond* strips to have appeared in the *Express* newspapers and been syndicated in non-UK newspapers.

STORY	WRITER	ARTISTS	DATE	SERIAL No.
Serialised in the *Daily Express*				
Casino Royale	IF/AH	JM	7.7.58–13.12.58	1–138
Live and Let Die	IF/HG	JM	15.12.58–28.3.59	139–225
Moonraker	IF/HG	JM	30.3.59–8.8.59	226–339
Diamonds Are Forever	IF/HG	JM	10.8.59–30.1.60	340–487
From Russia With Love	IF/HG	JM	3.2.60–21.5.60	488–583
Dr. No	IF/PO	JM	23.5.60–1.10.60	584–697
Goldfinger	IF/HG	JM	3.10.60–1.4.61	698–849
Risico	IF/HG	JM	3.4.61–24.6.61	850–921
From A View To A Kill	IF/HG	JM	25.6.61–9.9.61	922–987
For Your Eyes Only	IF/HG	JM	11.9.61–9.12.61	988–1065
Thunderball	IF/HG	JM	11.12.61–10.2.62	1066–1128*

Series aborted prematurely

STORY	WRITER	ARTISTS	DATE	SERIAL No.
(Series Two)				
On Her Majesty's				
Secret Service	IF/HG	JM	29.6.64–17.5.65	1–274
You Only Live Twice	IF/HG	JM	18.5.65–8.1.66	275–475

STORY	WRITER	ARTISTS	DATE	SERIAL No.
(Series Three)				
The Man With				
the Golden Gun	IF/JL	YH	10.1.66–10.9.66	1–209
The Living Daylights	IF/JL	YH	12.9.66–12.11.66	210–263
Octopussy	IF/JL	YH	14.11.66–27.5.67	264–428
The Hildebrand Rarity	IF/JL	YH	29.5.67–16.12.67	429–602
The Spy Who Loved Me	IF/JL	YH	18.12.67–3.10.68	603–815
The Harpies	JL	YH	4.10.68–23.6.69	816–1037
River of Death	JL	YH	24.6.69–29.11.69	1038–1174
Colonel Sun	KA/JL	YH	1.12.69–20.8.70	1175–1393
The Golden Ghost	JL	YH	21.8.70–16.1.71	1394–1519
Fear Face	JL	YH	18.1.71–20.4.71	1520–1596
Double Jeopardy	JL	YH	21.4.71–28.8.71	1597–1708
Starfire	JL	YH	30.8.71–24.12.71	1709–1809
Trouble Spot	JL	YH	28.12.71–10.6.72	1810–1951
Isle of Condors	JL	YH	12.6.72–21.10.72	1952–2065
The League of Vampires	JL	YH	25.10.72–28.2.73	2066–2172
Die With My Boots On	JL	YH	1.3.73–18.6.73	2173–2256
The Girl Machine	JL	YH	19.6.73–3.12.73	2257–2407
Beware of Butterflies	JL	YH	4.12.73–11.5.74	2408–2541
The Nevsky Nude	JL	YH	13.5.74–21.9.74	2542–2655
The Phoenix Project	JL	YH	23.9.74–18.2.75	2656–2780
The Black Ruby Caper	JL	YH	19.2.75–15.7.75	2781–2897
Till Death Do Us Part	JL	YH	7.7.75–14.10.75	2898–2983
The Torch–Time Affair	JL	YH	15.10.75–15.1.76	2984–3060
Hot-Shot	JL	YH	16.1.76–1.6.76	3061–3178
Nightbird	JL	YH	2.6.76–4.11.76	3179–3312
Ape of Diamonds	JL	YH	5.11.76–22.1.77	3313–3437

STORY	WRITER	ARTISTS	DATE	SERIAL No.
Serialised in the *Sunday Express*				
(Series Four)				
When the Wizard Awakes	JL	YH	30.1.77–22.5.77	1–54

STORY	WRITER	ARTISTS	DATE	SERIAL No.
Syndicated strips not featured in newspapers in the UK				
Sea Dragon	JL	YH	not applicable	55–192
Death Wing	JL	YH	not applicable	193–354
The Xanadu Connection	JL	YH	not applicable	355–468
Shark Bait	JL	YH	not applicable	469–636

STORY	WRITER	ARTISTS	DATE	SERIAL No.
Serialised in the *Daily Star*				
(Series Five)				
Doomcrack	JL	HN	2.2.81–19.8.81	1–174
The Paradise Plot	JL	JM	20.8.81–4.6.82	175–378
Deathmask	JL	JM	7.6.82–8.2.83	379–552
Flittermouse	JL	JM	9.2.83–20.5.83	553–624
Polestar	JL	JM	23.5.83–15.7.83	625–719*

Series stopped publishing in the Daily Star at 673

STORY	WRITER	ARTISTS	DATE	SERIAL No.
Syndicated strips not featured in UK newspapers				
The Scent of Danger	JL	JM	not applicable	720–821
Snake Goddess	JL	YH	not applicable	822–893
Double Eagle	JL	YH	not applicable	894–965

GLOSSARY

KEY TO CREATORS

IF: IAN FLEMING
AH: ANTHONY HERN
HG: HENRY GAMMIDGE
PO: PETER O'DONNELL
JL: JIM LAWRENCE
KA: KINGSLEY AMIS
   (under pseudonym Robert Markham)
JM: JOHN MCLUSKY
YH: YAROSLAV HORAK
HN: HARRY NORTH

SERIAL NUMBERS

Each serial number represents a day. However, in Scotland, some strips were published in the *Daily Express* on days when there were Bank Holidays in England and Wales; these were designated by the suffix 'a' after the serial number on the strips.

JAMES BOND 007 WILL RETURN.....

COMING SOON FROM TITAN BOOKS!